HUMAN LEARNING

AND MEMORY

Human Learning and Memory ◇ SELECTED ◇ READINGS

EDITED BY NORMAN J. SLAMECKA

NEW YORK

OXFORD UNIVERSITY PRESS

LONDON • TORONTO 1967

Copyright © 1967 by Oxford University Press, Inc.

Library of Congress Catalogue Card Number: 67-15135

Fourth printing, 1972

PRINTED IN THE UNITED STATES OF AMERICA

PREFACE

This book makes available a substantial collection of some of the significant research articles in the area of human learning and memory. For several years I had hoped that the more frequently cited "key" articles would be collected and placed between two covers. This would have been a great personal convenience, as well as a convenience for my students. The rapid accumulation of research in verbal learning over the last fifteen years or so has made the classic McGeoch and Irion reference book obviously unrepresentative of the current state of the field. To some extent, the excellent verbal learning symposium reports edited by Cofer, and by Cofer and Musgrave, have filled that gap. Symposium papers, however, have a tendency to be higher-level excursions into a specific problem area, and they generally presuppose a detailed acquaintance with most of the relevant research already published. For this reason they are not well suited for an introductory reference role, at least at the undergraduate level.

The present collection is designed as a basic source for courses in verbal learning, and for other courses that consider the field of human learning. It is appropriate for use at the advanced undergraduate, as well as at the graduate, level. It forms the substance of my own graduate seminar in verbal learning at the University of Vermont, and some parts of it are also incorporated into the advanced undergraduate course in learning. Among other things, it is a practical solution to the problem encountered when a dozen or more students, all seeking the same article, converge simultaneously upon the library.

The fifty articles have been partitioned into ten sections of five articles each. Each section concerns itself with a different specific problem or phenomenon in human learning. Whenever possible, an attempt has been made to arrange the articles so as to reflect fairly the chronological development of the problem, and to convey some sense of the continuity to be found in the scientific enterprise. Further, each section is introduced by some relevant remarks about the area in question, together with five additional pertinent references for those who wish to study the problem more extensively. With one exception, each article is republished in its entirety. The one exception is Lashley's comprehensive contribution to the problem of serial order, from which eleven pages (pp. 122-7, 131-5) have been omitted because of its great length. Trying to select only fifty articles out of the great number published in the field was an arduous personal task, and necessarily somewhat arbitrary. It is hoped that my choices will prove to be acceptable to others in the field, and that my omissions will be forgiven. Except for Lashley's paper, all articles were picked from the journal literature of psychology. Papers that were mainly reviews of the literature were excluded, and relatively recent work was favored.

All of the proceeds from sales of this book will be given to the Humane Society of the United States.

N.J.S.

Burlington, Vermont
February 1967

CONTENTS

III THE SERIAL POSITION EFFECT   111

IV CONTINUITY VERSUS DISCONTINUITY   149

V FREE RECALL   217

VI SHORT-TERM MEMORY

VII DETERMINANTS OF SPECIFIC TRANSFER

VIII PSYCHOLINGUISTICS

IX CONCEPT FORMATION 443

X CONDITIONING OF VERBAL RESPONSE CLASSES 493

HUMAN LEARNING

AND MEMORY

THE INTERFERENCE THEORY OF FORGETTING

THIS section focuses upon the progress of certain recent developments in the theory of forgetting. The brunt of the explanation for forgetting phenomena within the traditional associationistic framework had, until lately, rested mainly upon the concept of retroactive inhibition (RI). This refers to the interference produced by new learning (IL), interpolated between the original learning (OL), and recall of that original learning. The magnitude of the retroactive inhibition effect is assessed against the performance of a control group which has only the original learning and its recall, without any interfering learning task interpolated within the retention interval. Numerous laboratory studies have verified the reality of the phenomenon, and have studied the influence of several variables that govern its magnitude (Slamecka & Ceraso, 1960). In short, forgetting was explained by appealing to subsequent learning of other material.

As a consequence of the work of B.J. Underwood, the potentially greater importance of a related concept, that of proactive inhibition (PI), came to the fore. Proactive inhibition refers to the interference generated by previous learning, with the retention of subsequent learning. The magnitude of proactive inhibition is assessed against the performance of a control group which does not experience the previous learning task. In short, forgetting can also be attributed to the effects of old learning. A stress upon this latter concept, together with demonstrations of verbal unlearning and assumptions about spontaneous recovery, formed the basis for a revised theory of forgetting. The following readings, arranged in chronological order of appearance, are a good illustation of the action and reaction which characterize the progress of scientific development in this, as well as in other fields.

Underwood's paper is a classic of scientific detective work. Re-examining the data from a wide range of previous studies, Underwood showed that the degree of retention of a list after 24 hours was very strongly influenced by the number of previous lists learned. With heavily practiced subjects, retention of the last list learned was only 25 per cent or even less, whereas with naïve subjects, 75 per cent was remembered. This was a striking illustration of the importance of proactive inhibition.

The paper by Barnes and Underwood provided clearcut confirmation of the hypothesis that with the A–B, A–C interference paradigm, the learning of the second list produces substantial unlearning of the first-list items. Such an hypothesis was tentatively suggested several years before by Melton and Irwin (1940), to account for retroactive inhibition effects. With the A–B, A–B' paradigm, there was no interference, and mediation was the probable mechanism for second-list learning.

The stage was now set for the elaboration of a theory which would embody the above findings within the context of everyday language habits. The paper by Underwood and Postman focused upon the key role of extra-experimental associations in forgetting. It was assumed that competing extra-experimental associations, stemming from a subject's language habits, were unlearned during the acquisition of a laboratory list. With the passage of time these unlearned associations were presumed to recover spontaneously in strength, and eventually to provide proactive interference at recall of the laboratory list. Thus, forgetting of even a single list could be attributed to proactive inhibition coming from the recovery of natural associations the subject had carried with him to the laboratory. These extra-experimental associations were of two kinds: item-sequence habits, which referred to word associations, and letter-sequence habits, which referred to letter associations.

Subsequent papers reported tests of deductions from the theory, and initial results were fairly promising at the item-sequence level (Postman, 1961), but failed to provide support at the letter-sequence level (Underwood & Keppel, 1963). At this time also, a closer examination of the underlying assumptions took place.

A process of spontaneous recovery, akin to that found with animal learning, was also assumed applicable to verbal learning, and some data were available to show that *relative* recovery could be obtained (Briggs, 1954). Koppenaal's paper presented a thoroughgoing test for the detection of absolute spontaneous recovery of unlearned verbal associations, and failed to find it, thereby casting doubt upon the reality of the hypothesized phenomenon.

Slamecka's paper described several direct tests of the assumption that pre-experimental associations at the item-sequence level are unlearned as a result of the acquisition of a competing laboratory list. The results gave no support to that assumption, but suggested instead that pre-experimental associations are highly resistant to extinction.

The outcomes of the latter two investigations constitute indirect evidence against the validity of the theory as it had been presented, and imply that some revision is indicated. The theory is undeniably attractive in its compelling description of the important role of language habits, and it is likely that a revised form of it will be developed in the near future.

BRIGGS, G. E. Acquisition, extinction, and recovery functions in retroactive inhibition. *J. exp. Psychol.*, 1954, **47**, 285-93.

MELTON, A. W., & IRWIN, J. McQ. The influence of degree of interpolated learning on retroactive inhibition and the overt transfer of specific responses. *Amer. J. Psychol.*, 1940, **53**, 173-203.

POSTMAN, L. The present status of interference theory. In C. N. Cofer (Ed.), *Verbal learning and verbal behavior.* New York: McGraw-Hill, 1961. Pp. 152-79.

SLAMECKA, N. J., & CERASO, J. Retroactive and proactive inhibition of verbal learning. *Psychol. Bull.*, 1960, **57**, 449-75.

UNDERWOOD, B. J., & KEPPEL, G. Retention as a function of degree of learning and letter-sequence interference. *Psychol. Monogr.*, 1963, **77**, No. 567.

1 / Interference and Forgetting

BENTON J. UNDERWOOD, *Northwestern University* [1]

I know of no one who seriously maintains that interference among tasks is of no consequence in the production of forgetting. Whether forgetting is conceptualized at a strict psychological level or at a neural level (e.g., neural memory trace), some provision is made for interference to account for at least some of the measured forgetting. The many studies on retroactive inhibition are probably responsible for this general agreement that interference among tasks must produce a sizable proportion of forgetting. By introducing an interpolated interfering task very marked decrements in recall can be produced in a few minutes in the laboratory. But there is a second generalization which has resulted from these studies, namely, that most forgetting must be a function of the learning of tasks which interfere with that which has already been learned (19). Thus, if a single task is learned in the laboratory and retention measured after a week, the loss has been attributed to the interference from activities learned outside the laboratory during the week. It is this generalization with which I am concerned in the initial portions of this paper.

Now, I cannot deny the data which show large amounts of forgetting produced by an interpolated list in a few minutes in the laboratory. Nor do I deny that this loss may be attributed to interference. But I will try to show that use of retroactive inhibition as a paradigm of forgetting (via interference) may be seriously questioned. To be more specific: if a subject learns a single task, such as a list of words, and retention of this task is measured after a day, a week, or a month, I will try to show that very little of the forgetting can be attributed to an interfering task learned outside the laboratory during the retention interval. Before pursuing this further, I must make some general comments by way of preparation.

Whether we like it or not, the experimental study of forgetting has been largely dominated by the Ebbinghaus tradition, both in terms of methods and materials used. I do not think this is due to sheer perversity on the part of several generations of scientists interested in forgetting. It may be noted that much of our elementary knowledge can be obtained only by rote learning. To work with rote learning does not mean that we are thereby not concerning ourselves with phenomena that have no counterparts outside the laboratory. Furthermore, the investigation of these phenomena can be handled by methods

From the *Psychological Review,* 1957, **64**, 49-60, with permission of the author and publisher.

1. Most of the data from my own research referred to in this paper were obtained from work done under Contract N7 onr-45008, Project NR 154-057, between Northwestern University and The Office of Naval Research.

which are acceptable to a science. As is well known, there are periodic verbal revolts against the Ebbinghaus tradition (e.g., 2, 15, 22). But for some reason nothing much ever happens in the laboratory as a consequence of these revolts. I mention these matters neither by way of apology nor of justification for having done some research in rote learning, but for two other reasons. First, it may very well be true, as some have suggested (e.g., 22), that studies of memory in the Ebbinghaus tradition are not getting at all of the important phenomena of memory. I think the same statement—that research has not got at all of the important processes—could be made about all areas in psychology; so that the criticism (even if just) should not be indigenous to the study of memory. Science does not deal at will with all natural events. Science deals with natural events only when ingenuity in developing methods and techniques of measurement allow these events to be brought within the scope of science. If, therefore, the studies of memory which meet scientific acceptability do not tap all-important memorial processes, all I can say is that this is the state of the science in the area at the moment. Secondly, because the bulk of the systematic data on forgetting has been obtained on rote-learned tasks, I must of necessity use such data in discussing interference and forgetting.

Returning to the experimental situation, let me again put in concrete form the problem with which I first wish to deal. A subject learns a single task, such as a list of syllables, nouns, or adjectives. After an interval of time, say, 24 hours, his retention of this list is measured. The explanatory problem is what is responsible for the forgetting which commonly occurs over the 24 hours. As indicated earlier, the studies of retroactive inhibition led to the theoretical generalization that this forgetting

was due largely to interference from other tasks learned during the 24-hour retention interval. McGeoch (20) came to this conclusion, his last such statement being made in 1942. I would, therefore, like to look at the data which were available to McGeoch and others interested in this matter. I must repeat that the kind of data with which I am concerned is the retention of a list without formal interpolated learning introduced. The interval of retention with which I am going to deal in this, and several subsequent analyses, is 24 hours.

First, of course, Ebbinghaus' data were available and in a sense served as the reference point for many subsequent investigations. In terms of percentage saved in relearning, Ebbinghaus showed about 65 per cent los over 24 hours (7). In terms of recall after 24 hours, the following studies are representative of the amount forgotten: Youtz, 88 per cent loss (37); Luh, 82 per cent (18); Krueger, 74 per cent (16); Hovland, 78 per cent (11); Cheng, 65 per cent and 84 per cent (6); Lester, 65 per cent (17). Let us assume as a rough average of these studies that 75 per cent forgetting was measured over 24 hours. In all of these studies the list was learned to one perfect trial. The percentage values were derived by dividing the total number of items in the list into the number lost and changing to a percentage. Thus, on the average in these studies, if the subject learned a 12-item list and recalled three of these items after 24 hours, nine items (75 per cent) were forgotten.

The theory of interference as advanced by McGeoch, and so far as I know never seriously challenged, was that during the 24-hour interval subjects learned something outside the laboratory which interfered with the list learned in the laboratory. Most of the materials involved in the investigations cited above were nonsense syllables, and the subjects were college students. While realizing that I am viewing these results in the light of data which Mc-Geoch and others did not have available, it seems to me to be an incredible stretch of an interference hypothesis to hold that this 75 per cent forgetting was caused by something which the subjects learned outside the laboratory during the 24-hour interval. Even if we agree with some educators that much of what we teach our students in college is non-sense, it does not seem to be the kind of learning that would interfere with nonsense syllables.

If, however, this forgetting was not due to interference from tasks learned outside the laboratory during the retention interval, to what was it due? I shall try to show that most of this forgetting was indeed produced by interference—not from tasks learned outside the laboratory, but from tasks learned previously in the laboratory. Following this I will show that when interference from laboratory tasks is removed, the amount of forgetting which occurs is relatively quite small. It then becomes more plausible that this amount could be produced by interference from tasks learned outside the laboratory, although, as I shall also point out, the interference very likely comes from prior, not interpolated, learning.

In 1950 a study was published by Mrs. Greenberg and myself (10) on retention as a function of stage of practice. The orientation for this study was crassly empirical; we simply wanted to know if subjects learn how to recall in the same sense that they learn how to learn. In the conditions with which I am concerned, naive subjects learned a list of ten paired adjectives to a criterion of eight out of ten correct on a single trial. Forty-eight hours later this list was recalled. On the following day, these same subjects learned a new list to the same criterion and recalled it

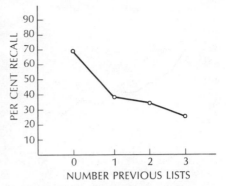

Fig. 1. Recall of paired adjectives as a function of number of previous lists learned (10).

after 48 hours. This continued for two additional lists, so that the subjects had learned and recalled four lists, but the learning and recall of each list was complete before another list was learned. There was low similarity among these lists as far as conventional symptoms of similarity are concerned. No words were repeated and no obvious similarities existed, except for the fact that they were all adjectives and a certain amount of similarity among prefixes, suffixes, and so on must inevitably occur. The recall of these four successive lists is shown in Fig. 1.

As can be seen, the more lists that are learned, the poorer the recall, from 69 per cent recall of the first list to 25 per cent recall of the fourth list. In examining errors at recall, we found a sufficient number of intrusion responses from previous lists to lead us to suggest that the increasing decrements in recall were a function of proactive interference from previous lists. And, while we pointed out that these results had implications for the design of experiments on retention, the relevance to an interference theory of forgetting was not mentioned.

Dr. E. J. Archer has made available to me certain data from an experiment which still is in progress and which deals with this issue. Subjects learned lists of 12 serial adjectives to one perfect trial

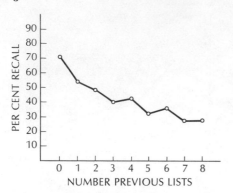

FIG. 2. Recall of serial adjective lists as a function of number of previous lists learned. Unpublished data, courtesy of Dr. E. J. Archer.

and recalled them after 24 hours. The recall of a list always took place prior to learning the next list. The results for nine successive lists are shown in Fig. 2. Let me say again that there is no laboratory activity during the 24-hour interval; the subject learns a list, is dismissed from the laboratory, and returns after 24 hours to recall the list. The percentage of recall falls from 71 per cent for the first list to 27 per cent for the ninth.

In summarizing the more classical data on retention above, I indicated that a rough estimate showed that after 24 hours 75 per cent forgetting took place, or recall was about 25 per cent correct. In viewing these values in the light of Greenberg's and Archer's findings, the conclusion seemed inescapable that the classical studies must have been dealing with subjects who had learned many lists. That is to say, the subjects must have served in many conditions by use of counterbalancing and repeated cycles. To check on this I have made a search of the literature on the studies of retention to see if systematic data could be compiled on this matter. Preliminary work led me to establish certain criteria for inclusion in the summary to be presented. First, because degree of learning is such an important variable, I have

included only those studies in which degree of learning was one perfect recitation of the list. Second, I have included only studies in which retention was measured after 24 hours. Third, I have included only studies in which recall measures were given. (Relearning measures add complexities with which I do not wish to deal in this paper.) Fourth, the summary includes only material learned by relatively massed practice. Finally, if an investigator had two or more conditions which met these criteria, I averaged the values presentation in this paper. Except for these restrictions, I have used all studies I found (with an exception to be noted later), although I do not pretend to have made an exhaustive search. From each of these studies I got two facts: first, the percentage recalled after 24 hours, and second, the average number of previous lists the subjects had learned before learning the list on which recall after 24 hours was taken. Thus, if a subject had served in five experimental conditions via counterbalancing, and had been given two practice lists, the average number of lists learned before learning the list for which I tabulated the recall was four. This does not take into account any previous experiments in rote learning in which the subject might have served.

For each of these studies the two facts, average number of previous lists learned and percentage of recall, are related as in Fig. 3. For example, consider the study by Youtz. This study was concerned with Jost's law, and had several degrees of learning, several lengths of retention interval, and the subjects served in two cycles. Actually, there were 15 experimental conditions and each subject was given each condition twice. Also, each subject learned six practice lists before starting the experimental conditions. Among the 15 conditions was one in which the learn-

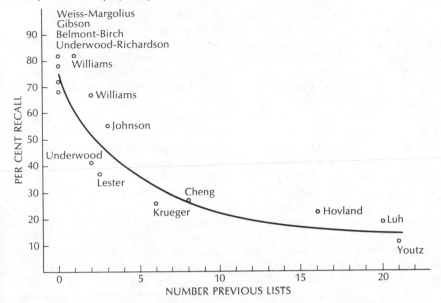

FIG. 3. Recall as a function of number of previous lists learned as determined from a number of studies. From left to right: Weiss and Margolius (35), Gibson (9), Belmont and Birch (3), Underwood and Richardson (33), Williams (36), Underwood (27, 28, 29, 30), Lester (17), Johnson (14), Krueger (16), Cheng (6), Hovland (11), Luh (18), Youtz (37).

ing of the syllables was carried to one perfect recitation and recall was taken after 24 hours. It is this particular condition in which I am interested. On the average, this condition would have been given at the time when the subject had learned six practice lists and 15 experimental lists, for a total of 21 previous lists.

The studies included in Fig. 3 have several different kinds of materials, from geometric forms to nonsense syllables to nouns; they include both paired-associate and serial presentation, with different speeds of presentation and different lengths of lists. But I think the general relationship is clear. The greater the number of previous lists learned the greater the forgetting. I interpret this to mean that the greater the number of previous lists the greater the *proactive*

interference. We know this to be true (26) for a formal proactive-inhibition paradigm; it seems a reasonable interpretation for the data of Fig. 3. That there are minor sources of variance still involved I do not deny. Some of the variation can be rationalized, but that is not the purpose of this report. The point I wish to make is the obvious one of the relationship between number of previous lists learned—lists which presumably had no intentionally built-in similarity—and amount of forgetting. If you like to think in correlational terms, the rank-order correlation between the two variables is −.91 for the 14 points of Fig. 3.

It may be of interest to the historian that, of the studies published before 1942 which met the criteria I imposed, I did not find a single one in which subjects had not been given at least one practice task before starting experimental conditions, and in most cases the subjects had several practice lists and several experimental conditions. Gibson's study (1942) was the first I found in which subjects served in only one condition and were not given practice tasks. I think it is apparent that the design proclivities of the 1920s and 1930s have been largely responsible for the exaggerated picture we have had of the rate of forgetting of rote-learned materials. On the basis of studies performed during the 1920s and 1930s, I have given a rough estimate of forgetting as being 75 per cent over 24 hours, recall being 25 per cent. On the basis of modern studies in which the subject has learned no previous lists—where there is no proactive inhibition from previous laboratory tasks—a rough estimate would be that forgetting is 25 per cent; recall is 75 per cent. The values are reversed. (If in the above and subsequent discussion my use of percentage values as if I were dealing with a cardinal or extensive scale is disturbing, I will say only that it makes the picture easier to grasp, and in my opinion no critical distortion results.)

Before taking the next major step, I would like to point out a few other observations which serve to support my general point that proactive inhibition from laboratory tasks has been the major cause of forgetting in the more classical studies. The first illustration I shall give exemplifies the point that when subjects have served in several conditions forgetting after relatively short periods of time is greater than after 24 hours if the subject has served in only 1 condition. In the Youtz study to which I have already referred, other conditions were employed in which recall was taken after short intervals. After 20 minutes recall was 74 per cent, about what it is after 24 hours if the subject has not served in a series of conditions. After two hours recall was 32 per cent. In Ward's (34) well-known reminiscence experiment, subjects who on the average had learned ten previous lists showed a recall of only 64 per cent after 20 minutes.

In the famous Jenkins-Dallenbach

(13) study on retention following sleep and following waking, two subjects were used. One subject learned a total of 61 lists and the other 62 in addition to several practice lists. Roughly, then, if the order of the conditions was randomized, approximately 30 lists had been learned prior to the learning of a list for a given experimental condition. Recall after eight waking hours for one subject was 4 per cent and for the other 14 per cent. Even after sleeping for eight hours the recall was only 55 per cent and 58 per cent.

I have said that an interpolated list can produce severe forgetting. However, in one study (1), using the A-B, A-C paradigm for original and interpolated learning, but using subjects who had never served in any previous conditions, recall of the original list was 46 per cent after 48 hours, and in another comparable study (24), 42 percent. Thus, the loss is not nearly as great as in the classical studies I have cited where there was no interpolated learning in the laboratory.

My conclusion at this point is that, in terms of the gross analysis I have made, the amount of forgetting which might be attributed to interference from tasks learned outside the laboratory has been "reduced" from 75 per cent to about 25 per cent. I shall proceed in the next section to see if we have grounds for reducing this estimate still more. In passing on to this section, however, let me say that the study of factors which influence proactive inhibition in these counterbalanced studies is a perfectly legitimate and important area of study. I mention this because in the subsequent discussion I am going to deal only with the case where a subject has learned a single list in the laboratory, and I do not want to leave the impression that we should now and forevermore drop the study of interference produced by previous laboratory tasks.

Indeed, as will be seen shortly, it is my opinion that we should increase these studies for the simple reason that the proactive paradigm provides a more realistic one than does the retroactive paradigm.

When the subject learns and recalls a single list in the laboratory, I have given an estimate of 25 per cent as being the amount forgotten over 24 hours. When, as shown above, we calculate percentage forgotten of lists learned to one perfect trial, the assumption is that had the subjects been given an immediate recall trial, the list would have been perfectly recalled. This, of course, is simply not true. The major factor determining how much error is introduced by this criterion-percentage method is probably the difficulty of the task. In general, the overestimation of forgetting by the percentage method will be directly related to the difficulty of the task. Thus, the more slowly the learning approaches a given criterion, the greater the drop on the trial immediately after the criterion trial. Data from a study by Runquist (24), using eight paired adjectives (a comparatively easy task), overestimated by about 10 per cent. In a study (32) using very difficult consonant syllables, the overestimation was approximately 20 per cent. To be conservative, assume that on the average the percentage method of reporting recall overestimates the amount forgotten by 10 per cent. If we subtract this from the 25 per cent assumed above, the forgetting is now re-estimated as being 15 per cent over 24 hours. That is to say, an interference theory, or any other form of theory, has to account for a very small amount of forgetting as compared with the amount traditionally cited.

What are the implications of so greatly "reducing" the amount of forgetting? There are at least three implications which I feel are worth pointing out. First, if one wishes to hold to an interference theory of forgetting (as I do), it seems plausible to assert that this amount of forgetting could be produced from learning which has taken place outside of the laboratory. Furthermore, it seems likely that such interference must result primarily from proactive interference. This seems likely on a simple probability basis. A 20-year-old college student will more likely have learned something during his 20 years prior to coming to the laboratory that will interfere with his retention than he will during the 24 hours between the learning and retention test. However, the longer the retention interval the more important will retroactive interference become relative to proactive interferences.

The second implication is that these data may suggest greater homogeneity or continuity in memorial processes than hitherto supposed. Although no one has adequately solved the measurement problem of how to make comparisons of retention among conditioned responses, prose material, motor tasks, concept learning, and rote-learned tasks, the gross comparisons have indicated that rote-learned tasks were forgotten much more rapidly than these other tasks. But the rote-learning data used for comparison have been those derived with the classical design in which the forgetting over 24 hours is approximately 75 per cent. If we take the revised estimate of 15 per cent, the discrepancies among tasks become considerably less.

The third implication of the revised estimate of rate of forgetting is that the number of variables which appreciably influence rate of forgetting must be sharply limited. While this statement does not inevitably follow from the analyses I have made, the current evidence strongly supports the statement. I want to turn to the final section of this paper which will consist of a review of the influence of some of the variables which are or have been thought to be related to rate of forgetting. In considering these variables, it is well to keep in mind that a variable which produces only a small difference in forgetting is important if one is interested in accounting for the 15 per cent assumed now as the loss over 24 hours. If appropriate for a given variable, I will indicate where it fits into an interference theory, although in no case will I endeavor to handle the details of such a theory.

Time. Passage of time between learning and recall is the critical defining variable for forgetting. Manipulation of this variable provides the basic data for which a theory must account. Previously, our conception of rate of forgetting as a function of time has been tied to the Ebbinghaus curve. If the analysis made earlier is correct, this curve does not give us the basic data we need. In short, we must start all over and derive a retention curve over time when the subjects have learned no previous materials in the laboratory. It is apparent that I expect the fall in this curve over time to be relatively small.

In conjunction with time as an independent variable, we must, in explanations of forgetting, consider why sleep retards the processes responsible for forgetting. My conception, which does not really explain anything, is that since forgetting is largely produced by proactive interference, the amount of time which a subject spends in sleep is simply to be subtracted from the total retention interval when predicting the amount to be forgotten. It is known that proactive interference increases with passage of time (5); sleep, I believe, brings to a standstill whatever these processes are which produce this increase.

Degree of learning. We usually say that the better or stronger the learning the more or better the retention. Yet,

we do not know whether or not the *rate* of forgetting differs for items of different strength. The experimental problem is a difficult one. What we need is to have a subject learn a single association and measure its decline in strength over time. But this is difficult to carry out with verbal material, since almost of necessity we must have the subject learn a series of associations, to make it a reasonable task. And, when a series of associations are learned, complications arise from interaction effects among associations of different strength. Nevertheless, we may expect, on the basis of evidence from a wide variety of studies, that given a constant degree of similarity, the effective interference varies as some function of the strength of associations.

Distribution of practice. It is a fact that distribution of practice during acquisition influences retention of verbal materials. The facts of the case seem to be as follows. If the subject has not learned previous lists in the laboratory, massed practice gives equal or better retention than does distributed practice. If, on the other hand, the subject has learned a number of previous lists, distributed practice will facilitate retention (32). We do not have the theoretical solution to these facts. The point I wish to make here is that whether or not distribution of learning inhibits or facilitates retention depends upon the amount of interference from previous learning. It is reasonable to expect, therefore, that the solution to the problem will come via principles handling interference in general. I might also say that a theoretical solution to this problem will also provide a solution for Jost's laws.

Similarity. Amount of interference from other tasks is closely tied to similarity. This similarity must be conceived of as similarity among materials as such and also situational similarity

(4). When we turn to similarity within a task, the situation is not quite so clear. Empirically and theoretically (8) one would expect that intratask similarity would be a very relevant variable in forgetting. As discussed elsewhere (31), however, variation in intratask similarity almost inevitably leads to variations in intertask similarity. We do know from a recent study (33) that with material of low meaningfulness forgetting is significantly greater with high intralist similarity than with low. While the difference in magnitude is only about 8 per cent, when we are trying to account for a total loss of 15 per cent, this amount becomes a major matter.

Meaningfulness. The belief has long been held that the more meaningful the material the better the retention—the less the forgetting. Osgood (21) has pointed out that if this is true it is difficult for an interference theory to handle. So far as I know, the only direct test of the influence of this variable is a recent study in which retention of syllables of 100 per cent association value was compared with that of zero association value (33). There was no difference in the recall of these syllables. Other less precise evidence would support this finding when comparisons are made among syllables, adjectives, and nouns, as plotted in Fig. 3. However, there is some evidence that materials of very low meaningfulness are forgotten more rapidly than nonsense syllables of zero association value. Consonant syllables, both serial (32) and paired associates (unpublished), show about 50 per cent loss over 24 hours. The study using serial lists was the one mentioned earlier as knowingly omitted from Fig. 3. These syllables, being extremely difficult to learn, allow a correction of about 20 per cent due to criterion overestimation, but even with this much correction the forgetting (30 per cent) is still appreciably more than the estimate we have

made for other materials. To invoke the interference theory to account for this discrepancy means that we must demonstrate how interference from other activities could be greater for these consonant syllables than for nonsense syllables, nouns, adjectives, and other materials. Our best guess at the present time is that the sequences of letters in consonant syllables are contrary to other well-established language habits. That is to say, letter sequences which commonly occur in our language are largely different from those in consonant syllables. As a consequence, not only are these consonant syllables very difficult to learn, but forgetting is accelerated by proactive interference from previously well-learned letter sequences. If subsequent research cannot demonstrate such a source of interference, or if some other source is not specified, an interference theory for this case will be in some trouble.

Affectivity. Another task dimension which has received extensive attention is the affective tone of the material. I would also include here the studies attaching unpleasant experiences to some items experimentally and not to others, and measuring retention of these two sets of items. Freud is to a large extent responsible for these studies, but he cannot be held responsible for the malformed methodology which characterizes so many of them. What can one say by way of summarizing these studies? The only conclusion that I can reach is a statistical one, namely, that the occasional positive result found among the scores of studies is about as frequent as one would expect by sampling error, using the 5 per cent level of confidence. Until a reliable body of facts is established for this variable and associated variables, no theoretical evaluation is possible.

Other variables. As I indicated earlier, I will not make an exhaustive survey of the variables which may influence rate of forgetting. I have limited myself to variables which have been rather extensively investigated, which have immediate relevance to the interference theory, or for which reliable relationships are available. Nevertheless, I would like to mention briefly some of these other variables. There is the matter of *warm-up* before recall; some investigators find that this reduces forgetting (12); others, under as nearly replicated conditions as is possible to obtain, do not (23). Some resolution must be found for these flat contradictions. It seems perfectly reasonable, however, that inadequate set or context differences could reduce recall. Indeed, an interference theory would predict this forgetting if the set or context stimuli are appreciably different from those prevailing at the time of learning. In our laboratory we try to reinstate the learning set by careful instructions, and we simply do not find decrements that might be attributed to inadequate set. For example, in a recent study (33) subjects were given a 24-hour recall of a serial list after learning to one perfect trial. I think we would expect that the first item in the list would suffer the greatest decrement due to inadequate set, yet this item showed only .7 per cent loss. But let it be clear that when we are attempting to account for the 15 per cent loss over 24 hours, we should not overlook any possible source for this loss.

Thus far I have not said anything about forgetting as a function of characteristics of the subject, that is, the personality or intellectual characteristics. As far as I have been able to determine, there is not a single valid study which shows that such variables have an appreciable influence on forgetting. Many studies have shown differences in learning as a function of these variables, but not differences in rate of forgetting.

Surely there must be some such variables. We do know that if subjects are severely insulted, made to feel stupid, or generally led to believe that they have no justification for continued existence on the earth just before they are asked to recall, they will show losses (e.g., 25, 38), but even the influence of this kind of psychological beating is short lived. Somehow I have never felt that such findings need explanation by a theory used to explain the other facts of forgetting.

Concerning the causes of forgetting, let me sum up in a somewhat more dogmatic fashion than is probably justified. One of the assumptions of science is finite causality. Everything cannot influence everything else. To me, the most important implication of the work on forgetting during the last ten years is that this work has markedly *reduced* the number of variables related to forgetting. Correspondingly, I think the theoretical problem has become simpler. It is my belief that we can narrow down the cause of forgetting to interference from previously learned habits, from habits being currently learned, and from habits we have yet to learn. The amount of this interference is primarily a function of similarity and associative strength, the latter being important because it interacts with similarity.

SUMMARY

This paper deals with issues in the forgetting of rote-learned materials. An analysis of the current evidence suggests that the classical Ebbinghaus curve of forgetting is primarily a function of interference from materials learned previously in the laboratory. When this source of interference is removed, forgetting decreases from about 75 per cent over 24 hours to about 25 per cent. This latter figure can be reduced by at least 10 per cent by other methodological considerations, leaving 15 per cent as an estimate of the forgetting over 24 hours. This estimate will vary somewhat as a function of intratask similarity, distributed practice, and with very low meaningful material. But the overall evidence suggests that similarity with other material and situational similarity are by far the most critical factors in forgetting. Such evidence is consonant with a general interference theory, although the details of such a theory were not presented here.

1. Archer, E. J., & Underwood, B. J. Retroactive inhibition of verbal associations as a multiple function of temporal point of interpolation and degree of interpolated learning. *J. esp. Psychol.*, 1951, **42**, 283-90.
2. Bartlett, F. C. *Remembering: a study in experimental and social psychology.* London: Cambridge Univer. Press, 1932.
3. Belmont, L., & Birch, H. G. Re-individualizing the repression hypothesis. *J. abnorm. soc. Psychol.*, 1951, **46**, 226-35.
4. Bilodeau, I. McD., & Schlosberg, H. Similarity in stimulating conditions as a variable in retroactive inhibition. *J. exp. Psychol.*, 1951, **41**, 199-204.
5. Briggs, G. E. Acquisition, extinction, and recovery functions in retroactive inhibition. *J. exp. Psychol.*, 1954, **47**, 285-93.
6. Cheng, N. Y. Retroactive effect and degree of similarity. *J. exp. Psychol.*, 1929, **12**, 444-58.
7. Ebbinghaus, H. *Memory: a contribution to experimental psychology.* (Trans. by H. A. Ruger, and C. E. Bussenius) New York: Bureau of Publications, Teachers College, Columbia Univer., 1913.
8. Gibson, Eleanor J. A systematic application of the concepts of generalization and differentiation to verbal learning. *Psychol. Rev.*, 1940, **47**, 196-229.
9. Gibson, Eleanor J. Intralist generalization as a factor in verbal learning. *J. exp. Psychol.*, 1942, **30**, 185-200.
10. Greenberg, R., & Underwood, B. J. Retention as a function of stage of practice. *J. exp. Psychol.*, 1950, **40**, 452-7.
11. Hovland, C. I. Experimental studies in rote-learning theory. VI. Comparison of retention following learning to same criterion by massed and distributed practice. *J. exp. Psychol.*, 1940, **26**, 568-87.
12. Irion, A. L. The relation of "set" to retention. *Psychol. Rev.*, 1948, **55**, 336-41.
13. Jenkins, J. G., & Dallenbach, K. M. Oblivescence during sleep and waking. *Amer. J. Psychol.*, 1924, **35**, 605-12.
14. Johnson, L. M. The relative effect of a time interval upon learning and retention. *J. exp. Psychol.*, 1939, **24**, 169-79.
15. Katona, G. *Organizing and memorizing: studies in the psychology of learning and teaching.* New York: Columbia Univer. Press, 1940.
16. Krueger, W. C. F. The effect of overlearning on retention. *J. exp. Psychol.*, 1929, **12**, 71-8.

17. Lester, O. P. Mental set in relation to retroactive inhibition. *J. exp. Psychol.*, 1932, **15**, 681-99.
18. Luh, C. W. The conditions of retention. *Psychol. Monogr.*, 1922, **31**, No. 3 (Whole No. 142).
19. McGeoch, J. A. Forgetting and the law of disuse. *Psychol. Rev.*, 1932, **39**, 352-70.
20. McGeoch, J. A. *The psychology of human learning.* New York: Longmans, Green, 1942.
21. Osgood, C. E. *Method and theory in experimental psychology.* New York: Oxford Univer. Press, 1953.
22. Rapaport, D. Emotions and memory. *Psychol. Rev.*, 1943, **50**, 234-43.
23. Rockway, M. R., & Duncan, C. P. Pre-recall warming-up in verbal retention, *J. exp. Psychol*, 1952, **43**, 305-12.
24. Runquist, W. Retention of verbal associations as a function of interference and strength. Unpublished doctor's dissertation, Northwestern Univ., 1956.
25. Russell, W. A. Retention of verbal material as a function of motivating instructions and experimentally-induced failure. *J. exp. Psychol.*, 1952, **43**, 207-16.
26. Underwood, B. J. The effect of successive interpolations on retroactive and proactive inhibition. *Psychol. Monogr.*, 1945, **59**, No. 3 (Whole No. 273).
27. Underwood, B. J. Studies of distributed practice: VII. Learning and retention of serial nonsense lists as a function of intralist similarity. *J. exp. Psychol.*, 1952, **44**, 80-87.
28. Underwood, B. J. Studies of distributed practice: VIII. Learning and retention of paired nonsense syllables as a function of intralist similarity. *J. exp. Psychol.*, 1953, **45**, 133-42.
29. Underwood, B. J. Studies of distributed practice: IX. Learning and retention of paired adjectives as a function of intralist similarity. *J. exp. Psychol.*, 1953, **45**, 143-9.
30. Underwood, B. J. Studies of distributed practice: X. The influence of intralist similarity on learning and retention of serial adjective lists. *J. exp. Psychol.*, 1953, **45**, 253-9.
31. Underwood, B. J. Intralist similarity in verbal learning and retention. *Psychol. Rev.*, 1954, **3**, 1960-66.
32. Underwood, B. J., & Richardson, J. Studies of distributed practice: XIII. Interlist interference and the retention of serial nonsense lists. *J. exp. Psychol.*, 1955, **50**, 39-46.
33. Underwood, B. J., & Richardson, J. The influence of meaningless, intralist similarity, and serial position on retention. *J. exp. Psychol.*, 1956, **52**, 119-26.
34. Ward, L. B. Reminiscence and rote learning. *Psychol. Monogr.*, 1937, **49**, No. 4 (Whole No. 220).
35. Weiss, W., & Margolius, G. The effect of context stimuli on learning and retention. *J. exp. Psychol.*, 1954, **48**, 318-22.
36. Williams, M. The effects of experimentally induced needs upon retention. *J. exp. Psychol.*, 1950, **40**, 139-51.
37. Youtz, Adella C. An experimental evaluation of Jost's laws. *Psychol. Monogr.*, 1941, **53**, No. 1 (Whole No. 238).
38. Zeller, A. F. An experimental analogue of repression: III. The effect of induced failure and success on memory measured by recall. *J. exp. Psychol.*, 1951, **42**, 32-8.

2 / "Fate" of First-List Associations in Transfer Theory

JEAN M. BARNES AND BENTON J. UNDERWOOD, *Northwestern University*

Theorists who attempt to arrive at an accounting of the facts of transfer and retroactive inhibition in verbal materials must inevitably make a decision concerning "what happens" to first-list associations when a second list is learned. The present study was designed to gather data which would make such decisions easier. Two transfer paradigms were used. One of these, A-B, A-C, is normally associated with production of negative transfer. In the other paradigm, A-B, A-B', stimuli are identical with responses highly similar; such an arrangement normally produces positive transfer.

The data from the present study allow an evaluation of three different conceptions concerning the fate of first-list (hereafter called List 1) associations during the learning of the second list (hereinafter called List 2). These three positions will be examined first as they apply to the A-B, A-C paradigm.

1. List 1 associations are unlearned or extinguished during the learning of the second list. While A-B, A-C is more comparable to the operations of counterconditioning than to extinction of conditioned responses, the term extinction will be used here in keeping with past practice. As a theoretical position, the unlearning or extinction hypothesis is associated with Melton and Irwin (1940) who used it to explain certain facts of RI. They suggested that at least part of RI could be accounted for by the loss of associative strength of List 1 responses resulting from extinction. It might also be assumed that negative transfer results from the interference accompanying the extinction process. A rather impressive amount of evidence could be marshalled in support of this extinction hypothesis. For present purposes, however, only an illustration of this evidence will be given. At various points in learning the second list, Briggs (1954) presented the stimuli common to both lists, one at a time, and asked S to give the first of the two re-

sponses which came to mind. The results showed that during the learning of List 2 there is a gradual decrease in frequency of List 1 responses, the curve being not unlike an extinction curve. A phenomenon analogous to spontaneous recovery of the List 1 responses was also found when retention was measured at various intervals of time after List 2 learning. Such evidence appears quite in line with the extinction hypothesis. However, as Briggs points out, a certain amount of ambiguity remains; the extinction curve does not necessarily mean that List 1 associations are extinguished in the sense that they are no longer available for recall. His results may mean only that List 2 associations become stronger than List 1 associations, hence, occur more and more frequently in recall. Such an increase in frequency of List 2 associations must necessarily be accompanied by a decrease in frequency of List 1 associations at recall. The question still remains, therefore, as to whether or not the A-B association is available after A-C is learned and this is one question the present study attempts to answer.

2. The system of associations in List 1 (A-B) remains relatively independent and intact throughout the learning of the associations in List 2 (A-C). This will be referred to as the independence hypothesis. The verbal stimuli are, of course, identical in the A-B, A-C paradigm, but there are other possible differentiating cues e.g., first list vs. second list) which would provide a means of having two independent response systems attached to the same apparent stimulus. Negative transfer could be said to occur in the process of establishing the independent response systems early in learning A-C. Retroactive inhibition could be attributed to loss of differentiation so that response competition occurs.

3. A third possible conception makes use of mediation. Having learned A-B in List 1, S retains this association so that List 2 items are learned with B as the mediator; S learns

From the *Journal of Experimental Psychology*, 1959, **58**, 97–105, with permission of the authors and publisher.

14

A—B—C. Negative transfer and RI could occur as a consequence of confusion on the part of S as to which response is used as the mediator and which response is mediated.

In the present study, different groups of Ss were stopped at various points in learning List 2 and were asked to give *both* List 1 and List 2 responses to each stimulus. If (as degree of List 2 learning increases) there is an increasing inability to give List 1 responses (over and above normal forgetting), the extinction hypothesis would be favored. If there was no such loss either the independence hypothesis or the mediation hypothesis would be favored. Provisions were included in the design to choose between these latter two if it became necessary. For example, if the mediation hypothesis is tenable it should be found that B is given before C more frequently than C before B when S is asked to write down both responses. The independence hypothesis would not predict such an ordering in response recall.

Turning next to the paradigm in which stimuli are identical but responses highly · similar (A-B, A-B′), the present study should again provide bases for choice among the three hypotheses.

1. Because retroactive facilitation is expected with this paradigm (e.g. Young, 1955) it might appear that an extinction hypothesis is not tenable. However, by the use of extinction plus other factors it is possible to account for retroactive facilitation. It is a fact that more List 1 instrusions occur in the learning of List 2 for this paradigm than for the A-B, A-C paradigm. Thus, the non-reinforcement of these responses makes extinction a very plausible mechanism. So, it could be assumed that in learning A-B′, A-B is extinguished. Retroactive facilitation could then be accounted for by mediation. It is known that highly similar items have high associative connection (Haagen, 1949). When S is asked to recall A-B after learning A-B′, even if A-B is extinguished the mediation sequence in recall could be A-B′-B, since there has been no extinction of the strong

association between B′ and B. However, without the addition of still more factors the positive transfer in learning A-B′ cannot be accounted for. Since the results of the present procedures do not make the extinction hypothesis a reasonable one for this paradigm, no attempt will be made here to suggest the additional factors needed to account for the positive transfer produced by this paradigm.

2. The independence hypothesis, used in conjunction with a theory of response generalization (Underwood, 1951), can be employed to account for both positive transfer and retroactive facilitation by the A-B, A-B′ paradigm.

3. The mediation hypothesis also provides an attractive alternative for this positive transfer paradigm. As noted above, items which have high similarity have high associative connection. Thus, having learned A-B, the learning of A-B-B′ should be very simple since B and B′ are already strongly connected. Therefore, positive transfer should occur. In learning List 2, if mediation occurs S will be given additional practice on A-B; hence, this association will be further strengthened during List 2 learning, and retroactive facilitation would be expected to occur.

In summary, two paradigms are used, one associated with the production of negative transfer, the other with production of positive transfer. By requiring S to recall both List 1 and List 2 responses at various points in the learning of List 2, it was expected that choice could be made among three conceptions (extinction, independence, mediation) of the fate of List 1 associations during the learning of List 2.

METHOD

General.—Two parallel experiments were conducted, one using the A-B, A-C transfer paradigm and one using the A-B, A-B′ paradigm. Within each experiment there were four groups of Ss. All Ss learned a first paired-associate list (List 1) of eight pairs to one perfect trial. Then List 2 was presented for a specified number of trials, namely 1, 5, 10, and 20 anticipation trials for the four groups in each experiment. After the specified number of trials for a given group, the memory drum was stopped, S was provided a sheet of paper on which the eight stimuli were printed, and he was asked to write down the two responses (one from the first list and one from the second) which were associated with each stimulus. This written recall provided the major source of data.

Lists.—Eight nonsense syllables of from 60% to 73% association value (Glaze, 1928) were used as stimuli for all lists. Intrastimulus similarity was low in that no consonant was repeated, and four vowels were used twice each. The responses were two-syllable adjectives taken from Haagen (1949). In the A-B, A-C lists there was no apparent interlist response similarity and intralist response similarity was as low as careful inspection procedure will produce. In the A-B, A-B′ lists the responses again had low interlist response similarity and intralist response similarity. The responses from each list which were paired with the same stimulus had similarity ratings ranging from .9 to 1.4 by Haagen's scale. These high-similarity response pairs were as follows: *insane—crazy; barren—fruitless; complete—entire; royal—regal; double—twofold; afraid—scared; tranquil—peaceful; spoken—verbal.* Three different pairings of stimuli and responses were used for both experiments to avoid the possibility that fortuitous associations between stimulus and response would bias the results. An equal number of Ss in each group was given each pairing. For each experiment for each condition a given list was used as List 1 for half the Ss and as List 2 for the other half. Four orders of items were used to minimize serial learning.

The lists were presented on a Hull-type drum at a 2:2-sec. rate. The intertrial interval was 4 sec. Anticipation learning was used for List 1 and for List 2 to the point at which written recall was given (after 1, 5, 10, or 20 anticipation trials). A 1-min. interval separated the learning of the two lists.

Subjects.—A total of 192 Ss was used. There were 24 Ss in each condition for each experiment, the conditions being the point at which S was asked for written recall. All Ss had previously served in at least one verbal-learning experiment. However, no other experiment had been run in which S

was asked to recall responses from both lists, so there is no reason to believe that S anticipated that he would be asked for such recall. It should be emphasized that each S was asked for written recall only once so that it is not believed that Ss made any special attempt to remember List 1 responses. In assigning Ss, a listing of 192 entries was made such that each of the eight conditions occurred 24 times. Within these limits the ordering was random and Ss were successively assigned in order of their appearance at the laboratory.

Written recall.—When the specified number of trials on List 2 had been given, the memory drum was stopped and the sheet for written recall given to S. The stimuli were listed on the sheet with two blank spaces under each. The Ss were first instructed to write down the responses from the two lists below the appropriate stimuli. They were further told to write these down as they came to mind, and not to attempt to recall all the responses from one list first and then all those from the other. Two minutes were then allowed for this initial recall. Following this, they were instructed to go through the responses they had written, and indicate, by assigning the numbers 1 and 2, from which list the responses had come. An additional 2 min. were allowed for this. The Ss were also told to write down any additional responses which they might think of while they were assigning list numbers.

After the recall papers were collected, a series of questions was asked to determine: (a) if S had written the responses as they came to mind or if there was deliberate attempt to recall the adjectives from a given list first, (b) whether or not S had used first-list responses to mediate the learning of the second-list responses.

RESULTS

Transfer.—The major concern in the present paper is with the written recall results. However, it will be worthwhile to note briefly the transfer facts and to show that random assignment of Ss to groups was effective. For all eight groups combined, the mean number of trials to learn List 1 to one perfect trial was 10.36, with the means for groups ranging from 9.17

to 12.00 trials. The F was less than 1. Lacking a precise control for transfer, some indication of the effects can be obtained by comparing the learning of List 1 with that of List 2. The total correct responses for the first three trials of the two lists were used as the response measure for the three groups having 5, 10, and 20 trials on List 2. For the A-B, A-B′ paradigm, more correct responses were given on List 2 than on List 1, indicating positive transfer. For all three groups combined, the mean number correct on the first list was 9.84, and for the second, 14.35. The t was 8.55. For A-B, A-C the mean number correct on the first list was 9.64, and on the second, 8.57. This t was 1.67. This result indicates that in a statistical sense no negative transfer was present, but this is not an unusual finding for this type of comparison since learning-to-learn and warm-up would counteract the negative effect. Finally, in keeping with previous studies (e.g., Underwood, 1951), the number of overt intrusions of List 1 responses during the learning of List 2 was much greater for A-B, A-B′ than for A-B, A-C.

Written recall.—There were several alternative ways by which the written recall could be scored. The most stringent method would be to count a response as correct only if it were placed with the appropriate stimulus and also correctly identified as to list. The most liberal method would be to count an adjective correct if recalled, regardles of whether it was placed with the correct stimulus and correctly identified as to list. The results for both methods are shown in Table 1. An inspection of this table will show that the differences produced by the two scoring methods are relatively small. The implication is that if S wrote down a response, he usually identified it correctly with stimulus and list.

Turning first to the results for the A-B, A-C paradigm, the results for the stringent scoring method have been plotted in

TABLE 1. *Mean number of responses recalled from each list for each transfer paradigm as scored by two methods* [a]

Method	List	Point of Written Recall (Trials)			
		1	5	10	20
Paradigm A-B, A-C					
1	1	6.67	5.38	5.00	4.12
	2	3.46	6.29	7.33	7.38
2	1	6.96	5.58	5.42	4.29
	2	4.12	6.71	7.71	7.42
Paradigm A-B, A-B′					
1	1	7.67	7.21	7.12	6.92
	2	7.21	7.25	7.83	7.79
2	1	7.75	7.33	7.25	7.08
	2	7.38	7.29	7.96	7.83

[a] In Method 1 the response is counted correct only if correctly identified with stimulus and list. In Method 2 it is counted correct if merely recalled.

Fig. 1. As would be expected, as the number of learning trials on List 2 increases, the number of correct responses given from this list increases. Responses from the first or A-B list, however, show a gradual decline as the number of trials on List 2 increases. It is as if the A-B associations are weakened or extinguished during the learning of A-C. The loss as a function of number of A-C trials cannot be attributed to a few Ss losing many responses since most Ss showed the decline. An analysis of variance of the four recall points for A-B gave an F of 8.86 ($F = 4.88$ for $P = .01$ with 3 and 92 df).

It was noted that Fig. 1 suggests that the A-B associations are extinguished. It might be suggested, furthermore, that not only are these associations extinguished, but also that the response per se is not available. This could be deduced from the fact that the two scoring methods did not differ much, implying that if S knew the response, he also knew what stimulus and what list it went with. However, this conclusion cannot be reached with complete confidence. The reason is that the instructions to S stressed the recall of the responses to the

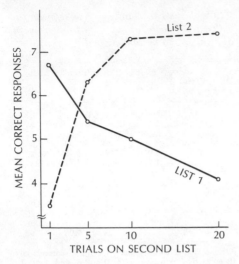

FIG. 1. Mean number of responses correctly recalled and identified with stimulus and list in the A-B, A-C paradigm.

specific stimuli; he was never told to put down a response even if he didn't know with which stimulus it was paired. It is therefore possible that Ss did not put down responses unless they were reasonably confident of its stimulus.

The objection might be raised that the decline in A-B associations seen in Fig. 1 is not to be attributed to the learning of A-C but rather represents simple forgetting. To make sure that this would not be a valid objection, a control group of 12 Ss was run. This group learned List 1 to one perfect trial and then rested for a period of time equivalent to that spent in learning A-C by the group given 20 trials. This period was 13 min. (including the 1 min. between lists). The rest interval was filled with S working on a pyramid puzzle. After the rest, Ss were given a written recall for the responses to the stimuli in the list they had learned. Counting only those responses which were appropriately paired with their stimuli, the mean recall was 7.75. Hence, it can be concluded that the decrement in recall of A-B associations as a function of trials on A-C cannot be attributed

to simple forgetting, but must result from the learning of A-C.

The results for the A-B, A-B' paradigm as given in Table 1 are quite different from those of A-B, A-C. It may first be noted that the recall of List 2 responses (A-B') is nearly perfect after only one anticipation trial and, of course, remains high throughout 20 trials. Indeed, by both scoring methods the median recall for all groups at all points is 8.0 items. The first-list associations (A-B) show no appreciable decline. By the stringent scoring method the mean recall, even after 20 trials on A-B', is nearly seven.

Order of recall.—The facts concerning the order of recall of the two responses can be used as evidence for or against a mediation hypothesis, as this hypothesis was discussed in the introduction. If S tends to recall List 1 responses first, it could be taken as evidence in support of a mediation hypothesis. Contrariwise, it would be evidence against mediation if List 2 responses tend to be recalled first. In this analysis data were not used from 12 Ss who admitted under questioning that they attempted to write down all responses from one list first and then all from the other. Of these, seven had learned A-B, A-C, and five, A-B, A-B'. Obviously, only cases in which both responses were recalled could be used. For A-B, A-B', there were 161, 159, 170, and 162 pairs of responses recalled for 1, 5, 10, and 20 trials, respectively. The corresponding percentages for the List 1 response being recalled before the List 2 response are 79%, 62%, 58%, and 53%. For A-B, A-C, the number of cases where both responses were recalled was 79, 113, 109, and 95 for 1, 5, 10, and 20 trials, respectively. The percentages of List 1 responses recalled first are 81%, 49%, 40%, and 43%. Assuming chance order as 50%, it can be seen that (excepting the conditions where only one trial was given on List 2 and where List 1 would be much stronger than List 2) with A-B, A-C the List 1 responses tend to be recalled first with chance or less than chance frequency. For A-B, A-B' first-list responses are recalled with greater than chance frequency although after 20 trials this frequency has nearly reached 50%.

Subject reports.—Of the 96 Ss who learned the A-B, A-B' paradigm, 94 said they had used the List 1 responses to mediate the learning of List 2. These Ss further reported that they tended to drop the use of these mediators as List 2 learning progressed. Of those 96 Ss who had learned A-B, A-C, only two reported attempts to use the B response to mediate A-C learning; both Ss further reported that this merely confused them.

DISCUSSION

The A-B, A-C paradigm.—Three conceptions of what might "happen" to A-B during the learning of A-C were given in the introduction. These three conceptions were extinction or unlearning, the maintenance of two independent S-R systems, and mediation. The present data give strong support to the conception of extinction and at the same time argue against the other two conceptions. The recall of List 1 associations decreased progressively throughout the learning of A-C with nearly a 50% loss after 20 trials on A-C. A hyperbolic equation fitted to this curve predicts an asymptote at 3.46. Thus, it does not seem that all items would be extinguished, even with an extremely large number of trials on A-C. This conforms to the fact that forgetting in the RI paradigm has not been shown to be complete with very high degrees of interpolated learning. Thus, while the present data strongly support an extinction hypothesis they do not indicate why all items are not, nor are likely not to be, extinguished.

It seems reasonable to reject the independence hypothesis. If this hypothesis is to be retained, some mechanism will have to be added to account for the loss in the A-B associations over and above normal forgetting. If it is said that the A-C associations were so dominant that S was unable to recall the A-B associations, then the conception becomes very similar to an extinction hypothesis.

The mediation hypothesis cannot be seriously considered in light of the evidence. If List 2 responses are learned through mediation of B (A—B—C) the A-B association should not be lost from S's repertoire. If it is said that the mediators drop out, then something like extinction must also be added to account for their loss from S's repertoire. Furthermore, Ss' reports did not indicate that mediation had taken place (as was true of the reports for A-B, A-B'). All in all, the results give strong support to an extinction-like process; they do not give much support to an hypothesis of independence nor one of mediation.

It was noted that if S could recall a response he could usually identify it correctly as to list. On the surface, such evidence seems contrary to conceptions which say that some RI may be attributed to competition resulting from a lack of differentiation as to which response belongs in which list (e.g., Underwood, 1949). However, two additional facts must be noted which are relevant to this matter. First, in the present study essentially unlimited recall time was given so that identification of responses with lists should be more accurate than when recall is paced by a memory drum at a 2-sec. rate. Secondly, this differentiation is assumed to be very high when recall is given immediately after interpolation; differentiation is assumed to decrease as a function of time between interpolated learning and recall (Underwood, 1949). It is quite possible that the high accuracy of identifying responses with lists would be lost even with the present method if, say, a 24-hr. interval occurred between interpolation and written recall. Nevertheless, the present results would strongly suggest that nearly all RI could be accounted for by unlearning or extinction if unlimited recall time is given immediately after interpolated learning. The lack of differentiation, leading to competition between responses, should become an additional component in RI only after the passage of time since interpolated learning. Indeed, in view of the findings suggesting spontaneous recovery of extinguished associations (Briggs, 1954), it can be held that after the recovery is complete, all RI is due to competition. This two-component conception of RI will incorporate the major facts.

The A-B, A-B′ paradigm.—The data for this paradigm have shown that the A-B associations were maintained at a high level throughout the learning of A-B′. The very slight decline noted over 20 trials could be attributed to the extinction of the A-B responses for those cases in which Ss did not know the meaning of a word or words, hence, similarity of the responses was ineffective and the results were the same as an A-B, A-C paradigm. However, while accepting this possibility, it can be omitted from further consideration. The question still remains as to whether it is or is not likely that the A-B associations were extinguished while S learned A-B′ even when similarity was effective. It was noted in the introduction that such an hypothesis was a plausible one; indeed, looking only at the basic results it remains plausible.

The possibility that A-B could be extinguished and the present results still be obtained (no apparent loss in the A-B associations) may be handled by mediation in which after learning A-B′ (and extinguishing A-B), S recalled the B response because of its high associative connection with B′. Thus, when asked to recall, the associations were A to B′ and then B′ to B. If this took place,

A-B could be extinguished and the present basic results would still be obtained. However, other findings argue against this interpretation and tend instead to support mediation in which A leads to B and B leads to B′ at recall.

1. If B is recalled via B′, B′ should be recalled before B. The data indicate that B is more often recalled first. It is true that after 20 trials B and B′ were recalled first about equally often. So, it is still possible that with high degrees of A-B′ learning, some extinction of A-B did occur.

2. Nearly all Ss report using B as a mediator to learn A-B′; none reported that B′ was used as a mediator in the recall of B. However, they did report that the use of B as a mediator tended to drop out as learning of A-B′ proceeded. Some extinction of A-B might have been a concomitant or cause of this drop out. But, the fact that that percentage of times in which A-B was recalled first (before A-B) never drops below 50% suggests that if extinction was occurring it was much less in amount than that which occurred in A-B, A-C.

The conclusion is, therefore, that while the possibility of extinction of A-B in the A-B′ paradigm cannot be completely ruled out, it does not appear as compelling an interpretation as does the mediation hypothesis in which A-B mediates B′.

Finally, what about the hypothesis of independent response systems in which response generalization is used to account for positive transfer and retroactive facilitation? The use of response generalization to explain certain facts of transfer has been of considerable help in organizing the facts of transfer. One particular statement of this formulation can be briefly summarized (Underwood, 1951). It is assumed that when A-B is being learned, all responses similar to B likewise develop some associative strength to A. The amount of such strength, developed through what has been called parasitic reinforcement, is directly related to similarity of the response with the B response. Positive transfer occurs, therefore, because less learning has to occur in the second list than in the first. Thus, in the present situation, if A-B' develops some associative strength as a consequence of learning A-B, positive transfer should occur when S is asked to learn A-B'. Retroactive facilitation would occur, since during the learning of A-B' the A-B association would be further strengthened. It should be noted that this hypothesis deals only with the associations between A and B, and between A and B'; it does not deal in any way with the already well-established association between B and B' which forms a central part of the mediation hypothesis.

The present evidence suggests that the response-generalization accounting of certain facts of transfer may well be abandoned in favor of a mediation hypothesis. The mediation hypothesis will account for the same general facts as will response generalization; furthermore, certain facts of the present experiment seem difficult to reconcile with the response-generalization hypothesis.

1. Almost without exception, Ss report mediation. While it may be possible to extend the theory of response generalization to account for this fact that Ss report mediation, the mediation per se can be used to account for the results, without further elaboration.

2. It was noted that after only one anticipation trial, recall of List 2 was nearly perfect. The theory of response generalization assumes a generalization gradient decreasing rather sharply as similarity decreases. The generalized association is not assumed to grow in associative strength at a rate comparable at all to the directly-reinforced association (A-B). To account for the extraordinarily rapid learning of A-B' would mean that there is essentially no gradient between B and B', or to say this another way, the gradient is flat. In previous experiments, no such rapid learning of A-B' was noted; learning was more rapid than for a control condition but nothing like

that shown here in the written recall. Indeed, in the present study for the groups having 5, 10, and 20 trials (before written recall), the mean number of items recalled on the second anticipation trial (comparable to the point at which written recall was asked for in the group having only 1 anticipation trial) was 5.04. This is to be contrasted with 7.75, obtained on written recall at the same point. The reason for this discrepancy, it is believed, is that under the standard procedures of anticipation learning S does not have time to mediate all items. Given more time, recall is nearly perfect right at the start of "learning" the second list. This finding is not compatible with the theory of response generalization.

The conclusion is that mediation of B' through A-B is a more appropriate formulation than response generalization to account for positive effects in transfer and retention when response similarity is involved with identical stimuli. As similarity between responses decreases, the associative connection between them will likewise decrease; thus, a gradient-like phenomenon will appear in transfer. With moderate similarity between responses, the associative connection between the two will be less than in the present case, and additional strengthening of the associative connection will be necessary before mediation is completely effective. Thus, positive transfer will be less than when the responses are highly similar. It is apparent that since no evidence for mediation could be found in A-B, A-C, the mediation hypothesis must be abandoned when the responses reach a certain level of dissimilarity (or a low level of similarity). It is at this point that extinction begins to occur with consequent negative transfer.

SUMMARY

The A-B, A-C and the A-B, A-B' transfer paradigms were studied in order to evaluate three conceptions concerning the fate of first-list associations in learning a second list; namely: extinction of first-list associations, maintenance of two independent S-R systems, and mediation of the learning of the second-list response by the first-list association. For each paradigm, different groups of 24 Ss each were stopped after 1, 5, 10, or 20 anticipation trials on List 2 and were asked to write down *both* List 1 and List 2 responses to the stimuli. Both lists contained eight pairs of nonsense syllables and two-syllable adjectives. List 1 learning was carried to one perfect trial.

For the A-B, A-C paradigm there was a gradual reduction in reproduction of List 1 responses as degree of List 2 learning increased. A control condition showed that this reduction could not be accounted for by normal forgetting. No successful mediation of the C response via A-B was reported. It was concluded that of the three alternative conceptions, extinction of the List 1 responses was clearly to be preferred. It appears that nearly all retroactive inhibition measured immediately after interpolated learning may be due to extinction or unlearning of first-list responses during the learning of the second list.

For the A-B, A-B' paradigm, the List 1 responses showed no appreciable loss over 20 trials and List 2 was given nearly perfectly after one anticipation trial. Of 96 Ss, 94 reported the use of the A-B association to mediate the B' response. The rapid learning

of List 2 is understandable by the mediation hypothesis, but some extinction of the A-B association in the A-B, A-B' paradigm cannot be ruled out completely by the present data. The A-B association may be extinguished and then mediation of the List 1 response occurs via A-B'-B. However, considering all evidence, it seemed most probable that mediation occurs most frequently in the order A-B-B'. Finally, the evidence suggests that transfer effects produced by variation in response similarity can be more simply accounted for by mediation than by a theory using response generalization.

BRIGGS, G. E. Acquisition, extinction, and recovery functions in retroactive inhibition. *J. exp. Psychol.*, 1954, **47**, 285-93.
GLAZE, J. A. The association value of nonsense syllables. *J. genet. Psychol.*, 1928, **35**, 255-69.
HAAGEN, C. H. Synonymity, vividness, familiarity, and association-value ratings for 400 pairs of common adjectives. *J. Psychol.*, 1949, **30**, 185-200.
MELTON, A. W., & IRWIN, J. McQ. The influence of degree of interpolated learning on retroactive inhibition and the overt transfer of specific responses. *Amer. J. Psychol.*, 1940, **53**, 175-203.
UNDERWOOD, B. J. Proactive inhibition as a function of time and degree of prior learning. *J. exp. Psychol.*, 1949, **39**, 24-34.
UNDERWOOD, B. J. Associative transfer in verbal learning as a function of response similarity and degree of first-list learning. *J. exp. Psychol.*, 1951, **42**, 44-53.
YOUNG, R. K. Retroactive and proactive effects under varying conditions of response similarity. *J. exp. Psychol.*, 1955, **50**, 113-19.

3 / Extraexperimental Sources of Interference in Forgetting [1]

BENTON J. UNDERWOOD, *Northwestern University*
AND LEO POSTMAN, *University of California*

This paper deals with sources of interference as related to the retention of serial verbal lists. More particularly, it is concerned with extraexperimental sources of interference. The presentation involves three steps: (a) the background facts and thinking which led to a conception of how extraexperimental sources of interference may influence retention; (b) the reporting of an experiment designed to evaluate certain implications of the conception; and (c) a reexamination

of the conception in light of the experimental evidence.

BACKGROUND

We will start with the premise that interference is a major cause of forgetting. The facts of retroactive and proactive inhibition show that much forgetting can be produced by having subjects learn lists which, due to specifiable

From the *Psychological Review*, 1960, **67**, 73-95, with permission of the authors and publisher.

similarity, will interfere directly with the recall and relearning of another list. But we also know that forgetting of verbal lists will be produced by other lists not designed to be particularly similar, and that the amount of such forgetting is directly related to the number of lists learned prior to the learning of the list to be recalled (Underwood, 1957a). From such facts it would seem that a reasonable empirical extension could be made to cover forgetting where no formal interfering tasks are used. That is to say, it does not seem an overgeneralization to suggest that forgetting which occurs without the presence of a formal interfering task might be due to extraexperimental sources of interference. These interferences may arise as a consequence of new learning which occurs during the retention interval (thus simulating retroactive inhibition), or they may occur as a consequence of learning which had occurred prior to the learning of the task to be recalled (proactive inhibition). This latter case requires further discussion.

How can habits learned previously (a month, a year, or 10 years ago) interfere with the retention of a task being learned at the present time? Two assertions seem necessary to make this situation comprehensible. First, it must be assumed that the verbal habits being learned at the present time require the breaking, extinction, unlearning, or inhibition of previously acquired habits. Secondly, the evidence indicates (e.g., Briggs, 1954) that extinguished verbal habits show at least a relative recovery (i.e., relative to the associations of the task to be recalled) in strength with the passage of time, and that this recovery may occur without the performance of these habits. Of course, if Habit A is extinguished in learning Habit B, and then if A is practiced again before a retention test for B is given, the recovery of A would be facilitated and the interference with B should be maximal. How-

ever, as noted, it appears that at least a relative recovery of an extinguished verbal habit will occur when it is not practiced By such mechanisms, forgetting due to sources of interference established prior to the learning of a task to be recalled can be accounted for.

It is apparent that if the above argument is allowed to remain as is, a clear gap is present. For we assert that the evidence from the formal proactive and retroactive operations leads to an interference conception of forgetting which in turn leads to the assertion that when *no* formal interfering task is given the forgetting observed must be due to extraexperimental sources of interference As plausible as this argument may seem, it is apparent that it would be highly desirable to specify possible sources of extraexperimental interference, and to specify these in such a way that experimental tests of their influence on forgetting are possible. We will suggest two such sources.

Letter-sequence interference

One source of interference is believed to come from well-established letter-sequence habits. By well-established letter-sequence habits we simply mean habits that are developed through the normal course of learning the language. It may be thought of as producing intra-unit interference or between-letter interference. As an extreme illustration, a low-association value consonant syllable such as JQB may be considered. If this syllable were in a list which the subject has to learn, it is assumed that: (a) Previously learned letter-sequence habits will make this particular sequence difficult to learn since the previously established habits will have to be extinguished. For example, Q never follows J in the language, but all the vowels do. These habits, we presume, must be extinguished or inhibited before the syllable can be learned. (b) With the passage of time following learning of the syllable, these older habits will recover and interfere at the time of the retention test. In addition, it is quite likely that the previously established letter habits will be used during the retention interval to augment the interference resulting from recovery.

If letter-sequence habits produce interference, the magnitude of this interference will decrease as the letter sequences more and more approximate the most frequent sequences in the language. Thus, we may conceive of a gradient of interference which diminishes in amount as the letter sequences whose retention is being tested come more and more in correspondence with those most frequently used in the language. When the letter sequences make up a very frequently used word, or even a frequently used sequence not forming a word (e.g., SOM), we would predict little among-letter interference either during learning or at recall. In Mandler's (1954) terminology, such sequences are said to be well integrated. To state the supposed relationship using this term it would be said that the greater the degree of integration of a verbal unit the less will that unit suffer from interference from previously established letter-sequence habits.

Unit-sequence interference

The second potential source of interference will be referred to as unit-sequence interference. By the *unit* we mean a word or sequence of letters appearing in a list as an independent unit. Each syllable in a list of nonsense syllables is a unit, as is each word in a list of words. The interference we are referring to, then, is the interference falling on sequential associations between units. Conceptually, it may be thought of initially in exactly the same way as the interference between letters within a unit. As an illustration, assume that the word *over* is a unit in a serial list. Assume further that, due to long existing language habits, there is a strong tendency for the *over* to elicit *there*. We presume that this association will have to be extinguished before a new association can be established, but that with the passage of time the original association will recover to interfere with retention. In addition, since the sequence *over-there* will probably occur (be said, or heard) during a retention interval, the recovery process of the interfering association will be augmented by its use.

While the above unit-sequence interference is believed to be reasonable, it would appear that a further source of such interference would occur if the units have pre-experimental associations are in the list being learned. To continue the above example, if both *over* and *there* were units in a serial list, but were not in adjacent serial positions, the strong association between them should interfere with whatever associations are required by the order of the items.

Generally speaking, the more frequently a word occurs in the language, the greater is the number of words with which it is associatively connected. This fact can be obtained directly from the production method of scaling meaningfulness (e.g., Noble, 1952). This means that if high-frequency words are used in a serial list, there will be a large number of pre-experimental associations existing among the items, many of which will have to be extinguished in order for the subject to achieve the particular order of items required by the experimenter. It would be expected, therefore, that the recovery of these pre-experimental associations over a retention interval would result in considerable interference at the time of the retention test. Thus, the unit-sequence conception of interference allows the derivation of a second gradient of interference from extraexperimental sources, with maximum interference being present with high-frequency words, and decreasing as the frequency of use of the units in the language decreases. It should be noted parenthetically that this assumed source of interference may actually facilitate retention under certain conditions. For example, such interitem associations should facilitate retention if the subject is *not* required to learn the items in any particular order and is *not* required to recall them in any particular order (Deese, 1959).

The operation of the two gradients of interference may now be summarized. The letter-sequence interference gradient will be at a maximum when the pre-experimental associative strength between letters is low. The amount of such interference will decrease as the pre-experimental associative connection between letters increases. When the associative connection between letters becomes of a strength found among letters in low-frequency words, another gradient, the unit-sequence gradient, begins to emerge. The amount of interference expected from this gradient continues to increase up to the point where very high-frequency words are present. Roughly speaking, this entire dimension, incorporating both gradients, can be thought of in terms of the classical dimension of meaningfulness. The letter-sequence interference gradient is maximal with low meaningfulness, the unit-sequence interference gradient maximal with high meaningfulness. Both decrease toward intermediate degrees of meaningfulness. The problem of the extent of the gradients, and the degree of overlap, we leave to a later section.

Do available data give support to the above conception? It should be noted that adequate tests of the hypothesis require careful selection of material. But, in addition, two procedural criteria must be adhered to. First, since the conception is concerned with extraexperimental interference, the subjects used must not have learned material in the laboratory which might interfere. Essentially, this means the use of subjects completely naive to verbal-learning experiments. The second criterion which must be met is that degree of learning before the retention interval must be properly assessed for the different materials. Differences in rate of learning might well be expected if materials of different difficulty (via meaningfulness) are involved. Since retention is a function of degree of original learning, and since rate of learning and strength at end of learning are related, whatever method is used must show that differences which occur in retention cannot be attributed to differences in degree of original learning.

Not many available studies meet the above requirements. But, even those that do, do not give much encouragement to the assumed operation of the two gradients. Two studies (Postman & Rau, 1957; Underwood & Richardson, 1956) indicate that within the range of meaningfulness of Glaze nonsense syllables, there is little difference in retention. Furthermore, in the Postman-Rau experiment, words (as scaled by Noble, 1952) differed only little from nonsense syllables. In short, these studies would give no support to either of the proposed gradients. Yet, for a number of reasons, these studies may not be appropriate tests. Primarily, these reasons center around materials and length of retention interval. We believe that the plausibility of such interference gradients is high enough to warrant a specific test in which materials are chosen in a fashion to maximize the effects of the gradients. In the present study, we propose to explore the full range of the unit-sequence gradient and, as it turns out, a part of the letter-sequence gradient.

METHOD

The lists

Two 12-unit serial lists were constructed of very high-frequency items. One of these lists consisted of three-letter words, the other of trigrams (three-letter units not forming words). The supposition was that the high-frequency words would have associative connections with other words in the list as well as with words not in the list. Thus, this list, according to the conception outlined above, would be subject to high interference from the unit-sequence gradient. The trigram list, on the other hand, would have relatively few associative connections with other units in the list or with units outside the list. However, both lists of items, because of their high frequency, should represent well-integrated letter sequences and thus be subject to minimal interference from the letter-sequence gradient. For these two lists the prediction is clear: the high-trigram list will be better retained than the high-word list.

To sample at another point on the unit-sequence gradient, two additional lists were constructed. Again, one of these consisted of three-letter words and the other of three-letter trigrams, but the frequency of occurrence in the language of the units in both lists was low. We did not in fact have a clear prediction concerning the retention of these lists simply because we did not have evidence concerning how far the letter-sequence gradient extends in an upward direction, nor how far the unit-sequence gradient extends in a downward direction along the meaningfulness scale. If the low-frequency trigrams are more subject to letter-sequence interference than the low-frequency words, and if the low-frequency words are but little subject to interference from the unit-sequence gradient, clearly the words should be better retained. But, it is also quite possible that the low-frequency words may be subject to interletter interference. Because of these unknowns, no specific prediction is made concerning the retention of these lists of low-frequency items. Rather, they were used in the hope that the results would give an indication about the likelihood of the gradients and, perhaps, their extent.

The four lists used are shown below. The lists are identified by frequency of items (Hi or Lo) and whether the units are trigrams (T) or words (W).

The words in List Hi-W are classified AA in the Thorndike-Lorge (1944) general count. The words in List Lo-W have a mean frequency of 2.75 per million in the same count. The Hi-T List consists of units whose average frequency in printed text is approximately the same as the frequency of the units in the Hi-W List when the frequency of the latter is counted both as to their occurrence as words and as parts of longer words. The same relationship holds for Lists Lo-W and Lo-T. The manner in which these frequencies were derived will be detailed in a forthcoming publication. However, one available source (Pratt, 1939) gives a rough approximation of the relative frequencies involved.

The choice of particular items for the lists was governed by two criteria in addition to frequency. The first dealt with formal intralist similarity, i.e., number of duplicated letters. By the nature of the materials involved we found it difficult to get an exact equation on this variable. The two high-frequency lists had a somewhat greater repetition of letters than did the low-frequency lists. The number of different letters used was 18, 17, 15, and 13,

List Hi-W	List Hi-T	List Lo-W	List Lo-T
AGE	ATI	ADO	ARP
END	EST	COB	COF
HIM	HAN	DOE	DOP
NOT	NES	DUN	DUR
OLD	OME	EFT	ERF
OUR	OUN	FAD	FUM
RAN	RON	HIE	HEO
SHE	SHO	HOD	HOK
TEN	TES	LAX	LAK
USE	UND	RUT	RHA
WAS	WER	SAC	SIL
WIN	WHI	WRY	WYE

for Lo-W, Lo-T, Hi-W, and Hi-T, respectively. The number of duplicated letters in each position was approximately the same for all lists. The higher repetition rate for the high-frequency list (as compared with low) occurred as a consequence of greater repetition of letters between first and second and between second and third positions.

The second criterion imposed in choosing items was that each be reasonably pronounceable. There was no attempt to equate lists on this variable; rather, the attempt was made to select items which were fairly easy to pronounce as opposed to items very difficult to pronounce.

During the course of running the experiment, other evidence suggested that pronunciability and rate of learning were positively related. Therefore, all 48 items were rated for pronunciability along a 5-point scale by 95 Ss, none of whom served in the learning experiment. The Ss were asked to rate the ease or difficulty of pronouncing each item relative to all the others, with a value of 1 representing the greatest ease, and 5 the greatest difficulty. The mean values for the four lists were 2.02, 2.74, 2.31, and 2.77, for Hi-W, Hi-T, Lo-W, and Lo-T, respectively. As will be seen, these ratings have some predictive value for learning.

One other characteristic of the units used has been obtained. In handling the results the term *wordness* will be used to identify *lists* made up of words vs. lists made up of trigrams. A unit was considered a word if it appeared among the 20,000 most frequently used words in the Thorndike-Lorge (1944) list. Now in fact, not all words were identified as such by Ss nor were all trigrams identified as *not* being words. Following relearning, each S was given a sheet on which all 24 trigrams and the 12 words from List Lo-W appeared in random order. The S was instructed to check each one which he thought was a word. Not a single word in List Lo-W was checked by all Ss ($N = 144$) as being words. The mean percent checking each word was 61%. The word FAD was checked by 98.6% of the Ss. At the other extreme, EFT was checked by 2.8%. Other relatively low percents were ADO, 41.0%, DUN, 39.6%, and HIE, 23.6%.

For List Lo-T every unit was checked by at least one S as being a word. The mean percent checking each unit was 5.7%. Those most frequently checked were FUM (13.9%), SIL (13.9%), and WYE (19.4%). For List Hi-T, on the other hand, four units were not checked by any subject. Omitting one unit from consideration, the mean percent checked was 1.0%. The one unit which was atypical was RON, which 68.1% of the Ss checked as being a word. Thus, these data are fairly clear in indicating that the high-frequency trigrams used are less likely to appear to be words than are the low-frequency trigrams.

For the learning and retention tests the lists were presented in constant serial order at a 2-sec. rate. The anticipatory cue for the first unit was a single asterisk. Two blank spaces came between the last unit in the list and the asterisk so that the inertial interval was 4 sec.

To avoid having the results tied to a particular serial order, six different orders were used. The rules used in constructing the orders were: (a) no unit appeared in the same serial position in different orders; (b) no two units appeared contiguously in more than one order; and (c) in none of the orders did adjacent units start with the same letter.

Subjects and procedure

A total of 144 Ss, all college students, were used in the experiment, being assigned to one of eight groups of 18 Ss each. With a few exceptions, all Ss were naive to verbal-learning experiments. A few Ss (estimated at 5% of the total) had previously served in a verbal-learning experiment, but in all cases this had occurred at least 12 months prior to their present service.

Two groups were assigned to each list. For one group for each list, retention was measured 30 sec. following original learning; for the other, retention was measured 1 week following original learning. All Ss in the 30-sec. groups also returned for a retention test after 1 week, but, of course, these retention data do not enter into the analysis. The original learning was carried to one perfect recitation for all groups for all lists.

The use of the 30-sec. retention interval provides a base for measuring forgetting over the week interval. If there are differences in rate of learning among the four lists, or if there are differences in the postcriterial drop (for any reason), the 30-sec. retention test provides a measure of degree of learning taken immediately after learning under conditions exactly comparable to the measurements made at 1 week. On both retention tests, relearning was carried to one perfect recitation or for five trials if the criterion was reached in less than five trials.

Instructions common to serial learning experiments were used with one exception. The Ss both spelled and pronounced the units in making anticipations. The spelling always preceded pronunciation and E did not score the anticipation wrong if the pronunciation was late, i.e., if it occurred after the end of the 2-sec. anticipation interval.

In assigning the Ss to lists, 18 blocks of eight entries each were used. Within each block, each list occurred twice, once as a 30-sec. retention condition, and once as a 1-week condition. Within the block the order was random. Each of the 6 orders used for each list was assigned to 3 Ss, this assignment being made on a random basis for the 18 Ss given a particular list and a particular retention interval.

The loss of Ss in the experiment was relatively heavy. Indeed, 206 Ss were run through at least part of the procedures in order to obtain 144 "good" Ss. Two Ss were lost for failure to learn, one of these

The final cause for loss of Ss was rehearsal during the 1-week retention interval. In an attempt to mask the possibility that retention would be measured after 1 week, two additional tasks were inserted after original learning. One task consisted of a 5-min. test on number series progressions, and the other consisted of 3 min. of work on a simple card trick. Before S left the experimental room he or she was informed that 1 week later they would be measured on additional tasks. After S had relearned the list after 1 week, a nonpunitive interview was conducted concerning rehearsal during the week interval. If S had practiced the list more than three times orally, the records were not used in the final results. If the S had written down the items once, the records were not used. A total of 16 Ss were rejected for such rehearsal. These were distributed as follows: Hi-W, 2; Hi-T, 4; Lo-W, 3; and Lo-T, 7.

Whenever an S was lost for any of the above reasons, the next S to appear was assigned to the list and retention interval of the S who was lost.

RESULTS

Speed of learning

Table 1 shows the mean numbers of trials to criterion for the four lists. Since

TABLE 1. *Trials to Criterion and Distribution of Overt Errors in Original Learnings*

List	Trials to Criterion		Overt Errors per Trial		Mean Per Cent of		
	Mean	SD	Mean	SD	Intralist Errors	Other Errors	Partial Responses
Hi-W	29.97	10.72	1.29	.57	81.8	1.9	16.3
Hi-T	31.53	11.10	1.21	.62	68.4	12.0	19.6
Lo-W	29.50	8.74	1.23	.63	70.4	9.4	20.2
Lo-T	36.94	12.39	1.26	.57	50.7	25.9	23.4

for failure to learn the Hi-T List, one for failure to learn the Lo-W List. Forty-four Ss were lost for miscellaneous reasons, e.g., not following instructions, failure to return for retention test, illness in the case of E, etc. The 44 Ss were divided among the conditions as follows: Hi-W, 30 sec., 3; Hi-W, 1 wk., 5; Hi-T, 30 sec., 5; Hi-T, 1 wk., 7; Lo-W, 30 sec., 5; Lo-W, 1 wk., 6; Lo-T, 30 sec., 4; Lo-T, 1 wk., 9.

there were no significant differences between the groups tested after 30 sec. and after one week, the results of the two samples were combined, and each of the means in Table 1 is based on 36 Ss. In spite of the diversity of the materials the variations in speed of learning are not extensive. Regardless of frequency, words are learned faster than trigrams

$(F=6.06$, 1 and 140 df, $.01<P<.02)$. Words of high and low frequency are learned at about the same rate. The Hi-T List has an advantage over the Lo-T List. Neither frequency nor the interaction of frequency with wordness (words vs. nonwords) is, however, significant. Two facts are worthy of emphasis. First, frequency of letter sequences in and of itself has only limited effects on speed of acquisition. Secondly, wordness overrides whatever effects of frequency are present. The rapid acquisition of the Lo-W List clearly supports these conclusions.

Speed of learning as a function of pronunciability

Why does wordness, regardless of the frequency of letter sequences, favor acquisition? Our results suggest that it is not the frequency of the letter sequences but the frequency with which the items occur as integral units in the language which determines speed of acquisition. The fact that the Lo-W List is learned more rapidly than either the Hi-T List or the Lo-T List is consistent with this interpretation. The same argument would, however, also lead us to expect a large difference between the Hi-W List and the Lo-W List. The items in the Hi-W List, which are among the most common words in the English language, certainly occur as units with vastly greater frequency than the items in the Lo-W Lists (which Ss often fail to recognize as words). The contradiction is removed if we assume that in the learning of the Hi-W List the beneficial effects of frequency of occurrence were masked by interference from pre-experimental associations. We dislike to deal with theoretical mechanisms which oppose and perhaps balance each other in the learning process. Yet, at the same time, it is apparent that we must necessarily cope with this situation when the data demand

it. A stage analysis (to be presented later) indicates that the items in Hi-W were more available than items in Lo-W, but the error analysis (also to be presented later) indicates that intralist unit interference was greater for Hi-W than for Lo-W. That we believe that these two opposing mechanisms were in balance in the present Hi-W list does not mean that such will inevitably be the case. That is, if a list were constructed in which the items were of the same frequency as those in the present Hi-W, but in which interunit associations were more numerous and stronger, we would clearly predict slower learning for such a list than for the present Hi-W.

The hypothesis that it is the frequency of occurrence of the units rather than of the letter sequences which is the critical variable in acquisition also receives support from an analysis of the relationship between pronunciability and speed of learning. Letter sequences which occur as integral units in the language are likely to be easier to pronounce than trigrams which occur as parts of other words. As we have seen, the lists of words were on the average rated as easier to pronounce than the lists of trigrams, and words were learned faster than trigrams. To establish a systematic relationship between pronunciability and speed of learning it is necessary to show, however, that the correspondence holds for individual items as well as lists. For this purpose, the 48 items included in the experimental lists were arranged in the order of their mean pronunciability ratings without regard to list membership. The total number of correct anticipations during learning was used to measure ease of acquisition for each item. To make these measures comparable across lists, the anticipation score of each item was expressed as a deviation, in *SD* units, from the mean anticipation score of all the items in a given list. Since there were only six orders per list, these

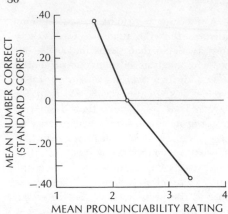

FIG. 1. Number of correct responses during learning (standard scores) for three groups of 16 items arranged in order of decreasing pronunciability.

standard scores are not entirely balanced for the effects of serial position. The resulting bias can be minimized, however, by a grouping of items. Figure 1 shows the relationship between pronunciability and ease of learning when the distribution of pronunciability ratings is divided into successive thirds. It is clear that the direct relationship found with total lists holds for individual items when list membership is ignored. The strength of this relationship is assessed by the coefficient of correlation between pronunciability ratings and anticipation scores. The correlation for individual items, which takes no account of serial-position biases, is .28 ($.02 < P < .05$). When the bias is reduced by computing the correlation for successive pairs of items arranged in order of pronunciability the value of r becomes .46 ($.01 < P < .02$). We conclude that (a) speed of learning is a function of pronunciability, and (b) the association between wordness and ease of pronunciation is one of the factors responsible for the observed differences in speed of learning.

Errors during learning

The mean numbers of overt errors per trial are presented in Table 1. Overt errors include intralist errors (correct units given in an incorrect position), three-letter responses not in the list ("other errors"), and partial responses. The rate of overt erors is virtually identical for the four lists. While the over-all error rate is the same, the relative frequencies of the different kinds of errors vary from list to list. The percentage which each kind of error was of the total errors was determined for each S, and the means of these percentages are shown in Table 1. The relative frequency of intralist errors is greatest for the Hi-W List and smallest for the Lo-T List, with the Hi-T and Lo-W Lists yielding intermediate values. Thus, the percentage of intralist errors is a function of both frequency and wordness. The rank order of the conditions suggests that the rate of intralist errors varies with the availability of the items as response units. Availability of the responses is also an essential condition of anticipation learning. To the extent that both correct anticipations and intralist errors depend on response availability, speed of learning and percentage of intralist errors should be positively related. Such a positive relationship does, in fact, obtain when words and trigrams are compared. The same pattern holds for the two lists of trigrams but not for the two lists of words. One possible interpretation is that when a serial list is composed of items from S's linguistic repertoire, the relative frequency of intralist errors will reflect not only the availability of the responses but also interferences from pre-experimental associations which compete with the prescribed responses. Thus, the items in the Hi-W List are not only the most available responses but also the most likely to be linked through pre-experimental learning. As a result, the percentage of intralist errors is higher for the Hi-W List than the Lo-W List but there is no corresponding difference in speed of learning.

The percentages of three-letter responses not in the list vary *inversely* with both frequency and wordness. Such errors hardly ever occur during the learning of the Hi-W List but constitute a substantial proportion of the errors made by Ss learning the Lo-T List, with the Lo-W and Hi-T Lists again yielding intermediate values. The rare cases which occurred during the learning of the Hi-W List could readily be identified as instances of response generalization (HER replacing SHE, HIS replacing HIM, etc.) or transpositions of letters during the spelling of a word. Many of the errors made during the learning of the other three lists, on the other hand, pointed to persistent difficulties of response integration. Occasionally four-letter responses were given, especially on the early trials of learning. If these errors are taken as evidence for interference from Ss' letter-sequence habits, the large difference between the Hi-T List and the Lo-T List readily falls into place. Response integration is also a source of some difficulty in the learning of the Lo-W List but the use of easily pronounceable units appears to make the problem much less severe than for the Lo-T List.

Partial responses may include slow correct responses as well as incomplete errors. Since a given letter could be correct in more than one position, a precise classification and interpretation of partial responses are not possible.

Stages of acquisition. Learning cannot occur unless the appropriate responses are available to S. At the same time, however, the probability of intralist errors may increase with response availability. In accounting for the correlation between the rate of correct responses and misplaced responses it is useful to make an analytic distinction between two successive stages of learning (Underwood, Runquist, & Schulz, 1959). The first stage is one of response integration during which the items in

the list becomes available to S as responses. If the items are not already in S's repertoire the prescribed letter sequences must be acquired during that stage. The greater the positive transfer from S's pre-experimental habits the shorter will be the stage of response integration. The trial on which a response is first given, whether in the correct or incorrect position, may be used to measure the speed of response integration. The second stage is an associative one in which the response is connected with the appropriate stimulus, e.g., in serial learning to the preceding item. The number of trials separating the first occurrence of the response anywhere in the list from its first occurrence in its correct position provides a measure of the difficulty of the associative stage. While the distinction is useful for analytic purposes, it is recognized that both stages are likely to proceed concurrently: associative connections begin to be built up during the integrative stage, and response integration continues during the associative stage.

The correlation between correct responses and intralist errors suggests that the lengths of the two stages need not necessarily be related. Figure 2 does, in fact, reveal such a lack of relationship. In that figure, we have shown for the four sets of material the mean trial on which responses were first given in any position and the mean trial on which they were first given in the correct position. There are substantial differences in the speed with which different kinds of responses become available. Words are given earlier than trigrams, and within each of these two classes high-frequency items are given more rapidly than low-frequency items. There are no comparable differences in the length of the associative stage. The time which elapses between the first appearance of a response and its first correct placement is roughly equal for all materials. The difference

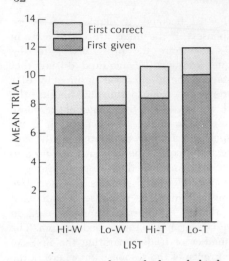

FIG. 2. Mean trial on which each kind of item was first given and mean trial of first correct anticipation.

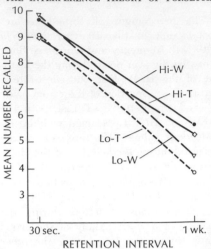

FIG. 3. Mean numbers of correct responses on first trial of relearning.

between the two measures is, in fact, smallest for the Lo-T List where response integration is believed to proceed most slowly. This pattern is fully consistent with the relationships found in the analysis of the errors.

Recall. The mean numbers of items anticipated correctly on the first trial of relearning are shown in Figure 3. The results of the 30-sec. test show clearly that attainment of a fixed criterion does not imply constant associative strength, and that the magnitude of the postcriterial drop must be taken into account in assessing long-term retention loss (Underwood, 1954). In agreement with the assumption that associative strength at criterion varies directly with rate of acquisition, immediate recall is higher for the two lists of words than for the two lists of trigrams. The correspondence between rate of acquisition and immediate recall also holds for the two lists of words: equal rates of acquisition are followed by equal amounts of recall after 30 sec. Comparison of the two lists of trigrams, however, reveals a discrepancy. Although the Hi-T List was learned faster than the Lo-T List, the amounts recalled

are virtually identical. This finding suggests that for the Hi-T List one perfect recitation represents a less stable criterion of performance than for the other lists. Internal evidence from the learning records which supports this conclusion will be presented below.

Retention after one week appears to be poorer for the two low-frequency lists than for the two high-frequency lists. For both words and trigrams, equal performance on the 30-sec. test is followed by a difference in favor of the high-frequency list after one week. At both levels of frequency, words and trigrams suffer comparable losses at recall. The mean differences between the 30-sec. and 1-week groups which represent the amount of retention loss are as follows: Hi-W, 4.11; Hi-T, 3.83; Lo-W, 5.39; Lo-T, 5.23. Analysis of variance fails to reveal any significant differences in the amount of retention loss as assessed by the interaction of lists with interval. The F ratio which approaches significance most closely is that for the interaction of frequency with interval. The obtained value of F is 3.29, whereas 3.91 is required at the .05 level with 1 and 136 *df*. The total recall scores suggest, therefore, that differences in letter-sequence interference influenced the amount of forgetting but the effect is at best of marginal significance.

The recall scores also fail to provide any clear evidence for differences in retention as a function of unit-sequence interference. At both levels of frequency the retention losses are slightly greater for words than for trigrams but the differences are small and not significant. Thus, the first measure of retention to be examined, viz., total amount recalled, yields inconclusive results with respect to letter-sequence interference and largely negative results with respect to unit-sequence interference. All the trends present in the total recall scores are, however, in the direction predicted by the theory. We shall now present further analyses which bring out these trends more clearly and significantly by means of measures which proved more sensitive to the variables manipulated in the experiment.

Recall as a function of serial position

Interference effects may be expected to vary as a function of the serial position of the items to be recalled. There are several reasons for this expectation. First, strength of learning at criterion varies as a function of serial position. After a given retention interval, the absolute level to which the items have been learned may determine the sensitivity of the recall test to the effects of interference. Pre-experimental habits may recover slowly, and items which have received relatively few reinforcements during acquisition are more likely to reveal interference from extraexperimental sources than those which have been substantially overlearned. Secondly, the recall trial is also a learning trial. The improvement which occurs in the course of that trial may facilitate the recall of different materials to unequal degrees. Thus, interference from intralist errors

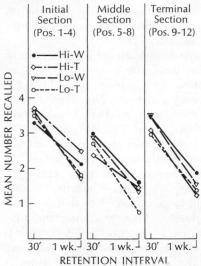

FIG. 4. Mean numbers of correct responses for different sections of the list on the first trial of relearning.

may be progressively reduced during the first re-exposure to the series whereas letter-sequence interference might not. Finally, the degree of sequential dependency among the items should critically influence the results of the recall test. The greater the degree of sequential dependency the more serious will be the cumulative effects of failures in the early part of the series.

In the light of these considerations, the results of the recall tests were examined separately for the initial (Serial Positions 1-4), middle (Positions 5-8) and terminal (Positions 9-12) sections of the lists. The relevant data are presented in Figure 4. Prior to statistical analysis, the recall scores for the three sections of the list were subjected to a Freeman-Tukey square-root transformation in order to remove heterogeneity of variance. Analysis of variance shows the higher-order interaction, Interval × Sections × Frequency × Wordness to be significant ($F = 3.34$, 2 and 136 *df*, $.02 < P < .05$.) The variations in relative retention loss which occur from section to section may therefore be considered reliable. Further tests of significance will be presented in connection with the discussion of the results for each section.

Initial section. In the initial section of the list the low-frequency materials are forgotten more rapidly than the high-frequency materials. The interaction of frequency with interval is significant ($F = 4.84$, 1 and 136 df, $.02 < P < .05$). The low-frequency items would (according to the theory) be more subject to letter-sequence interference than the high-frequency units. The latter, in turn, should be more subject to unit-sequence interference. Thus, this interaction may mean that letter-sequence interference is greater than unit-sequence interference at these serial positions. That there is some unit-sequence interference is suggested by the fact that the high-frequency trigrams are recalled better than the high-frequency words on both the immediate and the delayed test. Recall for the Hi-W List is, indeed, somewhat poorer than for any other material in spite of the fact that the Hi-W List was learned faster than the Hi-T and the Lo-T Lists and at about the same rate as the Lo-W List. A possible interpretation is that some of the strongest pre-experimental associations which gave rise to persistent intralist errors during learning were not extinguished sufficiently and recovered during the 30-sec. interval. Such interferences would be most detrimental to the recall of the early section of the list, i.e., before the context of the series had been re-established. If this interpretation is correct, some of the losses attributable to unit-sequence interference are reflected in the control measures rather than the long-term retention scores.

Middle section. In the center of the list, immediate recall is better for words than for trigrams. The difference found in the initial section between the Hi-W and the Hi-T List is reversed. The Lo-W List begins to show an advantage over the Lo-T List. With reference to this baseline, there is evidence for both kinds of interference. The high-frequency lists are retained better than the low-frequency lists. The interaction of frequency with interval is significant ($F = 4.27$, 1 and 136 df, $.01 < P < .05$). This finding is again consistent with the assumption of differential letter-sequence interference. As Figure 4 shows, however, it is primarily the superior retention of the high-trigram list which is responsible for this interaction. Indeed, the Hi-T List is retained better than any other list. The fact that the Hi-T List suffers less loss than the Hi-W List gives the most direct support thus far for differential unit-sequence interference.

Terminal section. In the terminal section of the list, words are recalled better than trigrams both after 30 sec. and after 1 week. Summed over the two intervals, the difference between words and trigrams is significant ($F = 6.12$, 1 and 136 df, $.01 < P < .02$). That words are better recalled than trigrams appears to be a function of differences in sequential dependencies, a matter to which we will turn shortly. There is a somewhat greater loss for the low-frequency words than for the other materials but there are no significant differences in the amount of forgetting.

The trends revealed by the sectional analysis may now be summarized. First, significant variations in the rate of forgetting as a function of the characteristics of the materials are limited to the first two sections of the list. The recall scores for these sections provide evidence for differences in both letter-sequence interference and unit-sequence interference. Secondly, as we proceed from the beginning to the end of the list, words gain an increasing advantage over trigrams in immediate recall. In the final section, this difference is most pronounced, is maintained after one week, and accounts for substantially all the observed differences in recall. Thus, as the end of the list is approached, wordness per se becomes the primary determinant of both immediate and delayed recall and overrides the influence of other variables. This interaction between list section and the other variables explains the inconclusive results obtained with total recall scores.

Sequential dependencies

The superiority of the words in the final section suggests that a list of words is characterized by a lower degree of sequential dependency than is a list of trigrams. That is, the correct anticipation of a word is less dependent on the context provided by correct reproduction of the preceding items than is the correct anticipation of a trigram. Two possible reasons for such a difference in sequential dependency may be mentioned. First, words which are well integrated and become readily available as responses may be more easily associated with specific serial positions than trigrams. Association between a single item and a *specific* serial position makes anticipation relatively independent of preceding responses. Secondly, to the extent that words have higher *m* value (Noble, 1952) than trigrams of comparable frequency, associations between adjacent words may be more independent of serial position than associations between adjacent trigrams. As a result, the loss of weakly learned items in the middle of the list would detract less from the recall of relatively strong terminal items in a list of words than in a list of trigrams.

To support our interpretation, independent evidence is required for the assumed difference in sequential dependency. Such support is provided by (a) an analysis of serial position effects in learning, and (b) evidence for differential degrees of sequential dependency in the recall of words and trigrams. Turning to learning first, we have used the number of increases between adjacent serial positions to quantify the degree to which linkages between successive items were independent of the serial context. As S progresses from the beginning to the end of the list, the probability of a correct anticipation typically decreases, until there is a rise in the terminal positions. In a list with a high degree of sequential dependency there should be few reversals in this trend, i.e., rises between positions in a falling section of the serial position curve. By the same token, a high degree of sequential dependency should delay the onset of the terminal rise. To the extent that successive associations are relatively independent of the preceding serial context, rises between adjacent serial positions should become more probable. The number of such rises was, therefore, determined for the serial position curve of each individual S. The mean numbers of rises per S for the four lists were as follows: Hi-W, 4.94; Hi-T, 4.30; Lo-W, 5.06; Lo-T, 4.47. The difference between words and trigrams is significant ($F = 8.43$, 1 and 136 *df*, $P < .01$). The difference in the frequency of rises is consistent with the hypothesis that associations between adjacent words are less influenced by the preceding context than are adjacent associations between trigrams. The same hypothesis leads to the expectation that for words the recall of items from the terminal section should be less contingent on prior recall of central items than for trigrams. The results of the one-week tests, which show a wider range of individual variations than the 30-sec. tests, were used to verify this implication. In Figure 5 the mean number of correct responses in Section 3 is plotted as a function of the number of responses obtained in Section 2. There is a clear positive correlation for the two lists of trigrams whereas for words recall of Section 3 is virtually independent of the number of correct responses in Section 2. This finding further

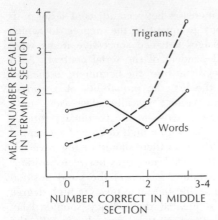

FIG. 5. Mean numbers of correct responses in terminal section as a function of the number of correct responses in the middle section (1-wk. recall tests).

supports the hypothesis of differences in the degree of sequential dependency between words and trigrams.

Relearning

The mean numbers of trials to criterion in relearning are shown in Figure 6. Inspection of the figure immediately calls attention to a salient feature of the results, viz., the divergence between the Hi-T List and all other lists. After 30 sec., the Hi-T List is relearned appreciably more slowly than the other lists. After one week, this relationship is completely reversed. As measured against the 30-sec. base-line, therefore, the relearning scores show very little forgetting of the Hi-T List and major losses for the other lists. The interaction of lists with interval is significant ($F = 3.33$, 3 and 136 df, $.01 < P < .02$). The finding that the high-frequency trigrams are relearned faster than any of the other materials is, of course, in full agreement with the prediction made by an interference theory of forgetting.

Before this result is accepted at face value, we must find an answer to the puzzle posed by the unexpectedly slow relearning of the Hi-T List after 30 sec.

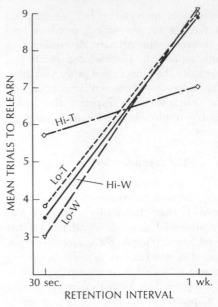

FIG. 6. Mean numbers of trials to relearn to criterion.

It must be shown that the results of the immediate relearning do, indeed, adequately represent the strength of the Hi-T List shortly after attainment of the criterion. Any conclusions concerning differential rates of long-term forgetting depend, of course, on the validity of the 30-sec. control measure. Our confidence in its validity rests, in turn, on our ability to relate the facts of relearning to those of original learning.

Further analysis shows that the relearning scores after 30 sec. reflect almost entirely differences in the difficulty of the center of the list. As may be seen in Figure 4, the Hi-T List falls substantially below all other lists in the amount recalled from the middle section and does so in the middle section only. The number of intralist errors at recall is highest and shows the sharpest peak in the center of the list for the Hi-T List (Figure 8). The pattern evident on the recall trial persists through subsequent relearning trials: the group relearning the Hi-T List has greater difficulty than any other

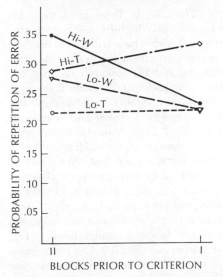

FIG. 7. Probability of repetition of intralist errors in last two blocks of five trials preceding criterion trial.

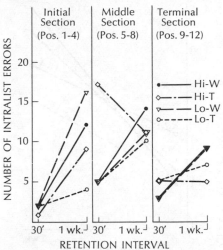

FIG. 8. Total frequency of intralist errors for different sections of the list on first relearning trial.

group in the center of the list and continues to make more intralist errors (Figure 9). The fact to be accounted for narrows down, therefore, to the persistent difficulty of the center of the Hi-T List in relearning after 30 sec.

Examination of the original learning records has led us to the conclusion that the instability of the Hi-T List at criterion stems from the combination of high response availability and low meaningfulness which is characteristic of these materials. The items in the Hi-T List represent extremely frequent letter sequences and, therefore, are readily integrated as responses. As nonwords, they may be assumed to have relatively low meaningfulness; certainly their m values must be substantially lower than those of the high-frequency words. Under these circumstances, the stability of the associative connections between successive items does not keep in step, as it were, with the rapid increases in response availability. It then becomes likely that S reaches criterion at a point in learning at which some of the associative connec-

tions, especially those in the center of the list, are still extremely unstable and liable to be lost on the postcriterial trial. Put differently, because of high response availability Ss learning the Hi-T List are likely to reach criterion by "overshooting the mark" in the final stages of learning but because of the low meaningfulness of the items they will have difficulty in regaining criterion during relearning.

Our interpretation finds support in a number of independent analyses. First, there are greater cyclical fluctuations during the learning of the Hi-T List than of the other lists. Cyclical learning curves similar to those described by Underwood (1957b) were plotted for each of the four lists. These curves clearly showed more extensive fluctuations in the magnitudes of the postcriterial drops for the Hi-T List than for the other lists. The observed differences in relearning appear to be consistent with the long-term trends characteristic of these curves. Secondly, a comparison between fast and slow learners shows that the relationship between speed of learning and relearning is quite different for the Hi-T List and the other lists. According to our analysis,

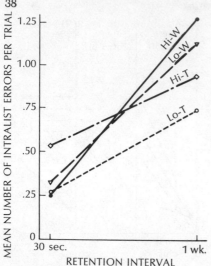

FIG. 9. Mean numbers of intralist errors per trial in relearning to criterion.

it is the fast learners of the Hi-T List who reach criterion during an exaggerated spurt and who are mainly responsible for the decrements in immediate relearning. Contrary to the usual relationship, therefore, fast learners of the Hi-T List should take longer to relearn and make more intralist errors than slow learners.

Table 2 presents a set of measures which is consistent with this interpretation. The percentage of the total learning

lists. Thus, in the learning of trigrams, and particularly high-frequency trigrams, the speed with which criterion is reached is correlated with a relatively rapid terminal stage. The opposite is true for words. As anticipated, Table 2 shows a pronounced negative relationship between speed of learning and relearning for the Hi-T List. A similar relationship obtains, though to a considerably lesser degree, for the Lo-T List. With words, the relationship between speed of learning and relearning is clearly positive. The differences between fast and slow learners in the rate of intralist errors during relearning follow a similar pattern, i.e., fast learners of the Hi-T List make more errors than slow learners, whereas the opposite is true for the other groups. As regards intralist errors, therefore, the group learning the Lo-T List no longer behaves like the group learning the Hi-T List. As was shown earlier, however, the rate of intralist errors is less critical in the learning of the Lo-T List than the Hi-T List. With the low frequency materials, other three-letter errors reflecting difficulties of integration are a more sensitive index. With respect to such errors, fast Ss do, in fact, surpass slow Ss (.28 vs. .11).

A final analysis is directed at an explanation of the unusually large number of intralist errors given during the recall of the Hi-T List after 30 sec. It appeared possible that the combination of high-frequency letter sequences and low meaningfulness would be conducive to a growth of error tendencies late in learn-

TABLE 2. *Measures of Performance of Fast and Slow Subjects in Learning and Relearning*

List	Per Cent Learning Time from 10/12 to 12/12		Trials to Relearn After 30 Sec.		Intralist Errors per Trial in Relearning	
	Fast Ss	Slow Ss	Fast Ss	Slow Ss	Fast Ss	Slow Ss
Hi-W	27.2	18.2	2.44	4.67	1.75	2.76
Hi-T	16.2	27.1	7.56	3.89	5.81	3.66
Lo-W	24.0	22.3	2.22	3.78	2.50	3.25
Lo-T	20.9	26.5	4.67	3.00	2.18	2.75

time required to go from a criterion of 10/12 to one perfect recitation was used to assess the degree of criterial end spurt. In the case of the Hi-T List, the percentage is considerably lower for fast than for slow Ss. The difference is in the same direction but smaller for the Lo-T List and is reversed for the two word ing when the appropriate responses were fully available to Ss but interitem associations were still weak. To test this possibility, the development of intralist errors during the last 10 trials preceding criterion on each of the lists was subjected to a detailed analysis. These 10 trials were divided into two blocks of five each. Within each block, the probability of repetition of an intralist error was investigated, i.e., the ratio of repeated intralist errors to total number of different errors was determined. The results are shown in Figure 7. As criterion is approached, the probability of an error being repeated declines in the word lists. It remains at a steady, relatively low level in the Lo-T List. It is only in the Hi-T List that the probability of error repetition actually increases in the final precriterial stage. During the last block of five trials, therefore, the probability is considerably higher for the Hi-T List than for the other three lists which yield virtually identical values. It may be noted that the two subsamples of 18 Ss learning a given list gave comparable results for all lists. The relative frequencies of intralist errors at 30-sec. recall, which are heavily weighted by responses in the middle section, are predicted reasonably well from the trends in Figure 7.

Examination of the internal evidence thus leads us to accept the interaction shown in Figure 5 as valid and to consider the losses measured by relearning a function of differential interference. The Hi-T List suffers some extremely rapid losses, the reasons for which we have attempted to trace back into the process of acquisition. Whatever is not lost immediately is, as predicted, relatively immune from long-term outside interferences.

DISCUSSION

The experiment was designed to examine the implications of two assumed interference gradients, namely, a unit-sequence gradient and a letter-sequence gradient. We will first examine the credibility of assuming a unit-sequence gradient in light of the results of the experiment.

The assumption was that List Hi-W would be more susceptible to unit-sequence interference in retention than would List Hi-T. The word list, made up of frequently used words, should have fairly strong associative connections among units within the list (e.g., OLD-AGE) as well as have strong associations with words not in the list. The high-frequency trigrams, on the other hand, should have relatively few such associations and yet at the same time they should be readily available because of their high frequency. If it is assumed that the pre-experimental associations of List Hi-W have to be extinguished during learning, and that these extinguished associations recovered during the retention interval, the retention of List Hi-W should be inferior to List Hi-T. The recovery of the associations during the retention interval should, furthermore, be augmented by the use of the words in List Hi-W in new and old contexts during the retention interval.

The question may be raised as to whether the assumed differences in the nature of the two lists are reasonable. We do not have association data to document our presumption that the units in the word list were more highly connected pre-experimentally than were the trigrams. Nor do we have data to indicate that the words had more associations outside the list than the trigrams. However, in addition to a fairly self-evident impression on these matters obtained from inspecting the list, and in addition to the known fact that the greater the frequency of a word the greater the number of associates it has, internal evidence in support of the different characteristics ascribed the two lists is available. The single most relevant datum is the greater number of intralist errors which occurred in learning List Hi-W than List Hi-T. Although we did not present the data, it can be reported that these intralist errors occurred with high frequency very early in learning List Hi-W and then gradually diminished in frequency as learning proceeded. This high initial occurrence of such errors may be attributed to the associative connections existing among the items at the start of learning. List Hi-T, on the other hand, was actually producing an increase in repetitive intralist errors as original learning approached termination.

In view of these trends in intralist errors, it might be asked why List Hi-T was not learned more rapidly than List Hi-W. There are two facts which suggest why this did not occur. First, there was some evidence that the high trigrams produced some integrative (letter-sequence) errors early in learning. Secondly, if it is accepted that items in List Hi-T have relatively few interitem associations at the start of learning, then, it follows that in Noble's sense (1952) they have low m value (a relatively small number of associates as such). Insofar as m is related to learning, the Hi-T List should be learned more slowly than the Hi-W List.

If it be assumed, in light of the above comments, that the Hi-W and Hi-T Lists do have the differential characteristics necessary to make a test of the item-sequence gradient of interference, the critical question is how well the retention results support the expectation from the theory. In terms of recall of correct responses, the only clear-cut support of the theory occurred in the middle serial positions. Here, the loss was greater for List Hi-W than for List Hi-T. In the initial serial positions the Hi-T List was better recalled than the Hi-W List at both retention intervals, but there was no difference in the amount lost over the

week. In the final serial positions, the Hi-W List was better recalled at both intervals but again there was no differential loss.

The argument that has been advanced would predict that the frequency of intralist errors should show a greater increase over the week for List Hi-W than List Hi-T. That this is the case is shown in Figure 8, where intralist errors at recall for all lists for both retention intervals are shown. In every section the increase in intralist errors is appreciably less for List Hi-T than for List Hi-W. In the middle serial positions there is actually a decrease in the frequency for List Hi-T, but since we have made no statistical tests it may be best to speak of no change in frequency.

If, as shown in Figure 8, intralist error tendencies recover less for the Hi-T List than for the Hi-W List, why is the overall forgetting (in terms of correct responses) of the Hi-T List not less than for List Hi-W? The answer is found, we believe, in the greater number of sequential dependencies built up in learning List Hi-T than in learning List Hi-W. In the results section it was shown that in the learning of the trigram lists correct anticipation of a given response is more dependent upon earlier correct anticipations than is true for the word lists. We have suggested that this is due to the differences in m value. But, whatever the reason, it can be seen that the failure to get one response at recall reduces the probability of recalling a subsequent response, and this reduction is greater for the trigram lists than for the word lists. This difference in sequential dependency was unexpected and, as far as we know, previously unreported, but it seems clearly to produce an outcome which works against the recall data showing clear confirmation of the unit-sequence gradient. Since relearning should be much less influenced by this factor than recall, we turn to these relearning data as being a more pure case of the operation of the unit-sequence interference gradient.

It will be remembered that the relearning data showed less forgetting of List Hi-T than of the other lists. Does the change in frequency of intralist errors correspond to the theory and hence to the relearning scores? The answer can be found in Figure 9. The increase in intralist errors over the week interval is apparently greater for the word lists than for the trigram lists. This plot gives intralist errors per trial during relearning to the criterion. After 30 sec., many of the Ss made no errors during relearning. In order to get some notion of the reliability of the change from 30 sec. to 1 week in these intralist errors, 30-sec. Ss and 1-week Ss were paired for a given type of list, the pairing being based on the random order used to assign Ss to lists originally. From these pairings change scores could be derived. For the 36 Ss learning the two word lists the mean change in intralist errors per trial was .91; for those learning the trigram lists the mean change was .45. The difference gives a *t* of 2.88, significant beyond the .01 level. It thus seems reasonable to conclude that intralist errors increase more rapidly for the word lists than for the trigram lists. We conclude, further, that this fact gives substance to the notion of the unit-sequence gradient in forgetting. The trigrams, having minimal pre-experimental associative connections among themselves or with units not in the list, are not subjected to interference from the unit-sequence gradient as much as are the word lists.

We turn next to an evaluation of the other assumed gradient—the letter-sequence gradient. Is there evidence for a recovery process leading to interference *within* the responses?

Letter-sequence interference would be documented by three-letter sequences which are more frequent in the language than the responses they replace. As an illustration, consider an error which occurred with some frequency in List Lo-T during learning. The correct response was LAK, the substituted response, LAC. LAC is a much more frequent letter sequence in the language than is LAK. Thus, this might be considered a relatively pure case of letter-sequence interference. Other kinds of three-letter errors cannot be so easily interpreted. For example, ARF occurred very frequently as an error, apparently as a merger of ARP and ERF. ARF is a very low-frequency trigram, although RF is a much more frequent two-letter sequence than is RP. Thus, given AR, F is a more probable response than is P. But it is a fact that very few letters are imported and overtly produce interference, i.e., nearly all wrong sequences involve letters actually in the list. This means that evidence of overt interference must be limited to intra-unit interference from letters within the list. Many of these errors can be shown (as illustrated above) to consist of at least two-letter sequences which are more frequent (hence, are assumed to have higher associative strength) than the sequences they replace. Some cannot.

A consideration of the structure of the lists together with the error results may suggest that we are simply dealing with intralist formal similarity defined by letter duplication. It is known that for nonsense syllables intralist formal similarity has a greater effect in learning low-meaningful items than in learning high-meaningful items, but there is little differential effect on retention (Underwood & Richardson, 1956; Underwood & Richardson, 1958). In the present study the low-frequency lists (Lo-T and Lo-W) show a greater loss at recall over the week than do the high-frequency lists. The differences are significant statistically for the first two sections (Serial Positions 1-8, see Figure 4). The nature of the errors, as explained above, does not allow us to decide whether this effect is produced by error tendencies resulting from formal intralist similarity, by stronger letter-sequence habits, or both. It is worth pointing out, however, that List Hi-T had greater formal similarity than either Lo-T or Lo-W and yet we find little evidence for letter-sequence errors in retention. So, while we are inclined against formal intralist similarity as the critical factor, our data do not allow us to make a clear decision.

In spite of the interpretative problems, we can show that letter-sequence errors do increase over the retention interval. This increase is most clearly seen in the relearning data. Because many Ss gave no such errors at 30 sec., we have plotted the per cent of Ss giving such errors during relearning after 30 sec. and after 1 week. It should be clear that these errors plotted in Figure 10 are three-letter responses which are not responses in the list, i.e., they are not intralist errors.

Figure 10 shows that for List Lo-T and List Lo-W there is a clear increase in percentage of Ss making letter-sequence errors. For List Hi-T there is actually a slight decrease. For List Hi-W it is probably not correct to speak of these errors as letter-sequence errors for they consist in most cases of what we have called generalized responses, e.g., HER for SHE, WON for WIN, WERE for WAS. Finally, we may note that the higher frequency of letter-sequence errors in List Lo-T than in Lo-W is balanced by fewer intralist errors in Lo-T than Lo-W (Figure 9) and that relearning time is about the same in both instances.

Our conclusion concerning the letter-sequence gradient is that the evidence supports the plausibility of such a gradient but that we cannot rule out completely the possibility that the results could be attributable to formal intralist similarity without any need to appeal to letter-sequence habits which S brings

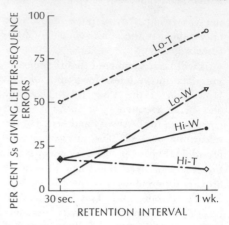

FIG. 10. Percentages of Ss giving letter-sequence errors in relearning.

to the situation. Only by using lists in which no duplicated letters occur can this separation be made clearly.

The present study has given some evidence that extraexperimental sources of interference can be treated analytically. The critical requirement is to know what associations the subject brings to the laboratory and then present him with a task where these associations will have to be broken, inhibited, or extinguished. The lists used in the present study were believed to meet this requirement, although, as pointed out earlier, it would be quite possible to show this more clearly than we have. We have suggested two sources of interference—two classes of associations—which S may bring to the laboratory. List Lo-T was primarily used to illustrate the letter-sequence habits which S brings with him; List Hi-W to illustrate the unit-sequence habits; List Hi-T the minimum of either kind of habits; and, as the data turned out, List Lo-W seems to have elicited a fair number of both types of habits.

The assumption of a recovery of inhibited or extinguished associations was a fundamental part of our thinking and of the analyses made. Will all types of habits recover at the same rate? Is one week long enough to expect an appreciable recovery to occur? These are merely suggestive of the questions which will need to be answered if extraexperimental sources of interference in forgetting are to be systematically evaluated.

SUMMARY

This paper examines two major sources of extraexperimental interference in long-term forgetting: (a) letter-sequence interference which is produced by well established associations between letters in S's language, and (b) unit-sequence interference which reflects pre-experimental associations among the units of a list. Both types of interfering associations must be extinguished during the acquisition of a serial list and are assumed to recover during the retention interval. Differential rates of forgetting are predicted for materials varying in susceptibility to the two kinds of extraexperimental interference.

An experiment testing these assumptions is reported. Four kinds of three-letter units were used in a serial learning task: high-frequency words, high-frequency nonsense items (trigrams), low-frequency words and low-frequency trigrams. Retention was tested 30 sec. after the end of practice and after one week. It was assumed that letter-sequence interference would be greater for low-frequency than high-frequency units whereas unit-sequence interference should be greater for words than nonwords. Speed of acquisition was greater for words than for trigrams. The differences in long-term retention, measured at recall and in relearning, and supplemented by an analysis of overt errors, gave support to the present analysis of the conditions of extraexperimental interference.

BRIGGS, G. E. Acquisition, extinction and recovery functions in retroactive inhibition. *J. exp. Psychol.*, 1954, **47**, 285-93.

DEESE, J. Influence of inter-item associative strength upon immediate free recall. *Psychol. Rep.*, 1959, **5**, 305-12.

MANDLER, G. Response factors in human learning. *Psychol. Rev.*, 1954, **61**, 235-44.

NOBLE, C. E. An analysis of meaning. *Psychol. Rev.*, 1952, **59**, 421-30.

POSTMAN, L., & RAU, L. Retention as a function of the method of measurement. *Univer. Calif. Publ. Psychol.*, Berkeley: Univer. California Press, 1957, **8**, 217-70.

PRATT, F. *Secret and urgent.* Indianapolis: Bobbs-Merrill, 1939.

THORNDIKE, E. L., & LORGE, I. *A teachers' word book of 30,000 words.* New York: Teachers College, Columbia Univer., 1944.

UNDERWOOD, B. J. Speed of learning and amount retained: A consideration of methodology. *Psychol. Bull.*, 1954. **51**, 276-82.

UNDERWOOD, B. J. Interference and forgetting. *Psychol. Rev.*, 1957, **64**, 49-60. (a)

UNDERWOOD, B. J. A graphical description of rote learning. *Psychol. Rev.*, 1957, **64**, 119-22. (b)

UNDERWOOD, B. J., & RICHARDSON, J. The influence of meaningfulness, intralist similarity and serial position on retention. *J. exp. Psychol.*, 1956, **52**, 119-26.

UNDERWOOD, B. J., & RICHARDSON, J. Studies of distributed practice: XVIII. The influence of meaningfulness and intralist similarity of serial nonsense lists. *J. exp. Psychol.*, 1958, **56**, 213-19.

UNDERWOOD, B. J., RUNQUIST, W. N., & SCHULZ, R. W. Response learning in paired-associate lists as a function of intralist similarity. *J. exp. Psychol.*, 1959, **58**, 70-78.

4 / Time Changes in the Strengths of A-B, A-C Lists; Spontaneous Recovery? [1]

R. J. KOPPENAAL, *University of Manitoba, Winnipeg, Canada*

In recent S-R transfer and interference explanations of forgetting there has been increasing emphasis on proactive interference. The increase of proactive interference with the length of the retention interval, in particular, occupies a prominent place in recent theorizing.

The time effects in question are illus-

From the *Journal of Verbal Learning and Verbal Behavior*, 1963, **2**, 310-19, with permission of the author and publisher, Academic Press, Inc.

1. This research was supported by two grants from the National Research Council of Canada, APBT-40 and APA-77, and by the University of Manitoba's Research and Publications Fund. The author is indebted to a number of students, Hannah Katz, Lorraine Wilgosh, Marcia Greenberg, and Lillian Corman, for testing subjects, and to the late Nelson O'Hara for help in the original conception of the study.

trated in the case where two lists of paired-associates with the same stimulus terms but different response terms (A-B, A-C) are learned consecutively. After a short retention interval (e.g., ½ hour) the retention of the second list learned will be far superior to the retention of the first list. This difference has been attributed to *unlearning* of the first list during second-list learning, with unlearning analogous to experimental extinction.

It is now well documented that after longer retention intervals (24 to 48 hours) there is equally good recall of first and second lists. To explain the change in relative strengths of the two lists with time, Underwood (1948a; 1948b) suggested that the first list spontaneously recovers strength lost during unlearning, extending the analogy with conditioning phenomena.

This development has brought about a fundamental change in the interference theory of forgetting. Forgetting happens over time, and for many years the variable presumed to be operating in time was interpolated learning (IL), producing retroactive inhibition (RI). Now, however, Underwood and Postman (1960) and Postman (1961a, b) have assigned the major role in forgetting to the spontaneous recovery of prior learning (PL), producing proactive inhibition (PI). Thus spontaneous recovery is the important variable operating in time.

There are two uncomfortable aspects of the explanation of the time effects in terms of spontaneous recovery. First, complete recovery would evidently be required if this concept alone is to explain the convergence of the two lists. Complete recovery would rob this concept of its analogy with conditioning phenomena. The second problem, one of parsimony, stems from Underwood's (1948b) suggestion that in addition to spontaneous recovery of the first list, both lists undergo "usual forgetting" over time. This suggestion was necessitated by the fact that

while the first list increases in relative strength, it evidently does not increase in absolute strength. Therefore, two opposed processes are presumed to act on the first list over time. Spontaneous recovery increases first-list strength, while usual forgetting decreases that strength, and the two effects are largely balanced out in the resulting behavior.

Koppenaal and O'Hara (1962) suggest that the time changes can be handled quite simply through the assumptions of negatively accelerated unlearning. The proposition is that unlearning is a negatively accelerated, increasing function of practice on relevant IL, with the resulting retention function decreasing with positive acceleration. This notion originated in a study of short-term retention where an increase in proactive intrusions, much like that noted over time, was produced by adding a third list to the standard PI learned A-B, A-C, A-D Lists and recalled the second list. More recent unpublished work by the author indicates that manipulation of IL in RIP conditions may produce increases in PI as well as in proactive intrusions.

In attempting to explain the similar effects of time and RIP in the same way it is immediately apparent that the notion of spontaneous recovery of the first list is inapplicable. There is no known basis for supposing that learning a third (A-D) list could aid the absolute recovery of the first (A-B) list. Instead further unlearning of the first list would be likely. Koppenaal and O'Hara suggested that the third list produced greater unlearning of the second list than of the already somewhat unlearned first list (negatively accelerated unlearning). The net result of third-list learning is a reduction in the difference between the strengths of the first and second lists.

Over time, it was argued, instead of a third list there is uncontrolled extra-experimental IL which produces unlearning of the two lists. However, the second list, stronger than the first following laboratory learning, loses strength at a faster rate until the two approach equal strength with time. The two central empirical time effects, relative increase of first-list responses and absolute decrease of responses from both lists, are accounted for by one process. Given that the concept of negatively accelerated unlearning can be used to account for both the time and RIP effects, and that it represents an economical explanation of the time effects alone, is there any reason to postulate spontaneous recovery of the first list?

One good reason for retaining the concept of spontaneous recovery would be direct evidence of absolute recovery. The usual specific recall employed in studies of RI and PI, and the modified free recall (MFR) of Underwood (1948b) and Briggs (1954) give results which can be attributed to either absolute or relative recovery of the first list with time. It is important in this context to formalize the differentiation of *relative* and *absolute* recovery. *Absolute* recovery refers to an increase in the absolute number of responses or associations (of a specified group) available to S at recall (other measures than frequency may be applicable, but this is the measure in common use). *Relative* recovery refers to an increase in the availability of one group of responses or associations in relation to another, regardless of the absolute changes in either. Recovery, of course, refers to either of the above changes taking place over an interval of time after cessation of formal learning of the responses or associations in question (hence "spontaneous").

"Availability" is a key term in the above definitions, and it is used here in the sense that Barnes and Underwood (1959) used it; i.e., availability is measured in a relatively free responding situation where S is encouraged and given ample time to recall all responses learned to each stimulus. This recall procedure was labelled MMFR by Melton (1961). As yet, both absolute and relative recovery, as defined, must be classed as inferred phenomena since the time effects under discussion have not been subjected to the availability measure. In using the MMFR measure, the purpose of the following study is to determine whether the recovery of the first of two A-B, A-C lists is absolute or relative, or both.

METHOD

Subjects and materials. The volunteer Ss were 168 students of introductory psychology at the University of Manitoba. All were naive with respect to laboratory verbal learning. In one part of the study 112 Ss, 16 in each of seven retention-interval conditions, each learned two lists of ten paired-associate two-syllable adjectives. The lists were presented on a Gerbrand memory drum at a 3:3 sec. rate, with a 9-sec. intertrial interval, and 1 min. between lists. The learning criterion on each list was one errorless trial. Two sets of two lists each (A-B, A-C; i.e., identical stimuli, unrelated responses) were used equally often in all subconditions. In each subcondition the two lists within a set were used equally often as the first list.

The stimulus words of a set of lists, with respective responses were presented in three different orders, alternating continuously for a given S within and between lists over all learning trials and the recall trial.

Each set of lists was constructed so as to minimize, by careful inspection, structural and meaningful similarities between words except, of course, for the identical stimuli.

Design. The seven retention intervals, measured from the conclusion of the criterion trial on the second list to the start of the recall trial, were: 1 min, 20 min, 90 (80-100) min, 6 (5-7) hours, 24 (22-26) hours, 72 (68-76) hours, and 1 week (± 6 hours). One MMFR-type recall trial was given to each S after the appropriate interval. On the recall trial the stimulus words were exposed on the memory drum in the appropriate order and S was instructed to give responses from both lists, and to give the responses in the order in which they occurred to him, not necessarily in the order he learned them. The S was allowed up to 60 sec (more than enough time by pilot data) to respond to each stimulus word on the recall trial, and was encouraged to guess.

There was one major deviation from the typical MMFR procedure. On the recall trial half of the Ss in each interval condition had the two correct responses exposed for 3 sec. after responding to each stimulus, an adaptation of the usual anticipation-correction procedure employed in specific recall. The other half of the Ss received no correction information on the recall trial.

This part of the study, then, was a $2 \times 7 \times 2$ factorial, with List $\times$ Retention Interval $\times$ Correction-at-Recall, respectively. In addition another 7 groups of 8 Ss each learned just one list and recalled it after the various retention intervals. The four lists used in the two-list conditions were used equally often in each one-list condition. As with the two-list groups, half of each one-list group were shown the correct responses after responding on the recall trial, and half were not. No special free-recall instructions were required for the one-list Ss but the 60-sec. responding period and the mild encouragement to guess were maintained.

The Ss in the 20-min. recall conditions were given coffee, conversation, or picture magazines in a different room during the retention interval. The Ss in longer recall conditions were dismissed from the laboratory for the retention interval. The cooperation of all Ss except those with 1-min. recall was requested in not deliberately rehearsing laboratory learning during the retention interval.

The Ss were randomly assigned to conditions as they appeared at the laboratory. The randomization was accomplished by the use of a shuffled stack of data sheets pre-assigned to specific conditions and counterbalancings. However, an attempt was made to reassign S to a different retention interval if he could not possibly appear at the desired time for recall. Several devices were employed to make this an infrequent occurrence. (1) Original appointments at the laboratory were made only if S had at least 1½ hours free, to allow for the 20-min. interval. (2) Original learning sessions were conducted primarily in the mornings, to allow

for the 6-hour interval. (3) Small deviations from the designated intervals were allowed (as indicated earlier). Reassignment was necessary in only 13 cases, and in each of these cases the next data sheet in the shuffled stack was used. Only the 1-min. interval was free of these cases, the 24- and 72-hour conditions having 3 cases each, the 20- and 90-min. and 6-hour conditions having 2 each, and the one-week condition just one case. Judging by the original learning data no sizable inequalities between conditions resulted from this virtually inescapable situation. Through care taken in reminding Ss of appointments, the number of failures to reappear for the recall session was negligible.

An afterthought resulted in an addition to the study after it was underway. The last 6 Ss in each retention interval of the two-list experiment were asked, after recalling to each stimulus, which list (first or second) each of their recalled responses was from.

RESULTS

Original learning. The number of trials to criterion for the two-list experiment was subjected to an analysis of variance, with Lists (within Ss) $\times$ Retention Interval (between Ss) $\times$ Correction-at-Recall (between Ss) as the effects. The F for the List main effect was 17.89 ($p < .001$); no other F exceeded 1.3. The mean number of trials on the first list was 12.8 ($SD = 6.75$), on the second, 10.6 ($SD = 4.90$). This small positive transfer in trials to criterion is common with the materials and procedures employed.

The mean number of trials to criterion in the one-list experiment was 11.5 ($SD = 5.87$), with no significant differences due to retention intervals or correction-at-recall.

Recall, two-list experiment. Since the recall scores were by nature proportions of small numbers of possible responses (10, for any one list), they were transformed to radians (Walker and Lev, 1953) before analysis of variance. The three-way analysis of the transformed scores showed the correction-at-recall

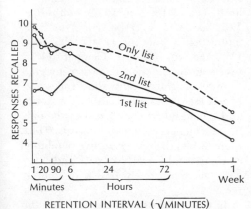

RETENTION INTERVAL ($\sqrt{\text{MINUTES}}$)

FIG. 1. Retention curves for the first, second, and only lists.

variable associated with $F < 1.00$. This variable was not associated with significant variations in any other measure in this study and so will be largely ignored from this point on. Significant variations were associated with Retention Intervals ($F=9.03$, $df=6/98$, $p<.001$), Lists ($F=$

nature of the interaction between lists and retention intervals. The general picture is as expected; List 2 was clearly stronger immediately following learning, with this difference diminishing over time. To lend more precision to the picture several t-test comparisons were made between pairs of conditions, employing overall error estimates from the analysis of variance. The differences between Lists 1 and 2 were significant beyond the .01 level at 1, 20, and 90 min., and exactly at the .05 level at 6 hours. At 24 hours, 72 hours, and one week Lists 1 and 2 did not differ significantly.

Analysis of the effect of the retention interval for the two lists separately (within-groups error estimate from the three-way analysis above) revealed significantly reduced recall of both lists over the one-week period. The finding of particular note here was that the increase in List-1 responses from 90 min. to 6 hours generated a non-significant t of 1.18.

Table 1 shows which list response was

TABLE 1. *Mean number of first responses from each list when both responses were recalled, and mean number of responses from each list when only one was recalled: Two-list experiment*

				Retention Interval			
	1	20 min.	90 min.	6 hours	24 hours	72 hours	1 week
			First Response When Both Recalled				
List 1	2.94	2.75	2.88	3.25	2.69	2.94	1.44
List 2	3.25	3.19	3.07	2.81	2.06	1.00	.94
			Only Response Recalled to Stimulus				
List 1	.44	.75	.50	1.37	1.69	2.19	2.62
List 2	3.25	2.94	3.00	2.44	2.63	2.38	1.81

55.00, $df=1/98$, $p<.001$) and the interaction of these two variables ($F=8.25$, $df=6/98$, $p<.001$). The mean number of responses recalled from each list at each retention interval is presented in Fig. 1. The SDs corresponding to these means, based on the raw scores, varied from .79 to 2.48 and were correlated with the means.

Figure 1 gives a clear indication of the

given first when S gave two responses to a stimulus, and the number of times a response from each list was the only response to a stimulus. The greater strength of the second list at short retention intervals was reflected only in a greater frequency of single responses from that list. There was no pronounced tendency for S to give the List-2 responses first when both were available.

There was a tendency for List-1 responses to be given first at longer retention intervals, but since the frequencies were so small no statistical analysis was attempted.

The list-identification data (representing only the last 6 Ss run in each interval condition) were subjected to a three-way analysis of variance after transformation of the proportion scores to radians. No F exceeded 1.25, and examination of means revealed no large differences either between lists or retention intervals. The mean proportions of recalled responses which were identified with the correct list were, for the seven intervals from 1 min. to 1 week: .96, .94, .86, .95, .87, .88, .88. It has long been assumed that time decreases list differentiation and thus produces the sizable increase with time of interlist intrusions in the recall of a specific list. It should be noted, however, that in the recall of a specific list S normally has only 2 or 3 sec. to respond. The leisurely pace of the MMFR procedure may make it insensitive to changes in differentiation which do affect more hurried recall. In addition, the number of intrusions, although sometimes doubled or tripled from short to long retention intervals, is typically quite small relative to the total responses recalled. Thus even small reductions in the accuracy of list identification could contribute a substantial part of the increase of interlist intrusions with time.

Recall, one-list experiment. The mean number of responses correctly recalled at the various intervals is presented in Fig. 1. The statistical analysis of this data is presented in the next section.

Comparison of one-list and two-list recall. For a statistical comparison here two simple two-way analyses of variance (Lists × Retention Intervals) were used, comparing the recall of the only list with each of the two-list recalls in turn.

The analysis comparing the only list with the second list resulted in Lists and Intervals effects significant at the .001 level ($Fs=7.18$ and 16.33, with $df= 1/54$ and $6/154$, respectively) and the interaction significant at the .05 level ($F=2.83$, $df=6/154$). Comparison by t-tests at the different retention intervals showed non-significant differences between lists up to and including 6 hours, and significantly better recall of the only list at all longer retention intervals. Thus, there evidently was proactive inhibition of the second list at 24 hours and after, even under relatively free and leisurely recall.

In the comparison of the only list and the first list, some of the data were not used because of non-comparability of the actual retention intervals. That is, the "1-min." recall of the first list on the average was actually 20 min. after cessation of first-list learning. For this analysis, then, the 1-min. recall of the first list and the 20-min. recall of the only list were matched, and the 20-min. recall of the first list and 1-min. recall of the only list were discarded. The analysis showed both the Lists and Intervals main effects significant beyond the .001 level ($Fs= 33.17$ and 6.21, with $df=1/32$ and $5/132$, respectively), and the interaction non-significant ($F=1.30$, $df=5/132$, $p > .20$).

Errors at recall. Table 2 gives a breakdown as to source of the overt recall errors in both experiments. The numbers in the table are per 8 Ss. Most of the overt errors were misplaced responses; i.e., responses from the list(s) learned, but recalled to the wrong stimulus. More detailed analysis showed that at shorter retention intervals these misplaced responses tended to be primarily, though not exclusively, from the first list. At longer intervals the two lists contributed approximately equal numbers of misplaced responses.

There appears to have been some increase in all types of overt errors with increasing length of the retention inter-

TABLE 2. *Errors at recall for two-list and one-list experiments*

Retention Interval	Two-list Experiment [a]			One-list Experiment		
	Misplaced Responses	Stimulus Words	Extra-experimental	Misplaced Responses	Stimulus Words	Extra-experimental
1 min.	10	1	0	1	0	0
20 min.	11.5	1.5	1	3	1	0
90 min.	9	2	3	4	0	0
6 hours	8	1.5	1	0	0	1
24 hours	15	3.5	2.5	4	1	0
72 hours	14.5	2.5	3	4	0	0
1 week	15	3	6.5	5	7	3

[a] The N per condition differed for the two experiments (two-list = 16, one-list = 8). For ease of comparison the total errors for the two-list conditions were halved.

val. However, the most striking difference in overt errors was related to the number of lists learned. Misplaced responses, in particular, were rare in one-list conditions compared to two-list conditions. The difference was too large to have simply resulted because there were twice as many list responses to misplace in the two-list conditions. Learning competing A-B, A-C lists increased intralist generalization at recall.

DISCUSSION

Comment is in order on the absence of any effects of correction-at-recall under the MMFR procedure, and under the leisurely recall of a specific list in the one-list experiment. The MMFR procedure was designed with a view to explaining results obtained in the recall of specific lists (Barnes and Underwood, 1959). Recall of specific lists of paired-associates has almost universally involved the same anticipation-correction procedure as is used during learning. MMFR as used thus far has not involved any correction or knowledge of results. This difference was viewed as a possible source of error in theoretically integrating evidence from MMFR and recall of specific lists. Two theoretical points were used to predict opposite results of correction-at-recall. If seeing or rehearsing other responses in a list constitutes an important part of the stimulus context to which a response becomes associated during learning, then recall performance should be superior

when the other responses are exposed on the recall trial. On the other hand, if seeing or rehearsing other responses exerts an interference effect then recall performance should be poorer with correction-at-recall. Since this variable had no discernible effect on recall it could be that these two predicted processes balanced each other out. In view of the complete lack of effects on any measure in the entire study it seems more likely than neither predicted process was in operation.

We turn now to the nature of the retention losses observed. It was indicated earlier that the 20 min. recall of the only list represents the best estimate of what the "1-min." recall of the first list would have been, had the second list not been learned. The loss of first-list strength attributable, then, to second-list learning was 2.88 of 9.50 responses, or 30%. Over the next week only an additional 1.62 first-list responses were lost (17% of 9.50). By comparison, the second list did not lose significantly in the first 20 min., but suffered greater losses than the first over the next week (53% of 20-min. recall). The effect of these different rates of loss was to reduce and finally eliminate the difference between the first and second lists. This, of course, is the time effect which has been well-documented with other measures. Consideration of other aspects of the present data, however, results in a picture of this time effect which is quite different than expected.

The most unexpected finding was the difference between the second and the only lists at longer retention intervals. In fact, this difference was probably underestimated because the second list was learned faster and therefore to a higher criterion. Under a recall procedure which has been presumed to eliminate response competition and thus proactive interference, the effects of interference from experimental prior learning appear sizable and very likely permanent. Even with recall of a specific list Underwood (1950) found that increasing the time allowed S for responding from 2 to 8 secs. eliminated PI. Underwood employed a 20-min. retention interval and in the present study the difference between the second and only lists appeared only at 24 hours and longer, so there is no real contradiction in the two sets of data. PI does increase with time. The present results imply that long-term PI is not due simply to the type of response competition that MMFR can be presumed to eliminate. This is a most radical suggestion. Interference theory (two-factor) has assumed that all interference effects are due to unlearning or to competition at recall. Prior learning (PL) cannot produce unlearning, as PL and unlearning are presently understood, and MMFR appears to satisfy all requirements of the operations necessary to eliminate response competition at recall.

Whatever the explanation for it, the finding of long-term PI of response availability (MMFR) augments the current emphasis on PI as the major source of forgetting. The implication relevant to the purposes of this study is that increasing PI of response availability contributes to the temporal changes in the relative strength of first and second lists. In fact, this is the only discernible process which produced the convergence of the two lists with time in this study. There is no satisfactory evidence that the first list recovered absolutely or even relatively when the standard was a proper control, the only-learned list.

While there was no clear-cut evidence of absolute recovery of the first list the retention curve (Fig. 1) does rise considerably at 6 hours. Chance ups and downs are to be expected, of course, but the observed rise is large enough to preclude a firm conclusion that there is no absolute recovery under the conditions of this study. Even if the increase in the first-list responses at 6 hours does represent actual absolute recovery, however, it is apparent that this recovery could not be considered as the only process responsible for the convergence of the first and second lists with time. In fact, the absolute recovery of, at the most, one response would represent little more than one-third of the amount of eventual recovery relative to the second list.

The lack of recovery relative to the only list is even more crucial to the understanding of the interaction of time and interference effects. The only sizable trend in the direction of relative recovery occurred at the one-week interval. It must be concluded that either the results at one week were due to error, or that recovery is extremely slow compared to that suggested by the observation of first and second lists. In view of the latter possibility, future studies of the interaction of time and interference effects would do well to explore retention intervals longer than one week. Of course, even if the recovery of the first list relative to an only list is found to occur at intervals of one week and longer, this would have little relation to the 24-48 hour convergence of first and second lists.

In order further to explore the theoretical implications of the present findings, it may be instructive to re-examine the nature of the hypotheses of spontaneous recovery and negatively accelerated unlearning. Essentially these hypotheses, both based on two-factor theory, attempted an analysis of the Time × PL interaction in the recall of a specific list by postulating a level of behaviour, response availability, where PL would have no effect. At this level time would interact with IL effects, causing temporal changes in the relative availability of first and second lists. Only when the available response competed at recall (specific or MFR) would the effects of PL and the Time × PL interaction appear. The results of this study could hardly have been more contrary to this view. Time did not interact with IL, but did interact with PL.

In order to preserve the notion that PI is due only to competition at recall it must be assumed that MMFR availability is subject to competition effects. Furthermore, the divergence of the retention curves of the second and only lists with time strongly suggests a multiplicative function involving competition and some variable operating over the retention interval. It appears reasonable and consistent with interference theory to identify the time variable as extra-experimental IL which has unlearning effects but over intervals of less than a week provides little in the way of strong responses to compete at the recall of the list. It can then be postulated that the inhibition of response availability is some multiplicative function of unlearning and response competition. For an only list the competition which interacts with unlearning over time would have to be primarily from extra-experimental sources, mostly PL, with some competition probably arising from intralist generalization. The second list would have additional strong competition from experimental PL (first list). Thus as unlearning increased with time, the inhibition of availability would increase at a faster rate for the second list.

It may be fruitful briefly to speculate on the molecular basis of this interaction of unlearning and competition. Unlearning may be viewed as a tendency to avoid an association, this tendency being built up in situations where the association is inappropriate. However, when the association is again specifically called for, the generalized avoidance tendency is effective only to the extent that there are competing responses to channel the input away from the association. If there are not, the well-directed input rapidly overcomes the generalized avoidance. The competing responses may be recognized as inappropriate and not performed. Their function is to divert the input at a stage previous to testing for appropriateness.

This interpretation has the advantage of being compatible with the interaction of experimental IL and PL reported by Koppenaal and O'Hara (1962), and of identifying the processes operating over time with experimentally manipulable variables. The disadvantage is some difficulty with the retention function of the first list over time. The immediate inhibition of the first list is not a problem, since the second-list IL produces unlearning *and* strong competing responses. However, the interference factors from experimental IL must be supposed to have had their total effect by the end of second-list learning, and not to interact with unlearning over time. The only defense for this complication is that the data insist on it; after second-list learning the first list shows no further effect of experimental IL.

There are alternative interpretations. Absolute or relative recovery of the first list could be postulated at a more fundamental level of response strength than MMFR availability, but this would result in substantial problems of balancing effects on the first list. The fact of the matter is that the only and first lists appear to be affected equally by the same time process(es). However, balancing must still be entertained seriously, as any interpretation presently available faces problems with the curve of first-list retention over time.

The interpretation in terms of an interaction of unlearning and competition, since it identifies the time processes with variables that can be manipulated somewhat independently of time, is quite amenable to investigation. For example, experimental IL that provides opportunity for substantial unlearning but does not provide strong competing responses (like time?) should produce only minor RI, but should interact with experimental PL in the manner that time did in this study. Such experimental IL could be produced by having a number of IL lists practiced for only a few trials each. On the other hand, there should not be the same pronounced interaction if the nature of PL and IL is reversed, with the poorly practiced lists as PL. Further, the speculation about the molecular nature of the interaction leads to the prediction that when the avoidance tendency (unlearning) and the diverting tendency (competition) are overcome by input which is very strongly directed to the association (e.g., a recognition test), both IL and PL should have much reduced inhibiting effects (relative to control recognition).

SUMMARY

This study examined the availability (MMFR) of responses from two (A-B, A-C) consecutively-learned lists of paired-associate adjectives, and from an only-learned list, after seven retention intervals varying from 1 min. to one week.

As expected, the retention of the first of the two lists was far poorer than the second at short retention intervals, but the two were approximately equal after retention intervals of 24 hours and more. However, contrary to expectation, the first list showed neither absolute recovery, nor even relative recovery when the standard was the only-learned list. Comparison of the retention of the second list and the only list showed that the second list suffered proactive inhibition of response availability at longer retention intervals (24 hours and more). Both of these developments were seen as contrary to existing conceptions in two-factor interference theory, and some revisions were suggested.

BARNES, J. M., AND UNDERWOOD, B. J. Fate of first-list associations in transfer theory. *J. exp. Psychol.*, 1959, **58**, 97-105.

BRIGGS, G. E. Acquisition, extinction, and recovery functions in retroactive inhibition. *J. exp. Psychol.*, 1954, **47**, 285-93.

KOPPENAAL, R. J., AND O'HARA, G. N. The combined effect of proaction and retroaction. *Canad. J. Psychol.*, 1962, **16**, 96-105.

MELTON, A. W. Comments on Professor Postman's paper. In C. N. Cofer (Ed.) *Verbal learning and verbal behavior.* New York: McGraw-Hill, 1961.

POSTMAN, L. Extra-experimental interference and the retention of words. *J. exp. Psychol.*, 1961, **61**, 97-110. (*a*)

POSTMAN, L. The present status of interference theory. In C. N. Cofer (Ed.) *Verbal learning and verbal behavior,* New York: McGraw-Hill, 1961. (*b*)

UNDERWOOD, B. J. Retroactive and proactive inhibition after 5 and 48 hours. *J. exp. Psychol.*, 1948, **38**, 29-38. (*a*)

UNDERWOOD, B. J. "Spontaneous recovery" of verbal associations. *J. exp. Psychol.*, 1948, **38**, 429-39. (*b*)

UNDERWOOD, B. J. Proactive inhibition with increased recall-time. *Amer. J. Psychol.*, 1950, **63**, 594-9.

UNDERWOOD, B. J. Interference and forgetting. *Psychol. Rev.*, 1957, **64**, 49-60.

UNDERWOOD, B. J. and POSTMAN, L. Extra-experimental sources of interference in forgetting. *Psychol. Rev.*, 1960, **67**, 73-95.

WALKER, H. M., and LEV, J. *Statistical inference.* New York: Holt, 1953.

5 / Differentiation Versus Unlearning of Verbal Associations [1]

NORMAN J. SLAMECKA, *University of Vermont*

Underwood and Postman (1960) theorized that learning of a list requires the unlearning of competing preexperimental associations to the list items. 3 experiments tested this assumption. Experiments I and II showed that obtained extralist and intralist preexperimental associations were not unlearned following the learning of one or two competing lists. Experiment III showed no weakening of natural associations after competing list learning, by latency measures. It was concluded that preexperimental associations were inhibited but not unlearned during list acquisition. The hypothesis was developed that strong associates are differentiated before they can be unlearned, and weaker associates are unlearned more rapidly than they can become differentiated.

Underwood and Postman (1960) offered a theoretical account of verbal learning and recall which is based upon the traditional interference model, but which lays stress upon the role of existing language habits. Basic to their theory is the hypothesis that memorization of a list requires the unlearning of competing preexperimental associations to the list items. They recognize that S is no associative *tabula rasa*, but that he brings to the laboratory prepotent associative tendencies to the stimuli that will be encountered in the learning task, by virtue of long-standing language habits. If S must acquire new responses to items in the list, it is asserted that he must first break the older, preexperimental, associative bonds. To quote from Underwood and Postman (1960):

As an illustration, assume that the word *over* is a unit in a serial list. Assume further that, due to long existing language habits, there is a strong tendency for the *over* to elicit *there*. We presume that this association will have to be extinguished before a new association can be established, but that with the passage of time the original association will recover to interfere with retention [p. 75].

Other statements of this assumption are found in articles by Postman (1961b, p. 167; 1962b, p. 361).

Deductions from the theory have been tested (Postman, 1961a, 1962a; Underwood & Postman, 1960), and the re-

sults leave something to be desired, especially in predicting recall of lists as a whole. Limited support has come in the form of apparent recovery of intra-list errors which were regarded as pre-experimental associations. However, in testing the theory's applicability to letter-sequence recall, Underwood and Keppel (1963) found no confirmation.

The plausibility of the theory rests critically upon the adequacy of the unlearning hypothesis, and the hypothesis itself merits closer scrutiny. This paper presents evidence pertinent to the question of whether natural associations are, in fact, unlearned during competing laboratory list acquisition.

Barnes and Underwood (1959) showed that associations formed in the laboratory were unlearned after competing list learning. Using paired associates in the A-B, A-C paradigm, they found that availability of first-list responses at recall declined as a function of degree of second-list learning, under conditions of unlimited recall time. Failure to recall the original response was evidence for extinction or unlearning of the association. However, it may be hazardous to assume

From the *Journal of Experimental Psychology*, 1966, 71, 822-8, with permission of the author and publisher.
1. This work was supported by National Science Foundation Grants G-14,721 and B-14,999. The author gratefully acknowledges the assistance of Ernest Lemay and Edina Oldham. Experiment II was conducted during the author's tenure as Visiting Associate Professor at Dartmouth College.

that the phenomenon occurs with strong preexperimental associations. As Russell (1961) noted,

. . . there may be substantive differences in the antecedents of natural language habits which give them properties which are quite different from those normally produced in laboratory settings. . . . Furthermore, what little can be guessed at concerning the antecedents of natural language habits does not on the surface support their claim to comparability to experimentally acquired habits [p. 117].

EXPERIMENT I

This was a direct test of the assumption that learning a list necessitates the concomitant unlearning of competing extralist preexperimental associations. It was direct in that the availability of preexperimental associations generated by S was measured, following the learning of a prescribed list or lists. It also measured the extinction undergone by prescribed associations. The criterion of unlearning was that used by Barnes and Underwood (1959), viz., failure to recall the response when allowed unlimited time.

The design, seen in Table 1, incorporated two parallel retroactive inhibition experiments, one contained within the other. Group 2 was a control for assessing degree of unlearning of List I resulting from the second-list task for Group 1, and Group 3 was a control for assessing degree of unlearning of preexperimental

associations resulting from the prescribed list tasks of Groups 1 and 2.

Method.—Thirty-six students of general psychology at the University of Vermont served as naive Ss, divided into three groups of 12. Each S gave 50 free associations, 5 to each of 10 stimulus words. The word appeared on a memory drum and S was to say the first word that occurred in response to it, and then asked again 4 more times in succession. Instructions forbade repeating an associate to the same word, and no S did so. Four orders of stimulus presentation were used. The words were two-syllable nouns from lists used by Postman (1962a). Five were of high Thorndike and Lorge (1944) frequency (1,000–3,000 in L count) and five were of low frequency (1-3 in L count). Although free associations vary with the method used to elicit them, the particular responses given in this context will be defined as preexperimental associations. It can be assumed that they were the strongest associations to those stimuli. Then Group 1 learned two paired-associates lists in succession from the memory drum by the anticipation method. There was a 3:3-sec. rate of presentation and a 6-sec. intertrial interval.

The lists were of the A-B, A-C paradigm, with stimuli being the same words used in the free-association task. Responses were two-syllable nouns of intermediate Thorndike and Lorge frequency (10-33 in L count), from lists used by Postman (1962a). No S gave a free associate that was one of the prescribed responses. There were four orders of presentation of pairs, list sequence was counterbalanced, and there were two different pairings of stimuli and responses. Acquisition criteria were one errorless trial

TABLE 1. *Design of Exp. I and II*[a]

Group 1	Preexperimental Associations (A-P)	Learn List 1 (A-B)	Learn List 2 (A-C)	Recall Pre-experimental Associations (A-P)	Recall List 1 and List 2 Responses (A-B, C)
Group 2	Same as Group 1	Same as Group 1	Rest Task	Same as Group 1	Recall List 1 Responses (A-B)
Group 3	Same as Group 1	Rest Task	Rest Task	Same as Group 1	

[a] For Exp. II the prescribed list designations are A-Pr, since preexperimental responses were re-paired with other stimuli.

for List 1, and one errorless plus four trials for List 2. Group 2 learned one list (to one errorless trial), and then had a rest activity (the Meier art judgment test), for 11 min. Group 3 learned no lists, but spent 22 min. on the rest activity. These intervals were based upon the learning time for Group 1. Next, Ss recalled their preexperimental associations. The stimuli were on the drum, and unlimited recall time was allowed. Following this, Groups 1 and 2 were given unlimited time to recall the prescribed responses, with Group 2 recalling one response per stimulus, and Group 1, both responses.

Results.—Acquisition and recall data are seen in Table 2. There was no sig-

first three levels of associative strength, and then became irregular. Mean recall of the first response to each stimulus was 8.92, 9.00, and 9.58, for Groups 1, 2, and 3, and an F of 1.88 still indicated no unlearning even for primary associates. In fact there were no noteworthy differences across groups at any level of associative strength.

Of 165 intrusion errors committed in learning both lists (by both Groups 1 and 2) 157 were intralist response. Of the remainder, 6 were intralist stimulus, 1 was unintelligible, and the other was a distortion of the correct word.

TABLE 2. *Results of Exp. I and II*

Group	List 1		List 2		Preexperimental Associations	
	M	SD	M	SD	M	SD
Exp. I						
Acquisition Trials						
1	8.58	3.60	10.83	2.62		
2	9.08	1.77				
Recall Scores						
1	6.58	2.47	9.75	.44	41.42	3.55
2	9.75	.60			40.17	4.62
3					40.50	3.88
Exp. II						
Acquisition Trials						
1	6.75	2.32	6.25	3.19		
2	7.00	4.26				
Recall Scores						
1	6.17	2.14	9.42	1.09	18.00	4.97
2	9.92	.10			18.67	5.17
3					17.17	5.10

nificant difference between Groups 1 and 2 in learning of List 1, $t(22)=.42$. List 1 recall was significantly less for Group 1 than for Group 2, $t(22)=4.12$, $p<.01$, indicating unlearning of some prescribed responses. Relative retroactive inhibition was 32.51%. In sharp contrast to this, recall of preexperimental associations did not even approach significance among the three groups, $F(2, 33)=.28$. Further, there were no significant differences in recall of preexperimental associations to either the high-frequency or the low-frequency stimuli, $F(2, 33)=.07$ and .45, respectively. Within each group, probability of recall decreased over the

Thus, no known extralist preexperimental associates intruded themselves.

The above results provided no support for the hypothesis that extralist preexperimental associations *must* be unlearned for a competing list to be memorized. However, under the same conditions, a prescribed list suffered unlearning through the competition of a subsequent list. Since extralist associates did not intrude, it might be argued that they had no opportunity to be unlearned. Therefore, another experiment was performed under conditions where competing preexperimental associations were intralist. In light of evidence for a "selector mechanism" (Underwood & Schultz, 1960, p. 305), which recognizes that extralist intrusions are rare in verbal learning, a test involving intralist competing associations was essential.[2]

The design of Exp. II was basically that of Exp. I, with two changes. The first was in the free-association phase, where S was now allowed to repeat an associate previously given. A set against repetition of earlier responses might otherwise have been established (as in Exp. I), and carried to prescribed learning. If extinction requires unreinforced emission of responses, such a set might have worked against unlearning. Another change was in the construction of the lists. Each list had the same stimuli that were used in the free-association phase, but the responses were determined by each S's individual associations. The first list had as responses the first associates given by S, but paired with other stimuli. If the free associates are designated A-P, the first list would be A-Pr. The second list was also A-Pr, using the second associates. Thus, the strongest preexperimental response would necessarily be included in the lists, and not be cut out by a selector mechanism.

Experiment II

Method.—Thirty-six introductory psychology students at Dartmouth College served as naive Ss, divided into three groups of 12. The S gave five free associations to each of 10 words. Each word was shown on a separate card, and the cards were presented in haphazard order 50 times. The stimuli were the same as those of Exp. I. Next, Group 1 learned two paired-associates lists to a criterion of two consecutive correct trials by the method of alternate training and testing trials. On training trials each pair was shown on a card for 2 sec. On test trials the stimulus member was shown and S had unlimited time to recall the prescribed response. All cards were shuffled before each presentation. Lists were of the A-B, A-C

paradigm, with stimuli being the words used in the free-association task. List 1 responses were the primary associates given by S, re-paired with other stimuli. Preparation of the pairs took about 2 min. List 2 responses were the second associates, again re-paired. In cases where the first and second associates were the same, the response was retained and re-paired with another stimulus. Group 2 learned one such list to the same criterion and then had a rest activity (the Meier art judgment test), for 15 min. Group 3 Ss simply spent 30 min. on the rest activity. These intervals were based upon the learning time for Group 1.

Finally, S recalled his free associations. Each stimulus was shown once and unlimited recall time allowed. Then, similarly, Groups 1 and 2 recalled the prescribed responses.

Results.—Acquisition and recall data are shown in Table 2. There was no significant difference in learning List 1, $t(22) = .17$. Significant unlearning of List 1 occurred as a function of interference from List 2, $t(22) = 5.68$, $p < .01$. Relative retroactive inhibition was 37.8%. The mean number of different associates given was 19.17, 20.00, and 18.50, for Groups 1, 2, and 3, $F(2, 33) = .20$, with no difference in their recalls, $F(2, 33) = .24$. Nor was there a difference at recall as a function of high- or low-frequency stimuli, $F(2, 33) = .16$ and .50, respectively. Mean recall of primary associates was 9.75, 9.50, and 9.58, for Groups 1, 2, 3, respectively. Of 546 intrusion errors committed in learning both lists (by both Groups 1 and 2), 450 were intralist response with 54 specific to their original preexperimental stimuli. There were 49 extraneous intrusions (including 12 interlist), and the rest were intralist stimulus. Thus there were numerous overt competing responses and ample opportunities for their unlearning.

2. The importance of intralist preexperimental associations was recently reiterated by Underwood (1964): ". . . if a verbal unit not in the list is strongly associated with one in the list, the amount of interference it produces is less than for a unit which is equally strongly associated and is in the list [p. 58]."

Clearly, Exp. II produced no evidence that intralist preexperimental associations were unlearned following interfering learning, but they showed that under the same conditions, a prescribed list was substantially unlearned. Failure to detect retroactive inhibition of extra- or intralist preexperimental associations by the exacting criterion of unavailability led to consideration of a more sensitive measure. It was felt that latencies might indicate a weakening effect as a result of direct interference. Accordingly, Exp. III measured reaction latencies of primary associates to stimulus words, which associates were then re-paired for prescribed learning, followed by latency measures at recall of the original associates. A control group without prescribed learning provided the necessary comparisons. The design embodied the A-P, A-Pr paradigm of Exp. II, which theoretically provided maximum opportunity for weakening of intralist intrusions. Increased recall latencies would be evidence for weakening of associations.

EXPERIMENT III

Method.—Thirty-six students of general psychology at the University of Vermont served as naive Ss, divided into two groups of 18. Each S gave one associate to each of 14 words. Response latency was measured to the nearest hundredth of a second on a Standard electric timer. The words were two-syllable nouns of low Thorndike and Lorge frequency (1–3 in L count), from lists used by Postman (1962a), and were shown on separate cards. The experimental group learned an interfering list of paired associates by the method of alternate training and testing trials to a criterion of two consecutive errorless trials. This list had the same stimuli as in the free-association task, and responses were associates given by S re-paired. The control group had a rest activity (Meier art judgment test) for 20 min. Then, both groups recalled their original associations to the stimuli, with latencies measured.

Results.—Mean original response latencies of 2.76 sec. and 2.93 sec. (SD = .86 and 1.02) for the experimental and control groups, respectively, did not differ statistically, $t(34) = .53$, $p > .05$. Mean recalls of original associations were 13.17 and 13.39 (SD = .91 and .74), again showing no differential unavailability. Of 202 intrusion errors committed in learning, 182 were intralist response, of which 24 were specific to their original preexperimental stimuli. The remainder were intralist stimulus, with no extraneous errors. There were thus ample opportunities for weakening of inappropriate associations. Nevertheless, mean latencies of correctly recalled free associates were 1.82 sec. and 1.70 sec. (SD = .64 and .57) for the experimental and control groups, respectively. The difference was statistically insignificant, $t(34) = .60$, $p > .05$. Nor did a comparison of difference scores between original and recall latencies show any effect, $t(34) = .47$. These data offer no confirmation for the hypothesis that preexperimental associations were even weakened after a competing learning task.

DISCUSSION

The outcomes of these experiments point to the conclusion that, since no demonstrable unlearning or even weakening of preexperimental associates occurred after competing prescribed learning, the Underwood and Postman (1960) hypothesis is without direct support.

If the natural associations were not extinguished, what happened to them during prescribed learning? Evidently they were simply inhibited. They were recognized as inappropriate to their original stimuli in the context of the new task and were quickly withheld from utterance to those stimuli, but remained available for recall. This differential probability of utterance reflected a differentiation based upon contextual cues which delineated the learning situation from the recall situation. The learning context was the S^Δ where emission of the natural response was not reinforced, and the recall context was the S^D where it was appropriate. The thoroughness with which differentiation among contexts became effective is indicated by the rarity of extraneous intrusions in all three experiments, and by the rarity of intralist-response intrusions of natural associates specific to their original stimuli in Exp. II and III. Most of the latter were to stimuli *other* than the preexperimental ones, in accord with the changed task requirements. If unlearning had occurred, the original associations would have been unavailable in the recall context, or at least have had longer latencies.

The distinction between differentiation and unlearning has critical relevance to the Underwood and Postman position. Those authors have hypothesized that after learning of a list, extinguished natural associations will recover spontaneously and provide interference with recall of the list. However, if preexperimental associates are not extinguished, but only inhibited, there is nothing *from* which to recover, and therefore the spontaneous recovery assumption is untenable as an explanation for forgetting. In fact, there is no convincing and consistent evidence for true spontaneous recovery of verbal associations (Koppenaal, 1963; Slamecka, in press; Slamecka & Ceraso, 1960).

Why were the prescribed associates so vulnerable to unlearning? The different fates of prescribed vs. natural associates can be attributed fundamentally to their different strengths. The preexperimental associates in the above experiments were among the strongest ones to those stimuli, whereas the prescribed associates were far weaker. This is not to say that the prescribed associations all involved "raw" learning, since many were probably mediated by preexperimental connections. But on the average it is likely that the prescribed associates were much weaker than the older, preexperimental ones. Assuming that resistance to extinction is a positive function of associative strength, the experimental data can be explained as follows. The natural associates, being very strong, could be sufficiently differentiated from the prescribed list context and inhibited *before* any appreciable unlearning of them occurred. Their strength tended to assure that many extinction trials would have been needed to produce unlearning. However, differentiation took place before extinction could be accomplished, thus effectively removing the associations from any further possibility of unlearning, no matter how many more competing lists were given.

In contrast, the prescribed first-list associations were relatively weaker at the end of learning, and needed few extinction trials to render them unavailable. Thus, they were not all able to be differentiated from the second-list context in sufficient time to prevent a substantial number from being unlearned. The rest were differentiated and remained available at recall. The great vulnerability of weak associations to unlearning can be inferred from the data of Barnes and Underwood (1959). An eight-pair list was learned to bare mastery, followed by a competing list. After only one anticipation trial on the competing list, recall of first-list associates was down to 6.67 items, compared to an expected control recall of 8 (judged from an obtained control recall of 7.75, taken after a 13-min. period). Associative strength is thus a probable determiner of the time available for differentiation, before unlearning obliterates the association.

It is well known that susceptibility to retroactive inhibition is a negative function of first-list strength. It is also known that increased second-list learning increases retroactive inhibition only up to a point. Even with large numbers of second-list trials, first-list recall is never completely obliterated (Slamecka & Ceraso, 1960). The assumption that differentiation of an item makes it resistant to unlearning could accommodate such observations. On the other hand, any factor which makes differentiation difficult should decrease recall. Increased similarity might be one, and it is known that interference rises with more similar contexts, whether at the level of stimulus-items, testing procedures, or extra-list environments (Slamecka & Ceraso, 1960). It also follows that correctly recalled items should be correctly differentiated as to context. Barnes and Underwood (1959), Koppenaal (1963), and Slamecka (in press), have all reported that when a response was remembered its list membership was almost always properly identified. Such facts are certainly consistent with this rationale, and suggest that the differentiation concept deserves further consideration.

BARNES, J. M., & UNDERWOOD, B. J. Fate of first-list associations in transfer theory. *J. exp. Psychol.*, 1959, **58**, 97-105.

KOPPENAAL, R. J. Time changes in the strengths of A-B, A-C lists; spontaneous recovery? *J. verbal Learn. verbal Behav.*, 1963, **2**, 310-19.

POSTMAN, L. Extra-experimental interference and the retention of words. *J. exp. Psychol.*, 1961, **61**, 97-110. (a)

POSTMAN, L. The present status of interference theory. In C. N. Cofer (Ed.), *Verbal learning and verbal behavior.* New York: McGraw-Hill, 1961. Pp. 152-79. (b)

POSTMAN, L. The effects of language habits on the acquisition and retention of verbal associations. *J. exp. Psychol.*, 1962, **64**, 7-19. (a)

POSTMAN, L. The temporal course of proactive inhibition for serial lists. *J. exp. Psychol.*, 1962, **68**, 361-9. (b)

RUSSELL, W. A. Assessment versus experimental acquisition of verbal habits. In C. N. Cofer (Ed.), *Verbal learning and verbal behavior.* New York: McGraw-Hill, 1961. Pp. 110-23.

SLAMECKA, N. J. A search for spontaneous recovery of verbal associations. *J. verbal Learn. verbal Behav.*, 1966, in press.

SLAMECKA, N. J., & CERASO, J. Retroactive and proactive inhibition of verbal learning. *Psychol. Bull.*, 1960, **57**, 449-75.

THORNDIKE, E. L., & LORGE, I. *The Teacher's word book of 30,000 words.* New York: Teachers College, Columbia University, 1944.

UNDERWOOD, B. J. The representativeness of verbal learning. In A. W. Melton (Ed.), *Categories of human learning.* New York: Academic Press, 1964. Pp. 47-78.

UNDERWOOD, B. J., & KEPPEL, G. Retention as a function of degree of learning and letter-sequence interference. *Psychol. Monogr.*, 1963, **77**, (4, Whole No. 567).

UNDERWOOD, B. J., & POSTMAN, L. Extra-experimental sources of interference in forgetting. *Psychol. Rev.*, 1960, **67**, 73-95.

UNDERWOOD, B. J., & SCHULZ, R. W. *Meaningfulness and verbal learning.* New York: Lippincott, 1960.

SERIAL LEARNING PROCESSES

How does a person manage to learn a succession of responses in a fixed order? The pianist who must play the proper series of notes, or the experimental subject who must master the appropriate sequence of verbal items, is faced with much the same task. What are the processes which underlie the accomplishment of such tasks? This is the problem of serial learning, and it has been studied with human subjects mainly through the presentation of lists of nonsense syllables or unconnected words on a memory drum, using the method of anticipation.

The traditional and intuitively appealing view, associated with the pioneer work of Ebbinghaus (1964), is that each item in a list comes to serve as the stimulus for the next item, and so on in turn, so as to eventuate in the triggering of a chain of direct, adjacent associations. In addition, Ebbinghaus established the concept of remote associations. This asserts that during serial learning, associative bonds are also formed between items which are nonadjacent, or remote from each other in the list. The latter are presumed to be weaker than the adjacent associations. The supposed interfering effect of remote associations was invoked to explain the serial position curve, that is, the fact that the items at and just beyond the middle of a list are the most difficult to learn (Bugelski, 1950).

As plausible and compelling as this theoretical structure appeared, it did not satisfy all students of the problem. Asch, Hay, and Diamond (1960), for instance, studied serial learning under conditions in which the items not only had a certain temporal order, but also had various spatial locations. Their study showed that spatial arrangement had a marked influence upon the course of learning, and that a simple chaining hypothesis could not gracefully accommodate this fact. A recent experiment by Slamecka (1967) also utilized the device of providing spatial cues which were independent of the temporal serial order, and the results clearly failed to support expectations based upon the chaining view.

The papers in this section present analytic and experimental developments which have seriously challenged the traditional assumptions, and which have forced a reconsideration of the entire process of serial learning.

Lashley's classic paper on the problem of serial order stands as one of the earliest influential analyses of the problem. Ranging from linguistics to neurophysiology, Lashley skillfully limned out the complexities of a question which had initially seemed straightforward. He rejected an associationistic explanation and tentatively concluded that a serial performance, once mastered, has the properties of an integrated whole, rather than being a collection of independent responses.

The important paper by Young was one of the first direct tests of the traditional associationistic interpretation of serial learning. Utilizing a simple and clever experimental approach, Young found that the stimulus for a serial item was neither the preceding item nor a cluster of preceding items, but that it might have something to do with the position of the item in the list. This paper served to galvanize considerable interest in the serial order problem.

Ebenholtz's paper indicated that a pure position learning task, where the only clue to an item's identity was its position in a spatial array, strongly facilitated a subsequent serial learning task when the identical items retained their same positions. When the subsequent task involved changed positions, transfer declined.

Later, Ebenholtz (1963) also showed that learning was much easier if an item maintained its absolute position in the list, as compared to the case in which its position was varied. Again, knowledge of an item's position was seen as an important determinant of serial learning.

Slamecka's paper re-examined the validity of the doctrine of remote associations. Each of the methods by which remote associations have been studied, i.e. derived lists, method of association, and anticipatory and perseverative errors, was shown to be artifactual, or at least amenable to an equally attractive alternative explanation. Since the traditional view that serial learning consists in the formation of adjacent and remote associations was not upheld, a two-process conception was instead stressed, one that involved learning of the items and learning of their positions in the list.

The paper by Jensen and Rohwer contains a valuable critical summary of theoretical positions and work performed to date, as well as an experiment on transfer from serial to paired-associates learning. The data supported neither the chaining nor position hypotheses, and the authors appealed to Lashley's original suggestions as pointing in the most fruitful direction. Thus, the problem of serial order is still very much alive, and future work will probably continue to explore the role of position learning in serial tasks.

Asch, S. E., Hay, J., & Diamond, R. M. Perceptual organization in serial rote-learning. *Amer. J. Psychol.*, 1960, 73, 177-98.

Bugelski, B. R. A remote association explanation of the relative difficulty of learning nonsense syllables in a serial list. *J. exp. Psychol.*, 1950, 40, 336-48.

Ebbinghaus, H. *Memory: A contribution to experimental psychology.* New York: Dover Publications, 1964.

Ebenholtz, S. M. Serial learning: Position learning and sequential associations. *J. exp. Psychol.*, 1963, 66, 353-62.

Slamecka, N. J. Serial learning and order information. *J. exp. Psychol.*, 1967, in press.

6 / The Problem of Serial Order in Behavior

K. S. LASHLEY, *Harvard University and the Yerkes Laboratories of Primate Biology*

The previous speakers have approached our common problem by considering the properties of the elementary units of which we believe the cerebral structure to be built up. They have considered the kinds of neural integration or behavior which can be anticipated from those properties. The remaining members of the symposium have in their research been concerned chiefly with the analysis of complex behavior, seeking to derive general principles of neural integration from the infinitely complex products of that integration. Our common meeting ground is the faith to which we all subscribe, I believe, that the phenomena of behavior and of mind are ultimately describable in the concepts of the mathematical and physical sciences. In my discussion here, I have deliberately turned to the opposite extreme from the neuron and have chosen as a topic, one aspect of the most complex type of behavior that I know; the logical and orderly arrangement of thought and action. Our discussion so far has dealt chiefly with the conditions of input and of immediate switching in the nervous mechanism, without explicit consideration of what is already going on within the system.

My principal thesis today will be that the input is never into a quiescent or static system, but always into a system which is already actively excited and organized. In the intact organism, behavior is the result of interaction of this background of excitation with input from any designated stimulus. Only when we can state the general characteristics of this background of excitation, can we understand the effects of a given input.

The unpronounceable Cree Indian word "kekawewechetushekamikowanowow" is analyzed by Chamberlain (7) into the verbal root, *tusheka,* "to remain," and the various particles which modify it as follows: *ke(la)wow,* the first and last syllables, indicating second person plural; *ka,* a prefix of the future tense; *we,* a sort of imperative mode expressing a wish; *weche,* indicating conjunction of subject and object; *mik,* a suffix bringing the verb into agreement with a third person subject and second person object; and *owan,* a suffix indicating that the subject is inanimate and the object animate. A literal translation: "You will I wish together remain he-you-it-man you" or, freely, "may it remain with you." This difference in structure between Cree and English illustrates an outstanding characteristic of verbal behavior; the occurrence of predetermined, orderly sequences of action which are unique for each language. In English the adjective precedes, in French it follows the noun which it modifies. In English the movement or action of the subject is expressed as early as possible after the subject; in German the expression of action may be postponed until all qualifying thoughts have been expressed. In a sentence discussing this subject, Pick (20) introduces fifty-five words between the subject and the principal verb. Each Chinese word, and to a lesser extent, each English word, stands as an unchanging unit. In the highly inflective languages, such as Sioux, the form of almost every word in the sentence may be altered, according to some attribute of the subject, as when two objects rather than one or several are discussed.

The study of comparative grammar is not the most direct approach to the physiology of the cerebral cortex, yet

Abridged from *Cerebral Mechanisms in Behavior,* edited by L. A. Jeffress, New York: Wiley, 1951, pp. 112-36, by permission of the California Institute of Technology.

Fournié (10) has written, "Speech is the only window through which the physiologist can view the cerebral life." Certainly language presents in a most striking form the integrative functions that are characteristic of the cerebral cortex and that reach their highest development in human thought processes. Temporal integration is not found exclusively in language; the coordination of leg movements in insects, the song of birds, the control of trotting and pacing in a gaited horse, the rat running the maze, the architect designing a house, and the carpenter sawing a board present a problem of sequences of action which cannot be explained in terms of successions of external stimuli.

Associative Chain Theories

In spite of the ubiquity of the problem, there have been almost no attempts to develop physiological theories to meet it. In fact, except among a relatively small group of students of aphasia, who have had to face questions of agrammatism, the problem has been largely ignored. It is not even mentioned in recent textbooks on neurophysiology or physiological psychology, nor is there any significant body of experimental studies bearing upon the problem. The spinal animal scarcely exhibits serial activity, so the physiologist may be excused for overlooking the phenomenon. On the other hand, psychologists have been concerned chiefly with the question of whether or not the organizing processes displayed in serial action are conscious, and very little with the organization itself. I have chosen to discuss the problem of temporal integration here, not with the expectation of offering a satisfactory physiological theory to account for it, but because it seems to me to be both the most important and also the most neglected problem of cerebral physiology. Temporally integrated actions do occur even among insects, but they do not reach any

degree of complexity until the appearance of the cerebral cortex. They are especially characteristic of human behavior and contribute as much as does any single factor to the superiority of man's intelligence. A clearer formulation of the physiological problems which they raise should be of value, even though a solution of the problems is not yet in sight.

I shall consider first some of the questions raised by the structure of language, then turn to other forms of serial action for indications of the nature of the nervous mechanisms involved.

To the best of my knowledge, the only strictly physiological theory that has been explicitly formulated to account for temporal integration is that which postulates chains of reflexes, in which the performance of each element of the series provides excitation of the next. This conception underlay the "motor theories" of thinking which were advocated by several psychologists early in this century. Watson (26) sought to identify thought with inaudible movements of the vocal organs, linked together in associative chains. The peripheral chain theory of language was developed in greatest detail by Washburn (25). She distinguished what she called "successive movement systems" and, although she drew her examples from memorized series of nonsense syllables, her implication was that such series are typical of all language behavior. She defined a movement system as "a combination of movements so linked together that the stimulus furnished by the actual performance of certain movements is required to bring about other movements." She described speech as a succession of vocal acts in which the kinesthetic impulses from each movement serve as a unique stimulus for the next in the series (25, pages 11 ff.). Attempts to confirm these peripheral theories by mechanical (Thorsen, 23) or electrical (Max, 19) recording of muscular tensions have given no valid evidence in support of them. It should be noted that, at the time when the theories were proposed, it was generally believed that conduction in the nervous system is always downstream from sense organ to muscle, and that muscular contraction must always follow promptly on stimulation. The existence of reverberatory circuits which could maintain activity was scarcely suspected.

The introspective psychology which objected to such peripheral theories did not explicitly formulate an alternative neurological theory, but there is implicit in it a view that verbal thought is a simple chain of central processes in which each element serves to arouse the next by direct association. Titchener, for example, maintained that the meaning of a word (or of an auditory image in his system) consists of the chain of associations which it arouses; that it has no meaning until such a sequence has occurred. From this it must be inferred that he was thinking in terms of a simple associative chain, since no other relating process is suggested.

OBJECTIONS TO THE ASSOCIATIVE CHAIN THEORY

A consideration of the structure of the sentence and of other motor sequences will show, I believe, that such interpretations of temporal organization are untenable and that there are, behind the overtly expressed sequences, a multiplicity of integrative processes which can only be inferred from the final results of their activity. There is an extensive controversial literature dealing with this inferred integrative activity. Pick (20) devotes almost his entire book, *Die agrammatischen Sprachstörungen*, to reviewing discussions of the subject. Most of this literature deals with the question of whether or not the integrative processes are conscious. Much of this is irrelevant to the present topic, but the advocates of

so-called imageless thought did present a great deal of material indicative of the complexity of the problem of thought structure. From this, and other evidence which I shall present, I believe that the production of speech involves the interaction of at least three, possibly four, major neurological systems which are interrelated but somewhat independently variable.

Let us start the analysis of the process with the enunciation of the word. Pronunciation of the word "right" consists first of retraction and elevation of the tongue, expiration of air and activation of the vocal cords; second, depression of the tongue and jaw; third, elevation of the tongue to touch the dental ridge, stopping of vocalization, and forceful expiration of air with depression of the tongue and jaw. These movements have no intrinsic order of association. Pronunciation of the word "tire" involves the same motor elements in reverse order. Such movements occur in all permutations. The order must therefore be imposed upon the motor elements by some organization other than direct associative connections between them. So, for the individual movements in writing or typing the word, finger strokes occur in all sorts of combinations. No single letter invariably follows *g*, and whether *gh*, *ga*, or *gu* is written depends upon a set for a larger unit of action, the word.

Words stand in relation to the sentence as letters do to the word; the words themselves have no intrinsic temporal "valence." The word "right," for example, is noun, adjective, adverb, and verb, and has four spellings and at least ten meanings. In such a sentence as "The mill-wright on my right thinks it right that some conventional rite should symbolize the right of every man to write as he pleases," word arrangement is obviously not due to any direct associations of the word "right" itself with other words, but to meanings which are determined by some broader relations.

It has been found in studies of memorization of nonsense syllables that each syllable in the series has associations, not only with adjacent words in the series, but also with more remote words. The words in the sentence have, of course, associations with more remote words as well as with adjacent ones. However, the combination of such direct associations will not account for grammatical structure. The different positions of the word "right" in the illustrative sentence are determined by the meanings which the positions in relation to other words denote, but those meanings are given by other associations than those with the words in the spoken sentence. The word can take its position only when the particular one of its ten meanings becomes dominant. This dominance is not inherent in the words themselves.

From such considerations, it is certain that any theory of grammatical form which ascribes it to direct associative linkage of the words of the sentence overlooks the essential structure of speech. The individual items of the temporal series do not in themselves have a temporal "valence" in their associative connections with other elements. The order is imposed by some other agent.

This is true not only of language, but of all skilled movements or successions of movement. In the gaits of a horse, trotting, pacing, and single footing involve essentially the same pattern of muscular contraction in the individual legs. The gait is imposed by some mechanism in addition to the direct relations of reciprocal innervation among the sensory-motor centers of the legs. The order in which the fingers of the musician fall on the keys or fingerboard is determined by the signature of the composition; this gives a set which is not inherent in the association of the individual movements.

The Determining Tendency

What then determines the order? The answer which seems most in accord with common sense is that the intention to act or the idea to be expressed determines the sequence. There are, however, serious difficulties for this solution. There is not much agreement among psychologists concerning the nature of the idea. The structuralist school, under the leadership of Titchener, held that the idea consists of mental images, often the auditory images of words, and the meanings are nothing but sequences of such images. Describing the role of images in his lecturing, Titchener wrote (24) "When there is any difficulty in exposition, a point to be argued *pro* and *con* or a conclusion to be brought out from the convergence of several lines of proof, I hear my own voice speaking just ahead of me." What solution of the lecture problem for the lazy man! He need not think but only listen to his own inner voice; to the chain of associated auditory images. A behaviorist colleague once remarked to me that he had reached a stage where he could arise before an audience, turn his mouth loose, and go to sleep. He believed in the peripheral chain theory of language. (This clearly demonstrates the superiority of behavioristic over introspective psychology. The behaviorist does not even have to listen to his own inner voice.)

Seriously, such positions offer no solution for the problem of temporal integration. Titchener finds his grammar ready made and does not even raise the question of the origin of the succession of images. The chain-reflex theory, while definite, is untenable.

The third view of the nature of the idea was developed by a group known as the "Würzburg School" (see Boring, 4); exponents of imageless thought. It held that some organization precedes any expression that can be discovered by introspective or objective means. Thought is neither muscular contraction nor image, but can only be inferred as a "determining tendency." At most, it is discovered as a vague feeling of pregnancy, of being about to have an idea, a Bewusstseinslage. It is not identical with the words which are spoken, for quite frequently no word can be recalled which satisfactorily expresses the thought, and we search a dictionary of synonyms until a word or phrase is found which does seem appropriate.

In his discussion of the relation of thought to speech, Pick (20) accepts this point of view, but he asserts further that the set or the idea does not have a temporal order; that all of its elements are cotemporal. Evidence in support of this conclusion comes, for example, from translation of one language into another which has a different sentence structure. I read a German sentence, pronouncing the German words with no thought of their English equivalents. I then give a free translation in English, without remembering a single word of the German text. Somewhere between ·the reading and free translation, the German sentence is condensed, the word order reversed, and expanded again into the different temporal order of English. According to Epstein (9), the polyglot shifts readily from one language to another, expressing the same thought in either, without literal translation. The readiness with which the form of expression of an idea can be changed, the facility with which different word orders may be utilized to express the same thought, thus is further evidence that the temporal integration is not inherent in the preliminary organization of the idea.

THE SCHEMA OF ORDER

The remaining alternative is that the mechanism which determines the serial activation of the motor units is relatively independent, both of the motor units and of the thought structure. Supporting evidence for this may be found in the mistakes of order, the slips and interferences which occur in writing and speaking. For some time I have kept records of errors in typing. A frequent error is the misplacing or the doubling of a letter. *These* is typed t-h-s-e-s, *look* as l-o-k-k, *ill* as i-i-l. Sometimes the set to repeat may be displaced by several words. The order is dissociated from the idea. Earlier, in preparing this paper, I wrote the phrase, "maintain central activities." I typed *min*, omitting the *a*, canceled this out and started again; *ama*. The impulse to insert the *a* now dominated the order. I struck out the *a* and completed the phrase, only to find that I had now also dropped the *a* from *activities*. This example suggests something of the complexity of the forces which are at play in the determination of serial order and the way in which conflicting impulses may distort the order, although the primary determining tendency, the idea, remains the same.

The polyglot, who has become proficient in a secondary language, who thinks in it and even dreams in it, may still tend to use the grammatical structure of his native tongue. If, as in French, that tongue applies gender to inanimate things, the English pronouns referring to them may take the gender of the French equivalents, though the French nouns are not thought. The German postponement of the verb or the Magyar use of the past infinitive may be incorporated in the new language. In such cases, the structuring seems to be dissociated both from the content and from the simple associative connections of the words themselves.

The ease with which a new structure may be imposed on words is illustrated by the quickness with which children learn hog Latin. The form which I learned involved transposing the initial sound of each word to the end of the word and adding a long *a*. Thus—at-thay an-may oes-gay own-day e-thay eet-stray. Some children become very facile at such inversions of words, and re-structure new words without hesitation. From such considerations it seems to follow that syntax is not inherent in the words employed or in the idea to be expressed. It is a generalized pattern imposed upon the specific acts as they occur.

"PRIMING" OF EXPRESSIVE UNITS

There are indications that, prior to the internal or overt enunciation of the sentence, an aggregate of word units is partially activated or readied. Evidence for this comes also from "contaminations" of speech and writing. The most frequent typing errors are those of anticipation; the inclusion in the word being typed of some part of a word or word structure which should properly occur later in the sentence. It may be only a letter. Thus I wrote, *wrapid* writing, carrying the *w* from the second word to the first. Not infrequently words are introduced which should occur much later in the sentence, often five or six words in advance.

In oral speech, Spoonerisms illustrate the same kind of contamination. The Spoonerism is most frequently an inversion of subject and object: "Let us always remember that waste makes haste." But it may be only a transposition of parts of the words: "Our queer old dean" for "our dear old queen." The frequency with which such contaminations occur is increased by haste, by distraction, by emotional tension, or by uncertainty and conflict as to the best form of expression. In some types of aphasia the tendency to disordered arrangement of words is greatly increased, and, in extreme cases, the attempt to speak results in a word hash with complete loss of grammatical organization. Professor Spooner, after whom such slips are named, was probably suffering from a mild form of aphasia. In these contaminations, it is as if the aggregate of words were in a state of partial excitation, held in check by the requirements of grammatical structure, but ready to activate the final common path, if the effectiveness of this check is in any way interfered with.

In his *Psychopathology of Everyday Life*, Freud has given numerous examples of similar contaminations of action outside the sphere of language. We do not need to accept his theories of censorship and suppression to account for such slips. They are of the same order as misplacements in typing and represent contaminations of co-existing, determining tendencies to action.

Such contaminations might be ascribed to differences in the relative strength of associative bonds between the elements of the act, and thus not evidence for pre-excitation of the elements or for simultaneous pre-excitation. However, the understanding of speech involves essentially the same problems as the production of speech and definitely demands the postulation of an after-effect or after-discharge of the sensory components for a significant time following stimulation. Thus, in the spoken sentence, "Rapid righting with his uninjured hand saved from loss the contents of the capsized canoe," the associations which give meaning to righting are not activated for at least 3 to 5 seconds after hearing the word.[1] I shall refer later to other evidence for such long after-discharge of sensory excitations. The fact of continued activation or after-discharge of receptive elements and their integration during this activation justifies the assumption of a similar process during motor organization. The processes of comprehension and production of speech have too much in common to depend on wholly different mechanisms.

1. Dr. Lashley ingeniously laid the groundwork for this three paragraphs earlier, when he mentions "wrapid writing." The audience all heard, "Rapid writing with his uninjured hand," etc. "Capsized canoe" required a complete and amusing about-face. EDITOR.

INTERNAL AND OVERT SPEECH

One other point with respect to the organization of speech: The earlier literature on aphasia emphasized the distinction of internal and overt speech. The aphemia of Broca and the pure motor aphasia of Wernicke and later writers were held to be a loss of the ability to enunciate without loss of ability to think in words and without paralysis of the organs of speech. The brain insult was assumed to affect only the transition from the thought to the enunciation of the word. We may doubt the existence of instances of such "pure" defects and question the reliability of the early clinical examinations in view of the more careful analyses that have been made since 1917, but the distinction of internal and overt speech is still valid and the transition still unexplained. Watson interpreted internal speech as inaudible movements of the vocal organs, and Jacobsen (15) and Max (19) have given evidence of changes in muscular tonus during verbal thinking or thought of movement. This is far from proving that the motor discharge is essential for the internal formation of words, however.

I once devised an instrument to record small movements of the tongue. Within the limits of its sensitivity, it showed that in silent thinking the tongue usually drops to the back of the mouth and shows no detectable movement. Verbal problems, such as the correct squaring of three-place numbers, could be carried out with no trace of overt movement. If, however, I urged the subject to hurry or if I slapped his face, his tongue came forward and showed movements corresponding to the syllabification of internal speech or of the computation he was performing. This I interpret as indicating that internal speech may be carried out wholly by processes within the nervous system, with some unessential discharge upon the final common path for vocal movements. Facilitation of the motor path, either by increased emotional tension or by "voluntary" reinforcement, increases its excitability until the same central circuits whose activity constitutes internal speech are able to excite the overt movements. This aspect of the language function is irrelevant to the problem of syntax or serial order, but is important as illustrating a further point in the dynamics of the cerebrum. Many activities seem to require for their performance both a specific patterning and also a general facilitation, a rise in dynamic level. There are, I think, indications that hemiplegia and motor aphasia are primarily expressions of a low level of facilitation rather than a loss of specific integrative connections which are involved in the use of language or in the patterning of our movements. A monkey, for example, after ablation of the precentral gyrus may seem unable to use the arm at all, but if emotional excitement is raised above a certain level, the arm is freely used. As soon as the excitement dies down, the arm is again hemiplegic. I have seen something of the same sort in a human hemiplegic. The problem of the availability of memories, which was raised earlier in the discussion here, may find a partial solution in such fluctuations in dynamic level. In many of the organic amnesias the pattern of integration seems to be retained but can be reactivated only by an abnormally intense sensory or central reinforcement.

GENERALITY OF THE PROBLEM OF SYNTAX

I have devoted so much time to discussion of the problem of syntax, not only because language is one of the most important products of human cerebral action, but also because the problems raised by the organization of language seem to me to be characteristic of almost all other cerebral activity. There is a series of hierarchies of organization; the order of vocal movements in pronouncing the word, the order of words in the sentence, the order of sentences in the paragraph, the rational order of paragraphs in a discourse. Not only speech, but all skilled acts seem to involve the same problems of serial ordering, even down to the temporal coordination of muscular contractions in such a movement as reaching and grasping. Analysis of the nervous mechanisms underlying order in the more primitive acts may contribute ultimately to the solution even of the physiology of logic.

It is possible to designate, that is, to point to specific examples of, the phenomena of the syntax of movement that require explanation, although those phenomena cannot be clearly defined. A real definition would be a long step toward solution of the problem. There are at least three sets of events to be accounted for. First, the activation of the expressive elements (the individual words or adaptive acts) which do not contain the temporal relations. Second, the determining tendency, the set, or idea. This masquerades under many names in contemporary psychology, but is, in every case, an inference from the restriction of behavior within definite limits. Third, the syntax of the act, which can be described as an habitual order or mode of relating the expressive elements; a generalized pattern or schema of integration which may be imposed upon a wide range and a wide variety of specific acts. This is the essential problem of serial order; the existence of generalized schemata of action which determine the sequence of specific acts, acts which in themselves or in their associations seem to have no temporal valence.

INTERACTION OF TEMPORAL AND SPATIAL SYSTEMS

Integration ascribed to the spatial distribution of excitations in the nervous system has been much more intensively studied than the temporal aspects of nervous activity. Theories of integration are based almost exclusively upon space properties, time entering only in theories of facilitation, inhibition, and after-discharge. In cerebral functions, however, it is difficult to distinguish between spatial and temporal functions. The eye is the only organ that gives simultaneous information concerning space in any detail. The shape of an object impressed on the skin can scarcely be detected from simultaneous pressure, but the same shape can readily be distinguished by touch when traced on the skin with a moving point or when explored by tactile scanning. The temporal sequence is readily translated into a spatial concept. Even for vision it might be questioned whether simultaneous stimulation gives rise directly to space concepts. The visual object is generally surveyed by eye movements, and its form is a reconstruction from such a series of excitations. Even with tachistoscopic exposures, the after-discharge permits a temporal survey, and, with visual fixation, shifts of attention provide an effective scanning.

Since memory traces are, we believe, in large part static and persist simultaneously, it must be assumed that they are spatially differentiated. Nevertheless, reproductive memory appears almost invariably as a temporal sequence, either as a succession of words or of acts. Even descriptions of visual imagery (the supposed simultaneous reproductive memory in sensory terms) are generally descriptions of sequences, of temporal reconstructions from very fragmentary and questionable visual elements. Spatial and temporal order thus appear to be almost completely interchangeable in cerebral action. The translation from the spatial distribution of memory traces to temporal sequence seems to be a fundamental aspect of the problem of serial order.

I spoke earlier of the probability of a partial activation or priming of aggregates of words before the sentence is actually formulated from them. There is a great deal of evidence for such preliminary facilitation of patterns of action in studies of reaction time and of word association. Reaction time, in general, is reduced by preliminary warning or by instructions which allow the subject to prepare for the specific act required. In controlled association experiments, the subject is instructed to respond to the stimulus word by a word having a certain type of relation to it, such as the opposite or a part of which the stimulus is the whole; black-white, apple-seed. The result is an attitude or set which causes that particular category to dominate the associative reaction. Whether such preliminary reinforcement is to be ascribed to accumulation of excitatory state, as defined by Sherrington (21), or to some other physiological process, the facts of behavior assure that it is a genuine phenomenon and plays a decisive role in determining the character of the response.

Once the existence of such states of partial activation is recognized, their possible role in temporal integration must be considered. There are indications that one neural system may be held in this state of partial excitation while it is scanned by another. Here is an example. A series of four to six numbers is heard: 3-7-2-9-4. This is within the attention or memory span and is almost certainly not remembered in the sense in which one's telephone number is remembered, for memory of it is immediately wiped out by a succeeding series of numbers. While it is retained in this unstable way, subject to retroactive inhibition, the order of the numbers can be reassorted: 3-7-2-9-4, 3-2-7-9-4, 4-9-2-7-3, and the like. It is as if, in this case, a rhythmic alternation can suppress alternate items, or a direction of arousal can be applied to the partially excited system. Another example which illustrates even more clearly

the spatial characteristics of many memory traces is the method of comultiplication, used in rapid mental calculation. In attempts to play a melody backward, we have a further illustration. I find that I can do it only by visualizing the music spatially and then reading it backward. I cannot auditorily transform even "Yankee Doodle" into its inverse without some such process, but it is possible to get a spatial representation of the melody and then to scan the spatial representation. The scanning of a spatial arrangement seems definitely to determine, in such cases, the order of procedure. Two assumptions are implied by this. First, the assumption is that the memory traces are associated, not only with other memory traces, but also with the system of space coordinates. By this I do not mean that the engram has a definite location in the brain; our experiments show conclusively that such is not the case. Rather, when the memory trace is formed, it is integrated with directional characters of the space system, which give it position in reference to other associated traces. Second, the assumption is that these space characters of the memory trace can be scanned by some other level of the coordinating system and so transformed into succession.

This is as far as I have been able to go toward a theory of serial order in action. Obviously, it is inadequate. The assumptions concerning spatial representation and temporal representation may even beg the question, since no one can say whether spatial or temporal order is primary. Furthermore, such determining tendencies as the relation of attribute to object, which gives the order of adjective and noun, do not seem to be analyzable into any sort of spatial structure or for that matter, into any consistent relationship. I have tried a number of assumptions concerning the selective mechanism of grammatical form (spatial relations, the relative intensity or prominence of different words in the idea, and so on) but I have never been able to make an hypothesis which was consistent with any large number of sentence structures. Nevertheless, the indications which I have cited, that elements of the sentence are readied or partially activated before the order is imposed upon them in expression, suggest that some scanning mechanism must be at play in regulating their temporal sequence. The real problem, however, is the nature of the selective mechanism by which the particular acts are picked out in this scanning process, and to this problem I have no answer.

Such speculations concerning temporal and spatial systems do little more than illustrate a point of view concerning nervous organization which is, I believe, more consistent both with what is known of the histology and elementary physiology of the brain and also with behavior phenomena than are the more widely current theories of simple associative chains of reactions.

Nearly forty years ago Becher (2, page 243) wrote: "There is no physiological hypothesis which can explain the origin and relations of temporal forms in mental life; indeed, there is no hypothesis which even foreshadows the possibility of such an explanation." The situation is little better today, but I do feel that changing conceptions of the fundamental organization of the nervous system offer more hope for a solution of such problems than did the physiological knowledge available when Becher wrote. However, we are still very far from being able to form an explicit explanation of temporal structure.

1. AKELAITIS, A. J. Studies on the corpus callosum. ii. The higher visual functions in each hononymous field following complete section of the corpus callosum. *Arch. Neurol. Psychiat.*, 1941, **45**, 788-96.

2. BECHER, E. *Gehirn und Seele.* Heidelberg, 1911.

3. BETHE, A. Plastizität und Zentrenlehre. *Handb. d. norm. u. path. Physiol.*, 1931, **15** (zweite H.), 1175-1220.

4. BORING, E. G. *A history of experimental psychology.* New York: Century Co., 1929.

5. BROWN, T. G. On the nature of the fundamental activity of the nervous centers. *J. Physiol.*, 1914, **48**, 18-46.

6. BUDDENBROCK, W. v. Die Rhythmus der Schreitbewegungen der Stabheuschrecke Dyxippus. *Biol. Centralb.*, 1921, **41**, 41-8.

7. CHAMBERLAIN, A. F. Indians, North American. *Enc. Brit.*, 1911, **14**, 452-82.

8. CLARK, W. E. LeGros. Observations on the associative fiber system of the visual cortex and the central representation of the retina. *J. Anat. London*, 1941, **75**, 225-36.

9. EPSTEIN, I. *La pensée et la polyglossie.* Paris: Payot et Cie (no date).

10. FOURNIÉ, *Essai de psychologie.* Paris, 1887.

11. FRITSCH, G., & HITZIG, E. Ueber die elektrische Erregbarkeit des Grosshirns. *Arc. f. Anat. u. Physiol.*, 1870, pp. 300-32.

12. GOLDSTEIN, K. *The organism.* Boston: Ginn & Co., 1939.

13. HOLST, N. v. Vom Wesen der Ordnung im Zentralnervensystem. *Die Naturwissenschaften*, 1937, **25**, 625-31; 641-7.

14. INGEBRITZEN, O. C. Coordinating mechanisms of the spinal cord. *Genet. Psychol. Monogr.*, 1933, **13**, 483-555.

15. JACOBSEN, E. Electrophysiology of mental activities. *Amer. J. Psychol.*, 1932, **44**, 677-94.

16. LASHLEY, K. S. The accuracy of movement in the absence of excitation from the moving organ. *Amer. J. Physiol.*, 1917, **43**, 169-94.

17. LASHLEY, K. S. The mechanism of vision. xvii. Autonomy of the visual cortex. *J. Genet. Psychol.*, 1942, **60**, 197-221.

18. LASHLEY, K. S. The mechanism of vision. xviii. Effects of destroying the visual "associative areas" in the monkey. *Genet. Psychol. Monogr.*, 1948, **37**, 107-166.

19. MAX, L. W. Experimental study of the motor theory of consciousness. IV. *J. Comp. Psychol.*, 1937, **24**, 301-44.

20. PICK, A. *Die agrammatischen Sprachstörungen.* Berlin, 1913.

21. SHERRINGTON, C. S. *The integrative action of the nervous system.* London: Constable, 1906.

22. SHERRINGTON, C. S. Some functional problems attaching to convergence. *Proc. Roy. Soc.*, B, 1929, **105**, 332-62.

23. THORSEN, A. M. The relation of tongue movements to internal speech. *J. Exp. Psychol.*, 1925, **8**, 1-32.

24. TITCHENER, E. B. *Lectures on the experimental psychology of the thought processes.* New York: The Macmillan Co., 1909.

25. WASHBURN, M. F. *Movement and mental imagery.* Boston: Houghton Mifflin, 1916.

26. WATSON, J. B. Is thinking merely the action of the language mechanisms? *Brit. J. Psychol.*, 1920, **11**, 86-104.

7 / Tests of Three Hypotheses about the Effective Stimulus in Serial Learning [1]

ROBERT K. YOUNG, *University of Texas*

The items of a serial task are presented in a constant order; because of this the effective stimulus for a specific response may possibly be one of several alternatives: It may be: (*a*) the item immediately preceding the response to be learned; (*b*) a combination of several items preceding the response to be learned; (*c*) the position which the item holds in the list; (*d*) some combination of these; or (*e*) something else entirely.

The present paper reports a series of three experiments designed to help identify the effective stimulus in serial verbal learning. The first alternative (*a*), called the specificity hypothesis (Young, 1961), is tested in Exp. I by measuring transfer from a serial list to a subsequent paired-associate (PA) list composed of pairs taken from adjacent items in the serial list. If associations are formed between adjacent items in serial learning, positive transfer should obtain from the serial to the PA list and the PA transfer pairs should be learned faster than control pairs which have not been previously learned in serial order.

The second alternative (*b*), called the compound-stimulus hypothesis, is tested in Exp. II by measuring transfer from a serial list to a PA list composed of items taken from the serial list. Positive transfer from the serial to the PA task would be taken as evidence favorable to a compound-stimulus interpretation of the effective stimulus in serial learning.

The third alternative (*c*), called the serial-position hypothesis, is tested in Exp. III by observing transfer from one serial list to a second composed of the same items as the first. The serial position hypothesis assumes that items holding the same serial position in both lists (S items) would show positive transfer

from the first to the second list while items holding different positions in both lists (D items) would show negative transfer from the first to the second list. The reason for this is that S items constitute an A-B, A-B paradigm of positive transfer in which the stimulus (A) would be the constant serial position, and the response (B) would be the same item from list to list. The D items would constitute an A-B, A-Br paradigm of negative transfer (Porter & Duncan, 1953) in which the response to be learned to a constant position stimulus would be rearranged from the first list to the second.

GENERAL METHOD

In the three experiments all Ss were selected from introductory psychology classes at the University of Texas. All lists were constructed of dissimilar adjectives taken from Melton (Hilgard, 1951), and all were learned by the anticipation method. The lists were displayed by a filmstrip projector. The PA lists were learned at a standard 2:2-sec. rate with a 4-sec. intertrial interval while the serial lists were learned at a standard 2-sec. rate with a 6-sec. intertrial interval. When serial and PA lists were learned in an experiment, a 5-min. interval was employed between lists to allow time to change film strips and to read PA instructions; and when two serial lists were learned, a 1-min. interval between lists was needed to change film strips. All lists (with the exception of Exp. Ia) were learned to one errorless recitation and all PA lists had four orders of presentation to reduce the possibility of serial learning.

From the *Journal of Experimental Psychology*, 1962, **63**, 307-13, with permission of the author and publisher.
1. The research reported in the present paper was supported in part by the National Science Foundation (G-4850) and in part by a grant from the Graduate School of the University of Texas.

Experiment I

Method.—Each S learned a serial list and then a PA list. One-half the items in the PA list were experimental pairs obtained from adjacent items in the previously learned serial list, and the other half of the PA items were control pairs. The ordering of the experimental pairs in the PA list was exactly the same as in the serial list. That is, for these pairs the same stimulus elicited the same response in both serial and PA learning

To reduce the possibility of differences due to intrinsic differences in difficulty in the pairs themselves, the items which served as experimental pairs for half the Ss served as control pairs for the other half. Subgroups of 18 Ss learned one of two serial lists and then the common PA list containing items from both serial lists (Total $N=36$). Two 14-item serial lists (plus a cue symbol) were constructed and one 14-pair PA list was derived from the two lists.

Results.—The PA list may be thought of as being composed of two seven-pair sublists. The mean trials to learn the experimental and control sublists to one errorless recitation were 10.06 and 9.06, respectively ($F=.97$, $df=1/34$). The mean correct responses per S during learning for the experimental and control sublists were 62.58 and 63.22, respectively ($F=.17$, $df=1/34$).

As in a previous experiment measuring transfer from a serial to a PA list (Young, 1959), positive transfer occurred early in learning and then disappeared later in learning. The mean number of trials to attain successive criteria are plotted in Fig. 1. The Fs obtained between the experimental and control sublists for criteria of one, two, three, and four correct responses ($df=1/34$ in each case) were 4.86 ($P=.05$), 5.25 ($P=.05$), 10.50 ($P=.01$), and 7.61 ($P=.01$), respectively. Beyond a criterion of four correct responses, the two sublists do not differ with respect to mean trials to successive criteria.

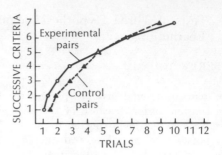

Fig. 1. Trials to successive criteria curves for the experimental and control sublists during PA learning in Exp. I.

The associations of the experimental pairs were differentially reinforced during serial learning. For example, Item 2 in the serial list was correct .84 times per trial; in contrast, Item 10 was given .39 times per trial. This difference reflects, of course, the bowed serial-position curve commonly found in serial learning. Since adjacent pairs were taken from the serial list and used in the PA learning, serial position effects should transfer to the PA learning if associations are formed between adjacent items. Where the pairs in the two PA sublists were arranged according to position in their respective serial lists, the mean percentage frequencies with which these experimental and control pairs were correct during PA learning are shown in Fig. 2. Of the seven comparisons made, one significant difference was obtained. As can be seen in Fig. 2, the last pair in the experimental sublist was given correctly more often than its control ($F=28.73$, $df=1/34$, $P<.001$).

The PA error data were analyzed in two ways. The stimuli in the PA list can be classified either as experimental or as control, and the data were analyzed according to this classification. The mean numbers of errors per trial elicited by experimental and control stimuli were .52 and .39, respectively. This difference is significant ($F=5.87$, $df=1/34$, $P<.05$). Secondly, the mean numbers of

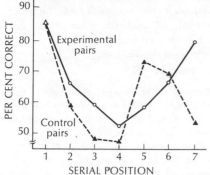

FIG. 2. Mean percentage correct in PA learning for the experimental and control sublists in Exp. I with the responses being ordered along the baseline as they were in the serial lists.

incorrect experimental items per trial elicited by an experimental stimulus and the mean numbers of control items per trial elicited by a control stimulus were .44 and .32, respectively ($F = 7.05$, $df = 1/34$, $P < .05$). It is noteworthy that the remainder of the errors per trial, .08 and .07, is small and constant across conditions.

EXPERIMENT IA

The associations formed during serial learning may not have been of sufficient strength to transfer to the subsequent PA task. Experiment Ia was conducted to control for this possibility. The design of this experiment is exactly the same as Exp. I with one exception: the serial learning criterion was increased to one errorless recitation plus an additional 10 trials. A total of 22 Ss were employed with 11 per subgroup.

The mean numbers of correct responses per S given to the even items during serial learning, arranged in serial position, may be summarized as follows: 36.36, 27.09, 25.36, 19.59, 22.55, 24.68, and 31.77. These even items were the response members of the seven experimental pairs in the subsequent PA learning. If it can be assumed that number of correct responses is a measure of associative strength, then the present experiment permits the formation of associations between sucessive items in the serial list.

The mean trials to learn the experimental

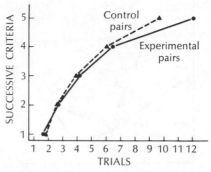

FIG. 3. Trials to successive criteria curves for the experimental and control sublists during PA learning in Exp. II.

and control PA sublists to one errorless recitation were 8.86 and 8.14, respectively ($F = .85$, $df = 1/20$). The mean correct responses per S during learning for the experimental and control sublists were 49.59 and 51.91, respectively ($F = .84$, $df = 1/20$). As in Exp. I, transfer of serial position effects, transfer during early learning, and overt errors were analyzed. In none of these analyses was a significant difference obtained.

EXPERIMENT II

Method.—The only difference between Exp. II and Exp. I was in the construction of the PA list. Two 15-item serial lists (plus a cue symbol) were constructed and a 10-item PA list was constructed from the two serial lists. Each stimulus in the PA list was composed of two items. These items were arranged one over the other and were in the same sequence (from top to bottom) as they were in the serial list. Forty-six Ss served in the experiment with 23 learning each serial list before learning the PA list.

Results.—As in Exp. I, the PA list may be thought of as being composed of two five-pair sublists. The mean numbers of trials required to reach one errorless recitation of the experimental and control sublists were 12.04 and 9.63, respectively ($F = 8.35$, $df = 1/44$, $P < .01$). As can be seen from the data on trials to successive criteria presented in Fig. 3, negative transfer obtained from the serial to the PA list.

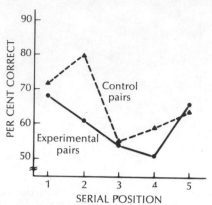

FIG. 4. Mean percentage correct in PA learning for the experimental and control sublists in Exp. II with the responses being ordered along the baseline as they were in the serial lists.

The mean numbers of correct responses per S given during learning of the experimental and control sublists were 41.13 and 46.91, respectively ($F = 7.27$, $df = 1/44$, $P < .01$). Both response measures are in agreement that prior serial learning retards subsequent PA learning.

As in Exp. I, the pairs in the two PA sublists were arranged according to position in their respective serial lists and the mean percentage frequencies correct for the experimental and control pairs are presented in Fig. 4. Only one of the five comparisons was significant. The second experimental pair was more difficult than was the comparable control pair ($F = 20.49$, $df = 1/44$, $P < .001$).

The results of the error analysis in Exp. II are comparable to the error data obtained in Exp. I. Experimental stimuli elicit more overt errors than do control stimuli ($F = 19.70$, $df = 1/44$, $P < .001$) with mean errors per trial being .61 and .34 for the experimental and control sublists, respectively. In addition, more experimental items are elicited incorrectly by experimental stimuli (.56 per trial) than is the case for control stimuli eliciting control items (.29 per trial) ($F = 23.91$, $P < .001$). Again it should be

noted that the remainder of the errors per trial, .05 and .05, is small and constant across conditions.

EXPERIMENT III

Method.—Experiment III differs from Exp. I and II in that transfer from one serial list to a second was studied and, in addition, a control group was employed. Four 13-item serial lists were constructed (with the first item serving as a cue symbol) for use in the experiment. Lists A and B were experimental lists and List C was a control list. Each S learned one of these lists and then all Ss learned the test list. Comparing List A with the test list, the even items in List A held the same serial position as they did in the test list while the odd items were randomly rearranged from List A to the test list. In List B the odd items held the same serial position as they did in the test list while the even items were randomly rearranged. In this manner test-list differences between those items with the same serial positions (S items) and those items with different serial positions (D items) are attributable to transfer effects rather than to differential difficulty due either to specific items or to serial position. The Control List C had no items in common with the test list, and test-list learning in the two experimental conditions may be compared to that in the control condition to evaluate transfer effects. Sixty-three Ss served in the experiment, 21 Ss in each condition.

Results.—The mean numbers of trials to learn the test list in Conditions A, B, and C were 12.43, 13.86, and 9.71, respectively ($F = 6.50$, $df = 2/60$, $P < .01$). Orthogonal comparisons (Senders, 1958) between the three conditions indicate that the experimental conditions did not differ ($F = 1.50$) while the test list in the control condition was learned faster than in the experimental conditions ($F = 11.51$, $df = 1/60$, $P < .01$). Negative transfer obtained from the experimental to the test lists and these data are comparable to transfer data obtained by Irion (1946).

The test list may be thought of as being composed of two six-item sublists—

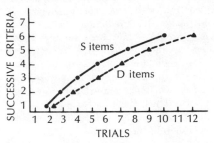

FIG. 5. Trials to successive criteria curves for the S- and D-item sublists during test-list learning in Exp. III.

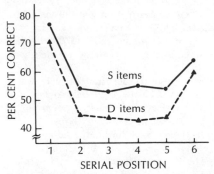

FIG. 6. Mean percentage correct in test-list learning for the S- and D-item sublists with the items being ordered along the baseline as they were in the test list.

the S items and the D items. Trials to reach a criterion of one errorless recitation for each of these sublists in the experimental conditions were analyzed. The mean trials to learn the S-item sublist was 10.17, while the mean for the D-item sublist was 12.14 ($F=14.97$, $df=1/40$, $P<.001$). The mean numbers of trials to attain sucessive criteria are plotted in Fig. 5.

The mean numbers of correct responses per S during test-list learning for the S- and D-item sublists were 46.86 and 39.90, respectively ($F=35.24$, $df=1/40$, $P<.001$). Both response measures are in agreement that the S-item sublist was easier to learn than the D-item sublist.

The S and D items were arranged according to their respective serial positions in the test list and, as can be seen from Fig. 6, differences obtained as a function of serial position. Only the first and last items did not differ between the S-item and D-item sublists. The Fs for Serial Positions 2, 3, 4, and 5 ($df=1/40$ in each case) were 6.82 ($P=.05$), 6.54 ($P=.05$), 10.59 ($P=.01$), and 6.79 ($P=.05$), respectively. Thus the items in the middle of the list were learned faster when the serial position was retained than when it was changed while such differences were not observed for the items at the ends of the list.

DISCUSSION

Experiment I tested the hypothesis that associations are formed between successive items within a serial list. This hypothesis, called the specificity hypothesis, was tested by constructing pairs taken from successive items in a serial list and measuring transfer from the serial list to a PA list composed of the serial pairs. The analyses of the data indicated that, aside from positive transfer early in learning, the experimental pairs were learned no faster than the control pairs.

It may be argued that the absence of an overall difference between the two sublists was due to interference resulting from the change of tasks. However, when the arrangements of the items between serial and PA task is such as to expect negative transfer, zero transfer also occurs (Young, 1961).

On the other hand, the serial-position hypothesis assumes that the position the item holds in the list is the effective stimulus rather than the item immediately preceding the response to be learned. If such were the case, no transfer would be expected from the serial to the PA list because the stimulus in the PA learning would be different from the effective stimulus in serial learning. Thus, according to the serial-position hypothesis, the transfer paradigm employed in Exp. I would be an A-B, C-B paradigm of zero transfer. In this case the A stimulus would correspond to the serial position of the item in the serial list, the C stimulus would correspond to the nominal stimulus in the PA list, and the B response would be the response to be learned in both lists. Thus, while the specificity hypothesis predicts positive transfer from the serial to the PA list, the serial-position hypothesis predicts zero transfer.

Positive transfer occurred early in learning in Exp. I. This could be taken as evidence favoring a specificity notion, or it could be accounted for in terms of gross differentiation. Such an interpretation would state that following serial learning S was able to differentiate between those items which were learned previously and those which were not. When presented with a prefamiliarized item, S would restrict his responses to some other prefamilarized item. Some of these guesses would be correct (significantly more than the control early in learning) and some would be incorrect (significantly more than the control errors).

The hypothesis that the two items preceding the response to be learned is the effective stimulus in serial learning was tested in Exp. II. Contrary to expectations from the compound-stimulus hypothesis, negative transfer occurred. While these data could be explained in terms of interference between the stimulus items (specificity interpretation) or in terms of interference arising from the similarity of the PA stimulus items to the initial serial positions (serial-position interpretation), the results of Exp. II do not permit serious consideration of the compound-stimulus hypothesis as a useful explanation of the stimulus in serial learning at this time.

The hypothesis tested in Exp. III was that the position the item holds in the serial list is the effective stimulus in serial learning. This hypothesis was tested by observing transfer from one serial list to another. The same items were employed in both lists and were arranged so that S items retained the same serial position in both lists while D items were randomly rearranged from the first to the second list. If the serial position were the effective stimulus, positive transfer would be expected for the S items and negative transfer would be expected for the D items. The results of the experiment show that the S items were easier to learn than the D items and that the test list in the experi-

mental conditions was learned slower than in the control. The specificity hypothesis would make the prediction that no differences would obtain between the S and D items in the test list. According to this position, each item was associated to a response in the first list; but in no case were the same two items learned successively in both lists. Thus, the transfer paradigm for all items becomes an A-B, A-Br paradigm of negative transfer.

The addition of a mediation construct would permit interpretation of the results of Exp. III in terms of the specificity hypothesis. The only requirement would be the assumption that during test-list learning an S item acts as a stimulus and elicits the next (missing) item, which in turn correctly elicits the next (S) item. Such a mediation assumption would enable the specificity hypothesis to predict that the S items would be learned faster than the D items.

The data of the present experiments provide no final answer to the question of the effective stimulus in serial learning. They are, for example, difficult to integrate into the extensive literature on remote associations (e.g., McGeoch, 1936) which may best be interpreted in terms of the specificity hypothesis. However, the serial position curves of Exp. I and III (Fig. 2 and 6) may be used to formulate a tentative hypothesis which employs both the specificity and the serial-position hypotheses. Evidence from Exp. I and elsewhere (Young, 1961) indicates that learning in accordance with the specificity hypothesis occurs at the extremes of the serial list but not in the middle. In addition, data from Exp. III indicate that position learning has an important cue function in the middle of the list but not at the extremes. It then may be that specificity learning occurs at the extremes and that position learning occurs in the middle of the test list. Some difficulties are immediately apparent with this formulation: the middle of the list is the point of greatest "position confusion" (Schulz, 1955), i.e., position learning should be less likely to occur; and when degree of serial learning is increased as in Exp. Ia, evidence for specificity learning is not apparent.

SUMMARY

Three hypotheses regarding the effective stimulus in serial learning were tested. If associations are formed between items of a serial list, then these associations should transfer to a subsequent PA list composed of the serial items with the S-R arrangement of the PA list being consistent with the ordering of the items in the serial learning. Positive transfer was observed only early in learning. If the effective stimulus in serial learning is the two preceding items in the list, then when sets of two items are used as stimuli, positive transfer should be observed in a subsequent PA task. In this case, negative transfer occurred. Finally, if the position of the item in a serial list is the effective stimulus, positive transfer should obtain from one serial list to another when the item retains the same serial position; and negative transfer should obtain when the serial position is changed. It was found that items retaining the same serial position were learned faster than items which had their serial positions changed from one list to another.

HILGARD, E. R. Methods and procedures in the the study of learning. In S. S. Stevens (Ed.), *Handbook of experimental psychology*. New York: Wiley, 1951. Pp. 517-67.

IRION, A. L. Retroactive inhibition as a function of the relative serial position of the original and interpolated items. *J. exp. Psychol.*, 1946, **36**, 262-70.

McGEOCH, J. A. The direction and extent of intraserial associations at recall. *Amer. J. Psychol.*, 1936, **48**, 221-45.

PORTER, L. W., & DUNCAN, C. P. Negative transfer in verbal learning. *J. exp. Psychol.*, 1953, **46**, 61-4.

SCHULZ, R. W. Generalization of serial position in rote serial learning. *J. exp. Psychol.*, 1955, **49**, 267-72.

SENDERS, V. L. *Measurement and statistics*. New York: Oxford Univer. Press, 1958.

YOUNG, R. K. A comparison of two methods of learning serial associations. *Amer. J. Psychol.*, 1959, **72**, 554-9.

YOUNG, R. K. The stimulus in serial verbal learning. *Amer. J. Psychol.*, 1961, **74**, 517-28.

8 / Position Mediated Transfer Between Serial Learning and A Spatial Discrimination Task

SHELDON M. EBENHOLTZ, *Connecticut College*

In a position learning task (PL) Ss learned to discriminate between 10 spatial locations arranged in a vertical array, by associating a nonsense syllable with each position. Transfer from serial learning (SL) to PL and from PL to SL was studied. In Condition C the temporal order of syllables in SL (i.e., from beginning to end) corresponded with the spatial location of the same syllables in PL (i.e., from top to bottom). The relative positions of the syllables was random in Condition D. In Condition R the relative syllable positions were displaced, however adjacent items in SL were at contiguous locations in PL. Transfer in both directions was highest in the 1st condition. With one exception, the results of Conditions D and R did not differ from each other. Results yield evidence for position learning in SL and raise the question of the role of sequential association.

Recent attempts to isolate the effective stimulus in serial learning (Ebenholtz, 1961, 1963; Horowitz & Izawa, 1963; Young, 1962) suggest the operation of two variables. These may be referred to as sequential association and temporal position. Although it is most probable that the formation of specific associations between successive terms is a sufficient condition for mastery of a serial list, present evidence does not warrant the same statement with regard to knowl-

From the *Journal of Experimental Psychology*, 1963, **65**, 603-8, with permission of the author and publisher.

edge of the positions of the component items.

The present experiment sought to isolate the role of position and to test the effectiveness of knowledge of position as a mediator of serial learning.

METHOD

A situation was sought which might represent a pure case of position learning; viz., one with minimum possibility of forming sequential associations. A spatial position learning task was devised with this purpose in mind.

The Ss were trained to discriminate between a vertical array of 10 small rectangular "windows" such that given any window S could supply the syllable appropriate to it. On the assumption that serial learning entails the ordering of syllables with respect to temporal location, both tasks involve a common process; i.e., position learning. Transfer from one task to the other should occur readily providing the syllables are ordered in similar fashion; viz., providing Syllable 1 in serial learning has to be associated with the top position in position learning, etc. If serial learning does *not* entail position learning, then the relative placement of syllables across the tasks should not effect the degree of transfer. A control condition, therefore, was introduced in which the relation of the positions of syllables across the tasks was random; e.g., the first syllable in serial learning appeared toward the center of the spatial array, etc. A second control was introduced in which the items maintained their relative order on the two tasks but were displaced from their absolute positions. This condition permitted the evaluation of the extent to which transfer may be mediated by specific associations between adjacent items.

PROCEDURE

Position learning (PL).—The S was seated in front of a column of $10\frac{1}{4} \times \frac{1}{2}$ in. rectangular windows cut in a large white cardboard screen. There was an interspace of $\frac{3}{4}$ in. between windows. Behind the display was a large revolving drum 14 in. high and 18 in. in diameter. Nonsense syllables were placed on the drum so as to appear in predetermined order in one window at a time. The apparatus functioned much like a traditional memory drum turned on its side with the long axis in vertical position.[1]

The purpose of the position learning task was to have S respond on the basis of spatial location. This condition may, therefore, be regarded as a paired-associate task with window location as the stimulus and nonsense syllable as response. In order to indicate the window to which S was to respond, a red patch was presented, all other windows remaining blank. After a fixed interval the red patch disappeared and the syllable appropriate to that position took its place.

The temporal order of presentation of syllables was determined by five orders of a 10-item Latin square. Items which occurred at spatially contiguous locations were never presented in temporal succession. After five trials the first five orders of presentation were repeated.

The S was allowed 3 sec. to respond with the prescribed syllable while the red patch was in view. The syllable itself appeared for an additional 3 sec. There was a 12-sec. intertrial interval. The Ss learned to a criterion of one perfect anticipation of all 10 items.

Serial learning (SL).—The conventional method of serial learning was used. However, conditions were made as similar to those of PL as possible. A red patch appeared prior to the first item and between each of the succeeding items. The Ss were instructed to respond with the succeeding term while the red patch was in view. Both the patch and the item were presented for 3 sec. each. The criterion, presentation rate, and intertrial interval were identical in PL and SL. In both conditions S was requested to pronounce the syllables and to correct himself in the event of a wrong response or no response. The syllables in both PL and SL were from the Glaze (1928) list of 80–100% association value. Intralist similarity was minimal.

DESIGN

A transfer design was employed to study the effects of PL on SL and of SL on PL.

1. The author wishes to thank Otto Hebel for his aid in the design and construction of the apparatus.

Two groups of Ss learned in the order of SL-PL. Under Cond. C the syllables in SL and PL were maintained at *coordinate* positions in both tasks. That is Syllables 1 through 10 in SL appeared at Windows 1 through 10, respectively, in PL.[2] However, the temporal order of presentation of syllables in PL was systematically varied and never corresponded with the temporal order of syllables in SL. In short, the temporal position of syllables in SL corresponded with their spatial position in PL.

Under Cond. D the items were presented at *disparate* locations across the tasks. In this condition Syllables 1 through 10 in SL appeared in PL at Windows 8, 6, 4, 10, 1, 9, 7, 2, 5, and 3, respectively. Two additional groups learned in the order PL-SL. One group learned under Cond. C and the other learned under Cond. D. There was a 2-min. interval between tasks. In order to facilitate comparisons between Cond. C and D it was necessary to counterbalance lists across these conditions. For this purpose two forms of an SL and PL list were used. The relations between the two SL and the two PL lists are summarized in the following paradigm:

The subscripts refer to the different forms of the lists used in SL and PL, respectively. When SL and PL have common subscripts Cond. C is indicated (viz., SL_1-PL_1 and SL_2-PL_2); where subscripts differ the relation between items is that of Cond. D. The net result of the counterbalancing procedure was that the first learned lists of Cond. C and D, respectively, were identical as were the lists learned secondly. Two additional groups of Ss constituted a third condition (R) in which the *relative* order of items on SL and PL was preserved. These were run after Cond. C and D had been completed. One group learned in the order SL-PL, the other in the order PL-SL. The PL list was identical with one of the forms used in Cond. C and D. The present SL list contained the same terms as those used previously, however, the presentation sequence differed. Items 1 through 10 occurred at Windows 8, 9, 10, 1, 2, 3, 4, 5, 6, and 7, respectively, in PL. Thus except

for the sequence between Items 3 and 4 in SL all terms which appeared in temporal succession in SL now appeared in spatially contiguous locations in PL. It may be noted that Cond. R and C were similar in that the *relative* order of terms was maintained across tasks. They differed, however, in that under Cond. R items occurred at disparate positions on SL and PL, respectively, e.g., Item 5 in SL occurred at Position 2 in PL, etc. In this latter respect Cond. R was similar to Cond. D.

The purpose of Cond. R was to check on the possibility of the transfer of specific associations between the temporally adjacent items of SL and the spatially contiguous terms of PL. If such associations may be assumed to occur under Cond. C (e.g., by rehearsal of groups of items in sequence) then high transfer to SL-C and low transfer (or interference) to SL-D is to be expected. The same possibility holds in the case of transfer from SL to PL.

Since position mediated transfer is excluded under Cond. R and D, the present view requires maximum transfer to occur under Cond. C. If performance under Cond. R and D is equivalent then the role of specific association must be assumed to be negligible.

SUBJECTS

A total of 40 Connecticut College students took part in Cond. C and D and 28 others in Cond. R. None had previous experience with rote learning in the laboratory. Of the former group 20 Ss had learned in the order SL-PL and 20 in the order PL-SL. Ten Ss in each of these groups learned under Cond. C and D, respectively, with half of the 10 Ss learning either Form 1 or Form 2 of their SL or PL lists. The Ss were assigned to Cond. C and D alternately, as they appeared at the laboratory. Those Ss taking part in Cond. R were assigned alternately to task order SL-PL or PL-SL.

RESULTS

The results of Cond. C and D are based upon the combined data of the two forms of the SL and PL lists.

---

2. The numbers represent the order of windows from top to bottom.

First list.—On the basis of *t* tests all comparisons within SL and PL, respectively, between Cond. C, D, and R revealed no significant differences in original learning. Inspection of Table 1 indicates, however, that the PL task was apparently more difficult than SL.

D and R did not differ significantly in either trials to criterion or errors per trial. On both indices Cond. C proved favorable in comparison with both Cond. D and R. Comparing PL-C with PL-D, t (18)=4.19, $p < .01$, and t (18)=4.92, $p < .01$, for trials to criterion and errors

TABLE 1. *Mean trials to criterion and errors per trial on initial list*

Cond.	Mean Trials to Criterion				Mean Errors Per Trial			
	SL		PL		SL		PL	
	M	SD	M	SD	M	SD	M	SD
C	7.00	2.36	9.40	2.87	3.94	1.28	4.63	.98
D	7.10	2.84	9.80	2.44	3.20	1.02	4.53	1.00
R	7.50	2.94	10.42	2.17	3.53	.75	4.67	.60

Evaluation was accomplished by pooling the data of all three groups on PL and SL, respectively. For trials to criterion t (66)=4.23, $p < .01$. Comparison of errors per trial yielded t (66)=8.15, $p < .01$.

Second list (transfer).—The results of the transfer task are represented in Table 2. When SL is the transfer task, Cond. C is learned with significantly fewer trials to criterion and less errors

per trial, respectively. Condition PL-C required significantly fewer trials, t (22) =3.45, $p < .01$ and less errors per trial, t (22)=4.08, $p < .01$, than Cond. PL-R.

It is of some interest to note that the mean scores of Cond. R consistently fall between Cond. C and D (see Table 2). The same is true in comparisons of percent transfer. This may be represented by comparing performance on the transfer list (T) with performance on the same

TABLE 2. *Mean trials to criterion and errors per trial on transfer list*

Cond.	Mean Trials to Criterion				Mean Errors Per Trial			
	SL		PL		SL		PL	
	M	SD	M	SD	M	SD	M	SD
C	1.60	.48	5.10	2.38	.40	.37	2.22	1.08
D	4.20	.97	10.00	2.60	2.66	1.01	4.19	.60
R	3.35	1.99	8.42	2.02	1.44	1.01	3.73	.59

per trial than Cond. D; t (18)=7.22 and 6.64, in each case $p < .01$. Similarly performance under SL-C was superior to SL-R, comparisons yielding t (22)=2.36, $p < .05$ and t (22)=3.71, $p < .01$ for trials and errors per trial, respectively. Condition D did not differ significantly from Cond. R in trials to criterion, however, the latter did produce significantly fewer errors per trial; t (22)=2.97, $p < .01$.

Considering PL as transfer task, Cond.

task as initial list (I). The formula (I-T) /I × 100 with trials to criterion as index, yielded 77.14, 55.33, and 40.84, for Cond. SL-C, SL-R, and SL-D, respectively, and 45.74, 19.19, and—2.04 for PL-C, PL-R, and PL-D in that order. These results indicate more transfer to SL than to PL under each condition, with the conditions arranging themselves in the order C-R-D.

Position effects.—Both SL and PL

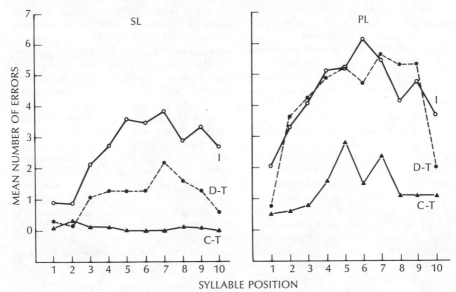

Fig. 1. Mean errors per position under SL and PL, Cond. C and D, respectively, and initial (I) and transfer (T) tasks.

lend themselves to analysis of errors by position. This is shown in Fig. 1. In order to plot the data, the top window in PL was arbitrarily designated as No. 1, the second from the top as No. 2, etc.

The curves of the initial SL and PL lists are based upon the combined data of Cond. C and D. The SL and PL curves are similar in that under both conditions end items are learned rapidly, central items yielding maximum errors. Such similar distributions are to be expected if identical processes (i.e., position learning) underlie both tasks.

The large amount of transfer under SL-C virtually eliminated the serial position curve. Nine of the 10 positions in SL yielded fewer errors when transfer occurred under Cond. C as compared with Cond. D. Condition PL-C yielded fewer errors than PL-D at all positions. Although not plotted, the error data of Cond. R fell between the curves of Cond. C and D. This was true of both SL and PL.

Discussion

In comparing Cond. C and D it was demonstrated that prior SL facilitated subsequent PL and vice versa, and that this occurred more readily when items appeared at coordinate positions on both tasks (Cond. C) rather than at disparate locations (Cond. D). This result suggests that knowledge of position is a significant factor in serial learning. This conclusion is valid only to the extent to which the operations defining PL exclude the forming of associations between spatially contiguous items. With one exception (SL-R) the results of Cond. R indicated that the preservation of the relation of contiguity between adjacent items in SL and PL, respectively, produced transfer which was not significantly greater than when the temporally contiguous terms of SL appeared at nonadjacent locations in PL (Cond. D). Since Cond. R produced little or no transfer beyond that of Cond. D, it follows that the facilitative effects of Cond. C were mediated primarily by the common positions of the items across the tasks.

The fact that transfer from PL to SL exceeded that from SL to PL raises a question. If both tasks entailed the learning of position, then transfer should have been equal in both directions. One explanation is that while both tasks involved position learning to a common criterion they differed in the degree to which the positions were discriminable at the time of transfer. Differences in position discriminability may also have contributed to initial differences in task difficulty. The fact that the initial tasks were of unequal difficulty, thereby producing differences in practice and item familarity, must also be considered as possible explanations. Another question relates to the fact that transfer was less than perfect. This may have been due to a number of variables. Some loss may be attributable to the shift from the spatial to temporal modalities, and to the small time interval between tasks. In addition it is possible that the degree of learning of the initial tasks may have been inadequate for maximum transfer. A more important consideration, however, is that position learning may *not* be adequate to account *completely* for serial learning. To the extent to which specific associations are required, the present conditions cannot yield complete transfer. The fact that Cond. R consistently produced transfer data which fell midway between Cond. C and D is support for the assumption that to some extent sequential associations are formed in serial learning.

It is of some interest to compare the effects of transfer obtained by Young (1959) with those of the present study. Young's Ss first learned paired associates and then transferred to a serial list in which pairs of successive terms were identical with those of the paired- associate list. If specific associative bonds were sufficient to master the serial list, then ideally Young's Ss should have learned within one trial. Actually a mean of 8.08 trials was required to reach one correct recitation of the entire list. Since in the present study transfer to SL-C was likewise less than perfect, it appears reasonable to conclude that neither position nor association are sufficient to explain serial learning. It seems most likely that both processes play a role.

The question remains as to the actual utilization of each process in the course of learning a serial list. Available evidence has not clarified this problem. There is some evidence (Ebenholtz, 1961) to suggest that responding on the basis of an association is more difficult than responding to position. On this assumption one may conceive of serial learning as proceeding on the basis of temporal position (i.e., at the ends of the list) up to the point where position discrimination is too poor to produce additional correct anticipations (i.e., at the center of the list). The Ss must then form consecutive associations between the terms at these poorly differentiated positions. The bow-shaped serial position curve may be understood as a consequence of this analysis by assuming position discrimination to be most difficult at the center of the list (see Schulz, 1955, for corroborative evidence). Error analysis of the spatial position task (see Fig. 1 and also Jensen, 1962) supports this view, as well.

It is important to note that the present formulation is contradictory to that offered by Young (1962) that "specificity learning occurs at the extremes and that position learning occurs in the middle of the list" (p. 313). Thus there is need for further clarification although there is good agreement as concerns a dual process theory of serial learning.

EBENHOLTZ, S. M. The relative roles of position learning and sequential association in the serial learning process. Unpublished doctoral dissertation, New School for Social Research, 1961.

EBENHOLTZ, S. M. Serial learning: Position learning and sequential associations. *J. exp. Psychol.*, 1963, in press.

GLAZE, J. A. The association values of nonsense syllables. *J. genet. Psychol.*, 1928, 25, 255-69.

HOROWITZ, L. M., & IZAWA, C. Comparison of serial and paired-associate learning. *J. exp. Psychol.*, 1963, 65, 351-62.

JENSEN, A. R. Temporal and spatial effects of serial position. *Amer. J. Psychol.*, 1962, 75, 390-400.

SCHULZ, R. W. Generalization of serial position in rote serial learning. *J. exp. Psychol.*, 1955, 49, 267-72.

YOUNG, R. K. A comparison of two methods of learning serial associations. *Amer. J. Psychol.*, 1959, 72, 554-9.

YOUNG, R. K. Tests of three hypotheses about the effective stimulus in serial learning. *J. exp. Psychol.*, 1962, 63, 307-13.

9 / An Inquiry into the Doctrine of Remote Associations [1]

NORMAN J. SLAMECKA, *University of Vermont*

The essential validity of the doctrine of remote associations was assessed. The findings of three original derived-list experiments supported a hypothesis of perception of list patterning, and were incompatible with predictions based upon remote associations. A fourth experiment supported the hypothesis that the association method produces its results through an artifact of serial position. Findings based upon the method of anticipatory and preservative errors were explained consistently by an alternative rationale that excluded remote associations. It was concluded that the doctrine of remote associations is of doubtful validity, and that serial memorization involves acquisition of the items per se, and then the learning of their positions in the list.

In his now classic monograph on rote verbal learning and retention, Ebbinghaus (1885) established the concept of remote associations. His investigations led him to believe that during the memorization of a serial list of items, functional associative bonds were established not only between immediately adjacent items but also directly, and at the same time, between items farther separated from each other in the list. These latter direct connections between noncontiguous items were designated as remote associations. They presumably arose automatically as part of the ordinary process of serial memorization, with no special effort on the part of the subject to bring them about. They were conceptualized as being formed both in the forward and backward directions, that is, an item in the middle of the list could develop a forward connection with the last item and a backward connection with one of the first items. As memorization of the series proceeded, it was thought that each and every item tended to form such a connection with every item in the list, thereby resulting in a complex bundle of associative interconnections among all the individual members of the series, as depicted in Figure 1. Numbers represent the sequential positions of the items as they occur in the list and arrows indicate associative bonds, with remote forward associations lying above, and remote backward lying below the item sequence. Furthermore, the strength of any given

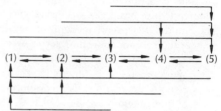

FIG. 1. Schematic illustration of associative bonds among the items of a memorized serial list, according to the concept of Ebbinghaus.

associative bond was asserted to be a negative function of its degree of remoteness. The bond between Items 1 and 5, above, represents a third degree of remoteness (since it spans three intervening items), and it would be of lesser strength than the bond from 1 to 3, a first degree of remoteness (since it spans only one intervening item). Also, all backward associations were considered to be much weaker than their counterparts in the forward direction. Thus, the remote bacward linkage from 4 to 1, above, would be weaker than the remote forward linkage from 1 to 4. To summarize our description of the essential properties of his concept, here is a statement from Ebbinghaus (Woodworth & Schlosberg, 1954):

With repetition of the syllable series not only are the individual terms associated with

From the *Psychological Review*, 1964, **71**, 61-76, by permission of the editor and publisher.
1. This work was aided by National Science Foundation Grant No. G-14, 721. The author is grateful for the assistance rendered by Ernest Lemay and Muriel Whalen.

their immediate sequents but connections are also established between each term and several of those which follow it. . . . The strength of these connections decreases with the number of the intervening (syllables). . . . Certain connections of the members are . . . actually formed in a reverse as well as in a forward direction. . . . The strength . . . was however considerably less for the reverse connections than for the forward ones [p. 710].

Since its inception some 77 years ago this formulation has remained, for all intents and purposes, essentially unchanged and has been accorded rather solid and widespread recognition in the conceptual armamentarium of the verbal learning theorist. Contemporary reference works in the experimental area discuss remote associations as an important part of the phenomena of serial learning (Hovland, 1951; McGeoch & Irion, 1952; Woodworth & Schlosberg, 1954), and recognition of the concept is also given in several introductory psychology texts (Geldard, 1962; Kimble, 1956; Morgan, 1961).

After a close appraisal of the pertinent literature and after conducting several experiments of our own, we have been forced to the conclusion that such widespread acceptance is definitely ill-advised, since there is much room for reasonable doubt about the validity of the remote associations doctrine (in our estimation it has indeed become a doctrine), and that it serves no necessary purpose in the conceptualization of serial verbal learning.

Experimental data from the remote associations literature have usually been regarded as proof that there indeed are such functional connections between each item and all others in a serial list. However, it will be demonstrated that certain necessary deductions from the remote associations position are not borne out empirically, and that these data are susceptible of other equally (if not more) plausible interpretations. Further, it will

be shown that phenomena previously attributed to the necessary influence of remote associations can be produced in the absence of any serial learning whatever. We shall present our supporting evidence in the sections to follow, sections delimited on the basis of the three types of experimental methods which have been utilized in the study of remote associations.

METHOD OF DERIVED LISTS

This method, originated by Ebbinghaus, provided the sole source of the data which he presented as evidence for remote associations. An original list is memorized, then the same items are arranged in a different serial order and presented to the same subject again for learning. The latter is the derived list, and it usually involves a patterned rearrangement of the items with respect to their original arrangement. A first-order derived list is formed by skipping every other item from the original list, a second-order list skips two items at a time, and so on. If the sequence of appearance of items in the original list is designated as 1, 2, 3, 4, 5, 6, 7, 8, 9, then a first-order derived list would have a sequence of 1, 3, 5, 7, 9, 2, 4, 6, 8, and a second-order list would be 1, 4, 7, 2, 5, 8, 3, 6, 9. The first-order list brings together items which were linked by a first degree remote association in original learning, and the second-order arrangement brings together items which were previously related by a second degree association. Keeping in mind that remote associations of the lowest orders are strongest, it then follows that a first-order list should be learned faster than one of second-order, and the latter still faster than a scrambled or control list whose items are in a random sequence. Ebbinghaus (1885) tested such a hypothesis and, indeed, found it supported by his data in terms of percentage savings in learning time.

We cannot agree, however, that his

experiment proved the existence of remote associations, for at least three reasons. First, Ebbinghaus learned by the method of whole presentation, wherein the entire list was always in view. It is possible that, inadvertently, he formed "remote" associations directly, by attending to nonadjacent items in direct succession. Secondly, he read the lists in a regular rhythmical manner, and such an imposed organization itself probably influenced the ease with which certain associations were formed, as shown by Müller and Schumann (Woodworth & Schlosberg, 1954). Third, and perhaps the more important objection, Ebbinghaus was his own subject. Since he prepared his own lists and was fully aware of the principle of their construction, it is quite possible that such knowledge could have produced the results, in spite of whatever other precautions he did take.

We turn, then, from this pioneering work to the subsequent experimental literature on remote associations using the method of derived lists, and find relatively few references.[2] Cason (1926) found no significant facilitation in the learning of first-order lists and concluded that "when a series of items is well learned and practiced until the recitation is very smooth, the forward associations between the adjacent items are the only associations that are formed [p. 316]." But we are left with some misgivings since the materials used were very long prose passages and a poem, and it is possible that the sequential dependencies and contextual constraints found in such material served to mask any effects of remote associations. A study by Hall (1928) must be ruled out of serious consideration because her peculiar method of constructing derived lists precluded any meaningful conclusions about remote associations. (McGeoch and Irion [1952] are also of this general opinion.) By far the best designed and

controlled study was carried out by Lepley (1934), who used first-order lists and comparable control lists of 12 nonsense syllables at six different retention intervals. Unfortunately, in no case was any first-order list easier to learn than its original list, and the same applied to a majority of the control lists as well. Such heavy and consistent negative transfer, resulting in a finding of no savings, renders the meaning of the results inconclusive for our purposes. Leply (1934) himself wrote: "Apparently, the potent factors at work in the present study are factors of interference of some sort and the only evidence of remote excitation we have results from a lesser degree of interference in the test lists at the end of the thirty minute forgetting interval [p. 16]." Such words are hardly calculated to convince the disinterested reader of the reality of remote associations.

Goldstein (1950), with relatively naive subjects, reported substantial savings over the original list in the learning of both a first-order list and a control list, but failed to find any savings advantage of the former over the latter arrangement, contrary to the results of Ebbinghaus. Apparently, degree of acquaintance with the materials used is a factor in the outcomes to be expected.

We will now describe our own experimental efforts to clarify the question of the meaning of derived list data. One common characteristic of all materials used in previous studies is that, with the exception of the control condition, there was always a rigidly patterned arrangement of items in the derived lists. That is, the ordering of the items in a derived list with respect to their original order was always regular or systematic. It is therefore conceivable that the subject, given a derived list, might actually per-

---

2. Since we are concerned only with derived-list studies in which remote associations were sought, we are not including a discussion of two studies in which the focus was upon adjacent backward associations, even though derived lists were used.

ceive the orderly relation that it bore to the original (such as skipping every other item), and proceed to "learn" it by (for instance) a process of mediation. This might take the form of uttering aloud every other item, and bridging the gaps by silent utterance of the intervening items. If his retention of the original list was perfect he could "learn" the derived list on the first recitation trial and earn an impressive savings score. If such were the case, his behavior certainly would not constitute proof of remote associative bonds, but only of perceptual alertness. Degrees of remoteness beyond the first would be progressively more difficult to perceive, and thus progressively fewer savings would be the inevitable result. Certain statements from previous studies are provocative in this regard. Cason (1926), who found no savings, wrote: "When the third and last part of the procedure had been completed, the subject was asked a number of questions about the experiment. None of the subjects noticed the way the lists had been constructed . . . [p. 309]." On the other hand, in a report where substantial savings were obtained in a study of adjacent backward associations, Garrett and Hartman (1926) commented: "When the reversed lists appeared, every S immediately guessed the order of the new arrangement, while the order of the reversed-pairs was at once evident to three Ss . . . [p. 245]."

Clearly, what is needed is some way of minimizing the possibility that the subject will have such an insight, while at the same time permitting savings due to truly remote associations. There is nothing whatever in the general rationale of the derived list method that requires the use of a regularly patterned list, just so long as it allows remote associations to demonstrate their facilitating effects upon learning. Therefore, a modified type of derived list which is of the first-order *on the average,* should produce just as much

savings as the regularly arranged first-order list, but without allowing the subject to benefit from perception of patterning. But if perception of patterning is the critical variable, then the modified first-order list should be learned just as slowly as a control list.[3] Experiment I was designed to test these divergent hypotheses.

EXPERIMENT

A total of 36 students served as subjects as part of the general psychology course requirements. Each subject learned one original list and then three derived lists in immediate succession, all to a criterion of one perfect recitation. The order of the derived lists was counterbalanced across subjects. Learning was by serial anticipation on a memory drum with a 3-second rate of presentation and a 6-second intertrial interval. The original list items were 14 letters of the alphabet in alphabetical sequence, from A to N for half the subjects, and from M to Z for the other half. The three derived lists were: (a) a control list with items in haphazard order, (b) the usual patterned first-order list with every other item skipped, and (c) a modified first-order list with 0, 1, and 2 items skipped in an irregular fashion, but with an overall mean of one skipped item. For the A to N list, it looked like this: A, D, E, G, H, K, M, B, C, F, I, J, L, N, corresponding to a skip sequence of 2, 0, 1, 0, 2, 1, (2), 0, 2, 2, 0, 1, 1. The necessary gap from M to B (indicated by the number in parentheses) also occurred in the regularly patterned arrangement, and is a common feature of derived list construction, in order that all the items be

---

3. The importance, in a learning situation, of identifying patterns of events is attested to in a paper by Bruner, Wallach, and Galanter (1959) when they write: "learning and problem-solving may be more profitably viewed as identification of temporally or spatially extended patterns . . . [p. 209]." Also, the well-known "discrimination hypothesis" is based upon the organism's perception of regular sequences of events (Tyler, Wortz, & Bitterman, 1953).

used. All lists retained the same first and last items of the original arrangement. The results presented in terms of mean total acquisition trials are found in the top row of Table 1. Original learning (OL) was 1.06 trials because, oddly enough, two subjects needed two trials

list pattern. On the other hand, we would predict that an original list of relatively unfamiliar items, such as nonsense syllables, would not produce facilitation in either type of first-order derived list. Although Ebbinghaus used nonsense syllable lists and reported savings in ac-

TABLE 1. *Mean trials for OL and derived lists for experiments I, II, and III*

Experiment	OL		Patterned list		OL		Modified list		OL		Control list	
	M	SD	M	SD	M	SD	M	SD	M	SD	M	SD
I	1.06	.23	4.94	3.22	1.06	.23	7.61	3.59	1.06	.23	7.94	2.51
II	20.45	8.22	13.30	4.40	19.95	8.01	12.95	7.31	20.60	6.27	13.55	5.17
III	19.90	4.42	10.90	4.71	20.25	7.32	12.05	3.28	20.80	4.81	14.10	5.02

each to recite the alphabet, in spite of the fact that all subjects were told the initial letter and that there was an alphabetical sequence. The overall F of 10.43 was significant beyond the .01 point $(df = 2/35)$, and Tukey's test showed that the patterned list was more rapidly learned than either the modified first-order, or the control list (.01 level gap $= 1.86$), with no difference between the latter two lists. Furthermore, 10 subjects learned the patterned list on the very first recitation trial, but this did not occur even once for the other two lists! It seems undeniable that such extremely rapid acquisition must have been the result of perception of the pattern. We feel that these data definitely provide strong support for the perception of patterning hypothesis, and at the same time stand against the remote associations doctrine, since the latter would maintain that the modified list should have produced savings equivalent to those of the patterned list.

The fact that savings were not consistently obtained in all past studies may be attributed to the subject's failure to perceive the particular derived list patterning. The familiar alphabet series used for OL in Experiment I was deliberately chosen in order that it would facilitate rapid perception of the derived

cord with remote association expectations, it can hardly be said that, for him, those materials were unfamiliar, since he invented them and was fully cognizant of their patterning. A truly naive subject would less likely have insight into the systematic rearrangement used for the patterned list, and consequently would show no savings over the control or modified lists. The remote associations position would predict that since the original list was learned, remote associations must have been formed and subsequent savings of equal degree should be obtained for both the patterned and modified lists, over the control. Experiment II tested these hypotheses.

EXPERIMENT II

A total of 60 naive subjects drawn from the same source as before was divided into three groups of 20 subjects each. Each subject learned a single original list to a criterion of two successive correct recitations, followed immediately by acquisition of a single derived list to the same criterion. The same presentation rate and intertrial interval were used as before. The lists were made up of 12 nonsense syllables with m' values from 3.03 to 3.12 (Noble, 1961). Two forms of the original list were made up, using the same syllables but in different order, to lessen inadvertent sequence effects. The three derived lists were of the same types as those used before: (a) a control list, (b) a patterned first-order list, and (c) a modified first-order (on the average) list with the following sequence of skipped syllables: 2, 0, 1, 2, 0 (2), 0, 2, 1, 0, 2. Prior to exposure to the derived list, each subject was told that it consisted of the same items as those in the original list, but in a different order. (The subjects of Experiment I were also told this.) Results of Experiment II are shown in the second row of Table 1. It requires no statistical analysis to conclude that there were no significant differences in the rates of learning among the three derived lists. No subject gave any evidence of having detected the principle of arrangement of List b. Goldstein (1950) also found that a patterned list was learned no more rapidly than a control list.

It is clear that simply arranging a derived list in patterned low-order form for learning by a naive subject does not automatically produce more rapid acquisition in comparison to the random or control arrangement. This fact is in contradiction to the specific expectation from the doctrine of remote associations, as is the finding of no savings for the modified list, as well. Some knowledge of the patterning must be present, it would seem, before facilitation can reasonably be expected.

What would the outcome of Experiment II have been if each subject did have knowledge of the principle of construction of his second list? We would predict that such knowledge would most benefit the group having the regularly patterned list, would least benefit the control group (knowing that the list is a haphazard rearrangement does not reduce much uncertainty), and might conceivably benefit the modified list group to some extent (knowing that the next item is either 0, 1, or 2 items away in the original list should reduce some uncertainty). Experiment III was performed to answer this question.

EXPERIMENT III

Another 60 naive subjects were used from the same source as before. Essentially, Experiment II above was repeated, with the identical nonsense syllable lists, the three types of derived lists, and the same presentation conditions and acquisition criteria. But these subjects were given full knowledge of the nature of their respective derived lists. This was achieved by: numbering each syllable on the original list in consecutive order from 1 to 12 and retaining these same numbers when the list appeared in derived form, and informing the subject, just before presentation of the second list, of the precise principle underlying its rearrangement. Results are shown in the bottom row of Table 1. Duncan's Multiple Range Test indicated significantly faster learning of the patterned list than of the control list (Rp3=3.02, df =57, p<.05). The modified list occupied an intermediate position in mean trials but was not significantly different from either of the other two lists (Rp2 =2.86, df=57, p>.05). Thus, with knowledge of the arrangement principle available to them, the subjects did best on the traditional Ebbinghaus type of list. Without such knowledge, as shown in Experiment II, they did no better than control subjects, favorable "remote" associations notwithstanding. Such a distinction would be foreign to the remote associations position, since it views formation of remote bonds as an *automatic* accompaniment of serial learning.

For purposes of control it was necessary to check that the three types of derived lists used in Experiments II and III were of equal difficulty in and of themselves, apart from any transfer effects from the original learning. Thirty naive subjects, from the same source as before, were each given one of the three list types to learn to a criterion of one errorless trial. Mean trials and subjects *SD*'s for the patterned, modified, and control lists, respectively, were: 18.3 (5.14), 20.1 (5.90), and 19.2 (5.81). The *F* was .23 (*df*=2/27), certainly not significant. It can be concluded that the derived lists per se did not differ in difficulty.

We conclude from the above experiments that the derived list method in fact fails to provide convincing support for the doctrine of remote association, and instead, serves to give plausibility to an alternative account based upon the subject's perception of list patterning. We will next consider the second method of studying remote associations.

ASSOCIATION METHOD

This method was introduced by Wohlgemuth (McGeoch & Irion, 1952) and later elaborated by others. After having learned a serial list, the subject is presented with each item individually and required to react with the first response that occurs to him. In order to reduce extraneous responses the subject may be instructed to restrict his associations by responding only with a list item. In any event, the production of an item response which was not adjacent to the stimulus item in OL is taken prima facie as representing a remote association established through serial learning. If Item 2 is the stimulus and the subject responds with Item 6, this is construed as a third degree remote forward association. McGeoch and Irion (1952) appear to have no doubts about the essential superiority and validity of this technique when they assert that:

Results obtained by the association method provide a more direct picture of the specific remote associations formed, are freer than the method of derived lists from the possible masking influences of associative inhibition, and leave no doubt that forward remote associations occur in relatively large numbers [p. 96].

McGeoch (1936) conducted an experiment using this technique, where, in addition to the associations, he also measured the reaction times of each. His results showed that there was a fairly steady decrease in the absolute number of associations (both backward and forward) as their degree of remoteness increased. Such a finding is in accord with expectations, since more remote associations are presumed to be weaker than less remote ones, and consequently less probable of emission. However, the forward reaction latencies themselves clearly contradicted such a position, since they tended to have shorter durations as they became more remote. Thus there is a nagging inconsistency in the findings as they relate to the doctrine of remote associations.

Later, Raskin and Cook (1937) added a logical refinement to the analysis of data generated by this method, and their paper appears to be the last significant word on the development of the technique. They pointed out that it is improper to tabulate only the absolute number of remote associations given, since the opportunities for their occurrence necessarily lessen as the degree of remoteness increases. A correction for opportunity must be made on the absolute totals. In their experiment they found, in agreement with McGeoch, that the absolute totals showed a steady decline with increasing degrees of remoteness, but when corrected for opportunity there was a rise starting at the fourth degree, resulting in an overall U-shaped function. They attributed this rise to summative effects of both backward and forward remote associations impinging upon the same item. They concluded that:

remote forward association are formed in the learning of a series of nonsense syllables, but . . . backward associations, also, are formed during the learning of such a series. As in the case of forward associations, the associations in a backward direction are formed between nonadjacent as well as adjacent syllables . . . [p. 393].

We vigorously dispute this conclusion and challenge the validity of the technique on which it was based, on the grounds that the association method involved a serious artifact which renders the results at least ambiguous with respect to the interpretation to be placed upon them. This flaw consists in completely neglecting the decisive implications of the serial position function. It is a well-established empirical fact that the initial items of a list are most easily learned, the last items next most easily, and those just beyond the middle are the last to be mastered. Since serial learning proceeds by complete trials, wherein the entire list is always run through in succession, it follows that the subject will have differential amounts of practice in giving the correct responses to different items. That is, by the time the list is mastered the subject will have had considerable overlearning on the first items, less so on the last items, and only bare mastery of the middle ones. Now, generalizing from the important work of such authors as Goldiamond and Hawkins (1958) and Underwood and Schulz (1960, Ch. 6), a relationship between the prior frequency of a response and its degree of availability may be stated as follows. Prefamiliarization of a response, or the degree to which it has been previously emitted, determines the probability of its emission in a subsequent free-responding situation. We suggest that the association method embodies the essential aspects of such a prefamiliarization procedure, in that the subject gets differential practice on the various OL items (because of their different serial positions), and is later tested for the relative dominance or availability of his responses. Such a state of affairs should

logically, in and of itself, produce the pattern of results commonly reported with the use of the association method, and heretofore singly attributed to the operation of true remote associative bonds. We contend that results such as those of McGeoch (1936) and Raskin and Cook (1937) could be obtained with no serial learning entering into the picture whatever, and that therefore they would not bear critically upon the question of whether remote associations are a valid by-product of serial learning. Experiment IV tested this hypothesis.

EXPERIMENT IV

Fifty-four naive psychology students participated as subjects. Each subject was given a controlled amount of differential practice on six nonsense syllables. The syllables, ranging in m' value (Noble, 1961) from 3.51 to 3.53, were: CIV, LAT, KEN, DIS, MOR, HAL. Each syllable was typed on a separate card, and after the deck of cards was well shuffled, the subject went through it, looking carefully at each card, spelling the syllable aloud and then pronouncing it. The frequencies of appearance in the deck of the six syllables were 25, 10, 3, 1, 3, 10. This was an approximation to the general shape of a serial position curve, and the subject went through this deck of 52 cards just once. There were three different arrangements of syllable-frequency pairings in order to control for idiosyncratic properties of any given syllable. Upon completion of this differential practice, the subject was tested by the association technique. In order to avoid the emission of unusable, extraneous responses, the subject was asked to respond with the first syllable that came to mind from those he had seen, but not to repeat the stimulus term he was being given. He was presented with each of the six syllables in haphazard order, one time each. The results are displayed in Table 2.

TABLE 2. *Total frequencies of associations obtained in experiment IV*

Stimulus items	Response items						Total
	1 Practiced 25 times	2 Practiced 10 times	3 Practiced 3 times	4 Practiced 1 time	5 Practiced 3 times	6 Practiced 10 times	
(X)	15	11	7	4	8	9	
1		21	8	2	9	14	54
2	24		7	4	8	11	54
3	14	9		6	14	11	54
4	13	14	10		9	8	54
5	26	8	6	5		9	54
6	17	13	12	6	6		54
Total	94	65	43	23	46	53	324

We may regard the items across the top margin of Table 2 as representing the sequence of items in a serial list which had, respectively, 25, 10, 3, 1, 3, and 10 mean total correct anticipations in OL. Along the left-hand margin are the stimuli presented during the association test, and the cells contain the total frequencies of particular responses given as associates. One diagonal row of cells is blank, since instructions forbade responding with the given stimulus syllable. Entries in the top row were not obtained empirically but were derived from the marginal totals of 54, divided according to the proportions required by the obtained column totals and are not included in the grand totals. The (X) represents what would have been the starting symbol for a serial list, that tells the subject to anticipate item number one. Since we lacked the foresight to include such an item during the association test, we decided, for completeness' sake, to synthesize its effect in the controlled manner

described in order to provide one more level of forward remoteness for the presentation in Table 3.

The frequencies within any column in Table 2 display some degree of unaccounted-for variability, but an inspection of the overall column totals shows that the attempt to achieve a serial position function through manipulation of the practice frequencies alone was reasonably successful. By the same token, our original statement relating degree of prefamiliarization to the subsequent degree of response availability was confirmed. Table 3 shows the distribution of these same remote associations arranged in degree of remoteness, according to the customary analysis of association method data. For instance, to obtain the total immediate forward responses (zero degree of remoteness), the frequencies in Table 2 running from the upper left corner down to the right through 15, 21, 7, 6, 9 and 9 were summed and appear as an absolute total of 67 in Table 3. To

TABLE 3. *Absolute totals and corrected totals of associations in Experiment IV, according to degrees of remoteness*

Forward associations				Backward associations			
Degree of remoteness	Absolute totals	Correction factor	Corrected totals	Degree of remoteness	Absolute totals	Correction factor	Corrected totals
0	67	6/6	67	0	54	5/5	54
1	45	6/5	54	1	40	5/4	50
2	28	6/4	42	2	33	5/3	55
3	24	6/3	48	3	39	5/2	97
4	22	6/2	66	4	17	5/1	85
5	9	6/1	54				

obtain the immediate backward responses, the frequencies running from the lower right corner of Table 2 up to the left through 6, 5, 10, 9, and 24 were summed and appear as a total of 54 in Table 3. The corrections suggested by Raskin and Cook, and the resulting totals, are also presented. The "absolute totals" columns show steady decreases in the totals of remote associations as degree of remoteness increases, in good agreement with McGeoch (1936) and Raskin and Cook (1937). The "corrected totals" columns also tend to approximate the U-shaped function described by Raskin and Cook.

Since it has now been shown that the overall results of the association method can be brought about without any previous serial learning, it follows that data gathered by that method are not at all conclusive with regard to the question of remote associations, and constitute no clear proof of their existence. Although the responses obtained in Experiment IV may be said to be associations to the stimulus items, they are certainly not the result of any *serial* learning procedure, and are not, therefore, remote associations in the true meaning of the term.

The last of the three methods used in the study of remote associations is discussed below.

METHOD OF ANTICIPATORY AND PERSEVERATIVE ERRORS

When one attempts to recite a serial list from memory, he may omit a few items and give a response further ahead in the sequence, or he may repeat an item that occurred earlier in the sequence. These responses are customarily designated, respectively, as anticipatory and perseverative errors. The method of anticipatory and perseverative errors consists essentially in analyzing the pattern of such errors committed during serial memorization. It has been presumed, rather uncritically, that such errors represent genuine remote associations formed by serial learning. The apparent advantages of this method, according to McGeoch and Irion, (1952), are:

The anticipatory error method has certain advantages over the two other methods. The remote associations, whatever their degree of remoteness, are overt and specific, which is not the case under the method of derived lists, though it is by the association method. Remote associations may be observed as a function of amount of practice in a single group of subjects. This cannot be done with the method of derived lists, and can be done with the association method only if an association test is made after each practice trial or after selected blocks of trials [p. 98].

Studies by Lumley (1932), Mitchell (1934), and Bugelski (1950) are representative of the use of this method, and their major findings may be summarized as follows: (a) anticipatory errors are much more frequent than perseverative errors, (b) frequency of such errors is inversely related to their degree of remoteness, even when corrected for opportunity of occurrence, and (c) as learning progresses, the number of far remote associations declines both absolutely and in proportion to the number of near remote associations.

In order to verify such findings from some of our own data, we present in Table 4 an analysis of the OL performance, up to one perfect trial, of the 60 subjects from Experiment II, above. Our data do indeed show the same pattern as those of previous reports: (a) out of a total of 1077 remote errors, only 62, or 5.8%, are in the backward direction; (b) there are fewer errors the higher their degree, even after correction; and (c) as fourths of learning increase, far remote errors drop off faster than near remotes. There is even a tendency, as Lumley (1932) observed, for near remotes to increase somewhat, at least up to the second fourth of learning.

TABLE 4. *Total number of remote associations (forward and backward combined) according to degree of remoteness for each fourth of learning, from OL of Experiment II*

Fourths of learning	Degree of remoteness									Total
	1	2	3	4	5	6	7	8	9	
1st	110	67	40	31	18	11	7	9	3	296
2nd	188	86	26	24	11	2	5	2	1	345
3rd	160	61	15	14	5	1	1	2	2	261
4th	128	27	14	4	1	1	0	0	0	175
Total	586	241	95	73	35	15	13	13	6	1077
Corrected total	586	265	116	100	55	28	29	36	22	

However, as may by now be suspected, our view of the meaning of data such as these is quite different from the usual interpretations that have been put upon them in the past. We choose, in order to test the strength of the traditional doctrine, to reject the assumption that these responses are true remote associations, according to the sense of that concept. Simply because the subject makes an intralist error does not necessarily mean that it represents an association that has been built up specifically through *serial* learning any more than if he were asked to utter the first number between 1 and 10 that ocurs to him when the stimulus "go" is given. It might be a response made prepotent through much prior practice of it alone. The presumption that such errors indicate serially learned, *direct* connections between spatially and temporally separated items is gratuitous and highly questionable. Rather, they can be more simply and compellingly explained as being the joint result of serial position effects and educated guesses on the part of the subject in the following manner.

As he learns, the subject must acquire the responses themselves (the "response-learning" phase of Underwood and Schulz, 1960), as well as their *relative* positions in the list (somewhat akin to the "hookup" phase of Underwood and Schulz). During the early stage of acquisition the subject has probably mastered only the first few (and possibly the last) items, thus reflecting the serial position influence, and has but a very sketchy grasp on the identity of the remaining items. There is, for him, an uncertain region in the central area of the list, the order of whose items has as yet not been fixed. However, the subject does his best to follow instructions and occasionally makes a guess as to the next item, uttering any one he happens to know except those he has just seen (therefore, very few backward associations), and those (probably the first ones) whose identity and position have been fixed. At this early stage he is more likely to emit remote associations of higher degree than later, since his ignorance of the list is maximal, and his guesses are less constrained. As learning proceeds, the uncertain region of the list shrinks in extent, leaving fewer unplaced items to be guessed, thus logically insuring that the resulting total errors, as well as their degrees of remoteness, will be smaller. It can be seen in Table 4 that the error total for the second fourth of learning is higher than for the first fourth, and yet, according to the account thus far, it should be lower. This may readily be understood on the presumption that the response-learning phase has reached completion during the second fourth of learning, and therefore the subject has more responses available to him for potential guesses than he has during the first fourth.

The preceding rationale predicts the

obtained overall pattern of errors in Table 4 and in those of other studies of this type, without drawing upon any dubious assumptions concerning the development of any remote associations. Such a rationale seems to us more parsimonious and somehow more promising than its alternative. For instance, it would be forced to predict that the distribution of the actual serial position sources of intralist errors would show a tendency, as learning proceeded, toward a greater concentration beyond the middle of the list, because of the progressive shrinking of the uncertain region. In other words, the variability of these errors should show a steady decline across successive fourths of learning, as acquisition progressed. The remote associations doctrine would, of necessity, be silent on this question, since it could deduce nothing specific from its premises alone.

A test of this prediction was made from the OL data (up to a criterion of one perfect trial) of Experiment II. The variances of the distributions of intralist errors from the first to the last fourths of learning were, respectively: 7.29, 6.07, 5.20, and 3.91. Thus, the predicted decline in variability was obtained, and the mean location in thé list from which the errors came was about the eighth item, which lies precisely in the region last to be mastered. That part of our hypothesis which asserts that the subject guesses at items he has not yet learned, but refrains from naming items that have already gone by, has received empirical confirmation from a recent study by Peterson, Brewer, and Bertucco (1963). Those authors tested the possibility

that the occurrence of remote associations is strongly influenced by a guessing strategy on the part of the Ss. In the ideal case, after the S had learned what the responses were, if he could remember what items had already appeared on a given trial, then he could confine his guesses to the remaining items [p. 258].

Their experimental results supported such a hypothesis.

At this point we are convinced that data generated by the method of anticipatory and perseverative errors yield more fully to the above stated rationale than to the alternative account invoking remote functional connections.

DISCUSSION

The major conclusion to be drawn is that the classical doctrine of remote associations is doubtful, in the sense that the data upon which the doctrine was dependent do not in fact unequivocally support it, but rather tend to support more strongly other explanatory hypotheses. These other hypotheses must be regarded, at the very least, as being strong alternatives to the classical doctrine in the light of the experiments described above. Nevertheless, what heuristic benefits has the classical doctrine been able to achieve? The main noteworthy use that has been made of it has been its application toward an explanation of the serial position function. Thus, Hull (1935) used it when he spoke in terms of trace-conditioned responses, and later Bugelski (1950), when he made direct use of the method of anticipatory and perseverative errors in developing a serial position rationale. We must maintain, however, that since the premise upon which such explanations rest (that is, the assumption of the existence of true remote associations) has been shown to be open to question it follows that such explanations themselves are not highly likely to survive future investigation. Judging by the evidence already marshalled above, it might be more prudent to say that the serial position function goes a long way toward explaining data usually attributed to the operation of remote associations, and not the other way around. Whatever the ultimately accepted explanation of the serial position curve will be (and papers are still being published about that problem), it is unlikely that remote associations will play any part in it.

What more positive statements can be made at this time about the conceptualization of serial memorization? Certainly, we feel that remote associations are out of the question, but it would be tempting at least to agree that adjacent connections between items are formed. However, even such an assumption cannot be made with confidence, since recent developments have rendered it highly questionable. Young (1961, 1962) has presented a great deal of convincing data to the effect that the stimulus for an item in a serial list is not the preceding item at all, but that it may instead be the serial position of that item. Also, Ebenholtz (1963) has demonstrated clearly that a serial list *can* be learned quite satisfactorily without the necessity of forming adjacent sequential connections in the list, but rather through associating the items with their spatial positions. With these developments to guide us, the most promising (and challenging) statement we can offer to describe serial learning is that it involves acquiring of the items per se, and then the fixing of their relative positions in the list, through associating them, not with each other, but with a self-generated sequential or spatial symbol (such as first, second, etc.). Both of these processes probably overlap in time with the response-learning stage being initiated first, and the position-learning stage starting shortly thereafter, in much the same manner as the two phases discussed by Underwood and Schulz (1960). It should be emphasized that this position does not deny the existence of associative bonds, but it does deny that serial learning proceeds by a process that results in simple chaining whereby one item is the stimulus for

the next, and it also denies the necessity for postulating any remote associations. Rather, the associations formed are more likely to be between the item and some distinctive symbol designating its relative position in the list, and are the result of an active searching process on the part of the subject. An apposite summarization of the serial learning situation was made many years ago by Woodworth (1938):

We may well be struck also with the importance of perception or apprehension in the learning process—perception of relations, patterns and meanings. To look at a list of numbers or nonsense syllables, you would think that the thing to be done was to forge links between the adjacent terms, but the actual learning proceeds largely in quite another way. It does not start with elements and unite these, but it starts with groups, or even with the whole series, and proceeds largely by analysis and the finding of parts and relations [p. 35].

SUMMARY

Previous studies relating to the doctrine of remote associations were reviewed, and several new experiments testing the validity of the concept were presented.

The overall results of Experiments I, II, and III served to support an hypothesis based upon perception of derived-list patterning, and were essentially incompatible with predictions based on the doctrine of remote associations.

Experiment IV gave support to a hypothesis that the association method produces its results because of an artifact, namely, differential practice on the correct responses because of the serial positions of list items. It was concluded that the association method was totally inconclusive with regard to the question of the reality of remote associations.

Findings based upon the use of the method of anticipatory and perseverative errors were consistently accounted for by a rationale based on serial position effects and the subject's guessing pattern, and a further prediction based on that rationale was confirmed.

It was concluded that the doctrine of remote associations is doubtful, and that other alternative hypotheses merit serious consideration. It was suggested that serial memorization involves the acquiring of the items per se, and then the fixing of their positions in the list through associating them with self-generated sequential or spatial symbols.

BRUNER, J. S., WALLACH, M. A., & GALANTER, E. H. The identification of recurrent regularity. *Amer. J. Psychol.*, 1959, **72**, 200-209.

BUGELSKI, B. R. A remote association explanation of the relative difficulty of learning nonsense syllables in a serial list. *J. exp. Psychol.*, 1950, **40**, 336-48.

CASON, H. Specific serial learning; a study of remote forward association. *J. exp. Psychol.*, 1926, **9**, 299-324.

EBBINGHAUS, H. Memory: *A contribution to experimental psychology.* (Trans. by H. A. Ruger, & C. E. Bussenius.) New York: Teachers College, Columbia University, 1913.

EBENHOLTZ, S. M. Position mediated transfer between serial learning and a spatial discrimination task. *J. exp. Psychol.*, 1963, **65**, 603-8.

GARRETT, H. E., & HARTMAN, G. W. An experiment on backward association in learning. *Amer. J. Psychol.*, 1926, **37**, 241-6.

GELDARD, F. A. *Fundamentals of psychology.* New York: Wiley, 1962.

GOLDIAMOND, I., & HAWKINS, W. F. Vexierversuch: The log relationship between work-frequency and recognition obtained in the absence of stimulus words. *J. exp. Psychol.*, 1958, **56**, 457-63.

GOLDSTEIN, N. Saving in the learning of scrambled lists as influenced by degree of familiarity with nonsense syllables. *J. gen. Psychol.*, 1950, **42**, 87-96.

HALL, M. E. Remote associative tendencies in serial learning. *J. exp. Psychol.*, 1928, **11**, 65-76.

HOVLAND, C. I. Human learning and retention. In S. S. Stevens (Ed.), *Handbook of experimental psychology.* New York: Wiley, 1951.

HULL, C. L. The conflicting psychologies of learning: A way out. *Psychol. Rev.*, 1935, **42**, 491-516.

KIMBLE, G. A. *Principles of general psychology.* New York: Roland Press, 1956.

LEPLEY, W. M. Serial reactions considered as conditioned reactions. *Psychol. Monogr.*, 1934, 46,(1, Whole, No. 205).

LUMLEY, E. H. Anticipation as a factor in serial and maze learning. *J. exp. Psychol.*, 1932, **15**, 331-42.

McGEOCH, J. A. The direction and extent of intra-serial associations at recall. *Amer. J. Psychol.*, 1936, **48**, 221-45.

McGEOCH, J. A., & IRION, A. L. *The psychology of human learning.* (2nd ed.) New York: Longmans, Green, 1952.

MITCHELL, M. B. Anticipatory place-skipping tendencies in the memorization of numbers. *Amer. J. Psychol.*, 1934, **46**, 80-91.

MORGAN, C. T. *Introduction to psychology.* New York: McGraw-Hill, 1961.

NOBLE, C. E. Measurements of association value (a), rated associations (a'), and scaled meaningfulness (m') for the 2100 cvc combinations of the English alphabet. *Psychol. Rep.*, 1961, Monograph Supplement 3-V8, 487-521.

PETERSON, L. R., BREWER, C. L., & BERTUCCO, R. A guessing strategy with the anticipation technique. *J. exp. Psychol.*, 1963, **65**, 258-64.

RASKIN, E. & COOK, S. W. The strength and direction of associations formed in the learning of nonsense syllables. *J. exp. Psychol.*, 1937, **20**, 381-95.

TYLER, D. W., WORTZ, E. C., & BITTERMAN, M. E. The effect of random and alternating partial reinforcement on resistance to extinction in the rat. *Amer. J. Psychol.*, 1953, **66**, 57-65.

UNDERWOOD, B. J., & SCHULZ, R. W. *Meaningfulness and verbal learning.* New York: Lippincott, 1960.

WOODWORTH, R. S. *Experimental psychology.* New York: Holt, 1938.

WOODWORTH, R. S., & SCHLOSBERG, H. *Experimental psychology.* (Rev. ed.) New York: Holt, 1954.

YOUNG, R. K. The stimulus in serial verbal learning. *Amer. J. Psychol.*, 1961, **74**, 517-28.

YOUNG, R. K. Tests of three hypotheses about the effective stimulus in serial learning. *J. exp. Psychol.*, 1962, **63**, 307-13.

10 / What Is Learned in Serial Learning? [1]

ARTHUR R. JENSEN AND WILLIAM D. ROHWER, JR., *University of California, Berkeley, California*

Serial learning is usually conceived of psychologically as the acquisition of a chain of S-R units: each item in the series is the stimulus for each succeeding item. With sufficient repetition the learner's own verbal responses become the only stimuli necessary to elicit each successive response. This simple and appealing conception of serial learning

From the *Journal of Verbal Learning and Verbal Behavior*, 1965, 4, 62-75, with permission of the authors and publisher, Academic Press, Inc.
1. This research was aided by a National Science Foundation grant to the Institute of Human Learning, University of California, Berkeley.

(if we ignore the unessential complications added by Hull) has prevailed to
the present time. The only trouble is
that, empirically, serial learning has not
yielded to this particular analysis. As a
result, the chief preoccupation of present
researchers in this field has been the
search, thus far without much success, for
the so-called "functional stimulus" in
serial learning. The problem was first
noted by Primoff (1938), who, in studying transfer from paired-associate to
serial learning, came to the following
conclusion: "A serial response seemed
to be different from and less difficult to
establish than a chained series of its
component connections: a serial association differed from a series of S-R
bonds" (1938, p. 394). Full recognition
of this problem was given by Underwood
(1963) in his review and discussion of
the relevant research, the gist of which
is that the sum of the experimental
evidence shows the S-R chain formulation to be either totally incorrect or at
best far from adequate.

This formulation fails most drastically
in its power to make predictions concerning transfer between serial and paired-
associate learning. While the usual interpretation of the S-R chain theory must
lead to the prediction of a substantial
amount of positive transfer from serial
to paired-associate learning (and vice
versa) when both lists have a number of
S-R units in common, in actual fact, no
appreciable transfer occurs under these
conditions. Since much of this evidence
has been previously summarized in
Underwood's paper as well as in previous articles (Jensen, 1962; Keppel and
Saufley, 1964), it need not be reiterated
in detail. It all highlights the central
question: If what is learned cannot be
conceptualized adequately as a chain of
S-R units, then just what does take place
in serial learning? What would constitute
a satisfactory psychological model of
serial phenomena?

The S-R chain theory of serial learning
has also been criticized on more purely
theoretical grounds by psychologists
who have been critical of S-R formulations in general. The most elaborate and
far-reaching discussion of serial phenomena in non–S-R terms is the paper by
Lashley (1951). Though Lashley pointed
out many of the difficulties an S-R theory
would have to encounter in dealing with
serial learning, he did not propose any
clear alternative theory. His emphasis,
however, seemed to be on central integrative processes which organize sequential behavior and which are not highly
dependent upon a sequential input of
conditioned stimuli. A more explicitly
Gestalt approach to serial learning has
been advocated by Asch, Hay, and Diamond (1960), whose experiments in this
field have emphasized the spatial and
configurational properties of the serial
list. Their suggestion that serial *position*
may function as a "cue" can, of course,
be quite divorced from Gestalt conceptions and can be comprehended within
the S-R framework and subjected to experimental test.

This is precisely the concern of the
present study: does serial *position* per
se, or some symbolically mediated
equivalent thereof, act as the functional
stimulus in serial learning? Since there
have also been previous attempts to
answer this question, a review of the
current situation is in order. The state of
research on this topic has grown quite
complicated, and it will be easier to summarize if we adopt a consistent terminology and organize the details by means
of some simple schemata.

The major hypotheses

Sequential hypothesis. There are three
major S-R hypotheses concerning what is
learned in serial (Ser) learning. The first
will be labeled the *sequential* hypothesis.
It states that each item in the list is the
functional stimulus for each adjacently

succeeding item, and it assumes that, as learning takes place, the learner's verbal responses themselves become the stimuli for successive responses.

This hypothesis, or an elaboration of it which will be called the *compound sequential* hypothesis, has been the prevailing conception of Ser learning. The *compound sequential* hypothesis states that two or more of the preceding items serve as the effective stimulus for each successive item in the series. It is usually assumed that the more remote one item is from another in the series, the weaker is its stimulus function. Backward associations are also assumed to occur and to result in some degree of response competition or interference with the forward associations.

Position hypothesis. The second major conception will be labeled the *position* hypothesis. It states that what is learned are associations between the items and their ordinal positions. One difficulty with this conception which is seldom recognized is how *position* acts as the functional stimulus, since in the usual anticipation method of Ser learning, in which each item appears singly in one window of the memory drum, serial position per se has no objective stimulus characteristics. Therefore, if position is to be regarded as the functional stimulus, one of two assumptions must be made: either absolute temporal position acts directly as the stimulus, or the temporal order gives rise to some symbolically mediated representation of serial position. The first alternative seems highly improbable, since alteration of the pacing interval in the course of Ser learning has not been shown to produce large decremental effects on performance; under certain conditions it can even facilitate performance. The second alternative, therefore, seems more tenable. Exactly how temporal order might mediate serial position is an open question. Mediation could take the form of temporal position eliciting the ordinal numerals in the learner; the numerals then serve as the "stimuli" for the "paired-associate" learning of the items in the list. Something of this nature was proposed by Schulz (1955), who required Ss, immediately after learning a serial list, to designate the ordinal number of the serial position occupied by each syllable when the syllables were presented in a random order. The Ss were able to designate ordinal position, and their accuracy was a function of serial position, the middle positions being the most difficult. If what the S had actually learned was an S-R connection between ordinal position and syllable, Schulz's task would represent a test of the formation of backward associations, since the syllables were given as the stimuli for the responses of naming ordinal position. On the other hand, it is possible that such associations are not acquired during the course of Ser learning, but once the list is mastered the S may be able to mediate these connections through his "knowledge" of the list, whatever that may consist of psychologically.

Dual-process hypothesis. The third major formulation, which grew out of discouragement with the two previous ones and which is a combination of the two, is called the *dual-process* hypothesis. In its simplest form it states that both sequential *and* positional associations are acquired in Ser learning. As a result of certain empirical findings, which are apparently in conflict, however, there are now two versions of the dual-process hypothesis. The first, suggested by Young, Patterson, and Benson (1963), states that the extremes of the Ser list are learned predominantly by sequential associations while the middle items are learned predominantly by positional associations. The second version, suggested by Ebenholtz (1963b), states just the opposite, viz., that position learning occurs predominantly at the extremes and sequential learning occurs in the middle of the list. The associations assumed by either version of the dual-process hypothesis are not regarded in an all-or-none fashion. Both sequential and positional associations can be assumed to occur throughout the entire list; the disagreement concerns their relative strengths in various parts of the list.

Experimental Paradigms

The hypotheses outlined above have been subjected to a considerable number of experimental investigations, all of which, however, may be classified under three general transfer paradigms. We will describe each paradigm, along with the associated findings.

Transfer from paired-associative to Ser learning. The evidence from this paradigm, based on the traditional procedures of paired-associate (PA) and Ser learning, is largely negative, though there have been instances of a moderate degree (35–55%) of positive transfer (Young, 1959; Jensen, 1962). It can be argued, however, with some empirical support (Jensen, 1962), that PA to Ser transfer depends upon S's transferring his *set* for PA learning to the Ser task. When S's tendency to regard the Ser list as a continuation of the PA task is experimentally hindered, transfer does not occur, even though S is fully informed of the relationship between the PA and Ser lists.

The latest evidence from the PA to Ser paradigm is an experiment by Young, Milaukas, and Bryan (1963) which provides some interesting new facts. Young *et al.* varied the degree of prior PA learning (15 trials versus 30 trials) and used both positive and negative Ser transfer tasks (Group P and Group N). For Group P all the adjacent items in the Ser list were previously practiced as PAs. For Group N there was no correspondence between the PA and Ser adjacencies. Control Ss (Group C) practiced a PA list in which both S and R terms consisted of entirely different adjectives, and then learned the same Ser list as presented to Groups P and N. Generally, Group P showed no significant transfer, although the

subgroup which had 30 prior PA trials showed significant ($p < .05$) transfer (28%), while the subgroup which had only 15 prior PA trials showed no significant transfer. It should be noted that the Control Group in this experiment received the Ser list without prior response learning. If the Ser items had been prefamiliarized in the Control Group, it is possible that no transfer at all would have materialized. The transfer found by Young *et al.* represents a savings of only 2 out of approximately 7 trials needed to attain criterion; at least one of these trials might be assumed to be needed for the response-acquisition phase of the rather difficult list of adjectives used in this experiment. It is advisable in this type of experiment that the Control Group either be prefamiliarized on the items in the transfer list or that the list be composed of items which involve very minimal response learning, such as high-frequency one-syllable words.

The other major finding of this study by Young *et al.* is that Group N (both the 15 and 30 trial conditions), as compared with the Control Groups, showed highly significant ($p < .001$) *negative* transfer (approximately — 55%).

Ebenholtz (1963b) used the PA to Ser paradigm to investigate the positional hypothesis. The stimulus item of each pair consisted of a particular position in a vertical array of small "windows." The particular window to which S was to respond was indicated by the appearance of a red patch in the window; the response item (nonsense syllable) which followed after 3 sec would appear in the same "window." The ten items were presented in a more or less random order and S had to learn to associate each response item with a particular spatial position. One of three transfer tasks followed: (*a*) a Ser list in which the temporal serial order of the items corresponded to their spatial order in the PA task, (*b*) a Ser list in which the response terms had no systematic relationship to the spatial array, and (*c*) a Ser list in which the *sequence* of the items corresponded to the order of the items in the spatial array but the *positions* of the items in the Ser list did not correspond to their positions in the spatial array. Ebenholtz found that transfer condition *a* was superior to *b* and *c,* which did not differ significantly from each other. Since there was no proper control group, and since conditions *b* and *c* could be interpreted as negative transfer paradigms, it cannot be said for sure whether condition *a* produced any position transfer. Ebenholtz estimated the percentage of transfer by comparing performance on the same task by another group of Ss which had received no previous warm-up task. We know that warm-up and generalized practice effects from first to second task are very great; for example, Young, Patterson, and Benson (1963) found that a second, unrelated Ser list took only about half as many trials for mastery as the first Ser list. Thus, the transfer reported by Ebenholtz (77% for condition *a* and 41% for condition *b*) is undoubtedly grossly overestimated. Since the relative degree of transfer was greatest at the ends of the list and least in the middle, Ebenholtz concluded in favor of a dual-process hypothesis in which the extremes of the series are learned predominantly by positional associations, and the middle items of the series, where discrimination of position is presumably more difficult, are learned predominantly by sequential association. Again, without the proper control groups, this conclusion cannot be very firm. At most, what the PA to Ser paradigm in the Ebenholtz experiment does show is that it is possible for spatial position to *mediate* transfer to a Ser list. Thus, spatial position might serve as a mediating link between temporal-order cues and responses in Ser learning.

Transfer from Ser to PA learning. This paradigm overcomes the objection just pointed out in connection with PA to Ser transfer. If Ser learning transfers positively to derived PAs, it must mean either that specific sequential connections have been acquired in Ser learning or that Ss can rapidly repeat the Ser list to themselves to "find" the required response term for each PA.

Ser to PA transfer has always produced less apparent transfer than PA to Ser. For example, the Ebenholtz procedure described above was reversed to form the Ser to PA transfer situation (1963b). Under the condition producing the highest transfer (i.e., perfect congruence between serial position

and spatial position) there was only 46% transfer, as contrasted to 77% transfer in the corresponding condition of the PA to Ser paradigm. Again, there was no proper control group and 46% is almost certainly an overestimate of the amount of transfer, for the same reason mentioned previously.

In short, the literature contains no bona fide demonstrations of significant positive transfer in the Ser to PA situation. In one study by Young (1962), even 10 trials of overlearning of the Ser list produced no transfer. Young also tested the compound sequential hypothesis by using two adjacent items from the Ser list as the stimulus terms in the PA transfer task, but this only produced slight negative transfer. Young concluded that both in terms of trials to criterion and number of correct responses ". . . prior serial learning retards subsequent PA learning" (1962, p. 310).

Could it be that in going from a Ser to a PA list Ss try to transfer their knowledge of the Ser list to the PA task by tacitly going through the Ser list until they get to the stimulus item of the PA and thence to the required response? The Ss reported attempting this strategy (Erickson, Ingram, and Young, 1963) and attributed the failure of transfer to the fact that the PAs were presented at a rate too fast to permit consistently successful mental scanning of the Ser list. To determine the degree to which this strategy, if actually operative, might be facilitated by slowing the rate of presentation of the PAs, Erickson *et al.* had Ss first learn a Ser list (14 adjectives) at a 1.5-sec rate and then learn the list of derived PAs at one of three rates: 1.5:1.5, 2:2, or 4:4. Comparisons with the appropriate controls for the three rates of presentation revealed neither significant over-all transfer nor a significant increase in transfer as a function of presentation rate. The serial-position data revealed transfer only on the items in the last two positions of the Ser list; there was zero transfer for the items at the beginning of the series and negative transfer for the middle items. These findings seem to contradict the implications of the strategy which Ss purported to use in the Ser to PA situation. But there is an important detail of the procedure used by Erickson *et al.* which might well have stacked the cards against the success of the Ss' purported strategy, viz., only half the items in the PA transfer list consisted of PAs derived from adjacent items in the prior Ser list; the other PAs in the list were entirely new. Under these conditions it seems not unlikely that the strategy reported by the Ss proved to be too inefficient (at best it could mediate only half the PAs) and was therefore quickly abandoned.

Transfer to a derived serial list. In this paradigm the learning of the original Ser list is followed by the learning of a second Ser list which is different from, but in some way related to, the first list. Probably because it has the advantage of not forcing the S to change his set from a Ser to a PA procedure, it has been adopted in several of the most recent investigations, particularly those concerned with the role of serial position as the functional stimulus.

Ebenholtz (1963a) used variations of this paradigm in two experiments designed to test both the sequential and positional hypotheses. In one experiment a Ser list was presented to one group in the usual manner. Another group received the same list, but each trial always began at a different place in the series; thus the sequence of items remained the same from trial to trial, but the position of the items with respect to the intertrial interval varied from one trial to the next. Learning was significantly slower in the second condition, as would be predicted from the position hypothesis. The Ss in the second condition, being deprived of position cues, were *forced* to learn the series sequentially, and we know that such learning, of which PA learning is an instance, is generally more difficult than Ser learning. Others have used essentially the same procedure, with minor variations, and found the same result (Bowman and Thurlow, 1963; Winnick and Dornbush, 1963). So a point is scored in favor of the positional hypothesis. It would have been interesting in the Ebenholtz experiment to have had both groups finally learn a derived PA list; one would predict that the condition of Ser learning in which position was varied would produce markedly greater transfer to the PA list than the constant-position condition.

In another experiment, Ebenholtz (1963a) tested the positional hypothesis as follows:

Group I learned Ser List 1 followed by Ser List 2, as indicated below (K represents new items).

List 1: A B C D E etc.
List 2: K_1 B K_2 D K_3 etc.

The old items retained the same positions in List 2 that they had held in List 1. Group II learned first a Ser list composed of the same items as List 1, above, but in a different order, and then learned List 2; the relationship between the lists was such that the old items in List 2 were four positions removed from the positions they held in the prior list. A control group learned first an equivalent but irrelevant list and then learned List 2. The results clearly showed faster learning only for those items in List 2 which retained the same position they held in List 1. [Essentially the same experiment was performed earlier by Young (1962, Exp. III), with results which lead to essentially the same conclusions.] These results, however, still do not rule out the sequential hypothesis. A good reason for this reservation concerning these findings which seem to favor the position hypothesis is that the results can also be explained in terms of the sequential hypothesis by assuming that every other response (i.e., the old items) in List 2 was mediated by the associations learned in List 1. The highly systematic and simple relationship between Lists 1 and 2 should not have made such mediation at all difficult.

An experiment intended to overcome this weakness was performed by Keppel and Saufley (1964). In the List 2 used by Keppel and Saufley some of the items retained the same positions they held in List 1, but not in any systematic pattern that could be readily transposed or mediated from List 1 to List 2. However, the results were essentially the same as Ebenholtz's; more items in constant positions were given correctly in 10 transfer trials than items in different positions. Most of the transfer was attributable to the items at the end of the lists, which agrees with Ebenholtz' conclusion that position learning is more pronounced at the extremes and weakest in the middle of the list. Thus it seems probable that sequential mediation is not an adequate explanation of the positional transfer found in these experiments. It is interesting that, while constant position resulted in positive transfer, changed position did not result in more intrusion errors based on position. Overt errors were predominantly due to sequential transfer from List 1 and not from positional transfer. Sequential transfer means that stimulus n in the transfer list is followed by response $n + 1$ from the original list. It would appear that if sequential associations are formed in Ser learning, they are incidental and may create interference and intrusion errors in a negative transfer paradigm, without producing any appreciable positive transfer in a positive paradigm.

For reasons that are not at all clear, the positional hypothesis fared less well in a series of experiments by Battig, Brown, and Schild (1964). They used the Ser_1 to Ser_2 paradigm, with three variations of List 2: (a) 3 of the items (of a 12-item list) maintained the same positions and the same sequential adjacencies as in List 1, (b) 3 items maintained the same sequence but held different positions, and (c) 3 items maintained the same positions but the sequence was not maintained. Degree of List 1 learning and the location (beginning or middle of the list) of the crucial 3 items were also varied. While some aspects of these experiments are difficult to interpret, Battig *et al.* were able to conclude quite definitely that there was ". . . complete lack of support . . . for direct associations of individual items with their serial positions as a principal mechanism of serial learning." There was no facilitation of items appearing in the same serial position unless the items were also sequentially adjacent. Conditions *a* and *b* both resulted in greater transfer than condition *c*, a finding which is consistent with the sequential but not with the positional hypothesis. Other aspects of the findings suggest that different processes might play different roles at various stages of practice. A question which was not raised by Battig *et al.*, but which seems pertinent, is whether their results might easily be explained by the possibility that the cluster of 3 items retaining the same sequence creates a kind of von Restorff effect. The isolation effect would not be so great for the same three

items appearing at separate positions in the list.

"Backward" Ser learning. If Ser_2 consists of Ser_1 in reverse order, the sequential and positional hypotheses should have different implications regarding the amount of transfer as a function of serial position, or so it has been argued by Young, Patterson, and Benson (1963). Since the middle items would be changed least in position, the position hypothesis would predict relatively greater positive transfer in the middle of the list and possibly negative transfer at the extremes. Assuming the existence of backward associations, the sequential hypothesis would predict either approximately equal transfer throughout the series or greater transfer at the extremes due to relatively greater overlearning of the associations between items at the extremes. To test this hypothesis Young *et al.* performed the appropriate experiment and found the result predicted by the position hypothesis. Though the overall transfer was not statistically significant, the middle positions did show significant positive transfer. While these results are quite clearcut, they are nevertheless quite puzzling in view of the fact that other paradigms have suggested that positive transfer occurs at the extremes of the list.

Instructional Variables

In all but one of the transfer experiments we have reviewed (Jensen, 1962), Ss were never informed of the nature of the transfer situation. An experiment by Winnick and Dornbush (1963), in which the starting point for a continuous serial list varied from trial to trial, showed that instructions to the S indicating the possibility of a shift in starting position was a significant variable in speed of learning. In a transfer situation instructions would seem even more crucial, and we believe it is a methodologically important point in research on this problem that all Ss be made fully aware of the transfer aspect of the experiment. Otherwise the possibility exists that differences in the amount of transfer obtained by different paradigms and with different learning materials might be due to differential tendencies of various conditions to elicit self-instructions which may affect degree of transfer.

The present experiment, based on the Ser to PA paradigm, was designed to obtain further evidence concerning the relative and absolute amounts of transfer of sequential and positional cues in Ser learning.

METHOD

Design

The principal aim of the experiment was to measure the amount of transfer from a Ser list to a PA list under two different conditions of PA learning. In one condition of PA learning, *Pos.* (position learning), serial position alone served as the stimulus item of each pair. The S's task was to learn to associate each response item with a particular serial position. The other condition, *seq.* (sequential learning), consisted of a derived double-function PA list in which each item of the prior Ser list served as the stimulus for its immediately succeeding item. Here the S's task was to learn the derived PAs by the usual anticipation method.

The standard transfer design was used, with each condition of PA learning having an appropriate control group. Thus there were four groups in all: the Position Transfer group (Pos. T), the Position Control group (Pos. C), the Sequence Transfer group (Seq. T), and the Sequence Control group (Seq. C).

Materials

Since it seemed desirable to minimize the time spent in response learning in the present experiment, the 12-item Ser list (Task 1) for the transfer groups and the derived 12-item PA lists (Task 2) for both the transfer and control groups consisted of high frequency three-letter words with no initial letters duplicated: END, JOY, MAN, HAT, WIT, PIE, SUM, GAS, TIP, NET, ART, and BED. The 12-item Ser list (Task 1) for the control groups consisted of trigrams matched with the word list for trigram frequency (based on the table of trigram frequencies in Underwood and Schulz, 1960, pp. 326-69) and also having no duplicated

initial letters: COM, REL, ZIN, VEN, EST, FAC, TIS, MUL, PIM, NOP, BOT, and DAL. The Ser lists were preceded by a set of three asterisks which also served as one of the stimulus items in the derived PA list of the Seq. conditions.

Procedure

All lists were presented on a memory drum. The Ser lists were presented at a 2-sec rate with a 2-sec intertrial interval. The PA lists were presented at a 2:2 rate; there were three different orders of presentation of the pairs. In all conditions Ss were required to attain a criterion of one errorless trial. The time elapsing between successive tasks was about 2 min, which allowed E to change the tape in the memory drum and to read the instructions for the next task.

Task 1 (Ser list). The Ss were instructed to learn by the anticipation method. On the first presentation of the list for all groups, E pronounced the items aloud. (The purpose of this procedure was to insure more or less uniform pronunciation of the trigrams.)

Task 2 (PA list), group Pos. T. In this transfer condition the stimulus item of each pair consisted of a horizontal row of 12 frames ("boxes"), one of which contained a bright red dot. The particular position indicated by the dot in the set of 12 frames was considered the stimulus to which a particular word had to be associated. Following the 2-sec presentation of the set of frames containing the red dot, the frames were presented again for 2 sec, this time with the appropriate response printed in the previously designated frame.

Just before Trial 1 the S was shown a set of completely empty frames and E explained the relationship between Task 1 and Task 2: "Each of the words in the series you just learned has been paired with one of the 12 boxes arranged in a row like this. The first word in the series has been paired with the first box in the row [E points to the "box" on the S's extreme left], the second word with the second box, the third word with the third box, and so on to the last word with the last box in the row [E points to the "box" at S's extreme right]. Thus there are

12 pairs of boxes and words." This was followed by an explanation of the function of the red dot as the positional stimulus, along with the usual instructions for PA learning by the anticipation method. The Ss began anticipating on the first presentation.

Task 2 (PA List), group Pos. C. In this control condition the materials and procedure were identical to those of the transfer group, except, of course, that the instructions had to be modified as follows: "Each of the words in a series of 12 has been paired with one of 12 boxes arranged in a row like this. Thus there are 12 pairs of boxes and words." From here on all the instructions were the same as for the transfer group. The Ss began anticipating on the trial following the first complete presentation of the PA list.

Task 2 (PA List), group Seq. T. Here the PAs were presented in the traditional manner, with the stimulus item appearing in the left-hand window of the drum, followed by the pairing of both stimulus and response items. As in the Pos. T condition, Ss were explicitly informed of the relationship between Task 1 and Task 2: "Each of the words in the series you have just learned has been paired with the word that immediately followed it in the series. The asterisks are included so that there is a set of 12 pairs." This was followed by the usual PA instructions. The Ss began anticipating on the first presentation.

Task 2 (PA List), group Seq. C. This control condition received the usual PA instructions without reference to the prior Ser list. The Ss began anticipating after one complete presentation of the list. In all other respects the materials and procedure were the same as for the corresponding transfer group.

Subjects

There were 80 Ss in all, 20 Ss in each of the four groups. All Ss were female and were volunteers from summer session courses in a Catholic girls college. Fifty-three of the Ss were lay students and 27 were Catholic sisters. Their mean age was 23 years, 8 months; $SD = 6$ years, 8 months. Each S was assigned to one of the four groups cyclically in the order of their appearance at the laboratory.

RESULTS

Over-all transfer

Ser to PA. Table 1 presents the mean trials to criterion for each of the conditions of the experiment. It is immediately clear that the transfer (T) and control (C) groups do not differ by many trials on the transfer task for either the Pos. or Seq. condition. The percentage of transfer was measured by the standard formula: % Transfer $= 100 \times (C-T)/C$. The Pos. condition resulted in 2.6% transfer; the Seq. condition produced negative transfer (-10.9%). These amounts of

Table 1. Mean trials for mastery of serial and paired-associate tasks

Group	Task 1 (Ser)		Task 2 (PA)	
	M	SD	M	SD
Pos. T	14.10	7.45	14.85	9.37
Pos. C	15.90	6.82	15.25	7.46
Seq. T	13.05	6.31	23.25	9.32
Seq. C	15.30	7.87	20.95	9.33

transfer are indeed minute, and analysis of covariance shows them to be totally lacking in significance. In the analysis of covariance the control variable was trials to criterion on Task 1, which were converted to T scores within the T and C groups separately, so that each group's mean was 50, with a SD of 10. (This T conversion was necessary, since Task 1 was different for the transfer and control groups.) The covariance analysis revealed a highly significant Methods (Pos. *vs.* Seq.) effect $(F=16.38, df=1/75, p<.001)$, but no significance $(F<1)$ for Groups (T *vs.* C) or for Methods × Groups $(F<1)$. Since the Methods means differ, and since percentage transfer is based on relative savings in the transfer groups as compared with the control group, it could be that while the *absolute* differences between T and C within each Method are not significantly different, the methods might show a difference in the *proportion* of C/T. In other words, a distinction is made between *absolute* and *relative* amounts of transfer. The relative differences can be tested for significance by analysis of variance simply by transforming the data to $\log_{10}$, or, if the data include zeros, to $\log_{10}(x+0.5)$. When the data are thus transformed to a log scale, differences may be interpreted as ratios. The $\log_{10}(x+0.5)$ transformation was performed on the data used in the first analysis and the analysis of covariance was carried out on these transformed data. The results remained essentially unchanged; Groups and Methods × Groups were nonsignificant sources of variance ($F < 1$ in both cases).

Transfer on trial 1. Since transfer effects might rapidly dissipate with successive learning trials, possibly due to an increase in interference tendencies, the methods of learning were compared for amount of transfer on just the first learning trial of Task 2. The percentage of transfer for the Pos. method was 28.5; for the Seq. method, 23.1. An analysis of variance applied to the Trial 1 data showed that there was significant transfer on Trial 1 for both the Pos. and Seq. methods, but the amounts of transfer in the two methods did not differ significantly. It should be pointed out that some, possibly all, of Trial 1 transfer might be attributable to response learning rather than to the associative aspect of the prior Ser learning.

Transfer as a function of stage of learning

Since the Trial 1 data of Task 2 revealed significant Ser to PA transfer, it was decided to analyze amount of transfer as a function of stage of learning. For this purpose, the number of trials needed to attain successive criteria (from 1 to 12 correct anticipations) was obtained for every S. Since these data are constrained by the fact that the series must necessarily increase from Criterion 1 to Cri-

terion 12, a condition which makes analysis of variance impermissible, the data were converted to difference scores, i.e., the number of trials needed to go from one criterial level to the next, rather than the number of trials needed to attain each criterion. To obtain greater stability, these scores were summed for each S over criteria 1-4, 5-8, and 9-12, thus yielding a point for each one-third of the total trials to criterion. The means of these points for the various groups were used to obtain the percentage of transfer $[(100 \times (C-T)/)]$ at each of the three stages of learning. The results are shown in the left half of Fig. 1.

The data from which the percentage transfer was determined were subjected to analysis of variance, first in raw scores form and then as transformed to $\log_{10}(x+0.5)$, to test absolute and relative transfer for significance. The analysis shows that the amount of transfer differs significantly ($p < .01$) as a function of the stage of learning. As can be seen in Fig. 1, practically all the positive transfer occurs in the first stage of learning (i.e., in the first one-third of the trials needed to attain criterion). Both analyses agree in showing no significant differences between the Pos. and Seq. conditions in over-all amount of transfer or in the amount of transfer as a function of stage of learning.

Transfer as a function of serial position

Anticipation errors (overt errors + omissions) in Task 2 were analyzed as a function of their serial position in Task 1. To gain stability, the data were combined for positions 1-3, 4-6, 7-9, and 10-12. The percentage transfer as a function of position is shown in the right half of Fig. 1. Again, analysis of variance of these data showed no appreciable difference between the Seq. and Pos. methods in amount of transfer. The Positions × Groups interaction, being nonsignificant for the raw data and

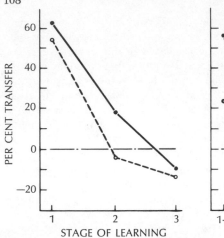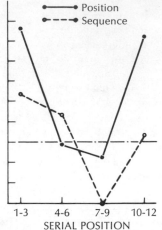

FIG. 1. Percentage transfer as a function of the stage of learning and of serial position (see text for full explanation).

highly significant $(p < .01)$ for the log-transformed data, indicates no difference between positions in absolute transfer but very significant differences in *relative* (percentage) transfer, as is indicated by Fig. 1. The Pos. and Seq. methods did not differ in the degree to which they show transfer as a function of serial position. The situation is quite clear in Fig. 1, and agrees perfectly with the stage analysis: items learned in the earlier trials are generally those in positions 1-3 and 10-12, and these are the positions showing the greatest transfer.

DISCUSSION

The present experiment was not intended to answer the question proposed in the title of this article, which, of course, is a theoretical problem and not an empirical one. Current hypotheses, however, do attempt to answer this question, and they lead to predictions which the present experiment was designed to test. The results indicate that the currently favored position hypothesis is hardly more adequate than the sequential hypothesis, which, as in many previous studies, again proved patently inade-

quate. And if the dual-process hypothesis is conceived of merely as the *summation* of positional and sequential learning, it, too, must be regarded as lacking, for the sum of two zeros is still zero.

Why is there no significant over-all transfer from Ser to PA learning for either the Sequential or Positional method, despite the fact that both methods clearly show positive transfer in the first few trials?

At least two essentially different types of explanation may be entertained.

(a) Any one or a combination of the above hypotheses is basically correct, but massive interference builds up in the second task which completely counteracts the associations that would make for positive transfer. It might even have to be assumed that, for some as yet unknown reason, these interference tendencies are greater in the transfer group than in the control group, since they must overcome the initial positive transfer. This hypothesis cannot be evaluated further until we know more about the variables of which interference in second-task learning is a function, particularly in the Ser to PA paradigm. Headway in solving this problem might be made by having Ser to PA transfer experiments in which the degree of associative interference is manipulated by the selection of list items, by varying the procedures of first-list learning, and by grouping Ss on the basis of individual differences in susceptibility to interference effects as established by performance in prior learning tasks. Since the von Restorff effect might be due to the relative immunity of the isolated item to interference effects within the list, for example, it would be interesting to know to what degree the von Restorff effect would transfer from a Ser to a PA list.

(b) The class of alternative hypotheses would state that Ser learning cannot be explained adequately by any of the previously described S-R hypotheses, but that it consists of something sufficiently different from the processes involved in PA learning, of either the sequential or positional type, as to lead to the prediction of no transfer from Ser to PA learning. The ephemeral position transfer occurring in the first few learning trials would be attributed to the S's attempt to maintain the *set* of the previous task or to the incidental learning of associations in the first task which the S tries to "use" in the second task. The maintenance of set or the intentional transfer of incidental learning, the argument continues, is so inappropriate to the second task, or so in conflict with the "natural" way of learning the second task, as to actually constitute an *interference* condition, which forces the S to abandon this approach and to learn the second task in the same manner as the control group. Thus the transfer group would show no overall advantage from having wasted time with an ineffectual strategy.

If the second alternative, which seems to be the most reasonable general conclusion to be drawn from all the available evidence, is favored, there remains the problem of how to conceptualize Ser learning. One possible approach, discussed in greater detail elsewhere (Jensen, 1962), would be to regard Ser learning as essentially a process of response integration rather than as the acquisition of specific S-R associations. (A similar notion was originally suggested by Lashley, 1951). An integrated response in this sense, for example, would be the reproduction of a digit series comprehended by the memory span in a single trial. When the number of items in the series exceeds the memory span, more than one trial is needed to attain the integration of the series. But psychologically this would not be conceived of as the acquisition of specific S-R connections among the items in the series. So far this idea has not been sufficiently formalized or detailed to have much predictive power for specific experimental outcomes. Indeed, the further elaboration of this hypothesis must precede the development of an appropriate experimental program. It seems hardly necessary that we should continue to be abashed by repeated demonstrations of empirical outcomes which current theories are obviously unable to predict and for which they must intemperately strain to produce even *ad hoc* explanations.

SUMMARY

A transfer experiment was performed under conditions that would permit Ss who first had learned a serial list to a criterion of mastery to "use" either *positional* associations or *sequential* S-R associations in the subsequent learning of paired associates (PAs) formally comprised of the same S-R connections existing in the prior Ser list. The principal results were as follows: (*a*) There was no significant over-all transfer from Ser to PA learning, in terms of total trials to criterion, for either the Positional or Sequential conditions. (b) There was significant Ser to PA transfer for both conditions only in the first third of the trials to criterion, after which transfer rapidly declined to zero. The Positional and Sequential conditions did not differ significantly in this respect. (c) The percentage of transfer is significantly related to serial position; those items at the beginning and end of the Ser list show positive transfer and those in the middle show zero or negative transfer.

The results were interpreted as supporting neither the position association nor the S-R "chain" association conceptions of Ser learning, and an alternative hypothesis was proposed for further consideration.

ASCH, S. E., HAY, J., AND DIAMOND, RHEA M. Perceptual organization in serial rote-learning. Amer. J. Psychol., 1960, 73, 177-98.

BATTIG, W. F., BROWN, S. C., AND SCHILD, M. E. Serial position and sequential associations in serial learning. J. exp. Psychol., 1964, 67, 449-57.

BOWMAN, R. E., AND THURLOW, W. R. Determinants of the effect of position in serial learning. Amer. J. Psychol., 1963, 76, 436-45.

EBENHOLTZ, S. M. Serial learning: Position learning and sequential associations. J. exp. Psychol., 1963, 66, 353-62. (a)

EBENHOLTZ, S. M. Position mediated transfer between serial learning and a spatial discrimination task. J. exp. Psychol., 1963, 65, 603-8. (b)

ERICKSON, C. C., INGRAM, R. D., AND YOUNG, R. K. Paired associate learning as a function of rate of presentation and prior serial learning. Amer. J. Psychol., 1963, 76, 458-63.

JENSEN, A. R. Transfer between paired-associate and serial learning. J. verb. Learn. verb. Behav., 1962, 1, 269-80.

KEPPEL, G., AND SAUFLEY, W. A. Serial position as a stimulus in serial learning. J. verb. Learn. verb. Behav., 1964, 3, 335-43.

LASHLEY, K. S. The problem of serial order in behavior. In Cerebral mechanisms in behavior. L. A. Jefress (Ed.), New York: Wiley, 1951. Pp. 112-36.

PRIMOFF, E. Backward and forward association as an organizing act in serial and in paired associate learning. J. Psychol., 1938, 5, 375-95.

SCHULZ, R. W. Generalization of serial position in rote serial learning. J. exp. Psychol., 1955, 49, 267-72.

UNDERWOOD, B. J. Stimulus selection in verbal learning. In C. N. Cofer and B. S. Musgrave (Eds.), Verbal behavior and learning: Problems and processes. New York: McGraw-Hill, 1963. Pp. 33-48.

UNDERWOOD, B. J., AND SCHULZ, R. W. Meaningfulness and verbal learning. Philadelphia: Lippincott, 1960.

WINNICK, W. A., AND DORNBUSH, R. L. Role of positional cues in serial rote learning. J. exp. Psychol., 1963, 66, 419-21.

YOUNG, R. K. A comparison of two methods of learning serial associations. Amer. J. Psychol., 1959, 72, 554-9.

YOUNG, R. K. Tests of three hypotheses about the effective stimulus in serial learning. J. exp. Psychol., 1962, 63, 307-13.

YOUNG, R. K., PATTERSON, JUDITH, AND BENSON, W. M. Backward serial learning. J. verb. Learn. verb. Behav., 1963, 1, 335-8.

YOUNG, R. K., MILAUKAS, E. W., AND BRYAN, J. D. Serial learning as a function of prior paired-associate training. Amer. J. Psychol., 1963, 76, 82-8.

THE SERIAL POSITION EFFECT

ONE of the best established and most pervasive phenomena in verbal learning is the serial position effect. This refers to the fact that with an ordered set of items those at the beginning are the easiest, those at the end next easiest, and those just beyond the middle are the hardest, to master. If item positions are plotted against errors, the function has a bowed shape resembling an inverted U, skewed to the left. Such curves have been obtained with an assortment of materials, under a wide variety of experimental conditions. The effect appears during recall as well as learning, and is reliable enough to be found even within individual subjects.

That the position of an item is such a strong determinant of its acquisition has posed a tantalizing challenge to psychologists. Considerable information is available about variables that influence the phenomenon, tasks other than serial learning which also produce it, and several theoretical offerings. For an excellent summary of earlier research and theory, the reader is referred to Chapter IV in McGeoch and Irion (1952). The following readings examine various aspects of the problem, and they are simply arranged in chronological order of publication.

The paper by McCrary and Hunter discusses an improved method of expressing errors in serial position curves. Instead of plotting mean errors on the ordinates, they used the percentage of total errors as the unit of measurement. As a result, curves representing different effective conditions of learning were practically identical. Variations in item difficulty, presentation rate, and learning ability failed to change the appearance of the curves.

Jensen's paper reports bowed curves under task conditions which departed markedly from usual serial learning procedures. Evidently it is not necessary to employ a serial anticipation method, nor a temporal sequence, nor even a consistent order of item presentation in order to obtain these curves. Along these lines, Murdock (1960) reported bowed error curves (lacking the usual skewness, however) in the course of discrimination learning, reflecting the distinctiveness of stimuli which varied unidimensionally. When serial position curves are plotted in free recall, random lists result in a skew to the right, indicating better recall of the last items. If the items are organized, as in prose passages, the curves assume the shape associated with serial tasks. Deese and Kaufman (1957) showed these changes by using materials of different degrees of organization.

Wishner, Shipley, and Hurvich (1957) presented a long serial list which was divided into distinctive segments by printing the items in different colors. Acquisition produced a separate bowed curve for each segment, which suggested that perceptual organization was a determining factor.

The Feigenbaum and Simon article presents a theory of the serial position function, based upon information processing, in which the subject is assumed to adopt a systematic strategy. The strategy involves using the first and last items as "anchors," which are learned first, and then working in toward the middle. Computer simulation data gave a close fit to empirical curves. Similarly, Ribback and Underwood (1950) attempted to account for the skewing of serial position curves by assuming that the list is learned from both ends, with the backward learning component being slower.

The paper by Glanzer and Dolinsky focuses upon the determinants of the serial list anchors. The experimental results suggested that any characteristic of a list may serve as an anchor point, and that suitable instructions can manipulate the point. Inhibition and facilitation interpretations of serial curves were rejected.

The article by Ebenholtz shows that serial position effects can be obtained in paired-associate learning, provided that the stimuli possess some positional relations among themselves. Thus, when the stimulus terms of the pairs are the numerals 1 through 10, the resulting error distribution has the familiar bowed shape, when plotted according to the ordinal sequence of the numbers. Such findings lend weight to the proposition that serial learning entails responding to the positional properties of items, however those properties are conveyed.

The above articles all have relevance to Section II as well, and it is highly likely that a valid theory of serial learning will also accommodate the serial position effect.

DEESE, J., & KAUFMAN, R. A. Serial effects in recall of unorganized verbal material. *J. exp. Psychol.*, 1957, **54**, 180-87.

McGEOCH, J. A., & IRION, A. L. *The psychology of human learning.* New York: Longmans, Green, 1952.

MURDOCK, B. B., JR. The distinctiveness of stimuli. *Psychol. Rev.*, 1960, **67**, 16-31.

RIBBACK, A., & UNDERWOOD, B. J. An empirical explanation of the skewness of the bowed serial position curve. *J. exp. Psychol.*, 1950, **40**, 329-35.

WISHNER, J., SHIPLEY, T. E., & HURVICH, M. S. The serial position curve as a function of organization. *Amer. J. Psychol.*, 1957, **70**, 258-62.

11 / Serial Position Curves in Verbal Learning

JOHN W. McCRARY, Jr., AND WALTER S. HUNTER, *Brown University, Rhode Island*

When a list of nonsense syllables is learned by a subject under conditions that require him to recall the following syllable as each one of the series is presented, it is found that the syllables in the middle of the list are learned more slowly than are those at the two ends, and that in general the initial syllables are learned more rapidly than are the final ones. When the results are plotted in terms of mean number of errors made at each serial position during learning, the graph has the form shown in Fig. 1.

Of the various theories proposed in explanation of the relatively slow rate at which the middle of the series is learned, that of Lepley (1) and Hull (2) has been the most ingenious and perhaps the best substantiated. The Lepley-Hull theory is that the bow-shaped serial position curve results from the large number of inhibitory processes present in the middle of a series of responses. It is known that during learning each syllable becomes associated not only with adjacent but also with remote syllables, so that both near and remote excitatory tendencies are set up. Progress toward mastery of the list involves a strengthening of the near excitatory tendencies and the weakening (or control) of the remote ones to the point where, when a given syllable is presented, the subject will report the next following syllable and not one farther along in the list, or none at all. A simple diagram can be constructed to show that remote excitatory tendencies pile up in the middle of the list. Proceeding from this point, an analogy is drawn between serial learning and conditioning. It is held that each succeeding syllable in the series becomes conditioned to the traces of preceding syllables so that remote associations are viewed essentially as trace-conditioned responses. Final

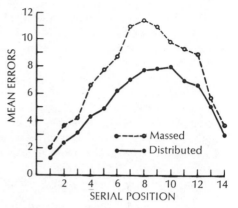

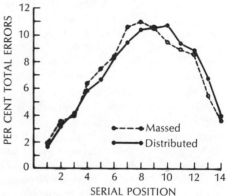

Fig. 1.

mastery is attained as a result both of the building up of internal inhibitions of the trace responses and of the strengthening of near excitatory tendencies. Inasmuch as the trace response tendencies are most numerous in the middle of the series, the inhibitory tendencies must be concentrated in the same location, to the relative neglect of the two ends. Many observations, particularly on the spontaneous recovery of extinguished responses, support the view that inhibitory tendencies dissipate more rapidly with the lapse of time than do excitatory tendencies. One

From *Science*, 1953, 117: 3032, 131-4, with permission of the authors and publisher.

can therefore make experimental tests of the effects of various manipulations of the time variable upon the serial position curve, looking for results that may or may not support the inhibition theory.

The most significant data on the serial position curve with respect to this theory come from experiments on massed vs. distributed practice and on changes in the rate of presentation of the syllables. In massed learning, practice periods follow one another with little or no rest between the periods, whereas in distributed learning there are rest periods of varying lengths at the close of each practice period. Within limits, distributed practice results in quicker learning than does massed practice. The inhibition theory predicts that the lapse of time involved in the rest periods of distributed practice will result in a relative loss of inhibitory tendencies and that, therefore, the serial position curve for distributed learning when compared with the massed learning curve will show a decrease in errors at each position but with the largest decrease in the middle portions of the curve, where the inhibitory effects have been greatest. Similar predictions are made for the effects of varying the rate at which syllables are presented, since, with a slow rate, inhibitory tendencies may be expected to dissipate more rapidly than with a faster rate of presentation.

Patten (3) and Hovland (4, 5) have conducted experiments of the above type. The upper half of Fig. 1 shows the essential results secured by Hovland (one of many experiments) when subjects learned a list of 14 syllables presented at a rate of 1 syllable each 2 sec. In the distributed practice series, there was a rest interval of 2 min 6 sec between successive presentations of the list, whereas in the massed practice series the rest period was only 6 sec. The decrease in mean errors brought about by distributed practice shows up at all serial positions, but it is

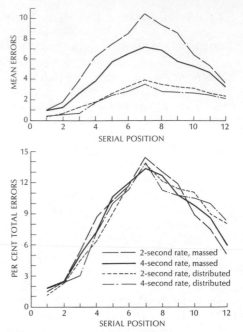

FIG. 2.

greatest in the middle of the series, as predicted by the inhibition theory. In another experiment, Hovland compared the serial position curves for the learning of 12-syllable lists under conditions of massed vs. distributed practice, using 2-sec and 4-sec rates of presentation per syllable. The mean number of errors per serial position under these various conditions is shown in the upper half of Fig. 2. Again there is evident a marked decrease in mean errors when distributed practice is compared with massed practice, with the greatest decrease in the central portion of the curve. The change from a 2-sec to a 4-sec rate of presentation has little effect under conditions of distributed practice, but a significant effect in massed practice.

The curves in the lower halves of Figs. 1 and 2 show the serial position curves of the upper halves of the figures plotted in percentages, with the mean errors at each position expressed as a percentage of the total mean errors made under a given practice condition. (Since we did not have access to Hovland's original data, the values are computed either from his curves or from his tables. In either case any errors in the calculations would be small.) The striking feature of the percentage plots is that there is essentially no difference in the curves for the different conditions of learning. This is also true for the percentage plots we have made of the data in eight other investigations by various authors. In all cases there was practically complete identity of the percentage serial position curves for the greater and lesser conditions of efficiency within a given experiment, with a rare maximum difference of 3.5% for a given serial position.

The reason for plotting percentage mean error curves is as follows, stated in terms of the experiment on massed vs. distributed practice: Since distributed practice is more efficient than massed practice, fewer errors are made during learning under the former than under the latter condition. Graphs of mean errors per syllable position, therefore, must give two curves which differ in their ordinate values much as is the case in Fig. 1, irrespective of the explanatory theory being investigated. When the absolute mean error curves are equated for area by plotting them in percentage terms, any essential differences in form are observable. The percentage curves of Figs. 1 and 2 show that the several serial positions have the same order of relative difficulty under the more and the less efficient methods of learning. From the standpoint of the Lepley-Hull inhibition theory, the percentage curves are more significant than the mean error curves, since they show that the reduction of errors brought about by the introduction of elapsed time intervals occurs throughout the series in proportion to the total errors made and in the same overall manner as where no elapsed time is introduced.

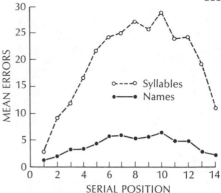

Fig. 3.

This does not prove the inhibition theory, but it is consistent with it.

In a further attempt to throw light on the serial position curve and on the relevancy of the inhibition theory, we have conducted an experiment on the serial learning of 14 nonsense syllables vs. 14 familiar names (an initial cue item was added to each list) by the conventional anticipation method counterbalancing the two series. In order to balance out any unevenness in difficulty of the specific items, each subject entered the list at a different point so that, for example, the syllable or name in serial positions 3 and 4 for one subject would be in positions 4 and 5 for another subject. The items were presented at a 2-sec rate, with the intertrial interval set at 8 sec. Learning was completed in one session, massed practice, to a criterion of one correct anticipation of each syllable in the course of one trial. The association values of the syllables were from 0 to 3% according to Hull's calibration (6). The names were the family names of the 16 graduate students who served as subjects and who, at this time, were well acquainted with each other. The mean number of trials required for learning the syllables was 39 and for learning the names, 11.

Fig. 3 gives the serial position curves for syllables and names plotted in terms of mean errors, and Fig. 4 replots the same data in terms of the percentage of

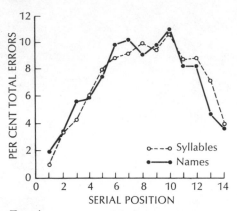

FIG. 4.

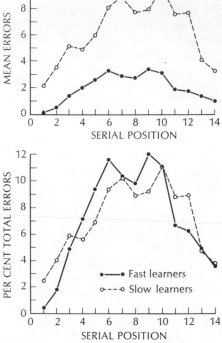

FIG. 5.

total errors made at each serial position. Again it is to be noted that (1) the curves are the familiar bow-shaped ones current in the literature, (2) the greatest gain in efficiency occurs in the middle of the series or just past the middle, and (3) the percentage plots are essentially identical. Items 2 and 3 above were brought about by the use of familiar names vs. nonsense materials as the material to be learned and not by the introduction of elapsed time, which might allow for a decrease of inhibitory tendencies as predicted by the Lepley-Hull theory.

The 16 subjects of the above experiment were classified as quick or slow learners on the basis of being in the upper or lower half of the group in total errors made during learning. The upper half of Fig. 5 presents the serial position curves for these two groups in learning familiar names as described above, and the lower half gives the curves on a percentage basis. Similar curves were found for quick vs. slow learners in the nonsense syllable learning of these 16 subjects, as well as in the experiment (not here reported) with 48 subjects in the learning of familiar and unfamiliar nonsense syllables.

The general conclusions from the above experiments and analyses are as follows: (1) Any experimental condition which increases the efficiency of serial verbal learning and which thereby decreases the total number of errors made will result in a serial position curve of mean errors which lies below the curve for a less efficient method of learning. (2) The reduction in mean errors per serial position, although greatest in the middle or just past the middle of the series, will be closely proportional at each position to the total number of errors made. It is in no sense surprising that, when one changes from a less to a more efficient method of learning, the greatest reduction of errors will occur in the central serial positions. This is not a confirmation of the inhibition theory but merely an evidence of the fact that significant gains in efficiency can only occur where serious errors have been made— namely, in the central part of the series. It is surprising, however, that the gains under a more efficient learning method should be as proportionately distributed as the percentage curves indicate.

The theoretical problem still remains of explaining why the serial position curves for verbal learning are bow-shaped. We can offer no solution ourselves, although we believe that a multiple- rather than a single-factor theory will finally be indicated. The Lepley-Hull inhibition theory is plausible only under the conditions discussed above, where lapses of time were introduced into the learning process. In order to rank as an adequate general theory it would need to be shown that *any* condition which increased the efficiency of serial verbal learning (including meaning, familiarity, and quick learning ability) decreased proportionately the inhibitory tendencies postulated in connection with the various serial positions.

1. LEPLEY, W. M. *Psychol. Monogr.*, 1934, **46**, (205).
2. HULL, C. L. *Psychol. Rev.*, 1935, **42**, 491.
3. PATTEN, E. F. *J. Psychol.*, 1938, **5**, 359.
4. HOVLAND, C. I. *J. exp. Psychol.*, 1938, **23**, 172.
5. IBID. 1940, **27**, 271.
6. HULL, C. L. *Amer. J. Psychol.*, 1933, **45**, 730.

12 / Temporal and Spatial Effects of Serial Position

ARTHUR R. JENSEN, *University of California, Berkeley*

With few exceptions, research and theory concerning serial rote-learning have developed within the S-R connectionist tradition of Ebbinghaus, Thorndike, and Pavlov.[1] Thus, the principal explanations of serial phenomena involve the concepts of S-R bonds, remote associations, stimulus-traces, trace-conditioned responses, inhibition of delay, gradient of reinforcement, stimulus-generalization, intralist interference, response-competition, proactive and retroactive inhibition, etc. The various S-R theories as explicitly formulated all have in common the assumption that serial learning consists essentially of the acquisition of connections between items in the series, each item in turn serving as the stimulus for the anticipation of the next item. The picture is that of a chain of S-R connections.

According to this view, the explanation of certain serial phenomena, such as the skewed bowing of the serial-position curve, is to be sought in the nature of the S-R connections, either in terms of their relative strengths as affected by the interaction of excitatory and inhibitory processes that are assumed to build up in the course of learning, or by interference or response-competition between the items resulting from the formation of remote associations or from stimulus-generalization. Generally regarded by theories based on a paradigm of conditioning as one of the variables responsible for the bowed shape of the serial-position curve is the *temporal aspect* of the serial list, controlled by presenting the individual items serially in the aperture of a memory-drum at a given rate.

PURPOSE

The following experiments were addressed to the question of whether the occurrence of the serial-position effect depends upon a temporal serial presentation of the items or if the bowing is a more general phenomenon which may also occur when the ordering of the items is predominantly spatial rather than tem-

From the *American Journal of Psychology*, 1962, 75, 390-400, with permission of the author and publisher.
1. A review of theories of the serial-position effect is found in J. A. McGeoch and A. L. Irion, *The Psychology of Human Learning*, 1952, 125-34.

poral and when S's response is not limited to serial anticipation. To answer this question, four experiments were performed. In Experiment I, nine stimuli in a row were presented simultaneously; the series was predominantly *spatial*. This arrangement admittedly would not rule out the possibility of temporal effects resulting from S's visually scanning the stimuli in a certain order. In Experiment II there was a one-at-a-time presentation of the nine stimuli, always in one location, but there was *no* serial order. The stimuli appeared in a *random* order, except for some restrictions made for methodological reasons to be explained later. The spatial serial arrangement was in the S's *response*-alternatives, which consisted of a row of nine buttons. The S had to learn by trial-and-error which button was associated with the particular stimulus presented at random on the screen in front of S. The reinforcement for pressing the correct button was the sound of a "bong." With this procedure, the idea of serial order probably never occurred to most of the S's. In Experiments III and IV, intended as controls, the stimuli were presented in the usual temporal serial manner.

Experiment I

Subjects. All Ss in these four experiments were upper-division and graduate students in the Department of Education. There were 30 Ss in Experiment I. They were naïve with respect to psychological theory and experimentation. The proportion of women to men was about two to one.

Apparatus. The stimulus-items consisted of nine brightly colored simple geometric forms made of plastic.[2] The objects are ¼ in. in thickness and approximately 1 in. in height or diameter; they appear subjectively of about equal size. The nine objects were: red triangle, green square, blue triangle, yellow diamond, red circle, yellow triangle, blue circle, pink square, and green diamond.

Procedure. S was first shown all the objects in a randomly scattered arrangement

and was told that the objects would be arranged in a row in front of him. He would be allowed to study the order for a period of 10 sec., after which the objects would be disarranged, and S would be required to try to arrange them in the proper order.

Flat on the table before S was taped a sheet of heavy white paper, 12 × 18 in. Centered on this sheet of paper was a 1½ × 12 in. rectangle, drawn in a heavy black line; the rectangle was in a horizontal position with respect to S. After E had displayed the objects to S and explained the task, E placed a black cardboard-screen in front of S so as to cut off S's view while the objects were arranged in a particular order within the rectangle on the sheet of paper. The objects were evenly spaced about ½ in. apart. When E said "Ready" and removed the screen, S studied the series for 10 sec. E then placed the screen in front of S and completely disarranged the objects in a haphazard manner. Then the screen was removed and S was told to reconstruct the order of the objects. There was no time limit, and S was required to guess when in doubt. If S's reconstruction was not perfect (it rarely was on the first trial), the entire procedure was repeated, until S attained the criterion of perfect reconstruction of the serial order. After each trial, while the screen was in front of S, E recorded S's performance. Never were S's mistakes pointed out to him; he was merely told that he would have to repeat the task until he got it perfect.

A different order of items was used for every S that effects arising from any particular order would tend to be randomized in the over-all results. A restriction was placed on the formation of the series: no two objects of the same shape or of the same color could be adjacent to each other.

Results

The Ss were able to learn this task quite easily. The mean number of trials to criterion was only 2.96; the mean number of errors was 9.06; and the mean percentage of errors was 33.96.

2. These objects are on the market as "Child Guidance Toys, No. 709, Primary Fit n' Form, Ages 1-3 yrs.," manufactured by Archer Plastics, Inc., Bronx 72, N.Y.

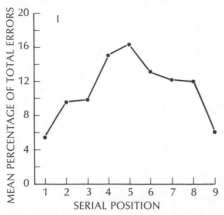

Fig. 1. *The Serial-position Curve in Experiment I.* The conditions were strictly spatial, *non*-temporal presentation of the serial list, with reconstruction as S's mode of response.

Since we are primarily interested in the *shape* of the serial-position curve, rather than its absolute position on the ordinate, the curves for all these experiments are based on the percentages of total errors that occur at each position. Thus the area under all the curves is the same. The percentage of total errors at each position was determined for each S individually, and these percentages were then averaged for the total group. The serial-position curve thus obtained for the data of Experiment I is shown in Fig. 1. The curve is quite typical of serial-position curves obtained by temporal serial presentation of the items. This curve is however, somewhat less skewed, although the greater proportion of errors still occurs beyond the middle position.

Experiment II

Apparatus. The apparatus used in this and the following experiments is described in the Apparatus Section of this JOURNAL.[3] The aspects of the apparatus essential to this experiment were: (a) the stimulus-display unit, and (b) the response-unit. On a table directly in front of S was the response-unit, consisting, in this experiment, of a straight row of nine buttons. The buttons, ⅜ in. in diameter, were evenly spaced 1½

in. apart, measured from the center of the buttons. All the buttons were identical and had no labels or other distinguishing cues. Directly behind the response-unit, in full view of S, was the stimulus-display unit, consisting of a 3×4 in. screen on which the stimuli appeared. The stimuli were nine brightly colored geometric figures which appeared one at a time in the center of the screen. The figures, approximately 2 in. in size, subjectively appear about equal in size. There were three forms in each of three colors—triangles (T), squares (Sq), and circles (C) colored red (R), yellow (Y), and blue (B). The stimuli appeared on the center of the screen one at a time in an order which throughout the experiment was *random*, with two exceptions: (a) each stimulus-object appeared once within every set of nine stimuli; (b) stimuli of the same shape or color never appeared in immediate succession. The first restriction on the randomness was imposed to insure equal exposure to all stimuli; the second restriction was imposed to make the presentation of stimuli consistent with the rules for presenation in the control experiments (Experiments III and IV), except for the variations that are directly germane to the purpose of the experiments.

Procedure. Twenty-five Ss served in the experiment. The S was instructed that his task was to learn by trial and error which button on the response-panel corresponds to each stimulus. When S pressed the correct button, he was reinforced by a "bong," following which the next stimulus appeared. If the wrong button was pressed, there was no "bong," but the next stimulus would appear. The S could not correct a mistake, since the instant one button was pressed, all others went "dead," so that pressing the correct button after an incorrect one had been pressed would produce no 'bong.' The rate of presentation of stimuli was governed by S, i.e. a new stimulus would not appear until S pressed a button, whether the right one or not. The stimulus would remain in view until the button was pressed, whereupon, after a 1-sec. delay, the next stimulus would appear. The purpose of this brief delay was to give S time to notice the S-R relationship. Also, the reinforcing "bong" occurred while the stimulus was still in view, but the "bong" never "overlapped" the presentation of the next stimulus.

The response-buttons were arranged in a straight row such that the order of the stimuli to which they corresponded was the same as the serial order of the stimuli used in Experiment III, which was intended as the control for comparative purposes. Going from the S's left to right, the stimulus corresponding to each button was: BSq, YT, RSq, BC, RT, YC, BT, YSq, RC.

Throughout the experiment E recorded S's responses in *sets of nine*. The S had to persist in the task until he attained the criterion of nine correct responses in succession all within a *set*. The criterion was established in this manner in order to have it correspond to the criterion in the other experiments, i.e. correct reproduction (or anticipation) of the serial list of nine items.

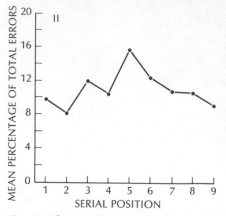

Fig. 2. *The Serial-position Curve in Experiment II*. The conditions were temporal, *non*-serial presentation of the stimuli, with serial spatial arrangement of the response-alternatives, and trial-and-error learning as S's mode of response. See text for method of deriving the curve.

RESULTS

This trial-and-error learning was by far the most difficult of all the tasks in the four experiments. To attain criterion, Ss required an average of 298.84 stimulus-presentations; they averaged 161.36 errors, and the mean percentage of errors was 53.98.

There was no systematic pattern in the number of errors or of correct responses made on each of the nine buttons. Individual Ss seemed to have preferences for particular buttons and used these much more than the others; these preferences may have been determined partly by which buttons happened by chance to give S his first few reinforcements. For the total group, however, these positional preferences averaged out, so that all the buttons received an approximately equal number of responses. The slight, unsystematic, and non-significant differences between the total responses for each button do not in any way resemble the usual serial-position curve.

But when the *percentage* of incorrect (i.e. non-reinforced) responses is computed for each button, thus ruling out the effect of absolute frequency of use of the button, a serial-position effect becomes evident. In other words, the terminal buttons are learned most readily and those in the middle are learned with the greatest difficulty. To compute the points for this curve properly, the percentage of errors for each button for each S must first be determined. Then, so as to weight each S equally in the totals, the percentage of errors on each button must be divided by the total of these percentages for all nine buttons; this is done for each S. These percentages are then averaged over all Ss for each button. The result is shown in Fig. 2. One point must be made clear: this curve does not represent the group's positional preferences for different buttons *per se*. It represents the relative difficulty of learning to match the buttons with their corresponding stimuli.

The data of this curve were subjected to an analysis of variance, which showed that the mean percentage of errors is significantly different for the different positions of the buttons. For the *Between*

Positions main effect, $F=3.11$, $df=8/192$, $p<0.01$. The most likely reason that the serial-position curve in Experiment II is so flat as compared with the other serial curves is that in the early stages of the trial-and-error learning the errors for the whole group were distributed more or less evenly over all the buttons. Such an admixture of "random errors" in any set of serial-learning data would produce a general flattening of the serial-position curve. Also, there was greater variability in the serial-position curves of individual Ss, due to the fact that, regardless of serial position, the button on which S chanced to receive his first reinforcement tended to be learned more readily than the other buttons. The fact that in trial-and-error learning S always hit upon his first success by chance introduced a good deal of "random error" into the results, and therefore the serial-position curve could not possibly emerge so conspicuously as it did in all the other experiments. There is no doubt, however, that a serial-position curve bearing the essential features was produced by a *non*-serial presentation of the stimuli and a purely spatial serial arrangement of the response-alternatives.

Experiment III

Procedure. Sixty Ss served in the experiment. The stimuli were presented on the screen, automatically paced by the machine at a 3-sec. rate, with a 6-sec. intertrial interval between each set of nine stimuli. The stimuli were presented repeatedly in a constant serial order. The series was preceded by a small white dot in the center of the screen which served as a signal to S to anticipate the first item in the serial list.

S was instructed to learn the list by the method of anticipation, responding by saying "blue square," "yellow triangle," etc., and was encouraged to guess when in doubt. He was also told what stimulus-items would appear—triangles, squares, and circles colored red, blue, and yellow—and that items of

the same shape or of the same color would never appear in immediate succession. The order of the stimuli was the same as the order of the response-buttons in Experiment II, viz. BSq, YT, RSq, BC, RT, YC, BT, YSq, RC. S began responding on the very first trial, and was required to attain the criterion of one perfect trial, i.e. anticipating correctly in immediate succession every item in the serial list.

RESULTS

This experiment, which followed the usual procedure of experiments on serial learning, viz. that of presenting the items in one location in a *temporal* sequence at a constant rate, serves as a basis for comparison with the results of Experiment II, which was a strictly *spatial* type of serial learning.

Since the percentage of errors in Experiment II was 53.98 and in Experiment III was only 44.22, it is evident that Ss in Experiment III were closer to the asymptote of complete mastery of the task than were Ss in Experiment II, even though both groups had attained the criterion of nine successive correct responses. The degree of bowing of the serial-position curve is in part a function of the stage of learning; it becomes increasingly peaked as S approaches the asymptote of mastery of the list. In view of this fact, it was decided that the serial-position curves produced in Experiment II and Experiment III should be compared, not on the basis of both groups having attained the same predetermined criterion of nine successive correct responses, but rather on the basis of the groups having attained the same degree of mastery of the task as represented by the percentage of errors. In other words, though fewer errors are made in the later stages of learning, they occur increasingly in the middle positions. Thus, while the total percentage of errors continues to decrease throughout learning, the greatest relative increase in errors is in the middle positions. Therefore, it seems reasonable to compare the serial-position curves of the two groups based on the data up to the largest number of trials on which both groups have approximately the same percentage of errors.

Since Experiment III produced the smaller percentage of errors, it was possible to find a point on the learning curve for the group at which they arrived at approximately the same percentage of errors as was reached in Experiment II by the time the criterion was attained. Inspection of the data of Experiment III revealed that the group attained approximately the same percentage of errors as Experiment II at a point that included three-fourths of the trials to the criterion. Therefore, the first three-fourths of the trials for each S were used in determining the serial-position curve. On this basis, the percentage of errors in Experiment III was 54.08, as compared with 53.98 in Experiment II. Thus, the serial-position curves for the two experiments are based on almost exactly the same level of mastery of the tasks in terms of the percentage of errors.

The serial-position curves in Experiment III, shown in Fig. 3, were determined in the same manner as in the other experiments. The solid line in Fig. 3 is the serial-position curve based on the first three-fourths of the trials, representing the same error percentage as in Experiment II. The broken line in Fig. 3 is the serial-position curve for all the trials up to the criterion on nine successive correct trials. It is, of course, more peaked. As would be expected, the bowed curves are typical of serial-position curves, with the greater proportion of errors occurring past the middle position in the series.

Experiment IV

Procedure. The procedure in this experiment, in which 60 Ss were used, was exactly

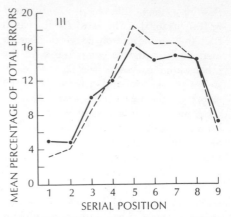

Fig. 3. *The Serial-position Curve in Experiment III.* The conditions were temporal serial presentation of the stimuli (machine-paced) and verbal anticipation as the mode of S's response. Solid line based on first three-fourths of trials in Experiment II; Broken line, all trials in Experiment III.

the same as in Experiment III, with two exceptions: (a) the rate of presentation of the stimuli was governed by S; each stimulus in the series appeared only after S had anticipated it. Thus, S was under no time-pressure and could take as long as he pleased in making each response. When S was in doubt as to the next anticipation, he was forced to guess, since the next item would never appear until S made a response. (b) Twenty different orders of stimuli were used, that each order was represented only three times in the over-all results. This procedure would tend to randomize any systematic interaction between the particular stimulus-items (or their arrangement) and their position in the series.

RESULTS

The average number of stimulus-presentations was only 27.14, the average number of errors was 8.83, and the average percentage of errors was 32.52. These figures are remarkably close to those of Experiment I, which were 26.70, 9.06, and 33.96, respectively. The *temporal* serial task appears to be of the same difficulty as the *spatial* serial task when S is allowed to respond at his own speed.

Since S began responding in Experiment IV on the very first trial without previous exposure of the serial order, the task was not comparable to Experiment I in this respect. In Experiment I S viewed the serial order for 10 sec. before attempting to reconstruct it on the first trial. Also, since so few trials were required to attain the criterion in Experiment IV, the first trial, which represents sheer guessing, constitutes a relatively large proportion of the total errors. Of course, the effect of serial position cannot emerge on the first trial when it is based on sheer guessing. Therefore, the serial-position curve, if it is to be properly compared with that of Experiment I, should be based only on all the errors made *after* the first trial. This was done, and the serial-position curves, shown in Fig. 4, were determined in the same manner as in the other experiments. The solid line is the curve of percentages of errors excluding the first trial. The broken line shows the percentage of errors for *all* trials. Of course, this curve is less peaked, since the errors on the first trial were more or less evenly distributed over all the positions, with the exception of the last position, which seems to show a marked "recency" effect. Actually, of course, this low percentage of errors in the last position, especially for the first trial, is not a true "recency" effect, but must be due to the fact that when S is not under time-pressure he can fairly well remember which item has not been used in the list up to the last item, which makes it easy for S to "guess" correctly the last item on his very first time through the series. Another interesting feature of the solid curve is the uniformly low percentage of errors in the first three positions, which indicates that most Ss were able to master the sequence of the first three items after just one exposure. Without time-pressure,

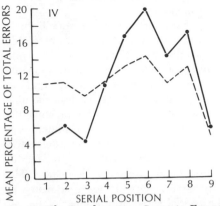

Fig. 4. *The Serial-position Curve in Experiment IV.* The conditions were temporal serial presentation of the stimuli (S-paced) and verbal anticipation as the mode of S's response. Solid line, percentage of errors excluding the first trial; Broken line, percentage of errors for all trials.

especially, one would expect immediate memory-span to play a part in learning the serial list, and it appears that this factor is represented by the equally low percentages of errors in the first three positions.

Summary

The essential features of the serial-position curve have been shown clearly to emerge under conditions involving neither serial anticipation, nor temporal order of the stimulus-items, nor even serial order of the stimulus-items.

In Experiment I, the stimuli (nine colored geometric forms) were presented for 10 sec. on each trial in a *spatial* serial arrangement (a straight row), all the stimuli appearing simultaneously. After each 10-sec. exposure, S had to reconstruct, without time-limit, the serial arrangement. The errors made in reconstruction were distributed in the typical bowed curve characteristic of serial-position curves produced under the usual conditions (represented in Experiments III and IV) of temporal serial presentation with verbal anticipation as the mode of response.

In Experiment II, the stimuli (nine colored geometric forms) were presented temporally, at a S-paced rate, in a *random* order. The S had to learn to match each of a set of nine identical buttons, arranged in a row, with each of the nine stimuli. Reinforcement for pressing the button corresponding to the stimulus appearing on the screen consisted of a "bong." Thus, S's mode of response was trial-and-error selective learning. The only *serial* aspect of the experiment was the *spatial* serial arrangement of the response-alternatives. When the percentage of errors made on each button for all trials up to the criterion of nine successive correct responses (the same criterion as in the other experiments) was determined, it was found that the relative difficulty of learning the buttons varied as a function of their position, the easiest to learn being those at the ends and the most difficult being those in the middle. In other words, the pattern of errors had the essential features of the usual serial-position curve. It did not, however, manifest the typical skewness of most serial-position curves. The distribution of the percentages of errors on the various buttons does not reflect positional preferences *per se*. While individual Ss showed positional preferences, reflected in the different numbers of total responses on each of the buttons, these preferences did not correspond to the serial-position curve, nor were they characteristic of the groups as a whole. The total responses on each button for the group were nearly equal.

Experiments III and IV were intended as control experiments; they involved the same type of stimuli and general procedures as the other experiments, except that they maintained the essential fea-

tures of temporal serial presentation and verbal anticipation on which S-R theories of serial rote-learning are based. In Experiment III, the stimuli were machine-paced as a 3-sec. rate, with a 6-sec. intertrial interval; in Experiment IV, the stimuli were S-paced, each stimulus appearing only after S had responded.

These findings would seem to have significance particularly for those S-R theories of the serial-position effect which depend upon a temporal sequence of the items and serial anticipation by S. The conditions of Experiments I and II, for example, completely lack the features which would permit one to invoke Lepley's hypothesis of "trace-conditioned responses" or Hull's hypothesis of "inhibition of delay" and its corollary that greater amounts of inhibitory potential span the middle items of the list.[4] The same can be said of Hull's theory of serial learning in 1952, which is based on the "gradient of reinforcement," i.e. the effectiveness of reinforcement in establishing an associative bond is assumed to decrease as a function of the delay in the reinforcement.[5] Yet, in Experiments I and II the conditions necessary for the operation of the variables postulated by Hull to explain the serial-position effect clearly do not exist. Still, however, the typical bowed serial-position curve comes forth. Apparently these theories of the serial-position effect either are incorrect or are not sufficiently general to explain the emergence of the bowed serial-position curve under conditions other than the learning of a temporal sequence by the method of serial anticipation.

4. W. M. Lepley, Serial reactions considered as conditioned reactions, *Psychol. Monogr.*, 46, 1934, No. 205, 40-45; C. L. Hull, *et al.*, *Mathematico-Deductive Theory of Rote Learning*, 1940, 110, 175-7.
5. Hull, *A Behavior System*, 1952, 156-91.

13 / A Theory of the Serial Position Effect

EDWARD A. FEIGENBAUM, *University of California, Berkeley*
AND HERBERT A. SIMON, *Carnegie Institute of Technology*

The paper proposes a theory of the well-known serial position effect that makes quantitative predictions, acceptable by non-parametric tests, of the observed amount of bowing of the serial position curve. The theory, which stems from viewing the central nervous system as an information-processing system, is compared with the Lepley-Hull hypothesis and Atkinson's theory of the serial phenomena, and is shown to be more satisfactory than the older explanations.

INTRODUCTION

Intraserial phenomena have been a major focus of interest in the study of serial learning. McGeoch (1942), for example, devoted 50 pages of his *Psychology of Human Learning* to such phenomena. And among intraserial phenomena, one of the most prominent is the serial position curve, depicting the relative number of errors made with the various syllables in a list while learning the list to some criterion.

McCrary & Hunter (1953) observed that if percentage of total errors is taken as the unit of measurement, then all the empirical serial position curves for lists of a given length are substantially identical. Earlier investigators, measuring number of errors, had concluded that relatively more errors occurred for the middle syllables when the lists were hard than when they were easy, more with slow learners than with fast learners, more with rapid presentation of syllables than with slow presentation, and so on. One can find in the literature numerous theoretical explanations of these differences.

The findings of McCrary & Hunter leave us in the embarrassing position of having explained phenomena that do not exist, i.e., the supposed differences in amount of the position effect, and of having failed to explain a striking uniformity that does exist—the substantial identity of curves derived under a variety of experimental conditions. McCrary &

Hunter themselves reach the peculiar conclusion that a single principle can hardly be expected to account for uniformity of effect under diversity of conditions, and hence that some multiple-factor is needed to explain the outcome.

The thesis of this paper is the opposite one—that if a uniformity underlies experiments performed under a wide variety of conditions, this uniformity should be traceable to a single simple mechanism that is invariant under change of conditions. We shall propose such a model of the information processing activity of a subject as he organizes his learning effort in a serial learning task. The serial position effect will be shown to be a consequence of the information processing strategy postulated in the model; the model predicts both qualitatively and quantitatively the shape of the curve and the percentages reported by McCrary & Hunter and by others.

SOME RELEVANT DATA

Before we state the theory of the serial position effect we shall review some important empirical findings on serial learning of nonsense syllables:

(1) Under the usual experimental conditions and with experienced subjects there is generally a characteristic curvilinear relation between number of errors to criterion for a given syllable and the

From the *British Journal of Psychology*, 1962, **53**, 307-20, with permission of the authors and the British Psychological Society.

serial position of that syllable in the list. The syllable with the largest number of errors is generally beyond the middle of the list, though this effect becomes less noticeable as the length of the list increases (Ribback & Underwood, 1950); the first syllable almost always exhibits the fewest errors (Hovland, 1938).

(2) McCrary & Hunter (1953) have shown that, for lists of a given number of syllables, all serial position curves obtained with the usual experimental procedures are virtually identical when errors are plotted on a percentage, rather than an absolute, basis. About the same degree of bowing is exhibited with nonsense syllables as with names, with massed as with distributed practice, with slow as with fast learners, with rapid as with slow presentation. Typical data for lists of 12 and 14 syllables are given in Tables 1 and 2.

(3) In spite of this uniformity under normal conditions, it is easy to produce large deviations from the characteristic curve. Such deviations can be produced in at least the following four ways: (a) by varying the difficulty of particular items in the list; (b) by introducing an item sharply distinguishable from those that precede it or follow it (McGeoch, 1942, p. 107); (c) by introducing distinguishable sublists within the main list (Wishner, Shipley & Hurvich, 1957); (d) by explicit instructions to the subjects (Krueger, 1932; Welch & Burnett, 1924). Not surprisingly, difficult items are learned with more errors than easy items in the same serial position; distinguishable items are learned with fewer errors; items that the subject is instructed to learn first are learned with fewer errors.

(4) For lists of a given length, average learning time per syllable is almost independent of: (a) the rate of presentation (though this result is not given explicitly by Hovland (1938), we have used his reported data to compute the average learning time per syllable; this constancy

has been independently reported by Wilcoxon, Wilson & Wise (1961)); and (b) the order in which subjects are instructed to learn the items (though this result is not given explicitly by Krueger (1932), we have computed it from his data). Hence, number of trials to criterion is inversely proportional to seconds per syllable.

(5) Distribution of practice reduces the number of trials to criterion, but not sufficiently to compensate for the additional total time. The advantages of distribution, measured in trials to criterion, almost disappears when the presentation rate is as slow as four seconds per syllable (Hovland, 1938).

In the next section we shall propose a theory of the serial learning process that accounts quantitatively for the data mentioned in items 1, 2, and 4, above, and qualitatively for the observation of item 3. In the present paper we shall not discuss the effects of distribution of practice, since these effects almost certainly derive from mechanisms that go beyond the simple theory proposed here. We wish merely to observe that when time to criterion is taken as the measure of learning rate these effects are of rather small magnitude compared with those we shall consider.

An information processing theory of serial learning

We hypothesize that serial learning is an active, complex process involving the manipulation and storage of symbols by means of an interacting set of elementary information processes; and that these processes are qualitatively similar to those used in problem solving, concept formation, and other higher mental processes (Newell, Shaw & Simon, 1958a). Thus, we shall argue that the stimulus-response sequences postulated by S-R theory are simple only in surface appearance—that beneath them lies an iceberg of complex information processing activity.

We shall not defend this viewpoint in detail here although it has proved exceedingly fruitful in research in which we and our associates have been engaged (see, for example, Feigenbaum (1959); Newell & Simon (1961); Newell *et al.* (1958*b*)). We should like to offer three brief observations to persuade the reader that our conjecture does not entirely fly in the face of common sense or previous psychological observation. First, expectancy and mediation theories, like those of Tolman (Hilgard, 1956, pp. 185-221), or of Osgood (Hilgard, 1956, pp. 464-5), attribute as much complexity to the stimulus-response connexion as does our conjecture; what they fail to indicate is the nature of the mechanisms that might provide the complexity. Secondly, equally elaborate and more explicit mechanisms are postulated in concept-formation theories like those of E. J. Gibson (1940), and the recent one of Bruner, Goodnow, & Austin (1956). Indeed, we shall see that one of our postulates involves a conception closely related to Bruner's notion of "cognitive strain." Thirdly, the time an experienced subject needs, per syllable, to memorize a list of a dozen nonsense syllables is of the order of thirty seconds. In comparison with the times required by familiar electronic systems for simple processes, this is an enormous time interval. It is large—by a factor of 500 or more—even in comparison with the 50 msec. or thereabouts required for the central processes in the simplest responses to stimuli. If a theory is to fill up this 30 sec. time interval in at all a plausible manner, it will have to attribute considerable complexity to the processes that take place. Feigenbaum (1959) reports on such a theory of verbal learning, dealing in a complete manner with discrimination learning, association learning, responding, etc. The theory predicts a variety

of the phenomena of rote learning of nonsense syllables in serial and paired-associate learning tasks.

Underlying assumptions of the model

For the purposes of this paper, we shall not need to examine the elementary information processes in detail, for the shape of the serial position curve will prove to be independent of their microstructure. This point is examined in detail by Feigenbaum (1959), where a distinction is drawn between macroprocesses of verbal learning and microprocesses. We require, instead, the assumption that in order for a connexion between a stimulus and a response to be formed, a certain (unspecified) sequence of elementary processes needs to be carried out, and that the execution of this sequence requires a definite interval of time, the length of the interval depending on the "difficulty" of the task and other parameters of the experimental situation.

We suppose the information processing mechanism to be operating predominantly in a serial rather than a parallel manner—it is capable of doing only one, or a few things at a time. The narrowness of the span of attention is a familiar aspect of conscious activity; we assume that it is also an attribute of the subconscious.

Information processing postulates

The structure of the theory is embodied in four postulates about the processing mechanism.

Postulate 1. Serial mechanism. The central processing mechanism operates serially and is capable of doing only one thing at a time. Thus, if many things demand processing activity from the central processing mechanism, they must share the total processing time available. This means that the total time required to memorize a collection of items, when there is no interaction among them, will be the sum of the times of the individual items. (In serial learning of syllables there is, in fact, interaction among individual items; and total learning time increases more than proportionately with number of items. We will not be concerned with this point in the present paper because we are dealing not with total learning time or total errors, but with the relative number of errors made on different syllables in a list.)

Postulate 2. Average unit processing time per syllable. The fixation of an item on a serial list requires the execution of a sequence of information processes that requires, for a given set of experimental conditions, a definite amount of processing time per syllable. The time per syllable varies with the difficulty of the syllables, the length of list, the ability of the subject and other factors. In a well-known series of experiments by Hovland (1938), for example, it averaged approximately 30 sec.

Postulate 3. Immediate memory. There exists in the central processing mechanism an immediate memory of limited size capable of storing information temporarily; and all access to an item by the learning processes must be through the immediate memory. There is a great deal of experimental evidence to support the concept of an immediate memory. The evidence points to a span of immediate memory of about five or six symbols (Miller, 1956). We postulate that each symbol stored separately in the immediate memory must be a familiar, well-learned symbol. For unfamiliar nonsense syllable materials, the familiar symbols are the letters. Thus, for the three-letter nonsense syllables ordinarily used, we postulate that the immediate memory has the capacity to hold two syllables (six letters). This means that it will ordinarily hold at any moment one S-R pair being learned.

Postulate 4. Anchor points. In the absence of countervailing conditions—the nature of which will be specified presently—the information processing will be carried out in a relatively systematic and orderly way which will limit the demands that are placed on the small immediate memory. This postulate is related to the generalization, which Bruner and his associates (1956) have tested in certain concept-forming experiments, that subjects develop strategies for limiting the "cognitive strain" involved in concept formation, and that these strategies involve handling newly acquired information in a systematic and orderly way.

We assume that subjects learning the syllables of a serial list will reduce the demands on memory by treating the ends of the list as "anchor points," and by learning the syllables in an orderly sequence, starting from these anchor points and working toward the middle. This procedure reduces demands on memory because, at each stage of the learning task, the next syllable to be learned is readily identified as being adjacent to a syllable that has already been learned. Thus, no special information about position in list needs to be remembered.

The idea of learning from anchor points is not new, though it does not seem to have been previously formalized. Woodworth (1938), for example, makes use of it in describing the process by which a list of digits is learned. Wishner *et al.* (1957) mention it in their discussion of the serial position curves obtained in their list-sublist experiment.

The first three postulates differ from the fourth in that the former describe built-in characteristics of the processing mechanism that are probably not learned or readily modified; while the latter describes a method of proceeding that is apparently habitual with most subjects, at least in our culture, but which is modifiable by experimental instructions, and by certain attention-directing stimuli.

It has been observed frequently that in serial memorization subjects not only develop associations between syllables, but also use various position cues and other cues. They learn, for example, that a particular syllable occurs in the early or in the late part of the list. (From this reliance on "irrelevant" cues, one can develop an explanation for such phenomena as anticipatory errors and "remote associations" that is much simpler than the usual one; but these topics would take us beyond the scope of our present task.) The use of position cues gives a unique status to the beginning and end of a serial list, for these items have the special property that they have no neighbours "before" and "after" respectively, i.e., the first item is always preceded, and the last item succeeded, by the intertrial activity. Once the items at the anchor points are memorized, the items contiguous to them become the first unlearned items "after" or "before" syllables already memorized; and so on, as the learning proceeds. More than this, the first two items are unique in that they represent the first S-R pair presented to the subject in the experiment. Thus, we can make out at least a plausible case that a learner can reduce the demands on immediate memory by memorizing in a more or less systematic fashion from the ends of the list toward the middle.

This postulate is sufficient to explain the bowed form of the serial position curve—although it says only a little more than the observed fact of the bowing. Its advantage over explanations like the Lepley-Hull hypothesis (which will be discussed later) is that it is not inconsistent with the ease (item 3, above) with which changes can be induced by the experimenter in the serial position curve.

In order to make quantitative predictions as to the amount of bowing that will be observed, we use the notion of anchor points to strengthen postulate 4, as follows:

Postulate 4a. Processing sequence. We postulate the following information processing strategy for organizing the serial learning task using anchor points: (a) the first two items presented in the experiment are learned first; (b) attention is next focused for learning on an item immediately adjacent to an anchor point. (In the ordinary serial list, this will be the third item or the last.) The probability that any specific item adjacent to an anchor point will be selected for learning next is $1/p$, where p is the number of anchor points (in the ordinary serial list, $p=2$. Thus, for example, the probability that the last item will be learned after the second item is $0 \cdot 5$); (c) attention is focused, and learning proceeds, item by item in this orderly fashion until the criterion trial is completed.

One can picture the subject building up over time an internal representation of the serial list he is learning. It will be seen, then, that the postulate specifies only a minimal amount of organizational activity: namely, the ability to add an item immediately after or immediately before an item already learned (or a "special" stimulus like the intertrial interval). Our explorations with other processing strategies have shown that this strategy reduces greatly the information processing demands on the learner.

Predictions from the postulates

The postulates describe a learning mechanism that memorizes serial lists in a prescribed way. This mechanism generates a serial error curve as it learns (i.e. some particular serial error curve is deduced as a consequence of the postulates). We wish to compute this serial error curve and compare it with the Mc-Crary & Hunter curve.

Computer simulation is the most general and powerful method for doing this.

We and others have used this method extensively in building theories of problem solving (Newell *et al.* 1958*a*), binary choice behaviour (Feldman, 1959), concept attainment (Hovland & Hunt, 1960), and other cognitive phenomena. It is described in detail elsewhere (Newell & Simon, 1961). Briefly the idea is this. The digital computer is a universal information processing device, capable of carrying out any precisely specified information process. Thus a computer can carry out exactly the information processing required by the postulates of the model. We programme the model on a computer, use it *qua* subject in verbal learning experiments (simulated inside the computer), observe the learning behaviour of the model, and thereby generate the consequences of the postulates in particular verbal learning situations. We have used this method in constructing and exploring an information processing theory of verbal learning (Feigenbaum, 1959). In particular, for the purposes of this paper, we have generated the serial error curve for a few simple serial learning experiments. We have done this in two different ways: first, following postulate 2, we introduced a unit processing time per syllable without specifying the microprocesses of the

learning that take place during this time interval; secondly, we removed the latter artificiality and substituted the full complement of microprocesses postulated by the more complete theory.

For the particular case of the serial position curve, the postulates are simple enough so that there is no real need to employ computer simulation to generate the predictions. The postulates can be formalized in a simple mathematical model, from which the quantitative predictions can be generated. As this method is likely to be more familiar to the reader, we give the mathematical model in the Appendix, and present the serial error curves which it predicts (for lists of twelve and fourteen syllables) in Tables 1 and 2. The results obtained by the computer simulation technique are substantially identical (though slightly more discontinuous).

What can we specifically say about the fit? First, the ordinates of the first and last syllable of the predicted curves are in almost exact agreement with those of the empirical curves. Secondly, the syllable position of the peak of the predicted curves is substantially the same as that of the observed curves. Thirdly, the ordinates of the predicted curves and the empirical curves at each syllable position

TABLE 1. *Table showing percentage of total errors made during acquisition at each syllable position of a 14-item serial list of nonsense syllables predicted and observed*

							Syllable position							
	1	2	3	4	5	6	7	8	9	10	11	12	13	14
Predicted	0·95	1·9	4·7	5·6	8·1	8·9	10·5	10·8	10·8	10·5	8·9	8·1	5·6	4·7
Observed °	1·0	3·5	4·3	6·0	8·0	8·9	9·2	10·0	9·5	10·6	8·8	8·9	7·2	4·0

° These values are approximate.
The data were taken from fig. 4 of McCrary & Hunter (1953, p. 133).

TABLE 2. *Table showing percentage of total errors made during acquisition at each syllable position of a 12-item serial list of nonsense syllables predicted and observed*

					Syllable position						
	1	2	3	4	5	6	7	8	9	10	11	12
Predicted	1·3	2·6	6·3	7·5	10·5	11·3	12·5	12·5	11·3	10·5	7·5	6·3
Observed °	1·5	2·3	4·5	7·0	10·3	11·6	14·0	12·4	11·0	10·0	8·5	7·0

° These values are approximate values for the median percentages at each position for the four curves presented in fig. 2 of McCrary & Hunter (1953, p. 132).

are very close, especially in the critical first and last third of each list, where very good agreement is important to any claims about goodness-of-fit. Furthermore, this fit was obtained without any arbitrary parameters, other than the specification of the sequence in which incoming syllables are processed.

The goodness-of-fit of the observed frequency distribution to the predicted distribution was tested by the Kolmogorov-Smirnov test of association. The test accepted the null hypothesis at the 99% level of significance.

ELABORATION AND DISCUSSION

In this section, we wish to compare the predictions of our information processing theory with those derived from the Lepley-Hull hypothesis, and extend our predictions to two important experiments, one of which was published after we had specified our model.

(1) *The Lepley-Hull hypothesis.* There have been few attempts to account for the serial position effect in quantitative terms. Hull *et al.* (1940) attempted to do so on the assumption of some inhibitory processes, or intralist "interference." Atkinson (1957), drawing on statistical learning theory, has exhibited a stochastic process which generates a curve of the general shape of the serial position curve. We shall discuss Hull's results in some detail, and comment briefly on Atkinson's.

Although Hull's equations provide a good fit to the empirical data, this fit is not a convincing test of the Lepley-Hull theory for the following reasons:

Hull's theory leads to a set of equations having three free parameters: the reaction threshold, the ratio of inhibitory potential to excitatory potential per trial, and the remoteness reduction factor. These are used to fit the serial error curve or, more precisely, the curve of number of repetitions to reaction threshold (see Hull *et al.* (1940, pp. 103-7)). Hull fits the theoretical curve by passing it through three points of the empirical curve. Since the empirical data form a relatively smooth, bow-shaped curve, it is not surprising that a three-parameter curve can be made to fit them closely; an equally good approximation can be obtained by fitting a parabola empirically to the data.

This means that Hull's hypothesis will fit almost any data (provided the serial position curve has the characteristic bowed pattern), and hence is almost impossible to disprove from the data. It is therefore an exceedingly weak hypothesis. By the same token—because of the three free parameters—Hull's theory does not predict the constancy on a percentage scale observed by McCrary & Hunter.

Conversely, given the constancy observed by McCrary & Hunter, we can draw certain conclusions from Hull"s theory regarding the growth of excitatory and inhibitory potential and the reaction threshold. For example, it can be shown by an examination of Hull's equations that the ratio of the increment in inhibitory potential per trial to the increment of excitatory potential must be a constant (independent, for example, of intra-list similarity). See Hull *et al.* (1940, pp. 104-5).

The McCrary & Hunter result implies that the Rs are related: they are proportional to each other. The variables q_i are homogeneous of degree two in R, and the D_i are homogeneous of degree one in R. The Js are homogeneous of degree zero in R. By equation (3) of p. 104, $\Delta e/\Delta k$ is homogeneous of degree zero in R, hence a constant.

This is surprising and contrary to the whole spirit of the Lepley-Hull hypothesis. For we would expect that with high intra-list similarity the inhibitory potential would rise more rapidly than with low intra-list similarity. On the contrary,

if Hull's model is correct the only parameter that changes as lists become more
difficult to learn is the ratio of the threshold to the increment of excitatory potential per trial (by equation 2, p. 104,
of Hull *et al.* (1940)). Finally, the
Lepley-Hull hypothesis does not explain
how a subject can voluntarily or through
a shift in his attention greatly alter the
shape of the curve.

There are four reasons, therefore, why
Hull's mathematical model for the serial
position effect is unsatisfactory: since it
contains three adjustable parameters its
predictions are very weak; it does not
predict the constancy in the percentage-
error curve; this constancy hardly seems
compatible with the mechanism assumed
as a basis for the model; and finally, the
model is difficult to reconcile with well-
known attention-shift and set-change
phenomena.

The preceding discussion of the curve-
fitting aspects of Hull's equations applies
also to Atkinson's equations. Atkinson
(1957) has available four free parameters.
He estimates these parameters from data
for an 18-syllable list, and uses these estimated values to make predictions for lists
of 8 and 13 syllables. However, a careful
examination of Atkinson's equations
shows that even after the parameters
have been estimated, there are enough
degrees of freedom left in the system
almost to insure a reasonably good fit to
the other curves. Thus, his theory suffers the same infirmity that we have
pointed out in Hull's.

Furthermore, to make workable the
difficult mathematics of the stochastic
process, Atkinson has had to introduce a
number of very constraining assumptions.
His equations hold only for serial lists
of highly dissimilar words which are
familiar and easily pronounced; the
presentation must be at a moderate rate,
with a long interval provided at the conclusion of each trial. Yet the same bowed
curve is obtained empirically when these

conditions are not met as when they are.
Finally, as in Hull's theory, there is difficulty in predicting the constancy observed by McCrary & Hunter. Given a
set of parameter values, Atkinson's theory
does not predict the constancy over the
experimental conditions reported by Mc-
Crary & Hunter. On the other hand, if
one admits that these values may change
from situation to situation, then one
must re-estimate them for each experimental condition, and therein the theory
loses much of its power.

(2) *The two-part list.* A simple extension of ordinary nonsense syllable experiments is to differentiate the first half
of the list from the second half by printing the former in one colour (say black)
and the latter in another colour (say red),
dividing the total list perceptually into
two smaller sublists.

What will be the shape of the serial
position curve? One can predict this
from Hull's theory by the unsatisfying
procedure of assuming that the total list
is learned as two separate sublists, and
by fitting each sublist with a three-
parameter curve such as we have discussed previously. The total fit will
have six free parameters.

We should like to be able to predict
the shape of the curve from the theory
we have already presented. There are
two important issues involved in making
such a prediction:

(i) Consider those subjects who perceive the total list as being constructed
of two sublists. One possible reasonable
strategy for dealing with the learning
task is to use the end points of each sublist as anchor points, in the type of learning process described earlier. Another
plausible strategy is to use as anchor
points the ends of the total list and one
point in the centre to identify the point
of bifurcation, say the first red syllable.

In making a prediction of the serial
position curve for the two-part list, we
have assumed simply that of those sub-

jects who perceived the list as being two sublists, one half used the first strategy and the other half used the second strategy. The assumption is, of course, a relatively crude one, but the prediction is not very sensitive to the actual percentages assumed. Alternatively, we could have estimated the percentage from the data.

(ii) In the experiment which we shall discuss shortly, we have no way of knowing precisely how many subjects perceived the task as one of memorizing two sublists and how many perceived it as learning one long serial list. In the absence of this knowledge, we can estimate these percentages from the observed ordinate of the first red syllable and weight our prediction at each syllable position appropriately using this estimate. This procedure essentially "fits" our predicted curve to the empirical curve at one point, the "break" between black and red syllables. But it guarantees nothing about the quality of the prediction at the other points.

As part of a larger experiment, Wishner *et al.* (1957) performed an experiment with a two-part list. They had an experimental group memorize lists of 14 syllables, half of which were printed in black capitals, the other half in red lower case letters. The experimental group was told that the object of the experiment was to discover how people learned two lists simultaneously.

In Table 3 the predicted values for the percentage of errors at each syllable position are compared with the observed values.

The predictions were generated by the methods previously described. Three anchor points were used. In the mathematical treatment the three-anchor-point predictions were corrected by a factor which insured an exact fit of the ordinate of syllable 9 (the middle anchor point). In the computer simulation method, whole-list and sublist strategies were both run and the predicted ordinates averaged in a weighted fashion such that the ordinate of syllable 9 fitted exactly. What this procedure comes down to is the assumption that approximately two-thirds of the subjects learned the list as two sublists and approximately one-third learned it as a single long list (note that these fractions were not assumed *a priori* but were obtained by working backwards from the observed ordinate of the ninth syllable).

The agreement at all syllable positions is very close. As contrasted with our other predictions, in this one we had available the one free parameter already mentioned. The goodness-of-fit of the observed frequency distribution to the predicted distribution was tested by the Kolmogorov-Smirnov test of association. The test accepted the null hypothesis at the 99% level of significance.

(3) *The experiments of Krueger.* We turn now to some important experiments, the results of which were alluded to previously, and which have important implications for the information processing theory.

In a well-known series of experiments, Krueger (1932) presented various kinds of lists of "easy" and "hard" paired nouns to subjects who either received instructions to learn the list in some specified order or no instructions at all. These studies demonstrated that the order in

TABLE 3. *Table showing percentage of total errors, predicted and observed, made at each syllable position during acquisition, for a two-colour, 14-item serial list of nonsense syllables*

	Syllable position													
	1	2	3	4	5	6	7	8	9	10	11	12	13	14
Predicted	1·9	3·1	4·7	6·7	9·1	10·1	8·9	5·9	6·0	8·3	8·7	9·8	9·9	5·5
Observed[*]	2·2	4·3	6·5	7·3	8·2	8·5	8·1	6·0	6·0	9·0	9·5	9·9	8·5	6·0

[*] These values are approximate, and were derived from data taken from Wishner *et al.* (1957, p. 260).

which the various items were learned was influenced markedly by the instructions given to the subjects. As McGeoch puts it (1942, p. 102), "The relation between rate of learning and position in the series is, then, a function of the direction of the subject's effort or attention." As we have indicated, this is entirely consistent with the information processing theory, which regards particular learning sequences as "strategies" for dealing with the learning problem—as adaptive response to task.

What about our more specific hypothesis that in the usual serial learning experiment the "end points" of the list will be taken as anchor points in the learning process? Krueger's experiments showed that subjects given *no* instructions produced essentially the same serial position curves as those subjects who were instructed to learn the *ends* of the list first.

Because the fixation of an item requires a fixed amount of processing time, and because the sequence of learning is considered a "strategy" and not a built-in characteristic of the learning process, our theory predicts that the total number of syllables learned will be proportional to the total learning time and independent of the order of learning. On this point Krueger reports, "When the attention given is constant, the total amounts learned are the same, irrespective of whether this effort is directed to the beginning, center, or the final sections of the unit which is to be memorized" (1932, p. 527).

Although we assume that there is a constant fixation time associated with each particular item on a list, items of different kinds (e.g., "easy" items against "difficult" items) will have different processing times. The theory we have proposed predicts that the total learning time will be the sum of these processing times per syllable, and as such will be independent of the order in which the syllables are learned. Confirming this prediction, Krueger reports, "When mate-

rials of unequal difficulty appear within the same unit to be mastered, the total number of trials required to memorize the unit is approximately the same whether attention is given at first to the more difficult or the easier sections of the unit" (1932, p. 527).

This is consistent with the McCrary & Hunter results. If one plots the Mc-Crary & Hunter curve by ordering the abscissa values not by serial position in the list but by the apparent order in which the syllables were learned, the ordinates lie on a straight line. This, of course, is in exact agreement with our model. Recent additional information on this phenomenon was obtained by Jensen (1962) for the learning of nonsense figures.

Thus, Krueger's experiments, though they were performed with serial lists of paired nouns rather than nonsense syllables, demonstrate (*a*) that the serial position curve can be "shaped" by the experimenter with suitable instructions to subjects, so that the order of learning syllables is itself a learned response; (*b*) that the total amount of material learned within a given time is independent of the order in which various items, sometimes heterogeneous with respect to difficulty, are learned.

SOME RECENT RESULTS

Subsequent to the specification of the model proposed in this paper, some important new experiments have been published on the effect of replacing syllables on a list during learning. Rock (1957) used the following procedure on his experimental groups: on each test trial, those syllables incorrectly responded to by the subject were removed and new syllables were substituted in their place for the next learning trial. Rock found no impairment of the rate of learning for the experimental groups (as compared with the control groups). This important result casts further doubt on Hull's incremental build-up hypothesis. Criticism of Rock's technique led Estes, Hopkins & Crothers (1960) to replicate and extend Rock's experiment, but their results substantiate Rock's.

Estes *et al.* say of these experiments, "No hitherto published theory with which we are familiar gives a reasonable account of our principal findings" (1960, p. 338). The information processing theory we have proposed here predicts the Rock result. A computer simulation of the Rock experiment using the information processing model generated behaviour substantially identical with that reported by Rock. In terms of our theory (postulate 4*a*) the explanation, of course, is that items on a list are learned one at a time in the processing sequence. Items presented when attention is focused on some other particular item are simply ignored by the learner, and are picked up on a later trial, as determined by the processing sequence. Hence, no time is lost by the learner if the experimenter replaces an item that has not yet been processed.

CONCLUDING REMARKS

In this paper we have surveyed the principal known facts about the shape of the serial position curve in serial learning of nonsense syllables by the anticipation method. We have examined the Lepley-Hull hypothesis as an explanation for the shape of the curve, and have concluded that the hypothesis is unsatisfactory. We have proposed an alternative hypothesis formulated in terms of information processes. We have shown that the hypothesis not only predicts the constancy of the serial position curve when the ordinates are plotted in percentage terms, but also predicts the quantitative values of the ordinates. Since the hypothesis allows no free parameters, its success in fitting the observed data provides rather persuasive evidence for its validity.

The information processing hypothesis is built on the following assumptions:

(1) that the brain is a serial processing mechanism with a limited span of processing attention;

(2) that the fixation of an item uses up a definite amount of processing time;

(3) that there is a small immediate memory which holds information to be processed;

(4) that the subject employs a relatively orderly and systematic method for organizing the learning task, using items with features of uniqueness as anchor points.

In this paper, we have offered no explanation of the fixation process itself, i.e., we have talked not at all about what occurs during the processing time assumed in item (2) above.

We are indebted to our colleague Allen Newell for numerous helpful discussions about this project, and to the Ford Foundation for financial assistance that made it possible.

APPENDIX

Given the unit processing time per syllable, one can, from the postulates, compute the average time after the beginning of a learning experiment that will pass before any specified syllable is learned. This time, in turn, determines uniquely the number of errors that will be made with that syllable. While the actual number of errors will be a function of the unit processing time, the percentage that this number represents of the expected total errors is independent of the unit processing time.

The numerical estimates given in the text tables were obtained as follows: By the postulates, the syllables will be learned in an orderly sequence, each syllable requiring a certain processing time, say k. Each syllable can be identified by its serial order, i, in the list as presented by the experimenter, and also by the order, r, in which it is learned by the subject. Since learning takes place from both ends of the list, these two orders will not, in general, be identical. Thus, s_i, the ith syllable in order of presentation, may be the same syllable as s'_r, the rth syllable in order of learning. (Technically, the list of syllables in order of learning is a permutation of the original list.) Let T'_r be the time that elapses before the first successful response to syllable s'_r—that is, until the rth syllable is learned. Then $T'_r = kr$. The number of errors, W'_r, the subject will make on the rth syllable is equal to the number of learning trials prior to the trial on which that syllable is learned and will be proportional to r:

$$W'_r = mr, \qquad (1)$$

where m is a proportionality constant, equal to k divided by the time per trial.

The numerical value of m is a function, of course, of the difficulty of the items, and the rate of presentation. However, we are only concerned with the fraction of total errors made on a given syllable, and this fraction is clearly independent of m. For let W be the total number of errors, summed over all syllables, and $w'_r = W'_r/W$, the fraction of total errors made on the rth syllable.

$$w'_r = mr \left/ \sum_{r=1}^{n} mr = r \left/ \sum_{r=1}^{n} r \right. \right.$$
$$= \frac{2r}{n(n+1)}, \qquad (2)$$

where n is the number of syllables in the list.

Suppose, for example, that we are dealing with a list of twelve syllables, then $\sum_{r=1}^{12} r = 78$. Hence, the fraction of total errors that will be made on the 4th syllable learned will be $4/78 = 0.051$.

Now, to obtain the serial position curve, we need merely to relabel the syllables from the order in which they are learned to their order of presentation. That is, if r_i is the rank, in order of learning, of the ith syllable in order of presentation, then the fraction of total errors for the ith syllable will be simply:

$$w_i = w'_{r_i} = r_i / \sum_r r_i. \qquad (3)$$

To apply this result, we must calculate the rank, r_i, of the ith syllable in order of presentation, as determined by postulate 4a. We assume (postulate 3) that the immediate memory capacity is two syllables and for simplicity in the calculation shall assume that the items are picked up pairwise in the processing sequence, and stored in the immediate memory for learning. The first two syllables in the list will be learned first (will have rank, $r = 1$, and $r = 2$, respectively), followed either by the last two syllables on the list, or by syllables three and four, each with probability one-half. The result is that in a list of 12 syllables the third syllable, for example, will have a probability of one-half of being the third syllable in order of learning, a probability of one-quarter of being the fifth syllable, a probability of one-eighth of being the seventh, and of one-sixteenth of being ninth or eleventh. Averaging these ranks, weighted by their respective probabilities, we find that the average rank of the third is $r_3 = 4 \cdot 875$. The fraction of total errors on the third syllable will then be $w_3 = 4 \cdot 875/78 = 0 \cdot 063$ (see Table 2). All the other predicted values in the tables were computed in the same way.

The fact that the third syllable has zero probability of learned fourth, sixth, eighth, etc., is artificially introduced by the calculation simplification introduced above of handling the syllables in pairs. It does not materially affect the serial position curve prediction, as is shown by the fact that the computer simulation (which does not use the pairwise learning simplification) generated the same serial position curve prediction.

References

Atkinson, R. C. A stochastic model for rote serial learning. *Psychometrika*, 1957, **22**, 81-95.

Bruner, J. S., Goodnow, J. J. & Austin, G. A. *A study of thinking*. New York: Wiley, 1956.

Estes, W. K., Hopkins, B. L. & Crothers, E. J. All-or-none and conservation effects in the learning and retention of paired associates. *J. Exp. Psychol.*, 1960, **6**, 329-39.

Feigenbaum, E. *An information processing theory of verbal learning*. The RAND Corporation, Paper P-1817, 1959.

Feldman, J. Analysis of behaviour in two choice situations. Unpublished doctoral dissertation, Carnegie Institute of Technology, 1959.

Gibson, E. J. A systematic application of the concepts of generalization and differentiation to verbal learning. *Psychol. Rev.*, 1940, **47**, 196-229.

Hilgard, E. R. *Theories of learning* (2nd ed.). New York: Appleton-Century-Crofts, 1956.

Hovland, C. I. Experimental studies in rote learning theory. III. Distribution of practice with varying speeds of syllable presentation. *J. exp. Psychol.*, 1938, **23**, 172-90.

Hovland, C. I. Human learning and retention. In

S. S. Stevens (ed.), *Handbook of experimental psychology*. New York: Wiley, 1951.

HOVLAND, C. I. & HUNT, E. B. The computer simulation of concept attainment. *Behavioral Science*, 1960, **5**, 265-7.

HULL, C. L. *et al. Mathematico-deductive theory of rote learning*. New Haven: Yale University Press, 1940.

JENSEN, A. R. Is the serial position curve invariant? *Brit. J. Psychol.*, 1962, **53**, 159-66.

KRUEGER, W. C. F. Learning during directed attention. *J. exp. Psychol.*, 1932, **15**, 517-27.

McCRARY, J. W. & HUNTER, W. S. Serial position curves in verbal learning. *Science*, 1953, **117**, 131-4.

McGEOCH, J. A. *The psychology of human learning*. New York: Longmans, Green, 1942.

MILLER, G. A. The magical number seven, plus or minus two; some limits on our capacity for processing information. *Psychol. Rev.*, 1956, **63**, 81-97.

NEWELL, A., SHAW, J. C. & SIMON, H. A. The elements of a theory of human problem solving. *Psychol. Rev.*, 1958a, **65**, 151-6.

NEWELL, A., SHAW, J. C. & SIMON, H. A. The processes of creative thinking. The RAND Corporation, Paper P-1320, 1958b.

NEWELL, A. & SIMON, H. A. Computer simulation of human thinking. *Science*, 1961, **134**, 2011-17.

RIBBACK, A. & UNDERWOOD, B. J. An empirical explanation of the skewness of the bowed serial position curve. *J. exp. Psychol.* 1950, **40**, 329-35.

ROCK, I. The role of repetition in associative learning. *Amer. J. Psychol.* 1957, **70**, 186-93.

WELCH, G. B. & BURNETT, C. T. Is primacy a factor in association-formation? *Amer. J. Psychol.*, 1924, **35**, 396-401.

WILCOXON, H. C., WILSON, W. R. & WISE, D. A. Paired-associate learning as a function of percentage of occurrence of response members and other factors. *J. exp. Psychol.*, 1961, **61**, 283-9.

WISHNER, J., SHIPLEY, T. E., JR., & HURVICH, M. S. The serial position curve as a function of organization. *Amer. J. Psychol.*, 1957, **70**, 258-62.

WOODWORTH, R. S. *Experimental psychology*. New York: Holt, 1938.

14 / The Anchor for the Serial Position Curve [1]

MURRAY GLANZER, *New York University,*
AND RICHARD DOLINSKY, *The University of Toledo*

Two experiments were carried out to determine the cue used by Ss to anchor the serial position curve in rote learning. Experiment I was designed to evaluate the role of starting position and facilitated (pretrained) syllable in lists that contained no other cues as to beginning or end (closed cycle lists). The results show that the Ss anchor the curve on the starting position. These findings contradict both facilitation and inhibition explanations of the serial position curve. On the basis of facilitation constructs it would be predicted that serial position curve should anchor on a facilitated syllable. On the basis of inhibition constructs it would be predicted that there should be no serial position effect in a closed cycle list. As an alternative to these it is suggested that the S makes a choice of anchor posiion and that any cue, position or list characteristic may serve as anchor for the curve. From this it follows that E should be able to instruct the S as to the anchor point. In Exp. II the E varied the indication of the beginning of the list by means of verbal instructions. The results show that the anchor point can be manipulated in this manner.

In rote learning S views a repetitive cycle of events—the series of syllables, a gap, the series of syllables, a gap, etc. The "beginning" of the list is ordinarily defined as the item that immediately follows the gap. The term "beginning" refers, therefore, to at least three factors associated with the repetitively appearing gap: (1) Primacy or first seen item. The first item that S sees (also, the first repeated item that he sees) appears next to the gap because E usually starts the list from the gap. (2) Spacing or reduction of presentation rate. The appearance of the gap coincides with a period during which E does not show S list items requiring a response. Presentation rate is, therefore, reduced during that period. (3) Association break. Every

From the *Journal of Verbal Learning and Verbal Behavior*, 1965, **4**, 267-73, with permission of the authors and publisher, Academic Press, Inc.
1. This investigation was supported by the U. S. Army Medical Research and Development Command, Department of the Army, under Research Contract DA-49-007-MD-1004.

item in the series functions as both a stimulus and response, except the two on either side of the gap. The item after the gap is solely a stimulus item; the item before the gap is solely a response item.

Glanzer and Peters (1962) carried out a series of experiments to determine the relative importance of these three factors —primacy, spacing, and association break—in generating the serial position effect. The results indicated that spacing was the most important single factor but that primacy, the first item seen, may play a part when spacing is not present. The results on the effect of spacing may be interpreted as agreeing with the explanations of the serial position effect in terms of inhibitory or interference factors. According to this type of explanation, the serial position curve results from the piling up of interference or inhibitory effects in the middle of the list (Hull, Hovland, Ross, Hall, Perkins, and Fitch, 1940). In order to have these interference or inhibitory effects pile up in the middle of the list, it is necessary that these effects occur only within each presentation of the list (e.g., that they do not extend from the last syllable of the list on trial n to the first syllable of the list on trial n + 1). The logical basis for this restriction, which is necessary to give the beginning syllables an advantage over the middle syllables, has usually not been given. It may, however, be derived by assigning a specific role to the intertrial interval or spacing. This interval may be viewed as a period during which these inhibitory or interfering effects decline or dissipate. Spacing is viewed, therefore, as acting as a buffer zone that protects some of the list items from inhibition or interference.

The effect of spacing can, however, be used to support another type of explanation—a facilitation explanation. It may be reasoned as follows: Slower presentation rates generally facilitate learning. In the case of serial learning, the local re-

duction in presentation rate that occurs between the "end" and "beginning" of the list facilitates the learning of the syllables that border it—the "first" and "last" syllables. The rapid learning of these syllables in turn facilitates the learning of their neighbors. The facilitative effect is thus generated forward and backward in the list to produce the full serial position effect. The skewing of the serial position curve can be accounted for by a mechanism suggested by Ribback and Underwood (1950). The facilitation type of explanation is discussed by Glanzer and Peters (1962) and Jensen (1962).

If this reasoning is correct, then it should be possible to use means other than spacing to facilitate the learning of particular items in a list and then generate a full serial position effect around those facilitated items. The first experiment below attempts to determine whether there is evidence to support this conclusion.

Experiment I

The term "closed cycle list" will be defined here as a list that has no gap in it. The S learning a closed cycle list views an unbroken, repetitive sequence of syllables. If a facilitation explanation of the serial position effect is correct, then pretraining S on a syllable that later appears in a closed cycle list should give a full serial position effect in the closed cycle list. The serial position effect would anchor on—i.e., have as its lowest point—the pretrained item. If an inhibition explanation is correct, then pretraining S on a syllable in a closed cycle list should give at most a local effect on the pretrained syllable but no serial position effect. Under the interpretation of the role of the intertrial interval given above, the closed cycle list does not have in it a buffer zone of space to give any syllables in the list special protection from inhibitory effects. The general procedure in this experiment was, therefore, to pretrain Ss on particular syllables, have them learn closed cycle lists containing those syllables, and then determine whether a serial position curve was generated about the pretrained syllables. It was also decided to determine whether further evidence could be found for a serial position effect anchored on the starting position. A serial position effect of this type would fit neither the facilitation nor the inhibition explanation.

Subjects. The Ss were 130 college students who were paid for their participation. A table of random numbers was used to assign the Ss to each of the conditions used (100 experimental conditions and 10 triple-replicated control conditions). There were, in addition, 7 Ss run (5 experimental and 2 control) who failed to complete the pretraining or failed to follow instructions. These Ss were dismissed and replaced by others to complete the group of 130 Ss.

Procedure. During a single session, the Ss learned three sets of material in the following order:

(1) A five-syllable, closed cycle serial list —DAT, COR, SEM, FIZ, HUL (Archer meaningfulness index between .81 and .90). This preliminary training was designed to acquaint the S with unbroken serial lists. The list was run to a criterion of one perfect trial on the complete list.

(2) A set of three paired associates. For the 100 experimental Ss the pairs were KIY-VAW, BOQ-JEX and a pair drawn from the final closed cycle list. For the 30 control Ss the pairs were KIY-VAW, BOQ-JEX, and WUC-FEK (Archer values between .16 and .27). The paired-associate training was continued to a criterion of five perfect trials on the complete set.

(3) A ten-syllable, closed cycle serial list (Archer values between .14 and .27)— MUB, GEC, RIH, ZUK, QAS, YOD, LIJ, PEF, XAN, TOV—run for 39 trials.[2]

All the material was presented on a memory drum at a 2-sec rate.

The 100 experimental Ss were run on each of the 100 possible combinations obtained by systematically varying the pretraining pair drawn from the final closed cycle list and by systematically varying the starting position in the final list. Thus 10 of the 100 experimental Ss were pretrained on the pair MUB-GEC. Of these 10 Ss, one was shown first, or started from, the syllable MUB in the final list. One was started from GEC. One

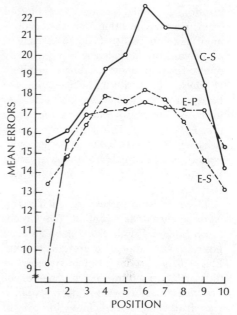

FIG. 1. Serial position curves for Experimental group with respect to the pretrained position. E-S is the same data, regrouped and plotted with respect to starting position. C-S is the curve with respect to starting position for the control group.

was started from RIH, etc. The 30 control Ss whose paired-associate pretraining did not include items from the final list, were equally divided among the 10 different starting positions in the final list.

Results. Serial position curves for the experimental Ss can be plotted either by grouping the data with respect to the pretrained position (E-P) or the starting position (E-S) in the final list. The curves obtained by these two groupings are shown in Fig. 1. Starting position gives a full serial position effect; pretraining position has a local effect, restricted almost completely to the pair involved in the pretraining. The curve for the control group (C-S) which can, of course, be plotted only with respect to the starting

2. The number of trials originally planned was 40. By error, however, the 40th trial was halted before completion for an early group of Ss. Rather than discard the data for these Ss it was decided to use 39 trials for all Ss.

position, is similar to the curve plotted from starting position for the experimental group (E-S). (The displacement downward of the E-S curve is primarily due to the pretrained syllables. The effect of these is distributed across the ten positions in the E-S curve, instead of being concentrated at two positions as in the E-P curve. The apparent greater peaking of the C-S curve is not supported by statistical analysis comparing the mean squares for position in the two curves.)

The data from the experimental group were analyzed as a set of ten Greco-Latin squares, with Ss, syllables, serial position with respect to pretrained syllables (PT), and serial position with respect to starting position (SP) as sources of variance. The between-subjects variance was further analyzed into the overall effect of particular starting positions and pretrained syllables. The data from the control group were analyzed as a replicated Latin square, with particular starting position (groups of Ss), syllables, and serial position with respect to starting position (SP) as sources of variance. The analyses were first carried out for the experimental and control groups separately. Comparison of the corresponding sums of squares in the two analyses indicated that it was appropriate to combine the two analyses into a single overall analysis. Unless indicated otherwise, the numerical values for F will be drawn from the overall analysis. The separate analyses give the same information.

All the within-Ss effects ($df=9/1143$) were significant at the .001 level—syllables ($F=11.233$), serial position with respect to starting position ($F=15.970$) and serial position with respect to pretrained item ($F=17.766$). The degrees of freedom listed above may be inflated, since repeated measures were used. Reduction of the degrees of freedom to 1 and 127, in line with the recommendation by Greenhouse and Geisser (1959), leaves

the effects significant at either the .005 or .001 level. The between-Ss effects—starting position, pretrained item, and their interaction were negligible and not statistically significant. (The residual between-Ss error from the control groups was used to evaluate the SP×PT interaction from the experimental groups.)

The serial position with respect to the pretrained item was also evaluated with the two syllables used in pretraining (stimulus and response) eliminated. This was done by computing the variance for the eight remaining positions. When this is done in the experimental group the F drops from 18.092 ($df=9/873$ $p<.001$) to less than 1.00 ($df=7/873$). If, however, the parallel elimination is carried out on the serial position effect with respect to the starting position, so that the two lowest points are excluded, the significance level remains the same. The F goes from 10.799 ($df=9/873$, $p<.001$) to 5.799 ($df=7/873$, $p<.001$).

Discussion. The results of the experiment go counter to both the facilitation and inhibition explanations of the serial position effect. They go against the facilitation explanation because the effect of pretraining is restricted almost entirely to the stimulus and response syllables used in pretraining (Fig. 1). They also go against the inhibition explanation. In a closed cycle list there is nothing to protect any part of the list from the hypothesized inhibition or interference effects. A full serial position effect is nevertheless generated about the starting position.

The results of this experiment and the preceding experiments (Glanzer and Peters, 1962) indicate that a change in the form of the serial list leads to a change by the Ss of the point to which they anchor the serial position curve. If the list is structured so that either spacing or starting position can be used, the Ss anchor the curve on the spacing. If only starting position is available, or starting position and pretrained syllables, the Ss anchor on starting position.

It may be argued therefore that the Ss choose the anchor point, their choice determined by the cues available or prominent in the experimental list. In general, however, any cue or characteristic of the list may be used by the Ss to anchor the curve. By appropriate structuring of the list, it should be possible, for example, to move the anchor for the serial position curve to a pretrained item. One way to do this is to eliminate the starting position, as Workman (1951) did, starting the list with a set of buffer items which appear only during the first presentation of the list and are thereafter omitted.

If the Ss choose the anchor point for the serial position curve—and any point in the list may serve as anchor—it is not useful to direct experimental analysis at the effect of particular items or characteristics of the list. This type of experimental analysis will generate (as it has in this and the preceding work) a sequence of experiments in which one list characteristic is important in one experiment and another characteristic is important in another experiment. It is necessary, rather, to direct the experimental analysis at the S's choice of the anchor for the serial position curve. In the next experiment an attempt is made to do this.

Experiment II

It appears as if S looks at the experimental list and on the basis of any one of several characteristics of the list instructs himself as to the beginning, middle, and end of the list. If this view is correct, then it should be possible to place this instruction under E's control. The present experiment was designed to do this.

Subjects. The Ss were 60 college students who were paid for their participation. A table of random numbers was used to assign them to each of the experimental conditions (two instructions, ten starting positions, three replications). There were, in addition, two Ss who were dismissed—one for failure

to learn the pretraining list and one for failure to follow instructions. These Ss were replaced by two others to complete the group of 60 Ss.

The Ss learned two closed cycle serial lists—a short five-syllable practice list followed by the main ten-syllable list. The lists were the same as the closed cycle practice list and main list used in Exp. I. The practice list was run to a criterion of one perfect trial. The main list was run for 40 trials. Both lists were presented at a 2-sec rate. Each S received the same type of instructions on his practice list as on his main list.

The starting position was systematically varied so that six Ss started at each of the ten syllables in the main list. As the first syllable appeared, half the Ss were told by E that it was the "beginning" of the list. Then, when the fifth syllable appeared, it was defined by E as the "middle" of the list. For the other half of the Ss the first syllable exposed was defined by E as the middle of the list, the fifth syllable was defined as the beginning of the list. Once E had made these definitions during the first presentation of the list, he made no further comments.

Results. The serial position curves plotted from the starting position are shown in Fig. 2.

The curve labeled B is for the group in which the first syllable presented was defined as the beginning by E. The curve is a standard serial position curve, except for a slight depression at the position defined as the middle by E. The curve labeled M is for the group in which the first syllable presented was defined as the middle by E. The curve is clearly bimodal with its lowest point the middle position, defined as the beginning by E.

The data were analyzed as forming two Latin squares, one at each level of verbal instruction. The variables that constituted the Latin squares were starting position, syllables and serial position with respect to starting position. The analysis of variance indicated that none of the between-Ss effects is significant. These are the overall effect of verbal instructions, starting position and their interaction. Of the within-Ss effects, all with $df = 9/360$, the following are significant at the .001 level: syllables ($F = 4.493$), serial position with respect to starting position ($F = 4.988$), and the interaction of serial position with verbal instructions ($F = 3.390$). The remaining interactions were not significant. Reduction of the degrees of freedom to obtain lower-bound significance levels, in line with the Greenhouse and Geisser recommendation, leaves the effects at the .05, .05, and .10 levels, respectively.

Examination of the curves for the individual Ss in the group whose first presented syllable was identified as the middle by E reveals three groups. About one-third of the Ss show a bimodal curve like that in Fig. 2, one-third show a standard unimodal curve anchored on the first syllable seen and one-third show a standard unimodal curve anchored on the fifth syllable seen (the syllable identified as the beginning by E).

Discussion. The findings give support to the following assertions: (1) that the S makes a choice as to the item or part of the list to be used as anchor; (2) that, in making his choice, he may make use of any item or part or characteristic of the list.

Experiment II, the attempt to use experimental instructions to determine the anchor point for the serial position was only partially successful. The average result was that the group of Ss made use of two anchor points, one determined by the starting position, the other by the instructions. This average result was produced by some Ss anchoring on the instruction beginning, some on the starting position, and some on both. As indicated earlier, it should be possible to have all Ss start from the instruction beginning by eliminating the starting syllable after the first trial.

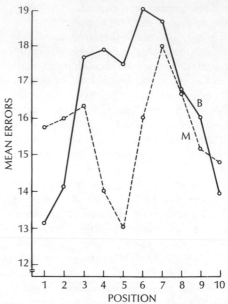

FIG. 2. Serial position curves for Exp. II. Both curves are plotted with respect to the starting position. The curve labeled B is for the group whose first syllable was defined by E as the beginning. The curve labeled M is for the group whose first syllable was defined by E as the middle.

The results of the two experiments indicate that simple inhibition or facilitation explanations cannot handle the serial position effect. Inhibition explanations, which assign a key role to a buffer zone of spacing between what E defines as the beginning and end of the list, are clearly ruled out. Facilitation explanations, in which the effect is automatically generated from a facilitated item, are also ruled out by the data.

The analysis of the serial position curve seems to fall into two parts. The first part is concerned with the S's definition of the beginning or definition of the order of the list items. This definition, it appears now, is not restricted to the use of any particular type of cue. It can be done on the basis of any characteristic chosen by the S. This does not mean that it cannot be brought under experimental control. It means, however, that the system through which the control works is not a simple one. The second part of the analysis is concerned with the ordering of the individual syllables once a beginning position has been chosen by S. Detailed examination of the nature of the learning of individual items in serial lists has begun (Jensen, 1962; Schulz, 1955; Young, 1961, 1962). The factors underlying the order in which the items are learned still remain to be discovered.

ARCHER, E. J. A re-evaluation of the meaningfulness of all possible CVC trigrams. *Psychol. Monogr.*, 1960, **74**, No. 10 (Whole No. 497).
GLANZER, M., & PETERS, S. C. Re-examination of the serial position effect. *J. exp. Psychol.*, 1962, **64**, 258-66.

GREENHOUSE, S. W., & GEISSER, S. On the methods in the analysis of profile data. *Psychometrika* 1959, **24**, 95-112.
HULL, C. L., HOVLAND, C. I., ROSS, R. T., HALL, M., PERKINS, D. T., & FITCH, F. B. *Mathematico-deductive theory of rote learning.* New Haven: Wale Univer. Press, 1940.
JENSEN, A. R. An empirical theory of the serial-position effect. *J. Psychol.*, 1962, **53**, 127-42.
RIBBACK, A., & UNDERWOOD, B. J. An empirical explanation of the skewness of the bowed serial position curve. *J. exp. Psychol.*, 1950, **40**, 329-35.
SCHULZ, R. Generalization of serial position in rote serial learning. *J. exp. Psychol.*, 1955, **49**, 267-72.
WORKMAN, W. G. An experimental investigation of cognitive factors as contrasted with noncognitive factors in rote serial learning. Unpublished doctoral dissertation, University of Chicago, 1951.
YOUNG, R. K. The stimulus in serial verbal learning. *Amer. J. Psychol.*, 1961, **74**, 517-28.
YOUNG, R. K. Tests of three hypotheses about the effective stimulus in serial learning. *J. exp. Psychol.*, 1962, **63**, 307-13.

15 / Serial-position Effect of Ordered Stimulus Dimensions in Paired-associate Learning [1]

SHELDON M. EBENHOLTZ,[2] *Connecticut College*

5 experiments supported the empirical generalization that the establishment of a differential response to each of a set of stimuli that are capable of being ordered along a sensory or conceptual dimension, is sufficient to produce a bowed error distribution. In 2 experiments the numerals 1 through 8 and 1 through 10 were used as stimuli in a paired-associates (PA) design. In 3 additional PA experiments stimuli were nonsense syllables, previously learned as members of a serial list. Response terms were disyllabic nouns or nonsense syllables. In all 5 experiments a serial-position effect (SPE) was obtained when mean percentages of errors in PA learning were plotted as a function of either stimulus number or stimulus position in prior serial learning (SL). Results support the propositions that (a) SL entails responding to positional cues, and (b) responding to the positional properties of items is sufficient to produce the SPE.

There is now a good deal of evidence to support the empirical generalization that discriminating [3] between stimuli that vary along some sensory dimension as from least to most or beginning to end, etc., is sufficient to produce a bow-shaped error distribution. Murdock's (1960) study supports this view with evidence from such dimensions as sound intensity, the areas of different-sized squares, the diameter of circles of varying size, weights, and time intervals. Further evidence of bowed curves under conditions

of discrimination learning has been obtained with spatial positions (Ebenholtz, 1963a; Jensen, 1962), line lengths, and percentage of reflectance of grays (Eben-

From the *Journal of Experimental Psychology*, 1966, **71**, 132-7, with permission of the author and publisher.
1. This investigation was supported in part by Public Health Service Research Grant MH07114-01, from the National Institute of Mental Health.
2. The author wishes to thank Barbara Brachman, Linda Foster, Anne Vicary, and Susan Thurston for their aid in collecting the data.
3. Discrimination is defined in the present context to mean the establishment of a differential response to each of a series of stimuli to some reliable criterion.

holtz, 1965). The present experiments were intended to determine whether the above generalization could be extended to include discrimination between stimuli varying along nonsensory, i.e., conceptual, dimensions as well.

METHOD AND PROCEDURE

Experiment I.—The numerals 1 through 10 were used as stimuli in a paired-associate design with disyllabic nouns as response terms. The latter (viz., ARROW, CURTAIN, DECOY, ENGINE, GIANT, HELMET, JACKET, LESSON, PILLOW, ZEBRA) were chosen from the Thorndike-Lorge (1944) word count and had frequencies of occurrence which ranged from 2 to over 50 per million words. Ten different lists of 10 number-noun pairs were used to counterbalance response terms equally over the 10 stimuli. Each of 20 Ss learned 1 of the 10 lists to a criterion of one perfect recitation. Learning and test trials alternated and items were presented at a 3-sec. rate with a 24-sec. intertrial interval. The order of presentation on successive learning and test trials was never the same; five different learning and test sequences were used on the first five trials and then repeated.

Experiment II.—The numbers 1 through 8 were used as stimuli (Group NS) to nonsense-syllable responses. Group NR learned the reverse pairs. Syllables were taken from the Glaze (1928) list of 87–100% association value and were chosen for minimal similarity. Syllables were counterbalanced over numbers such that for a block of eight Ss each number was paired with each syllable once. Eighteen Ss in each group learned by the method of anticipation at a 3:3-sec. rate. The intertrial interval was 6 sec. The order of presentation was varied on eight successive trials and then repeated. Learning was to a criterion of one perfect trial.

Experiment III.—The procedure and design were identical with those of Exp. I with the exception that instead of the numbers 1 through 10, stimuli were nonsense syllables which Ss first learned as members of a serial list. Previous studies (e.g., Ebenholtz, 1963a, 1963b; Young, 1962) have shown serial learning (SL) to entail learning the temporal positions of the items comprising the series. Thus one result of SL is that items may be presumed to represent the attribute of temporal position and therefore to constitute a sample of a dimension in which the items may be ordered from beginning to end. Discriminating between items learned previously as members of a serial list, should, therefore, produce a bowed error distribution in which stimuli from central portions of the serial list produce more errors than stimuli taken from extreme serial positions.

Ten syllables of minimal similarity were chosen from the Glaze (1928) list of 80–100% association value. A 10-item Latin square was used to compose 10 serial lists such that each item appeared at each position once and preceded and followed every other item once. The first 10 Ss each learned a different serial order, with Ss 11 and 12 repeating the serial order of the first 2 Ss. Since each syllable occurred at least once at each serial position and all 12 Ss learned the same set of 10 syllable-noun pairings, stimulus positions were counterbalanced over response terms. The criterion of PA learning, response terms, presentation rate, and intertrial interval were the same as in Exp. I.

Experiment IV.—Two groups of 10 Ss each learned 10 syllable-noun pairs after either free recall (FR) or SL of the stimulus syllables. Group SL was treated identically with Ss in Exp. III. Group FR differed only in that instead of serial learning prior to PA, Ss were instructed to free recall the syllables in any order until all 10 items could be recalled on a single trial. The Ss were presented with the syllables at a 3-sec. rate and asked to pronounce each term as it appeared. The presentation sequence was varied on each of 10 trials and then repeated. After pronouncing all 10 items S was allotted 30 sec. to recall as many as possible. Each S in group FR started the FR training with a different stimulus sequence in order to counterbalance items over presentation order. Both groups were treated identically in PA learning and conditions were the same as those of Exp. III.

Experiment V.—The conditions and procedures of Exp. III were replicated with the exception that the nonsense syllables were chosen from the Glaze (1928) lists of 27–33%

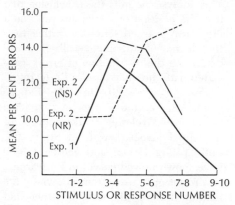

FIG. 1. Mean percentage of errors in PA learning as a function of stimulus (response) number.

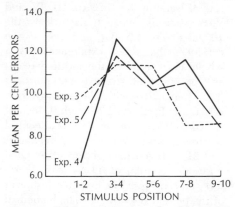

FIG. 2. Mean percentage of errors in PA learning as a function of stimulus position in prior SL.

association values. Ten Ss took part in this experiment.

None of the Ss had taken part previously in studies of verbal learning and all were unfamiliar with the purposes of the experiments.

RESULTS

Numbers as stimuli and responses.— Figure 1 represents the mean percentage of errors as a function of stimulus position.[4] Adjacent positions have been combined and averaged in order to reduce the inordinate influence of zero scores. The bowed curves are apparent in both experiments even though the averaging of errors at adjacent positions tended to flatten the curves.

In Exp. 1 the mean percentage of errors at Positions 1, 2, 9, and 10 (7.9%) was compared with the mean percentage of errors at Positions 4, 5, 6, and 7 (10.7%). The difference was significant, $p < .005$, by the Wilcoxon (1949) test for paired replicates. A similar comparison between the mean percentage of errors at Positions 1, 2, 7, and 8 (10.9%) and Positions 3, 4, 5, and 6 (14.1%) in Exp. II, Group NS, also yielded significance, $p < .05$, by the Wilcoxon test.

When numbers are used as responses in PA learning, the pairs containing lower numbers tend to be learned with fewer errors than those containing higher numbers. Group NR represents this trend in Fig. 1. The mean percentage of errors at Positions 1, 2, 3, and 4 was 10.2% in comparison with 14.8% for Positions 5, 6, 7, and 8. The difference of 4.6% was significant, $p < .01$, by the Wilcoxon test.

Serially learned items as stimuli.—In Fig. 2 are represented the mean percentage of errors in PA learning as a function of prior stimulus position for Exp. III, IV, and V. In each case the mean percentage of errors per position was less for pairs containing stimuli from extreme serial positions than for pairs whose stimuli were located at central serial positions. Comparison of the mean percentage of errors at combined Positions 1, 2, 9, and 10 with the mean percentage at Positions 4, 5, 6, and 7 showed, in each case, a higher average at central positions, the mean difference being 2.0, 4.5, and 2.1 for Exp. III, IV, and V, respectively. This finding in three independent experiments suggests that it is not a chance outcome; however, in no case was there a statistically significant difference. This is probably due to the relatively small sample size and extremely rapid

4. All serial-position curves were based upon percentages obtained for each S separately and then averaged over stimulus positions.

rate of learning, i.e., in Exp. III, IV, and V, respectively, mean trials to learn the 10 pairs were 4.5, 3.4, and 3.8. If one considers the three experiments as a whole and compares the mean percentage of errors at the extreme positions (i.e., 1 and 10) with the average percentage at Positions 2 through 9, then of the 32 Ss 9 averaged less errors at central positions, 2 yielded equal percentages and 21 averaged fewer errors at terminal positions. A total of 11 Ss may, therefore, be considered as negative instances of the present hypothesis. The binominal test (Siegel, 1956), however, shows this distribution of 11 and 21 to depart significantly from chance on the assumption of an equal split, $z = -1.59$, $p = .05$.

The effect of differential stimulus recall.—It is possible that the serial-position effect (SPE) as represented in Fig. 2 is due not to serial position as such but rather to the fact that the members of a serial list vary in terms of the frequency of correct recalls. From this point of view, items from central serial positions may be assumed to be less familiar than items at extreme positions. The SPE in PA learning may thus be understood as an effect of differential stimulus familiarity. The data of Exp. IV permit an evaluation of the effects of differential stimulus recall on subsequent PA learning.

The mean percentages of correct recalls for each of the 10 items on the free-recall task (Group FR) were rank ordered and correlated with the rank of the mean percentages of correct responses to the same 10 items in the subsequent PA task. The degree of correlation was not significant, $\rho (10) = -.006$, $p > .05$. In contrast, the data of Group SL revealed a significant correlation between the mean percentages of correct anticipations associated with each position in SL and the mean percentages of correct responses to pairs whose stimuli derived from these same positions, $\rho (10) = .746$, $p < .01$.

This analysis permits the conclusion that it is the *position* of a stimulus term on a previously learned serial list, rather than the degree of stimulus recall, that will determine the distribution of errors associated with the same term in PA learning.

Transfer from SL to PA.—Experiments III, IV, and V also bear on some of the issues relating to the transfer of sequential associations from SL to PA. Both Young (1962) and Jensen (1963) have shown bowed curves in PA learning as a result of transfer from SL, where the relation between the tasks was such that the PA list was composed of pairs of successive items from the previously learned serial list. Both authors have interpreted the SPE in terms of the transfer of relatively strong associations for pairs containing members derived from extreme serial positions, and the transfer of weak associations for pairs composed of items from central serial positions. The design of Exp. III, IV, and V precludes the possibility of positive associative transfer and, since all pairs were composed of new response terms, actually requires negative transfer in the form of a U-shaped error distribution. Thus, if the serial list is represented by the sequence: A-B-C-D-E-F-G-H-I-J, then the assumption of sequential associations in SL requires the PA task to be represented by: A-K_1, B-K_2, C-K_3, D-K_4, E-K_5, F-K_6, G-K_7, H-K_8, I-K_9, J-K_{10}. It follows that pairs containing stimuli from extreme serial positions (excluding Position 10) should be learned with maximum difficulty as these stimuli must produce the greatest associative interference, e.g., A-B should interfere more with A-K_1 than F-G can interfere with F-K_6 as the former (A-B) has been anticipated correctly in SL more frequently than the latter (F-G). This conclusion from the assumption of sequential associations in SL has not been confirmed and in fact the transfer data of Exp. III, IV, and V, represented in Fig. 2, show the exact opposite effect. This remains true even if the data of the pairs containing SL Item 10 are eliminated from the computation.

A further test of the same hypothesis can be made by comparing the rate of PA learning of Group FR with Group SL of Exp. IV. It can be assumed that in comparison to SL the FR of nonsense syllables produces relatively weak and unstable inter-item associations (Asch & Ebenholtz, 1962). It follows from the present paradigm that transfer from FR to PA should produce faster learning than transfer from SL to PA as the latter should lead to more associative interference than the former. The mean number of trials to criterion on the initial lists of Exp. IV was 8.0 and 4.9 in SL and FR, respectively, t (18)$=3.969$, $p<.01$. The mean number of correct recalls per item averaged over trials was 5.1 in SL and 3.9 in FR, the difference being nonsignificant, t (18)$=1.845$, $p>.05$ (two tails). Mean trials to criterion on the PA task was 3.4 for Group SL and 4.0 for Group FR. The difference was in a direction opposite to that predicted under the assumption of the transfer of sequential associations and was not significant, t (18)$=1.156$, $p>.05$. This outcome is consistent with the failure of a positive transfer paradigm to support the same hypothesis (e.g., Young & Casey, 1964).

DISCUSSION

All five experiments yielded an SPE. The data, therefore, support the generalization that the establishment of differential responses to each of a set of stimuli that are capable of being ordered along a sensory or conceptual dimension, is sufficient to produce a bowed error distribution. This outcome is consistent with the suggestion (Ebenholtz, 1963a, 1963b, 1965) that the occurrence of the SPE reflects the use of positional cues, a process which probably represents a fundamental mode of responding to the ordinal characteristics of stimuli.

The SPE resulting from the use of numbers as stimuli may help to account for some portion of the conflicting evidence regarding positional cues in SL. Jensen and Blank (1962) failed to support the position-learning hypothesis when Ss learned a nine-item serial list in which each item was labeled with a numeral indicative of the serial position of that item. In comparison with control Ss not given such positional cues, neither rate of learning nor shape of the SPE differed significantly. The present results indicate that responding to number stimuli is sufficient to produce an SPE even though the numerals are presented in random order. It follows that such stimuli cannot be expected to eliminate the SPE when they are presented in constant temporal order. More generally, the present data and those of Jensen and Blank suggest that the cue of serial position is not readily manipulatable, for, by definition, serial position is a relational characteristic of items within a series. Consequently, attempts to control the distinctiveness of positional cues will probably require the manipulation of relationships between the items and the terminal points of the series (e.g., Asch, Hay, & Diamond, 1960; Wishner, Shipley, & Hurvich, 1957).

Experiments I and II clearly support the present hypothesis, although other possible explanations remain to be examined. Recently, Battig and Spera (1962) determined the association value of numbers from 0 to 100. Their results indicate a general decrease in association value from 1 through 8 with an increase at 9 and 10. Their data, therefore, are consistent with an SPE for a 10-number experiment (e.g., Exp. I) but fail to account for a bowed curve brought about by a decrease in errors at Positions 7 and 8 as in Exp. II (Group NS). Thus the present data do not support the alternative that the SPE is an artifact of the association value of numbers.

When the numbers 1 through 8 were used as responses in Exp. II, Group NR, the higher numbers showed a significant tendency to produce greater errors than the low numbers, and an SPE was not obtained. This suggests that the SPE may be a function of *stimulus* rather than response order. However, this possibility is contradicted by the work of DeSoto & Bosley (1962). These authors obtained an SPE in a PA study in which male first names were stimuli and the response to each name was one of four chosen from the categories of college matriculation, i.e., freshman, sophomore, junior, and senior. Fewest errors were made when the correct response was freshman or senior, thereby producing an SPE with maximum errors at sophomore. The failure to obtain the SPE with numbers as responses may, therefore, reflect the special conditions of Exp. II, e.g., the use of unfamiliar nonsense syllables as stimuli.

An additional implication of the results of Exp. I and II is a methodological one concerning the use of single digit numbers in paired-associate studies. Unless these numbers are properly counterbalanced or avoided entirely, they may produce systematic artifacts. This may be the case in studies of discrimination learning and scaling as well.

The results of Exp. III, IV, and V have particular significance for the evaluation of the propositions (a) that SL entails responding to positional cues, i.e., SL represents one operation by which items, previously neutral with regard to order, come to possess ordinal and positional characteristics; (b) that responding to the positional properties of items is sufficient to produce the SPE. That stimuli previously learned in serial order produce the SPE in subsequent PA learning was the outcome in three independent experiments. This result lends confirmation directly to Proposition b and indirectly to Proposition a. This same result casts doubt on the interpretation that the SPE in PA learning (Jensen, 1963; Young, 1962), where the latter is made up of adjacent pairs of items from SL, reflects the positive transfer from SL to PA of sequential associations of differential strength. According to the present results the SPE obtained in such transfer studies can be interpreted as representing the effects of positional cues due to prior SL of the stimulus items. It is most likely, however, that both processes are operative, although unequivocal evidence supporting the assumption of sequential associations is relatively rare (e.g., Battig,

Brown, & Schild, 1964). It may be noted further that the failure to obtain a U-shaped error distribution in Exp. III, IV, and V suggests the conclusion that either positional cues are more potent than sequential associations, or that associative interference is a poor or unreliable indicator of associative processes.

Asch, S. E., & Ebenholtz, S. M. The process of free recall: Evidence for non-associative factors in acquisition and retention. *J. Psychol.*, 1962, **54**, 3-31.

Asch, S. E., Hay, J., & Diamond, R. M. Perceptual organization in serial rote-learning. *Amer. J. Psychol.*, 1960, **73**, 177-98.

Battig, W. F., Brown, S. C., & Schild, M. E. Serial position and sequential associations in serial learning. *J. exp. Psychol.*, 1964, **67**, 449-57.

Battig, W. F., & Spera, A. J. Rated association values of numbers from 0-100. *J. verbal Learn. verbal Behav.*, 1962, **1**, 200-202.

DeSoto, C. B., & Bosley, J. J. The cognitive structure of a social structure. *J. abnorm. soc. Psychol.*, 1962, **64**, 303-7.

Ebenholtz, S. M. Position mediated transfer between serial learning and a spatial discrimination task. *J. exp. Psychol.*, 1963, **65**, 603-8. (a)

Ebenholtz, S. M. Serial learning: Position learning and sequential associations. *J. exp. Psychol.*, 1963, **66**, 353-62. (b)

Ebenholtz, S. M. Positional cues as mediators in discrimination learning. *J. exp. Psychol.*, 1965, **70**, 176-81.

Glaze, J. A. The association value of nonsense syllables. *J. genet. Psychol.*, 1928, **35**, 255-69.

Jensen, A. R. Temporal and spatial effects of serial position. *Amer. J. Psychol.*, 1962, **75**, 390-400.

Jensen, A. R. Transfer between paired-associate and serial learning. *J. verbal Learn. verbal Behav.*, 1963, **1**, 269-80.

Jensen, A. R., & Blank, S. S. Association with ordinal position in serial rote-learning. *Canad. J. Psychol.*, 1962, **16**, 60-63.

Murdock, B. B., Jr. The distinctiveness of stimuli. *Psychol. Rev.*, 1960, **67**, 16-31.

Siegel, S. *Nonparametric statistics for the behavioral sciences.* New York: McGraw-Hill, 1956.

Thorndike, E. L., & Lorge, I. *The teacher's word book of 30,000 words.* New York: Teachers College, Bureau of Publications, Columbia University, 1944.

Wilcoxon, F. *Some rapid approximate statistical procedures.* (Rev. ed.) New York: American Cyanamid, 1949.

Wishner, J., Shipley, T. E., & Hurvich, M. S. The serial position curve as a function of organization. *Amer. J. Psychol.*, 1957, **70**, 258-62.

Young, R. K. Tests of three hypotheses about the effective stimulus in serial learning. *J. exp. Psychol.*, 1962, **63**, 307-13.

Young, R. K., & Casey, M. Transfer from serial to paired-associate learning. *J. exp. Psychol.*, 1964, **67**, 594-5.

CONTINUITY VERSUS DISCONTINUITY

A fundamental question about the nature of learning is examined in this section. Conceptually, the question appears to be a clear-cut and straightforward one, but in fact it has required considerable analytic and experimental ingenuity to bring it to anything resembling an empirical test. The problem may be put as follows: Is the associative bond between a stimulus and a response formed within a single trial at full strength, or does it grow gradually in strength over successive trials?

This question was first studied in the context of animal discrimination learning, and brought about the famous continuity-noncontinuity controversy, typified by the experiments of Krechevsky (1938) and of Spence (1945). The issue remained unsettled and virtually dormant for several years thereafter, but was eventually revived, this time within the domain of the verbal learning laboratory.

Again, sides have been drawn. The "all-or-none" theorist holds that a response is at zero strength until that trial on which it jumps to maximum strength. In short, the response is either fully learned or it is not learned at all. The "incremental" theorist holds that a response gradually gains increments of strength from each succeeding reinforced trial. Thus, it assumes any of a number of increasing strengths on its way to full development. Compromise positions between these extreme views are possible, and have in fact been suggested. On the face of it, the shape of the ordinary group learning curve would seem to provide evidence for the incremental view, since typically it rises gradually and progressively from zero to the maximum score. However, the smooth ascents of such curves can be the result of the averaging process itself, wherein individual stepwise jumps are obscured.

There are three major methods which have been utilized for the study of the all-or-none versus incremental question. The first is a transfer of training technique, which in the earlier animal studies was known as the discrimination reversal problem. For an illustration of the use of discrimination reversal problems in human concept formation tasks, the student is referred to Reading 41 in Section IX. With rote verbal learning, the technique takes the form of altering the composition of a list while learning is in progress, in order to detect possible negative transfer from partially learned responses. Rock's paper exemplifies this approach. The second method, introduced by Estes, consists in tracking the retention of individual responses across a number of unreinforced test trials, in order to measure their stability. The third method is associated with the development of mathematical models, and consists in detailed statistical analyses of the characteristics of responses made by subjects during the course of learning. All three methods will be encountered in the readings to follow, together with critical appraisals of their accuracy.

Rock's paper suddenly reopened the issue at the rote learning level. He found that there was no impairment in the rate of learning of a paired-associates list if, after every trial, new items were substituted for those not gotten correct on the previous trial. This implied that repetition had no influence upon learning.

Postman's paper is illustrative of the lively reaction initiated by the Rock experiment. Postman conducted two experiments using the Rock procedure, but with appropriate controls for item-selection included. His results failed to corroborate the all-or-none view and also indicated the difficulties inherent in such a procedure.

The paper by Estes displayed the force and elegance of the "miniature experiment" method. The data pointed clearly in the direction of the all-or-none position, and appeared to be safe against the kinds of weaknesses found in the Rock procedure.

The Underwood and Keppel paper reviewed the theoretical issues and reported experiments designed to assess Estes's "miniature experiment" method. The over-all results were such as to raise a reasonable doubt about the conclusiveness of the Estes *et al.* findings.

Bower's paper shows the impressive power of a mathematical model for predicting many aspects of paired-associates learning. It is one of the most successful models of its kind, and it is based upon an all-or-none assumption. Other examples of the mathematical model approach to learning are found in Readings 43 and 44.

An excellent detailed examination of a number of possible theoretical models of learning has led Restle (1965) to conclude that all-or-none findings are not decisive with respect to the viability of any of the theories considered. The fundamental issue about the stepwise or continuous nature of learning has yielded considerable data, but an unequivocal interpretation is still needed. For further commentary upon the complexities involved, the student is referred to Postman's article (1963) and to Ritchie's enlightening, and somewhat wry, analysis (1965).

KRECHEVSKY, I. A study of the continuity of the problem-solving process. *Psychol. Rev.*, 1938, 45, 107-33.

POSTMAN, L. One-trial learning. In C. N. COFER & B. S. MUSGRAVE (Eds.), *Verbal behavior and learning: Problems and processes.* New York: McGraw-Hill, 1963.

RESTLE, F. Significance of all-or-none learning. *Psychol. Bull.*, 1965, 64, 313-25.

RITCHIE, B. F. Concerning an incurable vagueness in psychological theories. In WOLMAN, B. B., & NAGEL, E. (Eds.), *Scientific psychology.* New York: Basic Books, 1965. Pp. 150-65.

SPENCE, K. W. An experimental test of the continuity and non-continuity theories of discrimination learning. *J. exp. Psychol.*, 1945, 35, 253-66.

16 / The Role of Repetition in Associative Learning *

IRVIN ROCK, *New School for Social Research*

Although repetition has long been regarded as essential in associative learning, there is some doubt as to how it achieves its beneficial effects. One possibility is that, in learning a list of items, the strength of association between each pair develops gradually, with each repetition adding an increment to the bond, until it is so strong that the first item produces recall of the second. According to this interpretation, repetition is a factor in the *formation* of associations. Another possibility is that repetition is essential because only a limited number of associations can be formed on any one trial. On each new encounter with a list of items we learn new ones, until finally we have learned them all. From this point of view, associations are formed in one trial, and improvement with repetition is only an artifact of work with long lists of items. Typical behavior in experiments on rote learning and in examples from everyday life indicate that some associations are formed in one trial, but such evidence does not prove conclusively that associations are not ordinarily formed by a process of gradual strengthening.

If associations are formed by a process of gradual strengthening based on repetition, it should be easier to form an association between items which have already been presented together on one or more previous trials, but which S has not yet been able to get right, than between items presented together for the first time. There are several ways of testing this assumption, but the method used in the experiments to be reported here seems most direct. A control group is given the task of learning a list of paired associates to a criterion of one errorless trial. An experimental group is handicapped by removing all pairs which S fails to get right after every trial and substituting new pairs for them. The new pairs are randomly selected from a pool of pairs prepared in advance and from which the initial lists for the two groups also are randomly selected. This means that the experimental group always has the same number of pairs to learn on any given trial—the same number as has the control group—but only some of them will have been seen previously (those already learned) and some will never have been seen previously. Training of the experimental group also is continued to a criterion of one errorless trial.

For the experimental group, then, a pair is either learned the first time it is seen, or it is removed, and S does not, therefore, have what might be presumed

From the *American Journal of Psychology*, 1957, 70, 186-93, with permission of the author and publisher.
* Received for publication May 29, 1956. The author is indebted to Mr. Walter Heimer for assistance in this study and to the many students and colleagues who helped in its course.

to be the benefit of repetition in *forming* associations. If a pair is learned on that first occasion, it will remain in the list as long as S continues to get it right. Thus pairs successfully mastered on one trial are repeated, but the repetition does not affect the formation of associations, although S gains whatever benefit may accrue from repetition *after* associations are formed. This critical distinction between the role of repetition in forming associations and the role in fixing or reinforcing associations already formed will be discussed later. For the present, it suffices to say that the experimental group has to form associations without benefit of repetition.

EXPERIMENT I

Method. Two groups, of 25 college students each, were required to learn a list of 12 letter-number pairs, which were printed on 3×5 in. cards. The left-hand member of each pair was either a letter of the alphabet or a double-letter. The right-hand member was a number from 1 to 50, since 50 such card-pairs were prepared corresponding to the 25 letters and double-letters, excluding the letter *I*. (The reason for using this type of pair will be discussed below.) The numbers were assigned to the letters by means of a table of random numbers, and the 12 pairs to be used for each S were randomly selected by shuffling. In the case of Ss in the experimental group, the remaining 38 cards were available as a pool from which new ones could be selected to replace unlearned pairs after each trial. It was thought unlikely that there would be a need for more than 38 substitute-pairs.

A metronome was used to time a 3-sec. exposure of each card and a 5-sec. interval between successive cards. S was instructed to associate the letter or letters on each card with the number, and that the serial order of cards would be randomly changed from trial to trial. In view of the procedure used with the experimental group (to eliminate a sense of surprise and lack of understanding of the task which might otherwise be expected), S was told in advance that new

pairs might be shown from trial to trial, although the total number would remain the same, and that it was his task to try to learn all those shown at any time.

A recall-test for paired associates was used after every trial. On the back of every card was printed only the first item of the letter-number pair. The 12 cards used in that learning trial were therefore reversed, shuffled, and presented at the rate of one every 5 sec., S's task being to respond with the correct number. In the case of the experimental group, the cards were sorted in two piles as S responded, depending upon whether he was right or wrong. New cards were then substituted for the wrong ones, and these were shuffled together with the right ones in preparation for the next trial. There was a 30-sec. interval between each test-trial and the subsequent learning trial.

After about three-fourths of the Ss had been tested, it was noted that the average first-trial performance of the experimental group was higher than that of the control group. To correct for this sampling error, the remaining Ss were not assigned to a group until they had completed the first trial. Those doing relatively well (four or more pairs correct) were then assigned to the control group and those doing relatively poorly (three or fewer correct) were assigned to the experimental group. Since the procedure is the same for both groups for the first trial, this was a perfectly good way of equating the groups. The result was that the two groups as finally constituted had virtually identical scores on the first trial.

Results.—It turned out that the number of extra pairs available for substitution in the lists of the experimental group was not sufficient in every case. For five Ss, the experiment had to be discontinued because there were insufficient new cards to substitute for unlearned pairs on the last trial given. These Ss were scored 10+ which means that they would have required at least 10 trials to reach the criterion. Similarly, there were three Ss in the control group who did so badly that work with them was discontinued before the criterion was reached, and they too were scored 10+.

The median number of trials to reach the criterion for the two groups was exactly the same; namely, 4.75. The semi-interquartile range also was identical for the two groups; namely, 1.45. If the cases scored as 10+ are excluded, the mean of the control group is 4.55 and the *SD* is 1.9, while the corresponding values for the experimental group are 4.35 and 1.2. As can be seen by inspection, the mean difference falls far short of statistical significance ($t=0.41$). The mean number of errors (no response *plus* wrong answers) to criterion was 17.9 for the control group ($SD=9.9$) and 17.2 for the experimental group ($SD=8.6$), and this difference too lacked statistical significance ($t=0.24$). A plot of the mean number of correct responses per trial yields highly similar curves for the two groups. There was thus no advantage for the control group.

The reason for using letter-number pairs instead of other material, e.g. nonsense-syllable pairs, in the first experiment was as follows. It was thought that, if nonsense-material were used, the control group might have an advantage unrelated to the hypothesis under investigation. Repetition for this group would certainly have had the effect of making each individual item familiar, and there was reason to suppose that it would be easier to form associations between familiar items than between unfamiliar ones, even though the familiar items had never in the past been associated with each other. Since one does not have to learn the items as such if they are familiar, one can concentrate on the associations to be formed. If nothing else, it ought to be easier to *recall* a familiar item than an unfamiliar one. By using pairs of letters and numbers which were already familiar, an attempt was made to eliminate this factor. Of course, even here one might argue that the control group had an advantage because of the additional familiarization in successive

trials with the material used. Nevertheless, the use of familiar material would minimize this factor, and the results suggest that, even if there were such an advantage, its effect was negligible. In using familiar items, however, the problem arises of finding material in sufficient quantity and in other respects suitable for this type of experiment. By using letters and double-letters with numbers, 50 pairs were obtained but, as noted above, even this number turned out to be insufficient. Primarily to overcome this shortcoming, and in spite of the objection mentioned above, it was decided to repeat the experiment with pairs of nonsense-syllables. There is also something to be said for using this more traditional material because of the greater possibility afforded for comparison with previous work.

EXPERIMENT II

Method—The procedure followed that of Experiment I, except that pairs of three-letter nonsense syllables were used. They were taken from Glaze's list of syllables of 47% and 53% association value.[1] Eighty pairs were made up, from which 8 were randomly selected as the starting list for Ss of both groups, and there remained a pool of 72 pairs from which pairs could be randomly drawn as needed to substitute for unlearned pairs in the case of the experimental group. A response was scored correct if S pronounced the syllable correctly, and partially correct responses were scored as wrong. It was not necessary in this experiment to assign Ss to one or the other group after determining their scores for the first trial, because it turned out that performance on this trial was not significantly different for the groups as they were randomly constituted. There were 15 adults of both sexes, mostly college students, in each group.

Results.—In addition to the 30 Ss, there were 8 Ss who did not succeed in learning the list to the criterion, 3 in the control group and 5 in the experimental group. In all these cases, E discontinued the experiment because it was obvious that there was little likelihood that S would master the task in the time available. Several of these Ss were evening-session students tested at night, after work, when they were tired. In a few cases, the students had to return to a class, and therefore could not continue to the criterion, and two were somewhat older people. The pool of 72 pairs turned out to be more than adequate and had nothing to do with the discontinuation of the experiment for the Ss of the experimental group.

Considering first the results for the 15 Ss of each group who did learn, the mean number of trials to reach the criterion turned out to be identical, namely, 8.1. The SD was 3.0 for the control group and 2.4 for the experimental group. The mean number of errors to criterion was 26.7 for the control group (SD = 11.4) and 29.2 for the experimental group (SD = 12.6). The difference is not statistically significant ($t = 0.55$). If the eight Ss who failed to reach the criterion are included, scoring them as 15+, the median number of trials also is identical for the two groups; namely, 8.5. The semi-interquartile range is 3.2 for the control group and 4.2 for the experimental group. The learning curves for the two groups are again similar.

Discussion

There were reasons for expecting superior performance in the control groups of these experiments, entirely apart from the question of repetition. The possible advantage of familiarity, which applies particularly to Experiment II, has been mentioned. A second reason is that a recall test rather than a matching test of recognition was used. In a matching test, S must recognize which item belongs with which, but he does not have the additional task of recalling the second item. He need only recognize it. It is,

therefore, an easier task, and it is reasonable to suppose that the strength of an association must be greater for recall than for matching. If so, there must have been many instances in which the Ss of both groups were scored wrong but would have succeeded in a matching test. In fact, the many cases where S gave a partially correct response (almost the right number in Experiment I or two of the three letters correct in Experiment II), but was scored wrong, point in this direction. No doubt in such cases as well, S would have been correct if he had the advantage of a matching test. This would mean that an association did in fact exist, and the Ss of the experimental groups were penalized by having such pairs eliminated. A matching test was not used because it entailed certain technical difficulties in the case of the experimental groups in view of the unpredictable change of items from trial to trial. That the control groups were not superior despite this possible advantage, however, makes the case against the incremental theory all the stronger.

Another reason that one might have expected superior performance of the control groups relates to the fact that wrong pairs were removed from the list for the experimental groups even if they had been correct on one or more previous trials, although that happened only occasionally (primarily during the first few trials). Since it may be assumed that an association has been formed once S gets a pair correct, it was not necessary to remove these pairs to test the hypothesis under consideration. Doing so consequently constituted something of a very strict procedure for the experimental groups. When the same thing happened to an S in the control group, he had what is no doubt the advantage of being pre-

1. J. A. Glaze, The associative value of nonsense syllables, *J. genet. Psychol.*, 35, 1928, 255-67. Cf. also E. H. Hilgard, Methods and procedures in the study of learning, in S. S. Stevens (ed.), *Handbook of Experimental Psychology*, 1951, 541-4.

sented with the same pair again. If the association continued to exist—and failure on the previous trial was a matter of momentary forgetting—he would not really have to learn the pair. The S in the experimental group, however, had to learn a new pair to take its place. Why the control groups do not learn more rapidly in view of these reasons is not clear, except that apparently they do not add up to an advantage of strength sufficient to reveal itself under the conditions employed.

There is one other difference between the conditions of the two groups which, however, might be said to favor the experimental group. It may be argued that for every S there are certain pairs which are easier to learn than others. That being the case, the easy pairs may be the ones which are learned on any given trial, while the difficult ones are eliminated by a process of "natural selection." The new pairs substituted are not necessarily easy, but the reconstituted list on the whole is not as difficult as that with which the control group is faced on a corresponding trial. It is not easy to deal with this objection experimentally if difficulty is defined idiosyncratically, because the only way of finding out about a pair is to present it to that S for learning. Work on this problem is now in progress. Even if it should turn out, however, that the difficulty factor does work to the advantage of the experimental group, the meaning of such an advantage must be seen in the proper perspective. As things now stand, there are the several factors, mentioned above, which tend to favor the control group, and which ought to counterbalance any such advantage, but even if control of difficulty were to impair the performance of the experimental group to some extent, the question of interpreting the magnitude of the superiority of the control group would remain. One might still be struck by the level of performance

achieved by the experimental group without benefit of repetition.

The present results seem to support the thesis that, in the classical multiple-item learning situation, associations are formed in one trial. Informal observations and introspective reports support this finding. Most Ss succeed in learning only a few pairs per trial, and many do so with the aid of some mnemonic device. The theoretical significance of the widespread use of such devices in rote learning experiments has not been sufficiently emphasized in the past. The successful use of such devices may mean that an idea suddenly occurs to S which enables him to link two items then and there; it has, to some extent, the character of insightful learning. Some Ss concentrate on one or two pairs and hardly even attend to the rest; other Ss do try to learn them all. With or without the use of devices, the difficulty in getting more than a few pairs correct in any one trial has to do with the presence of so many other pairs.

It follows from the argument that repetition is important only for the learning of *additional* associations that in situations with few associations to be formed, repetition would not be required at all. This deduction can easily be tested by presenting Ss with only one pair of items (under conditions of incidental learning which eliminate the possibility of "silent" repetition).[2]

Why, in multiple-item learning situations, it is not possible as a rule to learn more than a few associations on any one trial, remains to be investigated, but the following point must be considered: If, a few seconds after any given pair is exposed during learning, and before the next pair is shown, E were to test for retention, there is little doubt that most Ss would give the correct response.

_____
2. Preliminary results reported by F. B. Springfield (The learning and retention of a single pair of associates, B.A. thesis, New School for Social Research, 1955) indicate that almost all Ss do succeed in establishing an association in one trial.

Would this result not mean that an association was in fact formed, and that the failure to get all items right on a test following the entire series is a matter of forgetting of already formed associations? In that event, one could regard forgetting due to the presence of many items as an instance of retroactive inhibition. According to this conception, repetition would not be required to *form* associations, even in the case of long lists of items, but only to strengthen them sufficiently to resist interference. The present experiments rule out this type of explanation, since Ss do as well with substituted new pairs as with the original ones. It is as if pairs which are not retained by the time of the test leave nothing in the nervous system of any value for future use. The Ss frequently comment spontaneously that they do not recognize the items of a pair which they have seen several times before.

The question is really one of deciding on a criterion for the existence of a formed association. It probably makes more sense—in terms of what we usually mean by associative learning—not to define success by the easy test of immediate memory, but rather by the traditional delayed test. At any rate, it may be said that repetition is required in rote learning, as defined by this latter criterion (the traditional one), because for some as yet unknown reason or reasons the existence of many items interferes with the formation of more than a few associative connections of a nature which is of any value beyond immediate memory. The hypothesis of Von Restorff concerning loss of individuality of traces under conditions of crowding is relevant here, but leaves many questions unanswered.[3]

It seems clear that repetition plays another role in rote learning; namely, that of strengthening or reinforcing associations once they are formed. There is little question that, in everyday life, we have strong associations between items which have been experienced contiguously very often. Experiments on overlearning clearly demonstrate this point, but they do not distinguish between the role of repetition before associations are formed and after they are formed, the impression being that repetition serves continuously to build up the strength of the association from zero-value to a value far in excess of that required for initial recall on the test following the learning trial. The present results show that this is not the case; repetition does not seem to be of value in forming associations. Hence, it must be concluded that, in overlearning, only the repetition *after* the association is formed is effective in strengthening it.

The present findings are certainly compatible with the thesis that an association is essentially the after-effect of an organization of the items during the initial experience.[4] Interestingly enough, however, the exponents of this point of view have never denied the importance of repetition in associative learning, tending to believe that, in the case of nonsense material in monotonous series (as contrasted with meaningful material), repetition is needed to consolidate what would otherwise be very unstable or weak trace-interrelationships.[5] Thus, in the case of rote learning it was implicitly taken for granted that associations are formed by a process of gradual strengthening. On the other hand, the present findings are incompatible with incremental theories, including those which stress the law of effect.

Summary

In two experiments, the learning of paired associates was studied. In each case, the traditional procedure was used

3. Hedwig von Restorff, Ueber die Wirkung von Bereichsbildung im Spurenfeld, *Psychol. Forsch.*, 18, 1933, 299-42.
4. Wolfgang Köhler, On the nature of associations, *Proc. Amer. Phil. Soc.*, 84, 1941, 492.
5. Kurt Koffka, *Principles of Gestalt Psychology*, 1935, 556-71.

for a control group, while for the experimental group unlearned pairs were removed and new ones submitted after each trial. No significant differences in rate of learning were found. This result suggests that repetition plays no role in the formation (as distinct from the strengthening) of associations, other than that of providing the occasion for new ones to be formed, each on a single trial.

17 / Repetition and Paired-associate Learning [*]

LEO POSTMAN, *University of California, Berkeley*

The role of repetition in the formation of verbal associations has recently become the focus of considerable discussion. The issue has been joined between two conceptions of the associative process— growth by successive increments vs. all-or-none change. The incremental theory asserts that each successive trial adds to the strength of an association, provided the conditions required for the reinforcement of a habit are met. If frequency of exposure is considered a sufficient condition of learning, the associations between stimuli and responses should be strengthened during repeated presentations of a list. By contrast, the all-or-none theory asserts that on any one trial associations are either fully formed or do not grow at all.[1] The apparent beneficial effects of repetition apply to the acquisition of a series but not to the formation of individual associations. Only a limited number of associations can be established on a given trial, and successive exposures to the series provide opportunities for increasing numbers of associations to be established, each on a single trial.

The question at issue is not whether a verbal association *can* be learned on a single trial. In experiments on rote-learning correct responses are frequently observed after one exposure to the list. It is consistent with an incremental theory that the rate of growth for some associations is sufficiently rapid to produce a correct response after one trial. The point under dispute is whether *all* associations are formed on a single trial. The disagreement comes to a head when one considers the effects of trials on which S fails to give the correct response. An incremental theory would have to hold that some associative growth occurs on such trials. According to an all-or-none theory, on the other hand, trials resulting in failure contribute nothing to associative growth.

Evidence allegedly supporting the all-or-none theory has been presented in a series of studies by Rock.[2] In the basic experiment on paired-associate learning, Rock compared a control group which learned a constant list of pairs with an experimental group for which all pairs missed on a given test-trial were replaced by new ones. This procedure insured that all pairs mastered by the experimental Ss were learned in one trial whereas the control Ss were exposed

From the *American Journal of Psychology*, 1962, 75, 372-89, with permission of the author and publisher.
[*] This research was facilitated by a grant from the National Science Foundation.
1. For a general discussion of the two positions see W. K. Estes, Learning theory and the new "mental chemistry," *Psychol. Rev.*, 67, 1960, 207-23. Estes identifies reinforcement of a habit with "the operation that is supplied by the experimenter in order to produce learning" (*ibid.*, 209). Under this definition, paired presentation of a stimulus and response constitutes a reinforcement, regardless of S's response.
2. Irvin Rock, The role of repetition in associative learning, this JOURNAL, 70, 1957, 186-93; Irvin Rock and Walter Heimer, Further evidence of one-trial associative learning, this JOURNAL, 72, 1959, 1-16.

repeatedly to each pair. Using both letter-number pairs and pairs of nonsense-syllables, Rock found no differences between the two groups in the number of trials to a criterion of one perfect recitation of the list.[3] Rock concluded from these resutls that repetition does not contribute to the formation of associations.

Rock's findings, at least for the letter-number pairs, have been confirmed by Wogan and Waters, and by Clark, Lansford, and Dallenbach.[4] In discussing these results, both Rock and the other investigators recognized some important sources of bias inherent in the experimental design, and attempts were made to assess the effects of these biases in control-experiments.

A first critical question is whether Rock succeeded in controlling the frequency of repetitions under the conditions of his experiment. The validity of his conclusions hinges on the assumption that each of the pairs learned by the control Ss had been repeated more often. During the training trials each card was exposed for 3 sec., and there was a 5-sec. interval between successive cards. There was an interval of unspecified length between each training trial and test-trial, as well as a 30-sec. interval between each test-trial and subsequent learning trial. Thus, there was considerable opportunity for Ss to rehearse the pairs. To the extent that there was such uncontrolled repetition, the basic conditions of the experiment were not met. Clark, Lansford and Dallenbach report that Ss, in their experiment, used the intervals between exposures to construct and rehearse mnemonic devices; such rehearsal also took place between trials. These investigators also point out that the slow rate of presentation allowed an indeterminate number of repetitions.

To reduce the opportunities for uncontrolled repetition, Clark, Lansford, and Dallenbach performed an additional experiment in which the exposure-time for each pair was reduced to 1 sec., and the interval between successive pairs was eliminated. With a more rapid rate of presentation, the experimental

Ss learned the list significantly faster than did the control Ss. Clark, Lansford, and Dallenbach conclude that uncontrolled rehearsal was not responsible for Rock's results and attribute the reversal to greater intra-list interference for the control group.[5] In a more recent study, Lockhead increased the rate of presentation to 0.75 sec. (with 1.25 sec. between cards) and reduced the inter-trial interval to 12 sec. Under these conditions, he found a highly significant difference in favor of the control group, i.e. constant lists were learned faster than changing lists.[6] Regardless of rate, however, the question remains whether Ss in both groups respond to each pair on each successive training trial. The Ss are instructed to attend to all pairs presented during the training trials but there is no control over their responses. Thus, it would be quite possible for Ss to concentrate on a few pairs at a time, rehearse them and essentially ignore other pairs. Such a procedure would be especially plausible for experimental Ss who know that all pairs which they fail to learn will be removed from the list. This source of error can be reduced by achieving experimental control over Ss' responses during the training trials.

A second difficulty is that the experimental Ss may learn a list of easier items than the control Ss. The removal of all pairs which the experimental S fails to learn on a given trial certainly provides an opportunity for the selection of relatively easy items. Rock and Heimer report an experiment which was designed to determine whether the selection of items gives an advantage to the experimental group.[7] In the first phase of this experiment, the Ss were given one expo-

3. Rock, op. cit., 187-90.
4. Michael Wogan and R. H. Waters, The role of repetition in learning, this JOURNAL, 72, 1959, 612-13; and L. L. Clark, T. G. Lansford, and K. M. Dallenbach, Repetition and associative learning, this JOURNAL, 73, 1960, 22-40. A more recent study (J. C. Reed and W. D. Riach, The role of repetition and set in paired-associative learning, this JOURNAL, 73, 1960, 608-11) shows that Rock's results may be peculiar to the nature of the instructions used in his experiment. The control group was told to associate stimuli and responses whereas the experimental group was instructed to learn all the pairs shown on a given trial. When the instructions were equalized, the experimental groups made more errors than the control group.
5. Clark, Lansford, and Dallenbach, op. cit., 35-8.
6. G. R. Lockhead, A re-evaluation of evidence of one-trial associative learning, this JOURNAL, 74, 590-96.
7. Rock and Heimer, op. cit., 9-13.

sure to 7 paired numbers followed by a matching test in which each stimulus was presented along with all the responses included in the list. In the second phase, a list of 12 paired numbers was presented 4 times, and a matching test was again used to measure learning. In the final phase of the experiment, only those Ss were used who had learned no fewer than 2 but no more than 3 pairs of the short list, and no fewer than 3 but no more than 8 pairs of the long list. On a final critical trial these Ss were exposed to a list of 8 pairs, 4 from the short list and 4 from the long list, all of which they had failed to learn previously. These two sets of 4 pairs were said to be of equal difficulty since each was drawn from the most difficult two-thirds of a prior list. In spite of the difference in the frequency of prior exposure, the two kinds of pairs were recalled equally well.

This procedure failed in its purpose of controlling the difficulty of the pairs for several reasons. (1) It is not reasonable to treat as equivalent the "most difficult two-thirds" of lists unequal in length and exposed for different numbers of trials. Rate of learning varies inversely with length of list.[8] One certainly cannot compensate for the length-difficulty relationship by a difference in the number of trials and then treat this same difference as the independent variable in assessing the effects of repetition on items said to be of equal difficulty. (2) A matching test on which both the stimuli and the correct responses are presented, the latter repeatedly, provides considerable opportunity both for rehearsal and for increases in intraserial interference. The magnitudes of these effects may have differed for the long and short lists. (3) The long list was learned after the short list. With highly similar materials this sequence of tasks probably produced associative and proactive inhibition of the second list as well as retroactive inhibition of the first list. The relative amount of these interferences are not known. (4) "A considerable number" of Ss was dropped from the experiment because of failure to meet the criteria on the first two lists (2/7 and 3/12). Thus, if any conclusions can be drawn from this experiment, they would be limited to fast learners.

Clark, Lansford, and Dallenbach used a different procedure to evaluate the possible bias introduced by the selection of items.[9] One week after serving in a replication of Rock's first study, both experimental and control Ss learned a second list by the conventional method (i.e. without replacement of failed items). The materials presented to each experimental S consisted of the first 12 pairs which he had failed to learn during the first part of the experiment and which had, therefore, been dropped from his list after a single trial. The control Ss learned a list selected at random from the pool of letter-number pairs.[10] Since the lists of the experimental Ss were selected for difficulty whereas the lists of the control Ss were chosen haphazardly, a difference in favor of the latter might be expected. However, the number of trials to criterion on the second list was identical for the two groups. Clark, Lansford and Dallenbach conclude that idiosyncratic differences in difficulty among the pairs cannot account for either Rock's or their results.

Both the experiments which we have discussed used failure to be learned on the first few trials as the criterion of the difficulty of a pair. A supplementary, and perhaps more direct, attack on the problem of item-selection is to ask whether the total list finally mastered by an experimental S is easier than that of a control S. A study by Underwood, Rehula, and Keppel using this design with lists of letter-number pairs presents clear-cut evidence for the selection of easy items by the experimental Ss.[11] The present study uses such a design with lists of nonsense-syllables.

Still another difficulty which complicates comparisons between the experimental and control groups in Rock's design concerns the conditions of intra-list interference. Intra-list errors, particularly misplaced responses, account for a substantial proportion of fail-

8. J. A. McGeoch and A. L. Irion, *The Psychology of Human Learning*, 1952, 489 ff.
9. Clark, Lansford, and Dallenbach, *op. cit.*, 26-35.
10. Immediately after completion of the first part of the experiment, that list had been presented to the control Ss and after a recall-test had been followed by a supplementary list of 12 new pairs. The purpose of this procedure was to equalize prior experience and retroactive interference for the two test-lists.
11. B. J. Underwood, Robert Rehula, and Geoffrey Keppel, Item-selection in paired-associate learning, this JOURNAL, 75, 1962, 353-71.

ures in paired-associate learning. Such errors may be quite persistent, especially when stimulus-similarity is high. The removal of all pairs which S does not learn in a single trial may systematically reduce the extent of intra-list interference. Rock and Heimer describe an experiment in which they attempted to check on this possibility.[12] Instead of removing the pairs which S failed to learn on a given trial, these investigators interchanged the response-terms of all such pairs. Although such a procedure is conducive to intra-list interference, the new experimental group did not differ from the control group in the original study. These results cannot be considered conclusive. The procedure used by Rock and Heimer does not control the conditions of rehearsal, nor does it eliminate the possibility that experimental Ss selectively learn relatively easy pairs. Furthermore, the pattern of stimulus-response pairs changes from trial to trial, so that there is an opportunity for the selection of relatively easy *lists*. In contrast to the findings of Rock and Heimer, the results of Clark, Lansford, and Dallenbach indicate that intra-list interference is, indeed, greater for the control group than for the experimental group. Although there was no significant difference in the number of trials to criterion, the rate of errors was higher for control than experimental Ss, as was the probability of failures following a correct response.[13]

Rock has called attention to the fact that there are other possible biases in his procedure which give an advantage to the control group.[14] First, the opportunities for familiarization with the stimuli and responses are greater with a constant than a changing list. The difference between the experimental and control groups was, however, no greater with nonsense-syllables than with familiar letters and numbers. Secondly, in most of the critical comparisons between the two groups a recall-test was used which required greater associative strength than, say, a matching test. An easier test might have revealed the presence of associations where the recall-test did not. Rock suggests that the experimental groups "were penalized by having such pairs eliminated." The point is not obvious since an easier test would presumably have improved the scores of both

groups. Finally, missed pairs were removed from the list of an experimental S even if the failure was preceded by one or more correct responses. Thus, experimental Ss were penalized for momentary oscillations whereas control Ss were not. Rock states that such cases occurred only occasionally, and it should be possible to estimate the magnitude of the bias introduced by this procedure.

It is clear that the problems of control and interpretation in these experiments are exceedingly complex. Rock is disposed to argue that the biases operating for and against the experimental groups should balance each other. Even if they do not, "one might still be struck by the level of performance achieved by the experimental group without benefit of repetition."[15] It is difficult, however, to base any conclusions on either the absolute level of performance or the differences between the experimental and control groups as long as the magnitudes of the various biases are not known.

The purpose of the present study is to determine whether Rock's results obtained with lists of paired nonsense-syllables may reasonably be attributed to artifacts of procedure. When such materials are used, the mastery of the list requires the learning of unfamiliar responses as well as the association of these responses with the prescribed stimuli. Under these conditions the control group has a clear advantage since the integration of responses should be favored by repetition. Rock found that in spite of this bias the control group did not learn faster than the experimental group, and this finding was interpreted by him as strong evidence for one-trial learning. Actually, the lack of a difference is puzzling even if the one-trial hypothesis is assumed to be correct—since response-learning as well as association would appear to be independent of repetition.

12. Rock and Heimer, *op. cit.*, 1-5.
13. Clark, Lansford, and Dallenbach, *op. cit.*, 29-31.
14. Rock, *op. cit.*, 190 f.
15. *Ibid.*, 191.

Thus, it becomes important to assess the influence of some of the variables which remained uncontrolled in Rock's experiment. Our special concern will be with Ss' response to the list during the training trials and with a further assessment of experimental Ss.

METHOD

General. Two experiments were performed in which Rock's method of investigating one-trial learning was used. The major deviations from Rock's original procedure were (a) During the training trials the Ss were required to spell both stimuli and responses aloud. Thus, Ss were prevented from attending selectively to a few pairs at a time—a mode of attack which was possible under the conditions of the earlier studies. (b) Two Control Groups were included in the experimental design. Control Group I learned the lists presented initially to the Experimental Ss and thus corresponded to the control groups in Rock's studies. Control Group II learned the lists finally mastered by the Experimental Ss. A comparison between the two Control Groups permits a direct evaluation of the success of the Experimental Ss in selecting relatively easy pairs, at least to the extent that the basis of selection was not idiosyncratic.

These modifications of Rock's design were used in both the present experiments. The procedure used on the test-trials differed in the two experiments. In Experiment I, the Ss were reinforced on the test-trials, i.e., the correct pair was presented at the end of each anticipation-interval. This method of testing corresponds to that used in conventional studies of paired-associate learning. It has the advantage of counter-acting the fixation of errors during the test-trials. The correction of errors may be especially beneficial to Experimental Ss who are subject to cumulative associative interferences from discarded items. On the other hand, a second exposure to failed pairs may produce some learning which would be to the advantage of the Control Ss but might interfere with the acquisition of new pairs by the Experimental Ss. In view of these considerations no correction was given on the test-

trials of Experiment II.[16] A comparison between the two experiments will make it possible to assess the effects of correction.

Materials. Each S learned a list of eight paired nonsense-syllables. Syllables with association-values of 40.0%, 46.7%, 53.3% and 60.0% were used.[17] A total of 202 pairs was constructed. Stimuli and responses were drawn at random from the pool of syllables, with the restriction that the two members of a pair have no letters in common. The syllables were typed in capitals on white cards 3×5 in. in size. The stimulus and response appeared together on one side of the card, and the stimulus only on the other side.

Experimental design. The design for both experiments comprised 18 blocks of 3 Ss— one member each of the Experimental Group and Control Groups I and II per block. A different initial list, drawn at random from the pool of pairs, was used for each Experimental S. Pairs failed on a test-trial were replaced by new ones, also drawn at random, on the next training trial. Within each block, the member of Control Group I learned the initial list of the Experimental S, and the member of Control Group II learned the list on which the Experimental S reached the criterion of one perfect recitation. If the Experimental S failed to reach criterion, the list yielding the highest number of correct responses was used. If the highest score occurred on more than one trial, the earliest of these trials was used for selection of the list. The list of pairs remained constant, of course, for both Control Groups.

The member of Control Group II had to be run after the Experimental S. Thus, there were three possible orders of assignment to conditions within a block. The 18 blocks of the experiments were subdivided into 6 subgroups of 3 blocks each. Within a sub-group of blocks, each of the orders of assignment was used once, the sequence of orders being

16. It is not clear whether correction was given on the test-trials in Rock's first experiments. No reference to a correction is made in the original report. However, in describing a study which is said to have followed the original procedure in all respects, Rock and Heimer state that S was told whether he was right or wrong (*op. cit.*, 3).
17. The number of stimuli and responses of each association-value varied from S to S but tended to be proportional to the frequencies of these values in Glaze's norms. See J. A. Glaze, The association value of nonsense syllables, *J. genet. Psychol.*, 35, 263-64.

determined by a table of random numbers. Thus, each sub-group of 3 blocks constituted a complete replication of the experiment. All Ss were undergraduate students who did not know the purpose of the experiment.

Procedure. The instructions described the procedures of training and testing and also included a statement that some of the pairs might be replaced in the course of the experiment. The same instructions were given to all Ss, so that the groups did not differ in their initial set.

During the training trials each pair was presented for 6 sec., during which Ss spelled both the stimulus and the response letter by letter. A longer exposure was used than in the earlier studies in order to allow Ss adequate time to spell both members. The Ss readily adopted the appropriate rhythm so that each period of exposure was entirely filled by the spelling of the two syllables. The interval between successive pairs was 3 sec. There was an interval of 45 sec. between training trials and test-trials, during which the stimulus-cards were shuffled and

sented. In Experiment II no correction was given, and a new stimulus was presented 3 sec. after the end of the anticipation-interval.

Practice was continued to a criterion of one perfect recitation or for 12 trials, whichever took the longer. If S failed to reach criterion on the 16th test-trial, the experiment was discontinued. Thus, data from all Ss are available for 12 trials, regardless of whether and how fast they reached criterion.

RESULTS

(1) Learning to criterion. In Experiment I, 10 Ss in the Experimental Group, 17 Ss in Control Group I and all 18 Ss in Control Group II reached the criterion of one perfect recitation. The proportion of Ss reaching criterion is significantly lower in the Experimental Group than in the combined Control Groups ($\chi^2 = 12.15$, $df = 1$, $p < 0.01$).

The median numbers of trials to criterion are shown in Table I. The rate of

TABLE I. *Summary of learning scores*

Condition	Trials to criterion		Correct on Trials 1–12		Length integrative stage°	Length associative stage†
	Mdn	Q	M	SD		
Experiment I:						
Experimental	11.5	—‡	42.2	25.7	—	—
Control I	9.0	3.5	58.6	18.0	4.2	0.5
Control II	7.0	3.0	68.1	13.7	3.6	0.2
Experiment II:						
Experimental	>15.0	—‡	30.7	21.1	—	—
Control I	8.5	3.2	58.6	14.3	4.2	0.3
Control II	10.0	—‡	56.4	16.1	4.4	0.3

° Mean trial on which correct responses were first given anywhere in the list.
† Mean number of trials separating first occurrence of correct response anywhere and first correct anticipation.
‡ Indeterminate since 4 or more Ss failed to reach criterion.

the new order of presentation recorded by E. There was also a 45-sec. interval between a test-trial and subsequent training trial during which the cards were again shuffled and the necessary substitutions were made in the case of the Experimental Ss.

In both experiments a 3-sec. interval of anticipation was used on the test-trials, during which the stimulus-member of the pair was presented to S. In Experiment I each anticipation-interval was followed by a 3-sec. presentation of the correct pair, and 3 sec. thereafter the next test-stimulus was pre-

learning was slowest for the Experimental Group, and Control Group II surpassed Control Group I. Friedman's ranked analysis of variance shows the variation among the groups to be highly significant ($\chi^2 = 14.04$, $df = 2$, $p < 0.01$).[18] When the sign-test is used for individual comparisons, each group is found to differ significantly from the other two ($p = 0.05$ or less).

18. Frank Wilcoxon, *Some Rapid Approximate Statistical Procedures*, 1949, 7 f.

In Experiment II, 9 Ss in the Experimental Group, 15 Ss in Control Group I and 14 Ss in Control Group II reached criterion. The difference between the proportions of Ss in the Experimental Group and the combined Control Groups is again significant ($\chi^2 = 4.01$, $df = 1$, $0.02 < p < 0.05$).

The median numbers of trials to criterion in Experiment II are presented in Table I. The median score of the Experimental Group could not be determined exactly since half the Ss failed to reach criterion; it is, therefore, listed as > 15 (the score of the slowest S to reach criterion was 15). The Experimental Group again learned much more slowly than the Control Groups. However, the difference between the two Control Groups found in Experiment I is no longer present. The median of Control Group II is, in fact, slightly higher than that of Control Group I. The variations among groups is again significant by ranked analysis of variance ($\chi^2 = 6.24$, $df = 2$, $0.02 < p < 0.05$).[19] Sign-tests show the Experimental Group to differ significantly from both Control Groups ($p = 0.05$), whereas the difference between the latter is not significant.

(2) *Learning curves.* Fig. 1 shows the mean numbers of correct responses on the first 12 test-trials in Experiment I. The differences on Trial 1 are not significant. The three groups are clearly separated thereafter. The Experimental Group progressed most slowly and Control Group II fastest, with Control Group I occupying an intermediate position. The mean numbers of correct anticipations given during the 12 trials are shown in Table I. The Experimental Group not only gave fewer correct responses, but also was considerably more variable, than the Control Groups. Since there was significant heterogeneity of variance, nonparametric tests were used to evaluate the differences in the numbers of correct anticipations. The variation among the

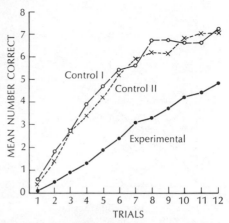

FIG. 1. Mean numbers of correct responses on Trials 1-12 in Experiment I.

groups is highly significant, as tested by a ranked analysis of variance ($\chi^2 = 12.36$, $df = 2$, $p < 0.01$). According to Wilcoxon's test for signed ranks, each group differs significantly from the other two at the 5% level or better.

The learning curves for Experiment II are shown in Fig. 2. The differences on Trial 1 are again not significant. As in Experiment I, the rate of improvement is clearly slowest for the Experimental Group. In contrast to the earlier results, however, the curves of the two Control Groups overlap closely. The mean numbers of correct anticipations are presented in Table I. Ranked analysis of variance again shows the variation among groups to be significant ($\chi^2 = 12.12$, $df = 2$, $p < 0.01$). The Experimental Group differs significantly from both Control Groups ($p < 0.01$ as determined by tests for signed ranks). There is no reliable difference between the two Control Groups.

Attention has been called to the fact that Experimental Ss are penalized by the procedure of removing failed pairs

---

19. In a few cases, two Ss in the same block failed to reach criterion. Ranks were then assigned on the basis of the highest criterion reached in learning. In the two cases involving an Experimental and Control S these criteria were 1 and 6, and 2 and 7, respectively.

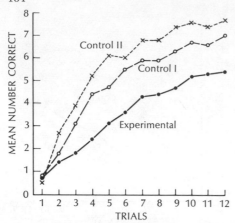

FIG. 2. Mean numbers of correct responses on Trials 1-12 in Experiment II.

which had been given correctly on earlier trials. To correct for this bias in the learning scores, an additional analysis of the data on acquisition was made. Table II shows the mean cumulative number of *different* correct responses given on Trials 1-12. In this tabulation,

the Control Groups. The two Control Groups differed only in Experiment I. Comparison between the two experiments indicates that the change from correction to non-correction during the test-trials was more detrimental to the Experimental Group than to Control Group I. The increase in the difference between the Experimental Group and Control Group I was accompanied by the loss of advantage for Control Group II.

(3) *Stage-analysis.* Since a significant difference between the two Control Groups was found in Experiment I, the question arises as to the specific characteristics of acquisition which are responsible for this difference. A stage-analysis was, therefore, performed on the data of the Control Groups in both experiments. In such an analysis, a distinction is made between two stages of acquisition, viz. (a) the integrative stage, and (b) the associative stage.[20] During the integrative stage the prescribed units are integrated

TABLE II. *Mean cumulative numbers of different correct responses on Trials 1-12*

Condition	Trial											
	1	2	3	4	5	6	7	8	9	10	11	12
Experiment I:												
Experimental	0.7	1.7	2.2	3.0	3.7	4.4	5.1	5.5	5.9	6.4	6.6	6.8
Control I	0.6	1.9	3.5	4.9	5.6	6.1	6.6	6.8	7.2	7.4	7.6	7.6
Control II	0.5	2.7	4.3	5.5	6.6	7.1	7.5	7.7	7.7	7.8	7.8	7.9
Experiment II:												
Experimental	0.2	0.7	1.4	1.7	2.4	3.2	4.1	4.7	5.2	5.7	6.0	6.4
Control I	0.6	1.8	2.9	4.3	5.5	6.3	6.9	7.1	7.2	7.3	7.3	7.4
Control II	0.4	1.4	2.9	4.2	5.1	5.9	6.7	7.1	7.3	7.6	7.6	7.8

Ss are given credit for each new correct response, regardless of whether or not it was given correctly again on subsequent trials. This analysis provides the most direct and unbiased test of the effects of repetition since it reflects the rate at which *new* associations are added under the various conditions. It is clear that the picture is the same as that obtained by the conventional method of scoring— the Experimental Group consistently falls below the Control Groups.

All the analyses agree in showing that in both experiments the Experimental Group learned much more slowly than

and become available as responses to S. The duration of this stage is estimated by the number of the trial on which a response is first given regardless of whether or not it is paired with the correct stimulus. The duration of the associative stage is estimated by the number of trials that elapse between the time the response is first given and the time it is paired with the correct stimulus. The two stages undoubtedly overlap, and there is good reason to believe that the integrative stage continues beyond the point of first

20. See B. J. Underwood and R. W. Schulz, *Meaningfulness and Verbal Learning*, 1960, 92-4.

correct association. However, the two indices make it possible to assess the relative importance of the two stages for different materials and conditions. Table I shows that in Experiment I there is a

were, however, substantial differences among the groups in the distribution of overt errors. Table III shows the mean percentages of the various classes of overt errors. The percentage of misplaced

TABLE III. *Mean percentages of different types of overt errors*

Condition	Misplaced responses	Stimulus-intrusions	Mixed errors	Partial responses
Experiment I:				
Experimental	19.7	3.0	56.7	20.6
Control I	39.9	8.9	38.6	12.6
Control II	26.7	3.8	52.6	16.9
Experiment II:				
Experimental	13.9	4.6	72.3	9.2
Control I	31.8	2.1	55.5	10.6
Control II	30.5	5.3	51.5	12.6

difference in favor of Control Group II in both stages of learning. However, by Wilcoxon's test for signed ranks only the difference in the duration of the associative stage is significant ($p < .05$). Thus, there appears to have been selection of pairs for ease of association, and probably for availability of responses. In Experiment II, the two Control Groups are all but indistinguishable by either measure.

(4) *Distribution of errors.* Incorrect responses were classified into failures to respond and overt errors. The latter were in turn divided into (a) misplaced responses, (b) stimulus-intrusions, (c) mixed errors, and (d) partial responses. A misplaced response occurred when a correct syllable was given to an inappropriate stimulus. An error was classified as a stimulus-intrusion when one of the stimuli in the list was given as a response. Mixed errors include all three-letter responses which were not items in the list. Partial responses consisted of either one or two letters.

For each S, the number of overt errors was expressed as a percentage of the total number of incorrect responses. In Experiment I, the mean percentage of overt errors was 49.0 for the Experimental Group, 41.3 for Control Group I, and 42.4 for Control II. Thus, the relative frequencies of overt errors were comparable for the three groups. There

responses is highest for Control Group I and lowest for the Experimental Group. Control Group II occupies an intermediate position but is closer to the Experimental Group than to the other Control Group. The pattern is the same for stimulus-intrusions although such errors occurred rarely. Mixed errors and partial errors occurred with relatively higher frequency for the Experimental Group and Control Group II than for Control Group I.

The variation in the percentage of misplaced responses is significant, as tested by ranked analysis of variance ($\chi^2 = 11.36$, $df = 2$, $p < 0.01$). Tests for signed ranks show that Control Group I differs from both the other groups at the 1% level. The difference between the Experimental Group and Control Group II is not significant.

In Experiment II, the relative frequency of overt errors was somewhat lower than in Experiment I but again comparable for the three groups. The mean percentage of overt errors was 38.7 for the Experimental Group, 36.7 for Control Group I, and 38.0 for Control Group II. The distributions of overt errors are presented in Table III. The percentage of misplaced responses is considerably lower for the Experimental Group than for both Control Groups. For mixed errors, the differences are in the opposite direction. The distributions of errors for the two Control Groups are quite similar. The significance of the differences in the percentages of misplaced responses was tested as before. The overall variation is significant ($\chi^2 = 8.36$, $df = 2$, $0.01 < p < 0.02$), and the Experimental Group differs significantly from Control Group I ($p < 0.01$) and Control Group II ($p < 0.05$).

(5) *Evidence for selection of items.* In the present design, the extent to which the Experimental Ss succeeded in select-

Groups are made *ex post facto,* and any conclusions drawn from the analysis are therefore, highly tentative.

The lists learned by the two Control Groups were compared on two task-variables, viz. (i) mean association-value and (ii) intra-list similarity. Each characteristic was evaluated separately for stimuli and responses. Table IV shows the distributions of differences between the two Control Groups on each characteristic, i.e. the frequency with which Control Group II was superior, equal, and inferior, to Control Group I.

TABLE IV. *Distribution of differences between lists of Control Groups I and II*
(Entries are numbers of cases)

Variable	Experiment I			Experiment II		
	CII>CI	CII=CI	CII<CI	CII>CI	CII=CI	CII<CI
Mean association-value of stimuli	11	—	7	13	—	5
Mean association-value of responses	15	—	3	8	1	9
Number different letters in stimuli	6	5	7	7	4	7
Number different letters in responses	10	2	6	7	—	11

ing relatively easy lists is gauged by a comparison of the two Control Groups. A difference in favor of Control Group II points to a systematic selection of items or lists. According to this criterion, there was systematic selection of items in Experiment I but not in Experiment II. Two problems now require attention: (a) the probable bases of selection where it did occur, and (b) the reason for the difference between the two experiments.

(a) *Characteristics of selected items.* A comparison of the lists learned by the two Control Groups may provide some information about the nature of the items selected by the Experimental Ss. Such an analysis is limited by the fact that about half the Experimental Ss failed to reach criterion. In such cases whatever selection occurred was only partial. The findings concerning the characteristics of selected items remain essentially the same, however, whether the entire Control Groups are considered or only those blocks in which the Experimental S reached criterion. Hence the tabulations to be presented below include the data for all Ss. It must be emphasized that the comparisons between the lists of the two Control

The opportunity for selection of items on the basis of association-value was limited since the total range of variation was between 40% and 60%. The distributions of differences in Table IV suggest that there was some selection of stimuli for association-value, especially in Experiment II. Selection of responses for association-value appears to have occurred in Experiment I but not in Experiment II. It is known that learning is influenced much more by meaningfulness of responses than of stimuli. Hence a larger difference in speed of learning between the two Control Groups would be expected in Experiment I than in Experiment II. The results are consistent with this expectation.

For both stimuli and responses, the number of different letters making up the eight items was used as the index of intra-list similarity. There is little evidence for systematic reduction in intra-list similarity, with the possible exception of response-similarity in Experiment I. In the learning of nonsense-syllables, similarity of responses has less pronounced effects than similarity of stimuli, and it is doubtful that it was an important basis of selection in Experiment I.

The one hypothesis which is clearly suggested by the comparison of the initial and terminal lists is the selection of pairs for meaningfulness of responses. The results of the stage-analysis are consistent with this hypothesis.

(b) Conditions of selection. There is some evidence for selection of items in Experiment I but not in Experiment II. This discrepancy between the two experiments, which had not been expected, cannot be attributed to the difference between the two Experimental Groups in speed of learning. The mean criteria finally reached, and hence the numbers of correct items used in the construction of the lists for Control Group II, were comparable in the two experiments —6.1 in Experiment I and 6.0 in Experiment II. The selection of items occurred later in Experiment II, but the opportunities for detecting the presence of selected items were equal in the two cases.

One possible reason for the apparent failure of selection in Experiment II may be a higher level of cumulative inter-trial interference in the absence of correction. For purposes of estimating the relative amounts of inter-trial interference for the two Experimental groups, a new analysis of errors was made. We considered all misplaced responses and stimulus-intrusions on the trials up to the terminal criterion, including errors from inside the list and from prior lists. The percentages of such errors coming from prior lists was 22.8 in Experiment I, and 36.1 in Experiment II. The contribution of inter-trial interference to other overt errors and failures to respond cannot be assessed, but these percentages suggest that it may well have been greater in Experiment II. Thus, the acquisition of new items in Experiment II may have been determined more by the conditions of inter-trial interference than by the intrinsic difficulty of the items themselves. Selection of items on this basis would, of course, not be reflected in the performance of Control Group II.

There may, of course, be other reasons for the discrepancy between the two experiments, nor can the possibility of a chance difference be discarded. The question can be settled only by manipulating the opportunities for selection systematically under different conditions of learning.

Discussion

Under the conditions of the present study the Experimental Group learned significantly more slowly than the Control Groups. Thus, the results are clearly contrary to those of Rock. If the earlier results are interpreted as positive evidence for the hypothesis of one-trial learning, that interpretation is called in question by our findings.

The major difference between Rock's procedure and ours lies in the control over Ss' responses during training. In Rock's experiment Ss merely observed the pairs; in the present study they were required to spell both stimuli and responses. The requirement that S respond overtly to each pair during training insures that the effective length of the list is the same for all Ss in both the Experimental and Control Groups. Without such a requirement, S can vary the number of pairs which he reads and rehearses at will from trial to trial. It is reasonable to assume that under Rock's conditions such selective rehearsal will occur more often in the Experimental Group than in the Control Group, especially when the learning materials are unfamiliar and difficult. Since time-per-item increases with length of list, the Experimental Group would have an advantage. The requirement of overt responses to each pair also reduces the opportunities for uncontrolled repetition of those pairs S is attempting to learn. In the present experiments such rehearsal remained possible, however, during the intervals separating training trials and test-trials.

The probable importance of uncontrolled rehearsal is indicated by a comparison between the corresponding groups in Rock's study using nonsense-syllables and the present Experiment II (in which the procedure was essentially similar to Rock's). In Rock's experiment the median number of trials to criterion was the same for both groups, viz. 8.5. In our Experiment II, the median of Control Group I was identical with that obtained by Rock, i.e. 8.5. On the other hand, the median of the Experimental Group exceeded 15 trials, with half the Ss failing to reach criterion. It is fair to conclude that our Ss in Control Group I behaved very much like Rock's, whereas our Experimental Ss clearly did not.

The analysis of errors supports the conclusion that the course of learning was essentially different for the Experimental and Control Groups. The Control Ss consistently gave a higher percentage of misplaced responses than did the Experimental Ss. The relative frequency of such errors is known to vary directly as a function of familiarization with the responses in a list of paired associates.[21] It is likely that the differences in the percentages of misplaced responses reflect a higher degree of response-learning by the Control Ss. In Experiment I, Control Group II gave relatively fewer misplaced responses than Control Group I. This finding points to selection of items for ease of associative connection. The results of the stage-analysis support these conclusions.

A significant difference in favor of the Control Groups is obtained whether or not correction is used on the test-trials. It had appeared possible that correction on the test-trials might bias the results against the Experimental Group since a second exposure to failed items could interfere with the acquisition of new pairs. The results suggest that correction reduced the fixation of errors and hence the amount of interference from prior discarded items. Thus, the net effect of correction seems to have been beneficial to the Experimental Group. The critical fact is, of course, that the differences between the Experimental Group and the Control Groups are significant in both experiments. Moreover, the size of the difference between the Experimental Group and Control Group II, which corrects for whatever normative selec-

tion of items does occur, is almost identical in the two cases. As measured by the mean numbers of correct responses on Trials 1-12 (Table I), this difference is 26.1 in Experiment I, and 26.3 in Experiment II.

The findings concerning the systematic selection of items by the Experimental Ss are ambiguous. Evidence for such selection, possibly based on meaningfulness of the responses, was obtained in Experiment I but not in Experiment II. It is obvious that the specific conditions under which the Experimental Ss are trained and tested will influence the amount and kind of selection that will occur. Analysis of the errors suggests that without correction cumulative interference from discarded prior items may become decisive in the selection of items, at the expense of relatively small variations in meaningfulness. Whether or not selection occurs, it fails to overcome the significant advantage of Control Group I over the Experimental Group. The same conclusion applies to possible selections based on idiosyncratic factors which could not be assessed in this study.

The results of the experiments throw serious doubt on the validity of Rock's evidence for one-trial learning, at least as far as his findings with nonsense-syllables are concerned. Our results cannot be interpreted, however, as evidence against the hypothesis or in favor of incremental theory. There is every reason to believe that the superiority of the Control Groups is at least in part a function of the degree of response-learning. With repeated presentations, responses become increasingly well integrated and available for association. We referred earlier to the distinction between the integrative and associative stages of learning. Rock's procedure gives an inevitable advantage to the Control Groups in the integrative stage. The one-trial hypothesis is, however, concerned exclusively with the associative stage. Thus, any experimental

21. Underwood and Schulz, *op. cit.*, 100-126.

comparison which can be influenced by differences in response-learning does not permit a clear-cut evaluation of the hypothesis. When letter-number pairs are used, response-integration may no longer be a critical factor, but with such materials there is now conclusive evidence for systematic selection of items.[22]

We conclude that the studies using Rock's design, including the present one, have yielded results which do not permit a decision between the one-trial hypothesis and the incremental hypothesis. A crucial experiment pitting the incremental hypothesis against the one-trial hypothesis remains to be designed.[23]

SUMMARY

Two experiments are reported investigating the role of repetition in the learning of paired nonsense-syllables. A procedure introduced by Rock was used: a control group learns a constant series of pairs, whereas for an experimental group all pairs failed on a given trial are removed and replaced by new ones. Two departures from the method used in the earlier study were introduced: (a) The Ss were required to spell the items during training whereas they had merely observed them in the previous experiment. (b) Two Control Groups were used, one of which learned the initial lists of the Experimental Ss, whereas the other learned the terminal lists. The second Control Group was used to assess the amount of systematic selection of easy items. In Experiment I correction was given on the test-trials. In Experiment II no correction was given.

In both experiments the Experimental Group learned significantly more slowly than the Control Groups. In contrast to Rock's results, repetition was found to have a significant effect on rate of learning. These findings underscore the importance of controlling Ss' responses to the materials during the training trials. Evidence for systematic selection of items was obtained in Experiment I but not in Experiment II. Comparison of the two experiments suggests that the amount and kind of item-selection varies with the conditions of inter-trial interference.

Analysis of Ss' performance indicates that the superiority of the Control Groups must be attributed, at least in part, to the beneficial effects of repetition on the integration of responses. The effects of repetition on the associative stage of learning remain indeterminate. Serious doubt is thrown on the validity of Rock's evidence for one-trial learning. The adequacy of his design for testing the hypothesis of one-trial learning is called in question.

22. Underwood, Rehula, and Keppel, *op. cit.*, this JOURNAL, 75, 1962, 353-71.
23. Recently Estes (*op. cit.*) has presented some challenging arguments and experimental data which he interprets as evidence for the one-trial conception. A discussion of this work is beyond the scope of this paper.

18 / Learning Theory and the New "Mental Chemistry" [1]

W. K. ESTES, *Indiana University*

Hovering in the background of our scientific enterprises is a question which we, as investigators, can afford neither to raise very often nor to overlook entirely. Namely, do we have good reason to believe that the general methods and working assumptions underlying our research can be counted on to lead in the long run

From the *Psychological Review*, 1960, 67, 207-23, with permission of the author and publisher.
1. This paper comprises, in substance, the writer's Presidential Address to the Division of Experimental Psychology, American Psychological Association, 1959. Several indebtednesses deserve acknowledgment: an unrestricted grant from the Ford Foundation supported portions of the experimental work; periods of relative freedom from academic routine in stimulating surroundings were made possible by the Department of Psychology, Northwestern Uni-

to satisfactory interpretations of our phenomena? In the psychology of learning, there has been a division of labor, with the experimentalists doing the overlooking, and each theorist having his turn at bringing up this question along with his answer. The answer is, of course, in each instance that the particular theorist's tactics point down the high road while those of the opposition lead into dark and forbidding *culs-de-sac*.

For my own part, although my hands are not entirely clean in the matter of theorizing, I had been content until very recently to go along with the single-minded "learning experimentalist," assuming that the Lord will look after those who remember their control groups and mind their Ps and Fs. The incident which jarred me out of this comfortable way of life began as a simple (in fact, as will be seen, unusually simple) bit of experimentation with no philosophical overtones. The original purpose of the experimentation was to provide more cogent empirical support than had hitherto been available for one of the central concepts of learning theory.

Several recent reviewers (e.g., Deese, 1958; Estes, 1956; Kendler, 1959; Restle, 1959) have noted that despite the popular stereotype of "learning theory" as virtually synonymous with "controversy," there has steadily, although unobtrusively, accumulated a body of concepts and assumptions which command relatively wide agreement and which contribute motivation and direction to a great part of the research being done in the field of learning. At the center of this core of communality one finds a concept which represents the distillation of centuries of theorizing about learning, not to speak of 70-odd years of experimentation in the tradition of functionalism and, later, behaviorism: the concept of associative strength. In the "mental mechanics" and "mental chemistry" of pre-experimental associationism,

this concept was verbalized in terms of the strength of associations between ideas; with Thorndike, it became strength of stimulus-response bonds; with Hull, the basic quantitative constructs of habit strength and excitatory potential. And it is in terms of this concept that contemporary learning theorists express the basic distinction between learning and performance, as well as their fundamental postulates relating the growth of habits to the number of training trials ("reinforcements").

There is little disagreement even in the precise quantitative form of these postulates, perhaps because our standards of acceptability come directly from the observed forms of empirical curves relating probabilities of learned responses, as well as measures of resistance to extinction or forgetting, to the number of training trials. Thus in a whole array of contemporary theories we find exactly the same equations expressing the effect of a reinforced training trial upon associative strength (cf. Restle, 1959). In Hull's system, this equation is

$$\Delta H = k \, (M - H)$$

where ΔH represents the change in habit strength (H) on any reinforced trial, M is the maximum value of habit strength, and k is a constant. Spence's (1955) revision of Hull's theory is based on the same postulate, although there is some question as to whether the H in the equation should be replaced by E, representing excitatory potential (Spence, 1955, 1958). Similarly, in statistical learning theory (Estes, 1959) the corresponding assumption has been expressed in the form

$$\Delta p = \theta \, (1 - p)$$

where Δp represents the change in the proportion of stimulus elements connected to a given response, and θ is a

versity and the Institute for Mathematical Studies in Social Sciences, Stanford University during the spring and summer, respectively, of 1959 while the paper was in preparation.

constant (the proportion of stimulus elements sampled on the trial). In the stochastic model of Bush and Mosteller (1955), the same linear function is assumed, "strength" being simply identified with response probability. For application to learning theorists, a well-known quotation may aptly be reversed to read, "In strength there is union." And with respect to the experimental literature, it seems fair to say that the assumptions that associative strength increases with reinforcement, decreases during retention intervals, and generalizes to new stimuli are the cornerstones of most contemporary treatments of conditioning and elementary verbal learning.

Areas of substantial agreement concerning either facts or interpretations, let alone both, are rare enough in the field of learning so that one might think we would do well to treasure the one we have located and carefully avoid doing anything to disturb it. This I (along with most of my fellow theorists and experimentalists) was happy to do, until my hand was forced by some purely experimental developments. The first of these was the, by now well-known, work of Kimble and his associates (1955, 1956; Dufort & Kimble, 1958) who, working with an eyelid conditioning situation, tried the novel procedure of omitting the CS on a substantial block of trials during an acquisition series. The rather surprising result of this variation was that the course of acquisition was virtually unaffected. Their interpretation was that only the first few reinforcements are actually effective in modifying the strength of associations between CS and CR, the rest of the "conditioning curve" actually reflecting some nonassociative process. The second development was contributed by Rock (1957), who found no retardation in the speed of paired-associate learning when he introduced the device of replacing missed items with new ones at the end of every trial. Rock

interpreted his findings as indicating that associations form on an all-or-none basis and that it is only associative strength in the sense of resistance to forgetting that grows as a function of number of reinforcements.

It seemed curious that both of these deviations from the usual experimental paradigms had yielded results which are in some respects sharply at variance with the generally accepted conception of the acquisition process. Of course these findings might turn out to have special explanations that would leave the established conception undisturbed. But then again, they might not. In the case of the Kimble, Mann, and Dufort (1955) study, counterexplanations and counterexperiments have already begun to pour into the literature (see, e.g., Goodrich, Ross, & Wagner, 1957) with the result so far of complicating matters still further rather than of clearing anything up. One might argue that concepts and assumptions which have been supported by a large accumulation of experimental findings cannot be seriously threatened by one or two apparently negative results. But this argument is weakened by the observation that all of the empirical support for the conceptualization of learning in terms of associative strength is quite indirect in character.

The basic concepts and assumptions of learning theory are universally supposed to refer to states and processes of the individual organism. Yet the existing evidence for the assumption that associative strength is an increasing function of number of reinforcements comes from performance curves representing average response measures over groups of learners, or from measures of resistance to extinction or retention scores averaged over groups of learners having different values of the independent variable. Even the few bits of negative evidence are indirect, depending on performance curves obtained under deviations from the usual experimental paradigms but still representing changes in average scores over series of trials for groups of subjects (Ss). It would seem that if our basic conceptions are sound, it should be possible to cut through the web of group performance curves and obtain more direct and compelling evidence for the existence of the assumed states and processes in individual organisms. This, in any event, is what I set out to accomplish for the concept of associative strength in a series of experiments now to be reported.

ON THE DEFINITIONS OF "REINFORCEMENT," "TEST TRIAL," AND "LEARNING"

In standard human learning situations, "learning" is almost universally defined and measured in terms of a change in the probability, or frequency, with which a given stimulating situation evokes a response (or instances of a response class) that has been designated as "correct" by the experimenter. With one reservation, to be noted below, I shall follow this usage. But the situation is quite different with "reinforcement," the same term being used in at least two quite different senses by different investigators and thus promoting no end of confusion. My own habitual usage is the "neutral definition" (Hilgard, 1956, p. 409) which identifies reinforcement empirically with the operation that is supplied by the experimenter in order to produce learning, as defined above, in any given situation. In a paired-associate situation, the reinforcing operation is the paired presentation of the stimulus and response members of an item; in classical conditioning it is the paired presentation CS and US; in verbal conditioning, the reinforcing operation for a given predictive response (e.g., predicting that the left light will appear) is the occurrence of the corresponding event (appearance of the left light)—in each case without regard to whether the S correctly anticipated the response member of the paired-associate item, gave a CR prior to occurrence of the US, or correctly predicted the event on the trial in question. The only property that different types of reinforcing operations are assumed to share is their common quantitative effect on the conditional probabilities of the possible alternative responses to the stimulating situation in which reinforcement occurs.

A narrower definition, favored especially by writers associated with a drive-reduction interpretation of reinforcement, would limit the term reinforcement to an operation that follows and is contingent upon the occurrence of the reinforced response on any trial. In this usage, reinforcement in paired-associate learning occurs only when the S has made a correct response in anticipation of the paired stimulus-response presentation, and reinforcement in verbal conditioning occurs only on trials when the S correctly predicts the trial outcome. Whether, according to this view, reinforcement occurs on only those trials of a classical conditioning experiment on which a CR occurs prior to the US depends upon theoretical decisions as to whether the CR and UR are "the same response" and whether reinforcement occurs at the onset or the termination of the US.

The primary advantage I see in the "neutral definition" is that it can be applied in an objective and consistent manner independently of one's position on systematic or theoretical issues. Learning certainly may occur prior to the first correct anticipation in a paired-associate experiment, prior to the first correct prediction in verbal conditioning, prior to the first CR in classical conditioning. The present usage permits us to speak, for example, about changes in probability of a response as a function of reinforcements on trials preceding its first occurrence, on the one hand, and changes as a function of reinforcements on trials including and following its first occurrence, on the other, without changing our definition of reinforcement.

It should be emphasized that the neutral definition does not beg such questions as whether presentation of a US following a CR constitutes the same reinforcing operation as presentation of a US on a trial when the CR did not occur; these two procedures represent instances of the same reinforcing operation if and only if they produce the same change in the probability of evocation of the CR by the CS. However, it seems strategic to avoid issues of this sort when, as in the present investigation, we are concerned with the nature of the changes in response tendencies during learning rather than with the conditions giving rise to these changes. Consequently, in the experiments to be reported, we have attempted so far as possible to avoid the customary confounding of reinforcement with antecedent response. In paired-associate situations, for example, we have deviated from the usual anticipation procedure by separating the reinforcement (paired-presentation of stimulus and response members of an item) from the test for learning (presentation of the stimulus member alone) so that an item may receive more than one reinforcement before the first test trial or may receive repeated test trials without intervening reinforcement.

For purposes of measuring retention, it would be ideal if one could give test trials on which no learning at all occurred. Indeed, so long as "learning" is conceived solely in terms of the definition given above (increase in probability of the "correct" response to a given stimulus), this goal is not too difficult to approximate. It seems intuitively clear, and can be demonstrated empirically (Estes, Hopkins, & Crothers, 1960), that no systematic increase in probability of correct responses to, say, paired-associate items will occur over a series of trials on which the stimulus members are presented alone and the S's responses receive no reward or informational feedback from the experimenter. We cannot, however, rule out the possibility that on these trials there might be learning in the sense of an increase in probability of whatever responses, correct or incorrect, actually occur. In fact, there is evidence that such learning does occur, but at a relatively low rate compared to the learning that occurs on reinforced trials (Estes et al., 1960). Consequently, in the analyses to follow, I shall assume that unreinforced trials can be treated, without serious error, simply as "neutral" test trials when primary interest is in measuring the effects of preceding reinforced trials.

UNITARY ASSOCIATION VS. HABIT HIERARCHY

If the stimulus-response relation established by reinforcement were a unitary, all-or-none connection of some sort, then the learning of a new response to a stimulus would automatically displace a previously associated response. Contrariwise, in every variant of the concept of associative strength, it is assumed that a number of different responses may simultaneously be associated with the same stimulus, the relative strengths of association depending primarily upon preceding frequencies of reinforcement of the different responses in the presence of the stimulus. This latter assumption has been embodied in Hull's "habit family hierarchy."

To spell out the question at issue in experimental terms, let us suppose that first Response A and subsequently Response B have been reinforced in the presence of a given stimulus (or stimulus complex—the nature of the stimulation does not matter so long as it is the same on each trial) for each member of a group of Ss and that a test trial now reveals an observed probability (relative frequency) of .5 for each response. Does this mean that for each S both Response A and Response B now have approximately equal habit strengths and therefore equal probabilities of evocation by the given stimulus? Such is the interpretation required by the conception of associative strength (habit strength, excitatory potential, proportion of conditioned elements, or whatever) as well as by any of the contemporary models formulated in terms of continuously variable response probabilities for individual Ss. Stated in these concrete terms, however, it does not seem that the assumption need depend for support only on extremely indirect evidence, as has hitherto been the case. To test these implications of the strength concept quite directly, we apparently need only reinforce two different responses to the same stimulus for an individual S, and then, by means of a series of unreinforced test trials, give the two responses an opportunity to exhibit their relative strengths—if such exist. The predictions under test would be straightforward. On the hypothesis of associative strength, or habit family hierarchy, we expect individual Ss to shift back and forth between the two previously reinforced responses over a series of tests. On the hypothesis of a unitary, all-or-none association between stimulus and response, we expect that an individual S who makes Response A, say, on the first test trial with a given stimulus will not shift to B on subsequent tests.

A paired-associate learning situation offered a number of convenient features for an empirical realization of the hypothetical experiment just described. The stimuli and reinforcements are readily controllable; and, by embedding a stimulus to which two different responses are to be reinforced in a conventional list, one can make S's task appear little different from familiar learning situations. For each of 20 Ss, the proce-

dures were replicated with six eight-item lists, all made up on the same principles.[2] The stimuli were all consonant syllables and the responses one-syllable words. Half of the items in each list had single correct responses; examples are:

STIMULUS	RESPONSE
HTX	wish
JFR	sped

These were simply "ballast" and will not be considered further. The other half of the items had two correct responses for each stimulus; examples are:

STIMULUS	RESPONSES
DGR	thaw, weep
BCG	pink, rule

The two correct responses to each stimulus were reinforced equally often for each S. By "reinforcement," in this context, we mean simply a paired presentation of stimulus and correct response to S; by "test," a presentation of the stimulus member of an item alone. In half of the replications, there were exactly two reinforcements preceding the test trials, one on each response; in the remaining replications, there were four reinforcements, two on each response, prior to the test trials. Following the reinforcements, a series of unreinforced test trials was given, the order of the stimuli being randomized anew for each test.

The critical data for our purposes are the proportions of cases in which the response given on the first test trial to a given stimulus was repeated on the second test. According to an interpretation in terms of associative strength, or habit family hierarchy, repetitions (AA or BB) and shifts (AB or BA) should have occurred with roughly

2. This experiment was conducted at Indiana University with the assistance of E. J. Crothers.

equal frequencies.[3] According to the notion of a unitary association, AA and BB should have each occurred about half of the time and the shifts AB and BA not at all. The results were as follows: Following two reinforcements, there were 85% repetitions and 15% shifts on the first two test trials, the percentages being based on all items that had correct responses on both tests. Following four reinforcements, these values were 89% for repetitions and only 11% for shifts. On later pairs of tests, the frequencies of AB and BA shifts were even smaller. Thus the results do not offer very impressive support for the assumption that a habit hierarchy exists in the individual S following the reinforcement of two different responses to the same stimulus. On the other hand, the data appear quite harmonious with an assumption of unitary association, since the proportions of AB and BA shifts appear small enough to be attributable to minor uncontrolled factors such, for example, as fluctuations in context (background stimulation, stimulus traces from preceding items) from one trial to the next.[4]

Although the present experiment failed to produce the anticipated direct support for the concept of associative strength, a "strength theorist," particularly one working within the framework of Hull's system, may not be too disturbed. With the benefit of an ad hoc assumption concerning the range of "behavioral oscillation," the model of Hull and Spence can be made to yield the prediction that, of two responses reinforced to the same stimulus, one or the other will dominate on test trials, thereby preventing shifts from one to the other on the part of individual Ss. In order to obtain a more decisive test of the strength conception, we evidently require an even simpler experiment in which only one response is ever reinforced.

With the hope of forestalling an indefinite regress through a series of progressively more refined experiments, suppose we ask what is the minimum set of operations and observations actually needed in order to demonstrate learning. Normally there must be a pretest in order to determine the initial probability of the to-be-learned behavior in the test situation; in practice the experimenter often has a priori information about initial response probabilities which makes the pretest dispensable. There must be a presentation of some reinforcing operation, and afterward a test to assess the change in performance produced by the reinforcement. If the function of response occurrences and nonoccurrences is to be determined, there will have to be a second test trial. And there we have it. Controlled comparisons relative to effects of the principal events occurring during an acquisition series can, in principle, be accomplished in an experiment running to about a trial and a half. By usual standards, this constitutes what can only be called a "miniature experiment." However, miniature experiments appeared to be what the tactical situation called for, and therefore miniature experiments are what we set out to run.

---

3. The response given on the first trial was the more recently reinforced response in approximately 60% of cases. Thus more instances of AA than BB would be expected; nevertheless the proportions of repetitions and shifts expected on the associative strength hypothesis are nearly equal (.52:.48).

4. It should be noted that these results cast doubt on the concept of habit hierarchy only as applied to response probabilities in the presence of a stimulus situation that has been manipulated as a unit over the series of reinforced test trials. M. S. Schoeffler (personal communication) and, in another unpublished study, Crothers and I have obtained positive evidence for the existence of a habit hierarchy associated with a compound stimulus, components of which have been separately correlated with reinforcements during the training trials. The results with compounding provide a control for the present experiment. If the very high proportions of repetitions reported above were attributable to learning that occurred on the first test trial, or to some nonassociative variable, then a similar excess of repetitions should have occurred over successive tests with stimulus compounds, however, no such excess was observed either in Schoeffler's study of compounding or in ours.

CONCEPTIONS OF THE ACQUISITION PROCESS: ASSOCIATIVE STRENGTH VS. ALL-OR-NONE MODELS

In the first of these experiments,[5] we used a paired-associate situation with consonant syllables as stimuli and numbers as responses. Forty-eight Ss were run with an eight-item list, yielding 384 observations on the first test trial. The principal portion of the experiment consisted simply in presenting each S once with each stimulus-response pair and then testing with each stimulus alone (in a new random order). Before proceeding to the results, let us examine the outcome expected on the basis of the notion of learning as a change in associative strength. In Figure 1 the situation is schematized in terms of a single item. The four squares at the left represent four hypothetical Ss, the emptiness of the squares indicating that all start the experiment with zero probabilities of making the correct response. Now we give a single reinforcement (paired presentation of the stimulus and correct response), the result of which is to raise the probability of the correct response (C) to, say, .25. The upper arrow leads to the theoretical state of affairs after this reinforcement, according to an interpretation based on the conception of associative strength. The strength of the association is increased for all of the Ss; and, neglecting for the moment possible individual differences, the probability of the correct response is now .25 for each individual, the one at the upper right who happened to make a correct response on the test, and the three who did not.

Suppose now that the interpretation based on the concept of strength were completely wrong and that stimulus-response associations really formed on an all-or-none basis. Then the state of affairs after the reinforcement should be as shown in the lower part of the figure. Again the probability of a cor-

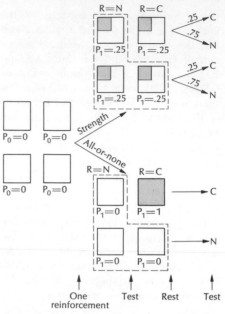

Fig. 1. Schema representing effects of a single reinforcement according to incremental (upper branch) vs. all-or-none (lower branch) theories. Squares represent Ss, with the proportion of darkened area in each indicating the probability of the correct response (C) for the given individual.

rect response increases from zero to .25, but the .25 now refers only to the group, not to any individual S. One S has formed the association (darkened square), and three have been unaffected by the reinforcement (empty squares).

To distinguish empirically between these two logically possible outcomes, we need only add the remaining half-trial to our trial-and-a-half, i.e., give another test without intervening reinforcement. Now, if the upper branch of the diagram is essentially correct, all Ss should have equal probabilities of making the correct response on the second test trial, regardless of what they did on the first test. But if the lower branch is correct, correct re-

5. This experiment was conducted at Indiana University with the assistance of B. L. Hopkins; for a full report of the method and results see Estes, et al. (1960).

sponses on the second test should come only from Ss who made correct responses on the first test. None should come from Ss who made incorrect responses (N) on the first test, for these Ss would not have profited at all from the learning trial.

There might be some attenuation of the expected proportions of correct responses on Test 2 by Ss making correct responses on Test 1 if there is any forgetting in this situation, but the proportions of correct following incorrect provide a critical comparison. If the all-or-none view is correct, then this proportion should be zero, or at least no greater than could be achieved by sheer guessing. But if any version of the strength conception is correct, then the proportion of correct following incorrect responses should be greater than chance. In order to make the outcomes that can be tolerated by the two interpretations sharply different, we need only choose our experimental materials and conditions so that the over-all proportions correct on both first and second tests are well above chance. It can be seen in Figure 2 that this has been achieved, for approximately 50% of the items were correct on the first test and nearly 40% on the second. Considering the critical lower branch of the diagram, leading from an incorrect response on the first test to a correct response on the second, we see that the results lean strongly in the direction prescribed by an all-or-none conception, for the 9% of correct following incorrect responses is less than the 12½% that could be achieved even by rather unintelligent guessing with an eight-item list if the reinforcement had no effect at all on these items. The difference between this value and the 71% of correct following correct responses is so large that a statistical test would be an empty formality.

A possible defense that might be advanced by a "strength theorist" is the hypothesis that the 51% of cases with incorrect responses on the first test simply represent preponderantly slower learners or more difficult items than the 49% of cases with correct responses. If so, then a control condition in which a second reinforcement is given between the first and second tests should yield a percentage of correct responses on Test 2 following incorrect on Test 1 that is much smaller than the percentage correct on Test 1. This control was run (with the same 48 Ss but different items), and the result is shown in Figure 3. The effect of the first reinforcement on the full set of Ss and items was to raise the probability of a correct response from near zero to .40; the effect of the second reinforcement on cases having incorrect responses on the first test was to raise the probability of a correct response from near zero to .46. Thus there seems to be no support forthcoming for the hypothesis of a large difference in learning rate between cases which did and cases which did not have correct responses on the first test.

Although it would be nice to claim credit for rare prescience in predicting the outcome of this little experiment, the fact is that the result came as a distinct jar to my preconceptions. In designing the study, our idea was not to undermine the strongly entrenched concept of associative strength, but to support it by showing that the results of Rock's experiments, apparently calling for an all-or-none interpretation, must be attributed to some artifact concealed in his ingenious but somewhat complex procedures. Thus when Hopkins and I examined the data from our initial group of 24 Ss and found the pattern shown in Figures 2 and 3, our first reaction was to replicate the whole thing with another group. But when the two replications turned out to agree

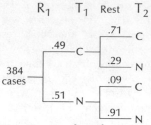

Fig. 2. Results of miniature experiment on acquisition of paired-associates. Empirical values are proportions of instance in which correct (C) and incorrect (N) responses on first test trial after a single reinforcement (paired presentation of stimulus and response members) were followed by C and N responses on a second test trial.

in every essential respect, we were left with no obvious course but to begin digesting an unanticipated and not entirely palatable conclusion. The most cleanly controlled comparisons we had managed to devise yielded no evidence that repeated reinforcements in this situation have any function other than to give repeated opportunities for the discontinuous formation of a learned association between observed stimuli and responses.

Still, it is well known that theoretical doctrines do not yield readily to negative evidence. One whose theories are based on a concept of strength will lose little ground if he can make a stand on the claim that all-or-none acquisition is simply a peculiarity of the paired-asso-

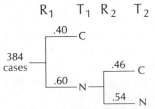

Fig. 3. Proportion correct on test after a second reinforcement for cases not having correct responses on first test compared with proportion correct on first test for the full set of Ss and items. The Ss and situation are the same as those represented in Figure 2.

Strength Model

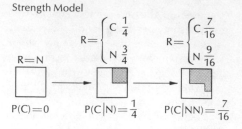

All-or-none Model

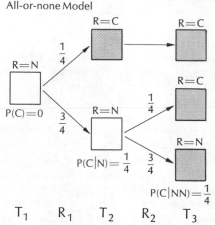

Fig. 4. Schema for first two trials of eyelid conditioning experiment showing changes in CR probability (proportion of darkened area in squares representing Ss) prescribed by incremental vs. all-or-none theories.

ciate experiment and not characteristic of human learning in general. To evaluate this possible defense of the strength concept, we clearly shall have to turn to some different situation that is quite different in the response mechanism and reinforcing operations from paired-associate learning. Eyelid conditioning meets these specifications, and it is convenient for our purposes since a colleague, I. Gormezano, has kindly made available his data from an intensive period of data collecting in the Wisconsin conditioning laboratory. Gormezano trained a sufficiently large group, approximately 170 Ss, under identical conditions so that the first few acquisition trials can be treated as one of our miniature experiments and analyzed in much the same way as the paired-associate study.

The situation obtaining over the first couple of trials is schematized in Figure 4. In the diagram, T_1 is the first CS presentation, prior to the first reinforcement, and we shall consider only Ss who made no CR on this test. Thus the initial probability of a CR is taken to be zero. Suppose now that the effect of the first reinforcement is to raise the probability of a CR to .25. According to the strength conception, shown in the upper panel, each S has his strength of conditioning increased by the same amount by this reinforcement and now has probability .25 of making a CR. Then the second reinforcement increases the conditioned strength for each S again; and, regardless of whether or not a particular S happened to make a CR on T_2, he now has a higher probability ($7\!/\!16$ if we apply the linear function mentioned earlier).[6] According to an all-or-none conception, the situation after the first reinforcement, shown in the lower panel, is that for ¼ of the Ss the CR has become associated with the CS and for the remaining ¾ of the Ss no conditioning has occurred. The effect of the second reinforcement is to give the unconditioned Ss another chance, and ¼ of these now become conditioned. The differential prediction, then, concerns the probability of a CR on the third test for Ss who made no CR on the second test (and similarly the probability of a CR on the fourth test for Ss who made none on any previous test, and so on). The strength conception requires this conditional probability to increase, whereas the all-or-none conception requires it to remain constant. The test seems quite sharp, for even with allowance for variation in conditioning rates among Ss, a model which assumes that associative strength increases with reinforcements cannot stand constancy

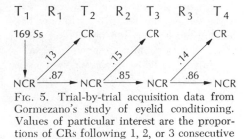

FIG. 5. Trial-by-trial acquisition data from Gormezano's study of eyelid conditioning. Values of particular interest are the proportions of CRs following 1, 2, or 3 consecutive non-CRs.

of this probability unless its assumptions are so restricted that it reduces to an all-or-none model.

The pertinent results of Gormezano's study are shown in Figure 5, carried through the first four trials, beyond which the number of cases begins to drop off too much for comfort. Inspecting the sequence of probabilities of CRs after 1, 2, or 3 consecutive NCRs—.13, .15, .14—we find the hypothesis of constancy appearing rather more attractive than the progressively increasing trend required by the strength interpretation. (According to a linear model, for example, the value .15 for a CR after an NCR should have been .24, and the .14 for a CR after two NCRs should have been .34.)

The consistency of these conditioning data with those of the paired-associate situation is almost too good to be true. In psychology we are not used to having quantitative tests of alternative theoretical notions yield such apparently decisive outcomes. Consequently, and considering the importance of the the oretical issue, perhaps we will not yet be accused of beating a dead hypothesis if we look for one more test with experimental arrangements differing from both of those preceding. We would like a situation similar to paired-asso-

---

6. For this example, the parameter θ in the function $\Delta p = \theta(1 - p)$ is equal to ¼ and after the first experiment p is also equal to ¼. Therefore we have

$$\Delta p = \tfrac14(1 - \tfrac14) = \tfrac{3}{16}$$

and for the new probability after the second reinforcement,

$$p + \Delta p = \tfrac14 + \tfrac{3}{16} = \tfrac{7}{16}$$

ciate learning in that unreinforced test trials can readily be given without disturbing the learners but one which eliminates the possibility of achieving substantial proportions of correct responses by guessing. A situation which meets these desiderata is the free verbal recall experiment used by Bruner, Miller, and Zimmerman (1955). For our present purposes the minimal experiment will consist of a single reinforcement followed by two recall tests. The reinforcement involves merely the experimenter's reading a list of words aloud to S. On a recall test, S is asked to write down as many words as he can remember (in any order). Then after an interval during which no additional reinfcrcement is given, S is (unexpectedly) tested again.

Results of two experiments [7] of this sort are shown in Figure 6. The upper tree represents an experiment with 35 Ss, each given a list of eight words at R_1. On the first test, T_1, 61% of the 280 opportunities for correct responses (C) yielded either incorrect responses or omissions (N), and of these less than 1% were followed by correct responses on the second test, T_2. In a replication conducted with some minor variations in procedure, 102 Ss were presented with eight words each on the reinforced trial. This time (lower tree in Figure 6) there were 72% N responses on the first test and less than 2% of these were followed by C responses on the second test. Clearly, if a word is not given correctly on the first test by a particular S, the chances are virtually *nil* that it will be correct on a second test.

This result does not, of course, *prove* that reinforcement has exerted no strengthening effect on the associations in the cases when the correct response failed to occur on the first test. But one whose theory requires him to assume that such strengthenings occur

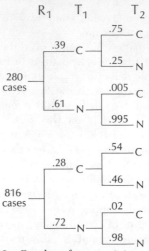

FIG. 6. Results of two miniature experiments on free verbal recall, showing near-zero proportions of correct responses on a second test trial for cases which did not have correct responses on the first test after a single reinforcement.

has a taxing assignment in producing a case for the existence of factors or processes which appear in just sufficient force to cancel out the hypothesized increments in response strength under each set of experimental procedures we have examined. Explanations depending on such factors as individual differences are not very prepossessing in the light of control comparisons of the type exhibited in Figure 3 (a similar control, with a similar result, was used for the free-verbal-recall situation). One might appeal to the effects of learning which occurs on the first test trial itself, arguing that an incorrect response which occurs on the first test receives a large increment in associative strength (from sheer contiguity or perhaps from some unspecified source of reinforcement) and therefore recurs with high probability on the next test. One important difficulty with this hypothesis is that the data do not support it. In the paired-

_____

7. These experiments, conducted at Indiana University with the assistance of Judith Crooks, will be reported in detail elsewhere.

associate study cited above, for example, the observed relative frequency with which an incorrect response occurring on the first test was repeated on the second test was only .24. Interpretations which preserve the incremental conception of associative learning should certainly be sought with all vigor; at the time of writing, however, none has come to my attention that seems at all plausible.

Retention as a Function of Reinforcement and Interspersed Test Trials

The story does not end here. Even if one is ready to grant that associations are made and broken in an all-or-none fashion, this concession, although by no means a minor one, does not exhaust the resources of the strength concept. It is possible that after an association has once formed, associative strength in the sense of resistance to forgetting continues to grow as a function of reinforcements. In fact the experimental situations we have used appear well suited to demonstrate such an effect.

It will not have escaped notice that although the three miniature experiments yielded sharply negative results relative to the conception of learning as a gradual strengthening of associations by reinforcement, they agree only in part with the usual notion of all-or-none learning (as, for example, defined by Voeks, 1955). The formation of learned associations appears to be discontinuous rather than gradual, but once a correct response (or conditioned response) has occurred to a given stimulus, it does not appear with certainty when the stimulus recurs after a rest interval. In fact, "forgetting" as measured by the proportion of shifts from a correct response on the first test to non-correct on the second test ranges from about 20% in the paired-associate situation to about 50% in free verbal recall. For the eyelid conditioning study, we did not report these proportions since the numbers of observations on which they were based were rather small; but for what it is worth, we might add that the proportions of CR to NCR shifts following the first three tests, despite the intervening reinforcement, fall well within the range given above for the other two experiments.

The minimum set of operations and observations required to test for a dependence of "resistance to forgetting" upon number of reinforcements is exhibited in Table 1. Following either

TABLE 1. *Design and results of minimal experiment on retention as a function of number of reinforcements*

Procedure	Amount of Retention	
	P-A	FVR
R T$_1$ T$_2$	.90	.54
R R T$_1$ T$_2$	.89	.52

one or two reinforcements, a sequence of two unreinforced test trials is given; and retention is measured in terms of the proportion of instances in which a correct response to a given stimulus on the first of these tests is repeated on the second test. Results of two such experiments are shown in the table.

The left-hand column of proportions represents data from a study conducted by the writer with the assistance of E. J. Crothers (Estes et al., 1960). Twenty Ss were each run on six eight-item paired-associate lists under each condition (number of reinforcements). The stimuli were nonsense syllables, and the responses were numbers in half the lists and familiar words in the other half. The right-hand column presents data from the free verbal recall experiment previously cited (102 Ss each tested with a list of eight items under each condition). The pattern of test proportions needs little comment. In each case the difference called for by the traditional conception of associative strength fails to appear.

This outcome is a little hard to swallow. It is well known that retention increases with overlearning. If the additional reinforcements given during the overlearning period do not produce the increased resistance to forgetting, then what does? We may obtain a clue as to the answer by introducing what might a priori seem to be very slight change in the design of our minimal experiment on retention. This variable is illustrated in Table 2. In the free

TABLE 2. *Design and results of minimal experiment on retention as a function of a test trial interposed between reinforcements*

Procedure	Amount of Retention
R R T₁ T₂	.52
R T₁ R T₂ T₃	.78

verbal recall experiment cited previously, we included, in addition to the condition shown in the upper row (which is the same as in Table 1), a condition with the same number of reinforcements but with an additional interspersed test trial. The idea was to give an opportunity for correct responses learned on the first reinforced trial to become conditioned to cues which arc present only on test trials and not on training trials—in other words to spread the effect of the first reinforcement over more stimuli. Retention is measured in terms of the proportion of correct responses repeated from T_1 to T_2 in the upper row and from T_2 to T_3 in the lower row. In contrast to the lack of effect on retention produced by increasing the number of reinforcements, note the large effect of the added test trial. Two reinforcements without an intervening test yield only 52% retention, whereas two reinforcements with an intervening test trial

yield 78% retention from the first to the second test following the second reinforcement.

Although the principle that retention increases with number of reinforcements is exceedingly well established in the lore of human learning, we must face the possibility that this empirical relation, like the classical acquisition curve, is an artifact of the confoundings inherent in the usual experimental paradigm.

Concluding Remarks

To recapitulate the box score: we have conducted a series of highly simplified experiments especially designed to provide relatively direct evidence for the widely accepted interpretation of learning and retention in terms of increments and decrements in associative strength. We noted that in virtually all contemporary learning theories, the concept of strength is assumed to have at least three different empirical manifestations—the habit hierarchy, the growth of associative strength in the sense of response probability as a function of number of reinforcements, and the increase in resistance to forgetting of once established associations with additional reinforcement. We tested for all three of these effects by means of the simplest controlled comparisons we could arrange, doing our utmost to eliminate the confoundings and the layers of statistical processing that shield the behavioral changes occurring on individual learning trials completely from view in conventional experimental designs. And under these presumably favorable circumstances, all three effects mysteriously evaporated, leaving a picture of unitary associations the learning and unlearning of which proceed on an essentially all-or-none basis.[8]

8. Several readers of a prepublication draft of this article have raised the question whether alternative measures, e.g., response latencies or recognition scores, might yield evidence of learning in cases

What is the import of these results for the question raised earlier concerning the strategic soundness of the general methods on which investigators of learning chiefly rely? The concept we have examined in detail epitomizes the intervening-variable paradigm for theory construction that has been popularized by Tolman and Hull, and their followers, to the point of dominating contemporary learning theory. The general technique is to postulate a hypothetical state or entity which is held to intervene in some sense between observed stimulus and response variables. Predictions derived from theories built around such constructs are checked against data from standard learning experiments. Thus the adequacy of the theories depends in turn on the adequacy with which essential aspects of learning are captured by standard experimental designs.

I have emphasized the term "standard" for despite the fact, decried by many critics, that psychologists in this field have resisted all admonitions to standardize their tasks, situations, and procedures, they have more than compensated for this lack by the degree to which they have standardized their experimental designs. Scanning the reference list of, say, Hilgard's *Theories of Learning* (1956),[9] one can find no more than a meager handful of studies which are not molded into a paradigm that might be termed the groups-by-trials design. The master blueprint requires the investigator to average some type of performance score, e.g., frequency of conditioned responses or of correct responses, over a series of trials for groups of Ss—the groups being differentiated on the basis of conditions obtaining over the series. Going back a few years in the experimental journals, one finds the customary output of this experimental paradigm to be a set of mean performance curves for experi-

mental and control groups; more recently the output is typically an array of analysis of variance tables, perhaps supplemented by some mean criterion scores. These observations in themselves do not constitute a criticism. No one would gainsay that the groups-by-trials design and its associated statistical techniques are useful tools for assaying the effects of various procedures and conditions upon performance. It is easy, however, to overlook the fact that the groups-by-trials design yields only information about relationships and trends which hold on the average over groups of Ss and series of trials. No accumulation of experiments, however large, all conducted and all analyzed in accord with this same general method can provide a sufficient empirical check on concepts and assumptions that refer to processes or events occurring in the individual learner. The findings we have considered in this paper suggest that in point of fact some of the most firmly entrenched concepts and principles of learning theory may be in a sense artifacts of a conventionalized methodology.

---

where the probabilities of conditioned responses or of correct recalls do not. Regardless of the answer, it is important to note that information about concomitant changes in other variables would have no logical bearing upon conclusions pertaining to the one actually chosen for analysis in a given experiment. To determine whether the behavior of recalling the correct response to a paired-associate item is learned in all-or-none fashion, we required an analysis according to the paradigm of Figure 2 with recall score as the dependent variable. To determine whether correct recognition of a previously viewed item is learned on an all-or-none basis, we would need a similar analysis with recognition score as the dependent variable. To determine whether the behavioral change associated with a decrease in latency is learned on an all-or-none basis, we would need a similar analysis with some criterion of change in latency as the dependent variable, and so on.

9. The harvest is even scantier if one consults the more monographic works, e.g., Tolman (1932), Hull (1943), or Spence (1955), associated with systems of intervening-variables in behavior theory; or, for that matter, my own theoretical writings (Estes, 1959). In the eclectic treatise of McGeoch and Irion (1952), deviant experimental designs appear in references with the earliest dates but disappear as one comes down to the contemporary literature.

The laboratory investigator of learning is used to going his own way more or less oblivious to the rattle of criticisms from textbook writers, educators, and other "outsiders." Traditionally the criticisms have always been to the same effect—that the "learning experimentalist" should push on from the worn out fields of conditioning and simple verbal learning, where there are really no unsolved problems of any importance remaining, and devote himself to richer, more complex, experiments that come closer to learning situations of real life (as contrasted with the unreal life found in the laboratory). Here we break with tradition, for the criticism generated by our work within the field suggests that progress toward a satisfactory theory of learning requires, not more complex, but simpler experiments. The conventional experiment, far from being oversimplified, represents such a complex and intricate confounding of stimulus and response variables over trials that once it has been done and reported in conventional form, no amount of study of the analysis of variance tables and Vincentized performance curves can disclose the effects exerted by specific causal variables on individual Ss upon particular occasions. Concepts depending solely upon the conventional experiment for support may turn out to belong, not to a psychology of learning, but only to a psychology of the criterion score, the mean performance curve, and the groups-by-trials design.

In concluding, I would like to indicate that I do not mean to offer the experimental findings reported in this paper as a crucial test of incremental vs. all-or-none theory. What does seem clear with respect to the former is that the kind of evidence heretofore adduced in support of incremental theories is inadequate to distinguish them from alternative conceptions. More penetrating experimental analyses are required. We have made a start in this direction, and from the early returns it appears that no extant theory of the incremental type can handle the pattern of results that is emerging. The temptation is great to indulge now in a bit of speculation as to whether the answer to this situation will prove to be a remodeling of one of the familiar incremental theories, or perhaps a quite different theory based on all-or-none assumptions—but this is a step I do not intend to take.

Since the earliest days of associationism, overdependence upon speculation and circuitous inference has impeded the interplay of theory with experiment. While I would not for a moment depreciate the role of imagination in science, I suspect that it will begin to serve us effectively in learning theory only as we begin to accumulate reliable determinations of the effects of single variables upon single learning trials in individual organisms. If by continual simplification of our experimental analyses and refinement of our mensurational procedures we can achieve these determinations, we may find that the long sought laws of association may be not merely "instigated," or even "suggested," but literally dictated in form by empirical data.

BRUNER, J. S., MILLER, G. A., & ZIMMERMAN, C. Discriminative skill and discriminative matching in perceptual recognition. *J. exp. Psychol.*, 1955, **49**, 187-92.

BUSH, R. R., & MOSTELLER, F. *Stochastic models for learning.* New York: Wiley, 1955.

DEESE, J. *The psychology of learning.* (Rev. ed.) New York: McGraw-Hill, 1958.

DUFORT, R. H., & KIMBLE, G. A. Ready signals and the effect of interpolated UCS presentations in eyelid conditioning. *J. exp. Psychol.*, 1958, **56**, 1-7.

ESTES, W. K. Learning. *Annu. Rev. Psychol.*, 1956, **7**, 1-38.

ESTES, W. K. The statistical approach to learning theory. In S. Koch (Ed.), *Psychology: A study of a science.* Vol. 2. New York: McGraw-Hill, 1959. Pp. 380-491.

ESTES, W. K., HOPKINS, B. L., & CROTHERS, E. J. All-or-none and conversation effects in the learning and retention of paired associates. *J. exp. Psychol.*, 1960, in press.

GOODRICH, K. P., ROSS, L. E., & WAGNER, A. R. Performance in eyelid conditioning following interpolated presentations of the UCS. *J. exp. Psychol.*, 1957, **53**, 214-17.

HILGARD, E. R. *Theories of learning.* (Rev. ed.) New York: Appleton-Century-Crofts, 1956.

HULL, C. L. *Principles of behavior.* New York: Appleton-Century, 1943.

KENDLER, H. H. Learning. *Annu. Rev. Psychol.*, 1959, **10**, 43-88.

KIMBLE, G. A., & DUFORT, R. H. The associative factor in eyelid conditioning. *J. exp. Psychol.*, 1956, **52**, 386-91.

KIMBLE, G. A., MANN, L. I., & DUFORT, R. H. Classical and instrumental eyelid conditioning. *J. exp. Psychol.*, 1955, **49**, 407-17.

McGEOCH, J. A., & IRION, A. L. *The psychology of human learning.* (Rev. ed.) New York: Longmans, 1952.

RESTLE, F. A survey and classification of learning models. In R. R. Bush and W. K. Estes (Eds.), *Studies in mathematical learning theory.* Stanford, Calif.: Stanford Univer. Press, 1959.

ROCK, I. The role of repetition in associative learning. *Amer. J. Psychol.*, 1957, **70**, 186-93.

SPENCE, K. A. *Behavior theory and conditioning.* New Haven: Yale Univer. Press, 1955.

SPENCE, K. A. Behavior theory and selective learning. In M. R. Jones (Ed.), *Nebraska symposium on motivation.* Lincoln: Univer. Nebraska Press, 1958.

TOLMAN, E. C. *Purposive behavior in animals and men.* New York: Appleton-Century, 1932.

VOEKS, V. W. Gradual strengthening of S-R connections or increasing number of S-R connections. *J. Psychol.*, 1955, **39**, 289-99.

19 / One-trial Learning?

BENTON J. UNDERWOOD AND GEOFFREY KEPPEL, *Northwestern University* [1]

A controversial theoretical issue has arisen in very recent years over the manner in which associations are formed. Controversies are not new in interpretations of learning phenomena, but it is a signal historical event when the controversies are based primarily on the interpretation of data from the verbal-learning laboratory rather than on data from the animal-learning laboratory. The history of verbal learning shows few instances in which the learning of a list of nonsense syllables became the center of affectively tinged and opposed conceptual assertions. But such seems to be the case in the current assertions which place in opposition what is called *incremental* or *gradual* development of associations and *one-trial* or *all-or-none* formation of associations.

As an illustration of the central points of disagreement, we may consider the learning of a single paired associate, VOF-CAT, which is one of several pairs in a list. The list is presented to a subject for alternate study and recall trials. That is, the subject is presented each pair singly for three or four seconds on a study trial under instructions to learn to associate the two members of each pair. Then he is given a test trial on which

the stimulus terms are shown singly and he is asked to try to give the response word that was paired with each. Thus, when VOF is shown on a test trial, the subject should try to give the response CAT. He is never shown the response terms on test trials. After the first test trial he is given another study trial, followed by another test trial, and so on. Now, let us assume that on the fourth test trial when VOF is shown, the subject first correctly gives the response in the time allowed him for this item.

We may now show schematically how "what has happened" is interpreted by a theory of one-trial learning as opposed to an incremental theory. In Figure 1 the four study trials are shown along the baseline, with associative strength on the ordinate. An incremental theory would say that with each successive study trial there has been a gradual increase in the associative strength between the stimulus and response term for the single pair under consideration (the linear relationship between trials and associative

From the *Journal of Verbal Learning and Verbal Behavior*, 1962, **1**, 1-13, by permission of the authors and publisher, Academic Press, Inc.

1. The experiments were supported by contract Nonr-1228 (15) between Northwestern University and the Office of Naval Research.

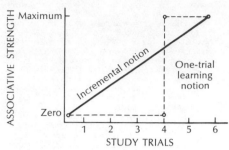

FIG. 1. Schematic representation of the learning of a single paired associate as interpreted by a one-trial theory and by an incremental theory. The single item was first given correctly following the fourth study trial.

ing. Our approach to the problem can best be understood by referring to a statement in the article by Estes, Hopkins, and Crothers (1960, p. 338):

Assuming that possible artifacts have been adequately handled by our various control measures, the results on acquisition appear incompatible with any theory which expresses learning in terms of increments in associative strength, excitatory potential, or simply response probability in individual Ss.

strength is used merely to simplify matters). The one-trial notion, on the other hand, says "nonsense"; no learning occurred until the fourth study trial at which time the association was established at maximum strength. Thus, Figure 1 represents the interpretation of the learning of a single paired associate by the two contrasting notions.

Two investigators have independently put forth the notion that associations are formed in one trial. One is Irwin Rock, who first published his ideas on the matter in 1957, and the other is William Estes who advanced his ideas in his Division-3 Address in 1959, the substance of his remarks subsequently being published in the *Psychological Review* (Estes, 1960). An evaluation of the methods used by Rock to investigate one-trial learning has been presented elsewhere (Underwood, Rehula, and Keppel, in press), the conclusion being that since the methods used by Rock did not control for item selection, hence item difficulty, the results of his investigations could not be used to arbitrate between one-trial and incremental-learning notions. Other investigators have also questioned the adequacy of Rock's procedures (Lockhead, 1961; Postman, in press). Therefore, the present paper will be concerned with the Estes version of one-trial learn-

The initial part of the present paper revolves around two main points. First, we do not believe that critical artifacts have been removed in the procedures of Estes *et al*. Secondly, even if the artifacts could be ruled out, we believe that the data presented could be interpreted handily by certain extant incremental theories. Before elaborating these two points, we wish to make our position clear on certain matters to avoid any possible misunderstanding. It will be seen that we are critical of the methods of research of a very small segment of the great amount of research with which Estes has been associated since the early 1940's. We may well be wrong in our assessment of these methods; if we are, we are sure that replies will be given in the same spirit as the present critique, namely, to try to get at the true state of affairs concerning the experimental facts. Our interest in the issues stems not from a strong theoretical commitment but from a commitment to the use of the best methods of research available. We have probably always accepted implicitly the validity of an incremental theory; indeed, the results of experiments we shall report tend to support such a theory. In spite of this, it is not the major purpose of this paper to promulgate an incremental theory nor to deny a one-trial theory. But, we *will* look critically at the methods of research from which data are obtained to support one or the other theories.

THE CRITICISMS

Procedures used by Estes et al. (1960). We will evaluate the first experiment presented in this article since it is implied that the results of this experiment provide the most critical data for separating one-trial and incremental-learning theories. A list of eight paired associates was used. The stimulus terms were consonant syllables, the response terms single-digit numbers. The list was presented first for a single study trial, followed by a test trial. Then, for each subject, four of the pairs were drawn randomly from the eight. These four pairs were given a second study trial, and finally, a second test trial was given for all eight items. From these simple procedures the data to deny incremental learning and to support one-trial learning were derived. We will look first at the data.

The first fact is that on the first test trial 49% of the stimuli were responded to correctly. This fact has no immediate theoretical implications. Of course, it might be said that for the average subject about half the items were indeed learned on one trial. But the issue before us is not whether one trial learning ever occurs but whether or not this is typical of *all* learning. And yet, as a baseline, the 49% figure becomes important. For now, the investigators ask the question of whether this value means that for a given item the probability of being correct is approximately .5 for each subject, or whether it represents a probability of 1.0 for half the subjects and zero for the other half. The former interpretation, namely, that it represents a .5 probability for each subject, is asserted to be an interpretation made by incremental theories, whereas the latter would be expected by a one-trial theory. So, of course, the intent is to make a choice between the two conceptions. The choice, according to these investigators, is made as follows. Assume there are four subjects. The fact reported earlier showed that approximately 50% of the items were correct. If the all-or-none notion is correct, each of two subjects had a probability of 1.0 for a given item and the other two subjects each had a probability of zero for the item. If this is true, a second test trial should demonstrate this state of affairs. Items which were correct on the first test trial should be correct on the second (without intervening study), and those not correct on the first should not be correct on the second (without intervening study). The data show that 71% of the items which were correct on the first trial were also correct on the second, and only 9% of those not correct on the first test trial were correct on the second. Strictly speaking, from a one-trial theory the values should be 100% and 0%. These are matters for later discussion. For the moment it is sufficient to report that Estes *et al.* conclude that the one-trial position is supported, the incremental position is not.

Application of an incremental theory. Let us consider how the above data may be handled by an incremental theory. Certain incremental theories do not set associative strength and performance isomorphic. More particularly, these theories make use of a threshold notion. This threshold is said to be reached at a certain level of associative strength, and it is only at this point that excitatory potential, necessary for a response to occur, comes into use; or, to keep the language consistent, only after the threshold is attained do these theories start considering probabilities of performing a response. Zero probability is set at threshold, not at zero associative strength. Thus, for the results of the experiment by Estes *et al.*, it could be said that if an item were incorrect on the first test trial then it was below the performance threshold; there is no reason why it should be correct on the second test trial with no intervening study. Likewise, an item above threshold on the first test trial has a high probability of being correct on the second. Items which were correct on the first test trial but not on the second, and those which were not correct on the first but correct on the second, would be handled by some incremental theories via the notion of *oscillation*.

It is apparent that the incremental theory which we think can handle the data of Estes *et al.* is a Hull-type theory. The threshold notion, which implies a distinction between associative strength and performance has always been a part of Hull's system building. A single quotation may be used to make this point (Hull, 1952, p. 12): "The reaction threshold stands at an appreciable distance above the absolute zero of reaction potential."

The failure of Estes to attempt to interpret his data in terms of such a theory is puzzling. It is as if he is setting a trap for the unwary, and we may be the first quarry. By this we do not mean that Estes must use such a theory but rather, if assertions are made that incremental theories cannot handle the results, it is puzzling why a Hull-type theory did not enter into his thinking. For it seems to us that such a theory can readily accommodate the results of the original experiment.

To make an incremental theory more complete, one may add an individual-difference variable; both Hull (1952) and Spence (1956) have done this. While it does not seem that either of these theorists have firmly set their systems as to the method of handling individual differences, one method is to keep the threshold for a given association constant across all subjects and vary the rate of growth of the association to incorporate differences in rate of learning among subjects. A schematic presentation of such a conception is given in Figure 2. The display shows four subjects of dif-

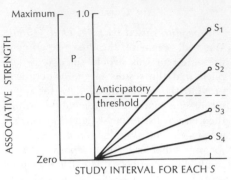

Fig. 2. Individual differences in rate of learning a single paired associate as interpreted by an incremental theory using an anticipatory threshold.

ferent learning abilities and the rate of growth of the associative connection for each as a function of a single study period. It will be noted that two ordinates are drawn. The one to the left is the same as that in Figure 1 and represents associative strength running from zero to some maximum strength. The other ordinate represents a performance measure; this measure starts at threshold with a probability of zero and increases as associative strength increases beyond the threshold. According to Figure 2, two subjects have developed associative strength above threshold and two have not. This conception leads to exactly the same prediction as that given by Estes *et al.* based on an all-or-none theory, namely, that without intervening reinforcement, the two items which were correct on the first test trial are likely to be correct on the second, and the two that were incorrect on the first test trial are likely to remain incorrect on the second.

It can also be seen that an incremental theory could handle differences in difficulty of items in the same manner that individual differences are handled in Figure 2. Thus, the four curves of Figure 2 could be thought of as representing four items of different difficulty for a single subject. With a constant period of study for each item the rate of growth varies because of differences in difficulty.

To summarize, we have been unable to see why a Hull-type incremental theory cannot handle the data Estes *et al.* present from this experiment. Futhermore, we have not found that any of the data presented by Estes (1960) from other experiments are resistant to interpretation by a theory of this type.

Questions of procedure. We turn next to procedural matters in an effort to show that artifacts have not been ruled out of the simple experiment outlined earlier. Two facts seem apparent. First, those items which were not gotten correctly on the first test trial must inevitably represent more difficult items on the average than those which were given correctly. Secondly, more incorrect items are represented in the protocols of slow-learning subjects than in those of fast-learning subjects, and, contrariwise, more correct items on the first test trial must be given by fast-learning subjects than are given by slow-learning subjects. Under these circumstances it seems quite out of the question that even Estes' interpretation of an incremental theory (i.e., that items which were incorrect and correct on the first test trial have equal probabilities of being correct on a second test trial), could receive confirmation.

Estes *et al.* were quite aware of the possibility of item differences producing the results we have discussed. But, in our opinion, their test of this was simply inappropriate. It will be remembered that after the first study trial four of the eight items were drawn at random for each subject, and the subject was given a second study trial for these four items, after which a second test of all eight items was made. Estes *et al.* show that 46% of the items which were incorrect on the first test trial, and then were given a second trial, were correct on the second test trial. Since the proportion correct on the first test trial was 49%, and since 46% is very close to that value, it is concluded that the two sets of items on which these values were determined are equivalent in difficulty. This comparison *assumes* that the first study trial produced no associative strength for items missed on the first test trial. But, an incremental theory could say simply that a certain amount of subthreshold strength had developed for these difficult items and that the second study trial resulted in about half of these being above the performance threshold. The fact that 49% and 46% are quantitatively above the same may well be an irrelevant, indeed, misleading fact, for theoretical inference. However, this is not the major point we wish to make, since we are concerned with methods.

It will be remembered that four items were given a second study trial. About half of these were incorrect on the first test trial, and it is these incorrect items to which attention is still directed. We have assumed that these items must necessarily be more difficult items than the full population of items, but no data are presented by Estes *et al.* which will test this assumption directly. However, such data would be available in their records. There were 48 subjects and by the nature of the design each subject learned two eight-item lists so that records on sixteen different pairs of items are available for each subject. The 48 subjects could be divided randomly into two subgroups of 24 subjects each. For each subgroup the number of times each of the sixteen items was responded to correctly on the first test trial could be determined. Finally, a correlation could be calculated between these two arrays for the sixteen items. The correlation must not differ significantly from zero to conclude that differences in item difficulty were of little relevance for the interpretation of the results of this experiment. Unless the experience in the

Northwestern University laboratory is completely atypical, it seems clear that a significant positive correlation will be found. The implication of such a correlation is that the items missed on the first test trial *were* more difficult than those given correctly and were consistently more difficult across subjects.

The second artifact of the experiment by Estes *et al.* concerns individual differences. Four items were drawn randomly from the eight presented on the first study trial, and those that were incorrect on the first test trial were examined to see what happened after a second study trial; the result was that 46% were correct. To take two extreme cases of individual differences, suppose first that a very slow subject got no items correct on the first test trial. On the second study trial he contributes four items to the pool from which the 46% statistic was derived. Secondly, suppose that a very fast learner got all items correct on the first test trial; such a subject will contribute no items to the pool from whence the 46% value came. It seems inevitable that the pool of missed items must be made up of the more difficult items and that these are more frequently represented in the protocols of slower-learning subjects than in the protocols of faster-learning subjects.

The third artifact contributing to the value of 46% comes from the method used to give the second study trial—the second reinforcement. The length of list was reduced from eight to four items; for the average subject two of these items were correct on the preceding test trial and two were incorrect. It is necessary, of course, to define operationally what is meant by a reinforcement. Estes *et al.* do this by specifying that a reinforcement is a single exposure of a given pair for a given time interval. These operations were identical for the first study trial where eight items were given and for the second where four were given.

Thus, the two trials differed only in terms of the number of items in the list. The assumption which underlies the evaluation of the 46% statistic made by Estes *et al.* is that the likelihood of an item being learned when in an eight-item list is equivalent to the likelihood of it being learned when in a four-item list. This is probably contrary to fact; the shorter the list into which an item is placed the greater is the likelihood that it will be given correctly. Two of the senior author's students (Fred Brown and Stephen Avard) have recently collected some data relevant to this point. Two conditions of a larger experiment will be considered. In one condition five pairs of items (consisting of bigrams as stimulus terms and common three-letter words as responses) were given a single study and test trial. For another group of subjects the same five items occurred as the first five items in a ten-item list which was also given a single study and test trial. What is the proportion correct for the five items common to both lists? The values were 75% for the five-item list and 59% for the ten-item list. It is conceivable that if the retention tests for the five-item lists had included five filler items (to make a ten-item list and thus more nearly simulate the Estes procedure), the recall of the five common items might have been equivalent for both lists, but this seems very doubtful.

To summarize: because of the problems of method outlined, we do not think the experiment by Estes, Hopkins, and Crothers is capable of deciding between an incremental theory and a one-trial theory.

How can investigation assess the merits of the two opposed conceptions? From the work of Estes *et al.*, and also from the work of Rock (1957), it would appear that there are at least three potential points or phases in learning an association where the insertion of empirical tests may be of value.

(1) The first phase occurs during a trial or trials during which an item is presented but is not given correctly on the test trial, i.e., no evidence of learning is given in the performance of the subject. The one-trial theory asserts that no associative strength has developed for such an item. An incremental theory would say that subthreshold associative strength may have developed, although we see no reason why an incremental theory is compelled to say that associative strength has developed for all such items.

(2) The second sensitive phase or point concerns the situation after an item has first been correctly anticipated. An unmodified one-trial theory must say that the probability of such an item being correct on a second test trial is 1.0; an incremental theory, using the oscillation principle and perhaps others, would expect variable probabilities depending upon the suprathreshold strength of the item.

(3) The third phase may be identified in classical terminology as the effect of overlearning on retention. One may not be able to measure changes in probability of performing an association over a series of trials simply because it is correct on every trial. Again, an unmodified one-trial theory would say that such overlearning is of no consequence, whereas an incremental theory might say that appropriate measures (e.g., long-term retention) would detect differences as a function of overlearning. Now, in fact, Rock (1957, p. 193) has said that "repetition *after* the association is formed is effective in strengthening it." He denies only that repetition was responsible in an incremental manner of forming the association. Thus, tests of Rock's one-trial theory versus an incremental theory must be confined to the first phase. Estes (1960), however, appears to make no such concession and intends to have his theory applied to all three phases. Each phase will now be considered in

turn, with major emphasis placed on the first phase.

PHASE 1

Have items given one or more study trials but never given correctly on test trials developed any associative strength? If the answer is "yes," support is given to an incremental theory; if the answer is "no," support is given to a one-trial theory. It is simple to pose the empirical question, but to get an unambiguous answer empirically is not so simple. At a philosophical level we tend to eschew the crucial experiment for the simple reason that they rarely turn out to be crucial. However, our philosophy was not quite strong enough to prevent our trying the two experiments which will be reported now.

Experiment I

Procedure. Twenty-two pairs of items were constructed. The stimulus terms were two letters with low associative connection between the two letters according to the Underwood-Schulz (1960) tables. The response terms were single letters. Each of 22 letters was used once as the first letter of a stimulus term, once as the second letter, and once as a response letter, with no letter repeated in a given pair.

Two groups of 44 Ss each were run, and a member from each group may be thought of as being run in pairs, an Experimental S and a Control S. For each of the 44 pairs of Ss the procedure was as follows. Eleven pairs were randomly selected from the 22-pair pool. These 11 pairs were presented to the Experimental S for a single study trial followed by a test trial. Those items that were missed (no response or an incorrect response) were now given immediately to S for a second study and test trial. We were asking, of course, whether or not any associative strength had developed on the first study trial for those items that were missed on the first test trial, the plan was to let such associative strength, if it existed, manifest itself by determining the influence of a further study trial. But what is the appropriate control for the learning which is shown by the second test trial? We need to compare the recall of the shortened list of items originally missed by the Experimental S with the recall of the same items when they had not been given the original study trial. A Control S must be presented the shortened list of items for a study and recall trial, but the study trial must be the first exposure the S has to the critical items. In addition, the Control S cannot be given the list "cold"; he must be at the same practice and warm-up level as the Experimental S. To accomplish this the Control S was given a study and test trial on the 11 items remaining in the pool after drawing 11 for the Experimental S. Immediately after the test trial, the Control S was given the shortened list given the Experimental S.

As noted, 11 pairs were drawn randomly from the pool of items and given to the first Experimental S. The remaining 11 items were given the Control S to equate practice and warm-up for the two Ss. For the next pairs of Ss, the two groups of 11 items were reversed so that the 11 given to the Control S of the first pair of Ss were now given the Experimental S in the second pair of Ss, and the 11 pairs given the first Experimental S were used as the warm-up and practice list for the second Control S. Thus, each item was used equally often as a control and experimental item when the results for the procedure for the four Ss are considered. Successive blocks of four Ss were handled in exactly the same way except that a new random drawing of 11 items was made for each block.

Items were presented by hand on cards at a 4-sec. rate, with 2 sec. between each card. On test trials only the stimulus was presented for 4 sec., with S instructed to give the response paired with it. All Ss were urged *not* to guess. Approximately 1 min. elapsed between the test trial for the first list and the start of the study trial for the shortened list. Any S was dropped if eight or more of the 11 items were given correctly on the first test trial. The reason for this was to avoid giving second lists so short that no discrimination between Control and Experimental Ss would be expected. The order of the items on the shortened-list study trial was different from the order in which these items had been presented the Experimental Ss on the original study and test trial but was the same for both Control and Experimental Ss. The test order for the shortened list was different from the order on the study trial but was again identical for both Control and Experimental Ss in a given pair of Ss. All Ss were given a second retention test on the shortened list immediately after the first.

Results. The results for the shortened list show a higher recall by the Experimental Ss than by the Control Ss. The Experimental Ss recalled 3.65 items, the Control, 3.10. This difference of .45 items is not significant statistically. However, it was noted that the Control Ss had better performance on the first list than did the Experimental Ss, the values being 3.75 and 3.63 for these 11-item lists. The use of covariance to adjust for the difference in learning of the first list produced a t of 2.19 for recall of the second list, a value which is beyond the 5% significance level. On the second test trial Experimental Ss gave an average of 3.40 items correct, the Control Ss gave 2.90 correct.

Another way to view the results is in terms of pairs; that is, let the 22 items rather than Ss be the entry. While these occurred with different frequencies in the shortened list the frequency of each was identical for Experimental and Control Ss. Using the direct-difference method of determining the t gave a value of 2.22, with greater frequency of recall by the Experimental Ss. It was noted that the 22 items were not equally represented in the second list. The reason is that there were consistent differences in item difficulty. The number of times each item was given correctly on the first test trial was determined for each subgroup of 44 Ss. The product moment correlation between these two arrays of 22 scores was .74. This high relationship was attained in spite of the fact that some attempt was made to construct homogeneous pairs.

Discussion. These results would tend to support an incremental theory; it appeared that the first study trial for the Experimental Ss was not irrelevant for the items missed on the first test trial. But we should not be too quick in reaching the conclusion that the relevancy of the first study trial comes about because of the subthreshold tendencies developed on that trial. One can always find fault with these crucial experiments and since the critical difference between the recall of the Experimental and Control Ss on the shortened list is not, in either an absolute or statistical sense, great, the effect of a possible confound cannot be gainsaid. For example, it is possible that the Control Ss may have suffered some interlist interference in learning the shortened list since each had been exposed to 11 stimuli in addition to the number of stimuli in the shortened list while the Experimental Ss had only been exposed to 11 different stimuli. However, if such differences in interlist similarity were operative it did not show up in the number of overt errors made in recalling the second list since both groups made exactly the same number, namely 89, or approximately two per S. (These errors were made in spite of the fact that Ss were instructed not to guess.) Still, it could be argued that errors are not an infallible index of amount of interference. Thus, the possibility that poorer performance of the Control Ss could be attributed to greater interlist interference cannot be entirely ruled out. On the other hand, there is a factor which would tend to favor the Control Group. We know that the missed items for an Experimental S are more difficult for him than are the items he anticipated correctly. But, in an absolute sense, the missed items for an Experimental S may be more difficult for him than would the same items be for a Control S. If any items are especially difficult for idiosyncratic reasons (which is quite possible since the intersubject agreement on item difficulty was not perfect), such items would not be as difficult for the Control S; or, to put this another way, some items which are difficult for an Experimental S for whatever reason may be easy for the Control S because of idiosyncratic reasons. This would facilitate the learning of the Control Ss. Our conclusion is that while the results tend to support an incremental theory we cannot be completely sure that the test is adequate. We therefore designed another experiment to avoid the difficulties noted.

Experiment II

Procedure. A single list of 11 pairs was used, with two-letter stimuli and the digits 1 through 11 as responses. No letters were duplicated among the 22 letters used in the stimuli. Eleven different lists were constructed such that each stimulus term was paired once with each response term. Of course, no given stimulus term nor a given response term appeared twice within a list. The eleven different lists represent 121 different pairs. Two Experimental Groups of 44 Ss each were run. Since 11 lists were available, and since no pair was repeated in the 11 lists, each list and each item was given to four different Ss in each group.

One Experimental Group (E1) was treated in exactly the same manner as was the Experimental Group in the previous experiment. That is, they were first given the 11 pairs for a study and test trial and then a study and test trial on the items missed on the first test trial. The second group (E2) provided the new twist. They were also given a study and test trial on the 11 items, and again the missed items became the critical ones. However, the stimulus and response members of the pairs of items missed by Ss in E2 were re-paired for the second study and test trial. Thus, the second list given the E2 Ss constituted a negative transfer paradigm. That is, it constituted a negative transfer paradigm if any associative strength had developed on the first study trial for the items missed on the first test trial. In short, we thought that a comparison of the performance of the two groups on the shortened list would maximize the effect of any associative tendencies developed on the first study trial, these tendencies pushing the performance of E1 up and the performance of E2 down.

Our basking in the beauty and simplicity of this experiment was abruptly terminated when we suddenly realized that this design possessed a very likely confound. By avoiding the difficulties produced by the design of the first experiment we had admitted a new problem. Consider the group (E2) in which the missed items are re-paired for the second study trial. The original items that were missed were difficult, relatively; we know this simply because they were missed. By re-pairing the stimulus and response terms we may very well be providing the Ss with easier pairs than would be the case for Ss in E1 who are "stuck" with the original pairs they missed. Thus, a direct comparison between the two groups on the recall of the shortened lists would be biased against an incremental theory. Nevertheless, we proceeded with the experiment as planned since we saw a way to test independently the difficulty of the shortened lists.

Details of the experimental procedures were the same as for Experiment I except that 2 min. elapsed between the test trial of the first list and the start of the study trial of the shortened list, this time being necessary for the experimenter to re-pair the missed items according to a prearranged random schedule.

Results. The two groups of 44 Ss each gave identical mean performance on the first list. This is important for it avoids having different lengths of lists as second lists for the two groups. The mean recall of the first list was 4.61 items out of the 11 presented. Therefore, the average length of the second list for both groups was 6.39 items.

In the recall of the shortened list the E1 Ss averaged 4.07 items, the E2 Ss averaged 3.75. This difference is not significant, giving a *t* of just over 1, but the difference is in the direction which would favor an incremental theory. On the second test trial the mean recall was 3.98 for E1 and 3.55 for E2. Our next step was to evaluate item difficulty for the two shortened lists.

Item difficulty was determined by evaluating the first recall—the recall of the 11 items presented initially. There are 121 different pairs. Each pair was given to four different Ss in each of the two groups of 44 Ss each. For each group separately we determined the number of times (out of a possible four times) that each item was correctly given on the first recall trial. The correlation between these two arrays of scores for the 121 items was .31, with .23 needed for the 1% significance level. This correlation, it should be clear, was obtained despite the fact that only four different Ss determined the score for an item in each group of Ss. When the items were grouped into 24 categories (23 groups of 5 items and 1 group of 6 items) to give more stability, the correlation became .61. But, by either value we may conclude that there is some intersubject agreement on easy and different items.

The next step was to assess the difficulty of the re-paired items given the E2 Ss as compared with the item difficulty of the second list given the E1 Ss. To make the determination a value was assigned each item in each list, and a mean list difficulty index determined for each S. The value assigned a given item was the number of times it was given correctly on the first study trial; these values could range from 0 to 4, since only 4 Ss determined the difficulty of an item within a group of Ss. Hence, a high mean list value indicates relatively easy items (easy list) and a low mean value indicates relatively difficult items. For the E1 Ss the mean list difficulty of the shortened list, consisting of pairs that had been missed on the first test trial, was 1.20. For the re-paired lists of the E2 Ss the mean list value was 1.51. The difference between these two means gives a *t* of

3.48, far beyond the 1% significance level.

The above comparison on item difficulty may not be quite fair. Item values for E1 Ss cannot be above three for a given item in the second list. For an item to appear in the second list for an E1 S, it had to be missed by that S on the first list; hence, a maximum value of three is all that is possible. For E2 Ss, on the other hand, a re-paired item in the second list could receive the maximum value of four. Indeed, for the 44 Ss in E2, there were 14 re-paired items which received a value of four. While this fact supports our contention that the re-paired items for E2 Ss are easier than the second-list items for E1 Ss, the comparison of mean list values may be biased by the admission of these items with values of four in determining mean list values for E2 Ss. Therefore, we rescored all re-paired lists in which items receiving a value of four appeared, assigning a value of three to all such items. Our earlier conclusion does not change; the mean value for the second lists for E1 Ss is 1.20, that for the E2 Ss, 1.-6. The difference produces a t of 3.13.

Discussion. From these analyses we conclude that the second or shortened lists learned by the E2 Ss (the re-paired lists) were constituted of easier items than the shortened lists learned by the E1 Ss. If no associative strength had developed for the missed items on the first study trial we would have expected the E2 Ss to learn their shortened re-paired lists significantly better than the E1 Ss would be expected to learn their shortened lists, since the E2 lists were easier than the E1 lists. In spite of this, the E1 Ss got more items than did the E2 Ss. Thus, it could be inferred that some associative strength had developed for items which were missed on the first test trial; the evidence could be interpreted as consonant with an incremental theory and as not supporting a one-trial theory.

In Experiment II we attempted to eliminate possible objections to procedures in Experiment I. We believe this was accomplished. And, although the interpretation of the results of Experiment II involved an indirect step, we can see no methodological problems which prevent this interpretation. Perhaps others can. In any event, we are not so untutored as to believe that these two experiments have settled a theoretical issue.

PHASES 2 AND 3

Phase 2 represents another point which may provide an evaluation of the two theoretical positions. The question is simply—what happens on a second recall trial to an item given correctly on the first, with no study intervening? As noted earlier, an unmodified one-trial theory must say that such items will be correct 100% of the time after they are first given correctly. In the study of Estes *et al.* (1960), discussed in detail earlier, the percentage repetition was 71%. In another study which Estes (1960) cites, the repetition value was 54%. Estes is quite aware of this disparity between his theory and the data; indeed, it causes him no little theoretical agony. His two mechanisms for resolving the contradiction are *guessing shrinkage* and *forgetting*. By guessing shrinkage is meant that if the subject guesses and gets a response correct on the first test trial no learning has occurred and this response is not likely to be given on the second test trial. We will not deny that some Ss may guess and that some of the guesses are correct. We do not see, however, that one can assign quantitative estimates to guessing shrinkage unless the S is *forced* to respond to all stimuli.

That forgetting may occur between two test trials seems clear, and certainly Estes *et al.* (1960) make matters difficult for themselves when they use the same Ss in more than one condition. If one uses naive subjects and lists of low intralist similarity the percentage of repetition increases appreciably. For example, in our Experiment I the percentage repetition of correct responses for the two test trials was 84% for the Experimental Ss, and 83% for the Control Ss. In Experiment II the values were 89% and 88% for E1 and E2, respectively. In the Brown-Avard experiment (mentioned in connection with the length of list issue), the percentage repetition was 91% for the 5-item list and 94% for the 10-item list. These values are much closer to the 100% than is shown in the studies of Estes. And yet, even under the most favorable circumstances (namely, subjects naive to the material in the laboratory, instructions not to guess, and low intralist similarity), the percentages do not attain 100%. In short, the Phase-2 facts do not give support to a one-trial learning theory. These facts do not, of course, require that the basic notion of one-trial learning be abandoned. But modifications seem necessary, and when these are made the basic postulate loses its uniqueness since these modifications must account at least for incremental changes in performance if not in learning. At this point the two opposed conceptions will not differ as starkly as they do when the basic notions are set in opposition as they were in Figure 1.

The question of Phase 3 is whether or not reinforcements (study trials) beyond the trial on which an item is first given correctly influences retention. The data presented by Estes *et al.* (1960) in their second experiment indicates that there is little effect of such further study. We shall not analyze this experiment nor attempt to defend a position that overlearning does influence retention. However, it should be noted that in the experiment the retention interval used by Estes *et al.* is a matter of a few minutes. It remains to be seen whether or not with longer retention intervals the same facts obtain, and hence that they may be considered as contradictory to the classical principle (as exemplified by Krueger's work, 1929) that overlearning enhances retention.

SUMMARY AND FINAL COMMENTS

We have taken the position that the data which have been used to support one-trial learning postulates have come from experiments with faulty methods. This position does not disavow the theory of one-trial learning. We have also taken exception to statements that the data of these experiments cannot be interpreted by available incremental learning theories. In addition, two experiments were reported which could be interpreted as supporting an incremental theory and as not supporting a one-trial theory, but we are under no illusions that these experiments settle the issue in the sense that they are crucial experiments. The consideration of the performance of subjects in verbal learning experiments after a response is first given correctly led to the conclusion that if one-trial learning is occurring, a system which uses this basic postulate must be modified to such an extent that it will closely approximate the incremental theories. In conclusion, certain additional statements are judged to be relevant.

(1) What constitutes "one trial" is quite an arbitrary matter. An 8-sec. rate of presentation for a pair of items constitutes four trials at a 2-sec. rate. We feel confident that shortening the anticipation interval on test trials will give data which, superficially at least, conform even more to an incremental notion than is the case when slow rates of presentation are involved (as has been the case in most of the experiments from which notions of one-trial learning have stemmed). Again, it should be clear that if such is true it does not mean a disproof of the one-trial theory, but rather it means that modification of it is needed. It is perhaps quite possible to add modifying performance

factors to the one-trial theories; if so, accounting for performance will become a major part of the theories. There is nothing wrong with this except that there will remain little difference between the theories which are now set in opposition.

(2) We have spoken earlier of the difficulties of deriving crucial experiments. Certain theories simply are not capable of disproof. Certain aspects of the incremental theory seem to be of this nature. To disprove the incremental theory in Phase 1 (to show that an item not given correctly has gained *no* associative strength) essentially requires proof of the null hypothesis. As long as experiments show a small, consistent, even though statistically insignificant effect in Phase-1 experiments, the incremental theory remains tenable. To disprove the incremental theory in this phase requires that a series of experiments show results which represent a random dispersion of effects around zero. This is not a virtue for a theory, but this characteristic seems to be inherent in the incremental theory.

(3) In the experiments dealing with one-trial learning the emphasis has been on the single association between a stimulus and a response term. The responses used have been readily available to the subjects; little if any response learning as such is involved. Learning a verbal list under these conditions takes place very rapidly. But, it should be clear that the association between the stimulus and response term in fact may not be representative of the other learning which occurs when heavy response learning is involved (e.g., integration of the letters of difficult syllables); certainly when heavy response learning is involved it requires the major portion of the learning time (Underwood and Schulz, 1960). One-trial theories have not included response learning in their discussion. It is quite possible that a theory of one-trial learning could be extended to cover response learning as well as learning the

association between the stimulus term and response term, but we believe it will be a very difficult job. In any event, the point we wish to make is that the issues as drawn by the one-trial theories cover only a small portion of the associations which must be established in many verbal-learning tasks.

(4) As noted in the introduction, the theoretical issues represent a curious twist in theorizing about learning in that the data to support the theories are sought in the verbal-learning laboratory. Not since Thorndike has the human subject been used consistently as a source of data to test basic theoretical notions about learning. The memory drum seems to have replaced the T-maze, at least temporarily. This may or may not be an appropriate trend. There is some evidence (Postman, in press) that human subjects may adopt certain strategies in learning which may completely prohibit theoretical tests of propositions of the kind discussed in this paper. For example, supposing a subject adopts a strategy to concentrate on one or two pairs out of a list of eight on a given trial, ignoring all the others. If this does happen, the arbitrary definition of "one trial" is sadly deficient for the theoretical purposes intended. Now in fact we do not really know in any systematic way how frequently such strategies, as well as others, may be adopted by a subject. But, if such strategies do occur, and if they make tests between alternative theoretical positions absurd, then perhaps the verbal-learning laboratory is not the place to seek data in support of so-called fundamental postulates of learning.

ESTES, W. K. Learning theory and the new "mental chemistry." *Psychol. Rev.*, 1960, **67**, 207-23.

ESTES, W. K., HOPKINS, B. L., AND CROTHERS, E. J. All-or-none and conservation effects in the learning and retention of paired associates. *J. exp. Psychol.*, 1960, **60**, 329-39.

HULL, C. L. *A behavior system.* New Haven: Yale Univer. Press, 1952.

KRUEGER, W. C. F. The effect of overlearning on retention. *J. exp. Psychol.*, 1929, **12**, 71-8.

LOCKHEAD, G. R., A re-evaluation of evidence of one trial associative learning. *Amer. J. Psychol.*, 1961, **74**, 590-95.

POSTMAN, L. Repetition and paired-associate learning. *Amer. J. Psychol.*, in press.

ROCK, I. The role of repetition in associative learning. *Amer. J. Psychol.*, 1957, **70**, 186-93.

SPENCE, K. W. *Behavior theory and conditioning.* New Haven: Yale Univer. Press, 1956.

UNDERWOOD, B. J., AND SCHULZ, R. W. *Meaningfulness and verbal learning.* Philadelphia: Lippincott, 1960.

UNDERWOOD, B. J., REHULA, R., AND KEPPEL, G. Item selection in paired-associate learning. *Amer. J. Psychol.*, in press.

20 / An Association Model for Response and Training Variables in Paired-associate Learning [1]

GORDON H. BOWER, *Stanford University*

This paper reports an attempt to apply a simple association learning model to the analysis of the influence of response and training variables on paired-associate learning. The issues under investigation are old ones but have not been resolved satisfactorily in the past. With the aid of the elementary learning model, the problems are posed clearly and, the data willing, adequately resolved by the use of a few simple and intuitively compelling assumptions about learning.

The first problem that led to this investigation concerns the relationship between the number of response alternatives (N) and error rate in paired-associate learning. Experimental results (Noble, 1955; Riley, 1952) are in agreement in showing that the number of errors subjects make before reaching some criterion of learning is greater the larger the number of response alternatives. There is little agreement, however, as to the interpretation of this fact.

Two possible factors could be involved. First, the effectiveness of a reinforced trial in increasing performance (i.e., the learning rate constant) may be influenced by N; and second, N may influence the probability of being correct by sheer guessing on items that are yet unlearned. It is a reasonably safe assumption that N has the second effect on chance guessing. Previous data are unclear on whether N also influences the first factor, the effectiveness of a reinforced trial. This is not an easy question to answer since it is difficult to separate the effects of these two factors in the data. Guessing occurs only on unlearned items but there is no way to tell by direct observation just how many items have been learned and how many have been guessed correctly on any given trial. Moreover, there appears to be little hope that more refined or ingenious experimental procedures will enable us to unconfound these two factors so that we may crucially test the hypothesis that N affects the learning rate.

This is the type of situation in which a theoretical model of learning can make a strategic contribution. Indeed, without the aid of some formal model of the learning process, the question of the effect of N can neither be posed clearly nor answered clearly. With the aid of a theory one can make suitable allowance for the guessing factor and thus make an assessment of the contribution of learning and guessing at every stage of the experiment.

The model to be presented has been formally treated in more detail in a previous paper (Bower, 1961). Here the theory will be presented informally and only those implications relevant to the present discussion will be introduced.

1. This investigation was supported in part by a grant, M-3849, from the National Institute of Health, United States Public Health Service. From the *Psychological Review*, 1962, 69, 34-53, with permission of the author and publisher.

For a more formal statement of the axioms and theorems, the reader may consult the prior report. The basic notion of the model is the assumption that each stimulus item and its correct response become associated on an all-or-none basis. Considering a single item, it can be in either of two states at the beginning of each trial: conditioned to its correct response or not conditioned. If the item is conditioned at the beginning of a trial, then the correct response occurs. If the item is not conditioned, then the probability of the correct response depends somewhat upon the experimental procedure. In experiments by the writer, the subjects were told the N responses (Integers 1, 2, . . .N) available to them and were told to respond on every trial regardless of whether they knew the correct answer. If the N numbers occur equally often as the to-be-learned responses to the items, then the probability that the subject will guess correctly on an unlearned item is $1/N$ on the simplest assumptions; [2] correspondingly, his probability of guessing incorrectly is $1-1/N$. The following discussion of the model is oriented specifically towards such an experimental procedure.

With the theory formulated in this way, one cannot uniquely specify the subject's state of conditioning on a given item from the knowledge that he made a correct response, since this correct response may have come about by guessing on an unlearned item. Thus, the theory does not imply that the first correct response will be followed by correct responses on all subsequent trials. However, if the subject makes an error, then we can make a determinate inference that the item was not conditioned at the beginning of the trial.

We have introduced the notions of the two states of conditioning and the probability of the correct response given the item's state of conditioning at the beginning of each trial. We assume that each

item in initially unconditioned and that the effect of successive reinforced trials is to provide repeated opportunities for the item to become conditioned. The single parameter of the theory is the learning rate constant (c) which represents the probability that an unconditioned item becomes conditioned as the result of a single reinforced trial. The probability that a reinforced trial fails to condition the correct response to an unlearned item is $1-c$. The probability that an item is still not conditioned after n reinforced trials is $(1-c)^n$. If c is larger than zero, then this probability approaches zero as n becomes large; that is, given a large number of reinforced trials, it is certain that the item will become conditioned on some one of these reinforced trials. When the item becomes conditioned, the probability of a correct response jumps from $1/N$ up to 1.

From the considerations above we may obtain an expression for q_n, the probability that the subject responds incorrectly to a given item on Trial n of the experiment. To obtain q_n we note that the probability that the item has failed to be conditioned during the preceding $n-1$ trials is $(1-c)^{n-1}$; and if the item is not conditioned then the probability of

---

2. The arguments to be developed apply only to those conditions in which the response alternatives are immediately available to the subject and he is permitted time to give a relevant response on each trial before the terminal event (e.g., reinforcement) occurs. This is the procedure most familiar to those who run animal subjects in choice situations. A more frequent procedure in human learning experiments has been to give the subject a fixed time interval in which he may respond, and the terminal event (e.g., correct response in paired associates, next item in a serial list) follows after that time interval regardless of whether the subject makes a relevant response. To remark on the sociology of experimenters, there seems to be an empirical correlation between the use of experimenter vs. subject-controlled exposure time and whether the relevant responses per se (as well as the S-R associations) must be learned in the experimental situation: when the responses must be learned, experimenters usually control exposure time; when the response alternatives are immediately available, either via instruction or construction, the subject is allowed to control exposure time. Clearly, however, there is no necessary entailment between these procedural aspects, and one may expect the empty cells of the 2×2 contingency table to be filled by future experimentation.

guessing incorrectly is $1-1/N$. Hence, the probability of an error on Trial n is given by the product of these two factors:

$$q_n = (1-1/N)(1-c)^{n-1} \qquad [1]$$

Using this elementary association model, the first question of this investigation can be restated in a clear manner: Is c independent of N? If c is independent of N, then, given an estimate of c obtained from one group, we should be able to predict in advance the performance of other groups trained with differing numbers of response alternatives by simply adjusting the N factor in Equation 1. To the extent that these free predictions are accurate, we would have good evidence for the assertion that N affects guessing probabilities but has no influence on learning rate per se.

The second question prompting this investigation concerns the relation between several different training conditions and performance in paired-associate learning. The two major conditions of training studied to date are the correction and noncorrection conditions. The more frequently used condition is the correction procedure in which subject is informed of the correct response on every trial regardless of whether he responds correctly. In noncorrection training, the subject is told right or wrong depending on whether his response is correct or incorrect. In the following, we will use the word "reinforcement" in the general sense intended by Estes (1960), viz., as operations exerting certain general quantitative effects upon response probabilities. In paired-associate experiments, the reinforcing operation is that of informing subjects of the correct response or in some way ensuring that this response is the last one to occur in the presence of a stimulus item. With this interpretation, then, on every trial under a correction procedure the correct response is reinforced. The noncorrection training procedure differs in that the correct response is reinforced only on those trials when it occurs; since all incorrect responses are followed by the experimenter simply saying "Wrong," no explicit reinforcement operation is involved. We will refer to such trials as nonreinforced trials.

Within the model, an account of the noncorrection procedure takes the form of specific assumptions about the formation of associations following reinforced and nonreinforced trials. Considerations of parsimony lead us to assume that the effect on conditioning of a reinforced trial is the same whether the reinforcement occurs in the context of a correction or noncorrection procedure, viz., the probability that an unlearned item becomes conditioned to its reinforced response is c, the same constant as in the case of the correction procedure. A new assumption that is required concerns the effect of a nonreinforced trial, when the experimenter says "Wrong" following an error. The assumption that has been made elsewhere (Thorndike, 1932) and that is made here also, is that a nonreinforced trial in this situation results in no net change in the probability of a correct response. This assumption is not offered as a universal interpretation of nonreinforcement; however, within the specific situation to which the model will be applied (i.e., the alternative responses are equiprobable initially and a number of different S-R events occur between successive presentations of any given stimulus) there is some basis for thinking that the no change assumption may be approximately correct.

From these assumptions about the noncorrection procedure, a difference equation can be derived expressing the change in the average probability of an error from Trial n to Trial $n+1$:

$$q_{n+1} = q_n[q_n] + (1-q_n)[(1-c)q_n] \qquad [2]$$

The first term on the right-hand side of

Equation 2 exhibits the assumption of no change (i.e., $q_{n+1}=q_n$) when the subject makes an error on Trial n, with probability q_n; the second term shows that if a success occurs (with probability $1-q_n$), then with probability c the item becomes conditioned (if it is not already) and with probability $1-c$ the reinforcement was ineffective and no change occurs on that particular trial. An explicit solution of Equation 2 is not available. However, Miller and McGill (1952; see also Bush & Mosteller, 1955, p. 181), have derived the following recurrence relation for Equation 2 (the constants have been changed appropriately):

$$q_n=(1-1/N)[1-(1-c)^{n-1}]q_{n-1}$$
$$+(1-1/N)(1-c)^{n-1} \qquad [3]$$

Equation 3 can be used to compute successive values of the average error probability once N and c are known. In general, the predicted learning curve is S shaped, a feature which is consistent with the expectation of a low rate of improvement early in training when the subject is trying to discover the correct response. The point of inflection of the S curve will be positively related to N. These features seem in qualitative agreement with noncorrection results reported by Noble (1955), although his experimental procedure was more complex than the one under present consideration.

At this point in the analysis, Experiment I was carried out with four groups of subjects learning the same list of 10 paired associates. The variables were the number of response alternatives (the first three or first eight integers) and correction vs. noncorrection training procedure. For brevity, the four groups will be referred to by the symbols 3-C, 8-C, 3-NC and 8-NC, where 3 or 8 represent the number of responses, and C and NC designate correction and noncorrection training, respectively. A more extensive discussion of the procedure and results of Experiment I will be deferred till

later; it will be sufficient here to note one critical result of Experiment I since it was this fact that led to Experiment II. The fact was that strong evidence was obtained to support the assumption of no change in success probability following a nonreinforced trial in the noncorrection training groups; that is, with either three or eight response alternatives, saying "Wrong" followed a subject's incorrect response had no effect on his probability of success on the next trial.

This no change result supports our earlier assumption about nonreinforced trials, but how are we to understand it? On rational grounds, one might expect that subjects would tend to eliminate a response which was followed by "Wrong." For example, if subjects in the 3-NC group tended to eliminate their first erroneous response, then the probability of the correct response on the next trial should be around one-half or at least greater than one-third. However, the results of Experiment I clearly showed that this increase did not occur, and we seek some explanation for why it did not occur.

An explanation may be found perhaps by attending to the responses evoked in the subject by saying to him "Wrong" after he has responded, e.g., "three." The reason for this inquiry is that, holding to a strict contiguity interpretation for the formation of association, it is these terminal reactions to the stimulus which have an opportunity to become conditioned. Often these implicit reactions to "Wrong" are primarily emotional; in this regard, it may be reported that subjects frequently volunteered the information, "I know I've been getting that item wrong, but I can't remember what number I said last time." Clearly, if the subjects' implicit reactions are primarily emotional, then we may expect no change in the recorded response probabilities on the next trial. However, if subjects implicitly react to "three is wrong" with the response "one or two is correct," when the contiguity interpretation would imply that the probability of response "three" would decrease and the probability of responses "one" and/or "two" would correspondingly increase.

According to this interpretation, the noncorrection procedures in Experiment I did not insure responses of the form, e.g., "one or two is correct" after the experimenter said "Wrong" to "three." For one of the groups in Experiment II, conditions were arranged to insure the occurrence of responses in this form following errors. There were three response alternatives and subjects were instructed that one and only one number was correct for each nonsense syllable. If, for example, the subject responded with "three," instead of saying "Wrong," the experimenter said "one or two is correct." It should be noted that, in a formal sense, the subject gains no more information about the correct response with this procedure than when the experimenter says "Wrong," as in the noncorrection procedure. Comparisons of the results of this procedure with the standard noncorrection procedure are given below.

The second condition run in Experiment II was aimed at a slightly different question. The question is whether there is some more basic way of specifying reinforcement contingencies in this situation rather than merely listing them, correction and noncorrection. The formulation proposed here is that this basic variable is the degree to which the experimenter specifies the correct response following an error by the subject; to describe it in another way, the variable is the size of the subset of alternatives within which the one correct alternative is said to lie. The correction and noncorrection procedures occupy the extreme poles of this dimension; in the correction procedure, the experimenter uniquely specifies the correct response; in the noncorrection procedure, when the experi-

menter says "Wrong," he implicitly specifies "one of the other $N-1$ alternatives is correct." [3] To illustrate the construction of intermediate values of this training dimension, suppose there were eight response alternatives and that the subject responds incorrectly with "one" to a given item; then the experimenter might say "three or six is correct," or "six or eight or two or five is correct," and so on. For the second group in Experiment II, with eight responses, the experimenter said two numbers following errors. The subjects were instructed that one of the numbers was correct and that the other number was a distractor, but there were no cues as to which number was the correct one. Of course, if the subject gave the correct number, the experimenter indicated this to him.

It is clear that such a continuum of training conditions can be constructed. It is also clear that variations in this training variable should produce graded variations in performance intermediate between the two extremes produced by the correction and noncorrection procedures. To describe some of the factors involved in this prediction, consider the reasons for expecting the partial correction group listed above (call it the 8-P group) to make fewer errors than the 8-NC group from Experiment I.

First, a subject in the 8-P condition is expected to make fewer errors before his first correct response because there is at least some likelihood that the correct association will be formed following an error. Specifically, we assume that before the first correct response the probability that the item becomes conditioned following an error is $c/2$, where c is the same learning constant as before. In general, if the subject is told k alternatives, one of which is correct, then we assume that the probability of the correct association being formed is c/k on each trial

---

3. However, see the related discussion above concerning the subject's reactions to "Wrong."

before the first success. This formulation is equivalent to assuming that the subject selects at random one of the k possibly correct responses to rehearse on a given trial, with probability $1/k$ he selects the correct response, and with probability c rehearsal of this correct response results in conditioning.

The preceding analysis applies on trials before the first correct response occurs. After the subject has been once informed of the correct response, his probability of recognizing it among the two numbers the experimenter says (following a subsequent error, if any) will be greater than one-half. If the subject recognizes the correct number and then rehearses it, the effect is much the same as a reinforced trial. In general, we may let r represent this recognition probability following the first correct response; because of implicit rehearsal, r is also the probability of a reinforced trial on incorrect trials following the first correct response. Specifically, we assume for the present case that r is unity; that is, following the first correct response, we assume that subject can recognize with Probability 1 the correct number among the two numbers that the experimenter says following an error. If the subject recognizes the correct response and rehearses it, then with probability c the conditioned association is formed.

To summarize the discussion for the partial correction groups, we have assumed that prior to the occurrence of the first correct response the probability of conditioning is $c/2$ on each trial; on the trial of the first correct response and those trials following the probability of conditioning is c. In a later section we suggest a number of ways to test the details of these assumptions.

In the experiments to be described there were six independent groups; if the model and theoretical assumptions are correct, then the data from the six groups can be reproduced after estimating the constant c from one of the groups selected arbitrarily. One can easily recognize the advantages of casting our theoretical assumptions in explicit form within such a model. Not only can we clearly pose the questions of how N and its interactions with training conditions affect error rate, but we have also developed a conceptual framework within which it is possible to get an answer to these questions. The basic learning parameter, c, plays a central role in the theory and is not just a curve-fitting constant; for a homogeneous population of subjects with the same learning materials, the underlying theory constrains c to be the same for all conditions. If indeed such parameter invariance obtains (i.e., if c can be transposed from one condition to the others), then a strong appeal can be made for the simplicity and power of the underlying theory within which c derives its meaning.

THE EXPERIMENTS [4]

The subjects, 88 Stanford undergraduates, were required to learn a list of 10 paired associates to a criterion of two successive correct runs through the entire list. The stimulus items were nonsense syllables of 0-5% association value chosen for low intralist similarity. The responses were the first three or first eight integers, paired randomly with the stimuli for each subject. With three response alternatives, two of the three responses were used for three stimuli each and the third response, selected randomly for each subject, was paired with the remaining four stimulus items. With eight response alternatives, all eight numbers were first paired with eight randomly selected syllables for each subject, and then the remaining two syllables were assigned to different but randomly selected numbers for each subject.

The subjects, run individually, were

4. This experiment was carried out with the assistance of Takao Umemoto.

instructed to learn a list of 10 nonsense syllables and their associated number responses, the response alternatives being either one, two, or three (or one, two, . . ., seven, or eight), and that the syllables and numbers had been paired off randomly. They were asked to respond within 2 or 3 seconds after the stimulus card was shown, and to guess a number if they didn't know the answer. The result of this practice is that the exposure time cannot be specified exactly; however, it was noted that the subjects followed instructions and responded within 2 or 3 seconds in the large majority of cases.

For all three training conditions, if the subject gave the correct number to a card, the experimenter repeated it, e.g., "three is correct." The three conditions differed on trials when the subject responded incorrectly: in the correction conditions, the experimenter said the correct number; in the noncorrection conditions, the experimenter said "Wrong" following errors; and in the partial correction condition, the experimenter said two numbers following errors, e.g., "one or three is correct." The subjects in the partial conditions were informed that only one of the numbers the experimenter said would be correct and the other number was a distractor (chosen at random) and that half the time the correct number would be said first and half the time it would be said second. The 10 stimulus cards were shuffled for 15 seconds between runs through the deck. The entire list was repeated until the subject went through two consecutive cycles without any errors.

The numbers of subjects in each group were 14 in the 3-C, 8-C, and 8-NC groups; 15 in the 3-P and 8-P groups; and 16 in the 3-NC group. Assuming that each item and each subject may be characterized by the same value of c, the data consist of 140, 150, or 160 sequences of correct and incorrect responses for the

various experimental conditions. Before the model could be evaluated, the learning rate constant, c, had to be estimated. The data from the 3-C group were selected for this purpose; the least squares estimate of $c = .218$ was obtained by fitting the learning curve (i.e., percentage correct vs. trials) for this group.

The first predictions concern the average total errors per item before achieving the learning criterion. The predictions for the correction and noncorrection groups were obtained by summing Equations 1 and 3, respectively, over trials. The predictions for the partial groups were obtained by calculating the average errors before the first success (using $c/2$ as the rate constant) and the average errors following the first success (using c as the rate constant) and then adding these two numbers. The observed means (M) and standard errors of the means (σ_M) are shown in Table 1 along with the predicted means (P).

It is clear from Table 1 that the theory performs adequately in predicting aver-

TABLE 1. *Average total number of errors per item observed and predicted*

Training condition	Response alternatives	
	3	8
Correction	$M = 2.94$	$M = 3.95$
	$P = 3.03$	$P = 4.00$
	$\sigma_M = .19$	$\sigma_M = .25$
Partial	$M = 3.74$	$M = 5.95$
	$P = 3.88$	$P = 5.80$
	$\sigma_M = .21$	$\sigma_M = .35$
Noncorrection	$M = 5.65$	$M = 9.42$
	$P = 5.59$	$P = 9.54$
	$\sigma_M = .34$	$\sigma_M = .61$

age total errors using the single estimate of c. In all six cases the predicted value falls within one standard error of the observed mean.[5] The differential effect

---

5. The standard errors for the 3-C and 8-C groups can be predicted by the theory and turn out to be somewhat larger than the observed values (predicted values were .24 and .30 for 3-C and 8-C groups, respectively). Deriving comparable variance predictions for the partial and noncorrection conditions presents complex mathematical problems which have not been solved to date.

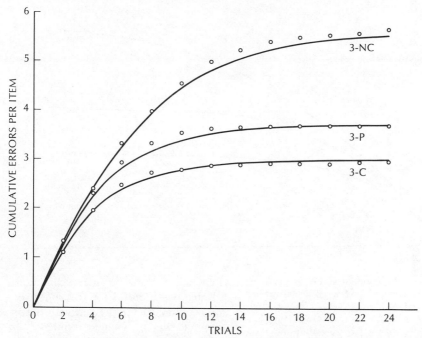

FIG. 1. Average cumulative errors per item plotted as a function of trials for subjects having three response alternatives. (The smooth curves represent predicted values; the dots near a curve represent the corresponding observed values.)

of N upon error rate is amplified as one proceeds from the correction through the partial to the noncorrection training procedures.

A second indication of the goodness of fit of the theory is shown graphically in Figures 1 and 2 which present observed and predicted values for cumulative errors as a function of trials. The smooth curves connect the predicted values while the unconnected points are the empirical values. The predicted values for the correction and noncorrection conditions were obtained by cumulating successive values of error probabilities calculated from Equations 1 and 3, respectively. The theoretical curve for the partial correction conditions is not expressible in a simple equation but successive values can be obtained. The first several values will

be derived here to illustrate the procedure. Define Q_n as the probability that the item is not yet conditioned by the beginning of Trial n. The probability of an error on Trial n would then be $(1-1/N)Q_n$. The first several values of Q_n for the partial correction conditions are:

by assumption

$$Q_1 = 1$$

$$Q_2 = \frac{1}{N}(1-c) + \left(1 - \frac{1}{N}\right)$$

$$\times \left(1 - \frac{c}{2}\right)$$

$$Q_3 = \frac{1}{N}(1-c)^2 + \left(1 - \frac{1}{N}\right) \qquad [4]$$

$$\times \left(1 - \frac{c}{2}\right)\frac{1}{N}(1-c)$$

$$+ \left(1 - \frac{1}{N}\right)^2\left(1 - \frac{c}{2}\right)^2$$

The value of Q_2 is the sum of two probabilities: (*a*) that a correct guess occurs on Trial 1 but conditioning failed to occur

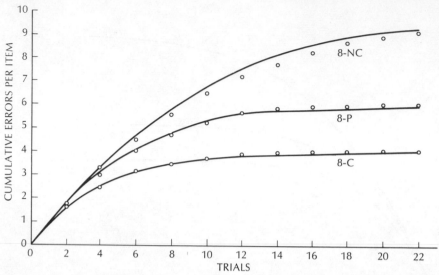

Fig. 2. Average cumulative errors per item plotted against trials for subjects having eight response alternatives. (The smooth curves represent predicted values; the dots near a curve are the corresponding observed values.)

with probability $1-c$, and (b) that subject guessed incorrectly on Trial 1 and fails to condition the correct response with probability $1-c/2$. The value of Q_3 is the sum of the joint probabilities of three events: (a) correct on Trial 1, fails to condition on Trials 1 and 2; (b) error on Trial 1, success on Trial 2, fails to condition after either trial; (c) errors on both trials, not conditioned on either trial. The general rule for obtaining Q_n is that prior to the first correct response the conditioning probability is $c/2$ and that on the trial of the first correct response and thereafter the conditioning probability is c. By multiplying these Q_n values by $1-1/N$ and summing them, the predicted curves for the partial correction conditions are obtained. As Figures 1 and 2 show, for five of the six groups the fit of predicted to observed values is satisfactory; the correspondence to the 8-NC points would not be impressive were it not for the fact that the same c constant was used in generating all the curves

under appropriate boundary conditions.

Equations 2 and 3 for the noncorrection conditions were derived with the assumption that no change resulted from nonreinforced trials. To the extent that these equations adequately describe performance in the noncorrection conditions, the assumption of no change is supported. However, additional data bearing upon this assumption may be obtained by analysis of the early trials before learning has occurred. Beginning with the first trial, consider the sequence of probabilities of a correct response following 0, 1, 2, . . . consecutive errors. As soon as a subject responds correctly to a given item, that item is dropped from later computations. If the randomization of responses to stimuli has been effective, then the first value of this series should be close to $1/N$, the probability of guessing the correct number by chance. Moreover, if the assumption of no change is correct, then the probabilities of a success following 1, 2, 3, . . . consecutive errors should remain around $1/N$ for the noncorrection groups, deviating from this value only by random sampling fluctuations. The results of this analysis are shown in Table 2 for the noncorrection groups. It should be realized that going

TABLE 2. *Probability of a success following n consecutive errors from the first trial for the noncorrection groups*

n	3-NC	8-NC
0	.34	.12
1	.31	.11
2	.28	.14
3	.31	.17
4	.31	.13
5	.37	.16

down the column these estimates become progressively less reliable because the number of cases involved (beginning with 160 or 140) decreases. These series of estimates for both three and eight response alternatives reveal no significant trends away from the first value. Hence, the results provide additional support for the assumption of no change following nonreinforced trials in the noncorrection conditions.

An analysis related to that above can be given for the correction and partial correction groups. Because the success rate was higher for these groups, there was insufficient data to obtain reliable estimates of single-trial probabilities such as shown in Table 2 for the noncorrec-

TABLE 3. *Predicted and observed conditional probabilities of success following an error on the preceding trial*

Training condition	Response alternatives			
	3		8	
	Ob-serve	Pre-dict	Ob-serve	Pre-dict
Correction	.48	.48	.35	.35
Partial				
Before first success	.35	.35	.21	.22
After first success	.46	.48	.38	.33

tion groups. However, this difficulty may be circumvented by considering over all trials the probability of a success given an error on the preceding trial. For the correction group, this probability should be a constant, $c+(1-c)p_o$ where p_o is the probability of guessing correctly. For the partial correction conditions, the

probability of a success following an error should be $c/2+(1-c/2)p_o$ before the first success and should be $c+(1c-c)p_o$ after the first success. Such predictions are very sensitive to small changes in p_o. Our efforts to randomly assign responses to stimuli were directed towards making p_o be close to $1/N$ in value. However, with even a moderate-sized sample, small deviations of the actual probability of correct guessing inevitably occur. Hence, a fairer test of the model (rather than a test of the randomization procedure) is provided by predictions based on empirical estimates of p_o. Using the first-trial estimates of p_o (which on the whole were close to $1/N$), the predicted probabilities of success following an error were obtained and are compared with the observed values in Table 3. The correspondence between predicted and observed values is quite satisfactory; we may note that the rather complex assumptions about conditioning in the partial correction conditions receive substantial support from these data.

Another way to test the assumptions of the model involves predicting the number of errors before the first success. Since for the partial and noncorrection groups the stochastic process is not complicated prior to their first success, it is possible to predict both the mean and variance of this statistic for these groups. Define F_1 to be the number of errors before the first success, and p_o to be the probability of a correct guess. Then it can be shown (Bower, 1961) that the mean and variance of F_1 for the noncorrection groups are:

$$M = \frac{1-p_o}{p_o}, \quad V = \frac{1-p_o}{p_o{}^2} \qquad [5]$$

Similarly, for the correction groups, the mean and variance of F_1 are:

$$M = \frac{1-p_o}{p_o+c(1-p_o)}, \qquad [6]$$
$$V = M + M^2(1-2c)$$

The expressions for the partial correction groups are the same as in Equation 6 except with c replaced by $c/2$.

The predicted values of the mean and standard error of F_1 for the six groups are shown in Table 4 along with the observed means and standard errors. For the noncorrection groups, p_0 was estimated as the average of the values in Table 2 since the theory says those values represent random fluctuations around p_0.

Inspection of Table 4 shows that in the six cases the predicted mean F_1 is within a standard error of the observed mean, and the predictions of the standard errors are also close to the observed standard errors. In general, the average

TABLE 4. *Observed and predicted mean and standard error of the number of errors before the first success*

Training condition	Response alternatives	
	3	8
Correction	$M = 1.33$ $F = 1.39$ $\sigma_M = .092$ $\sigma_F = .125$	$M = 2.25$ $F = 2.37$ $\sigma_M = .185$ $\sigma_F = .180$
Partial	$M = 2.12$ $F = 2.16$ $\sigma_M = .192$ $\sigma_F = .191$	$M = 4.15$ $F = 4.02$ $\sigma_M = .289$ $\sigma_F = .329$
Noncorrection	$M = 2.17$ $F = 2.15$ $\sigma_M = .201$ $\sigma_F = .206$	$M = 6.20$ $F = 6.38$ $\sigma_M = .511$ $\sigma_F = .558$

F_1 increases with N and the differential effect of N is amplified under the partial and noncorrection training conditions.

It should be noted that at an empirical level N has its primary influence upon errors before the first success, and has practically no influence upon errors following the first success. The reader may convince himself of this fact by subtracting the mean F_1 values in Table 4 from the mean total error values in Table 1. At first glance, this observation seems to invalidate the model by showing that N only influences the discovery stage but not the fixation stage of learning after

the first correct response has occurred. In fact, however, theoretical predictions of average errors following the first success correspond closely to the observed values; of course, this must be so since the theory predicts F_1 and total errors reasonably well. The reason we expect errors following the first success to be relatively constant over N is that, according to the theory, a sampling bias is involved in comparing the three and eight alternative conditions at this point. Errors following the first success will occur only for items whose first correct response came about by guessing, and for these guessed correct items we expect more errors with eight than with three response alternatives. Let g_N represent the probability that with N alternatives the first correct response comes about by guessing and let e_N represent the average number of subsequent errors for an item whose first correct response occurred by guessing. Then the expression for the average number of errors following the first correct response (call it w_N) is:

$$w_N = g_N e_N + (1 - g_N) \cdot 0 = g_N e_N \quad [7]$$

That is, a proportion g_N of first correct responses come about by guessing and we expect an average of e_N more errors for these items; a proportion $1 - g_N$ of the first correct responses come about by conditioning on the preceding trial and for these items we expect zero subsequent errors. According to the theory, e_8 will be larger than e_3; however, g_8 will be smaller than g_3; that is, given a first correct response, it is more likely to have occurred by guessing when N is three than when N is eight. Therefore, the fact that the products $g_3 e_3$ and $g_8 e_8$ are approximately equal is neither surprising nor a refutation of the theory.

DISCUSSION

The overall results provide strong support for the validity of the model and the specific hypotheses about experimental variables. The data of six independent groups were adequately reproduced using a single estimate of the learning rate constant obtained from one of these groups. The fact that in 24 independent predictions the model came close to the data is sufficient justification for exploring further consequences of the theory.

The initial problem that led to this investigation was whether the number of response alternatives could be shown to affect learning rate on reinforced trials in addition to contributing to differential error probabilities due to guessing on unlearned items. The data supported the assumption that learning rate on reinforced trials was a constant independent of the number of response alternatives, and that the effect of N upon error rate could be attributed to differential guessing probabilities on unlearned items. It should be noted that these conclusions are valid only for the experimental procedure used here in which the response alternatives are immediately available to the subject. For alternative procedures in which the subject is required to learn the responses (e.g., three or eight nonsense syllables) as well as the S-R associations, a number of complicating factors enter to obscure the picture and prevent resolution of the basic problem.

The second problem of this study was to account for the effect on performance of several training procedures. One may conceive of the correction, partial correction, and noncorrection procedures as varying in the degree to which the correct response is specified following an incorrect response by the subject. This variable in turn determines the probability that the correct response is reinforced following incorrect responses. Thus, in the correction condition, the reinforcement probability is 1 on every trial; under partial correction, the reinforcement probability is $1/k$ before the first correct response and is essentially 1

afterwards due to a high recognition probability; under noncorrection, the probability that the correct response is reinforced is essentially zero following errors. The data supported these hypotheses and gave additional support to the assumption that when the correct response was reinforced, the probability of conditioning was a constant, c, the same for all three conditions.

In addition to confirming these specific assumptions about N and training conditions, the results lend support to the learning model in which these assumptions are embedded. In this one-element model, the probability of the correct response can have only two values, $1/N$ or 1. The stimulus element begins in the unconditioned state and each reinforced trial provides an opportunity for the element to become associated in all-or-none fashion with the correct response. When conditioning finally occurs, response probability jumps from $1/N$ to 1. Discontinuous learning theories have been contrasted frequently with "response strength" theories which assume that an associative factor (habit strength in Hull's theory, proportion of conditioned elements in Estes' linear model) increases in a cumulative manner with successive reinforcements. According to a strength theory, response probability may take on a large (possibly infinite) number of values ranging from $1/N$ up to 1. It is frequently difficult to distinguish this theory from the one-element model since they predict the same average learning curve over a group of subjects and items. Indeed, the present results on average errors could be fit about equally well by the linear model. Since the discussion has been oriented towards the one-element model, perhaps it would be appropriate to record a few extra results which favor this model. For these purposes, let us consider two sequential statistics for which the two models deliver qualitatively different predictions.

The first statistic is the average number of errors (to perfect learning) following an error that occurs on Trial n of the experiment. The one-element model makes the rather counterintuitive prediction that this average number of subsequent errors is a constant independent of the trial number on which the leading error occurs. Thus, if we observe an error on Trial 10 we predict the same number of subsequent errors as if we had observed that error on Trial 1. The point of the matter is that when an error occurs on Trial n we know that the item was not conditioned before Trial n, and we can set the clock back to Trial 1 as far as the model is concerned in predicting future errors on that item. In contrast, the associative strength approach (specifically, the linear model) predicts that the number of errors following an error on Trial n is a decreasing function of n; that is, the greater the number of reinforced trials before a particular error, the higher the associative strength at that time, and hence the fewer the number of subsequent errors before perfect learning.

To obtain a sizable sample on which to test this critical point, data from 48 subjects in another 10-item paired-associate experiment [6] (with $N=2$) were pooled with the 3-C and 8-C groups of the present experiment. The varying N's will not affect the results on constancy vs. monotone decreasing aspects of errors following an error on Trial n. Using this pool of 760 response sequences (10 items for each of 76 subjects), the distributions of the number of errors following an error occurring on Trial 1, on Trial 2, . . . , on Trial 6 were obtained. The analysis was not carried beyond Trial 6 since the number of cases involved was decreasing so that estimates of means would be more unreliable. The estimates of the average number of errors following an error on Trial n are shown in Figure 3.

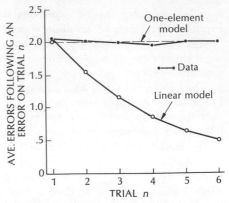

FIG. 3. Paired-associate data: average errors following an error that occurs on Trial n, for $n = 1, 2, \ldots, 6$. (Data points are filled dots; predictions of linear and one-element models are indicated.)

These data clearly favor the constancy prediction of the one-element model. Although the estimates fluctuate somewhat this can be attributed to sampling variability; even the largest difference (2.05 vs. 1.95) does not approach statistical significance ($t=0.49$). Also in Figure 3 is shown the rough order of magnitude of the numbers to be expected from the linear model. These predicted numbers are not exact because of different learning rates in the two experiments that were pooled. However, the average c value was .25 and this value was used to obtain the values on the graph. Clearly the curve predicted by the linear model is quite discrepant from the data; accordingly, the one-element model appears to give a more adequate description of these data.

A second example of this constancy effect is shown in Figure 4 which presents similar data collected in an experiment on verbal discrimination learning. In this experiment 34 subjects learned 20 items, an item consisting of two different nonsense syllables printed on a card. The subject's task was to read off each card that syllable arbitrarily

---

6. These experiments were carried out with the assistance of Norman Karns and James Colloran.

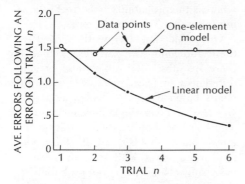

FIG. 4. Verbal discrimination data: average errors following an error that occurs on Trial n, for $n = 1, 2, \ldots, 6$. (Data points are the dots: predictions of linear and one-element models are indicated.)

designated as correct for that item; the subject repeatedly went through the items in random order until he achieved two consecutive errorless trials with the entire list. Since response learning per se is not involved in this situation, the one-element model was expected to apply. Since there were two response alternatives on each card, we make the natural assumption that the chance probability that subject selects the correct syllable is one-half. Detailed comparisons of predicted and observed statistics indicated excellent fit of the model; the results in Figure 4 are representative of the over-all accuracy of the predictions for this set of data. An additional set of paired-associate learning data providing a comparison of the linear and one-element models has been reported in a previous paper (Bower, 1961); there again the one-element model was clearly superior to the linear model in predicting details of the data.

A second measure suggested by Estes (1960) for differentiating the one-element and linear models concerns the probabilities of repetition and alternation of responses over a series of test trials following training. Consider a miniature experiment consisting of one or two reinforced trials followed by two test

trials (T_1 and T_2) on which the subject is not informed whether his response is right or wrong. The comparison differentiating the two theories is the probability of correct on T_2 given a correct and incorrect response, respectively, on T_1. According to the one-element model, the probability of correct following incorrect on T_1 should be around the chance guessing level ($1/N$); the probability of correct following correct on T_1 will be much higher, being somewhat less than one because we may expect some of the correct responses on T_1 to have occurred by guessing. The predictions of these conditional probabilities by the linear model depends upon whether there are substantial subject and/or item differences in learning rate. If for the moment we neglect such differences, as we have in testing the one-element model, then the linear model implies that the conditional probabilities of success following either a success or failure on T_1 will be equal.

Two experiments will be reported to this point. The first, performed with the assistance of Sharon Gadberry, consisted of 36 subjects learning two 10-item lists (nonsense syllables), the responses being the integers 1 to 10. Following two presentations of each S-R pair, the subjects received two test trials with the stimulus member of each pair. The pooled results of this experiment are shown in the first row of Table 5. Starting with 720 cases (36 subjects on two 10-item lists), the

TABLE 5. *Results of two experiments on the probability of correct on T_2 following correct and failure on T_1*

Experiment	Number of cases	Percentage correct on T_1	Percentage correct after correct	Percentage correct after failure
I. Nonsense syllables, 10 number responses	720	.586	.896	.163
II. Noun-noun pair.	320	.900	.995	.030

probability of correct on T_1 was .586; of those correct, 89.6% were correct on T_2; of those incorrect on T_1, only 16.3% were correct on T_2. These results support the one-element model. Two comments are required here: First, the value of .896 for correct following correct on T_1 is about what would be expected if 10% of the correct responses on T_1 had occurred by guessing; secondly, the value of .163 for correct following incorrect on T_2 is a little higher than the chance level of .100; however, this is likely an artifact of assigning stimuli and responses in one-to-one correspondence so that when k items are learned the probability of guessing correctly on the unlearned items may be close to one in $N-k$ instead of the a priori value of one in N.

The difference between probabilities of success on T_2 following a success and failure on T_1 should be increased above those in the previous study if one requires the responses per se to be learned (e.g., as in word-word pairs). Under these circumstances, the chance level of guessing will be practically zero. Thus, if the subject fails to respond correctly on T_1, the probability of being correct on T_2 is essentially zero; by the same reasoning, if a correct response occurs on T_1 it is most likely to have come about by conditioning so that the probability of correct on T_2 for this item should be essentially unity if forgetting is negligible in this situation. Row two of Table 5 reports the results of an experiment performed under these conditions with the assistance of Judith Slagter. Thirty-two subjects received three presentations on each of 10 noun-noun pairs (e.g., moon-pin) followed by two test trials. The percentage correct on T_1 was substantially higher than in the first experiment with nonsense syllable-number pairs. However, the important points of interest are that the probability of correct on T_2 given a correct on T_1 is essentially unity,

whereas the probability of correct following failure on T_1 is nearly zero.

One objection frequently raised to these foregoing comparisons is that if there are substantial subject and/or item differences in learning rates, then arguments based upon the pooled aggregate will tend to favor the one-element result. The point of the objection is this: if the linear model holds, and if differences in learning rates lead to a distribution over subjects of response probabilities, then considering the entire aggregate the conditional probability of a success following a success is expected to be higher than the conditional probability of success following a failure. This happens, according to the argument, because when we conditionalize upon the first success we are selecting predominately those protocols from the upper end of the distribution of response probabilities. However, granting that this argument is sound, it nevertheless helps not at all in rescuing the linear model from such data; it simply shifts the focus of the argument from conditional probabilities to joint probabilities of pairs of responses on T_1 and T_2. For convenience in the following, let p_{10} represent the point probability of a success on T_1 and a failure on T_2, and let p_{01} be the joint probability of failure on T_1 and success on T_2. It is a simple matter to show that if the linear model holds, then p_{10} should equal p_{01} *regardless* of possible differences between subjects and/or items in learning rates or initial probabilities. Data from four studies previously published by Estes (1960, 1961) show that the required identity of p_{10} and p_{01} fails to appear in any of the four studies. For example, in one study (Estes, 1960, Figure 2, p. 215) the value of p_{10} was .132 while p_{01} was .046; in another study (Figure 6, p. 218) p_{10} was .098 while p_{01} was .003. A variety of ad hoc hypotheses about individual differences to supplement the linear model have been considered in a paper by Estes (1961); the outcome of those investigations was that no simple ad hoc supplements could bring the linear model into correspondence with these elementary data which were collected to test it directly.

The question about individual differences raised by the objection above can be answered by comparison with the variability expected from the model. Suppose this question is considered in the context of a more extended experiment such as that described for the 3-C group in the preceding pages. A summary measure of an individual's performance might be the total errors (T) he makes over the 10 items. If we assume within the model that all subjects and items are characterized by the same learning rate constant, c, then a subject's T score represents the sum of 10 values sampled randomly and independently from a distribution which allegedly is the same for all subjects and items. The theoretical variance of these T scores may be calculated using our single estimate of c; this predicted variance may then be compared with the variance of the observed T scores by taking their ratio which will be distributed approximately as the F statistic. If the observed variance of T scores is much larger than that predicted, then we would tend to attribute the inflated variance to variations in c over subjects. This test has been applied to several sets of paired-associate learning data collected by the writer, including the data from the 3-C and 8-C groups of the present study for which the variance of T could be predicted. With the population of college students who have served as subjects in these various experiments, this test statistic has always yielded nonsignificant F values; that is, the variance of T between subjects does not differ significantly from what would be expected on the basis of random sampling from the stochastic process assumed by the model

to be common to all subjects. A similar statement can be made about analogous tests for differences in item difficulty; this outcome was expected, of course, since precautions were taken in selecting stimuli which appeared to be equal in intralist similarity and association value. Alternative procedures for handling this question regarding subject and/or item differences in the RTT experiment were considered in a paper by Estes, Hopkins, and Crothers (1960).

In concluding this report, it might be appropriate to add a few general comments concerning the issues under discussion lest some misunderstandings arise. First, it is misleading to cast the issues under discussion at the level of all-or-none theories versus response-strength theories of learning; rather the point at issue is whether the appropriate model for the present experimental situation is a two-state or a multistate process, where "state" here refers to a particular value of response probability. The continuous linear model is the limiting case of the class of multistate models. The all-or-none assumption about conditioning with respect to the available stimuli is not a differentiating feature of these two classes of models. Since the early writings of Guthrie (1930) it has been clear that the all-or-none conditioning assumption would imply gradual and cumulative changes in response probabilities provided there is sufficient variability in the stimulus samples from trial to trial. Within the framework of statistical learning theory, the feature differentiating the two classes of models is how many independent stimulus components one must assume to represent adequately the course of learning in this or that experimental situation. The two-state model proposed here for elementary association learning assumes that each item may be represented by a single stimulus element within the model and that this element can be in either of two states. That the number of elements is the critical assumption is illustrated by the fact that the statistics in Figures 3 and 4 and in Table 5 would not discriminate qualitatively between the linear model and a *two*-element model (i.e., where each item is represented by two stimulus components, with a random one being sampled on each trial). For more extensive discussions of small element models the reader may refer to a paper by Estes (1959) or a book by Suppes and Atkinson (1960).

Secondly, it should be recognized that in this report we have demonstrated only that the one-element model adequately describes results from elementary paired-associate learning experiments. The job of extending the range of applicability of a theory is an empirical project which must proceed piecemeal. In large part, the success in applying the model to a given learning situation will depend upon the simplicity of the situation and the degree of experimental control over stimulus variables. To cite a pertinent illustration: in training a rat to shuttle in response to a buzzer to avoid shock in a Mowrer-Miller shuttle box, conditioning is typically a gradual, "multi-stage" process (cf. Mowrer, 1960, p. 36); however, if experimental conditions are drastically simplified and precautions are taken to eliminate possible sources of interfering responses, then avoidance conditioning is a one-trial, "two-state" process (Maatsch, 1959). An analogous illustration for the eyelid conditioning situation has been reported by Voeks (1954).

In contrast to those situations in which a two-state behavioral process may possibly be achieved through experimental control, there is a large number of common learning situation for which such precise stimulus control probably can not be achieved, and it is unlikely that a simple two-state model could apply. These situations may be characterized generally as ones in which exposure to discriminative stimuli is subject-controlled; these situations range from those in which the critical cues are proprioceptive stimuli from the subject's current behavior, as in motor skill learning, to situations in which selected components of a complex stimulus array control behavior through the mediation of an overt or implicit observing response, as in complex concept learning. One example of this latter class would be that of a rat learning a black-white discrimination in a T maze; the stimuli effective at the moment of choice are multiple and vary from trial to trial depending upon the subject's vicarious trial and error behavior. For such situations more elaborate conceptual apparatus (cf. Audley, 1960; Bower, 1959; Spence, 1960) is required to analyze the interaction between observing behavior and instrumental, goal-directed behavior.

AUDLEY, R. J. A stochastic model for individual choice behavior. *Psychol. Rev.*, 1960, **67**, 1-15.

BOWER, G. H. Choice point behavior. In R. R. Bush & W. K. Estes (Eds.), *Studies in mathematical learning theory.* Stanford Univer. Press, 1959.

BOWER, G. H. Application of a model to paired-associate learning. *Psychometrika*, 1961, **26**, 255-80.

BUSH, R. R., & MOSTELLER, F. *Stochastic models for learning.* New York: Wiley, 1955.

ESTES, W. K. Component and pattern models with Markovian interpretations. In R. R. Bush & W. K. Estes (Eds.), *Studies in mathematical learning theory.* Stanford Univer. Press, 1959.

ESTES, W. K. Learning theory and the new mental chemistry. *Psychol Rev.*, 1960, **67**, 207-23.

ESTES, W. K. New development in statistical behavior theory: Differential tests of axioms for associative learning. *Psychometrika*, 1961, **26**, 73-84.

ESTES, W. K., HOPKINS, B. L., & CROTHERS, E. J. All-or-none and conservation effects in the learning and retention of paired associates. *J. exp. Psychol.*, 1960, **60**, 329-39.

GUTHRIE, E. R. Conditioning as a principle of learning. *Psychol. Rev.*, 1930, **37**, 412-28.

MAATSCH, J. L. Learning and fixation after a single shock trial. *J. comp. physiol. Psychol.*, 1959, 408-10.

MILLER, G. A., & McGILL, W. J. A statistical description of verbal learning. *Psychometrika*, 1952, **17**, 369-96.

MOWRER, O. H. *Learning theory and behavior.* New York: Wiley, 1960.

NOBLE, C. E. Compound trial-and-error learning as a function of response availability. *J. exp. Psychol.*, 1955, **49**, 93-6.

RILEY, D. A. Rote learning as a function of distribution of practice and the complexity of the situation. *J. exp. Psychol.*, 1952, **43**, 88-95.

SPENCE, K. W. Conceptual models of spatial and non-spatial selective learning. In K. W. Spence (Ed.), *Behavior theory and learning.* Englewood Cliffs, N. J.: Prentice-Hall, 1960.

SUPPES, P., & ATKINSON, R. C. *Markov learning models for multiperson interactions.* Stanford Univer. Press, 1960.

THORNDIKE, E. L. *The fundamentals of learning.* New York: Teachers College, 1932.

VOEKS, V. W. Acquisition of S-R connections: A test of Hull's and Guthrie's theories. *J. exp. Psychol.*, 1954, **47**, 137-47.

FREE RECALL

OF all methods utilized in verbal learning, free recall imposes the fewest external constraints upon the subject's performance. For this reason it is best suited for revealing whether, and to what extent, a person takes an active role in organizing the materials to be learned. Free recall learning is also of interest in its own right, for there is the task of identifying the variables to which it is responsive. The procedure involves presentation of a list of items, followed by the subject's attempt to recall as many as he can in whatever order they occur to him. If more than one trial is given, the items are usually presented in random sequence from trial to trial. However, even if items are presented in the same serial order on every trial, the amount and rate of recall are totally unaffected when compared to the random order mode of presentation. The procedure has the advantage of effectively separating training from testing trials, and allowing for a better measure of amount learned at any point. By contrast, anticipation procedures confound these two aspects, since every trial is both a training and a test trial. Free recall is unaided in that no distinctive stimuli are provided by the experimenter to guide the recall. By contrast again, both serial and paired-associates anticipation procedures provide a specific cue for each response. The question of what constitutes the effective stimulus that guides free recall performance poses a problem for classical associationistic theory.

Experiments utilizing free recall can be classified under two headings, depending upon the intent of the particular study. First, there are studies in which the focus is upon total amount recalled. Second, there are studies in which the focus is upon the *order* in which items are recalled. The following readings include both types of experiments, and they are presented according to that division, rather than chronologically.

The paper by Miller called attention to organizational processes that allow a person to exceed the limits of his memory span. Lists longer than about seven items can still be memorized through a process of "chunking," in which several items comprise one chunk. Storage of these informationally rich chunks is the key to extended memory performance. Miller and Selfridge (1950) varied the degree of sequential dependency within lists. By a clever generating technique,

217

lists embodying various orders of approximation to English were presented for free recall. Performance improved with higher orders of approximation. Later, Deese (1961) noted that the improvement did not necessarily imply a true increase in retention, but may instead have reflected increasingly successful attempts at *construction* of the material on the basis of language habits.

The paper by Deese investigated amount recalled as a function of the associative structure of the list. Previously, Jenkins, Mink and Russell (1958) reported that pairs of words that are strong free-associates tend to be recalled together, even though widely separated during initial presentation. Deese developed an index of inter-item associative strength, which measured the extent of free-associative strength among all of the items in a list, and showed that amount recalled was positively related to the size of the index.

Murdock's paper rigorously examined the properties of free recall through twelve closely related experiments. Amount recalled was studied as a function of various formal characteristics of the procedure, rather than of list composition. Two of the major findings were that the free recall method produced no practice effect, and that the amount recalled after one presentation was a multiplicative function of list length and rate of presentation. Thus, so long as total presentation time is constant, recall is invariant with changes in length and presentation rate. An equation was developed which could predict learning with fair accuracy.

The two remaining selections are representative of the type of study which focuses upon the order aspects of recall performance. The paper by Bousfield was the first in a series which demonstrated, and then systematically examined, a phenomenon called "category clustering." A list was constructed of words drawn from four categories: animals, names, professions, and vegetables. Although the items were presented in a random order, subjects showed a striking tendency to write them down in clusters, according to category membership. The previously cited article by Jenkins, Mink, and Russell exemplified "associative clustering," wherein clusters were formed on the basis of free-association linkages. The direction of subsequent research on the clustering phenomenon is aptly discussed by Cofer (1965).

The paper by Tulving goes one step further in the investigation of the tendency to rearrange the order of items in free recall. Even though a list of words has no apparent categorical structure, nor any appreciable inter-item associative bonds, it is nevertheless the case that a subject will tend to recall items in the same order on successive trials (with presentations randomized). Tulving developed a measure of this tendency, called SO, or "subjective organization." It was shown that SO increased progressively as learning increased. Thus, it has been the free-recall procedure which has provided the avenue through which a pervasive psychological attribute, the tendency to impose organization upon material in recall, has been recognized. Most recently, Mandler (1966) reported a series of experiments aimed at examining organizational processes under conditions that allow assessment of the effects of the number of sorting categories used by the subject. This approach is an extension of Miller's original chunking hypothesis, and appears quite promising.

COFER, C. N. On some factors in the organizational characteristics of free recall. *Amer. Psychologist*, 1965, **20**, 261-72.

DEESE, J. From the isolated verbal unit to connected discourse. In C. N. Cofer (Ed.), *Verbal learning and verbal behavior.* New York: McGraw-Hill, 1961. Pp. 11-31.

JENKINS, J. J., MINK, W. D., & RUSSELL, W. A. Associative clustering as a function of verbal strength. *Psychol. Rep.*, 1958, **4**, 127-36.

MANDLER, G. Organization and memory. In Spence, K. W., and Spence, J. T. (Eds.), *The psychology of learning and motivation: Advances in research and theory.* New York: Academic Press, 1966.

MILLER, G. A., & SELFRIDGE, J. A. Verbal context and the recall of meaningful material. *Amer. J. Psychol.*, 1950, **63**, 176-85.

21 / The Magical Number Seven, Plus or Minus Two: Some Limits on our Capacity for Processing Information [1]

GEORGE A. MILLER, *Harvard University*

My problem is that I have been persecuted by an integer. For seven years this number has followed me around, has intruded in my most private data, and has assaulted me from the pages of our most public journals. This number assumes a variety of disguises, being sometimes a little larger and sometimes a little smaller than usual, but never changing so much as to be unrecognizable. The persistence with which this number plagues me is far more than a random accident. There is, to quote a famous senator, a design behind it, some pattern governing its appearances. Either there really is something unusual about the number or else I am suffering from delusions of persecution.

I shall begin my case history by telling you about some experiments that tested how accurately people can assign numbers to the magnitudes of various aspects of a stimulus. In the traditional language of psychology these would be called experiments in absolute judgment. Historical accident, however, has decreed that they should have another name. We now call them experiments on the capacity of people to transmit information. Since these experiments would not have been done without the appearance of information theory on the psychological scene, and since the results are analyzed in terms of the concepts of information theory, I shall have to preface my discussion with a few remarks about this theory.

INFORMATION MEASUREMENT

The "amount of information" is exactly the same concept that we have talked about for years under the name of "variance." The equations are different, but if we hold tight to the idea that anything that increases the variance also increases the amount of information we cannot go far astray.

The advantages of this new way of talking about variance are simple enough. Variance is always stated in

From the *Psychological Review*, 1956, **63**, 81-97, with permission of the author and publisher.
1. Preparation of the paper was supported by the Harvard Psycho-Acoustic Laboratory under Contract N5ori-76 between Harvard University and the Office of Naval Research, U. S. Navy (Project NR142-201, Report PNR-174). Reproduction for any purpose of the U. S. Government is permitted.

terms of the unit of measurement—inches, pounds, volts, etc.—whereas the amount of information is a dimensionless quantity. Since the information in a discrete statistical distribution does not depend upon the unit of measurement, we can extend the concept to situations where we have no metric and we would not ordinarily think of using the variance. And it also enables us to compare results obtained in quite different experimental situations where it would be meaningless to compare variances based on different metrics. So there are some good reasons for adopting the newer concept.

The similarity of variance and amount of information might be explained this way: When we have a large variance, we are very ignorant about what is going to happen. If we are very ignorant, then when we make the observation it gives us a lot of information. On the other hand, if the variance is very small, we know in advance how our observation must come out, so we get little information from making the observation.

If you will now imagine a communication system, you will realize that there is a great deal of variability about what goes into the system and also a great deal of variability about what comes out. The input and the output can therefore be described in terms of their variance (or their information). If it is a good communication system, however, there must be some systematic relation between what goes in and what comes out. That is to say, the output will depend upon the input, or will be correlated with the input. If we measure this correlation, then we can say how much of the output variance is attributable to the input and how much is due to random fluctuations or "noise" introduced by the system during transmission. So we see that the measure of transmitted information is simply a measure of the input-output correlation.

There are two simple rules to follow. Whenever I refer to "amount of information," you will understand "variance." And whenever I refer to "amount of transmitted information," you will understand "covariance" or "correlation."

The situation can be described graphically by two partially overlapping circles. Then the left circle can be taken to represent the variance of the input, the right circle the variance of the output, and the overlap the covariance of input and output. I shall speak of the left circle as the amount of input information, the right circle as the amount of output information, and the overlap as the amount of transmitted information.

In the experiments on absolute judgment, the observer is considered to be a communication channel. Then the left circle would represent the amount of information in the stimuli, the right circle the amount of information in his responses, and the overlap the stimulus-response correlation as measured by the amount of transmitted information. The experimental problem is to increase the amount of input information and to measure the amount of transmitted information. If the observer's absolute judgments are quite accurate, then nearly all of the input information will be transmitted and will be recoverable from his responses. If he makes errors, then the transmitted information may be considerably less than the input. We expect that, as we increase the amount of input information, the observer will begin to make more and more errors; we can test the limits of accuracy of his absolute judgments. If the human observer is a reasonable kind of communication system, then when we increase the amount of input information the transmitted information will increase at first and will eventually level off at some asymptotic value. The asymptotic value we take to be the *channel capacity* of the observer: it represents the greatest amount of information that he can give us about the stimulus on the basis of an absolute judgment. The channel capacity is the upper limit on the extent to which the observer can match his responses to the stimuli we give him.

Now just a brief word about the *bit* and we can begin to look at some data. One bit of information is the amount of information that we need to make a decision between two equally likely alternatives. If we must decide whether a man is less than six feet tall or more than six feet tall and if we know that the chances are 50-50, then we need one bit of information. Notice that this unit of information does not refer in any way to the unit of length that we use—feet, inches, centimeters, etc. However you measure the man's height, we still need just one bit of information.

Two bits of information enable us to decide among four equally likely alternatives. Three bits of information enable us to decide among eight equally likely alternatives. Four bits of information decide among 16 alternatives, five among 32, and so on. That is to say, if there are 32 equally likely alternatives, we must make five successive binary decisions, worth one bit each, before we know which alternative is correct. So the general rule is simple: every time the number of alternatives is increased by a factor of two, one bit of information is added.

There are two ways we might increase the amount of input information. We could increase the rate at which we give information to the observer, so that the amount of information per unit time would increase. Or we could ignore the time variable completely and increase the amount of input information by increasing the number of alternative stimuli. In the absolute judgment experiment we are interested in the second alternative. We give the observer as much time as he wants to make his re-

sponse; we simply increase the number of alternative stimuli among which he must discriminate and look to see where confusions begin to occur. Confusions will appear near the point that we are calling his "channel capacity."

ABSOLUTE JUDGMENTS OF UNIDIMENSIONAL STIMULI

Now let us consider what happens when we make absolute judgments of tones. Pollack (17) asked listeners to identify tones by assigning numerals to them. The tones were different with respect to frequency, and covered the range from 100 to 8000 cps in equal logarithmic steps. A tone was sounded and the listener responded by giving a numeral. After the listener had made his response he was told the correct identification of the tone.

When only two or three tones were used the listeners never confused them. With four different tones confusions were quite rare, but with five or more tones confusions were frequent. With fourteen different tones the listeners made many mistakes.

These data are ploted in Fig. 1. Along the bottom is the amount of input information in bits per stimulus. As the number of alternative tones was increased from 2 to 14, the input information increased from 1 to 3.8 bits. On the ordinate is plotted the amount of transmitted information. The amount of transmitted information behaves in much the way we would expect a communication channel to behave; the transmitted information increases linearly up to about 2 bits and then bends off toward an asymptote at about 2.5 bits. This value, 2.5 bits, therefore, is what we are calling the channel capacity of the listener for absolute judgments of pitch.

So now we have the number 2.5 bits. What does it mean? First, note that 2.5 bits corresponds to about six

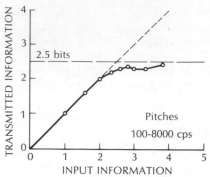

FIG. 1. Data from Pollack (17, 18) on the amount of information that is transmitted by listeners who make absolute judgments of auditory pitch. As the amount of input information is increased by increasing from 2 to 14 the number of different pitches to be judged, the amount of transmitted information approaches as its upper limit a channel capacity of about 2.5 bits per judgment.

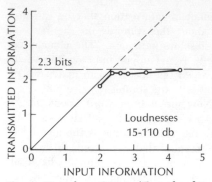

FIG. 2. Data from Garner (7) on the channel capacity for absolute judgments of auditory loudness.

equally likely alternatives. The result means that we cannot pick more than six different pitches that the listener will never confuse. Or, stated slightly differently, no matter how many alternative tones we ask him to judge, the best we can expect him to do is to assign them to about six different classes without error. Or, again, if we know that there were N alternative stimuli, then his judgment enables us to narrow down the particular stimulus to one out of N/6.

Most people are surprised that the number is as small as six. Of course, there is evidence that a musically sophisticated person with absolute pitch can identify accurately any one of 50 or 60 different pitches. Fortunately, I do not have time to discuss these remarkable exceptions. I say it is fortunate because I do not know how to explain their superior performance. So I shall stick to the more pedestrian fact that most of us can identify about one out of only five or six pitches before we begin to get confused.

It is interesting to consider that psychologists have been using seven-point

rating scales for a long time, on the intuitive basis that trying to rate into finer categories does not really add much to the usefulness of the ratings. Pollack's results indicate that, at least for pitches, this intuition is fairly sound.

Next you can ask how reproducible this result is. Does it depend on the spacing of the tones or the various conditions of judgment? Pollack varied these conditions in a number of ways. The range of frequencies can be changed by a factor of about 20 without changing the amount of information transmitted more than a small percentage. Different groupings of the pitches decreased the transmission, but the loss was small. For example, if you can discriminate five high-pitched tones in one series and five low-pitched tones in another series, it is reasonable to expect that you could combine all ten into a single series and still tell them all apart without error. When you try it, however, it does not work. The channel capacity for pitch seems to be about six and that is the best you can do.

While we are on tones, let us look next at Garner's (7) work on loudness. Garner's data for loudness are summarized in Fig. 2. Garner went to some trouble to get the best possible spacing of his tones over the intensity range from 15 to 110 db. He used 4, 5, 6, 7,

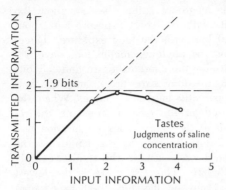

FIG. 3. Data from Beebe-Center, Rogers, and O'Connell (1) on the channel capacity for absolute judgments of saltiness.

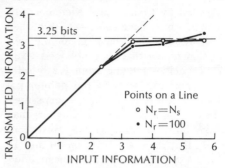

FIG. 4. Data from Hake and Garner (8) on the channel capacity for absolute judgments of the position of a pointer in a linear interval.

10, and 20 different stimulus intensities. The results shown in Fig. 2 take into account the differences among subjects and the sequential influence of the immediately preceding judgment. Again we find that there seems to be a limit. The channel capacity for absolute judgments of loudness is 2.3 bits, or about five perfectly discriminable alternatives.

Since these two studies were done in different laboratories with slightly different techniques and methods of analysis, we are not in a good position to argue whether five loudnesses is significantly different from six pitches. Probably the difference is in the right direction, and absolute judgments of pitch are slightly more accurate than absolute judgments of loudness. The important point, however, is that the two answers are of the same order of magnitude.

The experiment has also been done for taste intensities. In Fig. 3 are the results obtained by Beebe-Center, Rogers, and O'Connell (1) for absolute judgments of the concentration of salt solutions. The concentrations ranged from 0.3 to 34.7 gm. NaCl per 100 cc. tap water in equal subjective steps. They used 3, 5, 9, and 17 different concentrations. The channel capacity is 1.9 bits, which is about four distinct concentrations. Thus taste intensities

seem a little less distinctive than auditory stimuli, but again the order of magnitude is not far off.

On the other hand, the channel capacity for judgments of visual position seems to be significantly larger. Hake and Garner (8) asked observers to interpolate visually between two scale markers. Their results are shown in Fig. 4. They did the experiment in two ways. In one version they let the observer use any number between zero and 100 to describe the position, although they presented stimuli at only 5, 10, 20, or 50 different positions. The results with this unlimited response technique are shown by the filled circles on the graph. In the other version the observers were limited in their responses to reporting just those stimulus values that were possible. That is to say, in the second version the number of different responses that the observer could make was exactly the same as the number of different stimuli that the experimenter might present. The results with this limited response technique are shown by the open circles on the graph. The two functions are so similar that it seems fair to conclude that the number of responses available to the observer had nothing to do with the channel capacity of 3.25 bits.

The Hake-Garner experiment has been

repeated by Coonan and Klemmer. Although they have not yet published their results, they have given me permission to say that they obtained channel capacities ranging from 3.2 bits for very short exposures of the pointer position to 3.9 bits for longer exposures. These values are slightly higher than Hake and Garner's, so we must conclude that there are between 10 and 15 distinct positions along a linear interval. This is the largest channel capacity that has been measured for any unidimensional variable.

At the present time these four experiments on absolute judgments of simple, unidimensional stimuli are all that have appeared in the psychological journals. However, a great deal of work on other stimulus variables has not yet appeared in the journals. For example, Eriksen and Hake (6) have found that the channel capacity for judging the sizes of squares is 2.2 bits, or about five categories, under a wide range of experimental conditions. In a separate experiment Eriksen (5) found 2.8 bits for size, 3.1 bits for hue, and 2.3 bits for brightness. Geldard has measured the channel capacity for the skin by placing vibrators on the chest region. A good observer can identify about four intensities, about five durations, and about seven locations.

One of the most active groups in this area has been the Air Force Operational Applications Laboratory. Pollack has been kind enough to furnish me with the results of their measurements for several aspects of visual displays. They made measurements for area and for the curvature, length, and direction of lines. In one set of experiments they used a very short exposure of the stimulus—1/40 second—and then they repeated the measurements with a 5-second exposure. For area they got 2.6 bits with the short exposure and 2.7 bits with the long exposure. For

the length of a line they go about 2.6 bits with the short exposure and about 3.0 bits with the long exposure. Direction, or angle of inclination, gave 2.8 bits for the short exposure and 3.3 bits for the long exposure. Curvature was apparently harder to judge. When the length of the arc was constant, the result at the short exposure duration was 2.2 bits, but when the length of the chord was constant, the result was only 1.6 bits. This last value is the lowest that anyone has measured to date. I should add, however, that these values are apt to be slightly too low because the data from all subjects were pooled before the transmitted information was computed.

Now let us see where we are. First, the channel capacity does seem to be a valid notion for describing human observers. Second, the channel capacities measured for these unidimensional variables range from 1.6 bits for curvature to 3.9 bits for positions in an interval. Although there is no question that the differences among the variables are real and meaningful, the more impressive fact to me is their considerable similarity. If I take the best estimates I can get of the channel capacities for all the stimulus variables I have mentioned, the mean is 2.6 bits and the standard deviation is only 0.6 bit. In terms of distinguishable alternatives, this mean corresponds to about 6.5 categories, one standard deviation includes from 4 to 10 categories, and the total range is from 3 to 15 categories. Considering the wide variety of different variables that have been studied, I find this to be a remarkably narrow range.

There seems to be some limitation built into us either by learning or by the design of our nervous systems, a limit that keeps our channel capacities in this general range. On the basis of the present evidence it seems safe to say that we possess a finite and rather small capacity for making such unidimensional judgments and that this capacity does not vary a great deal from one simple sensory attribute to another.

ABSOLUTE JUDGMENTS OF MULTIDIMENSIONAL STIMULI

You may have noticed that I have been careful to say that this magical number seven applies to one-dimensional judgments. Everyday experience teaches us that we can identify accurately any one of several hundred faces, any one of several thousand words, any one of several thousand objects, etc. The story certainly would not be complete if we stopped at this point. We must have some understanding of why the one-dimensional variables we judge in the laboratory give results so far out of line with what we do constantly in our behavior outside the laboratory. A possible explanation lies in the number of independently variable attributes of the stimuli that are being judged. Objects, faces, words, and the like differ from one another in many ways, whereas the simple stimuli we have considered thus far differ from one another in only one respect.

Fortunately, there are a few data on what happens when we make absolute judgments of stimuli that differ from one another in several ways. Let us look first at the results Klemmer and Frick (13) have reported for the absolute judgment of the position of a dot in a square. In Fig. 5 we see their results. Now the channel capacity seems to have increased to 4.6 bits, which means that people can identify accurately any one of 24 positions in the square.

The position of a dot in a square is clearly a two-dimensional proposition. Both its horizontal and its vertical position must be identified. Thus it seems natural to compare the 4.6-bit capacity for a square with the 3.25-bit capacity

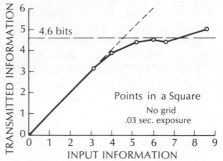

FIG. 5. Data from Klemmer and Frick (13) on the channel capacity for absolute judgments of the position of a dot in a square.

for the position of a point in an interval. The point in the square requires two judgments of the interval type. If we have a capacity of 3.25 bits for estimating intervals and we do this twice, we should get 6.5 bits as our capacity for locating points in a square. Adding the second independent dimension gives us an increase from 3.25 to 4.6, but it falls short of the perfect addition that would give 6.5 bits.

Another example is provided by Beebe-Center, Rogers, and O'Connell. When they asked people to identify both the saltiness and the sweetness of solutions containing various concentrations of salt and sucrose, they found that the channel capacity was 2.3 bits. Since the capacity for salt alone was 1.9, we might expect about 3.8 bits if the two aspects of the compound stimuli were judged independently. As with spatial locations, the second dimension adds a little to the capacity but not as much as it conceivably might.

A third example is provided by Pollack (18), who asked listeners to judge both the loudness and the pitch of pure tones. Since pitch gives 2.5 bits and loudness gives 2.3 bits, we might hope to get as much as 4.8 bits for pitch and loudness together. Pollack obtained 3.1 bits, which again indicates that the second dimension augments the channel capacity but not so much as it might.

A fourth example can be drawn from the work of Halsey and Chapanis (9) on confusions among colors of equal luminance. Although they did not analyze their results in informational terms, they estimate that there are about 11 to 15 identifiable colors, or, in our terms, about 3.6 bits. Since these colors varied in both hue and saturation, it is probably correct to regard this as a two-dimensional judgment. If we compare this with Eriksen's 3.1 bits for hue (which is a questionable comparison to draw), we again have something less than perfect addition when a second dimension is added.

It is still a long way, however, from these two-dimensional examples to the multidimensional stimuli provided by faces, words, etc. To fill this gap we have only one experiment, an auditory study done by Pollack and Ficks (19). They managed to get six different acoustic variables that they could change: frequency, intensity, rate of interruption, on-time fraction, total duration, and spatial location. Each one of these six variables could assume any one of five different values, so altogether there were 5^6, or 15,625 different ones that they could present. The listeners made a separate rating for each one of these six dimensions. Under these conditions the transmitted information was 7.2 bits, which corresponds to about 150 different categories that could be absolutely identified without error. Now we are beginning to get up into the range that ordinary experience would lead us to expect.

Suppose that we plot these data, fragmentary as they are, and make a guess about how the channel capacity changes with the dimensionality of the stimuli. The result is given in Fig. 6. In a moment of considerable daring I sketched the dotted line to indicate roughly the trend that the data seemed to be taking.

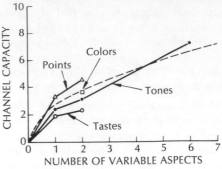

FIG. 6. The general form of the relation between channel capacity and the number of independently variable attributes of the stimuli.

Clearly, the addition of independently variable attributes to the stimulus increases the channel capacity, but at a decreasing rate. It is interesting to note that the channel capacity is increased even when the several variables are not independent. Eriksen (5) reports that, when size, brightness, and hue all vary together in perfect correlation, the transmitted information is 4.1 bits as compared with an average of about 2.7 bits when these attributes are varied one at a time. By confounding three attributes, Eriksen increased the dimensionality of the input without increasing the amount of input information; the result was an increase in channel capacity of about the amount that the dotted function in Fig. 6 would lead us to expect.

The point seems to be that, as we add more variables to the display, we increase the total capacity, but we decrease the accuracy for any particular variable. In other words, we can make relatively crude judgments of several things simultaneously.

We might argue that in the course of evolution those organisms were most successful that were responsive to the widest range of stimulus energies in their environment. In order to survive in a constantly fluctuating world, it was better to have a little information about a lot of things than to have a lot of information about a small segment of the environment. If a compromise was necessary, the one we seem to have made is clearly the more adaptive.

Pollack and Ficks's results are very strongly suggestive of an argument that linguists and phoneticians have been making for some time (11). According to the linguistic analysis of the sounds of human speech, there are about eight or ten dimensions—the linguists call them *distinctive features*—that distinguish one phoneme from another. These distinctive features are usually binary, or at most ternary, in nature. For example, a binary distinction is made between vowels and consonants, a binary decision is made between oral and nasal consonants, a ternary decision is made among front, middle, and back phonemes, etc. This approach gives us quite a different picture of speech perception than we might otherwise obtain from our studies of the speech spectrum and of the ear's ability to discriminate relative differences among pure tones. I am personally much interested in this new approach (15), and I regret that there is not time to discuss it here.

It was probably with this linguistic theory in mind that Pollack and Ficks conducted a test on a set of tonal stimuli that varied in eight dimensions, but required only a binary decision on each dimension. With these tones they measured the transmitted information at 6.9 bits, or about 120 recognizable kinds of sounds. It is an intriguing question, as yet unexplored, whether one can go on adding dimensions indefinitely in this way.

In human speech there is clearly a limit to the number of dimensions that we use. In this instance, however, it is not known whether the limit is imposed by the nature of the perceptual machinery that must recognize the sounds

or by the nature of the speech machinery that must produce them. Somebody will have to do the experiment to find out. There is a limit, however, at about eight or nine distinctive features in every language that has been studied, and so when we talk we must resort to still another trick for increasing our channel capacity. Language uses sequences of phonemes, so we make several judgments successively when we listen to words and sentences. That is to say, we use both simultaneous and successive discriminations in order to expand the rather rigid limits imposed by the inaccuracy of our absolute judgments of simple magnitudes.

These multidimensional judgments are strongly reminiscent of the abstraction experiment of Külpe (14). As you may remember, Külpe showed that observers report more accurately on an attribute for which they are set than on attributes for which they are not set. For example, Chapman (4) used three different attributes and compared the results obtained when the observers were instructed before the tachistoscopic presentation with the results obtained when they were not told until after the presentation which one of the three attributes was to be reported. When the instruction was given in advance, the judgments were more accurate. When the instruction was given afterwards, the subjects presumably had to judge all three attributes in order to report on any one of them and the accuracy was correspondingly lower. This is in complete accord with the results we have just been considering, where the accuracy of judgment on each attribute decreased as more dimensions were added. The point is probably obvious, but I shall make it anyhow, that the abstraction experiments did *not* demonstrate that people can judge only one attribute at a time. They merely showed what seems quite reasonable, that people are less accurate if they must judge more than one attribute simultaneously.

SUBITIZING

I cannot leave this general area without mentioning, however briefly, the experiments conducted at Mount Holyoke College on the discrimination of number (12). In experiments by Kaufman, Lord, Reese, and Volkmann random patterns of dots were flashed on a screen for ⅕ of a second. Anywhere from 1 to more than 200 dots could appear in the pattern. The subject's task was to report how many dots there were.

The first point to note is that on patterns containing up to five or six dots the subjects simply did not make errors. The performance on these small numbers of dots was so different from the performance with more dots that it was given a special name. Below seven the subjects were said to *subitize;* above seven they were said to *estimate.* This is, as you will recognize, what we once optimistically called "the span of attention."

This discontinuity at seven is, of course, suggestive. Is this the same basic process that limits our unidimensional judgments to about seven categories? The generalization is tempting, but not sound in my opinion. The data on number estimates have not been analyzed in informational terms; but on the basis of the published data I would guess that the subjects transmitted something more than four bits of information about the number of dots. Using the same arguments as before, we would conclude that there are about 20 or 30 distinguishable categories of numerousness. This is considerably more information than we would expect to get from a unidimensional display. It is, as a matter of fact, very much like a two-dimensional display. Although the dimensionality of the random dot patterns is not entirely clear, these results

are in the same range as Klemmer and Frick's for their two-dimensional display of dots in a square. Perhaps the two dimensions of numerousness are area and density. When the subject can subitize, area and density may not be the significant variables, but when the subject must estimate perhaps they are significant. In any event, the comparison is not so simple as it might seem at first thought.

This is one of the ways in which the magical number seven has persecuted me. Here we have two closely related kinds of experiments, both of which point to the significance of the number seven as a limit on our capacities. And yet when we examine the matter more closely, there seems to be a reasonable suspicion that it is nothing more than a coincidence.

THE SPAN OF IMMEDIATE MEMORY

Let me summarize the situation in this way. There is a clear and definite limit to the accuracy with which we can identify absolutely the magnitude of a unidimensional stimulus variable. I would propose to call this limit the *span of absolute judgment,* and I maintain that for unidimensional judgments this span is usually somewhere in the neighborhood of seven. We are not completely at the mercy of this limited span, however, because we have a variety of techniques for getting around it and increasing the accuracy of our judgments. The three most important of these devices are (*a*) to make relative rather than absolute judgments; or, if that is not possible, (*b*) to increase the number of dimensions along which the stimuli can differ; or (*c*) to arrange the task in such a way that we make a sequence of several absolute judgments in a row.

The study of relative judgments is one of the oldest topics in experimental psychology, and I will not pause to review it now. The second device, increasing the dimensionality, we have just considered. It seems that by adding more dimensions and requiring crude, binary, yes-no judgments on each attribute we can extend the span of absolute judgment from seven to at least 150. Judging from our everyday behavior, the limit is probably in the thousands, if indeed there is a limit. In my opinion, we cannot go on compounding dimensions indefinitely. I suspect that there is also a *span of perceptual dimensionality* and that this span is somewhat in the neighborhood of ten, but I must add at once that there is no objective evidence to support this suspicion. This is a question sadly needing experimental exploration.

Concerning the third device, the use of successive judgments, I have quite a bit to say because this device introduces memory as the handmaiden of discrimination. And, since mnemonic processes are at least as complex as are perceptual processes, we can anticipate that their interactions will not be easily disentangled.

Suppose that we start by simply extending slightly the experimental procedure that we have been using. Up to this point we have presented a single stimulus and asked the observer to name it immediately thereafter. We can extend this procedure by requiring the observer to withhold his response until we have given him several stimuli in succession. At the end of the sequence of stimuli he then makes his response. We still have the same sort of input-output situation that is required for the measurement of transmitted information. But now we have passed from an experiment on absolute judgment to what is traditionally called an experiment on immediate memory.

Before we look at any data on this topic I feel I must give you a word of warning to help you avoid some obvious associations that can be confusing.

Everybody knows that there is a finite span of immediate memory and that for a lot of different kinds of test materials this span is about seven items in length. I have just shown you that there is a span of absolute judgment that can distinguish about seven categories and that there is a span of attention that will encompass about six objects at a glance. What is more natural than to think that all three of these spans are different aspects of a single underlying process? And that is a fundamental mistake, as I shall be at some pains to demonstrate. This mistake is one of the malicious persecutions that the magical number seven has subjected me to.

My mistake went something like this. We have seen that the invariant feature in the span of absolute judgment is the amount of information that the observer can transmit. There is a real operational similarity between the absolute judgment experiment and the immediate memory experiment. If immediate memory is like absolute judgment, then it should follow that the invariant feature in the span of immediate memory is also the amount of information that an observer can retain. If the amount of information in the span of immediate memory is a constant, then the span should be short when the individual items contain a lot of information and the span should be long when the items contain little information. For example, decimal digits are worth 3.3 bits apiece. We can recall about seven of them, for a total of 23 bits of information. Isolated English words are worth about 10 bits apiece. If the total amount of information is to remain constant at 23 bits, then we should be able to remember only two or three words chosen at random. In this way I generated a theory about how the span of immediate memory should vary as a function of the amount of information per item in the test materials.

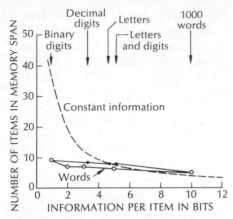

FIG. 7. Data from Hayes (10) on the span of immediate memory plotted as a function of the amount of information per item in the test materials.

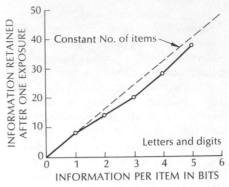

FIG. 8. Data from Pollack (16) on the amount of information retained after one presentation plotted as a function of the amount of information per item in the test materials.

The measurements of memory span in the literature are suggestive on this question, but not definitive. And so it was necessary to do the experiment to see. Hayes (10) tried it out with five different kinds of test materials: binary digits, decimal digits, letters of the alphabet, letters plus decimal digits, and with 1000 monosyllabic words. The lists were read aloud at the rate of one item per second and the subjects had as much time as they needed to give their responses. A procedure described by Woodworth (20) was used to score responses.

The results are shown by the filled circles in Fig. 7. Here the dotted line indicates what the span should have been if the amount of information in the span were constant. The solid curves represent the data. Hayes repeated the experiment using test vocabularies of different sizes but all containing only English monosyllables (open circles in Fig. 7). This more homogeneous test material did not change the picture significantly. With binary items the span is about nine and, although it drops to about five with monosyllabic English words, the difference is far less than

the hypothesis of constant information would require.

There is nothing wrong with Hayes's experiment, because Pollack (16) repeated it much more elaborately and got essentially the same result. Pollack took pains to measure the amount of information transmitted and did not rely on the traditional procedure for scoring the responses. His results are plotted in Fig. 8. Here it is clear that the amount of information transmitted is not a constant, but increases almost linearly as the amount of information per item in the input is increased.

And so the outcome is perfectly clear. In spite of the coincidence that the magical number seven appears in both places, the span of absolute judgment and the span of immediate memory are quite different kinds of limitations that are imposed on our ability to process information. Absolute judgment is limited by the amount of information. Immediate memory is limited by the number of items. In order to capture this distinction in somewhat picturesque terms, I have fallen into the custom of distinguishing between *bits* of information and *chunks* of information. Then I can say that the number of bits of information is constant for absolute judgment and the number of chunks of information is constant for immediate memory. The span of immediate memory seems to be almost independent of the number of bits per chunk, at least over the range that has been examined to date.

The contrast of the terms *bit* and *chunk* also serves to highlight the fact that we are not very definite about what constitutes a chunk of information. For example, the memory span of five words that Hayes obtained when each word was drawn at random from a set of 1000 English monosyllables might just as appropriately have been called a memory span of 15 phonemes, since each word had about three phonemes in it. Intuitively, it is clear that the subjects were recalling five words, not 15 phonemes, but the logical distinction is not immediately apparent. We are dealing here with a process of organizing or grouping the input into familiar units or chunks, and a great deal of learning has gone into the formation of these familiar units.

RECODING

In order to speak more precisely, therefore, we must recognize the importance of grouping or organizing the input sequence into units or chunks. Since the memory span is a fixed number of chunks, we can increase the number of bits of information that it contains simply by building larger and larger chunks, each chunk containing more information than before.

A man just beginning to learn radiotelegraphic code hears each *dit* and *dah* as a separate chunk. Soon he is able to organize these sounds into letters and then he can deal with the letters as chunks. Then the letters organize themselves as words, which are still larger chunks, and he begins to hear whole phrases. I do not mean that each step is a discrete process, or that pla-

teaus must appear in his learning curve, for surely the levels of organization are achieved at different rates and overlap each other during the learning process. I am simply pointing to the obvious fact that the dits and dahs are organized by learning into patterns and that as these larger chunks emerge the amount of message that the operator can remember increases correspondingly. In the terms I am proposing to use, the operator learns to increase the bits per chunk.

In the jargon of communication theory, this process would be called *recoding*. The input is given in a code that contains many chunks with few bits per chunk. The operator recodes the input into another code that contains fewer chunks with more bits per chunk. There are many ways to do this recoding, but probably the simplest is to group the input events, apply a new name to the group, and then remember the new name rather than the original input events.

Since I am convinced that this process is a very general and important one for psychology, I want to tell you about a demonstration experiment that should make perfectly explicit what I am talking about. This experiment was conducted by Sidney Smith and was reported by him before the Eastern Psychological Association in 1954.

Begin with the observed fact that people can repeat back eight decimal digits, but only nine binary digits. Since there is a large discrepancy in the amount of information recalled in these two cases, we suspect at once that a recoding procedure could be used to increase the span of immediate memory for binary digits. In Table 1 a method for grouping and renaming is illustrated. Along the top is a sequence of 18 binary digits, far more than any subject was able to recall after a single presentation. In the next line these same binary digits are grouped by pairs. Four possible pairs can occur: 00 is renamed 0, 01 is

TABLE 1. *Ways of recoding sequences of binary digits*

Binary Digits (Bits)		1	0	1	0	0	0	1	0	0	1	1	1	0	0	1	1	1	0

2:1	Chunks	10	10	00	10	01	11	00	11	10
	Recoding	2	2	0	2	1	3	0	3	2
3:1	Chunks	101		000	100		111	001		110
	Recoding	5		0	4		7	1		6
4:1	Chunks	1010			0010		0111		0011	10
	Recoding	10			2		7		3	
5:1	Chunks	10100			01001			11001		110
	Recoding	20			9			25		

renamed 1, 10 is renamed 2, and 11 is renamed 3. That is to say, we recode from a base-two arithmetic to a base-four arithmetic. In the recoded sequence there are now just nine digits to remember, and this is almost within the span of immediate memory. In the next line the same sequence of binary digits is regrouped into chunks of three. There are eight possible sequences of three, so we give each sequence a new name between 0 and 7. Now we have recoded from a sequence of 18 binary digits into a sequence of 6 octal digits, and this is well within the span of immediate memory. In the last two lines the binary digits are grouped by fours and by fives and are given decimal-digit names from 0 to 15 and from 0 to 31.

It is reasonably obvious that this kind of recoding increases the bits per chunk, and packages the binary sequence into a form that can be retained within the span of immediate memory. So Smith assembled 20 subjects and measured their spans for binary and octal digits. The spans were 9 for binaries and 7 for octals. Then he gave each recoding scheme to five of the subjects. They studied the recoding until they said they understood it—for about 5 or 10 minutes. Then he tested their span for binary digits again while they tried to use the recoding schemes they had studied.

The recoding schemes increased their span for binary digits in every case. But the increase was not as large as we had expected on the basis of their span for octal digits. Since the discrepancy increased as the recoding ratio increased, we reasoned that the few minutes the subjects had spent learning the recoding schemes had not been sufficient. Apparently the translation from one code to the other must be almost automatic or the subject will lose part of the next group while he is trying to remember the translation of the last group.

Since the 4:1 and 5:1 ratios require considerable study, Smith decided to imitate Ebbinghaus and do the experiment on himself. With Germanic patience he drilled himself on each recoding successively, and obtained the results shown in Fig. 9. Here the data follow along rather nicely with the results you would predict on the basis of his span for octal digits. He could remember 12 octal digits. With the 2:1 recoding, these 12 chunks were worth 24 binary digits. With the 3:1 recoding they were worth 36 binary digits. With the 4:1 and 5:1 recordings, they were worth about 40 binary digits.

It is a little dramatic to watch a person get 40 binary digits in a row and then repeat them back without error. However, if you think of this merely as a mnemonic trick for extending the memory span, you will miss the more important point that is implicit in nearly all such mnemonic devices. The point is that recoding is an extremely powerful weapon for increasing the amount of information that we can deal with. In one form or another we

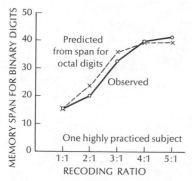

FIG. 9. The span of immediate memory for binary digits is plotted as a function of the recoding procedure used. The predicted function is obtained by multiplying the span for octals by 2, 3 and 3.3 for recoding into base 4, base 8, and base 10, respectively.

use recoding constantly in our daily behavior.

In my opinion the most customary kind of recoding that we do all the time is to translate into a verbal code. When there is a story or an argument or an idea that we want to remember, we usually try to rephrase it "in our own words." When we witness some event we want to remember, we make a verbal description of the event and then remember our verbalization. Upon recall we recreate by secondary elaboration the details that seem consistent with the particular verbal recoding we happen to have made. The well-known experiment by Carmichael, Hogan, and Walter (3) on the influence that names have on the recall of visual figures is one demonstration of the process.

The inaccuracy of the testimony of eyewitnesses is well known in legal psychology, but the distortions of testimony are not random—they follow naturally from the particular recoding that the witness used, and the particular recoding he used depends upon his whole life history. Our language is tremendously useful for repackaging material into a few chunks rich in information. I suspect that imagery is a

form of recoding, too, but images seem much harder to get at operationally and to study experimentally than the more symbolic kinds of recoding.

It seems probable that even memorization can be studied in these terms. The process of memorizing may be simply the formation of chunks, or groups of items that go together, until there are few enough chunks so that we can recall all the items. The work by Bousfield and Cohen (2) on the occurrence of clustering in the recall of words is especially interesting in this respect.

SUMMARY

I have come to the end of the data that I wanted to present, so I would like now to make some summarizing remarks.

First, the span of absolute judgment and the span of immediate memory impose severe limitations on the amount of information that we are able to receive, process, and remember. By organizing the stimulus input simultaneously into several dimensions and successively into a sequence of chunks, we manage to break (or at least stretch) this informational bottleneck.

Second, the process of recoding is a very important one in human psychology and deserves much more explicit attention than it has received. In particular, the kind of linguistic recoding that people do seems to me to be the very lifeblood of the thought processes. Recoding procedures are a constant concern to clinicians, social psychologists, linguists, and anthropologists and yet, probably because recoding is less accessible to experimental manipulation than nonsense syllables or T mazes, the traditional experimental psychologist has contributed little or nothing to their analysis. Nevertheless, experimental techniques can be used, methods of recoding can be specified, behavioral indicants can be found. And I anticipate that we will find a very orderly set of relations describing what now seems an uncharted wilderness of individual differences.

Third, the concepts and measures provided by the theory of information provide a quantitative way of getting at some of these questions. The theory provides us with a yardstick for calibrating our stimulus materials and for measuring the performance of our subjects. In the interests of communication I have suppressed the technical details of information measurement and have tried to express the ideas in more familiar terms; I hope this paraphrase will not lead you to think they are not useful in research. Informational concepts have already proved valuable in the study of discrimination and of language; they promise a great deal in the study of learning and memory; and it has even been proposed that they can be useful in the study of concept formation. A lot of questions that seemed fruitless twenty or thirty years ago may now be worth another look. In fact, I feel that my story here must stop just as it begins to get really interesting.

And finally, what about the magical number seven? What about the seven wonders of the word, the seven seas, the seven deadly sins, the seven daughters of Atlas in the Pleiades, the seven ages of man, the seven levels of hell, the seven primary colors, the seven notes of the musical scale, and the seven days of the week? What about the seven-point rating scale, the seven categories for absolute judgment, the seven objects in the span of attention, and the seven digits in the span of immediate memory? For the present I propose to withhold judgment. Perhaps there is something deep and profound behind all these sevens, something just calling out for us to discover it. But I suspect that it is only a pernicious, Pythagorean coincidence.

1. BEEBE-CENTER, J. G., ROGERS, M. S., & O'CONNELL, D. N. Transmission of information about sucrose and saline solutions through the sense of taste. *J. Psychol.*, 1955, 39, 157-60.
2. BOUSFIELD, W. A., & COHEN, B. H. The occurrence of clustering in the recall of randomly arranged words of different frequencies-of-usage. *J. gen. Psychol.*, 1955, 52, 83-95.
3. CARMICHAEL, L., HOGAN, H. P., & WALTER, A. A. An experimental study of the effect of language on the reproduction of visually perceived form. *J. exp. Psychol.*, 1932, 15, 73-86.
4. CHAPMAN, D. W. Relative effects of determinate and indeterminate *Aufgaben*. *Amer. J. Psychol.*, 1932, 44, 163-74.
5. ERIKSEN, C. W. Multidimensional stimulus differences and accuracy of discrimination. *USAF, WADC Tech. Rep.*, 1954, No. 54-165.
6. ERIKSEN, C. W., & HAKE, H. W. Absolute judgments as a function of the stimulus range and the number of stimulus and response categories. *J. exp. Psychol.*, 1955, 49, 323-32.
7. GARNER, W. R. An informational analysis of absolute judgments of loudness. *J. exp. Psychol.*, 1953, 46, 373-80.
8. HAKE, H. W., & GARNER, W. R. The effect of presenting various numbers of discrete steps on scale reading accuracy. *J. exp. Psychol.*, 1951, 42, 358-66.
9. HALSEY, R. M., & CHAPANIS, A. Chromaticity-confusion contours in a complex viewing situation. *J. Opt. Soc. Amer.*, 1954, 44, 442-54.
10. HAYES, J. R. M. Memory span for several vocabularies as a function of vocabulary size. In *Quarterly Progress Report*, Cambridge, Mass.: Acoustics Laboratory, Massachusetts Institute of Technology, Jan.-June, 1952.
11. JAKOBSON, R., FANT, C. G. M., & HALLE, M. *Preliminaries to speech analysis.* Cambridge, Mass.: Acoustics Laboratory, Massachusetts Institute of Technology, 1952. (Tech. Rep. No. 13.)
12. KAUFMAN, E. L., LORD, M. W., REESE, T. W., & VOLKMANN, J. The discrimination of visual number. *Amer. J. Psychol.*, 1949, 62, 498-525.
13. KLEMMER, E. T., & FRICK, F. C. Assimilation of information from dot and matrix patterns. *J. exp. Psychol.*, 1953, 45, 15-19.
14. KÜLPE, O. Versuche über Abstraktion. *Ber. ü. d. I Kongr. f. exper. Psychol.*, 1904, 56-68.
15. MILLER, G. A., & NICELY, P. E. An analysis of perceptual confusions among some English consonants. *J. Acoust. Soc. Amer.*, 1955, 27, 338-52.
16. POLLACK, I. The assimilation of sequentially encoded information. *Amer. J. Psychol.*, 1953, 66, 421-35.
17. POLLACK, I. The information of elementary auditory displays. *J. Acoust. Soc. Amer.*, 1952, 24, 745-9.
18. POLLACK, I. The information of elementary auditory displays. II. *J. Acoust. Soc. Amer.*, 1953, 25, 765-9.
19. POLLACK, I., & FICKS, L. Information of elementary multi-dimensional auditory displays. *J. Acoust. Soc. Amer.*, 1954, 26, 155-8.
20. WOODWORTH, R. S. *Experimental psychology.* New York: Holt, 1938.

22 / Influence of Inter-item Associative Strength upon Immediate Free Recall [1]

JAMES DEESE, *The Johns Hopkins University*

A number of recent studies have pointed to the associative strength of particular items within the context of the material presented to Ss as a fundamental determinant of the organization and amount of recall in immediate free recall. Of particular interest to the problems examined in the present study are those experiments dealing with clustering and association strength. Two experiments (3, 4) have demonstrated that when stimulus-response pairs from free association norms are randomly separated in presentation, they are reunited in recall and recalled in proportion to the strength of the association. The large and consistent clustering effects obtained in these experiments suggest that it may be fruitful to examine the more general case of associative relationships between all items, not just particular pairs of items.

The principal independent variable examined in the present study may be described as inter-item associative strength. The experiment examines the influence of this variable upon some characteristics of immediate free recall. Inter-item associative strength is defined as the average relative frequency with which all items in a list tend to elicit all other items in the same list as free associates. The hypotheses concerning inter-item associative strength which are examined in the present experiment are: (a) the number of items recalled is proportional to inter-item associative strength; (b) extraneous intrusions are inversely related to inter-item associative strength; and (c) the number of different intrusions is inversely related to inter-item associative strength. The last hypothesis stems from the results of an earlier experiment (2). In this experiment it was demonstrated that the frequency of occurrence of a particular intrusion was proportional to the probability of that intrusion's occurring as a free associate to items on the list. It turns out, for reasons explained below, that if inter-item associative strength is high, the items on the list tend to elicit the same free associates from outside of the list. Thus, the number of different high strength free associates from outside the list is relatively small. If the inter-item associative strength is low, on the other hand, there are few if any free associates in common between different items on the list. Thus, if intrusions are determined by associative strength to items on the list, there will be little overlap between different associations and the intrusions will be variable.

In general, these hypotheses may be described by the assertion that lists with high-item associative strength are more highly organized than those with low inter-item strength. High organization means that the number of items recalled is increased and that resistance to outside intrusion is relatively high.

One important question in the interpretation of the relationship between associative strength and recall concerns the immediacy of the influence of associative strength. There are at least two possibilities. Associative strength may have a direct influence upon recall; thus, in part, free recall may be described as free association. On the other hand, associative strength may be used, through the intervention of a secondary or mediating activity, as a mnemonic device. That is to say, Ss may deliberately seek appropriate associations and actively reject

From *Psychological Reports*, 1959, **5**, 305-12, with permission of the author and publisher.
1. This study was carried out while the author was at the University of California, Berkeley.

associations that are inappropriate. While a definitive test for any given situation as to whether Ss behave in one way or the other is almost impossible, a test was built into the present study which tells the extent to which Ss actually do use an associative mnemonic device available to them outside of the items to be remembered. This mnemonic device consists of a name given to each list, a name which Ss write down on their data sheets before beginning recall. Under certain conditions of the experiment the name provides an associative cue for items on the list; under other conditions the name provides no such cue. A comparison of recall with and without appropriate names suggests the extent to which Ss use such a device.

PROCEDURE

The experiment was conducted in two phases. In one phase data on immediate free recall for lists of words were obtained. In the second phase free association norms were established with a new sample of Ss for the words used in the recall experiment. The specific procedures were as follows:

Immediate free recall.—Eighteen lists of 15 words each were used for the free recall tests. Six of the lists consisted of words frequently given as associations to particular Kent-Rosanoff stimuli. Each list consisted of high frequency response items to a single Kent-Rosanoff stimulus. Six lists consisted of low frequency associations to the same six stimuli, and six lists consisted entirely of words never given as associations to those stimuli. The association frequencies were determined from the Minnesota norms (5). The lists were all matched for Thorndike-Lorge frequency on the L count (6). Associated with each list was a list name. For half of the Ss the list name was the appropriate Kent-Rosanoff stimulus; for the remaining Ss the name was an irrelevant word matched in Thorndike-Lorge frequency with the appropriate Kent-Rosanoff word. All lists together with their names are shown in Table 1. These particular lists were chosen because preliminary data suggested a great

range of variation in inter-item associative strength for the lists. Preliminary investigation had shown that in general high frequency response items to Kent-Rosanoff stimuli tend to elicit one another as free associates, while low and "zero" frequency response items do not tend to elicit one another as free associates.

Ss $(N = 144)$ drawn from the Introductory Psychology course at the University of California, Berkeley, were divided into six groups of 24 Ss each. Each group of Ss was given two high frequency lists, two low frequency lists and two zero frequency lists (as defined above). For half of the Ss the name given to the list was relevant (although, of course, the relevancy of the name was of no significance for the zero frequency lists), and for half of the Ss the name given the list was irrelevant.

All Ss were tested in groups. The following instructions were given after introductory remarks: I will read a short list of words to you. You are to listen carefully to the words and try to remember them. Immediately after I read the list, I will say "begin" and you are to write down, in the order in which you remember them, as many of the words as you can. It is extremely unlikely that you will remember all of the words, but on some lists you will probably remember a good many, and on other lists you will remember few. For the first list of words write the words in the first column. Then fold over this column and use the second column for the second list. If you are not sure about how to spell a word, write it down the best way you can. Each of the lists of words will have a name. I will read the name of the list first, and you are to write down the name of the list in the box at the top of each column before I begin reading the list. Do you understand?"

Word association tests.—The use of inter-item associative strength as a variable in this experiment made it necessary to obtain free association norms for the words used in the recall experiment. Therefore, the words presented in Table 1 were given to 50 Ss drawn from the same population as those Ss used in the recall tests. Previous evidence showed that a group this size yielded stable norms (2). The instructions given to Ss in this part of the study were those used in obtaining

TABLE 1. *Word lists used*

1. (Butterfly, Deliberate) HF.° Moth Insect Wing Bird Fly Yellow Net Pretty Flower Bug Cocoon Color Stomach Blue Bees.
2. (Butterfly, Deliberate) LF. Garden Sky Flutter Sunshine Nature Chase Spring Collection Beautiful Caterpillar Summer Light Wasp Colorful Grace.
3. (Butterfly, Deliberate) ZF. Book Tutor Government Study Early Velvet Winter Payroll Line Zebra Spray Arrow Help Arithmetic Typical.
4. (Slow, Sold) HF. Walk Speed Quick Lazy Drive Skid Run Work Fast Down Stop Snail Sign Poke Traffic.
5. (Slow, Sold) LF. Go Tortoise Drag Slide Late Crawl Country Motion Dull Steady Caution Stream Halt Sticky Accident.
6. (Slow, Sold) ZF. Home Exactly Step Devotion Morning Wave Fine Paper Improve Cat Glitter Company Weapon Watch Evening.
7. (Music, National) HF. Art Sweet Play Tone Soft Instrument Symphony Sing Note Song Sound Piano Noise Band Horn.
8. (Music, National) LF. Beautiful Heat Enjoyment Eat Nice Fun Cold Emotion String Silence Page Charm Ballet Pretty Drum.
9. (Music, National) ZF. Determine Person Story Depth Projection Desert Body Mood Check Headache Mongrel Rest Attract Force Various.
10. (Whistle, Propose) HF. Stop Train Noise Sing Blow Tune Sound Dog Song Shrill Boy Wolf Loud Mouth Woman.
11. (Whistle, Propose) LF. Ring Ear Low Watch Speech Game Signal Fellow Pierce Talk Tone Teeth Shout Music Referee.
12. (Whistle, Propose) ZF. Plant Nation Kindly Wish Student Chief Name Coat Indication Early Forget Opera Position Cut Hat.
13. (Command, Contract) HF. General Halt Voice Soldier Harsh Attention Sharp Navy Order Army Obey Officer Performance Tell Shout.
14. (Command, Contract) LF. Firm Head Direct Sword Change Stupid Agreement Forward Post Repeat Strong Chief Demand Yell Anarchy.
15. (Command, Contract) ZF. Fight Add Oven Shed Class True Library Report Matter Bank Ordinary Exhibit Dollar Tempo Optimistic.
16. (Chair, Possible) HF. Sofa Wood Cushion Stool Comfort Rest Pillow Rung Table Sit Legs Seat Soft Desk Arm.
17. (Chair, Possible) LF. Small Paint Straight Study Lazy Cozy Hard Couch Modern Upholstery Glue High Cloth Relax Rocker.
18. (Chair, Possible) ZF. Lake Ride Tonight Enemy Subtract Turtle Big Theary Legal Family Delicious Low School Race Insurance.

° The two words at the beginning of each list in parenthesis are the appropriate and inappropriate names for that list. The Code HF refers to high frequency (associates to appropriate name), LF to low frequency and ZF to zero frequency.

the Minnesota norms for the Kent-Rosanoff words. The test consisted of 260 items administered in two forms of 130 items each. Half of the Ss received each form first. The results of the test were tabulated as the percent frequency of every item on each list occurring as a free association to other items on the same list. These percentages were summed and averaged to obtain the index of inter-item associate strength. While the frequencies for any given item, particularly for low frequency responses, may be relatively unreliable, the inter-item association index itself is very stable (2).

RESULTS

Number of items recalled.—There is a larger number of items recalled for high frequency associates to Kent-Rosanoff stimuli than for low or zero frequency associates. However, the means and

standard deviations presented in Table 2 clearly show that giving Ss the appropriate Kent-Rosanoff stimulus as a name has *no* effect upon the number of items recalled. If the Kent-Rosanoff stimulus had been effective when presented at the beginning of the list, it should have produced an interaction in Table 2 such that there would have been a difference in mean number of items recalled between the relevant and irrelevant name conditions for the high frequency lists (and perhaps for the low frequency lists) but not for the zero frequency lists. No such interaction exists, however; in point of fact, recall for Ss given irrelevant names is very slightly superior for all lists.

The failure of the stimulus name to make a difference in number of items recalled suggests that the major variable

TABLE 2. *Means and standard deviations of numbers of items recalled for high frequency, low frequency and zero frequency lists of associates to appropriate list name*

	High Frequency		Low Frequency		Zero Frequency	
	Mean	SD	Mean	SD	Mean	SD
Appropriate Name	7.17	1.53	6.02	1.62	5.38	1.48
Inappropriate Name	7.52	1.44	6.14	1.54	5.61	1.41

associated with the different numbers of items recalled for the three kinds of lists is the inter-item associative strength of the individual lists. A direct examination of this variable can be seen in the correlation between the inter-item associative strength index and the number of items recalled per list. For this correlation, the two conditions of list name were combined.

The number of items recalled per list is shown in Column 2 of Table 3, while the inter-item associative strength is shown in Column 1. The *r* between these variables is .88, significant at beyond the 1% level for 17 *df*. This relationship is consistent with the clustering effects discovered by Jenkins, Mink, and Russell (3) with particular pairs of associates. The conclusion is that the likelihood of a particular item's occurring in free recall is a function of the associative strength of that item to other items in the list. This conclusion, of course, may be extended to words not actually presented by E but occurring as intrusions (2).

Extra-list intrusions.—The adjusted mean number of extra-list intrusions per list occurring in recall is shown in Column 3 of Table 3. The adjustment consisted of multiplying all occurrences of the appropriate Kent-Rosanoff stimulus as an intrusion by two. This was necessary since for half the Ss this word was artificially excluded as an intrusion. The correlation between the adjusted mean intrusions and inter-item associative strength is −.48, significant at between the 5% and the 1% level. The correlation is materially lowered by one list. This list consisted of low frequency associates to the Kent-Rosanoff word "Music." In the case of this list both the inter-item

TABLE 3. *Inter-item associative strength, items recalled per S, intrusions per S and commonality of intrusions for all lists*

List		Inter-item Assoc. Str.	N items Recalled	N Intrusions	Commonality
Butterfly	HF	28.3	7.9	.18	17.27
Butterfly	LF	4.3	6.7	.33	6.43
Butterfly	ZF	1.0	5.6	.50	7.51
Slow	HF	15.1	6.5	.40	5.80
Slow	LF	0.2	5.8	.59	11.09
Slow	ZF	2.7	5.8	.40	6.84
Whistle	HF	22.8	7.3	.39	7.79
Whistle	LF	4.0	5.6	.61	4.30
Whistle	ZF	2.3	5.4	.60	2.70
Music	HF	20.5	7.7	.21	9.09
Music	LF	9.3	6.1	1.14	3.70
Music	ZF	0.0	5.1	.69	3.79
Command	HF	13.0	7.1	.13	23.61
Command	LF	0.7	5.6	.53	4.17
Command	ZF	0.0	5.2	.57	6.31
Chair	HF	17.0	7.8	.43	14.04
Chair	LF	2.0	6.6	.82	4.39
Chair	ZF	0.0	6.1	.39	5.88

associative strength and the frequency of intrusion were relatively high. This case is so deviant from the general regression that it suggests this list may have unique properties. Thus, while we may accept the generalization implied in the obtained correlation, it can be applied to individual collections of items only with caution.

The fourth column in Table 3 shows an index of commonality for the extra-list intrusions given by different Ss. This index, which can vary from 0 to 100, expresses as a percentage the ratio of agreements in giving particular words as intrusions to the total number of possible agreements among all of the intrusions given by different Ss. This index is independent of the absolute number of intrusions, though its variance is not. The correlation between the commonality index and inter-item associative strength for the different lists in .55, significant at approximately the 1% level. Thus, not only is there a tendency for the intrusions to be somewhat less frequent for lists high in inter-item associative strength but also the intrusions given by different Ss tend more often to agree for such lists. This is in accord with other data (2). The absolute frequency of intrusions is considerably higher, however, and the absolute degree of commonality for particular intrusions is considerably less than that expected on the basis of earlier work (2).

DISCUSSION

Despite ample evidence for the importance of verbal associations in the recall process, there are many undecided questions about the exact role these associations play. Two related questions concern (a) whether or not the associations occur as deliberate mnemonic devices and (b) whether or not there is a selection process after the association such that Ss reject some associations but emit others as items in recall. In general, these questions involve a distinction as to whether associations in recall are primary or are secondary mediated processes. The present data bear on the adequacy of the alternate answers to these questions.

The possible influence of the list name upon recall is significant for the first question. The fact is that there is not an increase in recall frequency as a result of the availability of a list name which has high associative strength for the items on the list. Thus, it is clear that Ss in this study did not use an extra-list mnemonic device available to them. In view of their failure to use a well-labelled, high frequency associative device from outside of the list, it seems unlikely that they deliberately set about to improve recall by the use of considerably weaker intra-list associative connections. It is difficult to see how Ss would deliberately use a weaker associative mnemonic device from within the list rather than a stronger one readily available to them at the top of the recall data sheets.

Considerably more positive evidence bears on the question of selectivity after association has occurred. The greatest stumbling block to the view of association in recall as a primary, simple process of free association is the fact that recall is generally more appropriate or relevant than the purely associational view would seem to imply. Previous verbal associations that Ss bring into experiments on verbal processes are so strong and pervasive that it is impossible to avoid them, even if it is desired. Despite these associations, however, the responses in free recall of English words are fairly well restricted to the items given to Ss in the original presentation. In the category clustering phenomenon, for example, extraneous intrusions are few, despite the fact that the items presented to Ss by no means exhaust the categories involved (1). Thus, it has seemed likely that Ss edit their associations before producing them as overt items in recall. This implies that Ss must have available to them a faint copy of the original material or some general context imported by the material originally presented against which they may judge the relevancy of their associations.

This assumption proves to be quite unnecessary for the present data, however. In the present case it is only necessary to assume that Ss are able to reproduce from immediate memory a small core of items (the "immediate memory span") and that to these items free associations occur, the strongest of which are emitted as responses in recall. It is not necessary to assume that Ss pick and choose among their associations. The appropriateness or inappropriateness of recall will be determined by the list of words itself. If the list is an "organized" one (obtained, for example, by picking popular free associations to particular words, as was done in this experiment), the inter-item associations tend to converge on the items in the list and upon a few restricted responses outside of the list. If, on the other hand, the list of words is composed of items chosen randomly from the dictionary or a large word count, there is no convergence on items in the list, and only by rare chance will two words on the list elicit the same response as a strong association. In this case the total number of responses in recall is reduced slightly because the scattered associations given by the items on the list cannot jointly reinforce any particular response enough to make intrusions occur frequently enough to offset poor recall of items on the list. Those intrusions that do occur should be, more often than not, popular associations to particular individual items on the list. Because the number of different popular associations is large (equal to the number of items on the list if the most popular association defines popularity), the number of intrusions may be relatively large. Because these associations do not converge on common responses, however, the commonality of the intrusions will be low.

Thus, the results of the present study can be described by the assumption that recall consists of a small core of words directly available through immediate memory and of strong free associations to these. Recall is good or poor depending, then, upon the tendency of free associations from items within the list to converge upon other items within the list.

Will this assumption describe the results, say, of category clustering? It at least implies that frequency of intrusions (as well as tendency to cluster) will vary with inter-item associative strength within a category of items both within and without the list. Thus, it is implied that category clustering depends upon associative strength and should vary with it. Bousfield (1) has argued for an interpretation of category clustering in terms of superordinate functions, and it is possible that such an interpretation may lead to conclusions quite different from those implied by the free association hypothesis.

SUMMARY

Lists consisting of 15 words each were presented to Ss for immediate free recall. For each of the 18 lists a measure of inter-item associative strength was obtained; this consisted of the average relative frequency with which all items in a list tend to elicit all other items on the list as free associates. Inter-item associative strength was positively correlated (.88) with the number of words recalled per list, negatively correlated ($-.48$) with the number of extra-list intrusions in recall, and positively correlated (.55) with the commonality of the extra-list intrusions that did occur. In general, these results are consistent with an interpretation of free recall in terms of free association. Free association, as it occurs in recall, is probably a direct, unmediated activity with little or no active editing of the material being recalled. The data on intrusions from the present experiment are consistent with the assumption of lack of editing. The fact that Ss in the present experiment gave no evidence of using an extra-list associative mnemonic device made available to them suggests that the free association from item to item in recall is not the result of Ss' instructing themselves to free associate in order to increase recall.

1. BOUSFIELD, W. A. The occurrence of clustering in the recall of randomly arranged associates. *J. gen. Psychol.*, 1953, **49**, 229-40.
2. DEESE, J. On the prediction of occurrence of particular verbal intrusions in immediate recall. *J. exp. Psychol.*, 1959, **58**, 17-22.
3. JENKINS, J. J., MINK, W. D., & RUSSELL, W. A. Associative clustering as a function of verbal association strength. *Psychol. Rep.*, 1958, **4**, 127-36.
4. JENKINS, J. J., & RUSSELL, W. A. Associative clustering during recall. *J. abnorm. soc. Psychol.*, 1952, **47**, 818-21.
5. RUSSELL, W. A., & JENKINS, J. J. *The complete Minnesota norms for response to 100 words from the Kent-Rosanoff Association Test.* Tech. Rep. No. 11, Contract N8ONR-66216 between Office of Naval Research and Univer. of Minnesota.
6. THORNDIKE, E. L., & LORGE, I. *The teacher's word book of 30,000 words.* New York: Bureau of Publications, Teachers Coll., Columbia Univer., 1944.

23 / The Immediate Retention of Unrelated Words [1]

BENNET B. MURDOCK, JR., *University of Vermont*

Many group learning curves from rote-learning studies are approximately exponential in form. The present study started with an attempt to find a rote-learning task such that the results of individual Ss learning single lists would be a sufficiently close approximation to an exponential function so that this function could be used to describe the data. Describing the learning curves of individual Ss by a mathematical function should not only make possible a more exact description of the data but also facilitate the discovery of inter-relationships among variables.

It soon became apparent that in free-recall verbal learning the data of individual Ss learning single lists could adequately be described by an exponential function. In free-recall verbal learning a list of items is presented one at a time and after each presentation S recalls as many items as possible. The words may be recalled in any order, and the order of presentation is randomly varied from trial to trial. The exponential function that describes the data is $R = c(l - e^{-bn})$ where R is the number of items recalled after each presentation, c is an upper limit or asymptote, b is the rate constant or slope of the curve in a semilog plot, and n is the number of presentations. Thus, the exponential function shows how R varies as a function of n.

To avoid any confusion it is necessary to discuss briefly the relationship between learning and retention. The term "free-recall verbal learning" describes a type of rote-learning task in the same way that paired-associate learning or serial learning describe other types of rote-learning tasks. In free-recall verbal learning retention is measured after each presentation by the method of unaided recall. It is suggested that learning be considered the slope of the curve showing R as a function of n. Thus, learning would be the first derivative of R with respect to n, dR/dn. Such a distinction between retention and learning is analogous to the distinction between position and velocity in mechanics; just as velocity is the rate of change of position with respect to time so learning is the rate of change of retention with respect to the number of presentations. Such a definition of learning is of course consistent with the idea that is accepted by almost all

From the *Journal of Experimental Psychology*, 1960, **60**, 222-34, with permission of the author and publisher.

1. This article was facilitated by a Faculty Summer Research Fellowship from the University of Vermont. The author would like to thank Clinton D. Cook for invaluable advice at all stages of the project.

psychologists; namely, that learning is an improvement in performance. This definition sidesteps all problems as to why the improvement occurs; in so doing it makes possible a clear separation between the phenomenon itself and the factors on which the phenomenon depends.

The fact that the curve $R = f(n)$ is exponential in form means that the slope of the line, or learning, is proportional to the number of items yet to be recalled; thus, $dR/dn = b(c - R)$. The learning becomes slower and slower with each successive presentation. Since learning is considered to be the slope of the retention curve (i.e., retention as a function of number of presentations) the obvious measure of learning is b, the slope of the straight line obtained by plotting $\ln[(c - R)/c]$ as a function of n, where ln is log to the base e. Thus, the rate constant b replaces such traditional measures of learning as number of trials to criterion or number of correct responses. Finally, it is assumed that the exponential describes the results of all Ss in free-recall verbal learning; individual differences are assumed to be manifest in differing numerical values of the parameters b and/or c.

The present study reports a number of separate experiments, all of which dealt with the immediate retention of unrelated words. Some of the experiments studied retention after only one presentation, while others used repeated presentations. The experiments using repeated presentations were of course studies of free-recall verbal learning, but as has been pointed out, studies of free-recall verbal learning can be considered to be studying the phenomenon of retention. A number of the experiments were, either wholly or in part, designed to give evidence about practice effects. To allay any doubts as to the adequacy of the design used in many of the experiments it is necessary to state here that there are no practice effects, either warm-up or learning-how-to-learn. The preceding statement applies both to retention after one presentation and to free-recall verbal learning;

evidence to support these assertions will be presented in the Results section.

The two experimental variables that were studied most intensively were the length of the list and the presentation time (i.e., time per item). Some of the experiments investigated the effects of length of list and presentation time upon retention following a single presentation; other experiments studied the effects of these two variables on free-recall verbal learning. For the latter experiments, since the effect of repeated presentations could be described by an exponential function, the problem became one of determining the effects of length of list and presentation time upon the parameters b and c.

With two exceptions (Exp. IX and X) the learning material used in all the experiments were words drawn from the Thorndike-Lorge list of the 1,000 most common words in the English language (Thorndike & Lorge, 1944, pp. 267-70). As the words were essentially unrelated no attention was paid to the clustering of words during recall (Bousfield, 1953). Also, no attention was paid either to the rate at which the words were recalled during any given recall period (Bousfield & Sedgewick, 1944) or the order in which the words were recalled (Deese, 1957).

PROCEDURE

After Exp. I a set of standardized conditions was established for the study of free-recall verbal learning. The standardized conditions (abbreviated SC) facilitated comparisons among different experiments, and also served as a point of departure for the study of the effects of the several experimental variables. Enough data were collected under SC to present both normative data and data on reliability. Also, in several experiments there was some departure from SC. Since these departures had no noticeable effects on free-recall verbal learning it was possible to consider them as irrelevant (Underwood, 1957, pp. 284-7).

The SC were as follows: The stimulus material consisted of a list of 30 words randomly selected from the Thorndike-Lorge list of the 1,000 most common words in the English language. The words were presented at a presentation time of 2 sec./word, and after each trial S wrote down on a mimeographed data sheet as many words as he could recall. The data sheets were arranged in two columns of 13 spaces each with the letters of the alphabet running down the page at the left of each column. Each word was to be written in the space by the letter with which it began. Four trials were given, and the periods of time allowed for recall were 90, 120, 150, and 150 sec. for Trials 1-4, respectively. The 30-word test list was preceded by one trial on a 10-word practice list with a 45-sec. recall period. Group testing was used, the words were printed freehand on 4×6-in. index cards, and the cards were shuffled between trials to approximate a random order.

The unequal recall times (i.e., 90, 120, 150, and 150 sec. for Trials 1-4, respectively) were used to make the group testing as comparable to individual testing as possible. When Ss were tested individually (see Exp. V and VI) they were allowed as much time as they wanted for recall; it was found that they used progressively more time as the number of previous trials increased. The particular recall times selected for SC were based on rough averages obtained from the individual testing.[2]

To determine if the unequal recall times for Trials 1-4 would affect retention, a group of 22 Ss was tested under SC. Then they were retested under identical conditions except that they were given the same recall time (150 sec.) for all four trials. For total number of words recalled the mean difference between the two conditions was less than one word, and the difference did not approach statistical significance ($t = 0.32$). Thus, it would appear that the unequal recall times used under SC had little effect on the number of words recalled.

Since the words were randomly selected from the Thorndike-Lorge list it was assumed that, except for sampling fluctuations, lists of the same length were always of comparable difficulty. Therefore, within a given experiment lists were not counterbalanced among conditions. However, it should be noted that most of the conclusions are based on the results of two or more different experiments, and different lists were used in different experiments.

As has been mentioned there are no practice effects, either warm-up or learning-how-to-learn. Therefore in some (though not all) of the experiments to be reported the order in which Ss received the various treatments was not counterbalanced. In general the primary consideration was simplicity of design; lists were never counterbalanced, and order was counterbalanced only when it could be done without increasing the complexity of the experimental design.

Finally, as also will be shown, there is no difference between visual and auditory presentation. Therefore, while visual presentation was used under the SC, auditory presentation was used instead in any experiment which required a presentation time of 1 sec./word or less. With auditory presentation all homonyms were deleted from the population of words before the samples were drawn.

In the following descriptions of specific experiments, it is to be understood that in all experiments making use of repeated presentations the procedural details were as described under SC unless specific mention to the contrary is made. In addition to the abbreviations already mentioned (R, c, b, n, and SC) the following abbreviations will also be used: L (length of list), PT (presentation time/item), t (total time required for presentation of the complete list), and R_1 (number of words recalled after one presentation). Further, in any numerical designation of a specific list the first number indicates L and the second number indicates PT; thus, 30-2 means a list of 30 words presented at a rate of 2 sec./word.

Experiment I.—The purpose was to determine if a learning-set developed. The Ss were tested under the SC on five successive sessions each spaced one week apart. A total of 29 Ss participated in one or more of the five sessions plus two make-up sessions, but only 19 Ss participated in all five

2. Although the two experiments using individual testing are described as Exp. V and VI, they were actually the first experiments to be performed. The numbering of the experiments is based on expository convenience, not chronology.

regular sessions. In Exp. I and in all other experiments except where specifically noted the Ss were students of both sexes in the introductory psychology course who served as experimental Ss to fulfill a course requirement. No S served in more than one experiment.

Experiment II.—The purpose was to determine if a warm-up or fatigue effect occurred. All Ss ($N = 14$) learned six successive lists in one 2-hr. session. The first list was learned under the SC. Lists 1, 2, 4, and 5 were followed by a filler-task consisting of 10 short-answer questions made up specifically for this purpose (e.g., "Who is the Governor of Vermont?"). The Ss were allowed 15 sec. to answer each question. List 3 was followed by an 8-min. rest period during which time Ss were free to leave the room.

Experiment III.—The purpose was to determine the effects of L on R_1. In Exp. IIIa the lists were 15-2, 30-2, 45-2, 60-2, and 75-2. A different group was used for each list, and each list was presented once. Auditory presentation was used. One 75-word list was recorded on a tape recorder and, for each group, the tape was simply stopped after the appropriate number of words had been read. There were 14, 55, 19, 29, and 25 Ss for the five groups, respectively. The 55 Ss who were given a 30-2 list were also given one trial on a second 30-2 list as soon as the first list was finished. In Exp. IIIb seven additional groups were tested, and each group was given one trial on each of two to four lists. The lists and the order in which they were presented were as follows: first group ($N = 10$): 400-1, 5-1, 5-2; second group ($N = 17$): 100-1, 200-2, 6-1, 6-2; third group ($N = 15$): 200-1, 100-2, 8-1, 8-2; fourth group ($N = 24$): 45-1, 150-1, 10-1, 10-2; fifth group ($N = 30$): 75-1, 15-1, 30-1; sixth group ($N = 90$): 60-1, 60-2, 30-2; seventh group ($N = 13$): 60-1, 150-2. Thus, for Exp. IIIa and IIIb combined, there were at a PT of 2 sec./word Lists 5, 6, 8, 10, 15, 30, 45, 60, 75, 100, 150, and 200 words in length. For a PT of 1 sec./word there were all these lengths plus a 400-word list. In all a total of 260 Ss participated in Exp. III.

Experiment IV.—The purpose was to determine the effects of L on R_1 using the method of whole presentation. Three lists (25, 50, and 75 words long) were mimeo-

graphed. Three different groups of 18 Ss each were used. Each group was given one trial on each list, and the order in which the three groups learned the three lists was counterbalanced. For each list Ss were given 30 sec. to study the list in any way they wished, and then they were tested for recall.

Experiment V.—The purpose was to determine if the results of individual Ss learning single lists in free-recall verbal learning are adequately described by an exponential function. There were 18 Ss tested individually on a 30-2 list. Both practice and test list were carried to a criterion of one perfect trial except that the experimental session was limited to 1 hr.; if S did not reach criterion on the test list within the allotted time the experiment was terminated. Written recall was not used; S said aloud all the words he could recall and E recorded them on a check list.

Experiment VI.—The purpose was to determine the effect of L on b and c. One S was tested individually for 22 sessions, and at each session a different list was learned. There were six lists of 20-2, four lists each of 30-2, 40-2, and 50-2, and two lists each of 75-2 and 100-2. The order in which these 22 lists were learned was approximately counter-balanced. Both practice and test list were learned to a criterion of one perfect trial. As in Exp. V, E recorded the words recalled on a check list. The S was an undergraduate psychology major who volunteered for the experiment, and she was paid for her services.

Experiment VII.—The purpose was to determine the effect of L on b and, in part, to replicate Exp. VI with additional Ss. This experiment consisted of four sessions. On each session there was one trial of a 10-2 practice list, four trials of a test list, the filler task described under Exp. II, and then four trials of a second test list. The eight test lists were 15-2, 20-2, 25-2, 30-2, 35-2, 40-2, 50-2, and 60-2. The order was counterbalanced in that each session one "long" (35 words or more) and one "short" (30 words or less) list was used, and the order of long and short alternated on successive sessions. The first test list learned the first day was 30-2. There were 22 Ss in Exp. VII.

Experiment VIII.—The purpose was to determine the effect of PT on R_1 and b. The procedure was identical with that of Exp. VII except that the experimental variable was PT and not L. The eight lists were $30\frac{1}{2}$, $30\frac{3}{4}$, 30-1, $30-1\frac{1}{4}$, $30-1\frac{1}{2}$, 30-2, 30-3, and 30-4. The "fast" ($1\frac{1}{4}$ sec./word or less) and "slow" ($1\frac{1}{2}$ sec./word or more) rates were counterbalanced as in Exp. VII, and the first test list learned the first day was 30-2. Auditory presentation by a tape recorder was used. A total of 18 Ss participated in one or more sessions, but only 13 Ss participated in all four sessions.

Experiment IX.—The purpose was to determine the effect of frequency of usage on R_1 and b. The procedure was identical with that of Exp. VII except that the experimental variable was frequency of usage and not L. Frequency of usage was varied by dividing the 30,000 words of the Thorndike-Lorge list into eight subgroups, each subgroup containing approximately the same number of words. The frequency of usage of the eight subgroups were 100+/million, 50-99/million, 10-49/million, 4-9/million, 2-3/million, 1/million, 5-17/18 million, and 4/18 million. The "high" (4-9/million or more) and the "low" (2-3/million or less) groups were counterbalanced as in Exp. VII, and the 100+/million (comparable to the 1,000 most common words) was the first test list learned the first day. All lists were 30-2. A total of 22 Ss participated in one or more sessions, but only 20 Ss participated in all four sessions.

Experiment X.—The purpose was to determine the effect of emotional value on R_1 and b.[3] Each of 50 Ss (friends and sorority sisters of E) rated 30 words from Stagner's list (Stagner, 1933) on a 7-point scale of emotional value. For each S two lists were constructed, one of the 12 highest-rated and one of the 12 lowest-rated words. Each S then learned both lists to a criterion of one perfect trial. The Ss were tested individually, and the order in which the two lists was learned was counterbalanced. No practice list was used, E recorded the words that S was able to recall, and PT was 3 sec./ word.

Experiment XI.—The purpose was to replicate Exp. II, to determine R_1 as a joint function of L and PT, and to study the effects on R_1 and b of variations in L and PT holding total presentation time (t) constant.

In Exp. XIa (Session 1) the first half of Exp. II was replicated exactly except that the order of the lists was changed from 1, 2, 3, to 3, 1, 2. In Exp. XIb (Session 2) following a practice list R_1 was determined for 18 different lists. The lists were of three different lengths (15, 45, and 75 words) and six different presentation times ($\frac{1}{2}$, $\frac{3}{4}$, 1, $1\frac{1}{2}$, 2, and 3 sec./word). The order in which the lists were presented was determined by a table of random numbers. Auditory presentation was used, and there was a 2-min. rest after the sixth and after the twelfth list. In Exp. XIc (Session 3) there was a practice list, a 60-1 list, a filler task, a 20-3 list, a filler task, and a $40-1\frac{1}{2}$ list. Auditory presentation was used; for all three sessions $N = 16$.

Experiment XII.—The purpose was to replicate Exp. II and XIa, and to get further information on the effects of L on R_1. In Exp. XIIa (Session 1), following a practice list, Ss were tested for R_1 after four lists of 15-2, 30-2, 45-2, and 60-2 each. The order of these 16 lists was counterbalanced in blocks of four, and auditory presentation was used. In Exp. XIIb (Session 2), Exp. II and XIa were replicated exactly except that completely different lists were used. For the two sessions the Ns were 16 and 17, respectively.

RESULTS AND DISCUSSION

Instead of presenting the results of each experiment separately, the conclusions that have been drawn will be stated and, following each conclusion, its evidence. This method of presentation will be used because in most cases each conclusion is based on more than one experiment. In some cases corroborative evidence from other studies in the literature is available; such evidence will be cited where appropriate.

Conclusion 1.—The numerical value of the asymptote c is the number of words in the list. Evidence: (a) For each of the 22 lists learned by S in Exp. VI a least-squares solution of the exponential was used which gave a numerical value for

---

3. This experiment was designed and conducted by Cynthia Marvin in a course in experimental psychology taught by the author.

both *b* and *c*. Specifically, the least-squares solution was used on the approximation $\Delta R / \Delta n = bc - bR$ where ΔR was the upper envelope of the curve and R was the midpoint of each ΔR interval. The mean values for *c* were 21.0, 30.5, 40.5, 51.2, 80.2, and 101.3 words for the 20, 30, 40, 50, 75, and 100-word lists, respectively. The coefficient of determination (r^2) was 99.7%; thus practically all the variability in *c* can be attributed to *L*. (*b*) The same least-squares solution was used on the data of each of the 18 Ss in Exp. V. For all Ss the mean value of *c* was 31.0 words, and this did not differ significantly from the expected value of 30 words ($t = 1.03$, $P > .05$). (*c*) Bruner, Miller, and Zimmerman (1955) used the method of free-recall verbal learning with four lists of 8, 16, 32, or 64 words. Their recall data are plotted in percentages in the top half of their Fig. 1 (p. 188). All groups reached a criterion of at least 80% correct, and their curves suggest that, with a sufficient number of trials, all groups would reach or come close to 100% recall.

The fact that the asymptote *c* is the same as *L* means that one of the parameters in the exponential equation can be identified with an experimental variable which is under the control of *E*. Also, it greatly simplifies the work of fitting the exponential to the data. Knowing the value of the length, *L*, of a list substituting *L* for *c*, and writing the equation in the logarithmic form gives the equation $\ln[(L - R)/L] = -bn$. Thus, a plot of $\ln[(L - R)/L]$ against *n* gives a straight line with a slope of *b* and an intercept of zero.

A standard method has been used to solve for *b*. For SC there are actually five points to determine the curve. These are the number of words recalled after 0, 1, 2, 3, and 4 trials (when $n = 0$ then $R = 0$). It is necessary to use the least-squares formula for a straight line that passes through the intersection of the two axes (Bennett & Franklin, 1954, p. 232).

A least-squares solution for the exponential in log form does not minimize the sums of squares of deviations for the exponential form. In fact the log form introduces a systematic bias, weighting the last trial most heavily and the 0th trial least heavily (Murdock & Cook, 1960). In an attempt to correct for this bias, Trials 1, 2, 3, and 4 were weighted by a factor of 4, 3, 2, and 1, respectively. Although this weighting is arbitrary and does not result in a true least-squares solution for the exponential it is at least objective and simple to use; also, the data simply do not warrant a more precise treatment.

It is to be understood, then, that in all the analyses to follow, the parameter *c* in the exponential is assumed to have the numerical value of *L*. Furthermore, in all analyses to follow the numerical value of *b* was determined by the weighted least-squares method described in the preceding paragraph. Finally, in all cases a separate numerical value of *b* was always calculated for each list learned by each S. Thus, when mean values are presented, they will be mean *b* values and not the *b;* obtained from the mean trial-by-trial values.

Conclusion 2.—The data for individual Ss learning single lists is adequately described by an exponential function. Evidence: (*a*) There were a total of 101 Ss who learned under SC: 29 Ss from Exp. I, 14 Ss from Exp. II, 22 Ss from Exp. VII, 20 Ss from Exp. IX, and 16 Ss from Exp. XI. In all cases Ss were given four trials on a 30-2 list and, except for the practice list, it was the first list they had learned. After the value of *b* had been determined for each S a standard error of estimate, ($\sigma_{R \cdot n}$) was computed for each S. The distribution of $\sigma_{R \cdot n}$ for the 101 Ss was positively skewed with a median of 1.4 words and a semi-interquartile range of 0.5 words. Thus, on the average, two-thirds of the obtained values did not differ by more than 1.4 words from the best-fitting exponential. (*b*) For the 18 Ss of Exp. V, *b* was determined in the same manner (i.e., first four trials only), but the $\sigma_{R \cdot n}$ was computed from the total number of trials given each S. The median $\sigma_{R \cdot n}$

was 1.7 words and the semi-interquartile range was 0.4 words.

As no mathematical function ever describes experimental data perfectly, the question as to whether a given set of data is "adequately" described by a particular function is essentially a matter of judgment. In the present case the standard error of estimate has been used as a measure of goodness of fit. As has been shown, the deviations between the obtained data and the mathematical function average approximately 1.5 words; this would seem to be in adequate fit.

Another way of testing the appropriateness of a given function is to compare its goodness of fit with that of other possible functions. In the present case the most reasonable comparison is with the stochastic model of Bush and Mosteller (1955) which has also been suggested for free-recall verbal learning. For the Bush and Mosteller model it is necessary that Ss reach a criterion of one perfect trial in order to obtain an estimate of a_1. There were 13 Ss in Exp. V who reached criterion within the allotted time, and for each S the necessary parameters of the Bush and Mosteller model were determined. The value of p_0 was determined by the ratio $(N-1)/(N_0-1)$ and, for $a_1 T_2$ was the mean number of nonrecalls. As a measure of goodness of fit for these 13 Ss, the median $\sigma_{R \cdot n}$ for the Bush and Mosteller model was 2.2 words whereas for the exponential function the median $\sigma_{R \cdot n}$ was 1.6 words. A t test showed that the exponential function gave a significantly smaller $\sigma_{R \cdot n}$ than did the stochastic model ($t = 4.71$, $P < .01$). Therefore, insofar as it was possible to make a comparative test, it would seem that the exponential provides a more accurate description of free-recall verbal learning than does the Bush and Mosteller stochastic model.

Conclusion 3.—There is no difference between group testing with written recall and individual testing with oral recall. Evidence: (a) In Exp. V there were 18 Ss who were tested individually with oral recall. The mean value of b for these 18 Ss was 0.41, and this value did not differ significantly from the mean b value

of 0.39 obtained for the 101 Ss tested under SC ($t = 0.64$, $P > .05$).

Conclusion 4.—There is no difference between auditory presentation and visual presentation. Evidence: (a) In Exp. VIII there were 18 Ss who were tested under SC except that auditory presentation replaced visual presentation. The mean value of b for these 18 Ss was 0.37, and this value did not differ significantly from the mean b value of 0.39 obtained for the 101 Ss tested under SC ($t = 0.55$, $P > .05$).

The fact that individual testing with oral recall and auditory presentation do not affect the results makes it possible to combine the 18 Ss of Exp. V and the 18 Ss tested under SC. Since there is no learning-how-to-learn effect, and since their results do not differ significantly from the 101 Ss of SC ($b = 0.38$, $t = 0.13$, $P > .05$), the 17 Ss of Exp. XIIb can also be added. Thus, there were a total of 154 Ss who learned a 30-2 list either under SC or under conditions which were equivalent to SC; the data of these 154 Ss can be used to obtain norms for free-recall verbal learning.

Conclusion 5.—The distribution of the rate constant b is positively skewed, but its distribution is normalized by a logarithmic transformation. Evidence: (a) A histogram giving the distribution of b for all 154 Ss learning a 30-2 list is shown in Fig. 1 and, as can be seen, the distribution is positively skewed. This skewness is statistically significant ($t = 4.73$, $P < .001$) when tested by a method suggested by Snedecor (1956, pp. 199-200). (b) A logarithmic transformation of b results in a distribution that does not differ significantly from a normal distribution ($\chi^2 = 4.10$, $df = 6$, $P > .05$).

For all 154 Ss the mean value of the rate constant (obtained by taking the antilog of the mean of the transformed scores) was 0.39, and one SD covered the range from 0.26 to 0.57. As an indication of the stability of b, the 154 Ss came from eight different experiments and these different experiments were considered as separate samples. An analysis showed that with samples of the

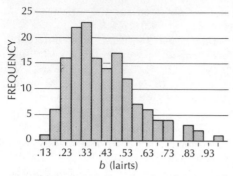

Fig. 1. Histogram showing distribution of b for 154 Ss.

TABLE 1. *Means and SDs of log 10b for Exp. I*

Session	Group A N = 19		Group B N = 9	
	Mean	SD	Mean	SD
1	.65	.16	.57	.19
2	.58	.17	.60	.21
3	.63	.16	.64	.20
4	.65	.16	.60	.16
5	.60	.14		

size used (approximately 15 to 20 Ss) two-thirds of the samples did not vary by more than 7% from the total mean of 0.39.

To discuss the nature of the rate constant more completely, it should be pointed out that b is a measure of the rate at which the curve approaches the asymptote c (L). The unit of measure of b is reciprocal trials; we would suggest the term "lairt." The reciprocal of the rate constant indicates the number of trials required to attain approximately 63% of L. Thus, to say that the total mean was 0.39 lairts indicates that, on the average, Ss required 2.6 trials to reach a criterion of 19 out of 30 words (i.e., 63% of L). Actually, b is like SD in that it can be used to specify any desired criterion of mastery. Thus, in $0.5/b$ trials S should reach 39% L, in $2/b$ trials 86% L, in $3/b$ trials 95% L, etc.

Because the distribution of b was positively skewed all statistical tests (including those already presented under Conclusions 3 and 4) are based on a logarithmic transformation of b. When means and SDs of b are reported it is to be understood that these values are the antilogs of the transformed scores.

Conclusion 6.—There is no learning-how-to-learn effect in free-recall verbal learning. Evidence: (*a*) In Exp. I there were 19 Ss (Group A) who participated in all five regular sessions. An analysis of variance showed that the effect of sessions was not statistically significant ($F = 2.01$, $P > .05$). The means and SDs of log $10b$ are shown in the upper part of Table 1

for each of the five sessions. (*b*) In Exp. I there were an additional nine Ss (Group B) who participated in at least four different sessions. An analysis of variance showed that with these Ss the effect of sessions was not statistically significant ($F < 1.00$). The means and SDs of log $10b$ are shown in the lower part of Table 1 for each of these four sessions. (*c*) As has already been indicated, the mean value of b for Session 2 of Exp. XII (i.e., Exp. XIIb) did not differ significantly from the mean value of b for SC.

Greenberg and Underwood (1950) found that recall following a 10-min. retention interval did not improve with practice. The present results are consistent with these findings; the slope of the retention curve did not vary systematically as a function of stage of practice.

Conclusion 7.—There is no warm-up effect in free-recall verbal learning. Evidence: (*a*) An analysis of variance of the results of Exp. II showed that the effect of lists *was* statistically significant ($F = 7.14$, $P < .001$). The means and SDs of log $10b$ are shown in Table 2 and of the six lists learned only List 2, according to Tukey's tests (Edwards, 1954, pp. 330-35) differed significantly from the rest.

TABLE 2. *Means and SDs of log 10b for Exp. III (N = 14)*

Measure	Session					
	1	2	3	4	5	6
Mean	.53	.66	.55	.55	.54	.49
SD	.15	.19	.21	.19	.20	.17

(b) Experiment XIa was an exact replication of the first half of Exp. II except that the order of the lists was 3, 1, and 2 instead of 1, 2, and 3. Again the effect of lists was statistically significant ($F = 14.16$, $P < .001$ and again, according to Tukey's tests, only List 2 differed significantly from the rest. However, in Exp. XIa List 2 was the third list learned, and for the second list learned (i.e., List 1) the mean value of b was actually lower (though not significantly so) than the first list learned. Thus it would appear that the significant Fs resulted from a particular list which was easier to learn and not from any warm-up effect. (c) As a further check, Exp. XIIb was an additional replication of the first half of Exp. II except that three completely different 30-2 lists were used. An analysis of variance showed that the effect of lists was not statistically significant ($F < 1.00$). (d) In Exp. X a number of Ss reached criterion so quickly that it was not possible to calculate a numerical value for b. Instead, trials to criterion was used as the measure of learning and the mean difference between the first and second list was a nonsignificant 0.3 trials ($t = 0.83$, $P > .05$).

With the large number of different lists used it was inevitable that some lists would be appreciably harder or easier than average. The List 2 of Exp. II seemed to be the only list of all those used that was sufficiently deviant so as to result in statistically significant differences in learning.

Conclusion 8.—The reliability of b is .77. Evidence: (a) The correlation coefficient of .77 is based on 76 Ss: 29 Ss from Exp. I, 14 Ss from Exp. II, 16 Ss from Exp. XIa, and 17 Ss from Exp. XIIb. The correlation was based on the first two 30-2 lists learned by each S except for the 14 Ss of Exp. II. In Exp. II the second list was the deviant list; therefore, the third 30-2 list was substituted for the second 30-2 list.

Conclusion 9.—The relationship between the rate constant b and frequency of usage (FU) as measured by the Thorndike-Lorge word count is given by the formula, $b = .048$ log $FU + 0.31$. Evidence: For the data of Exp. IX the coefficient of determination (r^2) was 66%, and the slope of the line differed significantly from zero ($t = 3.43$, $df = 6$, $P < .05$).

The linear relationship between b and log FU suggests that the same relationship which holds for perceptual recognition thresholds (Howes & Solomon, 1951) also holds for learning. The results are also in essential agreement with those of Hall (1954) for free-recall verbal learning.

Conclusion 10.—There is no warm-up effect for R_1, the number of items recalled after one presentation. Evidence: (a) There were 55 Ss in Exp. IIIa who were given one trial on each of two successive 30-2 lists. The mean R_1 difference was -0.3 words, and this difference was not significant ($t = 0.76$, $P > .05$). (b) In Exp. XIIa, Ss were given one trial on each of 16 lists. These 16 lists were divided into four quarters and the differences among the four quarters were not significant ($F = 1.44$, $P > .05$). (c) An analysis of variance of R_1 for the three lists of Exp. XIIb showed that the differences among lists were not significant ($F = 1.14$, $P > .05$).

The data of Exp. XIb cannot be used to test for warm-up because the order in which the lists were presented was randomized, not counterbalanced. However, in addition to the above evidence there is an unpublished experiment by A. J. Babick and the author which is relevant. This experiment tested R_1 for 18 successive 25-1 lists; each of 18 Ss was tested individually. The 18 lists were divided into six groups of three lists each, and an analysis of variance showed that the differences among lists were not significant ($F = 2.24$, $P > .05$).

Conclusion 11.—$R_1 = kt + m$ where $t = L \times PT$. Evidence: The evidence for Conclusion 11 is shown in Table 3 which gives the values of r^2, k, and m

TABLE 3. *Values of r^2, k, and m for $R_t = kt + m$*

Exp.	Ind. Var.	Range	N	r^2	k	m
IIIa	L	15–75 words	142	98%	.071	5.9
III	L	5–400 words	260	88%	.056	5.8
VII	L	15–60 words	22	72%	.063	6.3
VIII	PT	½–4 sec.	13	92%	.080	4.8
XIb	PT	½–3 sec.	16	98%	.025	6.3
XIIa	L	15–60 words	16	90%	.028	6.4
Median				91%	.060	6.1

for the six relevant experiments (considering Exp. IIIa and III as separate experiments even though five points from the former are included in the 25 points of the latter). One source of evidence for a linear relationship is the coefficient of determination, r^2; the median r^2 for the six experiments was 91%. Perhaps even more important it should be noted that the various experiments, despite different lists, different Ss, different methodologies, different conditions, and even different experimental variables, all gave numerical values for k and m that were of the same order of magnitude.

It appears that the effects of L and PT can be subsumed under the total time, t. Thus, t is the critical variable and it is a multiplicative function of L and PT. The numerical values for the entries of k and m in Table 3 were obtained by making use of this multiplicative relationship irrespective of whether L or PT was the variable actually manipulated in the experiment itself.

Since the slope k is positive, R_t increases either as PT increases or L increases, the other held constant. There is considerable supporting evidence from Woodworth (1938, pp. 19–20) for the general finding that the number of items recalled increases as the list gets longer. Nonetheless, it was still rather surprising to find, for instance, that while the average recall of a 400-word list was 35 words no S was able to recall more than 10 words out of a 15-word list. Incidentally, it should be pointed out that, according to our data, it is misleading to emphasize the fact that the percentage of words recalled decreases as L increases. Actually, the per-

centage of words recalled over and above m stays constant; specifically, $(R_t - m)/L = kPT$.

Since t is the critical variable, it should be possible to vary L and PT simultaneously while keeping t constant and obtain the same recall. In Exp. XI there was a 20-3, a 30-2, a 40-1½, and a 60-1 list. Since for all four lists t was the same (60 sec.) R_t should therefore be the same for all four lists. The mean values of R_t for the four lists were 9.3 words, 9.3 words, 9.6 words, and 8.4 words, respectively; the differences were not significant ($F < 1.00$).

It is suggested, then, that more words are recalled from a longer list because the longer list requires more time to present. If this is so, R_t for lists of different lengths presented for the same length of time by the method of whole presentation should not differ since t is the same. Experiment IV was conducted to test this and, as predicted, length was not a significant variable ($F = 2.48, P > .05$).

Using the median values of k and m shown at the bottom of their respective columns in Table 3 the formula becomes: $R_t = .06t + 6.1$, where t is measured in seconds. Assuming comparable samples it should be possible to predict results from other studies. Peters (1936) used a 10-1 list; $\tilde{R}_t = 6.7$ words, obtained $\bar{R}_t = 5.2$ words (Table 2, p. 575). Bousfield, Sedgewick, and Cohen (1954) used a 60-3 list; $\tilde{R}_t = 16.9$ words, obtained R_t at the end of 2 min. $= 16.2$ words. Deese (1957) used a 20-1 list; $\tilde{R}_t = 7.3$ words, obtained $\bar{R}_t = 5.7$ words. Deese and Kaufman (1957) used a 32-1 and a 10-1 list; $R_t = 8.0$ words and 6.7 words, and as best could be determined from their Fig. 1 (p. 182) obtained $R_t = 8.5$ words and 5.8 words, respectively. Unfortunately, several other studies which have tested R_t have either not used a fixed PT or else have not reported it. While the above predictions are fairly accurate, on the average they tend to be a little high. Most of these experiments selected the words from the 30,000 most common words, so the obtained values should be a little lower than would be predicted on the basis of the 1,000 most common words.

Given the linear relationship between R_t

and t and the exponential function for free-recall verbal learning, it is possible to state the relationship between b, L, and PT. This relationship can be written:

$$e^{-b} = 1 - kPT - \frac{m}{L} \quad [1]$$

To illustrate how Equation 1 works, for a 30-2 list $L = 30$ words and $PT = 2$ sec./word. Taking median values so $m = 6.1$ words and $k = .06$ words/sec. then $e^{-b} = .677$, or $b = .39$ lairts. The predicted value agrees perfectly with the mean value for b obtained under SC, even though four of the six experiments used to determine the median values which entered into the determination of $\tilde{b}$ were completely different from those experiments which entered into the determination of $\bar{b}$.

In Exp. VII, L was systematically varied, and this experiment can be used to test Equation 1. In Exp. VII, $PT = 2$ sec./word; assuming the median values for k and m Equation 1 becomes:

$$\tilde{b} = - \ln \left[.88 - \frac{6.1}{L} \right] \quad [1a]$$

The symbol "ln" represents log to the base e. The predicted and obtained results are shown in Fig. 2. The smooth curve gives the predicted values and midpoints of the vertical lines are the obtained group means. The extent of the vertical lines indicates the 99% confidence interval. All points show satisfactory agreement.

In Exp. VIII, PT was systematically varied, and this experiment can also be used to test Equation 1. In Exp. VIII, $L = 30$ words; assuming the median values for k and m Equation 1 becomes:

$$b = - \ln [.80 - .06\,PT] \quad [1b]$$

The predicted and obtained results are shown in Fig. 3 and, except for the two fastest presentation times, all points show satisfactory agreement.

Finally, in Exp. XI there were four lists in which L and PT were simultaneously varied but t was constant. With $t = 60$ sec. and again using the median values Equation 1 becomes:

$$\tilde{b} = - \ln \left[1 - \frac{9.7}{L} \right] \quad [1c]$$

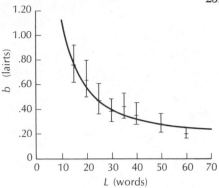

Fig. 2. Predicted and obtained results for b as a function of L.

The predicted and obtained values are shown in Fig. 4 and, except for the fastest presentation time (i.e., the 60-1- list) all points show satisfactory agreement. Considering the results as a whole, they seem to provide fairly convincing evidence in support of Equation 1.[4]

In conclusion, it should be understood that, although not explicitly stated, all proposed relationships only hold within certain limits. Thus, it seems reasonable to assume that a list can be so long that S could not master it completely; then c would no longer be identical with L. Or, PT could be so long or so short that R_1 would no longer be a linear function of t. No serious attempt to determine limits has been made; however, the results just presented suggest

4. Analyses of variance of Exp. VII, VIII, and XI showed that, in each case, group differences were significant beyond the .001 level.

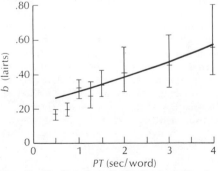

Fig. 3. Predicted and obtained results for b as a function of PT.

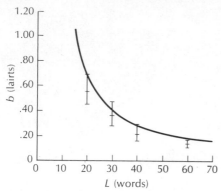

FIG. 4. Predicted and obtained results for b a function of L with t constant.

that the fastest presentation times used may have been at or near the limits.

Also, it is obvious that when $t = 0$ then $R_1 = 0$, so literally it makes no sense to assume a positive value for the intercept m. However, for the sake of simplicity the intercept has been treated as if the function were linear throughout the range. In all probability m is the memory span; this is its rational interpretation and the numerical value agrees with the conventional values reported in the literature. The parameter k is a measure of the rate at which R_1 changes as a function of t.

Finally, we have no evidence as to why R is an exponential function of n, or why R_1 is a linear function of t. An understanding of why these relationships take the form they do awaits further research.

SUMMARY

A number of experiments are reported which investigated the immediate retention of unrelated words. Some studied retention following a single presentation; others studied the changes in retention that occurred with repeated presentations. The latter experiments were in effect studies of free-recall verbal learning. The method of free-recall verbal learning was selected for investigation because it was found, the results of individual Ss learning single lists could adequately be described by an exponential function.

For the experiments on free-recall verbal learning a standard procedure and a stan-

dard method of fitting the exponential were used; normative data and data on reliability were presented. It was shown that there was no learning-how-to-learn or warm-up effect. Also, there was no difference between visual and auditory presentation or between individual and group testing. Learning was found to be a linear function of log frequency of usage.

The two experimental variables most intensively investigated were length of list and presentation time per item. The number of items retained after one presentation was a linear function of the total time required for presentation of the list, where the total time was a product of the length of list and the presentation time per item. Given this linear relationship and the exponential function for free-recall verbal learning it was possible to predict the learning of a list with a fair degree of accuracy given its length and presentation time.

BENNETT, C. A., & FRANKLIN, N. L. *Statistical analysis in chemistry and the chemical industry.* New York: Wiley, 1954.

BOUSFIELD, W. A. The occurrence of clustering in the recall of randomly arranged associates. *J. gen. Psychol.*, 1953, **49**, 229-40.

BOUSFIELD, W. A., & SEDGEWICK, C. H. W. An analysis of sequences of restricted associative responses. *J. gen. Psychol.*, 1944, **30**, 149-65.

BOUSFIELD, W. A., SEDGEWICK, C. H. W., & COHEN, B. H. Certain temporal characteristics of the recall of verbal associates. *Amer. J. Psychol.*, 1954, **67**, 111-18.

BRUNER, J. S., MILLER, G. A., & ZIMMERMAN, C. Discriminative skill and discriminative matching in perceptual recognition. *J. exp. Psychol.*, 1955, **49**, 187-92.

BUSH, R. R., & MOSTELLER, F. *Stochastic models for learning.* New York: Wiley, 1955.

DEESE, J. Serial organization in the recall of disconnected items. *Psychol. Rep.*, 1957, **3**, 577-82.

DEESE, J., & KAUFMAN, R. A. Serial effects in recall of unorganized and sequentially organized verbal material. *J. exp. Psychol.*, 1957, **54**, 180-87.

EDWARDS, A. L. *Statistical methods for the behavioral sciences.* New York: Rinehart, 1954.

GREENBERG, R., & UNDERWOOD, B. J. Retention as a function of stage of practice. *J. exp. Psychol.*, 1950, **40**, 452-57.

HALL, J. F. Learning as a function of word-frequency. *Amer. J. Psychol.*, 1954, **67**, 138-40.

HOWES, D. H., & SOLOMON, R. L. Visual duration threshold as a function of word probability. *J. exp. Psychol.*, 1951, **41**, 401-10.

MURDOCK, B. B., JR., & COOK, C. D. On fitting the exponential. *Psychol. Rep.*, 1960, **6**, 63-9.

PETERS, H. N. The relationship between familiarity of words and their memory value. *Amer. J. Psychol.*, 1936, **48**, 572-84.

SNEDECOR, G. W. *Statistical methods* (5th ed.) Ames: Iowa State Coll. Press, 1956.

STAGNER, R. Factors influencing the memory value of words in a series. *J. exp. Psychol.*, 1933, **16**, 129-37.

THORNDIKE, E. L., & LORGE, I. *The teacher's word*

book of 30,000 words. New York: Teachers College, Columbia Univer., 1944.

UNDERWOOD, B. J. *Psychological research.* New York: Appleton-Century-Crofts, 1957.

WOODWORTH, R. S. *Experimental psychology.* New York: Holt, 1938.

24 / The Occurrence of Clustering in the Recall of Randomly Arranged Associates

W. A. BOUSFIELD, [1] *University of Connecticut*

A. INTRODUCTION

The writer and Sedgewick (1) employed a simple technique to investigate the characteristics of sequences of associative responses. The procedure was to ask subjects to list items in specified categories, e.g., animals, birds, and cities in the United States. Inspection of the data at that time revealed a significant phenomenon which, while apparent, appeared too elusive for quantification. In the lists of birds, for example, there occurred many sequences of related items such as *hawk, eagle, vulture,* and *chicken, turkey, duck, goose.* The first three may be classed as birds of prey, and the latter as domestic fowl. We shall here refer to such groups as clusters, and define a cluster as a sequence of associates having an essential relationship between its members. An examination of kymographic records showing the temporal distribution of associates revealed an apparent tendency for the members of clusters to occur in relatively rapid succession. It turned out, however, that many of the temporally distinguishable groups of items revealed no obvious basis of relationship. For example, on one instance *hawk* was followed by *sparrow.* According to our definition this pair might be a cluster since there are several ways in which they could be related. Some hawks prey on sparrows, and sparrow hawk is the name of a bird. In this situation we cannot rely on the experi-

menter's subjective judgment, and we would prefer not to rely on the subject's introspections.

The purpose of this paper is to describe the results of the use of a technique for quantifying clustering as here defined. The theoretical significance of this undertaking derives in part from the assumption that clustering is a consequence of organization in thinking and recall. If clustering can be quantified, we are provided with a means for obtaining additional information on the nature of organization as it operates in the higher mental processes.

B. METHOD

A consideration of the following factors determined the choice of the method: (*a*) the subjects should produce sequences of verbal responses since previous work had apparently demonstrated the occurrence of clustering in data of this type; (*b*) the sequences should be of a nature to permit clustering within a wide range; (*c*) the identification of clustering should be objective. Because of the need for objectivity it was necessary to force restrictions considerably beyond those involved in the listing of items in a single general category. The method finally chosen was that of presenting

From the *Journal of General Psychology*, 1953, **49**, 229-40, with permission of the author and publisher.
1. The author wishes to acknowledge the assistance of Mr. Dallas Grover in the tabulation and treatment of the data of this study.

subjects a prepared list of nouns, and then having the subjects list serially as many as they could recall within a period of 10 minutes. The list used throughout the experiment comprised 60 nouns made up of 15 each of 4 different categories, namely, *animals, names, professions,* and *vegetables.* In order to insure at least a minimum of control over the associative values of the words, use was made of the Thorndike-Lorge tables (4). The four categories were matched as closely as possible on the basis of frequencies of occurrence per million of words in general. These words appear in Table 1. The mean frequencies of

Muskrat, blacksmith, panther, baker, wildcat, Howard, Jason, printer, chemist, radish, mushroom, Otto, plumber, pumpkin, chipmunk, Amos, Wallace, parsnip, milkman, druggist, leopard, woodchuck, Adam, grocer, Simon, Owen, lettuce, giraffe, turnip, garlic, rhubarb, typist, eggplant, Noah, zebra, donkey, Gerald, dentist, otter, parsley, spinach, Oswald, weasel, broker, waiter, florist, Bernard, dancer, reindeer, Byron, cabbage, melon, badger, mustard, diver, carrot, Sherman, camel, baboon, Moses.

The technique for obtaining data resembled that outlined in the earlier study (1) for group experimentation. The experiment took place in a large lecture

TABLE 1. *List of stimulus words*

Animals		Names		Professions		Vegetables	
Word	Freq.	Word	Freq.	Word	Freq.	Word	Freq.
giraffe	1	Amos	1	milkman	1	eggplant	1
baboon	2	Gerald	1	typist	1	parsnip	1
zebra	2	Byron	3	florist	2	garlic	3
panther	5	Oswald	4	plumber	2	rhubarb	3
wildcat	5	Jason	5	diver	4	radish	4
leopard	6	Otto	5	druggist	4	melon	5
reindeer	6	Noah	6	broker	7	mustard	7
chipmunk	7	Wallace	7	printer	7	spinach	8
muskrat	7	Owen	7	dentist	9	parsley	8
woodchuck	7	Bernard	9	baker	10	carrot	9
otter	8	Adam	10	chemist	10	mushroom	10
weasel	9	Sherman	10	dancer	10	turnip	10
badger	11	Simon	11	grocer	11	lettuce	12
donkey	16	Moses	12	waiter	13	pumpkin	13
camel	18	Howard	19	blacksmith	19	cabbage	16
Mean Freq.	7.33		7.33		7.33		7.33

occurrence are the same for each category, and the ranges of these frequencies approximately match. We chose two-syllable words on the assumption that they would be more recognizable in an auditory presentation than would one-syllable words. Having selected the words, they were randomized in the following way. Each word was written on a small piece of cardboard, ⅛ x 1 in. These cards were then repeatedly shuffled in a box, and then drawn one by one. The original items, thus randomized, occurred in the following serial order to make up the list of stimulus words:

room. Each subject had a piece of paper, 8½ x 11 in., and a pencil. Two groups (90 and 35 subjects respectively) of undergraduate students in psychology received the following instructions:

I shall read you a list of words, and you are asked to recall as many of them as you can after I have completed the reading. You are to start writing the words as rapidly as possible when I say, "*Go!*" Write the words in a column at the left side of the paper that has been given you. At intervals I shall say, "*Draw a line.*" On hearing this signal please draw a short horizontal line under the last word you have written, and then continue with more words. In the event you have thought of no additional words since the last instruction, *"Draw a line,"* you will draw another line just the same. Are there any questions?

After these instructions, the experimenter answered such questions as were relevant, and then read the stimulus list at a rate of three seconds per word, cues for these intervals being the barely audible click of a mechanical timing device. The signal for writing the words recalled was given three seconds after the reading of the last stimulus word. Thereafter the signals for drawing the demarcation lines were given at one-minute intervals for the period of 10 minutes. It may be noted that there was no mention in the instructions of the nature of the stimulus words. The subjects were asked only to list as many as they could recall, and to draw the demarcation lines when they heard the appropriate signal.

C. RESULTS

From the 125 lists of recalled items, 100 were selected at random. Four of the lists thus chosen were rejected because of obvious failure to follow instructions. Substitutes for these were also chosen at random. Thus 100 lists supplied the basic data of the experiment. The first step in the statistical treatment of the data was to determine the extent to which the subjects exceeded chance in their tendency to cluster their items in the four categories inherent in the list of stimulus words. The test of randomness was a derivation from the binomial theorem. In this frame of reference the problem was to determine, on the basis of chance expectation, how often we would expect an item (A, animal; N, name; P, profession; or V, vegetable) to be followed by another item in the same category. If a subject repeats n nouns, in one-fourth of all the cases there would be, by chance, a double symbol

AA, NN, PP, or VV. If we suppose there are r such repetitions, an appropriate measure of the tendency toward repetition, which we represent as y, is given by the following formula:[2]

$$y = \frac{4r}{\sqrt{3n}} - \sqrt{\frac{n}{3}}$$

We shall here refer to y as the index of repetition. In this formula, since n represents the total number of sequences, it must be the total number of items minus 1. The 4 is the number of categories in which repetitions can occur. It may be noted that y is distributed normally with unit standard deviation about zero, and that it is independent of the magnitude of n. Applying this formula to the list of randomized stimulus words, we have $n = 59$, and $r = 15$. In this case the index of repetition, y, is about .08. We are, therefore, justified in regarding the four categories of the stimulus words as randomly distributed.

The data, as expected, contained errors in the form of items not appearing in the stimulus words. When such items could be classed in the categories of the stimulus words they were labelled *categorical intrusions;* when they could not be so classed they were labelled *irrelevant intrusions.* Examples of the former were *bear, Allen, banker, clergy;* and of the latter, *number, atom, order,* and *bourbon.* Apparently, *clang* associations accounted for some of the irrelevant intrusions. In our analysis of clustering, the categorical intrusions were treated in the same way as the correct items.

Indices of repetition were computed not only for the data of the subjects, but also for data derived from a parallel artificial experiment. In this case the method involved drawing capsules at random and without replacement from a box containing 15 blue, 15 green, 15 orange, and 15 white capsules. A total of 100 such se-

---

2. The author is indebted to Dr. Geoffrey Beall for his suggestion of this formula.

quences were thus drawn with the number in each case matching the number of items listed by a corresponding subject. To test for possible bias in this method, 1,000 capsules were drawn with replacement. The result was 261 blues, 245 greens, 236 oranges, and 258 whites. These data yield a chi-square of 1.624. The corresponding probability value lies between .70 and .50 which is well within the limits of chance expectation.

The indices of repetition for the data of the subjects and for the drawings in the artificial experiment appear in Table 2. The differences between the two dis-

appreciable variability in the number of items they listed. The range was 12 to 36, with a mean of 24.97 and a standard deviation of 5.70.

A second method for appraising clustering was that of computing a simple *ratio of repetition*. This was the fraction representing the number of repetitions of items divided by the total items listed. For the subjects as a group this ratio was .45. The corresponding ratio for the artificial experiment was .24. The subjects, therefore, made nearly twice as many repetitions as were obtained in the artificial experiment.

TABLE 2. *Indices of repetition for subjects and for artificial experiment*

Indices		Subjects	Artificial experiment
6.25 to	6.74	1	—
5.75 to	6.24	2	—
5.25 to	5.74	—	—
4.75 to	5.24	1	—
4.25 to	4.74	9	—
3.75 to	4.24	11	—
3.25 to	3.74	7	—
2.75 to	3.24	6	—
2.25 to	2.74	16	1
1.75 to	2.24	9	3
1.25 to	1.74	9	5
.75 to	1.24	12	19
.25 to	.74	11	13
— .25 to	.24	4	14
— .75 to —	.26	1	17
— 1.25 to —	.76	1	16
— 1.75 to — 1.26		—	9
— 2.25 to — 1.76		—	2
— 2.75 to — 2.26		—	1
		100	100

tributions are obvious. The mean index for the subjects is 2.38 with a standard deviation of 3.11. For the artificial experiment the mean is −.04 and the standard deviation 1.03, which approximate the theoretical expectations of zero and 1.00 respectively. Thus the subjects as a group not only clustered their items beyond chance expectation, but they also showed greater variability. The correlation between the indices of repetition and the number of items listed by the subjects was .36 with a probable error of .06.

As was expected, the subjects showed

A third method was employed for comparing the clustering tendency of the subjects with that obtained by chance. This involved the tabulation of the incidence of single (unclustered) items, and the clusters of varying size. Table 3 shows the results of this analysis. It may be noted that whereas the subjects gave fewer single items and clusters of two than were found in the artificial experiment, they greatly exceeded the chance results in the incidence of higher order clusters.

It thus appears that the use of three separate methods for appraising cluster-

TABLE 3. *Incidence of single items and clusters of varying size for subjects and for artificial experiment*

	1's	2's	3's	4's	5's	6's	7's
Subjects	810	261	164	85	38	18	5
Artificial exp.	1,452	343	87	18	4	1	—

ing yielded measures showing that the subjects in recall tended to cluster their items beyond chance expectation. The use of the artificial experiment was in a sense gratuitous. To the experimenter, however, this simple expedient served as a useful check on the significance of the data.

In following through the foregoing analysis the question arose of possible changes in the clustering tendency during the course of recall. From *a priori* reasoning it appeared unlikely that clustering would remain constant. It would seem reasonable to suppose that the clustering tendency should diminish as the subjects approached exhaustion of their available supplies of items. In order to investigate this problem, the Vincent method was employed by dividing each of the 100 lists of items into successive decile intervals. The ratios of repetition (repeated items to total items) for these intervals appear in Table 4 and Figure 1 for both the data of the subjects and the data of the artificial experiment. These results reveal several interesting facts. The clustering tendency is initially above chance. It rises to a maximum in the region of the 4th decile, and then drops progressively to the range of chance. In so far as clustering represents organization in recall, this organization broke down as the subjects approached their limits of memory for the items. This

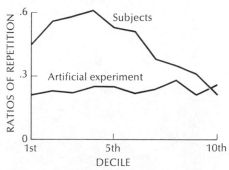

FIG. 1. Plots of ratios of repetition in successive deciles of items for subjects and for artificial experiment.

trend receives interesting general confirmation from a parallel analysis of the progressions of occurrence of single items and clusters. The data from this analysis are in Table 5. This confirmation is most marked for the single items and the clusters of 3. The former, representing lack of clustering, are at a minimum in the 4th decile, whereas the clusters of 3 have their maximum incidence in the same region. It is interesting to note that clusters of 2 have a consistently higher incidence in the artificial experiment than in the data of the subjects.

It was indicated earlier that the errors appearing in the data were of two types, namely, categorical intrusions and irrelevant intrusions. The totals of the categorical intrusions were as follows: 61 names, 54 animals, 43 professions, and

TABLE 4. *Ratios of repetition in successive deciles of items for subjects and for artificial experiment*

	1st	2nd	3rd	4th	5th	6th	7th	8th	9th	10th
Subjects	.45	.56	.58	.61	.53	.51	.38	.35	.31	.21
Artificial exp.	.21	.23	.22	.25	.25	.22	.24	.28	.21	.26

TABLE 5. *Progressive changes in the incidence of single items and clusters of varying size for subjects and for artificial experiment*

Decile	1's		2's		3's		4's		5's		6's		7's	
	S's	A. Exp.	S's	A. Exp.	S's	A. Exp.	S's	A. Exp.	S's	A. Exp.	S's	A. Exp.	S's	A. Exp.
1st	66	142	21	26	12	7	9	1	2	1	2			
2nd	47	152	23	31	21	5	7	4	9	1	6		1	
3rd	40	146	23	30	20	9	18	1	3		2			
4th	29	142	23	36	26	11	15	2	5		3			
5th	55	149	23	29	23	11	12	4	4	1	1		2	
6th	64	155	27	33	15	7	8	1	7		2		2	1
7th	102	141	30	44	15	6	6	1	2		1	1	1	
8th	110	126	31	38	9	11	4	3	3		1			
9th	119	146	34	38	12	6	4		2	1				
10th	178	153	26	38	11	14	2	1	1					
Totals	810	1,452	261	343	164	87	85	18	38	4	18	1	5	0

21 vegetables. There were 75 irrelevant intrusions. Since the subjects listed a total of 2,497 items, 7.17 per cent of these items were categorical intrusions and 3.00 per cent were irrelevant intrusions. It may be noted that two items classed as irrelevant intrusions were especially frequent. There were *auto* which was listed 21 times and *milk* which was listed 14 times. The former may have been a consequence of its phonemic similarity to the name *Otto* which was in the stimulus word list. This fact escaped detection until after the treatment of the data. We may further observe that the item *milk* may have derived from *milkman* which was also on the stimulus word list. Perhaps the items *auto* and *milk* should not be classed as completely irrelevant. They are irrelevant, however, to the categories of the stimulus words. The totals of all errors occurring in the successive deciles of items listed were as follows: 5, 13, 3, 15, 13, 20, 45, 32, 48, 60. It is apparent from these figures that the errors progressed at a positively accelerated rate. This trend is not changed when we subtract the irrelevant intrusions which were as follows for the successive deciles: 1, 6, 1, 3, 5, 7, 13, 6, 14, 19.

D. DISCUSSION

The results of this study have indicated that subjects, when given a list of randomly arranged items will in their recall show a greater-than-chance tendency to group the items in clusters containing members of the same general category. This implies the operation of an organizing tendency. The results further show that the extent of clustering varies in an orderly manner as a function of the number of items already recalled. The nature of this change is indicated in Figure 1 where the ratios of repetition initially exceed chance expectation, rise to a maximum, and then drop to the level of randomness. The assumptions necessary to account for this progression present a challenging theoretical problem. The following analysis is proposed tentatively and with full realization of its speculative character. To begin with, the progressive change in the clustering tendency as revealed in our data is too complex to be attributed solely to a unitary property of dynamic interrelationships between verbal habits or solely to the habit strengths of the individual items. If a single factor were sufficient, the curve of clustering tendency should probably be monotonic, and this does not appear to be the case. We can generate the curve of clustering tendency, however, from a minimum of two monotonic functions. This in turn implies the necessity of a minimum of two basic assumptions. These assumptions should account for the probability of occurrence of individual items. At present the most plausible assumptions would appear to be the following: (*a*) Habit strength (*HS*) deriving from the reinforcement an item has received both before and during the experiment. (*b*) Relatedness increment (*RI*) which is a hypothetical increment added to habit strength. An item by virtue of its occurrence adds this increment to other items to which it is related. A tentative method for distinguishing between these two types of strength is as follows. It may be recalled that the subjects were instructed to draw demarcation lines at the end of each successive minute of the 10-minute period allowed for recall. It was thus possible to construct a curve based on the means of the cumulative totals of the items produced in successive one-minute periods throughout the period of recall. We may regard the reciprocals of the latent periods of the successive deciles of items as measures of the combined habit strengths and relatedness increments operating within these deciles. As Hull (3) has indicated, the latent period is an index of habit strength. The addition of the re-

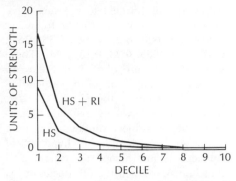

Fɪɢ. 2. Curves of hypothetical strengths of items in the successive deciles of recall. The upper curve (*HS* + *RI*) represents habit strengths plus relatedness increments; the lower curve (*HS*) represents habit strengths alone.

latedness increment to habit strength should not invalidate the use of the latent period as an index of availability of items. The reciprocals for the successive deciles were as follows: 16.68, 6.26, 3.33, 2.00, 1.25, 0.81, 0.53, 0.33, 0.19, 0.10. The curve of these reciprocals is shown in Figure 2 where it is labeled *HS* + *RI*. We now make the assumption that the amount of clustering that takes place is proportional to the strengths of the verbal habits. It is also reasonable to assume that the habit strengths of the items are randomly distributed with respect to the categories of the items. Using the ratio of repetition as the index of clustering, we may take the step of assuming the equality of the following ratios:

$$(1) \qquad \frac{HS+RI}{RRs} = \frac{HS}{RRc}.$$

In this formula *HS* is habit strength; *RI* is relatedness increment; *RRs* is the ratio of repetition for the decile obtained from the data of the subjects; *RRc* is the ratio of repetition derived by chance from the artificial experiment, and to which we assign the mean value of 0.24.

From the above formula we derive the equation for *HS* which is as follows:

$$(2) \qquad HS = \frac{RRc(HS+RI)}{RRs}.$$

Applying this formula to the successive deciles of items, we obtain the following values for HS: 8.90, 2.68, 1.38, 0.79, 0.57, 0.38, 0.33, 0.23, 0.15, 0.11. These values for HS are plotted in Figure 2. Considering any pair of corresponding points on the curves for HS and $HS + RI$, we may describe what is assumed to happen when a subject produces an item. Suppose, for example, a hypothetical subject has just named an animal, and that he has reached the 5th decile of his productions. Competing for the next place is another animal-item with a strength $(HS + RI)$ of 1.25 units and an item in a different category with an HS of 0.57 units. These strengths are supposedly subject to oscillation and their respective values may be regarded as probability weightings. It is more likely that the subject will list another animal-item than an item in a different category. The result is that the amount of clustering is raised from the chance-level of 0.24 to 0.53. Obviously HS and RI do not remain constant throughout the decile, but this does not alter the basic interpretation.

The assumptions of habit strength and relatedness increments can, it would seem, be meaningfully related to Hebb's (2) conception of cell assemblies. Within this framework full recognition is given to the necessity of stimulus-response constancy for the development of the habit strength of the assembly. On the other hand, the clustering tendency may derive from the overlap of assembly action.

This discussion may appropriately include mention of the somewhat surprising finding that the clusters made up of two similar items occurred at a lower-than-chance frequency throughout the lists. This is shown in Table 5. For the present we may venture only a partial explanation. The clustering tendency may have been so strong that the larger clusters precluded the occurrence of the small ones.

The possibilities for further research based on the measurement of the clustering tendency are extensive. There is a need for further study of the nature of the clustering tendency and the assumptions that may adequately account for it. Such research should be useful as already indicated for providing additional information on the nature of organization as it operates in higher mental processes. Among the more specific problems to which the method appears applicable are the development of verbal behavior, individual differences, consequences of emotion and frustration, consequences of mental disorders assumed to affect organization in higher mental processes, recall of different types of material, and influence of learning.

E. SUMMARY

1. Subjects were presented a randomized list of 60 items made up of 15 each of animals, names, professions, and vegetables. Immediately following the presentation, the subjects listed serially the items they were able to recall.

2. Analysis of the data from 100 subjects on the basis of three separate indices showed that the items were clustered in groups of similar categories appreciably beyond chance as indicated by a parallel artificial experiment.

3. The clustering tendency changed with the serial positions of the items on the lists in a way to indicate that it was initially above chance expectation, rose to a maximum, and then declined to randomness.

4. The progressive change in the clustering tendency is explained on the basis of two assumptions, namely, habit strength and clustering increment.

1. BOUSFIELD, W. A., & SEDGEWICK, C. H. W. An analysis of sequences of restricted associative responses. *J. gen. Psychol.*, 1944, **30**, 149-65.
2. HEBB, D. O. The organization of behavior. New York: Wiley, 1949. Pp. 335.
3. HULL, C. L. Principles of behavior. New York: Appleton-Century, 1943. Pp. 422.
4. THORNDIKE, E. L., & LORGE, I. The teacher's word book of 30,000 words. New York: Columbia University, 1944. Pp. 274.

25 / Subjective Organization in Free Recall of "Unrelated" Words [1]

ENDEL TULVING, *University of Toronto*

This paper is concerned with organization as a dependent variable in free recall learning. A method will be described for measuring the extent to which subjects' recall of verbal items presented in different orders on successive trials is structured sequentially. The method assumes no knowledge on the experimenter's part as to the sources of organization, and it is thus applicable to free recall learning of any list of verbal items. The effect of repetition on organization, and the relation of organization to amount of recall will be briefly examined in a simple experiment. The method and the data are discussed in terms of the problem of the role of repetition in free recall verbal learning.

VERBAL LEARNING AND ORGANIZATION

The fact that learning occurs under conditions of practice, often apparently through mere repetition of the material, is empirically well known, but theoretically not yet fully understood. Indeed, the question of why repetition leads to better recall has not been raised too often explicitly, although it has been implicit in much experimental and theoretical work.

The apparent lack of explicit interest in this problem seems to be related to the restricted aspects of subjects' behavior which are studied in verbal learning experiments. In a large majority of studies the dependent variables have been based on the operation of counting single unordered responses, assigned to categories such as "correct," "intralist intrusion," "remote backward association," and the like. Given but a single basic response variable of this kind, there is relatively little that can be done with the question of why repetition is effective, other than studying the effect of different independent variables on the rate of learning. One can be justifiably sceptical, however, of our chances of ever understanding the basic process of verbal learning by simply counting "correct" and various classes of "incorrect" responses under a variety of experimental conditions. Bolles' (1959) recent suggestion that, "If we are to understand human learning, we must determine what our Ss are really doing" (p. 580), can be regarded as an example of growing realization that a critical reappraisal of response variables in verbal learning is overdue.

An important contribution to our understanding of the basic acquisition process might well be provided by response variables based on ordered classifications of data (Miller & Frick, 1949). Such variables are particularly interesting the light of G. A. Miller's (1956a, 1956b, 1956c), conception of verbal learning as a direct consequence of the process of recoding or organization. Rehearsal or repetition, according to Miller, 1956b), has "the very important effect of organizing many separate items into a single unit" (p. 43). Repetition does not change the basic storage capacity of memory. Rather, organizing processes accompanying repetition lead to an apparent increase in this capacity by increasing the information load of individual units.

Miller's unitization hypothesis, if found tenable, has important implications for research strategy and theory in verbal learning. One of the difficulties in evaluating the hypothesis lies in the lack of appropriate measures of organization.

From the *Psychological Review*, 1962, **69**, 344-54, with permission of the author and publisher.
1. This research has been supported by the National Research Council of Canada under Grant Number APA-39.

Organization as a response variable has been investigated by many psychologists (e.g., Bousfield, 1953; Cofer, 1959; Jenkins & Russell, 1952; Rothkopf & Coke, 1961), but its measurement has always depended on the experimenter's knowledge of sources of organization present in the stimulus list. It is well known, however, that subjects are quite capable of memorizing materials which are not organized in any obvious manner, or for which the sources of organization cannot be readily specified. Thus, if the concept of organization is to have more general applicability, it seems necessary to develop methods that permit observation and quantification of organization as a response measure independent of the characteristics of the stimulus material. This is what the present paper attempts to do.

Behavioral manifestations of the hypothesized organizing process can best be studied under conditions where the order in which the subject recalls items is free to vary. Items which are organized into a single unit would then be expected to occur in close temporal contiguity in subject's recall. Repeated occurrences of such sequential patterns would indicate the existence of the organizing process, and the extent to which this occurs would provide an estimate of the degree of organization. Thus a quantitative analysis of sequential dependencies among items in subject's free recall on successive trials would yield measures of a response variable closely related to the hypothetical organizing process, independently of quantity of recall.

The method proposed in this paper is derived from information theory (Shannon & Weaver, 1949), and is quite similar to Miller and Frick's (1949) "index of behavioral stereotypy." It provides for a measure of sequential redundancy in repeated ordered samples of a set of items. As the experimental paradigm used here involves presentation of material completely free from any sequential redundancy, such redundancy or organization in subject's recall cannot be attributed to the input material. Rather, it is the subject who imposes a certain degree of organization on the material. For this reason such organization is called subjective organization (SO). In information theory terms, SO is "noise" produced by the channel, that is the subject; it is information in the output not found in the input (Miller, 1953).

MEASUREMENT OF SUBJECTIVE ORGANIZATION

Suppose we select L words, any words, and construct L different orders of these words such that each word appears in each of the L serial positions once and is preceded and followed by each other word just once. This can be done easily if $L+1$ is a prime number. We then represent each of these L ordered lists to the subject on L separate trials. Words are shown one at a time on the memory drum. After each trial the subject is asked to record all the words that he remembers from the list, in any order he wishes. After all L ordered lists have thus been presented we have L recall records from the subject, one for each trial. We then tabulate the frequency of all pairs of adjacent recall responses in a matrix consisting of $L+1$ rows and $L+1$ columns, and compute the measure of SO from the data in the matrix.

Table 1 shows a sample recall (output) matrix for a case where $L=16$ and where the subjects recall responses are pooled for all 16 trials. Symbols $x_1, x_2, \ldots x_{16}$ identifying the rows refer to the 1st, 2nd, ... 16th word in the nth position in the subject's recall list; symbols $y_1, y_2 \cdots y_{16}$ identifying the columns stand for the same words in the $(n+1)$th position in the subject's recall list. Thus x and y represent successive positions in the sub-

TABLE 1. *A sample recall matrix for an individual subject*

nth word	(n+1)th word																	n_i
	y_0	y_1	y_2	y_3	y_4	y_5	y_6	y_7	y_8	y_9	y_{10}	y_{11}	y_{12}	y_{13}	y_{14}	y_{15}	y_{16}	
x_0		1	1	2	2	1	3				2	1	1			1	1	16
x_1								1	1		9	1		2				14
x_2	1	2			1	2		2				2			2	2		12
x_3	2	1			1	2	1	2				2		1			1	13
x_4	1	2		1			1	5				3		1	1			15
x_5	1					2			1	8			1			2		15
x_6	1	1							1			1	1	11				16
x_7	1		1		2								1		7			12
x_8	2	2				3				2			1			4		14
x_9		1		1	1				10			1			1			15
x_{10}		1	1		1	1	3				1	2			1	1		13
x_{11}	1				6	1	2										4	14
x_{12}	2	1						2				1	1		1	1	4	13
x_{13}		2		9		1	2		1				1	1				16
x_{14}	1		9				1					2	1					14
x_{15}	2				1	3	1			5	1				1			14
x_{16}	1						2					1	5			1		10
n_j	16	14	12	13	15	15	16	12	14	15	13	14	13	16	14	14	10	N = 236

Note.—Recall is pooled over 16 trials.

ject's recall, and subscripts identify the contents of these positions, i.e., words. Symbol x_0 stands for the blank position (no word) immediately preceding the first word in the subject's recall list, and y_0 refers to the blank position immediately following the last word in the same list. The entries in the cells of the matrix show the frequency with which word i was followed by word j in the subject's recall on all 16 trials; their numerical values are symbolized as n_{ij}. Entries in the row labelled x_0 show the frequencies with which each word j stood at the beginning of the subject's recall lists on 16 trials, and similarly entries in the column y_0 show frequencies with which each word i was the last position of the recall lists on these trials. Zeroes have been omitted in the matrix. For instance, $n_{06}=3$, which means that Word Number 6 was in the first position (followed no other word) in the subject's recall on three trials; $n_{13}=0$, indicating that Word Number 3 never followed Word Number 1 during the 16 trials, and so forth. The numerical values of marginal totals of rows, n_i, show how many times each word i appeared in the subject's recall on all 16 trials. Marginal totals for corresponding rows and columns are of course identical. It is also to be noted that there are no entries in the cells along the main diagonal, from upper left to lower right, since normally no word follows itself in recall.

Given a recall matrix such as the one in Table 1, a number of different measures of second-order sequential organization could be used. The measure of sequential organization adopted in the present paper is essentially a measure of redundancy in a sequence of events when the probabilities of successive pairs of events are known or can be estimated:

$$C_x(y) = 1 - \frac{H_x(y)}{\max H_x(y)} \quad [1]$$

$H_x(y)$ here refers to the amount of information (uncertainty) in the event y when the preceding event x is known, and $\max H_x(y)$ stands for the maximum value of such uncertainty. This is Miller and Frick's (1949) second-order index of behavioral stereotypy. The formula for computing second-order SO involves a minor modification of the above formula,[2] simplifying calculations in addition to being somewhat more appropriate to the free recall learning situation. This formula is as follows:

$$SO = \frac{\sum_{i,j} n_{ij} \log n_{ij} - \min \sum_{i,j} n_{ij} \log n_{ij}}{\sum_i n_i \log n_i - \min \sum_{i,j} n_{ij} \log n_{ij}} \quad [2]$$

where n_{ij} represents the numerical value of the cell in the ith row and jth column, n_i represents the marginal total of the ith row, and $\min \sum_{i,j} n_{ij} \log n_{ij}$ represents the minimum value that $\sum_{i,j} n_{ij} \log n_{ij}$ can assume.

In cases where no marginal total n_i exceeds the length of the list L, $\min \sum_{i,j} n_{ij} \log n_{ij}$ is equal to 0, and Formula 2 reduces to the following relatively simple expression:

$$SO = \frac{\sum_{i,j} n_{ij} \log n_{ij}}{\sum_i n_i \log n_i} \quad [3]$$

In this formula $\sum_i n_i \log n_i$ can be regarded as a measure of maximum organization, $\sum_{i,j} n_{ij} \log n_{ij}$ represents the actual organization, and SO is simply a measure of actual organization relative to the maximum. Thus SO can assume all values between zero and unity, the former expressing the complete absence of second-order sequential organization, as in the case of the ordered stimulus lists presented to the subject, and the latter the maximum degree of such organization, as in the case of an imaginary subject who recalls all words on all trials exactly in the same order. SO for the data in Table 1, incidentally, is .397.

So far we have considered only second-order sequential organization, based on pairs of successive responses. The method can be easily extended to higher-order dependencies, even though the computational labors involved would be-

come quite prohibitive. However, estimates of higher-order organization can be obtained more easily. For instance, instead of setting up a three dimensional matrix for calculating third-order SO, we can tabulate data in a two dimensional matrix with nth items as rows and $(n+2)$th items as columns. In this case we also need two rows for blank spaces preceding the first word (x_0 and x_{0-1}), and two columns for blank spaces following the last word in each recall list (y_0 and y_{0+1}). This procedure amounts to collapsing the three dimensional matrix along the $(n+1)$th dimension. That is, we are computing an SO measure based on pairs of responses *separated* by one response. Such an SO is labeled SO (Lag 1), and it does provide an estimate of the third-order SO. In a similar manner, still higher order dependencies can be evaluated. SO (Lag 2) is an estimate of the fourth-order sequential organization, SO (Lag 3) is an estimate of the fifth-order SO, and so forth.

SO can be calculated for any block of trial, usually successive trials. Thus it is sometimes useful to indicate the size of the block on which the measure is based. For instance, SO (Blks=3) means SO calculated from blocks of three successive trials. SO for a single trial is not meaningful, as subjective organization is defined in terms of the subject's tendency to recall words in the same order on successive trials; in fact SO for a single trial, when calculated according to the formulas given, turns out to be 0, provided that the subject has not repeated any pairs of words.

---

2. Max $H_x(y)$ in Miller and Frick's index of behavioral stereotypy is defined as $max\ H(x,y) - max\ H(x)$. Thus it is based on the assumption that all responses are equally frequent. For the present problem, however, it may be somewhat more meaningful to compute $max'\ H_x(y)$ on the basis of the *given* frequency of individual responses, i.e., as determined by subject's recall:

$$max'\ H_x(y) = max\ H(x,y) - H(x)$$

If $max'\ H_x(y)$ is substituted for $max\ H_x(y)$ in Formula 1, that formula becomes mathematically equivalent with Formula 2, the measure of subjective organization as used in this paper.

Demonstration Experiment: Subjective Organization and Performance

The following simple experiment will serve as an illustration of how the method works, and the data from the experiment will provide tentative answers to three questions which can be raised in the context of the discussion of the concept of organization in the first section. The questions are as follows: First, do the subjects actually organize "unrelated" words when instructions are simply to recall as many words as they can? Second, does this subjective organization, if found in the data, increase with repetition of the material? Third, is there a systematic relation between subjective organization and more traditional measures of learning, such as the number of words correctly recalled?

Procedure. A list of 16 English words was adopted from another verbal learning experiment (List III in Tulving & Thornton, 1959). All words were disyllabic nouns, consisting of five, six, or seven letters. The words, here listed alphabetically, were as follows: ACCENT, BARRACK, DRUMLIN, FINDING, GARDEN, HOYDEN, ISSUE, JUNGLE, LAGOON, MAXIM, OFFICE, POMADE, QUILLET, TREASON, VALLEY, WALKER. Sixteen different sequences of these words were constructed such that, considering any block or all 16 orders of the stimulus list, there was no second-order or higher-order redundancy in the lists.

Sixteen female undergraduate students enrolled in the introductory psychology courses at the University of Toronto served as subjects. Their median age was 19 years. None of the subjects had previously participated in any verbal learning experiments.

Each subject was tested individually. In the instructions the subject was told that her task was to learn a list of 16 words, two-syllable English nouns, that would be presented to her on 16 separate trials. At the end of each trial she would write down as many words from the list as she remembered. Then she would be shown the same words again, in a different order, and at the end of the trial she would again write down

all the words that she was able to recall. The subject was also told that the order in which she recalled the words did not matter, her task was simply to recall as many of the words on each trial as she could.

The 16 different orders of the stimulus list were typed on white paper in lower case letters and presented to the subject on a memory drum. The rate of exposure was one word per second. At the end of the trial the subject was given 90 seconds to record her recall on sheets of paper lined with 16 consecutively numbered lines.

The order in which the 16 ordered lists were presented to the subjects was systematically counterbalanced among subjects. The method used for assigning the 16 orders of the stimulus list to the 16 subjects on the 16 trials was the same as that used in assigning the 16 words to 16 serial positions in 16 orders of the stimulus list.

Results. Two kinds of data are of interest in this experiment, performance (P) defined in terms of frequency of correct recall, and subjective organization (SO). Extralist intrusions and misspelled words from the list were ignored in computing both P and SO scores.[3] Repetitions of list words within a given trial were included in the recall matrix and thus entered the SO score, but not the P score. The mean number of extralist intrusions, together with misspelled words, was 0.13 per trial, the mean number of repetitions of list words was 0.09 per trial.

Second-order SO scores were calculated for successive blocks of two trials (SO, Blks$=2$), for running blocks of three trials, (SO, Blks$=3$), and for the total block of 16 trials (SO, Blks$=16$). SO (Blks$=2$) scores were also computed for 16 statistical subjects.[4]

3. Such extralist intrusions are of interest in their own right and may provide valuable information about the organizing process. In order to handle them in the present situation, the recall matrix can be simply extended. However, such intrusions can probably be better studied in different experimental situations (e.g., Deese, 1959).
4. IBM Model 650 Electronic Data Processing Machine was used in these calculations. Thanks are due to Albert S. Bregman for constructing the program. Data from statistical subjects, whose "per-

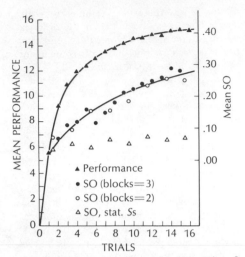

FIG. 1. Mean performance (upper curve) and mean SO (lower curve) as a function of trials. (Values of performance are to be read from the left ordinate, SO from the right ordinate. Mean SO for blocks of two trials from 16 statistical subjects are shown for comparison, open triangles. For further explanation see the text.)

The effect of repetition on both P and SO is summarized graphically in Figure 1. The values of P are to be read from the left, the values of SO from the right hand ordinate. The abscissa represents trials. The upper curve is the typical learning curve, showing performance as a function of trials. The lower curve, fitted by inspection to data points representing SO (Blks=3), could be called an "organization" curve. The SO for each block is plotted against the middle trial of the block. Thus there are 14 SO (Blks=3) scores. SO scores for successive blocks of size two are also shown for both the real and the statistical subjects, plotted against the midpoints of the trial blocks.

These data clearly demonstrate that subjects do in fact organize their recall sequentially even in the absence of such sequential organization in stimulus lists, and that this organization increases systematically with repeated exposures to, and recall of the material. Thus, in an

experimental situation such as the present one, repetition has two parallel effects: increasing frequency of recall is accompanied by an increasingly tighter sequential organization.

The slopes of the two curves depicted in Figure 1 seem to be different. When mean P scores are plotted against mean SO (Blks=3) for the 14 trials, the curvilinearity of the relation is obvious. However, the relation becomes quite linear when a logarithmic transformation is applied to the mean SO scores, suggesting that, as a first approximation, increase in performance is proportional to increase in log SO. The product-moment correlation between mean P and log mean SO (Blks=3) for Trials 2 to 15 was found to be +.96.

Estimates of higher-order SO were obtained in the form of SO scores for Lags 1, 2, and 3, for the total block of 16 trials. The mean SO (Blks=16) scores for these lags and their standard deviations are shown in Table 2, together with

TABLE 2. *Means and standard deviations of SO (Blks = 16) for various Lags*

Group	Lag 0	Lag 1	Lag 2	Lag 3
Experimental subjects				
Mean	.292	.224	.223	.216
Standard deviation	.054	.045	.034	.035
Statistical subjects				
Mean	.180			.169
Standard deviation	.017			.012

Note.—$N = 16$ for each group.

comparable data from the statistical subjects for Lags 0 and 3. Even though mean SO scores seem to decrease with increasing lags, it is interesting to note that SO (Lag 3, Blks=16) scores are higher than the same scores from the statistical subjects. The median test yielded a chi-square of 15.12, which is highly significant.

formance" was matched with that of individual experimental subjects, were collected as an attempt to estimate the amount of organization occurring by chance, since the sampling distribution of SO, under the null hypothesis of no organization, is not known.

The intercorrelations among SO (Blks = 16) scores for Lags 0, 1, 2, and 3, as well as correlations between these SO scores and several average P measures are shown in Table 3. These correlations are based on individual data from 16 subjects.

Certain orderly relations appear in Table 3. First, the correlations between

TABLE 3. *Intercorrelations among SO (Blks = 16) measures for Lags 0, 1, 2, and 3; and correlations between these SO scores and mean P scores on Trials 1 to 8, 9, to 16, and 1 to 16 for individual subjects*

Measures	SO			
	Lag 0	Lag 1	Lag 2	Lag 3
SO (Lag 1)	+.86			
SO (Lag 2)	+.62	+.85		
SO (Lag 3)	+.58	+.74	+.84	
P (Trials 1 to 8)	+.45	+.32	+.24	+.01
P (trials 9 to 16)	+.78	+.61	+.34	+.19
P (Trials 1 to 16)	+.63	+.47	+.30	+.08

Note.—$N = 16$.

any two adjacent SO measures on the lag dimension are reasonably high, all three listed in the table being approximately +.85. Second, with increasing distance on the lag dimension between any two SO measures the correlations decrease. Thus, for example, SO (Lag 0) has a correlation of +.85 with that for Lag 1, +.62 with Lag 2, and +.58 with Lag 3. Third, correlations between P and SO decrease with increase in the lag of the SO measure. The most important conclusion to be drawn from these data is that, within the limits of the present method, the second-order SO is about as useful a measure of sequential organization as that based on any combination of different orders, and more useful than any other single higher-order SO measure.

Positive correlations between SO and P scores in Table 3, where correlation is done on data from 16 subjects, support the observation of the same relation over trials. It is also interesting to note that on the basis of a single estimate of organization for each subject, that based on the total block of 16 trials, SO accounts for a larger amount of variance in the P variable for Trials 9 to 16 than for Trials 1 to 8.

All the above findings relate to organization as an intrasubject phenomenon. Commonality of organization between subjects, however, can also be investigated by using the same general method. That there might be such commonality became apparent in the inspection of recall data from different subjects. Recall matrices from individual subjects showed that quite often the patterning of response sequences was similar for many subjects. This phenomenon was investigated in two ways.

First, the recall data from all 16 subjects were pooled for all 16 trials and entered into an "intersubject recall matrix." If all subjects organized their recall differently, the distribution of cell entries in the group recall matrix would not be significantly different from the distribution under conditions where only chance factors are operating. To test the significance of the apparent deviation of the data in this matrix from chance distribution, the information function $T(x,y)$ was computed. It was found to be 0.352 bits which is significant at better than .01 level, using the method suggested by Miller (1955). This finding thus confirms the casual observation that there is a certain degree of commonality in the subject's recall.

The second method used to explore intersubject organization was as follows. For a single trial data were pooled in a recall matrix from all 16 subjects. For each such intersubject recall matrix SO was computed. This procedure results in 16 intersubject SO measures, one for each trial. These data are shown in Figure 2. Intersubject SO measures have been averaged for blocks of two trials, in order to smooth the curve. In view of

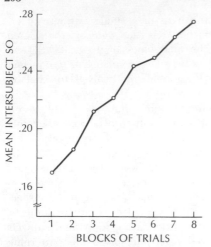

FIG. 2. Mean intersubject SO scores for 16 subjects on eight successive blocks of two trials.

the orderly increase in the intersubject SO measure with repetition, it would seem safe to conclude that the commonality of organized recall sequences between subjects increases with repetition of the material.

DISCUSSION

All three questions posed at the beginning of the experiment have been answered in the affirmative. It seems that the subjects do impose a sequential structure on their recall, that this subjective organization increases with repeated exposures and recall of the material, and that there is a positive correlation between organization and performance. None of these findings is very surprising, and all are in good agreement with related experimental evidence. Bousfield and his associates, as well as other investigators, have amply demonstrated that there is a strong tendency in subjects to recall randomly presented material in sequences of related words or clusters (Bousfield, 1953; Cohen & Bousfield, 1956; Jenkins & Russell, 1952). It has also been shown that repeated presentations of the stimulus word list in-

creases this clustering tendency (Bousfield & Cohen, 1953), and that there is a direct relation between the degree of clustering and the amount of recall (Bousfield & Cohen, 1955; Bousfield, Cohen, & Whitmarsh, 1958; Jenkins, Mink, & Russell, 1958; Sakoda, 1956). The findings of the present experiment extend the domain of these phenomena of organization from one trial recall and experimentally organized materials, as used in all the above experiments, to a learning situation, with several successive trials, and experimentally unorganized materials.

The finding that the organizing effects, well demonstrated in experiments on clustering, can be experimentally assessed even in case of unrelated words, is quite encouraging. Perhaps paradoxically this suggests that a list of completely *unrelated* words is probably as fictional as is a truly nonsensical nonsense syllable. It is for this reason that reference has been made throughout this paper to "unrelated" words, referring only to the fact that words are experimentally unselected as to their meaning.

The present method of quantifying sequential organization in free recall learning constitutes only a rather coarse net for capturing the process of organization in all its diversity. For one thing, the SO measure is most sensitive to rigid sequences of responses, or chunks (Miller, 1956c). It is quite likely, however, that a great deal of organization occurs in the form of clusters (Bousfield, 1953), in which items have no fixed order. This would tend not only to attenuate measures of SO, but also, through increased variability of SO, depress correlations with the performance variable.

It would be interesting, in view of Miller's utilization hypothesis, to look at organization in terms of its units. In many cases subjects undoubtedly impose a hierarchical organization on recall, or use a plan (Miller, Galanter, & Pribram,

1960). In other cases, particularly when the list to be learned is short and some coding device such as the alphabet can be employed, nonhierarchical organization may also occur. The present method does not lend itself to an identification of various strategies adopted by subjects, even though casual inspection suggests many diverse sources of organization; associative grouping, conceptual categories, assonance, grouping in terms of familiarity of items, and so forth.

The method provides only an over-all measure of organization. This measure is related to the size of the organizing units in a systematic manner, but the relation cannot be easily specified. The two extremes of the function, however, are determined by the definition of the SO measure, and the transition from one to the other must be gradual. In one case the units of organization are individual items in the list, resulting from previous response integration (Mandler, 1954) outside the laboratory. In this case the probability of two or more items being recalled consistently together is no greater than what might be expected by chance, and the numerical value of SO is approximately the same as that of statistical subjects. On the other extreme, the whole set of items is organized into one unit, and SO is at the maximum.

Assuming a systematic relation between the size of the organizing units and the numerical value of SO, the finding that the second-order SO accounts for a larger proportion of variance in individual P scores than do estimates of higher-order measures makes good sense. Some units of organization contain only two items, and, given a flexible order of units in recall, these are not tapped by the third-order and higher-order measures of SO, while the second-order measure is sensitive to all units of two or more items. This interpretation is also consistent with the observed intercorrelations among SO measures for different lags. Although these measures are all based on identical sequences of responses, the correlations are less than perfect. This probably reflects the fact that distributions of size of organizing units vary from subject to subject.

What is the significance of the method and the preliminary findings for the question originally posed about the effects of repetition on performance? It seems that response variables such as SO, based on ordered classifications of data, might be quite useful in our attempts to shed more light on the nature of the acquisition process in verbal learning. And the present findings seem to have contributed to the attractiveness of Miller's unitization hypothesis (1956a) as a serious beginning of a useful theory of free recall verbal learning. Even though intuitively there seems little doubt that performance depends on organization, the correlational design used in the present study does not yet permit such a conclusion and other kinds of experiments are necessary. Given a method of quantifying behavioral manifestations of the organizing process, it is quite possible to test many implications of the unitization hypothesis.

It is to be noted that the concept of repetition has been specified here rather loosely. There are at least two operationally distinguishable phases which should be studied separately, presentation of material and test for recall. A conceptual and experimental clarification of this important concept is clearly needed.

The observation of common recall sequences among different subjects and of increased stereotypy of such intersubject organization under conditions of practice very strongly suggests, or rather confirms the expectation, that sources of organization are discovered by subjects in the material, rather than invented idiosyncratically. Many task variables, therefore, are expected to influence both subjective organization and recall of the material, and a systematic exploration of these relations constitutes an important part of the research program designed to evaluate the tenability of the unitization hypothesis.

SUMMARY

A method for examining and quantifying sequential dependencies in the subjects' free recall of words on successive recall trials has been presented. Subjective organization as a dependent variable was defined in terms of the subject's tendency to recall items in the same order on different trials in the absence of any experimentally manipulated sequential organization among items in the stimulus list. In a preliminary experiment it was found that the subject's recall behavior manifests such subjective organization, that this organization increases with repetition, and that there is a positive correlation between organization and performance. These data were discussed with reference to the problem of the role of repetition in free recall verbal learning.

BOLLES, R. C. The effect of altering the middle of the list during serial learning. *Amer. J. Psychol.*, 1959, **72**, 577-80.

BOUSFIELD, W. A. The occurrence of clustering in the recall of randomly arranged associates. *J. gen. Psychol.*, 1953, **49**, 229-40.

BOUSFIELD, W. A., & COHEN, B. H. The effects of reinforcement on the occurrence of clustering in the recall of randomly arranged associates. *J. Psychol.*, 1953, **36**, 67-81.

BOUSFIELD, W. A., & COHEN, B. H. The occurrence of clustering in the recall of randomly arranged words of different frequencies-of-usage. *J. gen. Psychol.*, 1955, **52**, 83-95.

BOUSFIELD, W. A., & COHEN, B. H., & WHITMARSH, G. A. Associative clustering in the recall of words of different taxonomic frequencies of occurrence. *Psychol. Rep.*, 1958, **4**, 39-44.

COFER, C. N. A. study of clustering in free recall based on synonyms. *J. gen. Psychol.*, 1959, **60**, 3-10.

COHEN, B. H., & BOUSFIELD, W. A. The effects of a dual-level stimulus-word list on the occurrence of clustering in recall. *J. gen. Psychol.*, 1956, **55**, 51-8.

DEESE, J. On the prediction of occurrence of particular verbal intrusions in immediate recall. *J. exp. Psychol.*, 1959, **58**, 17-22.

JENKINS, J. J., MINK, W. D., & RUSSELL, W. A. Associative clustering as a function of verbal association strength. *Psychol. Rep.*, 1958, **4**, 127-36.

JENKINS, J. J., & RUSSELL, W. A. Associative clustering during recall. *J. abnorm. soc. Psychol.*, 1952, **47**, 818-21.

MANDLER, G. Response factors in human learning. *Psychol. Rev.*, 1954, **61**, 235-44.

MILLER, G. A. What is information measurement? *Amer. Psychologist*, 1953, **8**, 3-11.

MILLER, G. A. Note on the bias of information estimates. In H. Quastler (Ed.), *Information theory in psychology*. Glencoe, Ill.: Free Press, 1955.

MILLER, G. A. Human memory and the storage of information. *IRE Trans. inform. Theory*, 1956, **2**, 129-37. (a)

MILLER, G. A. Information and memory. *Scient. American*, 1956, **195**, 42-6. (b)

MILLER, G. A. The magical number seven, plus or minus two: Some limits on our capacity for processing information. *Psychol. Rev.*, 1956, **63**, 81-96. (c)

MILLER, G. A., & FRICK, F. C. Statistical behavioristics and sequences of responses. *Psychol. Rev.*, 1949, **56**, 311-24.

MILLER, G. A., GALANTER, E., & PRIBRAM, K. H. *Plans and the structure of behavior*. New York: Holt, 1960.

ROTHKOPF, E. Z., & COKE, E. U. The prediction of free recall from word association measures. *J. exp. Psychol.*, 1961, **62**, 433-8.

SAKODA, J. M. Individual differences in correlation between clustering and recall of meaningful words. *J. gen. Psychol.*, 1956, **54**, 183-90.

SHANNON, C., & WEAVER, W. *The mathematical theory of communication*. Urbana: Univer. Illinois Press, 1949.

TULVING, E., & THORNTON, G. B. Interaction between proaction and retroaction in short-term retention. *Canad. J. Psychol.*, 1959, **13**, 255-65.

SHORT-TERM MEMORY

Recently there has been a sharp rise of interest in the study of short-term memory, resulting in a number of worthwhile empirical and theoretical contributions. Previously, most studies of memory employed multiple trials on supra-span lists of items, with retention measured over periods of days. Such procedures characterize work in long-term memory. Although short-term memory studies cannot be absolutely separated from long-term memory work, short-term memory work characteristically utilizes sub-span lengths of material (even as little as one letter) presented once, with retention measured over seconds, or minutes at most. Keppel (1965) has discussed some basic methodological and design problems pertinent to long-term as well as short-term memory experiments and their bearing upon clear interpretations of data.

The increased focus upon short-term memory phenomena has undoubtedly been stimulated by several theoretical questions within the general area of retention. Foremost among these is the question of whether a memory trace is in effect permanent, unless obliterated by specific interference, or whether it is subject to a spontaneous decay process simply through the passage of time. McGeoch's (1932) now classic attack upon what was then known as the "law of disuse," was highly effective in establishing a theoretical framework based upon interference, at least for long-term forgetting. However, since that time, some promising possibilities for a decay-of-trace theory have developed within the domain of short-term memory effects, and it is upon that ground that the current quest is being carried on. For instance, Brown (1958) reported data that appeared more compatible with a decay hypothesis than with an interference hypothesis. Rehearsal of the items during the retention interval was assumed to be the mechanism which prevented decay of their traces. Apparently, even a brief suspension of the rehearsal process can lead to considerable forgetting. As an everyday example, if one has just glanced at a telephone number and then is momentarily distracted, he may find, to his consternation, that the number has been forgotten.

Another related issue is the question of memory storage, particularly whether a trace can pass through more than one state of availability. Some have contended that the initial perceptual or primary trace is highly transient and

271

subject to rapid decay. If it is encoded or rehearsed immediately, it then becomes consolidated and available for long-term storage. Hebb once entertained such a position, and several others do so today. (See Peterson, 1963.)

The following readings are representative of some of the most significant developments within short-term memory research, and are presented in their order of appearance in the literature. The Peterson and Peterson paper describes the technique that has become a basic methodology in the study of short-term retention. These authors showed that, under the proper conditions of rehearsal prevention, a singly presented trigram was virtually completely forgotten within a retention period of only 18 *seconds*. Such a pronounced drop in recall within such a short interval of time dramatically called attention to the possibilities of studying retention at a fine-grained level.

Murdock's paper (1961) reported a successful replication of the Peterson and Peterson results and showed that the number of "chunks" of information in the material was a significant factor in determining the degree of forgetting. Thus forgetting was not simply a function of time, even at the short-term level.

At about this time the issue of whether short- and long-term memory phenomena required separate theoretical explanations, or whether they could both be accommodated within an interference theory, came to the fore. The problem hinged on the likelihood that proactive inhibition was being generated in the short-term retention procedure. Peterson and Peterson found little evidence for such interference. The Keppel and Underwood paper described three experiments designed more explicitly to detect such effects, and the results did suggest that proactive inhibition followed the same laws in short-term and long-term retention, thus establishing some continuity between the two areas. In subsequent work, Wickelgren (1966) clearly demonstrated both proactive and retroactive inhibition effects in short-term memory, and also showed that the interference was a function of phonemic similarity of the items.

The excellent paper by Melton presents a comprehensive and eloquent statement of the issues concerning the relationship between short- and long-term memory, as well as additional relevant experimental data. Melton argued that the evidence strongly favored an explanation of both kinds of data in terms of a common theoretical structure. The explanation assumes a single storage mechanism and emphasizes the variables of frequency of repetition and informational chunking.

Finally, the recent Waugh and Norman paper develops and tests a theoretical model specific to short-term memory. The results of an experiment utilizing an interesting "probe-digit" technique, together with an analysis of data from other laboratories, supported the following conclusions: (a.) interference, rather than autonomous decay, is responsible for short-term forgetting, and (b.) there is a dual storage mechanism which allows an item to be retained in both states simultaneously.

At this stage of investigation it would appear that the weight of the evidence favors the essential continuity of long and short-term memory phenomena and the theory that interference, rather than decay, is the probable common forgetting mechanism.

BROWN, J. Some tests of the decay theory of immediate memory. *Quart. J. exp. Psychol.*, 1958, **10**, 12-21.

KEPPEL, G. Problems of method in the study of short-term memory. *Psychol. Bull.*, **1965**, 63, 1-13.

McGEOCH, J. A. Forgetting and the law of disuse. *Psychol. Rev.*, 1932, **39**, 352-70.

PETERSON, L. R. Immediate memory: Data and theory. In C. N. Cofer & B. S. Musgrave (Eds.), *Verbal behavior and learning: Problems and processes.* New York: McGraw-Hill, 1963, Pp. 336-53.

WICKELGREN, W. A. Phonetic similarity and interference in short-term memory for single letters. *J. exp. Psychol.*, 1966, **71**, 396-404.

26 / Short-term Retention of Individual Verbal Items [1]

LLOYD R. PETERSON AND MARGARET JEAN PETERSON, *Indiana University*

It is apparent that the acquisition of verbal habits depends on the effects of a given occasion being carried over into later repetitions of the situation. Nevertheless, textbooks separate acquisition and retention into distinct categories. The limitation of discussions of retention to long-term characteristics is necessary in large part by the scarcity of data on the course of retention over intervals of the order of magnitude of the time elapsing between successive repetitions in an acquisition study. The presence of a retentive function within the acquisition process was postulated by Hull (1940) in his use of the stimulus trace to explain serial phenomena. Again, Underwood (1949) has suggested that forgetting occurs during the acquisition process. But these theoretical considerations have not led to empirical investigation. Hull (1952) quantified the stimulus trace on data concerned with the CS-UCS interval in eyelid conditioning and it is not obvious that the construct so quantified can be readily transferred to verbal learning. One objection is that a verbal stimulus produces a strong predictable response prior to the experimental session and this is not true

of the originally neutral stimulus in eyelid conditioning.

Two studies have shown that the effects of verbal stimulation can decrease over intervals measured in seconds. Pillsbury and Sylvester (1940) found marked decrement with a list of items tested for recall 10 sec. after a single presentation. However, it seems unlikely that this traditional presentation of a list and later testing for recall of the list will be useful in studying intervals near or shorter than the time necessary to present the list. Of more interest is a recent study by Brown (1958) in which among other conditions a single pair of consonants was tested after a 5-sec. interval. Decrement was found at the one recall interval, but no systematic study of the course of retention over a variety of intervals was attempted.

EXPERIMENT I

The present investigation tests recall for individual items after several short

From the *Journal of Experimental Psychology,* 1959, *58*, 193-8, with permission of the author and publisher.
1. The initial stages of this investigation were facilitated by National Science Foundation Grant G-2596.

intervals. An item is presented and tested without related items intervening. The initial study examines the course of retention after one brief presentation of the item.

Method

Subjects.—The Ss were 24 students from introductory psychology courses at Indiana University. Participation in experiments was a course requirement.

Materials.—The verbal items tested for recall were 48 consonant syllables with Witmer association value no greater than 33% (Hilgard, 1951). Other materials were 48 three-digit numbers obtained from a table of random numbers. One of these was given to S after each presentation under instructions to count backward from the number. It was considered that continuous verbal activity during the time between presentation and signal for recall was desirable in order to minimize rehearsal behavior. The materials were selected to be categorically dissimilar and hence involve a minimum of interference.

Procedure.—The S was seated at a table with E seated facing in the same direction on S's right. A black plywood screen shielded E from S. On the table in front of S were two small lights mounted on a black box. The general procedure was for E to spell a consonant syllable and immediately speak a three-digit number. The S then counted backward by three or four from this number. On flashing of a signal light S attempted to recall the consonant syllable. The E spoke in rhythm with a metronome clicking twice per second and S was instructed to do likewise. The timing of these events is diagrammed in Fig. 1. As E spoke the third digit, he pressed a button activating a Hunter interval timer. At the end of a preset interval the timer activated a red light and an electric clock. The light was the signal for recall. The clock ran until E heard S speak three letters, when E stopped the clock by depressing a key. This time between onset of the light and completion of a response will be referred to as a

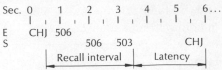

FIG. 1. Sequence of events for a recall interval of 3 sec.

latency. It is to be distinguished from the interval from completion of the syllable by E to onset of the light, which will be referred to as the recall interval.

The instructions read to S were as follows: "Please sit against the back of your chair so that you are comfortable. You will not be shocked during this experiment. In front of you is a little black box. The top or green light is on now. This green light means that we are ready to begin a trial. I will speak some letters and then a number. You are to repeat the number immediately after I say it and begin counting backwards by 3's (4's) from that number in time with the ticking that you hear. I might say, ABC 309. Then you say, 309, 306, 303, etc., until the bottom or red light comes on. When you see this red light come on, stop counting immediately and say the letters that were given at the beginning of the trial. Remember to keep your eyes on the black box at all times. There will be a short rest period and then the green light will come on again and we will start a new trial." The E summarized what he had already said and then gave S two practice trials. During this practice S was corrected if he hesitated before starting to count, or if he failed to stop counting on signal, or if he in any other way deviated from the instructions.

Each S was tested eight times at each of the recall intervals, 3, 6, 9, 12, 15, and 18 sec. A given consonant syllable was used only once with each S. Each syllable occurred equally often over the group at each recall interval. A specific recall interval was represented once in each successive block of six presentations. The S counted backward by three on half of the trials and by four on the remaining trials. No two successive items contained letters in common. The time between signal for recall and the start of the next presentation was 15 sec.

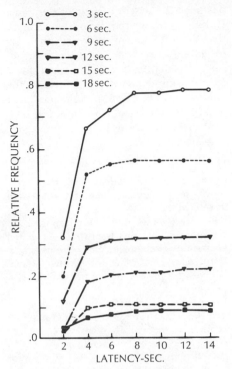

FIG. 2. Correct recalls as cumulative functions of latency.

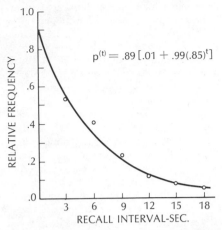

$$p^{(t)} = .89\,[.01 + .99(.85)^t]$$

FIG. 3. Correct recalls with latencies below 2.83 sec. as a function of recall interval.

Results and discussion

Responses occurring any time during the 15-sec. interval following signal for recall were recorded. In Fig. 2 are plotted the proportions of correct recalls as cumulative functions of latency for each of the recall intervals. Sign tests were used to evaluate differences among the curves (Walker & Lev, 1953). At each latency differences among the 3-, 6-, 9-, and 18-sec. recall interval curves are significant at the .05 level. For latencies of 6 sec. and longer these differences are all significant at the .01 level. Note that the number correct with latency less than 2 sec. does not constitute a majority of the total correct. These responses would not seem appropriately described as identification of the gradually weakening trace of a stimulus. There is a suggestion of an oscillatory characteristic in the events determining them.

The feasibility of an interpretation by a statistical model was explored by fitting to the data the exponential curve of Fig. 3. The empirical points plotted here are proportions of correct responses with latencies shorter than 2.83 sec. Partition of the correct responses on the basis of latency is required by considerations developed in detail by Estes (1950). A given probability of response applies to an interval of time equal in length to the average time required for the response under consideration to occur. The mean latency of correct responses in the present experiment was 2.83 sec. Differences among the proportions of correct responses with latencies shorter than 2.83 sec. were evaluated by sign tests. The difference between the 3- and 18-sec. conditions was found to be significant at the .01 level. All differences among the 3-, 6-, 9-, 12-, and 18-sec. conditions were significant at the .05 level.

The general equation of which the expression for the curve of Fig. 3 is a specific instance is derived from the stimulus fluctuation model developed by Estes (1955). In applying the model to the present experiment it is assumed that the verbal stimulus produces a response in S which is conditioned to a set of elements contiguous with the response. The elements thus conditioned are a sample of a larger population of elements into which the conditioned elements disperse as time passes. The proportion of conditioned elements in the sample determining S's behavior thus decreases and with it the probability of the response. Since the fitted curve appears to do justice to the data, the observed decrement could arise from stimulus fluctuation.

The independence of successive presentations might be questioned in the light of findings that performance deteriorates as a function of previous learning (Underwood, 1957). The presence of proactive interference was tested by noting the correct responses within each successive block of 12 presentations. The short recall intervals were analyzed separately from the long recall intervals in view of the possibility that facilitation might occur with the one and interference with the other. The proportions of correct responses for the combined 3- and 6-sec. recall intervals were in order of occurrence .57, .66, .70, and .74. A sign test showed the difference between the first and last blocks to be significant at the .02 level. The proportions correct for the 15- and 18-sec. recall intervals were .08, .15, .09, and .12. The gain from first to last blocks is not significant in this case. There is no evidence for proactive interference. There is an indication of improvement with practice.

Experiment II

The findings in Exp. I are compatible with the proposition that the after-effects of a single, brief, verbal stimulation can be interpreted as those of a trial of learning. It would be predicted from such an interpretation that probability of recall at a given recall interval should increase as a function of repetitions of the stimulation. Forgetting should proceed at differential rates for items with differing numbers of repetitions. Although this seems to be a reasonable prediction, there are those who would predict otherwise. Brown (1958), for instance, questions whether repetitions, as such, strengthen the "memory trace." He suggests that the effect of repetitions of a stimulus, or rehearsal, may be merely to

postpone the onset of decay of the trace. If time is measured from the moment that the last stimulation ceased, then the forgetting curves should coincide in all cases, no matter how many occurrences of the stimulation have preceded the final occurrence. The second experiment was designed to obtain empirical evidence relevant to this problem.

Method

The Ss were 48 students from the source previously described. Half of the Ss were instructed to repeat the stimulus aloud in time with the metronome until stopped by E giving them a number from which S counted backward. The remaining Ss were not given instructions concerning use of the interval between E's presentation of the stimulus and his speaking the number from which to count backward. Both the "vocal" group and the "silent" group had equated intervals of time during which rehearsal inevitably occurred in the one case and could occur in the other case. Differences in frequency of recalls between the groups would indicate a failure of the uninstructed Ss to rehearse. The zero point marking the beginning of the recall interval for the silent group was set at the point at which E spoke the number from which S counted backward. This was also true for the vocal group.

The length of the rehearsal period was varied for Ss of both groups over three conditions. On a third of the presentations S was not given time for any repetitions. This condition was thus comparable to Exp. I, save that the only recall intervals used were 3, 9, and 18 sec. On another third of the presentations 1 sec. elapsed during which S could repeat the stimulus. On another third of the presentations 3 sec. elapsed, or sufficient time for three repetitions. Consonant syllables were varied as to the rehearsal interval in which they were used, so that each syllable occurred equally often in each condition over the group. However, a given syllable was never presented more than once to any S. The Ss were assigned in order of appearance to a randomized list of conditions. Six practice presentations were given during which corrections were made of departures from instructions. Other details follow the precedures of Exp. I.

Results and discussion

Table 1 shows the proportion of items recalled correctly. In the vocal group recall improved with repetition at each of the recall intervals tested. Conditions

TABLE 1. *Proportions of items correctly recalled in Exp. II*

Group	Repetition Time (Sec.)	Recall Interval (Sec.)		
		3	9	18
Vocal	3	.80	.48	.34
	1	.68	.34	.21
	0	.60	.25	.14
Silent	3	.70	.39	.30
	1	.74	.35	.22
	0	.72	.38	.15

in the silent group were not consistently ordered. For purposes of statistical analysis the recall intervals were combined within each group. A sign test between numbers correct in the 0- and 3-repetition conditions of the vocal group showed the difference to be significant at the .01 level. The difference between the corresponding conditions of the silent group was not significant at the .05 level. Only under conditions where repetition of the stimulus was controlled by instructions did retention improve.

The obtained differences among the zero conditions of Exp. II and the 3-, 9-, and 18-sec. recall intervals of Exp. I require some comment, since procedures were essentially the same. Since these are between-S comparisons, some differences would be predicted because of sampling variability. But another factor is probably involved. There were 48 presentations in Exp. I and only 36 in Exp. II. Since recall was found to improve over successive blocks of trials, a superiority in recall for Ss of Exp. I is reasonable. In the case of differences between the vocal and silent groups of

Exp. II a statistical test is permissable, for Ss were assigned randomly to the two groups. Wilcoxon's (1949) test for unpaired replicates, as well as a *t* test, was used. Neither showed significance at the .05 level.

The 1- and 3-repetition conditions of the vocal group afforded an opportunity to obtain a measure of what recall would be at the zero interval in time. It was noted whether a syllable had been correctly repeated by S. Proportions correctly repeated were .90 for the 1-repetition condition and .88 for the 3-repetition condition. The chief source of error lay in the confusion of the letters "m" and "n." This source of error is not confounded with the repetition variable, for it is S who repeats and thus perpetuates his error. Further, individual items were balanced over the three conditions. There is no suggestion of any difference in responding among the repetition conditions at the beginning of the recall interval. These differences developed during the time that S was engaged in counting backward. A differential rate of forgetting seems indisputable.

The factors underlying the improvement in retention with repetition were investigated by means of an analysis of the status of elements within the individual items. The individual consonant syllable, like the nonsense syllable, may be regarded as presenting S with a serial learning task. Through repetitions unrelated components may develop serial dependencies until in the manner of familiar words they have become single units. The improved retention might then be attributed to increases in these serial dependencies. The analysis proceeded by ascertaining the dependent probabilities that letters would be correct given the event that the previous letter was correct. These dependent probabilities are listed in Table 2. It is clear that with increasing repetitions the serial dependencies increase. Again combining

TABLE 2. *Dependent probabilities of a letter being correctly recalled in the vocal group when the preceding letter was correct*

Repetition Time (Sec.)	Recall Interval (Sec.)		
	3	9	18
3	.96	.85	.72
1	.90	.72	.57
0	.86	.64	.56

recall intervals, a sign test between the zero condition and the three repetition condition is significant at the .01 level.

Learning is seen to take place within the items. But this finding does not eliminate the possibility that another kind of learning is proceeding concurrently. If only the correct occurrences of the first letters of syllables are considered, changes in retention apart from the serial dependencies can be assessed. The proportions of first letters recalled correctly for the 0-, 1-, and 3-repetition conditions were .60, .65, and .72, respectively. A sign test between the 0- and 3-repetition conditions was significant at the .05 level. It may tentatively be concluded that learning of a second kind took place.

The course of short-term verbal retention is seen to be related to learning processes. It would not appear to be strictly accurate to refer to retention after a brief presentation as a stimulus trace. Rather, it would seem appropriate to refer to it as the result of a trial of learning. However, in spite of possible objections to Hull's terminology the present investigation supports his general position that a short-term retentive factor is important for the analysis of verbal learning.

The details of the role of retention in the acquisition process remain to be worked out.

SUMMARY

The investigation differed from traditional verbal retention studies in concerning itself with individual items instead of lists. Forgetting over intervals measured in seconds was found. The course of retention after a single presentation was related to a statistical model. Forgetting was found to progress at differential rates dependent on the amount of controlled rehearsal of the stimulus. A portion of the improvement in recall with repetitions was assigned to serial learning within the item, but a second kind of learning was also found. It was concluded that short-term retention is an important, though neglected, aspect of the acquisition process.

BROWN, J. Some tests of the decay theory of immediate memory. *Quart. J. exp. Psychol.,* 1958, **10**, 12-21.

ESTES, W. K. Toward a statistical theory of learning. *Psychol. Rev.,* 1950, **57**, 94-107.

ESTES, W. K. Statistical theory of spontaneous recovery and regression. *Psychol. Rev.,* 1955, **62**, 145-54.

HILGARD, E. R. Methods and procedures in the study of learning. In S. S. Stevens (Ed.), *Handbook of experimental psychology.* New York: Wiley, 1951.

HULL, C. L., HOVLAND, C. I., ROSS, R. T., HALL, M., PERKINS, D. T., & FITCH, F. B. *Mathematico-deductive theory of rote learning: A study in scientific methodology.* New Haven: Yale Univer. Press, 1940.

HULL, C. L. *A behavior system.* New Haven: Yale Univer. Press, 1952.

PILLSBURY, W. B., & SYLVESTER, A. Retroactive and proactive inhibition in immediate memory. *J. exp. Psychol.,* 1940, **27**, 532-45.

UNDERWOOD, B. J. *Experimental psychology.* New York: Appleton-Century-Crofts, 1949.

UNDERWOOD, B. J. Interference and forgetting. *Psychol. Rev.,* 1957, **64**, 49-60.

WALKER, H., & LEV, J. *Statistical inference.* New York: Holt, 1953.

WILCOXON, F. *Some rapid approximate statistical procedures.* New York: Amer. Cyanamid Co., 1949.

27 / The Retention of Individual Items [1]

BENNET B. MURDOCK, JR., *University of Vermont*

The present paper reports a study of the short-term retention of individual verbal items. A study by Peterson and Peterson (1959) provided the starting point for the present experiments. In

From the *Journal of Experimental Psychology* 1961, **62**, 618-25, with permission of the author and publisher.

1. This study was supported by a research grant, M-3330, from the National Institutes of Health. Cynthia Marvin conducted many of the experiments and helped in the analysis of the results.

this study a single consonant syllable was presented to S, then immediately followed by a three-digit number. The S had to repeat the number, count backward by 3's or 4's at a 1-sec. rate for anywhere from 3 to 18 sec., then recall the original syllable. The results showed that the probability of recall decreased exponentially with duration of interpolated activity and approached an asymptote very close to zero.

Three experiments will be reported. Experiment I both replicated the original Peterson and Peterson (1959) study and investigated the effect of varying the nature of the to-be-remembered item. Experiment II was a study of short-term proactive inhibition (PI) which investigated the effect of varying the number of items preceding the to-be-remembered item. Experiment III studied the effect of varying the rate of the interpolated activity.

EXPERIMENT I

Method. This experiment was conducted in four successive sessions spaced about 4 weeks apart. Session 1 was a replication of the Peterson and Peterson (1959) study. The procedure was identical to theirs except for the following conditions: (*a*) the duration of the interpolated activity (i.e., counting backward) was 0, 3, 6, 9, 12, or 18 sec.; thus, we substituted the 0-sec. interval for the 15-sec. interval; (*b*) the metronome was set at rate of 1 beat/sec instead of 2 beats/sec; (*c*) the zero point of the interpolated activity was considered to begin with the first beat of the metronome following the presentation of the nonsense syllable; and (*d*) all Ss were given sufficient preliminary practice on the interpolated activity to enable them to count backward accurately. As in the Peterson and Peterson (1959) study both latency and accuracy of response were recorded, the consonant syllables were selected from the same pool, and the same controls (counterbalancing of syllables among conditions and conditions among stages of practice) were employed.

Session 2 was an exact duplication of Session 1 except for the to-be-remembered items. Instead of consonant syllables the items were single, monosyllabic, nonhomophonic words selected from the Thorndike-Lorge (1944) list of the 1000 most common words in the English language.

To test whether the large differences obtained between the results of Sessions 1 and 2 could be attributed simply to the number of "chunks" of information (i.e., three unrelated letters in the first session or one common word in the second session; see Miller, 1956) Session 3 was an exact duplication of Sessions 1 and 2 except that the to-be-remembered items were word triads. That is, on each trial S was presented three monosyllabic nonhomophonic words from the same pool as above. In selecting the word triads the only stipulation was that the three words could be clearly spoken in the same length of time (i.e, 1 sec.) required to say the three letters of the consonant syllables of Session 1.

As both accuracy and latency of recall were used as dependent variables, Session 4 was conducted to determine whether the duration of the interpolated activity itself would affect response latency. No stimulus item other than the three-digit number was presented; S was merely required to say "stop" as quickly as possible after the interpolated activity (counting backward) was terminated.

The same Ss were used in all four sessions; they were students of both sexes from the introductory psychology course who were fulfilling a course requirement. There were 24 Ss in each of the first three sessions and 20 Ss in the fourth session.

Results. The results of Session 1 clearly confirmed the results of Peterson and Peterson (1959). They presented their results in terms of the proportion of correct responses occurring with latencies less than 2.83 sec. (the over-all mean latency for all correct responses). We analyzed our results in the same way and compared them with the values predicted by the formula given in Peterson and Peterson (1959, Fig. 3, p. 195). The differences between the results predicted by this formula and the results actually obtained in Session 1 were small and nonsystematic; the mean (algebraic) difference in proportion was −.025.

The mean proportion recalled at each retention interval is shown in Table 1. These results include all correct re-

TABLE 1. *Mean proportion of correct recalls at each retention interval: Exp. I*

Retention Interval	Session 1 CCC Trigrams		Session 2 Words		Session 3 Word Triads	
	Mean	SD	Mean	SD	Mean	SD
0 sec.	.94	.11	.98	.04	.93	.10
3 sec.	.77	.15	.99	.03	.73	.21
6 sec.	.40	.18	.96	.07	.39	.23
12 sec.	.24	.14	.86	.11	.31	.22
18 sec.	.16	.12	.84	.14	.23	.16

sponses regardless of latency. To receive credit for a correct response in Sessions 1 and 3, S had to recall all three consonants or words in the correct order. Clearly, in all cases forgetting increased with the duration of interpolated activity, and with the longer retention intervals there was very little recall in Sessions 1 and 3.

As a simple statistical test, for each S we determined the total number of items recalled (maximum of 48) over all retention intervals. The mean values were 22.1, 44.3, and 23.0 items with SDs of 3.86, 1.99, and 5.98 for Sessions 1 to 3, respectively. The difference between Sessions 1 and 3 was not significant ($t=0.94$), but the difference between Session 2 and the other two combined was highly significant ($t=24.9$, $P<.001$).

An analysis of the latency data substantiated the above results. The mean latencies are shown in Table 2 and, in general, latencies increased with the duration of the retention interval. An analysis of variance of the results of Session 4 showed that the duration of the interpolated activity did have a significant effect ($F=25.14$, $P<.001$), but most of the difference was due to the 0-sec. retention interval. Thus, the "true" values for the 0-sec. interval for the first three sessions should be slightly lower than those reported. The corrections for differences among the remaining retention intervals are probably too slight to bother with.

To summarize the results of Exp. I: (a) they confirm the previous findings of Peterson and Peterson (1959); (b) they show that, for three types of items, forgetting, whether measured by accuracy or latency, increased with the duration of the interpolated activity; and (c) they show little difference between the retention of three consonants and three words but marked differences between the retention of three "chunks" and one word. The possible confounding of intersession practice effects will be considered with the results of the next experiment.

EXPERIMENT II

Method. This experiment was a study of short-term PI. As in Session 2 of Exp. I the stimulus items were single monosyllabic non-homophonic words. A given item was preceded by 0, 3, 6, 9, or 12 words, also from the Thorndike-Lorge list of the 1,000

TABLE 2. *Mean latency of correct recalls at each retention interval: Exp. I*

Retention Interval	Session 1 CCC Trigrams		Session 2 Words		Session 3 Word Triads		Session 4 Simple RT	
	Mean	SD	Mean	SD	Mean	SD	Mean	SD
0 sec.	1.91	0.97	1.13	0.30	1.63	0.28	1.06	0.26
3 sec.	2.01	0.64	1.32	0.31	2.02	0.67	0.85	0.17
6 sec.	2.45	1.01	1.51	0.55	2.32	0.74	0.86	0.18
9 sec.	3.16	1.21	1.61	0.58	2.40	0.72	0.90	0.18
12 sec.	2.49	0.91	1.59	0.62	2.63	1.06	0.92	0.19
18 sec.	3.04	1.18	1.69	0.65	2.79	1.20	0.92	0.25

most common words. The preceding words were read at a 1-sec. rate, but always S was asked to recall only the stimulus item. The interpolated activity was, as in Exp. I, counting backward for 0, 3, 6, 9, 12, or 18 sec. Each S was tested under all conditions. The 5 × 6 design (five levels of prior words, six retention intervals) required 30 trials (lists) for one replication, and there were eight replications in all. Thus, each S was given a total of 240 trials, 60 on each of 4 days. There were 24 Ss from the same population as before.

In all other respects the procedure was identical with that of Exp. I. There was complete counterbalancing of conditions within Ss and stimulus material across Ss. That is, there were eight blocks of 30 trials each so that the experimental conditions appeared equally often at all stages of practice. Within each block the order of the 30 trials was randomized. Each specific stimulus item was assigned equally often to each retention interval and, so far as possible, to each level of number of prior words. The specific words preceding the stimulus item were randomized by starting at a different place on the mimeographed word list for each S.

Results. An analysis of intersession practice effects showed that the proportion of words corectly recalled over the 4 days were .87, .87, .92, and .93, respectively. Although the magnitude of the improvement was relatively slight, it was consistent enough to be highly significant ($F = 9.12$, $P < .001$). In Exp. I the proportion of correct recalls for the first session (consonant syllables) was .46, and the proportion of correct recalls for the third session (word triads) was .48. Since the slight improvement was about what would be expected by practice effects alone, the confounding of practice effects and stimulus items probably does not affect the conclusion that consonant syllables and word triads were equally well recalled.

The mean proportion of correct recalls, regardless of latency, at each retention interval in Exp. II is shown in Table 3, and the mean latency of correct recalls

TABLE 3. *Mean proportion of correct recalls at each retention interval: Exp. II*

Retention Interval	Number of Prior Words					Mean
	0	3	6	9	12	
0 sec.	.995	1.000	.985	.985	.974	.988
3 sec.	1.000	.959	.927	.948	.969	.960
6 sec.	.953	.834	.896	.901	.865	.890
9 sec.	.938	.844	.860	.849	.875	.873
12 sec.	.938	.771	.834	.818	.860	.844
18 sec.	.907	.823	.802	.828	.823	.836
Mean	.955	.872	.884	.888	.894	

is shown in Table 4. Analyses of variance showed that, for each measure, both variables (number of prior words and retention interval) were significant at at least the .01 level. As the retention interval increased, accuracy decreased and latency increased. As the number of prior words increased, accuracy decreased from 0 to 3 words, then increased slightly but consistently from 3 to 12 words. As the number of prior words

TABLE 4. *Mean latency of correct recalls at each retention interval: Exp. II*

Retention Interval	Number of Prior Words					Mean
	0	3	6	9	12	
0 sec.	0.90	1.01	0.98	0.97	1.01	0.97
3 sec.	1.09	1.12	1.17	1.16	1.17	1.14
6 sec.	1.20	1.27	1.33	1.24	1.29	1.27
9 sec.	1.26	1.31	1.35	1.47	1.26	1.33
12 sec.	1.19	1.33	1.35	1.29	1.31	1.29
18 sec.	1.32	1.35	1.37	1.43	1.40	1.37
Mean	1.16	1.23	1.26	1.26	1.24	

increased, latency increased from 0 to 3 words but then stayed relatively constant from 3 to 12 words.

When the control condition (0 prior words) is omitted, there were in all 264 extralist intrusions, 161 intralist intrusions, and 81 omissions. Thus, the number of extralist intrusions, intralist intrusions, and omissions occurred in approximately the ratio 3:2:1. An intralist intrusion was considered to be one of the words preceding the to-be-remembered stimulus item, an extralist intrusion was any other word, and an omission was a failure to respond. An analysis of the intralist intrusions showed that almost half (74, or 46%) of these intrusions were the word immediately preceding the to-be-remembered stimulus item, and in general the percentage decreased with increasing remoteness from the stimulus item.

If the control group is included, there were in all 324 extralist intrusions. Of these 324 intrusions 98 (30%) were words that had been correct on one of the preceding trials, 86 were classified as having been mispronounced by S, 10 were obvious associations or synonyms of the correct response, and 130 were unclassifiable. Of the 98 intrusions from previous trials 58 had been correct on the immediately preceding trial, 13 on the preceding trial once removed, and the number decreased regularly with increasing remoteness. Thus, in general the analysis of the errors showed marked recency effects for both intralist and extralist intrusions.

To summarize, the results of Exp. II showed that proactive inhibition does occur in the short-term retention of individual items but (at least for accuracy) appears to be a U shaped function of number of previous words.

EXPERIMENT III

Method. This experiment was a study of the effect of different rates of interpolated activity on short-term retention of individual items. For this purpose counting backward did not seem to be a suitable type of interpolation; Ss could not easily count faster than a 1-sec. rate, and a slower rate might allow rehearsal of the original item. Therefore, a new procedure was devised. A list of words of unknown length was read to S, and S was instructed to remember both the first and the last three words in the list. Requiring S to remember the last three words seemed to prevent rehearsal of the first word.

A preliminary experiment was conducted to test the feasibility of this method. There were lists of six different lengths: 4, 7, 11, 16, 21, and 31 words, all nonhomophonic words from the Thorndike-Lorge 1,000 most common. There were 10 counterbalanced replications of the six lengths for a total of 60 trials (or lists) in all. Group testing was used, and all words were read in time with an electric metronome beating at a rate of 1 beat/sec. After each list had been read Ss had 20 sec. in which to write down the first and last three words of the list. A "ready" signal preceded by 2 sec. the start of each list. There were 29 Ss from the same population as before, all tested in a single session.

An analysis of the results of this preliminary experiment showed that, with one reversal, the proportion of correct recalls of the first word decreased as list length increased. The minimum proportion was .841 for the 31 word list. Statistically, the effect of list length was highly significant ($F = 5.81$, $P < .001$) and, in general, the results were quite comparable to the analogous data on single words in Exp. I and II. Therefore, it was decided to use this method to study the effect of rate of interpolation on short-term retention.

The main experiment was conducted in three sessions and followed closely the procedure of the preliminary experiment. In Session 1 there were six list lengths: 4, 7, 10, 13, 16, and 19 words. The metronome was beating at a rate of 2 beats/sec; starting with the second beat after the first word had been read the remaining words were read either at every beat, every other beat, or every fourth beat. Thus, in effect, the first word was presented for 1 sec. and the remaining words were read at a rate of either 2, 1, or 0.5 words/sec. List length and presentation rate were orthogonal to each other, and there were three replications for a total of 54 trials (or lists). The order of presentation was randomized within each replication.

In Session 2 (actually requiring 2 days to complete) there were three list lengths (7, 13, and 19 words) but five different rates. The metronome was set at a rate of 2.5 beats/sec, and starting with the second beat the remaining words were read at every beat, every other beat, every third beat, every fourth beat, or every fifth beat. Thus, the rates used ranged from 0.5 to 2.5

words/sec. There were eight replications for a total of 120 trials, 60 on each of the 2 days. The order of presentation was randomized within each replication.

In Session 3 there were six list lengths (4, 7, 10, 13, 16, and 19 words) but only two different rates. The metronome was set at a rate of 2.0 beats/sec, and the entire list was read either at a rate of one word every beat or one word every third beat. Thus, the two rates were 2.0 and 0.67 words/sec. These two rates were selected on the basis of the results of Session 2 as those which should yield maximum differences. At the slower rate Ss would have more time to rehearse the first word before the rest of the list started; this confounding was deliberately introduced in a further attempt to maximize the differences between the two rates. There were five replications for a total of 60 trials, and the order of presentation was randomized within each replication.

Group testing was used throughout. The same Ss were tested in all three sessions (though not in the preliminary experiment). They were 27 students from the same population as before; however, only 21 were tested in Session 3.

Results. In each of the three sessions the proportion of correct recalls decreased as the retention interval increased. Analyses of variance showed that the effect was statistically significant at beyond the .001 level in all three cases.

In Session 1, the proportions of correct recalls were .827, .860, and .829 for the rates of 0.5, 1, and 2 words/sec, respectively. An analysis of variance showed that the differences were not statistically significant ($F < 1.00$). In Session 2, the proportions of correct recalls were .909, .940, .918, .963, and .946 for words read every 1, 2, 3, 4, and 5 beats, respectively. Again, the differences were not statistically significant ($F = 2.10$, $P > .05$). In Session 3, the proportions of correct recalls were almost identical for the two conditions (.894 and .895). Thus, there seems little doubt that, under the conditions of this experiment, the rate of interpolation is not an effective variable

governing the short-term retention of individual items.

In Exp. III, Ss were asked to recall not only the first word but also the last three words. Since varying numbers of words preceded the last three words, an analysis of the recall data of the last three words as a function of number of preceding words can give further information about short-term proactive inhibition effects. The proportion of correct recall of the last three words is shown in Table 5. These results show exactly the

TABLE 5. *Mean proportion of correct recalls of the last three words: Exp. III*

Session	Number of Preceding Words					
	1	4	7	10	13	16
1	.938	.827	.846	.866	.863	.885
2	—	.874	—	.887	—	.898
3	.916	.867	.890	.895	.892	.905
Mean	.927	.856	.868	.883	.878	.896

same pattern as those of Exp. II (see Table 3): an initial drop followed by a gradual rise. The rise from 4 to 16 preceding words was reasonably linear, and the least-squares regression line of the means (bottom row of Table 5) had a slope significantly greater than zero ($t = 4.76$, $df = 3$, $P < .02$). Thus, these results confirm the conclusion of Exp. II; PI first increases but then decreases as the number of previous words increases.

An analysis of the errors showed omissions of 54%, 63%, and 64%; extralist intrusions of 28%, 25%, and 18%; and intralist intrusions of 18%, 12%, and 18%, each for Sessions 1, 2, and 3, respectively. Averaged across sessions the mean number of omissions, extralist intrusions, and intralist intrusions were 60%, 27%, and 12%, respectively. The corresponding values from Exp. II were 16%, 52%, and 32%, respectively. Thus, in Exp. III there were far more omissions and far fewer intrusions than in Exp. II. In Exp. II the interfering words preceded the to-be-remembered word while in Exp. III the interfering words followed the to-be-remembered word; this difference in procedure may have been responsible for the different ratios of omissions to intrusions found in the two experiments.

There was a definite serial position effect in the recall of the last three words. Table 6 shows the proportion of correct recalls of the first, second, and third of these last three words (the third word being the last word in the list). The data

TABLE 6. *Mean proportion of correct recalls of each of the last three words: Exp. III*

Session	Word		
	Last—2	Last—1	Last
Prelim. exp.	.784	.914	.977
1st Session	.761	.884	.966
2nd Session	.770	.916	.974
3rd Session	.801	.906	.974
Mean	.779	.905	.973

show the typical serial position effect of free recall (Deese & Kaufman, 1957); there appears to be rather little inter-experiment variability.

To summarize, the results of Exp. III showed no effect of rate of interpolation on short-term retention but confirmed the PI findings of Exp. II (and also see Rouse, 1959).

DISCUSSION

The results of the present experiments substantiate and extend the previous work of Peterson and Peterson (1959). With an appropriate interpolated activity, the forgetting of an individual item will increase over a retention interval measured in seconds. Further, the interpolated activity evidently need not be highly similar to the to-be-remembered stimulus item; there would appear to be little formal similarity between the three-digit numbers used in counting backward and the consonant syllables, single words, and word triads used in Exp. I and II.

Given this low similarity, it would seem unlikely that the interpolated activity would interfere with the retention of the stimulus item in the same sense that, for instance, an A-C list interferes with the retention of an A-B list in paired-associate learning. However, the interpolated activity presumably prevents rehearsal of the item, and the results consistently showed that the more time that elapsed without rehearsal the poorer the retention. Thus, the results of the various experiments using the counting backward as an interpolated activity would seem to be more compatible with a decay theory than with an interference theory of forgetting.

On the other hand, the results of Exp. III (using, of course, a quite different interpolated activity) showed that the rate of interpolation was not a significant variable determining forgetting. Given a constant number of interfering items, the total time required to present these items (and hence the time for decay to occur) could vary over a range of three or four to one and still produce the same amount of forgetting. Since in Exp. III it was the number of interpolated items and not their rate of presentation that was the critical variable, these results are more compatible with an interference theory than with a decay theory. Thus, taken as a whole, the present experiments do not provide unambiguous support for either a decay theory or an interference theory of forgetting.

The curvilinear PI function found in Exp. II and III may, at least partly, reflect the "behavioral strategy" (Pollack, Johnson, & Knaff, 1959) adopted by Ss. That is, in remembering the last word or words in a list of uncertain length, the more words that have been read the greater the probability that recall of the most recent word of words will be tested; Ss can react accordingly. Although such a possibility cannot be completely ruled out it seems unlikely for two reasons: (a) As Table 5 shows, the PI function in Exp. III was essentially the same in Session 2 as in Sessions 1 and 3. However, the uncertainty about list length was only half as great in Session 2 and, as Pollack, Johnson, and Knaff (1959) suggest, behavioral strategy would vary with degree of certainty. (b) During the course of each session Ss would gradually acquire a knowledge of the particular list lengths used, and this knowledge should facilitate the behavioral strategy. However, in Exp. III there was nothing approaching a significant practice effect, either in the preliminary experiment or in Sessions 1-3.

Finally, it is worth noting again the large differences in the retention of consonant syllables and word triads in one case, and individual words in the other case. Over the retention intervals studied, the proportion of correct recalls dropped to about .20 for the former and about .80 for the latter. It can be argued that the consonant syllables and word triads are three items to be remembered while an individual word is only a single item. If this is so, then, the number of items to be remembered would seem to be a significant variable in short-term retention.

SUMMARY

Three experiments were conducted on the short-term retention of individual items. Experiment I confirmed the findings of Peterson and Peterson (1959) and suggested that the number of items or "chunks" of information in the to-be-remembered stimulus item may be a significant variable in short-term retention. Experiment II demonstrated a significant proactive inhibition effect and suggested that the effect may be a U shaped function of number of preceding items. Experiment III showed that the rate of interpolated activity did not have a significant effect on short-term retention. The implications for a decay theory and an interference theory of forgetting were briefly discussed.

DEESE, J., & KAUFMAN, R. A. Serial effects in recall of unorganized and sequentially organized verbal material. *J. exp. Psychol.*, 1957, **54**, 180-87.
MILLER, G. A. The magical number seven, plus or minus two: Some limits on our capacity for processing information. *Psychol. Rev.*, 1956, **63**, 81-97.
PETERSON, L. R., & PETERSON, M. J. Short-term retention of individual verbal items. *J. exp. Psychol.*, 1959, **58**, 193-8.
POLLACK, I., JOHNSON, L. B., & KNAFF, P. R. Running memory span. *J. exp. Psychol.*, 1959, **57**, 137-46.
ROUSE, R. O. Proactive inhibition as a function of degree of practice on the two tasks. *Amer. Psychologist*, 1959, **14**, 385. (Abstract)
THORNDIKE, E. L., & LORGE, I. *The teacher's word book of 30,000 words.* New York: Columbia University, Bureau of Publications, 1944.

28 / Proactive Inhibition in Short-term Retention of Single Items [1]

GEOFFREY KEPPEL AND BENTON J. UNDERWOOD, *Northwestern University*

In 1959 Peterson and Peterson developed a technique whereby a single verbal item was presented to S for a learning trial of approximately .5-sec. duration, with retention being measured over intervals of up to 18 sec. These procedures produced a very systematic relationship between length of retention interval and percentage of items correct at recall, with 78% correct after 3 sec., and 8% after 18 sec. Thus, forgetting of the single item is nearly complete after 18 sec. The reliability of this forgetting curve is demonstrated by the fact that Murdock (1961) has repeated the Peterson-Peterson experiment and obtained nearly identical results.

The present experiments were designed to obtain data which would aid in interpreting theoretically the extraordinarily rapid forgetting of the single items which has been observed in the above experiments. The nature of the interpretative problem and how it arises, requires some background discussion.

The first distinction which must be made is between short-term retention procedures and long-term retention procedures. The short-term studies, as ex-

From the *Journal of Verbal Learning and Verbal Behavior*, 1962, **1**, 153-61, with permission of the authors and the publisher, Academic Press, Inc.
1. This work was supported by Contract Nonr-1228(15), Project NR 154-057, between Northwestern University and the Office of Naval Research.

emplified by Peterson and Peterson, involve retention of *single* items over very short intervals, say, 60 sec. or less. The long-term retention studies involve retention of *lists* of items over much longer intervals, such as 20 min., although usually hours or days are employed. Clearly no dichotomy is possible between the two types of studies based on length of retention interval, but in actual practice a working distinction between the two exists. We may identify the short-term studies as measuring short-term memory (STM) and the long-term studies as measuring long-term memory (LTM) with the understanding that the present usage also involves memory for singly presented items versus memory for lists of items.

The critical issue is whether or not LTM and STM will require fundamentally different interpretative principles. The resolution of this issue rests primarily on determining the role which proactive inhibition (PI) plays in STM. Interference theories of LTM use PI as a cornerstone paradigm (e.g., Postman, 1961); associations learned prior to the learning of associations for which retention is being tested may interfere with recall. However, a secondary fact reported by Peterson and Peterson (1959) and by Peterson (1963) is that little or no evidence is found for PI in STM. In addition, since little or no retroactive inhibition (RI) is believed to be produced by the activity used to prevent rehearsal in the studies of STM, it would appear that an interference theory, based on PI and RI, is quite incapable of handling the extraordinarily rapid forgetting observed in the studies of STM. Thus, we are faced with a potential theoretical schism, with one set of propositions being used for LTM and another possibly wholly different set for STM. In the interests of theoretical continuity, such a schism should be avoided if possible.

As noted above, the critical issue involved is the role which PI plays in STM. If PI is operative in STM, the variables which govern magnitude of PI in LTM should also have counterparts in the laws of STM. Some of these more critical variables will now be discussed.

Number of interfering associations. In LTM the greater the number of previously acquired associations the greater the PI (Underwood, 1945; 1957). It is the reported failure to reproduce this law in studies of STM that has led to the conclusion that there is little, if any, PI in STM. Actually, the procedure used in these studies of STM would seem to be ideal for obtaining PI. For example, in the Peterson-Peterson study, a counterbalancing technique was used in which each S served eight times at each of six retention intervals. Thus, each S at the termination of his conditions had been presented 48 different items. The items presented late in the session should be subject to a greater number of potentially interfering associations than would those items presented early in the session. Yet there appears to be little difference in the retention of items presented early in the session and those presented late in the session (but see later discussion).

Degree of learning. In LTM the higher the degree of learning to the list to be recalled the better the recall when the PI paradigm is used (Postman & Riley, 1959). This is not to say that the absolute PI is less with higher than with lower degrees of learning (when evaluated against a control group) of the list to be recalled, for according to Postman and Riley this relationship is complex. But, given a high degree of learning of a list, its recall will be higher than will the recall of a list with a low degree of learning when the proactive interference is constant on both lists. This fact has been used by Melton (1963) indirectly to suggest that PI is indeterminate in the available studies of STM. His reasoning is that as S proceeds through a series of conditions the learning-to-learn will serve to increase the degree of learning of items presented. This higher degree of learning, in turn, will counteract a decrement in retention which should occur as a function of the increasing number of potentially interfering associations which have been established as practice proceeds.

There is evidence that learning-to-learn does occur in STM studies (Peterson & Peterson, 1959). That it does occur requires a distinction between learning and retention in STM, a distinction which has not, in fact, been carefully maintained in the studies to date. Normally, we may use an immediate test (say, after 1 sec.) as a measure of degree of learning. Retention for longer intervals are assessed against the scores on the immediate test to determine the retention function. However, when percentage correct for immediate retention is essentially 100%, there is no way to derive a meaningful retention function. For, in a manner of speaking, the true degree of learning may be more than 100%. Thus, if STM of common words is to be compared with that of consonant syllables, and if the immediate test for words shows 100% correct recall and that for syllables 85%, comparison of the retention of the two materials at longer intervals may be both a function of underestimated differences in degree of learning and of differences in material. Latency measures at recall might be used as subsidiary indices of forgetting which occurs when the percentage correct remains near 100% for retention intervals of increasing length, but the moment recall falls substantially below 100% we have subject selection (those who do not get an item correct are not included in the measures) which may distort the mean of the natural distribution of latencies based on all Ss.

Length of retention interval. The logic of the PI situation demands an increase in PI as a function of the length of the retention interval (Underwood, 1948). So far as is known, no completely satisfactory test of this relationship has been made for LTM. Theoretically the increase in PI with increase in length of the retention interval may be accounted for by the recovery of extinguished interfering associations. Several studies strongly suggest such recovery (e.g., Briggs, 1954).

Interaction of variables. If the facts and theory of PI in LTM hold for STM, certain interactions among the above variables will be expected. Most critical among these is the interaction between the number of potentially interfering associations and the length of the retention interval. Theoretically it is assumed that the longer the retention interval the greater the recovery of interfering associations. If there are few or none such associations little or no decrement will be observed as a function of length of retention interval (i.e., forgetting will be very slow). If there are many potential associations which could interfere proactively, the longer the retention interval the greater the forgetting, since the longer the interval the greater the number of interfering associations which will have recovered.

We may now focus on the fact that PI is said not to be involved in the rapid forgetting in STM. In the Peterson-Peterson study Ss were tested on 48 successive items following two practice items. It has been suggested that PI reaches some maximum level rather quickly as a function of the number of previous items and that a constant amount of PI may occur thereafter. Thus, two practice items may "throw in" the maximum amount of PI and additional items may have no further decremental effects (Postman, 1962; Melton, 1963). While it seems apparent that there must be a limit to the number of previous items which will contribute to interference in

288

STM, it does not seem reasonable that all potential interfering associations would be established with only two items—the two practice items. It seems more reasonable to look at the Peterson-Peterson data from another point of view. If it is assumed that there is a practice effect in learning successive items, degree of learning for each successive item will be higher and higher. By principles of PI in LTM, the recall should also be higher and higher if amount of interference remains constant. But, of course, interference does not remain constant; more and more potentially interfering associations are acquired as testing continues. As noted earlier in the discussion, the question is how the positive effects of increased degree of learning with successive stages of practice balance out against the increased interference which accompanies the higher degree of learning. Some indication of the direction the answer may take is available in the Peterson-Peterson data.

These investigators divided the 48 experimental items into successive blocks of 12 items each so that Blocks 1 through 4 may reflect increasing degrees of learning of the items to be recalled and, simultaneously, increasing numbers of potentially interfering items. The percentage correct at recall by blocks was determined separately for two short intervals (3 and 6 sec.) and for two long intervals (15 and 18 sec.). The results are presented in Fig. 1. For the short retention intervals there is a consistent increase in recall from Block 1 to Block 4, the difference between the recall for the two extreme blocks being significant at the .02 confidence level. Peterson and Peterson identified this as a practice effect. Since there is no reason to believe that the practice effect occurs in the recall process it must mean that the degree of learning attained in the constant exposure period increases as trials pro-

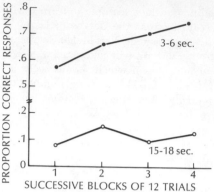

Fig. 1. Retention of single consonant syllables over short (3–6 sec.) and long (15–18 sec.) retention intervals as a function of number of preceding items. From Peterson and Peterson (1959).

ceed. For the longer retention interval there is no increase in recall. If only practice effects are involved, this curve should rise in exactly the same manner as the curve for shorter intervals. That it does not may indicate an increase in amount of PI as trials proceed. Thus, Fig. 1 gives indirect evidence for the critical interaction discussed earlier; that is, the interaction between amount of interference and length of the retention interval. With short retention intervals the practice effects more than compensate for increased interference; with long retention intervals the interference is of sufficient magnitude to mask the practice effects.

The evidence for the interaction between number of previous items and length of retention interval as inferred from Fig. 1 is not entirely satisfactory. Not only is the magnitude of the interaction small, but the failure to find a change in retention over blocks for the longer retention intervals must be interpreted as due to a balance between practice and interference effects. We believe it is possible to devise situations which will destroy this balance and thus give more direct evidence for the role of PI. Furthermore, studies are needed in which STM is examined for Ss without prior practice so that the rate of onset of PI as a function of 0, 1, 2, 3, etc., previous items is observed. The present experiments were designed to study these two issues.

EXPERIMENT 1

Method

Subjects. A total of 108 Ss from introductory psychology classes at Northwestern University served in Exp. 1. Most Ss had served in one or more verbal-learning experiments but in no case did an S have prior experience with the specific materials of the present experiment.

Procedure. Three retention intervals were used, namely, 3 sec., 9 sec., and 18 sec. A single consonant syllable was used for each retention interval. The procedure of Peterson and Peterson (1959) was followed, in which E spelled a syllable aloud and S attempted to recall it after the appropriate retention interval. The interval was timed from the moment the last letter of the syllable was spoken to the point at which S was instructed to recall. During the retention interval S counted backward by threes from a three-digit number spoken immediately after the presentation of the syllable, the rate of counting being one three-digit number per sec. Half the Ss were given a short practice period in counting backwards prior to being given the first syllable. However, since this practice had no discernible effect on the scores, the variable has not been maintained in presenting the results.

The three trigrams or consonant syllables were KQF, MHZ, and CXJ. Each has a 4% association value in the Witmer list (Underwood & Schulz, 1960). The retention for each S was measured over all three intervals with, of course, a different trigram being used for each interval. The three intervals were completely counterbalanced and three different orders of the trigrams were used such that each occurred equally often as the first, second, and third trigram presented. Thus 18 Ss are needed to fill the 18 different trigram-interval orders. Since 108 Ss were used, the design was replicated six times.

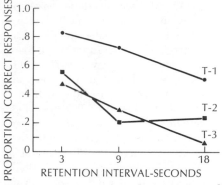

FIG. 2. Retention of single consonant syllables as a function of length of interval and number of prior syllables. Experiment 1.

The design allows retention to be determined for the three retention intervals after 0, 1, and 2 prior trigrams. Recall for the first trigram will be referred to as Test 1 (T-1), that of the second T-2, and the third, T-3.

Results

The results in terms of proportion of items correct for T-1, T-2, and T-3 for each retention interval are shown in Fig. 2. Each point is based on 36 Ss. Forgetting is apparent for all three tests. There is a large drop in proportion correct from T-1 to T-2, suggesting a severe proactive effect produced by a single prior item. There is no strong evidence that T-2 differs from T-3; thus, this may suggest a steady state or a constant amount of PI after the initial drop from T-1 to T-2. However, two facts relative to this point should be noted. First, at 3 sec. and at 18 sec., proportion correct is higher for T-2 than for T-3; only at 9 sec. is there a reversal. The fact that performance is better at 18 sec. than at 9 sec. (forgetting decreases between 9 and 18 sec.) suggests the possibility that for some unknown reason the 9 sec. T-2 estimate of retention is too low. Secondly, it is noted that the absolute number of Ss recalling correctly at T-2 and T-3 for the 9- and 18-sec. intervals is very low. At none of these points is retention above 25% and on T-3 at 18 sec. forgetting is virtually complete. At these low levels of performance it may be very difficult to show consistent differences. Nevertheless, it must be concluded that there is no evidence for an increase in PI between T-2 and T-3. Furthermore, there is no evidence for an interaction between tests and retention intervals; the curves for T-1 and T-3 are essentially parallel, although here again it must be noted that on T-3 at 18 sec. forgetting is virtually complete, a situation which may preclude the appearance of an interaction. If, however, retention at 3 sec. is used as a base and if percentage of items lost between 3 sec. and 18 sec. is calculated, there is a 40% loss (from 30 items to 18 items) for T-1, and an 88% loss (from 17 to 2 items) for T-3. This method of evaluating the results clearly shows the expected interaction. While we do not believe that this response measure (proportion lost) can be judged inappropriate, it was our expectation that the interaction would be of such magnitude as to be measurable by the direct recall measures. Therefore, we will conclude only that the results are not unfavorable to the interaction hypothesis.

The retention exhibited on T-1 falls from 83% at 3 sec. to 50% at 18 sec. The difference between these two proportions is highly significant ($z=3.00$). Only 83% of the Ss could correctly reproduce the trigram shown them 3 sec. later, and this was the first trigram shown. This suggests that degree of learning was low. However, to account for this we have no evidence to choose between failure to hear the letters and letter sequence correctly, as opposed to true forgetting over 3 sec. In any event, with a low degree of learning, STM should be easily interfered with. If interference via PI is responsible for the forgetting on T-1, it must come from associations acquired

in previous laboratory experiments, from conflicting letter-sequence habits, or both.

EXPERIMENT 2

Except for one major change, Exp. 2 was very similar to Exp. 1. The change made was toward increasing the degree of initial learning by using a 2-sec. visual exposure of the items for learning. As previously noted in presenting the results for Exp. 1, recall was very poor for T-2 and T-3 for the 9- and 18-sec. retention intervals. With such low recall it is doubtful that any clear interaction between tests and intervals could have been observed. Therefore, it was believed that by increasing the degree of learning a greater range of forgetting could be observed for T-2 and T-3.

Method

A total of 216 Ss served in Exp. 2. Some had served in previous laboratory experiments on verbal learning and some had not. The three trigrams used in Exp. 1 also were employed in Exp. 2. However, each trigram was presented visually for a 2-sec. learning trial before the retention interval. Each trigram was printed with a lettering set on a 3×5-in. card, the letters being ½ in. high. Following the presentation of a card for 2 sec., E spoke a number as the card was removed and S counted backward by threes as in Exp. 1. Practice in number counting was given prior to presentation of the first trigram.

Each S again served in all three retention-interval conditions. Intervals were completely counterbalanced as were also the three trigrams; thus, 36 Ss were required for each possible interval-trigram order.

Results

The proportions correct at each test for the three retention intervals are shown in Fig. 3. Each proportion is based on 72 Ss. It is apparent that the level of recall is appreciably higher than

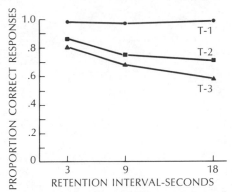

FIG. 3. Retention of single consonant syllables as a function of length of interval and number of prior syllables. Experiment 2.

in Exp. 1. This is due, we believe, to the longer exposure of the item on the learning trial. On T-1 only four responses (out of a possible 216) were incorrect; obviously, therefore, no forgetting is measurable across intervals on T-1. Proportion correct falls sharply from T-1 to T-2, with a continued but smaller decrease from T-2 to T-3. However, the drop from T-2 to T-3 is significant statistically. For each successive block of 18 Ss the interval order is perfectly balanced and each item has occurred equally often with each interval. Therefore, we may treat each group of 18 Ss as an independent experiment, thus giving 12 experiments. We may determine the total correct responses on T-2 and T-3 for each experiment separately, thus deriving two distributions of 12 entries each, one distribution representing number correct on T-2 and the other on T-3. The mean total items recalled per experiment for T-2 was 13.92, for T-3, 12.42. The mean difference (1.50±.54) gives a *t* of 2.78, which, with 11 *df*, is significant beyond the 5% level.

Although the forgetting over time for T-2 and T-3 is not as precipitous as in Exp. 1, it is clearly evident. Since there is no forgetting on T-1, it might appear that Fig. 3 shows the expected interaction between tests and intervals. How-

ever, such a conclusion is unwarranted. Whether or not forgetting "above" 100% correct occurred across intervals for T-1 is indeterminate from the correct-response measure. In recording the scores, note was made of all correct responses with latencies of 3 sec. or less. On T-1 almost all responses had latencies shorter than 3 sec. and there was no change in frequency of such responses with increasing intervals. This might be taken to indicate no forgetting across 18 sec. for T-1, hence that the interaction apparent in Fig. 3 is real. Experiment 3 would support such an interpretation.

The fact that Exp. 2 produced a difference between T-2 and T-3 in retention indicated that no "bottom" or steady state of PI had been reached. To test more fully the course of PI as a function of number of prior items, Ss in Exp. 3 were tested on six successive items.

EXPERIMENT 3

Method

A total of 96 Ss was used, divided into two subgroups of 48 each. Two retention intervals were employed, 3 sec. and 18 sec. One subgroup received the retention intervals in the order 3-18-3-18-3-18, and the other in the reverse order. This procedure permitted determination of retention after 3 sec. and after 18 sec. following 0, 1, 2, 3, 4, and 5 previous items.

Six new trigrams were chosen having a Witmer association value of 21%. This was the lowest association value from which six trigrams could be chosen so that no letter was duplicated among the 18 used. The six trigrams were: CXP, GQN, HJL, KBW, SFM, and ZTD. Six different orders of the trigrams were used such that each trigram occurred equally often on each successive test and, of course, equally often with each retention interval for each subgroup. None of the Ss used had served previously in laboratory experiments of verbal learning. The presentation procedures were exactly the same as in Exp. 2.

Results

The proportions of correct responses for both interval patterns are combined in Fig. 4. In this figure the six successive tests are given along the abscissa, with one curve representing retention after 3 sec. and the other retention after 18 sec. The trend of proactive interference which was initiated by the three tests in Exp. 2 is extended and clarified by Fig. 4. It may be noted that retention on T-1 is lower than in Exp. 2 for the 3-sec. interval. Since the procedures were identical in the two experiments, the differences must arise from the samples of Ss and from differences in materials. Actually, the trigrams of Exp. 2 had lower association value than those of Exp. 3. Whatever the cause, it is clear that degree of learning is lower in Exp. 3 than in Exp. 2. This unexpected turn of events, however, produces the very desirable effect of removing any problem of a "ceiling" effect in response measurement, at least for Tests 2 through 6.

It may be noted first that the recall on the very first item presented Ss does not differ for the 3-sec. and the 18-sec. retention intervals. However, with each successive test the differences increase, thus demonstrating the interaction between tests (number of prior interfering associations) and length of retention interval. Severe PI builds up over 18 sec. with successive tests but this does not happen over 3 sec. For T-1 through T-6, the z's for the difference between proportions for 3 and 18 sec. are: .47, 1.17, 2.17, 2.17, 4.51, and 4.23.

Significant forgetting is shown for the 3-sec. interval between T-1 and T-4 ($z = 2.33$). The rise between T-4 and T-5 is not significant statistically but may indicate that practice effects are more than counteracting interference effects produced by prior tests (see later).

The question as to whether a steady state of a constant amount of PI is being

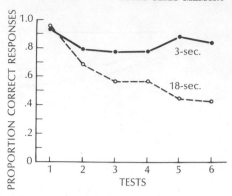

Fig. 4. Retention as a function of number of prior syllables and length of retention interval. Experiment 3.

approached in the 18-sec. curve is not clearly answered by Fig. 4. The question can be more easily answered by replotting Fig. 4 to separate the two independent groups. That is, the 3-sec. curve in Fig. 4 is based on two different groups of Ss, one having the 3-18-3-18-3-18 order of intervals, the other the reverse. We may, therefore, plot the 3- and 18-sec. curves separately for each group. This is done in Fig. 5. The solid lines represent the group given the 3-18 etc. order, the dotted lines representing the group given the reverse order. The filled circles represent the 3-sec. retention, the open circles the 18-sec. retention.

For the 18-sec. curves, the 3-18 Group shows no evidence of leveling off and the 18-3 Group shows only slight evidence of negative acceleration. In short, it would appear that extrapolation of these curves beyond the six tests used would give further continued larger and larger decrements in recall over 18 sec. That this is not so apparent in Fig. 4 appears to be due to the fact that this figure combines two groups of slightly different ability levels. It also should be noted that for both groups there is a rise in retention between the second and third tests for the 3-sec. interval. Although neither rise is significant statistically, the trend

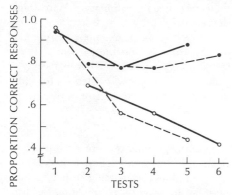

Fig. 5. Retention as a function of number of prior syllables and length of retention interval (solid circles, 3 sec.; open circles, 18 sec.) for Ss having intervals in the order 3-18-3-18-3-18 (solid lines) and in the reverse order (dotted lines). Experiment 3.

may be reliable in view of the Peterson-Peterson data shown in Fig. 1 where performance does systematically improve as a function of successive tests for short retention intervals.

Discussion

The results of the present experiments give strong support to the presumption that short-term retention of single items and long-term retention of lists of items are subject to the same laws of proactive inhibition. The parallelism of the results for STM and LTM when common variables are manipulated may be briefly summarized.

(1) In LTM, number of potential interfering associations and amount of PI are directly related. The same relationship occurred in Exps. 2 and 3; reasons for the failure of the evidence from Exp. 1 to support the principle were discussed earlier.

(2) Length of retention interval and magnitude of PI are directly related in LTM given a constant amount of interference. This relationship was observed in all experiments except for T-1 in Exps. 2 and 3, where interference was pre-

sumed to be low, and degree of learning high.

(3) In LTM, combining the effects of the above two variables leads to an interaction between number of potential interfering associations and length of retention interval. The interaction was clearly apparent in Exp. 3.

(4) In LTM, given constant interference, magnitude of PI decreases as degree of learning of list to be recalled increases. The degree of learning was not systematically manipulated in the present studies. However, since there is no reason to believe that auditory presentation intrinsically gives more PI than visual presentation, it may be inferred that the 2-sec. visual presentation in Exp. 2 produced a higher degree of learning than did the shorter auditory presentation in Exp. 1. Greater forgetting was observed in Exp. 1 than in Exps. 2 and 3. However, this is not a "clean" result, since the degree of learning of potentially interfering items in Exps. 2 and 3 would be higher than that of comparable items in Exp. 1. Nevertheless, the forgetting on T-1 over 18-sec. in Exp. 1 may be taken as an indication that the lower the degree of learning of the item to be recalled the more retention is influenced by proactive interference from sources outside the immediate experimental situation (associations developed in previous experiments or "natural" letter-sequence associations). It is a fact that on T-1 in Exp. 1 the intrusion of letters increased from 5% to 8% to 14% of all letters given for the 3-, 9-, and 18-sec. intervals, respectively. This suggests a recovery over time of interfering associations.

No data on letter intrusions occurring for tests beyond T-1 have been given. The reason for this is simply that by the nature of the designs used it is impossible to isolate variables which may be involved in producing intrusions. In the present studies, time between successive recalls differ; degree of learning of items given previously differ for different intervals; whether or not a previously presented item was correct or incorrect at recall should influence overt intrusions on subsequent items. If systematic laws concerning evocation of letter intrusions are to be derived, experiments must be explicitly designed for the purpose. For these reasons we have not presented intrusion data.

If the conclusion of the present experiments are sound, that is, the conclusion that the laws of proaction are the same for STM as for LTM, some economy in time may be gained by working out further laws of PI on STM rather than on LTM. For example, interitem similarity (e.g., letter duplication) should clearly influence STM. But there is reason to believe that this relationship may be complex. Specifically, in the present results it was noted that many intrusions consisted of a letter from a previous item replacing a letter at recall which occupied the same serial position, e.g., the middle letter. This suggests the operation of an A-B, A-C interference paradigm in which A is the common serial position. Such intrusions also represent the evidence needed to support the notion of spontaneous recovery of extinguished or partially extinguished associations over short intervals. If, however, serial position does constitute a common stimulus from item to item, identical letters in the same position for different items may produce a positive effect—i.e., proactive facilitation may result.

Finally, it may be noted that PI measured with a short recall interval (2 sec.) in LTM may disappear with longer intervals (Underwood, 1950). In all the STM studies reported thus far, recall intervals of from 10 sec. to 14 sec. have been used. A reduction in the time allowed for recall may increase the apparent PI, thus allowing work with higher degrees of learning of single items

than has been customary. With high degrees of learning and long recall intervals (as in Exp. 2), no measurement of forgetting is possible for initial items tested. Very short recall intervals might produce systematic evidence for forgetting for such degrees of learning.

SUMMARY

Three experiments were performed to determine the relationship between certain variables influencing proactive inhibition in long-term retention of lists of verbal items and the influence of these variables on short-term retention of single items. More particularly, retention of single items over 18 sec. should, if the laws of long-term retention are applied, decrease with number of previous items to which S has been exposed. In addition, amount of forgetting should be a direct joint function of number of previous items and length of the retention interval.

In Exp. 1 each S was presented consonant syllables singly, with retention being measured after 3, 9, and 18 sec. Forgetting of the first item presented (T-1) was less than for the second (T-2) or third (T-3) item, but forgetting of the latter (T-2 vs. T-3) did not differ. On all three tests forgetting was directly related to length of retention interval, but no interaction was evident between number of previous items and length of retention interval.

In Exp. 2 a higher degree of initial learning of the items was achieved. Forgetting increased directly as a function of number of previous items presented. The predicted interaction was indeterminate since retention was essentially 100% on T-1 for all retention intervals.

Experiment 3 tested retention of six successive items over 3- and 18-sec. intervals. Retention after 3 sec. showed an initial drop and then a rise over the six tests, the rise suggesting a practice effect. Forgetting over 18 sec. increased directly from T-1 to T-6 and there was no indication that a constant amount of proactive interference had been reached. The interaction between length of retention interval and number of potential proactively interfering items was very evident.

The results were interpreted to mean that proactive inhibition in short-term memory of single items follows the same laws as proactive inhibition in long-term memory of lists of items.

BRIGGS, G. E. Acquisition, extinction and recovery functions in retroactive inhibition. *J. exp. Psychol.*, 1954, **47**, 285-93.

MELTON, A. W. Discussion of Professor Peterson's paper. In C. N. Cofer (Ed.) *Problems and processes in verbal behavior and learning.* New York: McGraw-Hill, 1963.

MURDOCK, B. B., JR. The retention of individual items. *J. exp. Psychol.*, 1961, **62**, 618-25.

PETERSON, L. R. Immediate memory: Data and theory. In C. N. Cofer (Ed.) *Problems and processes in verbal behavior and learning.* New York: McGraw-Hill, 1963.

PETERSON, L. R., AND PETERSON, M. J. Short-term retention of individual verbal items. *J. exp. Psychol.*, 1959, **58**, 193-8.

POSTMAN, L. The present status of interference theory. In C. N. Cofer (Ed.) *Verbal learning and verbal behavior.* New York: McGraw-Hill, 1961.

POSTMAN, L. Short-term memory and incidental learning. Paper read at ONR conference, Ann Arbor, Michigan, February, 1962.

POSTMAN, L., AND RILEY, D. A. Degree of learning and interserial interference in retention. *Univer. Calif. Publ. Psychol.*, 1959, **8**, 271-396.

UNDERWOOD, B. J. The effect of successive interpolations on retroactive and proactive inhibition. *Psychol. Monogr.*, 1945, **59**, No. 3.

UNDERWOOD, B. J. Retroactive and proactive inhibition after five and forty-eight hours. *J. exp. Psychol.*, 1948, **38**, 29-38.

UNDERWOOD, B. J. Proactive inhibition with increased recall time. *Amer. J. Psychol.*, 1950, **63**, 594-9.

UNDERWOOD, B. J. Interference and forgetting. *Psychol. Rev.*, 1957, **64**, 49-60.

UNDERWOOD, B. J., AND SCHULZ, R. W. *Meaningfulness and verbal learning.* Philadelphia: Lippincott, 1960.

29 / Implications of Short-term Memory for a General Theory of Memory [1]

ARTHUR W. MELTON, *University of Michigan*

Memory has never enjoyed even a small fraction of the interdisciplinary interest that has been expressed in symposia, discoveries, and methodological innovations during the last five years. Therefore, it seems probable that the next ten years will see major, perhaps even definitive, advances in our understanding of the biochemistry, neurophysiology, and psychology of memory, especially if these disciplines communicate with one another and seek a unified theory. My thesis is, of course, that psychological studies of human short-term memory, and particularly the further exploitation of new techniques for investigating human short-term memory, will play an important role in these advances toward a general theory of memory. Even now, some critical issues are being sharpened by such observations.

The confluence of forces responsible for this sanguine prediction about future progress is reflected in this AAAS program on memory (see other articles in this issue of this JOURNAL). Advances in biochemistry and neurophysiology are permitting the formulation and testing

From the *Journal of Verbal Learning and Verbal Behavior*, 1963, **2**, 1-21, with permission of the author and publisher, Academic Press, Inc.

1. This paper comprises, in substance, the author's Vice-Presidential Address to Section I (Psychology) of the American Association for the Advancement of Science, 1962. The author is particularly indebted to the Center for Human Learning, University of California, Berkeley, where a research appointment during the Fall semester of 1962-1963 gave the freedom from academic routine and the stimulating discussions that led to the repetition of the Hebb experiment and also supported the preparation of this paper. Early exploratory studies on short-term memory and the experiment on the recall of different sized verbal units were supported by Project MICHIGAN under Department of the Army Contract DA-36-039-SC-78801, administered by the United States Army Signal Corps. Reproduction for any purpose of the United States Government is permitted.

of meaningful theories about the palpable stuff that is the correlate of the memory trace as an hypothetical construct (Deutsch, 1962; Gerard, 1963; Thomas, 1962). In this work there is heavy emphasis on the *storage* mechanism and its properties, especially the consolidation process, and it may be expected that findings here will offer important guide lines for the refinement of the psychologist's construct once we are clear as to what our human performance data say it should be.

Within psychology several developments have focused attention on memory. In the first place, among learning theorists there is a revival of interest in the appropriate assumptions to be made about the characteristics of the memory traces (engrams, associations, bonds, $_sH_r$'s) that are the products of experiences and repetitions of experiences. Thus, Estes (1960) has questioned the validity of the widespread assumption (e.g., Hull, 1943; Spence, 1955) that habit strength grows incrementally over repetitions, and has proposed an all-or-none conception as an alternative. More recently, he has examined (Estes, 1962) in detail the varieties of the incremental and all-or-none conceptions and the evidence related to them. Already, some defenders of the incremental concept (Jones, 1962; Keppel and Underwood, 1962; Postman, 1963) have taken issue with Estes' conclusions, and it would appear that this fundamental question about memory will loom large in theory and experiments for some time to come. At a somewhat different level, the revival of experimental and theoretical interest in the notion of perseveration or consolidation of the memory trace (Glickman, 1961), and attempts to embody it in a general theory of learning (Hebb, 1949; Walker, 1958), have also focused attention on a theory of memory as a fundamental component of a theory of learning.

A second strong stimulus to research on memory from within psychology are several findings of the last few years that have forced major revisions in the interference theory of forgetting and consequently a renaissance of interest in it (Postman, 1961). First, there was the discovery by Underwood (1957) that proactive inhibition had been grossly underestimated as a source of interference in forgetting. Then, the unlearning factor as a component of retroactive inhibition was given greater credibility by the findings of Barnes and Underwood (1959). And finally, the joint consideration of the habit structure of the individual prior to a new learning experience, the compatibility or incompatibility of the new learning with that structure, and the unlearning factor (among others) led to the formulation of the interference theory of forgetting in terms that made it applicable to all new learning (Melton, 1961; Postman, 1961; Underwood and Postman, 1960). Thus, this development focuses attention on the interactions of memory traces during learning as well as their interactions at the time of attempted retrieval or utilization in recognition, recall, or transfer.

But perhaps the most vigorous force directing attention within psychology to the need for a general theory of memory is the spate of theorizing and research on immediate and short-term memory during the last five years. In 1958, and increasingly thereafter, the principal journals of human learning and performance have been flooded with experimental investigations of human short-term memory. This work has been characterized by strong theoretical interests, and sometimes strong statements, about the nature of memory, the characteristics of the memory trace, and the relations between short-term memory and the memory that results from multiple repetitions. The contrast with the preceding thirty years is striking. During those years most research on short-term memory was concerned with the memory span as a capacity variable, and no more. It is always dangerous to be an historian about the last five or ten years, but I venture to say that Broadbent's *Perception and Communication* (1958), with its emphasis on short-term memory as a major factor in human information-processing performance, played a key role in this development. Fortunately, many of the others who have made important methodological and substantive contributions to this analysis of short-term memory have presented their most recent findings and thoughts in these Meetings on Memory, and they thus adequately document my assessment of the vigor and importance of this recent development. Therefore I will refrain from further documentation and analysis at this point, since the impact of some of these findings on our theory of memory is my main theme.

THE DOMAIN OF A THEORY OF MEMORY

A theory of memory is becoming important for a number of different reasons, and somehow all of these reasons properly belong to a comprehensive theory of memory. Its storage mechanism is the principal concern of biochemists and neurophysiologists; the morphology of its storage—whether as a multiplexed trace system with one trace per repetition, or a single trace system subjected to incremental changes in "strength" by repetition—is becoming a principal concern of learning theorists; its susceptibility to inhibition, interference, or confusion both at the time of new trace formation and at the time of attempted trace retrieval or utilization is the concern of forgetting and transfer theorists; and the perhaps unique properties of its manifestation in immediate and short-term retention is the principal concern of psychologists interested in human information-processing performance. One

knows intuitively that all of these different approaches emphasize valid questions or issues that must be encompassed by a general theory of memory, but nowhere—with perhaps the exception of Gomulicki's (1953) historical-theoretical monograph on memory-trace theory—will one find explicit systematic consideration of these several different facets of the problem of memory.

Since my present intention is to marshal some data relevant to one of the main issues in a general theory of memory—namely, the question of whether single-repetition, short-term memory and multiple-repetition, long-term memory are a dichotomy or points on a continuum—I feel compelled to discuss briefly what I believe to be the proper domain of a theory of memory and to differentiate it from a theory of learning.

After some exclusions that need not concern us here, learning may be defined as the modification of behavior as a function of experience. Operationally, this is translated into the question of whether (and, if so, how much) there has been a change in behavior from Trial n to Trial $n+1$. Any attribute of behavior that can be subjected to counting or measuring operations can be an index of change from Trial n to Trial $n+1$, and therefore an index of learning. Trials n and $n+1$ are, of course, the presentation and test trials of a so-called test of immediate memory or they may be any trial in a repetitive learning situation and any immediately subsequent trial. By convention among psychologists, the change from Trial n to Trial $n+1$ is referred to as a learning change when the variable of interest is the ordinal number of Trial n and not the temporal interval between Trial n and Trial $n+1$, and the change from Trial n to Trial $n+1$ is referred to as a *retention* change when the variable of interest is the interval, and the events during the interval, between Trial n and Trial $n+1$. Learning and retention observations generally imply that the characteristics of the task, situation, or to-be-formed associations remain the same from Trial n to Trial $n+1$. When any of these task or situation variables are deliberately manipulated as independent variables between Trial n and Trial $n+1$, the object of investigation is *transfer* of learning, i.e., the availability and utilization of the memorial products of Trial n in a "different" situation.

Now, these operational definitions of learning, retention, and transfer are completely aseptic with respect to theory, and I think it is important to keep them so. In part, this is because it is useful to keep in mind the fact that *learning* is never observed directly; it is always an inference from an observed change in performance from Trial n to Trial $n+1$. Furthermore—and this is the important point for theory—the observed change in performance is always a confounded reflection of three theoretically separable events: (i) the events on Trial n that result in something being stored for use on Trial $n+1$; (ii) the storage of this product of Trial n during the interval between Trials n and $n+1$; and (iii) the events on Trial $n+1$ that result in retrieval and/or utilization of the stored trace of the events on Trial n. For convenience, these three theoretically separable events in an instance of learning will be called *trace formation, trace storage*, and *trace utilization*.

Obviously, a theory of learning must encompass these three processes. However, it must also encompass other processes such as those unique to the several varieties of selective learning and problem solving. Some advantages will accrue, therefore, if the domain of a general theory of memory is considered to be only a portion of the domain of a theory of learning; specifically, that portion concerned with the *storage* and *retrieval* of the residues of demonstrable instances of association formation.

This seems to me to fit the historical schism between learning theories and research on memory and the formal recognition of this distinction may well assist in avoiding some misconceptions about the scope of a theory of memory. Historically, our major learning theories have not felt compelled to include consideration of the question whether storage of the residue of a learning experience (Trial n) is subject to autonomous decay, autonomous consolidation through reverberation, or to even consider systematically the memory-span phenomenon. On the other hand, much of the controversy between learning theorists surrounds the question of the necessary and sufficient conditions for association (or memory trace) formation. And even though most learning theories must say something about the conditions of transfer, or utilization of traces, they do not always include explicit consideration of the interference theory of forgetting or alternative theories. As for those who have been concerned with memory theory, they have, following Ebbinghaus (1885), employed the operations of rote learning, thus avoiding in so far as possible the problems of selective learning and insuring the contiguous occurrence of stimulus and response under conditions that demonstrably result in the formation of an association. Their emphasis has been on the storage and retrieval or other utilization of that association, i.e., of the residual trace of it in the central nervous system (CNS), and on the ways in which frequency of repetition and other learning affect such storage and retrieval.

The implication of this restriction on the domain of a theory of memory is that the theory will be concerned with post-perceptual traces, i.e., memory traces, and not with pre-perceptual traces, i.e., stimulus traces. It seems to me necessary to accept the notion that stimuli may affect the sensorium for a brief time and also the directly involved CNS segments, but that they may not get "hooked up," associated, or encoded with central or peripheral response components, and may not, because of this failure of being responded to, become a part of a memory-trace system. This view is supported by the recent work of Averbach and Coriell (1961), Sperling (1960), and Jane Mackworth (1962) which shows that there is a very-short-term visual pre-perceptual trace which suffers rapid decay (complete in .3 to .5 sec.). Only that which is reacted to during the presentation of a stimulus or during this post-exposure short-term trace is potentially retrievable from memory. While it is not necessary to my argument to defend this boundary for memory theory, because if I am wrong the slack will be taken up in a more inclusive theory of learning, it is of some interest that it is accepted by Broadbent (1963) and that it is consistent with a wealth of recent research on "incidental learning" in human subjects (Postman, 1964).

What, then, are the principal issues in a theory of memory? These are about either the storage or the retrieval of traces. In the case of the storage of traces we have had four issues.[2] The first is whether memory traces should be given the characteristic of *autonomous decay* over time, which was dignified by Thorndike (1913) as the Law of Disuse and which recently has been vigorously defended by Brown (1958). The antithesis is, of course, the notion that associations, once established, are permanent—a position initially formulated by McGeoch (1932) and incorporated in a radical form in Guthrie's (1935) theory of learning.

The second storage issue is again an hypothesis about an autonomous process, but one involving the *autonomous enhancement* (fixation, consolidation) of the

memory trace, rather than decay. The hypothesis was first formulated in the perseveration theory of Müller and Pilzecker (1900), with emphasis on the autonomous enhancement, or strengthening, of a memory trace if it was permitted to endure without interruption. As such, the emphasis was on a property of automatic "inner repetition" if repetition and duration are given a trade-off function in determining the strength of traces. More recently, the hypothesis has been that the memory trace established by an experience *requires* consolidation through autonomous reverberation or perseveration if it is to become a stable structural memory trace in the CNS (Deutsch, 1962; Gerard, 1963; Glickman, 1961; Hebb, 1949). Presumably, the alternative view is that every experience establishes a structural memory trace without the necessity of consolidation through reverberation or perseveration, but also without denying that such reverberation or perseveration, if permitted, may strengthen the trace.

The third issue about storage is the one previously referred to as *morphological* (at the molecular level) in our brief reference to the current controversy about the all-or-none versus the incremental notions of association formation. The all-or-none notion implies that the increment in the probability of response on Trial $n+2$ is a consequence of establishment of independent and different all-or-none trace systems on Trials n and $n+1$; the incremental notion implies that the same trace system is activated in some degree on Trial n and then reactivated and strengthened on Trial $n+1$. It is, of course, possible that both notions could be true.

2. For the purposes of this discussion, I am ignoring the hypothetical property of autonomous, dynamic changes within memory traces in the directions specified by gestalt laws (Koffka, 1935). While the need for such an hypothetical property is not yet a dead issue (Duncan, 1960; Lovibond, 1958), it has had very little support since the classical treatment of the matter by Hebb and Foord (1945).

The fourth issue about trace storage is actually one that overlaps the issues about retrieval or utilization of traces, and is perhaps the most critical current issue. This is the question whether there are two kinds of memory storage or only one. A duplex mechanism has been postulated by Hebb (1949), Broadbent (1958), and many others, and on a variety of grounds, but all imply that one type of storage mechanism is involved in remembering or being otherwise affected by an event just recently experienced, i.e., "immediate" or short-term memory for events experienced once, and that a different type is involved in the recall or other utilization of traces established by repetitive learning experiences, i.e., long-term memory or habit. Since a clean distinction between "immediate" memory and short-term memory is not possible (Melton, 1963), we shall henceforward refer to these two manifestations of memory as short-term memory (STM) and long-term memory (LTM).

Some principal contentions regarding the differences between the two memory mechanisms are that: (a) STM involves "activity" traces, while LTM involves "structural" traces (Hebb, 1949; 1961); (b) STM involves antonomous decay, while STM involves irreversible, non-decaying traces (Hebb, 1949); and (c) STM has a fixed capacity that is subject to overload and consequent loss of elements stored in it, for nonassociative reasons, while LTM is, in effect, infinitely expansible, with failure of retrieval attributable mainly to incompleteness of the cue to retrieval or to interference from previously or subsequently learned associations (Broadbent, 1958; 1963). On the other hand, the monistic view with respect to trace storage is one which, in general, accepts the characteristics of LTM storage as the characteristics of STM storage as well, and thus ascribes to the traces of events that occur only

once the same "structural" properties, the same irreversibility, the same susceptibility to associational factors in retrieval, as are ascribed to LTM.

The bridge to the theoretical problems of trace retrieval and utilization as major components of a theory of memory is obviously wrought by the issue of memory as a dichotomy or a continuum. Those who accept a dichotomy do so on the basis of data on retention, forgetting, or transfer that suggest two distinct sets of conditions for retrieval and utilization of traces; those who accept a continuum do so on the basis of data that suggest a single set of conditions or principles.

The history of our thought about the problems of retrieval and utilization of traces reveals three main issues. The first is the question of the dependence of the retrieval on the completeness of the reinstatement on Trial $n+1$ of the stimulating situation present on Trial n. Psychologists have formulated several principles in an attempt to describe the relevant observations, but all of them may be subsumed under a principle which asserts that the probability of retrieval will be a decreasing function of the amount of stimulus change from Trial n to Trial $n+1$. Changes in directly measured and manipulated cue stimuli, like the CS in a classical conditioning experiment, that result in decrement in response probability are generally referred to a sub-principle of stimulus generalization (Mednick and Freedman, 1960); changes in contextual stimuli that result in forgetting are usually referred to a sub-principle of altered stimulating conditions or altered set (McGeoch and Irion, 1952); and stimulus changes that occur in spite of all attempts to hold the stimulating situation constant are referred to a sub-principle of stimulus fluctuation (Estes, 1955). Since these are all principles of transfer, when they are employed to interpret failure of retrieval on Trial $n+1$, it is clear that all principles of transfer of learning, whether they emphasize the occurrence of retrieval in spite of change or the failure of retrieval in spite of some similarity, are fundamental principles of trace retrieval and utilization. At this moment I see no necessary difference between the dual- and single-mechanism theories of memory with respect to this factor of stimulus change in retrieval, but there may be one implicit and undetected.

The second issue relates to the interactions of traces. Here, of course, is the focus of the interference theory of forgetting which has, in recent years, led us to accept the notion that retrieval is a function of interactions between prior traces and new traces at the time of the formation of the new traces, as well as interactions resulting in active interference and blocking of retrieval. This theory was given its most explicit early expression in the attack by McGeoch (1932) on the principle of autonomous decay of traces, and has been refined and corrected in a number of ways since then (Postman, 1961). In its present form it accepts the hypothesis of irreversibility of traces and interprets all failures of retrieval or utilization as instances of stimulus change or interference. Therefore, it implicitly accepts a one-mechanism theory of memory. However, it has been recognized (Melton, 1961) that the principal evidence for the theory has come from the study of retrieval following multiple-repetition learning, and that the extension of the theory to STM is not necessarily valid. Since dual-mechanism theorists assert that retrieval in STM is subject to disruption through overloading, but not through associative interference, a prime focus of memory theory becomes the question of associative interference effects in STM.

A third important issue related to retrieval is the relationship between repetition and retrieval probability. While the fact of a strong correlation between repetition and probability of retrieval seems not to be questionable, there are two important questions about repetition that a theory of memory must encompass. The first of these is the question of whether repetition multiplies the number of all-or-none traces or whether it produces incremental changes in the strength of a trace. This has already been listed as a problem in storage, but it is obvious that the alternative notions about storage have important implications for the ways in which repetitions may be manipulated to increase or decrease probability of retrieval. The second is the question of whether there is a fundamental discontinuity between the characteristics of traces established by a single repetition and those established by multiple repetitions (or single repetitions with opportunity for consolidation). This appears to be the contention of the dual-mechanism theorists; whereas, a continuum of the effects of repetition in the establishment of "structural," permanent traces seems to be the accepted position of the single-mechanism theorists.

In summary so far, when the domain of a theory of memory is explicitly confined to the problems of the storage and retrieval of memory traces, it becomes possible to formulate and examine some of the major theoretical issues under the simplifying assumption that the formation of the associations or memory traces has already occurred. Then it becomes clear that the conflicting notions with respect to the properties of trace storage and the conflicting notions with respect to the principal determinants of trace retrieval, or failure thereof, converge on the more fundamental issue of the unitary or dual nature of the storage mechanism. My plan is to examine these alleged differences between STM and LTM in the light of some recent studies of human short-term memory, and then return to a summary of the implications these studies seem to have for the major issues in a general theory of memory.

STM AND LTM: CONTINUUM OR DICHOTOMY?

The contrasting characteristics of STM and LTM that have led to the hypothesis that there are two kinds of memory have not, to my knowledge, been considered systematically by any memory theorist, although Hebb (1949), Broadbent (1957; 1958; 1963), and Brown (1958) have defended the dichotomy.

The decay of traces in immediate memory, in contrast to the permanence, even irreversibility, of the memory traces established through repetitive learning, is the most universally acclaimed differentiation. For Hebb (1949) this rapid decay is a correlate of the non-structural, i.e., "activity," nature of the single perception that is given neither the "fixation" effect of repetition nor the opportunity for "fixation" through reverberation. For Broadbent (1957; 1958) and Brown (1958) this autonomous decay in time is a property of the postulated STM mechanism, and attempts have been made (e.g., Conrad and Hille, 1958) to support the notion that time per se is the critical factor in decay. Obviously, this autonomous decay can be postponed by rehearsal—recirculating through the short-term store (Broadbent, 1958)—and Brown (1958) has maintained that such rehearsal has no strengthening effect on the structural trace. However, the decay of a specific trace begins whenever rehearsal is prevented by distraction or overloading of the short-term store (Broadbent, 1957; 1958). A corollary of the decay process, by dislodging the trace from the short-term store, is not dependent on new learning and therefore not on the associative interference principles which account for most if not all of the forgetting of events that reach

the long-term store through repetition, reverberation, or both (Broadbent, 1963).

These characteristics contrast sharply with those attributed to LTM by the interference theory of forgetting which has dominated our thinking since McGeoch's (1932) classical attack on the Law of Disuse and which has gained new stature as a consequence of recent refinements (Melton, 1961; Postman, 1961). This theory implies: (a) that traces, even those that result from single repetitions, are "structural" in Hebb's sense, and are permanent except as overlaid by either the recovery of temporarily extinguished stronger competing traces or by new traces; and (b) that all persistent and progressive losses in the retrievability of traces are to be attributed to such associative interference factors, and not to decay or to a combination of nonassociative disruption plus decay. And, as a consequence of these two implications it is assumed that the effect of repetition on the strength of the single type of trace is a continuous monotonic process. On this basis a continuum is assumed to encompass single events or sequential dependencies between them when these events are well within the span of immediate memory and also complex sequences of events, such as in serial and paired-associate lists, that are far beyond the span of immediate memory and thus require multiple repetitions for mastery of the entire set of events or relations between them.

My discussion of the question: "STM or LTM; continuum or dichotomy" will therefore examine some experimental data on STM to see (a) whether they are interpretable in terms of the interference factors known to operate in LTM, and (b) whether the durability of memory for sub-span and supra-span to-be-remembered units is a continuous function of repetitions.

The reference experiments that provide the data of interest are those re-

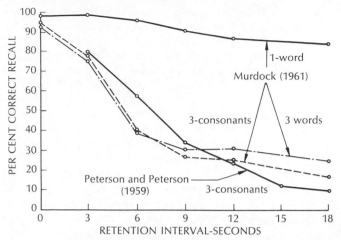

FIG. 1. Percentage frequency of completely correct recall of 3-consonant trigrams (Peterson and Peterson, 1959; Murdock, 1961), and 1-word and 3-word units (Murdock, 1961).

cently devised by Peterson and Peterson (1959) and Hebb (1961), with major emphasis on the former. While a number of ingenious techniques for investigating STM have been invented during the last few years, I believe that the Petersons' method is the key to integration of retention data on immediate memory, STM, and LTM. This is because, as you will see, it can be applied to to-be-remembered units in the entire range from those well below the memory span to those well above it, and the control and manipulation of duration and frequency of presentation are essentially continuous with those traditionally employed in list memorization.

In what must have been a moment of supreme skepticism of laboratory dogma, not unlike that which recently confounded the chemist's dogma that the noble gases are nonreactive (Abelson, 1962), Peterson and Peterson (1959) determined the recallability of single trigrams, such as X-J-R, after intervals of 3, 6, 9, 12, 15, and 18 sec. The trigrams were presented auditorily in 1 sec., a 3-digit number occurred during the next

second, and S counted backward by 3's or 4's from that number until, after the appropriate interval, he received a cue to recall the trigram. The S was given up to 14 sec. for the recall of the trigram, thus avoiding any time-pressure in the retrieval process. The principal measure of retention was the frequency of completely correct trigrams in recall.

The results of this experiment are shown in Fig. 1. It is noteworthy that the curve has the Ebbinghausian form, even though the maximum interval is only 18 sec., and that there is an appreciable amount of forgetting after only 3 and 6 sec. Other observations reported by the Petersons permit us to estimate that the recall after zero time interval, which is the usual definition of immediate memory, would have been 90%, which is to say that in 10% of the cases the trigram was misperceived, so that the forgetting is actually not as great as it might appear to be. Even with this correction for misperception, however, the retention after 18 sec. would be only about 20%, which is rather startling when one remembers that these trigrams were well below the memory span of the college students who served as Ss.

The rapid deterioration of performance over time is not inconsistent with the decay theory, nor is it necessarily inconsistent with the notion that traces from single occurrences of single items are on a continuum with traces from multiple items learned through repetition. However, additional data with the same method were soon forthcoming. Murdock (1961) first replicated the Peterson and Peterson experiment with 3-consonant trigrams, and then repeated all details of the experiment except that, in one study he used single common words drawn from the more frequent ones in the Thorndike-Lorge word lists, and in another study he used word triads, i.e., three unrelated common words, as the to-be-remembered unit.

Murdock's results from these three experiments are shown alongside the Petersons' results in Figure 1. His replication of the Petersons' study with trigrams gave remarkably similar results. Of considerable significance, as we will see later, is his finding that single words show less forgetting than did the trigrams, but that *some* forgetting occurs with even such simple units. Finally, the most seminal fact for theory in these experiments is his discovery that word triads act like 3-consonant trigrams in short-term retention.

Murdock's data strongly suggested that the critical determinant of the slope of the short-term retention function was the number of Millerian (1956) "chunks" in the to-be-remembered unit. Of even greater importance, from my point of view was the implication that, other things being equal, the rate of forgetting of a unit presented once is a function of the amount of intra-unit interference, and that this intra-unit interference is a function of the number of encoded chunks within the item rather than the number of physical elements, such as letters, or information units.

The first of several projected experimental tests of this hypothesis has been completed.[3] The to-be-remembered units were 1, 2, 3, 4, or 5 consonants.

The unit, whatever its size, was presented visually for 1 sec., and read off aloud by S. Then .7 sec. later a 3-digit number was shown for 1 sec. and removed. The S read off the number and then counted backward aloud by 3's or 4's until a visual cue for recall, a set of 4 asterisks, was shown. The delayed retention intervals were 4, 12, and 32 sec., and a fourth condition involved recall after only .7 sec., hereafter referred to as the zero interval. The Ss were given 8 sec. for the recall of each item. In the course of the experiment each S was tested four times at each combination of unit size and interval for a total of 80 observations. Every condition was represented in each of 4 successive blocks of 20 observations, and there was partial counterbalancing of conditions within the blocks and of to-be-remembered units between the blocks. Through my error, the to-be-remembered units of each specific size were not counterbalanced across the four retention intervals. Thanks only to the power of the variable we were investigating, this did not, as you will see, materially affect the orderliness of the data.

The results for the last two blocks of trials are shown in Figure 2. Again, the measure of recall performance is the percentage of completely correct recalls of the to-be-remembered unit, i.e., the single consonant had to be correct when only one was presented, all five consonants had to be correct and in the proper order when the 5-consonant unit was presented. The same relationships hold when Ss are not as well-practiced in the task, i.e., in Blocks 1 and 2, although the absolute amounts of forgetting are greater. The data in Figure 2 are to be preferred to those for the earlier stages of practice, because all five curves in this figure have their origin very near to

3. This study and a subsequent one are graduate research projects of David Wulff and Robert G. Crowder, University of Michigan, and will be reported under the title: Melton, A. W., Crowder, R. G., and Wulff, D., *Short-term memory for individual items with varying numbers of elements.*

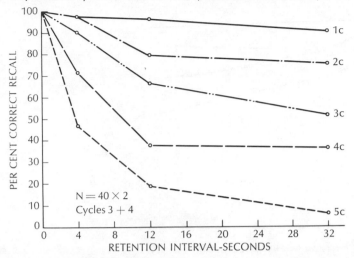

Fig. 2. Percentage frequency of completely correct recall of units of 1 to 5 consonants with well-practiced Ss (Blocks 3 and 4).

100% recall. That is, in all cases it is possible to assume that Ss had, in fact, learned the to-be-remembered unit during the 1-sec. presentation interval.

Aside from the self-evident generalization that the slope of the short-term forgetting curve increases as a direct function of the number of elements in the to-be-remembered unit, two features of these data are worthy of special attention. First, it should be noted that the slope of the curve for the 3-consonant units is not as steep as was reported by both Peterson and Peterson (1959) and by Murdock (1961). We do not know why there is this discrepancy, although it occurs consistently in our work with the Petersons' method.

The other point of interest is the obvious forgetting of the one-consonant unit. This curve looks very much like the one obtained by Murdock for single words. Both findings have significance for theory because they represent instances of forgetting when the intra-unit interference is at a minimum for verbal units. But before giving additional consideration to this point, a further set of data from this experiment needs to be

presented and a more general statement of the observed relationships deserves formulation.

If the increased slopes of the forgetting curves shown in Figure 2 are attributed to an increase in intra-unit interference, it is of some importance to show that the more frequent breakdown of complete recall as one increases the number of letters in the to-be-remembered unit is not merely a breakdown in the sequential dependencies between the letters, but is also reflected in the frequency of correct recall of the first letter of the unit. In Figure 3 are shown the percentages of first-letter recalls in the last two blocks of our experiment. Although they are lacking in the monotonic beauty of the curves for whole units correct, I am willing to accept the generalization that first-letter recall suffers interference as a function of the number of other letters in the to-be-remembered unit. Thus, what Peterson (1963) has called "background conditioning," and is measured by the recall of first letters, and what he has called "cue learning," and is represented by sequential dependencies in recall, are affected alike by the number of elements in the to-be-remembered unit. This is expected in so far as there is functional parallelism between "free" recall and

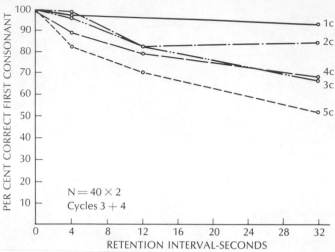

Fic. 3. Percentage frequency of correct recall of the first letter in 1- to 5-consonant units with well-practiced Ss (Blocks 3 and 4).

serial or paired-associate recall with respect to the effect of learning and interference variables (Melton, 1963).

In Figure 4 the results obtained so far have been generalized and extrapolated. This set of hypothetical curves will be used as the conceptual anchor for three points that are related to the question whether short-term and long-term memory are a dichotomy or points on a continuum. The first, and most obvious, point about the figure is that it reaffirms the notion that intra-unit interference is a major factor in the short-term forgetting of sub-span units, but now the parameter is the number of encoded chunks, instead of the number of physical elements or information units. This is consistent with Miller's (1956) cogent arguments for the concept of chunk as the unit of measurement of human information-processing capacities. It is also the unit most likely to have a one-to-one relationship to the memory trace. Obviously, it is also the concept demanded by the parallelism of the findings of Murdock with 1 and 3 words and our findings with 1 to 5 consonants, even though it cannot, of course, be asserted that the

number of elements beyond one in these experiments, be they words or consonants, stand in a one-to-one relationship to the number of chunks. Even though the strings of consonants in our experiment were constructed by subtracting from or combining consonant trigrams of Witmer (1935) association values less than 60%, there were surely some easy-to-learn letter sequences and some hard-to-learn letter sequences. That such differences in meaningfulness are correlated with chunkability is well known (Underwood and Schulz, 1960). Also, Peterson, Peterson, and Miller (1961) have shown, although on a limited scale, that the meaningfulness of CVC trigrams is positively correlated with recall after 6 sec. in the Petersons' situation. But perhaps the greatest gain from the use of the chunk as the unit of measurement in formulating the otherwise empirical generalization is a suggestion this yields about how we may get a handle on that intervening variable. It suggests to me that we may be able to establish empirical bench marks for 1, 2, 3, . . ., n chunks in terms of the slopes of short-term memory functions and then use these slopes to calibrate our verbal learning materials in terms of a chunk scale.

The evidence that the slope of the

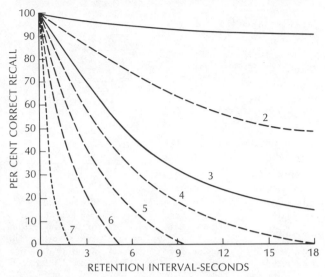

FIG. 4. The expected relationship between the number of recoded units ("chunks") in the to-be-remembered unit, the duration of the short-term retention interval, and the percentage frequency of complete correct recall, when each to-be-remembered unit is presented once, i.e., with just sufficient duration for one completely correct perceptual encoding. The solid-line curves represent some of the empirically determined functions; the dashed lines represent extrapolated functions; the dotted line represents the expected short-term memory function for a to-be-remembered unit that is at memory-span length for the individual S.

short-term forgetting curve increases dramatically as a function of the number of encoded chunks in the unit is evidence against autonomous decay being a major factor, but it does not deny that such decay may occur. It is evidence against decay as a major factor because: (a) a single consonant *was* remembered with very high frequency over a 32-sec. interval filled with numerical operations that surely qualify as overloading and disrupting activities (if one grants that the Petersons' method adequately controls surreptitious rehearsal); and (b) the major portion of the variance in recall is accounted for by intra-unit interference, rather than time. It does not deny that

decay may occur, since there was *some* forgetting of even the single consonant (and of the single word in Murdock's experiment) even though only one "chunk" was involved, and intra-unit interference was at a minimum.

The reason for the forgetting of the single chunk is, I believe, to be found in the other sources of interference in recall in this type of experiment. In the first place, I presume that no one will argue that counting backward aloud is the mental vacuum that interference theory needs to insure the absence of retroactive inhibition in the recall of the to-be-remembered unit, nor is it necessarily the least interfering, and at the same time rehearsal-preventing, activity that can be found for such experiments. However, we must leave this point for future research, because we have none of the systematic studies that must be done on the effects of different methods of filling these short retention intervals, and we also have no evidence, therefore, on the extent to which retroactive interference and intra-unit interference interact.

On the other source of interference which may explain the forgetting of the single chunk—namely, proactive interference (PI)—we do have some evidence. Peterson (1963) has maintained, on the basis of analysis of blocks of trials in the original Peterson and Peterson (1959) study, that there is no evidence for the build-up of proactive inhibition in that experiment, only practice effects. However, this evidence is unconvincing (Melton, 1963) when practice effects are strong, and if it is assumed that proactive inhibition from previous items in the series of tests may build up rapidly but asymptote after only a few such previous items. Such an assumption about a rapidly achieved high steady-state of PI is given some credence by the rapid development of a steady-state in frequency of false-positives in studies of short-term recognition memory (Shepard and Teghtsoonian, 1961).

A second, and powerful, argument for large amounts of PI throughout the Peterson type of experiment is the frequency of overt intrusions from previous units in the series during the attempt to recall an individual unit. Murdock (1961) found such intrusions in his studies of short-term retention of words, and there was the strong recency effect among these intrusions that is to be expected if the steady-state notion is valid. The analysis of such intrusions in studies involving letters rather than words is limited by the identifiability of the source of the intrusions, but all who run experiments with letters become convinced that such intrusions are very common and usually come from the immediately preceding units.[4]

More systematic evidence for strong PI effects in STM in the Petersons' situation is given by Keppel and Underwood (1962). A representative finding is shown in Figure 5. A three-consonant item which is the first item in the series is recalled almost perfectly after as long as 18 sec., and PI builds up rapidly over items, especially for the longer retention interval. These data support the notion

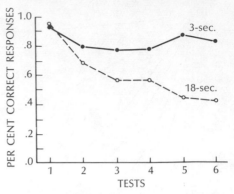

Fig. 5. Percentage frequency of completely correct recall of 3-consonant trigrams after 3 and 18 sec., as a function of the ordinal position of the test in a series of tests. The decline in recall reflects the buildup of proactive inhibition (Keppel and Underwood, 1962).

that there is substantial PI in the Peterson and Peterson experiment on short-term memory for single verbal units. As such, they, as well as the other evidence cited, indicate that the small amount of forgetting of single consonants or single words over short intervals of time may be partly, if not entirely, attributable to the PI resulting from sequential testing of recall of such items. Keppel and Underwood's results do not, however, support the view that the PI reaches a steady state in as few as five items, but this does not necessarily deny the steady-state notion. Also, a careful study of these data and the data on intra-unit interference suggests some strong interactions between PI, intra-unit interference (II), and the retention interval, all of which would support the interference interpretation, but discussion of these interactions would be tedious and unrewarding until properly designed experiments have been performed.

4. Apparent intrusions from preceding to-be-remembered units were very common in the 1- to 5-consonant experiment reported here, but the experimental design did not counterbalance first-order sequence effects over conditions and nothing meaningful can be said about such intrusions except that they occur with substantial frequency.

My conclusion from all this is that there is sufficient direct or inferential evidence for PI, RI, and II in the short-term retention of single sub-span verbal units, and that the PI and potential RI may account for the observed forgetting of one-chunk units, that is, when II is minimal. So much for interference.

The other line of investigation that needs to be considered before the question of continuum versus dichotomy can be properly assessed has to do with the effect of repetition on the short-term memory for sub-span and just supra-span strings of elements or chunks.

The concept of the memory span is rather important in this discussion because it is the boundary between the number of elements, or chunks, that can be correctly reproduced immediately after a single repetition and the number of elements, or chunks, that require two or more repetitions for immediate correct reproduction. Interestingly enough, the short-term forgetting curve for a unit of memory-span length turns out to be the limiting member of the hypothetical family of curves that has been used to generalize the relationship between the slope of the forgetting curve and the number of chunks in the to-be-remembered unit. The extrapolated forgetting curve for a unit of memory-span length is shown as the dotted-line curve of Figure 4.

The origin of this limiting curve on the ordinate will, of course, depend on the statistical definition of the span of immediate memory, but in order to be consistent I have placed it in Figure 4 at or near 100% recall after zero interval. It is also assumed that the presentation time for this and all other smaller numbers of chunks is just sufficient for one perceptual encoding of each element, i.e., for one repetition. For a unit of span length it is not surprising that precipitous decline of completely correct recall to zero is expected when only very short,

but filled, delays are introduced before recall begins. No experiment in the literature fits exactly these operational requirements, but the prediction is a matter of common experience in looking up telephone numbers, and we also have Conrad's (1958) evidence that Ss show a radical reduction in correct dialing of 8-digit numbers when required merely to dial "zero" before dialing the number.

At this point we are brought face to face with the question of the effects of repetition of sub-span and supra-span units on their recall. Such data are important for at least two reasons. In the first place, the argument for a continuum of STM and LTM requires that there be only orderly quantitative differences in the effects of repetition on sub-span and supra-span units. In the second place, if repetition has an effect on the frequency of correct recall of sub-span units, such as consonant trigrams, this must certainly have some significance for the conceptualization of the strength of a memory trace—whether it is all-or-none or cumulative.

The effect of time for rehearsal of a set of items before a filled retention interval was first studied by Brown (1958). His negative results led him to the conclusion that recirculation of information through the temporary memory store merely delays the onset of decay, but does not strengthen the trace. However, the original Peterson & Peterson (1959) report on the retention of consonant trigrams included an experiment which showed a significant effect of instructed rehearsal on short-term retention.

Fortunately, we now have available a report by Hellyer (1962) in which consonant trigrams were given one, two, four, or eight 1-sec. visual presentations before retention intervals of 3, 9, 18, and 27 sec. His data are shown in Figure 6 and require little comment. Obviously, a consonant trigram is remembered better with repetition even though it is com-

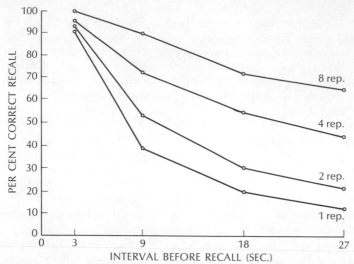

INTERVAL BEFORE RECALL (SEC.)

FIG. 6. Percentage frequency of completely correct recall of 3-consonant trigrams as a function of the frequency of 1-sec. presentations of the trigram before beginning the retention interval (Hellyer, 1962).

pletely and correctly perceived and encoded after only one repetition, as judged by the immediate recall of it. The slopes of the retention curves in our hypothetical family of curves based on the number of chunks in the to-be-remembered unit are, therefore, a joint function of chunks and repetitions. Or perhaps a better say that repetition reduces the number of theoretical statement of this would be to chunks in the to-be-remembered unit. This is why one word and one consonant have the same rate of forgetting.

As for the effect of repetition on just supra-span units, we have no data directly comparable to those of Hellyer for sub-span units, but we have data from a much more severe test of the repetition effect. I refer to the method and data of Hebb's (1961) study in which he disproved to his own satisfaction his own assumption about "activity" traces. In this experiment he presented a fixed set of 24 series of 9-digit numbers. Each of the digits from 1 to 9 was used only once within each to-be-remembered unit. The

series was read aloud to S at the rate of about 1 digit/sec., and S was instructed to repeat the digits immediately in exactly the same order. The unusual feature of the experiment was that exactly the same series of digits occurred on every third trial, i.e., the 3rd, 6th, 9th . . . 24th, the others varying in a random fashion.

His results are shown in Figure 7. Hebb considered the rising curve for the repeated 9-digit numbers, when contrasted with the flat curve for the non-repeated numbers, to be sufficient basis for concluding that some form of structural trace results from a single repetition of an associative sequence of events. Further, he properly considers this to be a demonstration of the cumulative structural effects of repetition under extremely adverse conditions involving large amounts of RI.

Hebb's method in this experiment may well be another important invention in the analysis of human memory. But I was not completely satisfied with his experiment and the reliability of his findings, for reasons that need not be detailed here. As a consequence of these uncertainties, I have repeated and extended Hebb's experiment by giving each

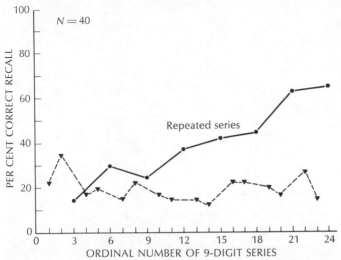

Fig. 7. Percentage frequency of completely correct recall of 9-digit numbers when tested immediately. The "repeated series" was a specific 9-digit sequence that occurred in the 3rd, 6th, 9th . . . 24th position in the series of tests. Other points represent non-repeated 9-digit numbers (Hebb, 1961).

of 32 women Ss two practice numbers and then 80 tests for immediate recall of 9-digit numbers. Within these 80 tests there were 4 instances in which a specific 9-digit number occurred 4 times with 2 other numbers intervening between successive trials, 4 in which a specific number occurred 4 times with 3 intervening numbers, 4 for 4 trials with 5 intervening numbers and 4 for 4 trials with 8 intervening numbers. In addition, there were 16 9-digit numbers that occurred only once. I will not try to describe the interlocking pattern of events that was used to achieve this design, but the design chosen was used in both a forward and backward order for different Ss, and the specific repeated numbers were used equally often under the different spacings of repetitions. Furthermore, within the entire set of 32 different 9-digit numbers used in this experiment, inter-series similarities were minimized by insuring that no more than two digits ever occurred twice in the same order. The numbers

were presented visually for 3.7 sec. and S recorded her response by writing on a 3×5 in. card which contained 9 blocks. Recall began .7 sec. after the stimulus slide disappeared, and 8.8 sec. were allowed for recall.

Unfortunately, my Ss behaved in a somewhat more typical fashion than did Hebb's, in that they showed substantial nonspecific practice effects. This complicates the determination of the effects of specific repetition, because later trials on a particular 9-digit number must always be later in practice than earlier trials, and also because this confounding of specific and nonspecific practice effects is more serious the greater the interval between repetitions of a specific number. This confounding has been eliminated, at least to my satisfaction, by determining the function that seemed to be the most appropriate fit to the practice curve based on first occurrences of specific numbers. This function was then used to correct obtained scores on the 2nd, 3rd, and 4th repetitions of a specific number in a manner and amount appropriate to the expected nonspecific practice effect.

A preferred measure of the effect of repetition in this situation is the mean number of digits correctly recalled in

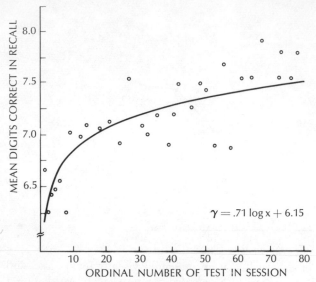

$$\gamma = .71 \log x + 6.15$$

FIG. 8. The nonspecific practice effect in the recall of new and different 9-digit numbers in the course of the experiment.

their proper positions. In Figure 8 is shown the mean number of digits correctly recalled, as a function of ordinal position of the first occurrence of a 9-digit number within the experimental session. This merely confirms my statement about practice effects; exhibits the equation used for corrections for general practice effects; and permits observation of the large variability of mean performance in this type of experiment.

The principal data from the experiment are shown in Figure 9. The effect of repetition of a specific 9-digit number is plotted, the parameter being the number of other different 9-digit numbers that intervened between successive repetitions of the specific number. In these curves the points for first-repetition performance are obtained points, and those for performance on the 2nd, 3rd, and 4th repetitions have been corrected for nonspecific practice effects. In Figure 10 these last data are expressed as gains in performance over performance on the first occurrence of a number. Compa-

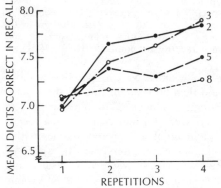

FIG. 9. Mean number of digits correctly recalled, as a function of the number of repetitions of the specific 9-digit number and of the number of other 9-digit numbers that intervened between repetitions. The data points for the first repetition are obtained values; the data points for the second, third, and fourth repetitions reflect corrections for nonspecific practice effects.

rable data for gains in the frequency with which entire 9-digit numbers were correctly recalled show the same relationships.

These data not only confirm the Hebb data, they also add material substance to an argument for a continuum of immediate, short-term, and long-term memory.

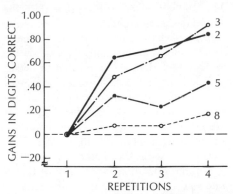

FIG. 10. Mean gains in number of digits correctly recalled, as a function of the number of repetitions of a specific 9-digit number and of the number of other 9-digit numbers that intervened between repetitions. All gain scores have been corrected for nonspecific practice effects.

Just as a continuum theory would have predicted Hebb's results with two intervening numbers between repetitions of a specific number, it also would predict that the repetition effect would be a decreasing function of the number of intervening numbers because between-repetition retroactive inhibition is being increased. Even so, I am not sure that any theory would have predicted that one would need to place as many as 8 other 9-digit numbers in between repetitions of a specific 9-digit number before the repetition effect would be washed out. Surely, the structural memory trace established by a single occurrence of an event must be extraordinarily persistent.

With respect to our hypothetical family of retention curves based on the number of chunks in the to-be-remembered unit, we can now with some confidence say that events which contain chunks beyond the normal memory span can be brought to the criterion of perfect immediate recall by reducing the number of chunks through repetition. If this empirical model involving chunks and repetitions to predict short-term forgetting is valid, it should be possible to show

that a supra-span 9-chunk unit that is reduced to 7 chunks through repetition, would have the short-term forgetting curve of a 7-chunk unit, and one reduced through repetition to a 3-chunk unit should have a 3-chunk short-term forgetting curve. Even though this prediction is probably much too simple-minded, it now requires no stretch of my imagination to conceive of the "immediate" or short-term memory for single units and the memory for memorized supra-span units, like 12 serial nonsense syllables or 8 paired associates, as belonging on a continuum.

IMPLICATIONS

We may now turn to the implications these data on short-term memory seem to me to have for a theory of memory. I will attempt no finely spun theory, because such is neither my talent nor my interest. Also, I can be brief because, aged Functionalist that I am, I would be the first to admit—even insist—that my inferences are stated with confidence only for the storage and retrieval of verbal material demonstrably encoded by adult human Ss.

The duplexity theory of memory storage must, it seems to me, yield to the evidence favoring a continuum of STM and LTM or else come up with an adequate accounting for the evidence presented here. My preference is for a theoretical strategy that accepts STM and LTM as mediated by a single type of storage mechanism. In such a continuum, frequency of repetition appears to be the important independent variable, "chunking" seems to be the important intervening variable, and the slope of the retention curve is the important dependent variable. I am persuaded of this by the orderly way in which repetition operates on both subspan units and supra-span units to increase the probability of retrieval in recall, and also by the parallelism between STM and LTM that is revealed as we look at STM with the conceptual tools of the interference theory of forgetting which was developed from data on LTM.

The evidence that implies a continuum of STM and LTM also relates, of course, to some of the other issues about the characteristics of memory storage. While it is perhaps too early to say that the autonomous decay of traces has no part in forgetting, whether short-term or long-term, I see no basis for assuming that such decay has the extreme rapidity sometimes ascribed to it or for assuming that it accounts for a very significant portion of the forgetting that we all suffer continually and in large amounts. On the contrary, the data from both STM and LTM tempt one to the radical hypothesis that every perception, however fleeting and embedded in a stream of perceptions, leaves its permanent "structural" trace in the CNS.

Insofar as I can understand the implications of the consolidation hypothesis about memory storage, I must concur with Hebb's (1961) conclusion that his experiment demonstrates the fixation of a structural trace by a single repetition of an event and without the benefit of autonomous consolidation processes. In fact, I think that our repetition and extension of his experiment establishes that conclusion even more firmly, because it shows that the retrievability of the trace of the first experience of a specific 9-digit number is a decreasing function of the amount of reuse of the elements in the interval between repetitions. Therefore, as far as our present data go, it seems proper to conclude that a consolidation process extending over more than a few seconds is not a necessary condition for the fixation of a structural trace. This does not, of course, deny that consolidation may be a necessary condition in other types of learning or other types of organism, nor does it deny that types of experience (e.g., Kleinsmith and Kap-

lan, 1963; Walker, 1963) other than the mundane remembering of nonsense strings of letters or words may benefit from such autonomous consolidation processes if they are permitted to occur.

The issue as to whether memory traces are established in an incremental or all-or-none fashion can be refined, but not resolved, on the basis of our observations on short-term memory. In all of the experiments with the Petersons' method, the initial operation was to insure that S encoded, i.e., learned, the to-be-remembered unit in a single 1-sec. presentation of it before the retention interval was introduced. This is "one-trial" learning in a more exact sense than has been true of various attempts to demonstrate the all-or-none principle in associative learning (Postman, 1963). Yet forgetting was rapid and strongly a function of the amount of potential intra-unit interference in the to-be-remembered unit. Also, this unit that was perfectly remembered after one repetition was better remembered after multiple massed repetitions. The proper question in the case of verbal associative learning seems, therefore, to be the characteristics of the trace storage that reflect the effects of repetitions on performance, rather than the question whether such associative connections reach full effective strength in one trial. The question of whether repetitions multiply the number of traces leading to a particular response or produce incremental changes in specific traces seems to me to be subject to direct experimental attack. Perhaps again because of my Functionalist background, I am inclined to believe that future research will show that both the multiplexing of traces and the incremental strengthening of traces results from repetition. Which mode of storage carries the greater burden in facilitating retrieval will depend on the variability of stimulation from repetition to repetition and the appropriateness of the sampling of this prior stimulation at the time of attempted retrieval.

Finally, with respect to the retrieval process, the theory of which is dominated by transfer theory for LTM, it seems that the placing of STM and LTM on a continuum—and the reasons for doing so—forces the interference theory of forgetting to include the prediction of forgetting in STM within its domain. At least, the testing of the theory in that context will extend its importance as a general theory of forgetting, if it survives the tests, and will quickly reveal the discontinuity of STM and LTM, if such is in fact the case.

Whatever may be the outcome of these theoretical and experimental issues in the next few years, of one thing we can be certain at this time. The revival of interest in short-term memory and the new techniques that have been devised for the analysis of short-term memory will enrich and extend our understanding of human memory far beyond what could have been accomplished by the most assiduous exploitation of the techniques of rote memorization of lists of verbal units. In fact, our evidence on STM for near-span and supra-span verbal units suggests that the systematic exploration of the retention of varying sizes of units over short and long time intervals will give new meaning to research employing lists.

ABELSON, P. H. The need for skepticism. *Science*, 1962, **138**, 75.

AVERBACH, E., AND CORIELL, A. S. Short-term memory in vision. *Bell Syst. Tech. J.*, 1961, **40**, 309-28.

BARNES, J. M., UNDERWOOD, B. J. "Fate" of first-list associations in transfer theory. *J. exp. Psychol.*, 1959, **58**, 97-105.

BROADBENT, D. E. A mechanical model for human attention and immediate memory. *Psychol. Rev.*, 1957, **64**, 205-15.

BROADBENT, D. E. *Perception and communication.* New York: Pergamon, 1958.

BROADBENT, D. E. Flow of information within the organism. *J. verb. Learn. verb. Behav.*, 1963, **2**, 34-9.

BROWN, J. Some tests of the decay theory of immediate memory. *Quart. J. exp. Psychol.*, 1958, **10**, 12-21.

CONRAD, R. Accuracy of recall using keyset and telephone dial and the effect of a prefix digit. *J. appl. Psychol.*, 1958, **42**, 285-8.

CONRAD, R., AND HILLE, B. A. The decay theory of immediate memory and paced recall. *Canad. J. Psychol.*, 1958, **12**, 1-6.

DEUTSCH, J. A. Higher nervous function: The physiological bases of memory. *Ann. Rev. Physiol.*, 1962, **24**, 259-86.

DUNCAN, C. P. Controlled fixation of the stimulus-figure in a study of autonomous change in the memory-trace. *Amer. J. Psychol.*, 1960, **73**, 115-20.

EBBINGHAUS, H. *Das Gedächtnis: Untersuchungen zur experimentellen Psychologie.* Leipzig: Duncker & Humbolt, 1885.

ESTES, W. K. Statistical theory of distributional phenomena in learning. *Psychol. Rev.*, 1955, **62**, 369-77.

ESTES, W. K. Learning theory and the new "mental chemistry." *Psychol. Rev.*, 1960, **67**, 207-23.

ESTES, W. K. Learning theory. *Ann. Rev. Psychol.*, 1962, **13**, 107-144.

GERARD, R. W. The material basis of memory. *J. verb. Learn. verb. Behav.*, 1963, **2**, 22-33.

GLICKMAN, S. E. Perseverative neural processes and consolidation of the memory trace. *Psychol. Bull.*, 1961, **58**, 218-33.

GOMULICKI, B. R. The development and present status of the trace theory of memory. *Brit. J. Psychol., Monogr. Suppl.*, 1953, Whole No. 29, 94 pp.

GUTHRIE, E. R. *The psychology of learning.* New York: Harper, 1935.

HEBB, D. O. *The organization of behavior.* New York: Wiley, 1949.

HEBB, D. O. Distinctive features of learning in the higher animal. In J. F. Delafresnaye (Ed.) *Brain mechanisms and learning.* London and New York: Oxford Univ. Press, 1961. Pp. 37-46.

HEBB, D. O., AND FOORD, E. N. Errors of visual recognition and the nature of the trace. *J. exp. Psychol.*, 1945, **35**, 335-48.

HELLYER, S. Supplementary report: Frequency of stimulus presentation and short-term decrement in recall. *J. exp. Psychol.*, 1962, **64**, 650.

HULL, C. L. *Principles of behavior.* New York: Appleton-Century-Crofts, 1943.

JONES, J. E. All-or-none versus incremental learning. *Psychol. Rev.*, 1962, **69**, 156-60.

KEPPEL, G., AND UNDERWOOD, B. J. Proactive inhibition in short-term retention of single items. *J. verb. Learn. verb. Behav.*, 1962, **1**, 153-61.

KLEINSMITH, L. J., AND KAPLAN, S. Paired-associate learning as a function of arousal and interpolated interval. *J. exp. Psychol.*, 1963, **65**, 190-93.

KOFFKA, K. *Principles of gestalt psychology.* New York: Harcourt, Brace, 1935.

LOVIBOND, S. H. A further test of the hypothesis of autonomous memory trace change. *J. exp. Psychol.*, 1958, **55**, 412-15.

McGEOCH, J. A. Forgetting and the law of disuse. *Psychol. Rev.*, 1932, **39**, 352-70.

McGEOCH, J. A., AND IRION, A. L. *The psychology of human learning* (2nd ed.) New York: Longmans, Green, 1952.

MACKWORTH, J. F. The visual image and the memory trace. *Canad. J. Psychol.*, 1962, **16**, 55-9.

MEDNICK, S. A., AND FREEDMAN, J. L. Stimulus generalization. *Psychol. Bull.*, 1960, **57**, 169-200.

MELTON, A. W. Comments on Professor Postman's paper. In C. N. Cofer (Ed.) *Verbal learning and verbal behavior.* New York: McGraw-Hill, 1961. Pp. 179-93.

MELTON, A. W. Comments on Professor Peterson's paper. In C. N. Cofer and B. S. Musgrave (Eds.) *Verbal behavior and learning: Problems and processes.* New York: McGraw-Hill, 1963. Pp. 353-70.

MILLER, G. A. The magical number seven, plus or minus two: Some limits on our capacity for processing information. *Psychol. Rev.*, 1956, 63, 81-97.

MULLER, G. E., AND PILZECKER, A. Experimentelle Beiträge zur Lehre vom Gedächtnis. *Z. Psychol.*, 1900, 1, 1-300.

MURDOCK, B. B., JR. The retention of individual items. *J. exp. Psychol.*, 1961, 62, 618-25.

PETERSON, L. R. Immediate memory: Data and theory. In C. N. Cofer (Ed.), *Verbal learning and behavior: Problems and processes.* New York: McGraw-Hill, 1963.

PETERSON, L. R., AND PETERSON, M. J. Short-term retention of individual verbal items. *J. exp. Psychol.*, 1959, 58, 193-8.

PETERSON, L. R., PETERSON, M. J., AND MILLER, A. Short-term retention and meaningfulness. *Canad. J. Psychol.*, 1961, 15, 143-7.

POSTMAN, L. The present status of interference theory. In C. N. Cofer (Ed.) *Verbal learning and verbal behavior.* New York: McGraw-Hill, 1961. Pp. 152-79.

POSTMAN, L. One-trial learning. In C. N. Cofer (Ed.) *Verbal learning and behavior: Problems and processes.* New York: McGraw-Hill, 1963.

POSTMAN, L. Short-term memory and incidental learning. In A. W. Melton (Ed.) *Categories of human learning.* New York: Academic Press.

SHEPARD, R. N. AND TEGHTSOONIAN, M. Retention of information under conditions approaching a steady state. *J. exp. Psychol.*, 1961, 62, 302-9.

SPENCE, K. W. *Behavior theory and conditioning.* New Haven, Connecticut: Yale Univer. Press, 1955.

SPERLING, G. The information available in brief visual presentations. *Psychol. Monogr.*, 1960, 74, Whole No. 498.

THOMAS, G. J. Neurophysiology of learning. *Ann. Rev. Psychol.*, 1962, 13, 71-106.

THORNDIKE, E. L. *Educational psychology: II. The psychology of learning.* New York: Teachers College, Columbia Univer., 1913.

UNDERWOOD, B. J. Interference and forgetting. *Psychol. Rev.*, 1957, 64, 49-60.

UNDERWOOD, B. J., AND KEPPEL, G. One-trial learning? *J. verb. Learn. verb. Behav.*, 1962, 1, 1-13.

UNDERWOOD, B. J., AND POSTMAN, L. Extraexperimental sources of interference in forgetting. *Psychol. Rev.*, 1960, 67, 73-95.

UNDERWOOD, B. J., AND SCHULZ, R. W. *Meaningfulness and verbal learning.* Philadelphia: Lippincott, 1960.

WALKER, E. L. Action decrement and its relation to learning. *Psychol. Rev.*, 1958, 65, 129-42.

WALKER, E. L. Memory storage as a function of arousal and time. *J. verb. Learn. verb. Behav.*, 1963, 2, 113-19.

WITMER, L. R. The association-value of three-place consonant syllables. *J. genet. Psychol.*, 1935, 47, 337-60.

30 / Primary Memory [1]

NANCY C. WAUGH, *Harvard Medical School*

AND DONALD A. NORMAN, *Center for Cognitive Studies, Harvard University*

A model for short-term memory is described and evaluated. A variety of experimental data are shown to be consistent with the following statements. (a) Unrehearsed verbal stimuli tend to be quickly forgotten because they are interfered with by later items in a series and not because their traces decay in time. (b) Rehearsal may transfer an item from a very limited primary memory store to a larger and more stable secondary store. (c) A recently perceived item may be retained in both stores at the same time. The properties of these 2 independent memory systems can be separated by experimental and analytical methods.

It is a well-established fact that the longest series of unrelated digits, letters, or words that a person can recall verbatim after one presentation seldom exceeds 10 items. It is also true, however, that one can nearly always recall the most recent item in a series, no matter how long the series—but only if this item may be recalled immediately, or if it may be rehearsed during the interval between its presentation and recall. Otherwise it is very likely to be lost. If we may assume that attending to a current item

From the *Psychological Review*, 1965, 72, 89-104, with permission of the authors and the publisher.

1. This research was supported in part by Research Grants No. MH 05120-02 and MH 08119-01 from the National Institutes of Health, United States Public Health Service, to Harvard University, Center for Cognitive Studies and to Harvard Medical School, respectively. The second author was supported by a National Science Foundation Postdoctoral Fellowship at the Center for Cognitive Studies.

precludes reviewing a prior one, we can say that the span of immediate memory must be limited in large part by our inability to rehearse, and hence retain, the early items in a sequence while attempting to store the later ones. Our limited memory span would then be but one manifestation of our general inability to think about two things at the same time.

Why should an unrehearsed item in a list be forgotten so swiftly? Is its physiological trace in some sense written over by the traces of the items that follow it? Or does this trace simply decay within a brief interval, regardless of how that interval is filled? Tradition, in the guise of interference theory, favors the first explanation (McGeoch, 1932; Postman, 1961), although some psychologists now think that new memory traces must fade autonomously in time (Brown, 1958; Conrad, 1957; Hebb, 1949). Until now, no one has reported any data which clearly contradict either of these ideas. In fact, when we first considered the problem of the instability of recent memory traces, we thought it entirely possible that both decay and interference operate over brief retention intervals to produce forgetting, and we therefore designed an experiment to weigh their respective effects. The results of this experiment were unexpectedly straightforward—and seemingly inconsistent with certain other existing data on immediate retention. We have been able, however, to formulate a simple quantitative model which relates our results to those reported by other investigators. What began as an attempt to evaluate two very general hypotheses about the forgetting of recent events has therefore resulted in a specific theory of short-term memory.

We shall describe our experiment in Section I below. A major portion of this paper, Section II, will be concerned with the description and application of our model. In Section III we shall discuss this model in relation to the general question of whether short- and long-term retention represent distinguishably different psychological processes.

I. PROBE-DIGIT EXPERIMENT

Our experiment was designed to measure the recall of a minimally rehearsed verbal item as a joint function of the number of seconds and the number of other items following its presentation. The general procedure was as follows. Lists of 16 single digits were prepared with the aid of a standard table of random numbers, under the constraint that no digit should appear more than twice in a row. The last digit in every list was one that had occurred exactly once before, in Position 3, 5, 7, 9, 10, 11, 12, 13, or 14. On its second appearance, this "probe-digit" was a cue for the recall of the digit that had followed it initially.

The lists were recorded on two magnetic tapes; they were read in a monotone voice by a male speaker at a constant rate of either one or four digits per second. Each of the nine possible probe-digit positions was tested 10 times. The two tapes accordingly contained 90 tests lists (plus 8 practice lists) apiece, all read at the same rate. The last digit in every list, the probe-digit, was accompanied by a high-frequency tone to aid the subject in detecting the end of the list. The position of the initial presentation of the probe varied randomly from list to list on each of the two tapes.

The subject's task was to write down the digit that had followed the probe digit in the list, guessing if he did not know. Since the probe-digit was unique in Positions 1 through 15, there was only one possible correct answer on any trial. Every subject listened to the list through earphones for a total of 12 experimental sessions, 6 with each tape, alternating between fast and slow lists. The first session under each condition and the first eight lists listened to in each session were considered to be practice and, unknown to the subject, were not scored.

The subjects received explicit instructions to control rehearsal by "thinking only of the last digit you have heard and never of any of the earlier ones." These instructions were repeated before the second session, and occasional reminders were given throughout the course of the experiment. Thus, the subjects were to rehearse every item during the interitem interval immediately following it. Our instructions were not designed to eliminate the rehearsal of single items as such, but rather to eliminate the rehearsal of *groups* of digits. The experiment actually tested the retention of a digit pair, the probe-digit and its successor. The retention of this pair should be independent of the interitem interval, if the instructions to avoid grouping were followed faithfully. We hoped, in effect, to test the retention of unrehearsed pairs of digits under two rates of presentation.

The subjects were four Harvard undergraduates, three males and one female.

The responses were scored and analyzed to yield a serial position curve for each rate of presentation, relating the relative frequency of an item's correct recall to its distance from the end of the list. A comparison of the two functions allows us to assess the relative effects of decay and interference on short-term forgetting, according to the following line of reasoning. Consider the recall of Item i from the end of the line. If the list was read at the rate of one item per second, then i items would have intervened, and i seconds would have elapsed between the time the subject heard the item and the time he attempted to recall it. (We count the second appearance of the probe-digit as an intervening event.) If the items were read at the rate of four per second, on the other hand, then only $i/4$, rather than i, seconds would have elapsed between the occurrence of Item i and the subject's attempt to recall it. A total of i other items would, of course, still have intervened between these two events. Therefore, if the probability of recalling Item i from the end of a slow list were identical with the probability of recalling Item $4i$ from a fast list, we could conclude that recent memory traces decay in time, independently of one another. Conversely, if the probability of recalling Item i were invariant with rate of presentation, we could conclude that rapid forgetting is caused primarily by retroactive interference.

The results of the experiment are shown in Figure 1. The scores for the

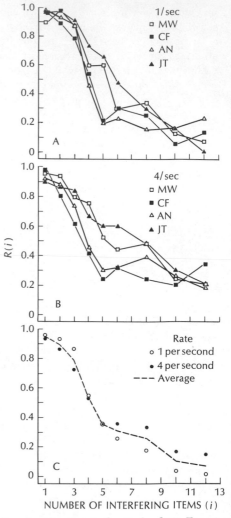

FIG. 1. *Results of the Probe-digit Experiment.* (Figures 1A and 1B represent retention functions for individual subjects under two rates of presentation; in Figure 1C these data have been pooled.)

individual subjects are presented in Figures 1A and 1B. The pooled data, corrected for guessing, are shown in Figure 1C.[2] Each point in Figures 1A and 1B

2. The response set—the 10 digits—was known to the subjects, and they knew that the probe would not be the same as the test digit. Thus the probability of correctly guessing the answer, g, was $1/9$. A standard normalizing technique was used to eliminate the effects of guessing from the data, namely, $p(\text{recall}) = [p(\text{correct}) - g]/(1 - g)$.

is based on 50 observations; each point in Figure 1C, on 200. It is evident that there are consistent differences among subjects, but little interaction between subjects and serial positions. Furthermore, although there appears to be a slight interaction between relative frequency of recall, or $R(i)$, and rate of presentation, it is clear that the effect of rate is relatively small compared to the effect of serial position. The main source of forgetting in our experiment was interference.

The differences between the two sets of points shown in Figure 1C are not statistically reliable, according to an analysis of variance performed on the number of items recalled by each subject at each value of i under the two rates of presentation ($F < 1$ for the mean square between rates tested against the interaction between subjects and rates). This conclusion is borne out by the results of nine Kolmogorov-Smirnov two-sample tests, one for each value of i, performed on the distributions of number of items recalled per subject per session under the two rates of presentation. We have therefore fitted the points shown in Figure 1C with a function that represents the probability of recalling Item i from the end of a series, estimated across rates of presentation. This function decreases monotonically with i, attaining a value of about .07 at $i = 12$.

II. MODEL FOR PRIMARY MEMORY

When we compared the foregoing results with the typical outcome of the first trial in a standard list-learning experiment, we found ourselves facing two dilemmas. In the first place, it often happens that an item in a long list is recalled after 10 or 20, or even more, items have followed it. But in our experiment, probability of recall was effectively zero for the eleventh item in from the end of a list. In the second place, various investigators have shown that probability of recall increases with presentation time (see Posner, 1963), yet in our experiment this probability, for all practical purposes, was independent of the rate at which the digits were read.

In seeking for a way to account for these discrepancies, it occurred to us that one difference between our experiment and previous ones in this area is that we instructed our subjects not to think about any item in a list once the next had been presented. This instruction to avoid rehearsal is, to be sure, rather unorthodox, although not completely without precedent (Underwood & Keppel, 1962). In order to minimize rehearsal, many experimenters try to keep the subject so busy that he does not have time to rehearse; but we think it highly likely that a well-motivated subject who is trying to learn a list will rehearse unless specifically enjoined from doing so. The typical subject's account of how he learns a list (Bugelski, 1962; Clark, Lansford, & Dallenbach, 1960) bears us out on this point. In fact, it is probably very difficult *not* to rehearse material that one is trying to memorize.

We shall assume here that rehearsal simply denotes the recall of a verbal item—either immediate or delayed, silent or overt, deliberate or involuntary. The initial perception of a stimulus probably must also qualify as a rehearsal. Obviously a very conspicuous item or one that relates easily to what we have already learned can be retained with a minimum of conscious effort. We assume that relatively homogeneous or unfamiliar material must, on the other hand, be deliberately rehearsed if it is to be retained. Actually, we shall not be concerned here with the exact role of rehearsal in the memorization process. We are simply noting that, in the usual verbal-learning experiment, the likelihood that an item in a homogeneous list will be recalled tends to increase with the amount of time available for its rehearsal. The probe-digit experiment has shown, conversely, that material which is not rehearsed is rapidly lost, regardless of the rate at which it is presented. It is as though rehearsal transferred a recently perceived verbal item from one memory store of very limited capacity to another more commodious store from which it can be retrieved at a much later time.

We shall follow James (1890) in using the terms *primary* and *secondary memory* (PM and SM) to denote the two stores. James defined these terms introspectively: an event in PM has never left consciousness and is part of the psychological present, while an event recalled from SM has been absent from consciousness and belongs to the psychological past. PM is a faithful record of events just perceived; SM is full of gaps and distortions. James believed that PM extends over a fixed period of time. We propose instead that it encompasses a certain number of events regardless of the time they take to occur. Our goal is to distinguish operationally between PM and SM on the basis of the model that we shall now describe.

Consider the general scheme illustrated in Figure 2. Every verbal item that is attended to enters PM. As we have seen, the capacity of this system is sharply limited. New items displace old ones; displaced items are permanently lost. When an item is rehearsed, however, it remains in PM, and it may enter into SM. We should like to assume, for the sake of simplicity, that the probability of its entering SM is independent of its position in a series and of the time at which it is rehearsed. Thus, it would not matter whether the item was rehearsed immediately on entering PM or several seconds later: as long as it was in PM, it would make the transition into SM with fixed probability. (Our PM is similar to Broadbent's, 1958, P system. One difference between our two systems is

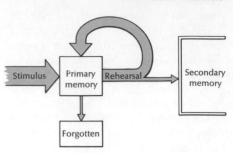

FIG. 2. *The Primary and Secondary Memory System.* (All verbal items enter PM, where they are either rehearsed or forgotten. Rehearsed items may enter SM.)

that ours relates rehearsal to longer term storage, whereas his does not.)

Finally, we shall assume that response-produced interference has the same effect on an item in PM as does stimulus-produced interference. That is, the probability that an item in PM will be recalled depends upon (*a*) how many new items have been perceived plus (*b*) how many old ones have been recalled between its presentation and attempted recall. Thus, if an item appears in Position *n* from the end of a list and the subject attempts to recall it after recalling *m* other items, it is as if the item had appeared in position $i = n + m$ in the list, and recall was attempted at the end of the list. This assumption is rather strong, but recent studies by Murdock (1963) and by Tulving and Arbuckle (1963) have, in fact, failed to reveal any consistent differences between stimulus- and response-induced interference in the retention of paired associates. It may not be unreasonable to suppose, therefore, that the two sources of interference exert equivalent effects on free and serial recall.

According to our hypothesis, then, the probability of recalling an item which has been folowed by *i* subsequent items is given by the probability that it is in PM, in SM, or in both. Assuming that these probabilities combine independently,

$$R(i) = P(i) + S(i) - P(i)S(i) \qquad [1]$$

where $R(i)$ is the probability that Item i will be recalled, $P(i)$ is the probability that it is in PM, and $S(i)$ the probability that it is in SM. The probability that this item is in PM is then given by

$$P(i) = [R(i) - S(i)]/[1 - S(i)]. \qquad [2]$$

We assume that $P(i)$ is a monotonic decreasing function of i and that

$$\lim_{i \to \infty} P(i) = 0.$$

We should like specifically to test the hypothesis that $P(i)$ is independent of the value of $S(i)$ and, in fact, varies with i in the manner of the probe-digit data. (This hypothesis is stated more formally in the Appendix.) In order to do so, we need data on verbal retention that meet the following requirements.

1. They should come from an experimental situation where at least some of the items are retrieved from PM.

2. The subject should have been allowed to rehearse, so that $S(i) > 0$.

3. The value of $S(i)$ should preferably be constant and independent of i.

4. The experimental lists should be long enough to let us estimate $S(i)$ for $i > 12$.

5. We should know the location of a given item in the stimulus list (n) and in the recall list (m), so as to be able to estimate the total number of interfering items $(i = n + m)$.

Free recall. The free-recall experiment is well suited to our purposes. Subjects can (and usually do) recall the last few items in a list right away, and the middle portion of the serial position curve (after the first three and before the last seven items) is effectively flat, thereby providing a convenient estimate of $S(i)$ (Deese & Kaufman, 1957; Murdock, 1962; Waugh, 1962).

Testing our hypothesis against data collected in a free-recall experiment therefore involves the following steps:

1. First, we estimate $S(i)$ from the average proportion of items recalled from the middle of a long list.

2. We then estimate $P(i)$ for each of the last seven items in the list by Equation 2.

3. We plot this estimate against $n + m = i$ and compare the resulting function with that shown in Figure 1.

Fortunately, we did not have to perform a free-recall experiment especially for this purpose: several such studies have been carried out and reported in sufficient detail to enable us to test our hypothesis against their results. We have chosen to analyze four sets of data collected by three different investigators: Deese and Kaufman (1957), Murdock (1962), and two as yet unpublished experiments conducted by Waugh. The two principal variables that affect $S(i)$ in free recall appear to be length of list (the amount of material that is to be retained) and presentation time (the amount of time available for the rehearsal of a given item). Manipulating these variables results in orderly changes in the value of $S(i)$, so that our estimates range from .08 to .45 across the four experiments.

1. In Deese and Kaufman's study, the subjects listened to lists of 32 unrelated English words read at a rate of one per second, and began recalling them immediately after the last had been spoken. Deese and Kaufman have presented a serial position curve based on these data and have also reported the relation between an item's serial position in recall and its position in the original list. We can thereby estimate i for each item in their lists, letting an item's average position in recall be our estimator of the amount of response interference

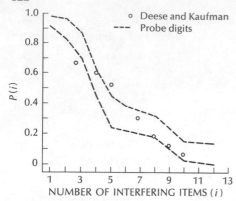

FIG. 3. Free-recall data from Deese and Kaufman (1957), corrected for asymptote and response interference.

(m).[3] We estimated $S(i)$ by the proportion of items recalled after the first three and before the last seven serial positions in the original list.[4] (This same general procedure will be followed in our subsequent analyses.)

The last seven points of Deese and Kaufman's serial position curve, taken from their Figure 1 and corrected for asymptote according to Equation 2, are plotted as a function of i in Figure 3. The dashed lines in Figure 3 represent the 99% confidence limits for the probe-digit function: a standard error for each point was estimated across subjects and experimental sessions. The uncorrected data are shown in Table 1.

2. Waugh's experiments were concerned with determining the number of items freely recalled from long lists as a function of presentation time. In her first experiment, 24, 30, 40, 60, or 120 different monosyllabic English words were read to the subjects at a rate of one per second. The proportion of items recalled varied inversely with list length, so that for each length of list there is a different serial position function. The asymptotes of these functions range from approximately .08 to .20. Median serial position in recall $(m+1)$ was calculated for each of the last six items in a list; Figure 4 shows $S(i)$ as a function of i for each of these items. The uncorrected data appear in Table 2.

In Waugh's second experiment, the subjects listened to 30 different words presented at a rate of 1, 2, 3, 4, or 6 seconds per word. In each case the presentations were either massed—that is, each word was read one, two, or three times in a row, at a rate of one word per second or of one word every two seconds—or they were distributed—each word was read once at one, two, three, four, or six different places in a list, at a

3. It is not really correct to use the average of the serial positions in recall as an estimate of $m+1$: the total effect of response interference should depend on the variance of this distribution as well as on its mean or median. It is the only alternative open to us, however, since our correction for asymptote must be applied to the average proportion of items retained, estimated across serial position in recall.

4. In estimating $S(i)$, we ignored the recall of the first three items on a list because they invariably show a primacy effect, perhaps the result of selective attention and rehearsal.

TABLE 1. *Proportion of items freely recalled as a function of serial position and total time per list*

Number of intervening items	List length × seconds per item						
	32×1	40×1	20×2	30×1	15×2	20×1	10×2
0	.72	.96	.95	.97	.97	.96	.95
1	.67	.85	.88	.89	.88	.84	.83
2	.60	.71	.75	.74	.80	.76	.71
3	.42	.51	.57	.52	.62	.62	.67
4	.32	.40	.43	.39	.58	.39	.58
5	.27	.27	.38	.33	.49	.30	.45
6	.22	.22	.38	.24	.42	.26	.45
6 + [a]	.17	.12	.27	.19	.38	.15	.45

Note.—Deese and Kaufman (1957), Column 1; Murdock (1961), Columns 2–6.
[a] Entries in this row represent the asymptotic value of $R(n)$.

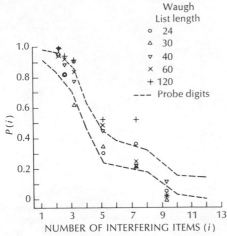

FIG. 4. Free-recall data from Waugh corrected for asymptote and response interference.

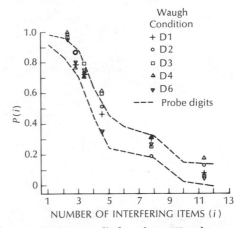

FIG. 5. Free-recall data from Waugh corrected for asymptote and response interference (1–6 distributed presentations per word).

rate of one word per second. The results of this experiment indicate that whether the repetitions are massed or distributed is of no importance; the probability that a word will be recalled is determined simply by the total number of seconds for which it is presented. Since this probability increases as a negatively accelerated function of presentation time,

TABLE 2. *Proportion of items freely recalled as a function of stimulus interference and number of items per list*

Number of intervening items	List Length				
	24	30	40	50	120
0	.95	.97	1.00	.95	1.00
1	.85	.85	.90	.93	.95
2	.92	.69	.81	.86	.92
3	.42	.46	.51	.53	.57
4	.47	.35	.31	.32	.57
5	.21	.17	.22	.14	.14
5 + [a]	.15	.17	.16	.12	.08

[a] Entries in this row represent the asymptotic value of $R(n)$.

the asymptotic values of the serial position function obtained in this experiment ranged from approximately .14 (for 30 words each read once) to .45 (for 30 words each read six times). Average serial position in recall was again calcu-

lated for each of the last six items in a list. The retention functions for massed and distributed repetitions, corrected for asymptote and response interference, are shown in Figures 5 and 6, respectively, along with the PM function obtained in our probe-digit experiment. The uncorrected data are shown in Table 2.

3. In Murdock's experiment, the subjects listened to lists of 20, 30, or 40 words read at a rate of 1 word per second and to lists of 10, 15, and 20 words read at a rate of 1 word every 2 seconds. Murdock found, as has Waugh (1963), that the probability of recalling a word that has been listened to for 2 seconds is almost exactly twice the probability of recalling a word that has been listened to for 1 second. Murdock's data can therefore be grouped into three pairs of serial position curves: 10 words read at a rate of 1 every 2 seconds versus 20 words read at a rate of 1 per second; 15 words read at a rate of 1 every 2 seconds versus 30 read at a rate of 1 per second; and 20 words read at a rate of 1 every 2 seconds versus 40 read at a rate of 1 per second. Within each pair, there are two asymptotes, one of which is approximately twice the value of the other.

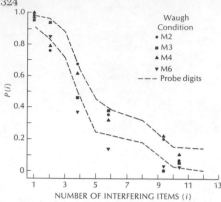

FIG. 6. Free-recall data from Waugh corrected for asymptote and response interference (2–6 massed presentations per word).

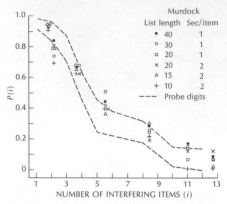

FIG. 7. Free-recall data from Murdock (1961), corrected for asymptote and response interference.

We have corrected Murdock's curves for asymptote—that is, for $S(i)$—and since he did not calculate serial position in recall for his words, we have plotted these corrected values of $P(i)$ against the avreage values of i calculated by Waugh for words recalled under similar conditions in the experiment just described (see Figures 5 and 6).[5] Murdock's uncorrected data are shown in Table 1.

It is clear that an appreciable number of the points displayed in Figures 3 through 7 fall outside the confidence limits we have set for the probe-digit function. In general, the discrepancies between theoretical and observed values of $P(i)$ appear to be unsystematic. They may have resulted from either of two possible sources which would not be reflected in the variance of the probe-digit function.

In the first place, we assume that $S(i)$ is constant for all i. While $S(i)$ does not in fact seem to vary systematically with i in the middle of a list, individual words do differ greatly in their susceptibility of storage in secondary memory: the serial position function for free recall is haphazardly jagged rather than perfectly flat. Thus, even one anomalously easy word in Location n, for instance, can greatly inflate our estimate of $R(n)$ and

hence $P(n)$. The probe-digit data would presumably not be subject to this kind of variability.

A second source of errors may lie in our estimation of i, or $m+n$. We have used average position in recall—call it $\bar{m}+1$—as our estimate of $m+1$. Even a small error in this estimate can lead to a sizable discrepancy between a theoretical and an observed value of $P(i)$, especially around the steep early portion of the function. Errors of this sort would be reflected in Figures 4–7, where i and $P(i)$ are derived from either partially or completely independent sets of data (in Figures 4–6 and Figure 7, respectively). Furthermore, we should in any case expect some discrepancy on purely mathematical grounds between $P(i)$, where (i) is the mean of a point distribution, as in the probe-digit experiment, and $P(\bar{m}+n)$, where m can assume any of a number of values, as in the free-recall data we have analyzed. Unfortunately, we are unable to specify the magnitude of this expected discrepancy.

In view, therefore, of the likelihood of the errors we have just described, we believe that the fit between the probe-digit function and the free-recall data is

5. The asymptotes for Murdock's curves were obtained by complementing his tabulated values for v (shown in his Table 2).

fairly good and is, in fact, probably too close to attribute to chance. Actually, in one respect it is surprising that the probe-digit function should describe the free-recall data as well as it does. The probe-digit experiment tested the retention of digit pairs, whereas the free-recall experiments tested the retention of individual items. How are we justified in equating the two? One possibility is to assume that in the probe-digit experiment the subjects perceived and stored the digits as a series of overlapping pairs, rather than as single digits. In this case, the measure of interference would be given by the number of digit-pairs that follow any given pair, which is, of course, equal to the number of single digits that follow it. In the free-recall experiment, on the other hand, the subjects may have perceived the words as independent units, and the effective interference would then consist of single words, as we have in fact been assuming. The problem, then, can be restated as follows: why do pairs of digits and single words exert equal amounts of retroactive interference on like items in primary memory? There is little in the existing literature that sheds much light on this point.

Paired associates. Our model should, of course, be able to describe ordered as well as free recall. We face serious problems, however, in attempting to apply it to serial learning: if a list is long enough to furnish a stable estimate of $S(i)$, the probability that a given item will be in PM at the time of testing is negligible, since serial items are customarily tested in the order in which they were presented. We must therefore turn to paired associates. In a recent study, Tulving and Arbuckle (1963) systematically varied the positions of the items on the recall list, and we have therefore applied our hypothesis to their data in the manner described above.

Tulving and Arbuckle presented number-word pairs to their subjects and then tested for the recall of each word by presenting only the number with which it had been paired. They were interested in measuring probability of recall after one trial as a function of an item's serial position in both the original list and the test list. We have estimated $S(i)$ by averaging the recall probabilities for $i > 13$, excluding Items 1 and 2. The value of their serial position curve is fortunately constant in this region, as it was for free recall. Note that in this task, each pair presented after a given number and before the cue for its recall actually consists of *two* interfering items: a word plus a number. We have counted all items occurring between the test item and its recall—including the test number—as interfering items. We have analyzed the proportion of items presented in Positions 1 through 6 from the end of the stimulus list and tested in Positions 1 through 6 of the response list. These proportions are shown in Tulving and Arbuckle's Tables 2 and 4; we have pooled those that correspond to a given value of i. Thus i, or $n + m$ (where $n = j$ and $m = i - j$), ranges from 1 to 11. These data are presented in Figure 8, along with our own estimate of $P(i)$. Again, considering the variability of $S(i)$ that is not taken into account by our model, the fit between data and theory appears to be reasonably good.

In sum, then, we believe we can say that the similarity between our probe-digit function and the various other, initially disparate, serial position curves shown in Figures 3–8 is consistent with the hypothesis that there is a primary memory store that is independent of any longer term store. The capacity of the primary store appears to be invariant under a wide variety of experimental conditions which do, however, affect the properties of the longer term store.

Single-item retention. Much of the experimental work on memory in the past 5 years has focused on measuring the re-

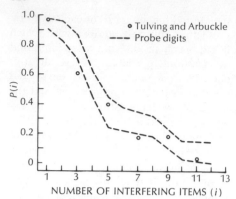

Fɪɢ. 8. Paired-associate data from Tulving and Arbuckle (1963) corrected for asymptote and response interference.

tention of a single verbal item—or of a brief list of items—over short intervals. A widely used procedure which was introduced by Peterson and Peterson (1959) is to expose an item (for example, a meaningless three-letter sequence) to a subject; have him perform some task that presumably monopolizes his attention (such as counting backwards by three's) for a specified number of seconds; and, finally, at the end of this interval, have him attempt to recall the critical item. The universal finding has been that retention decreases monotonically with the length of the retention interval. It has generally been assumed that the subject does not rehearse during the retention interval, that a number spoken by him does not interfere with a trigram previously spoken by the experimenter, and that therefore the observed decline over time in the retention of such an item reflects the pure decay of its memory trace. This general conclusion is clearly inconsistent with our results, since we have found that the length of the retention interval as such—within the limits we tested, naturally—is of relatively little importance in determining retention loss.

In seeking for a way to account for this discrepancy, it occurred to us to question the assumption that, in an experiment of the sort described above, the numbers spoken by the subject during the retention interval do not interfere with the memory trace of the item he is supposed to retain. Some experimenters have, after all, reported that dissimilar items seem to interfere with one another just as much as do similar ones in the immediate recall of very short lists (Brown, 1958; Pillsbury & Sylvester, 1940). What would happen, therefore, if we were to define a three-digit number uttered by a subject in the course of a simple arithmetic calculation—counting backwards—as one unit of mnemonic interference? Could our model then describe the forgetting of single items over brief intervals? We have attempted to fit the data of two experimenters, Loess (in press) and Murdock (1961), by converting the retention interval into a corresponding number of interfering items. Murdock's subjects were trained to count at a steady rate of one number per second, so the number of interfering items in his experiment is equal to the retention interval in seconds. Loess' subjects counted at a rate of one number every 1.5 seconds; we have therefore multiplied the length of his retention intervals by ⅔ in order to obtain the equivalent number of interfering items. We estimate $S(i)$ in both cases by the relative frequency of recall at $i = 18$.[6]

The two sets of data, corrected for asymptote, are shown in Figure 9, along with the probe-digit function. The correspondence between them is reasonably close. It is possible, of course, that this agreement between theory and fact is simply a matter of luck, depending, as it does, on the arbitrary assumption that a three-digit number generated by the subject himself is psychologically equivalent to a one-digit number presented by the

6. We have also tried to analyze the results of Peterson and Peterson (1959) but without success. Part of the difficulty may result from the fact that their subjects may not have adhered strictly to a prescribed rate of counting during the retention interval (L. Peterson, personal communication, 1964).

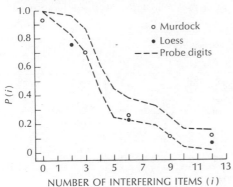

Fɪɢ. 9. The retention of three-item lists compared with the probe-digit function. (Loess' data denote the proportion of consonant trigrams recalled after various retention intervals; Murdock's data represent the average proportion of trigrams and word triads retained after a given interval.)

experimenter during the retention interval (as in the probe-digit study). Obviously we cannot draw any firm conclusions about the effect of interference on the retention of single items until this assumption is justified empirically. We can only point out that the results of Murdock and Loess do not necessarily contradict our model.

Dɪsᴄᴜssɪᴏɴ

We should at this point like to consider the general question of whether all verbal information is stored in the same system or whether, as we have assumed here, there are two independent mnemonic processes that contribute to retention even over very short intervals. The proponents of a unitary theory of memory, eloquently led by Melton (1963), have argued that recall after a few seconds is affected in very similar ways by the variables that govern recall over much longer intervals; and that therefore the distinction between a short-term memory mechanism, on the one hand, and a longer term mechanism, on the other, is purely arbitrary. The following facts

have been cited in support of this argument:

1. Short-term retention improves, just as does long-term retention, when the material to be recalled is repeated before a test of retention, or when it is repeated between successive tests (Hebb, 1961; Hellyer, 1962).

2. Retention after a brief delay is subject to proactive interference, as is retention after a long delay (Keppel & Underwood, 1962; Loess, in press). Why, asks the unitary theorist, should we distinguish between short- and long-term retention if we cannot find any quantitative and experimentally manipulatable differences between them? This question might well be disturbing if one took the position that the two processes have sharply defined non-overlapping temporal boundaries such that items recalled within some critical interval after their initial occurrence must have been retrieved from one system, whereas items recalled beyond this interval must have been retrieved from another. (Such a view would imply, interestingly enough, that an item would have to remain in a short-term storage for some specified number of seconds before passing into longer term storage, if it did so at all.)

But what if we do not require that the two systems be mutually exclusive? Then the probability that an item will be recalled will depend on both the probability that it is still in PM and the probability that it has entered into SM in the interval between its presentation and the start of the interfering sequence (or even during this sequence, if the subject is able to rehearse). All those variables that determine $S(i)$ for a given item—such as its position in a closely spaced series of tests, or the number of times it has been repeated —will then determine the observed proportion recalled after a brief inter-

TABLE 3. *Proportion of items freely recalled as a function of stimulus interference and presentation time*

Number of intervening items	Seconds per item								
	Distributed					Massed			
	1	2	3	4	5	2	3	4	6
0	.96	.99	.97	1.00	.97	.98	.97	1.00	1.00
1	.82	.90	.91	.86	.89	.82	.96	.87	.91
2	.76	.81	.86	.82	.87	.75	.63	.76	.63
3	.54	.64	.73	.76	.65	.51	.58	.58	.50
1	.38	.40	.50	.57	.60	.40	.31	.51	.44
5	.21	.36	.36	.49	.48	.27	.36	.45	.44
5 + [a]	.14	.26	.32	.38	.45	.25	.31	.38	.42

[a] Entries in this row represent the asympototic value of $R(n)$.

val. We believe we have shown, however, that $P(i)$ depends only on i and remains invariant with changes in $S(i)$; and we submit that most of the published data on short-term retention actually reflect the properties of both memory systems.

We would like to make one final point: the existence of some rather compelling introspective evidence in favor of two distinct mnemonic systems. PM, as we have defined it here, is best illustrated by a person's ability to recall verbatim the most recent few words in a sentence that he is hearing or speaking, even when he is barely paying attention to what is being said, or to what he is saying. Given that the flow of speech is intelligible, failures in the immediate recall of words we have just heard—errors of either omission, transposition, or substitution—are probably so rare as to be abnormal. Indeed, we believe that it would be impossible to understand or to generate a grammatical utterance if we lacked this rather remarkable mnemonic capacity. In order to recall a sentence verbatim at a later time, however, we usually have to rehearse it while it is still available in PM.

The same effect holds for meaningless arrangements of verbal items. If we present a subject with a random string of words, letters, or digits, and ask him to reproduce them in any order he chooses, he can maximize the number he recalls by "unloading" the last few items immediately. Most subjects in free-recall experiments report that these very late items tend to be lost if they are not recalled immediately, whereas items that came earlier in the list can be retrieved at leisure, if they can be recalled at all. In the colorful terminology of one such subject (Waugh, 1961), the most recent items in a verbal series reside temporarily in a kind of "echo box," from which they can be effortlessly parroted back. When an experienced subject is trying to memorize a list of serial items, moreover, he "fills up" successive echo boxes as the list is read to him and attempts to rehearse the contents of each. He will invariably lose some items if rehearsal is delayed too long or if he attempts to load his echo box with more than it can hold. We think it very likely that the PM function describes the (variable) capacity of this mechanism. We would remind you in this connection that, within very broad limits, the rate at which someone is speaking does not affect your ability to follow his words—just as differences in the rate at which meaningless lists of digits are presented do not exert any profound effect on the PM function.

CONCLUSIONS

We have tried to demonstrate the existence of a short-term or PM system that is independent of any longer term or secondary store by showing that one function relating probability of recall to number of intervening items can describe a number of seemingly disparate sets of experimental results. In doing so, we have deliberately avoided discussing a number of problems raised in our analyses. Foremost in our list of problems is the definition of an item. Certainly the idea of a discrete verbal unit is crucial to our theory. The interference effect that we have studied seems to be invariant over a broad class of units and combinations of units—single digits, nonsense trigrams, and meaningful words. How long a string of such primitive units can we combine and still have one item? Is an item determined by our grammatical habits? It is determined by the duration of the verbal stimulus? Is it determined by both? We do not know.

We have also avoided discussing the possible rules whereby items now in PM are displaced by later items. Are items lost independently of one another, or do they hang and fall together? It may perhaps prove difficult to answer this question experimentally, but it should not be impossible.

Finally, at what stage in the processing of incoming information does our PM reside? Is it in the peripheral sensory mechanism? Probably not. The work of Sperling (1960) indicates that "sensory memory"—to use Peterson's (1963) phrase—decays within a matter of milliseconds, whereas we have dealt in our analysis with retention intervals on the order of seconds. Does storage in PM precede the attachment of meaning to discrete verbal stimuli? Must a verbal stimulus be transformed into an auditory image in order to be stored in PM, even if it was presented visually? We refer the reader to a recent paper by Sperling (1963) for some thoughts on the latter question.

APPENDIX

A formal discussion of the interaction between PM and SM can be provided by a simple three-state Markov process. The assumptions of the model are:

1. There are three states of memory: S, P, and the null state, G.
2. The probability of recalling an item from either State S or State P is unity: items cannot be recalled from the null state, but they may be guessed with Probability g.
3. Items can only pass into State S when they are rehearsed and, for the experiments discussed in this paper, we assume that items are rehearsed only when they are presented. The probability that an item is stored in S, given that it was successfully rehearsed, is a.
4. Items in P are interfered with by later presentation of different items: the probability that an item returns to the null state on the presentation of the ith interfering item is δ_i.

The following equivalents hold between the terms defined for the Markov model and the terms defined in the body of the paper:

1. $P_i(S)$ is equivalent to $S(i)$.
2. $P_i(P)$ is equivalent to $P(i)[1 - S(i)]$.
3. δ_i is equivalent to $1 - P(i)$.

Now, define the random variable π with Value 1 if the test item is presented, and with Value 0 if some other (interfering) item is presented. (We can also let π be a probability—namely, the probability that the test item is presented. The formal statement of the model does not change with this redefinition.)

The transition probabilities for any given stimulus item (the test item) are specified by the matrix.

$$\begin{array}{c} \\ S \\ P \\ G \end{array}\begin{array}{c} S \\ \left[\begin{array}{c} 1 \\ a\pi \\ a\pi \end{array}\right. \end{array}\begin{array}{c} P \\ 0 \\ (1-\pi)(1-\delta_i)+\pi(1-a) \\ (1-a)\pi \end{array}\begin{array}{c} G \\ 0 \\ \left.(1-\pi)\delta_i\right] \\ 1-\pi \end{array}$$

Unfortunately, it is difficult to work with transition matrices of this form (with time-varying parameters). One approximation would be to let $\delta_i = \delta$, independent of i. This approximation yields an exponential decay function of the form $P_i(P) = (1 - a)$ $(1 - \delta)^{i-1}$. This is clearly not correct for the results of our experiment (Figure 1); but, for some purposes, it may not be a bad approximation. A model very similar mathematically to that produced by this simple approximation for δ_i has been studied by Atkinson and Crothers (1964), who found it to be quite good for certain types of paired-associates experiments. Their model, however, is derived from quite different considerations.

For any experiments with controlled rehearsals, the probability that an item reaches State S (or SM) is completely independent of the properties of the short-term state (P or PM). This is true because, as far as State S is concerned, the general transition matrix can be reduced by combining States P and G to form the "lumped" State P'. The new matrix is

$$
\begin{array}{cc}
 & \begin{array}{cc} S & \quad P' \end{array} \\
\begin{array}{c} S \\ P' \end{array} & \left[\begin{array}{cc} 1 & 0 \\ a\pi & 1 - a\pi \end{array} \right].
\end{array}
$$

This is a simple one-element Markov model. This means that although the complete description of the verbal learning process requires a description of the short-term state, a study of only the long-term retention of items can ignore the short-term memory.

REFERENCES

ATKINSON, R. C., & CROTHERS, E. J. A comparison of paired-associate learning models having different acquisition and retention axioms. *J. math. Psychol.*, 1964, **1**, 285-315.

BROADBENT, D. E. *Perception and communication.* New York: Pergamon Press, 1958.

BROWN, J. Some tests of the decay theory of immediate memory. *Quart. J. exp. Psychol.*, 1958, **10**, 12-21.

BUGELSKI, B. R. Presentation time, total time, and mediation in paired-associate learning. *J. of exp. Psychol.*, 1962, **63**, 409-12.

CLARK, L. L., LANSFORD, T. E., & DALLENBACH, K. M. Repetition and associative learning. *Amer. J. Psychol.*, 1960, **73**, 22-40.

CONRAD, R. Decay theory of immediate memory. *Nature*, 1957, **179**, 831-2.

DEESE, J., & KAUFMAN, R. A. Sequential effects in recall of unorganized and sequentially organized material. *J. exp. Psychol.*, 1957, **54**, 180-87.

HEBB, D. O. *The organization of behavior.* New York: Wiley, 1949.

HEBB, D. O. Distinctive features of learning in the higher animal. In J. F. Delafresnaye (Ed.), *Brain mechanisms and learning.* London: Oxford Univ. Press, 1961. Pp. 37-46.

HELLYER, S. Supplemental report: Frequency of stimulus presentation and short-term decrement in recall. *J. exp. Psychol.*, 1962, **64**, 650.

JAMES, W. *The principles of psychology.* Vol. 1. New York: Holt, 1890. Ch. 16.

KEPPEL, G., & UNDERWOOD, B. J. Proactive inhibition in short-term retention of single items. *J. verb. Learn. verb. Behav.*, 1962, **1**, 153-161.

LOESS, H. Proactive inhibition in short-term memory. *J. verb. Learn. verb. Behav.*, in press.

McGEOCH, J. A. Forgetting and the law of disuse. *Psychol. Rev.*, 1932, **39**, 352-370.

MELTON, A. W. Implications of short-term memory for a general theory of memory. *J. verb. Learn. verb. Behav.*, 1963, **2**, 1-21.

MURDOCK, B. B., JR. The retention of individual items. *J. exp. Psychol.*, 1961, **62**, 618-25.

MURDOCK, B. B., JR. The serial position effect in free recall. *J. Exp. Psychol.*, 1962, **64**, 482-8.

MURDOCK, B. B., JR. Interpolated recall in short-term memory. *J. exp. Psychol.*, 1963, **66**, 525-32.

PETERSON, L. R. Immediate memory: Data and theory. In C. N. Cofer, & Barbara Musgrave (Eds.), *Verbal behavior and learning: Problems and processes.* New York: McGraw-Hill, 1963. Pp. 336-53.

PETERSON, L. R., & PETERSON, M. J. Short-term retention of individual verbal items. *J. exp. Psychol.*, 1959, **58**, 193-8.

PILLSBURY W. B., & SYLVESTER, A. Retroactive and proactive inhibition in immediate memory. *J. exp. Psychol.*, 1940, **27**, 532-45.

POSNER, M. I. Immediate memory in sequential tasks. *Psychol. Bull.*, 1963, **60**, 333-49.

POSTMAN, L. The present status of interference theory. In C. N. Cofer (Ed.), *Verbal learning and verbal behavior.* New York: McGraw-Hill, 1961. Pp. 152-79.

SPERLING, G. The information available in brief visual presentations. *Psychol. Monogr.*, 1960, **74** (11, Whole No. 498).

SPERLING, G. A model for visual memory tasks. *Human Factors*, 1963, **5**, 19-36.

TULVING, E., & ARBUCKLE, T. Y. Sources of intratrial interference in immediate recall of paired associates. *J. verb. Learn. verb. Behav.*, 1963, **1**, 321-334.

UNDERWOOD, B. J., & KEPPEL, G. An evaluation of two problems of method in the study of retention. *Amer. J. Psychol.*, 1962, **75**, 1-17.

WAUGH, N. C. Free versus serial recall. *J. exp. Psychol.*, 1961, **62**, 496-502.

WAUGH, N. C. The effect of intralist repetition on free recall. *J. verb. Learn. verb. Behav.*, 1962, **1**, 95-9.

WAUGH, N. C. Immediate memory as a function of repetition. *J. verb. Learn. and verb. Behav.*, 1963, **2**, 107-12.

DETERMINANTS OF SPECIFIC TRANSFER

What is the effect of learning one set of items upon the rapidity of learning the next? The consequences of a learning experience are not confined to the specific material of a task, but are carried over via the altered state of the subject, to influence the conduct of subsequent tasks. The direction of that influence, and the identification of variables governing its magnitude, are the topics of these readings. It is customary to distinguish two broad classes of transfer, namely nonspecific and specific. Nonspecific transfer of learning refers to the facilitative results of experience with a given class of materials, irrespective of their *particular* composition. Practice effects and warm-up effects are nonspecific transfer phenomena, distinguished by the fact that the former are more enduring, and the latter are more likely to dissipate through time. A beautiful empirical example of this distinction is shown by Thune (1951). Quite the opposite results are characteristic of retention data, where memory for a given list gets poorer as a function of the number of previous lists memorized. That is, of course, the phenomenon of proactive inhibition. Thus, nonspecific transfer in learning is usually positive, and in retention it is usually negative. However, a complication arises whenever retention performance is measured between groups which display different learning rates. The problem lies in the likelihood that the terminal acquisition levels were unequal. Underwood (1964) presents a careful and lucid discussion of the procedure to be adopted in such circumstances.

Specific transfer refers to those consequences of previous learning which are traceable to the particular stimulus-response relations between the tasks involved. Its detection requires a more detailed analysis of the materials, both within and between lists. Nonspecific and specific effects operate simultaneously in any learning task, and their mutual influence has, until recently, been inadequately explored. However, Postman has embarked upon a number of thoroughgoing studies designed to reveal the interaction of practice level with various specific transfer paradigms (Postman, 1964). Proper quantitative assessment of specific transfer requires appropriate control over the concurrent nonspecific effects. This is presently accomplished by comparing the common-second-list performance of experimental groups (which differ in the S-R relations obtaining between their lists), to that of a control group which learns unrelated lists. In this fashion, practice and warm-up effects are equated across groups, allowing any learning differences to be attributed to the specific transfer paradigms involved. However, acquisition of an unrelated second list (AB-CD) means that the control group is necessarily exposed to more *new* items than are the other transfer groups (for instance, AB-AC and AB-CB), and therefore it differs in this respect as well as in the S-R *relations*. Such complications must be overcome in any attempt to develop a rational quantification of specific transfer.

The following readings are some of the landmarks in the contemporary study of specific transfer. They are ordered in a manner that reflects the increased interest in analysis of mediational mechanisms. The trend from an empirical single-stage to a mediational approach is discernible, and roughly parallels the publication dates. Reading 2 in Section I is also quite relevant here.

The paper by Osgood is a classic unification of the facts of transfer available at the time, integrated into a coherent predictive framework. The famous "transfer and retroaction surface" is a diagrammatic construction that encompasses the full range of S-R similarity relations possible between two lists, and the transfer outcomes to be expected. It predicts both direction and relative degree of transfer. It does not, of course, predict in quantitative terms, since other variables would influence the exact amounts of transfer generated in any experiment.

Since the Osgood surface was an *ad hoc* generalization from a limited number of different experiments, it was a necessary next step to test it systematically at more points. One of the better designed tests was conducted by Dallet (1962), and it tended to confirm the surface's predictions.

The paper by Twedt and Underwood compares transfer obtained by the mixed list method of presentation, with the unmixed list method. In a mixed list, different transfer paradigms are represented within the same list, whereas the unmixed list method used a separate list for each paradigm. Results showed absolutely no differential effects upon transfer, and implied a remarkable capacity of mixed list subjects to differentiate among the various paradigms.

The Russell and Storms paper is a convincing example of a mediational process producing positive transfer. Advantage was taken of word-association norms to construct paired-associates lists which eventuated in associative chains between the two lists. Two of the links in the chain were inferred, and not present as list items. This type of transfer effect is not explicitly provided for in the Osgood surface, and represents a new dimension of transfer phenomena.

The paper by Bastian investigates the efficacy of semantic similarity versus associative connection in producing positive transfer. With an AB-AC paradigm, maximum transfer occurred when the response items were associatively connected. Such results suggest that the Osgood surface might be recast in terms of associative strengths, rather than meaningful similarity. For an excellent extended discussion of mediation research, see Jenkins (1963).

Martin's paper represents the latest extension of the Osgood surface approach to transfer phenomena, incorporating the additional knowledge gained since the original surface was proposed. Martin's analysis eventuates in *three* transfer surfaces, reflecting three aspects of paired-associate learning; response availability, forward associations, and backward associations.

DALLETT, K. M. The transfer surface re-examined. *J. verb. Learn. verb. Behav.*, 1962, **1**, 91-4.

JENKINS, J. J. Mediated associations: Paradigms and situations. In C. N. Cofer & B. S. Musgrave (Eds.), *Verbal behavior and learning: Problems and processes.* New York: McGraw-Hill, 1963. Pp. 210-45.

POSTMAN, L. Studies of learning to learn: II. Changes in transfer as a function of practice. *J. verb. Learn. verb. Behav.*, 1964, **3**, 437-47.

THUNE, L. E. Warm-up effect as a function of level of practice in verbal learning. *J. exp. Psychol.*, 1951, **42**, 250-56.

UNDERWOOD, B. J. Degree of learning and the measurement of forgetting. *J. verb. Learn. verb. Behav.*, 1964, **3**, 112-29.

31 / The Similarity Paradox in Human Learning: A Resolution

CHARLES E. OSGOOD, *University of Connecticut*

Behavior is a continuous, fluid process, and activities learned in the laboratory are as much a part of it as a trip to the county fair. The segments which an experimenter arbitrarily selects for analysis are inextricably imbedded in this expanding matrix and are interpretable only in terms of its interactions. Transfer and retroaction experiments are explicit attempts to gauge these interactions, and the similarity variable— that is, the homogeneities existing among the materials successively practiced— turns out to be the most important factor as well as the most puzzling.

The classic statement of the relation between similarity and interference in human learning, as found in most textbooks in psychology, is that "the greater the similarity, the greater the interference." Although this law is traceable mainly to the work of McGeoch and his associates (10, 13, 14), there are many other experiments which superficially appear to substantiate it. When carried to its logical conclusions, however, this law leads to an impossible state of affairs. The highest degree of similarity of both stimulus and response in the materials successively practiced is that where any simple habit or S-R association is learned. The stimulus situation can never be precisely identical from trial to trial, nor can the response, but they are maximally similar—and here the greatest facilitation (ordinary learning) is obtained. *Ordinary learning, then, is at once the theoretical condition for maximal interference but obviously the practical condition for maximal facilitation.* Here is the fundamental paradox, and this paper suggests a resolution.

From the *Psychological Review*, 1949, **56**, 132-43, with permission of the author and publisher.

EMPIRICAL LAWS OF TRANSFER AND RETROACTION AS FUNCTIONS OF SIMILARITY

Transfer and retroaction in human learning are among the most extensively cultivated fields in experimental psychology, yet there are no clear-cut generalizations which satisfactorily bind the data together. The difficulty may be traced in part to the bewildering variety of procedures, materials and experimental designs employed by different investigators, a phenomenon perhaps characteristic of a young science. But some of the confusion can also be laid to the fact that in a large proportion of experiments the theoretically relevant relations are patently unspecifiable: the subjects merely learn List A and then List B, or Maze I and then Maze II, and either positive or negative effects may result, depending upon quite unanalyzable conditions. The purpose of this paper is to clarify the similarity function in human learning, and to accomplish this end only those experiments can be utilized wherein the *locus* of similarities is specifiable, as being between stimulus members, response members, or both. This analytic approach, although it may be considered inappropriate by some theorists and makes use of only part of the data, does give rise to a coherent and consistent picture.

When *transfer* is studied, one is interested in the effect of a specifiable prior activity upon the learning of a given test activity. When *retroaction* is studied, one is interested in the effect of a specifiable interpolated activity upon the retention of a previously learned activity. In both cases the experimenter arbitrarily "lifts" segments of a continuing process for analysis, and it would be expected that common laws would apply to both samplings. In the present context it can be shown that identical functions of similarity apply to both

Transfer and Retroaction Paradigms
TRANSFER

Paradigm A	$S_1 \rightarrow R_1$	$\underline{S_2} \rightarrow R_1$	$S_1 \rightarrow R_1$
Paradigm B	$S_1 \rightarrow R_1$	$S_1 \rightarrow \underline{R_2}$	$S_1 \rightarrow R_1$
Paradigm C	$S_1 \rightarrow R_1$	$\underline{S_2} \rightarrow \underline{R_2}$	$S_1 \rightarrow R_1$

RETROACTION

FIG. 1. Paradigms indicating the locus of variation among the successively practiced materials. A, stimulus variation; B, response variation; C, simultaneous stimulus and response variation.

transfer and retroaction data, which simplifies the theoretical task considerably. Figure 1 gives symbolic representation to three basic learning paradigms, *A* that in which stimulus members are varied in the materials successively practiced while responses are functionally identical, *B* that in which responses are varied and stimuli are functionally identical, and *C* that in which both stimulus and response members are simultaneously varied. It will be seen that in so far as similarity relations are concerned, the test for transfer is simultaneously the interpolated activity when the entire retroactive sequence is followed. The term "functional identity" is used here to make explicit the fact that *true* identity among either stimulus or response processes is a will-o-the-wisp, approached but never attained. Functional identity of stimuli in successive trials or tasks exists when the situation is objectively constant (i.e., when the same stimulus nonsense syllable appears on the screen or the same choice point is approached on repeated trials in the maze); functionally identical responses are those which the experimenter, at any given level of analysis, scores as being the same (i.e., no matter how the subject says CYF or how the rat maneuvers about a turn, it is scored "correct"). Functional identity thus becomes the limiting case of maximum similarity.

1. Let us first consider *paradigm A*, the condition in which stimulus similarity is variable and responses are func-

tionally identical. The transfer portion of this paradigm will be recognized as nothing other than a symbolic statement of *stimulus generalization*. In Hovland's classic study (9), for example, a galvanic skin response is first conditioned to a tone of a certain frequency $(S_1\text{-}R_1)$, then the test tone is presented and the extent to which the same response is made to it measured $(S_2\text{-}R_1)$. Hovland found that the greater the similarity between practice and test stimuli, the greater the amount of generalization (or positive transfer). The same results are regularly found wherever this paradigm can be identified, whether the materials be motor or verbal, meaningful or nonsense, or of any other nature. McKinney (15) required subjects to respond with a correct letter upon seeing each of four geometrical designs and then measured transfer of the same responses to alterations of these designs; when Yum (25) varied the similarity of visually presented nonsense-syllable stimuli, positive transfer was the result, the magnitude increasing with stimulus similarity.

While retroaction data derived from this paradigm are not so extensive, the available evidence is consistent in revealing *facilitation*. Hamilton's (7) subjects learned lists of paired-associates in which the stimuli were geometrical forms and the responses were nonsense syllables. Although responses were "identical" on original and interpolated lists, the stimulus forms varied from "identity" through two degrees of similarity, as independently indexed in terms of generalization, to complete neutrality. The magnitude of retroactive facilitation decreased regularly as similarity among the stimulus members decreased, effects of approximately zero magnitude being obtained with neutral stimuli. The empirical law for this paradigm is: *where stimuli are varied and responses are functionally identical, positive transfer and retroactive facilitation are obtained, the magnitude of both increasing as the similarity among the stimulus members increases.*

2. The situation in which stimuli are constant and responses are varied, *paradigm B*, is the standard associative and reproductive inhibition paradigm and, as might be expected, a large number of experiments (cf. 1, 6, 21) testify to the fact that *interference* is produced under these conditions. However, there is also a large body of evidence showing positive transfer under the same conditions. The latter evidence may be discounted on two grounds: (a) In many cases the so-called transfer response has been *learned previous* to the experimental situation. In many of Tolman's sign-learning studies, for example, animals trained to traverse the route to a goal by one path or means, such as running, will shift readily to another means, such as swimming, if the original behavior is blocked. Similarly, Wickens (23) has shown that a human subject who has learned to avoid the shock which follows a tone by an extensor movement of his finger, when his palm is down, "transfers" immediately to a flexion movement when his hand is then placed palm up. In such cases, the new learning in the experimental situation is the sign-value or meaning of the distinctive cue. A variety of overt behaviors has previously been associated with this mediation process—the human subject brings to the experiment a rich repertoire of pain-avoiding movements, and he would lift his head without new training if his nose were inserted between the electrodes! (b) In other cases what is measured as positive transfer under conditions fitting this paradigm can be shown to be attributable to "*practice effects*," i.e., the subject is learning how to learn nonsense syllables or learning how to learn mazes, and these general skills or habits counteract the interference inherent in the de-

sign. Siipola (20), for example, obtained small amounts of positive transfer for a code-substitution task, yet concluded from the large numbers of intrusions that actual negative transfer was being masked by a general "practice effect."

Bugelski (2) required his subjects to learn an original list of 10 paired nonsense syllables (such as *toc-nem*) and then interpolated three additional lists, the experimental subjects having identical stimuli and varied responses (such as *toc-rul*) and the control subjects having both members varied (such as *cos-rul*). Although insignificant amounts of positive transfer to successive lists were obtained in both conditions, the inherent interfering character of the stimuli-identical paradigm was revealed in the fact that the experimental subjects showed a marked decrement upon relearning the first list while the controls showed continued facilitation. Clearest evidence for negative transfer and retroactive interference under the conditions of this paradigm is offered in a recent monograph by Underwood (21). In measuring transfer, subjects learned 0, 2, 4, or 6 lists of meaningful paired-associates *prior* to learning a test list; in measuring retroaction, 0, 2, 4 or 6 interpolated lists were learned *after* the original learning of the same test list; in both cases, recall of the test list was measured after a delay of 25 minutes. Both negative transfer and retroactive interference were found, increasing in magnitude with the number of prior or interpolated lists having the same stimulus members but different responses.

But what about the *degree* of similarity among the varied responses in this paradigm? Perhaps because of the difficulty in defining response similarity, there are relatively few data here. In a recent experiment by Osgood (17), original learning of a set of paired letter-pairs and meaningful adjectives (such

as *c.m.—elated*) was followed by three types of interpolated items, each subject serving as his own control by learning an equal number of items in each similarity relation (such as *c.m.—high, c.m. —left* or *c.m.—low*); all subjects finally relearned the original list. Although interference was obtained under all conditions, it was significantly *less* for similar meaningful relations. One of the conditions of Bruce's (1) extensive investigation with nonsense-syllable paired-associates substantiates this finding. We may now state the empirical law for this paradigm: *where stimuli are functionally identical and responses are varied, negative transfer and retroactive interference are obtained, the magnitude of both decreasing as similarity between the responses increases.*

3. *Paradigm C,* where both stimuli and responses are simultaneously varied, is directly generated when the standard memory drum is used and lists of material are learned in constant serial order. Similarities are between items having the same serial position on successive lists, and each item serves simultaneously as a response to the preceding item and a stimulus for the succeeding item. Whatever interpolated lists are given, stimulus and response similarities must be simultaneously varied through the same degrees. McGeoch and McDonald (13) and Johnson (10) have employed this procedure with meaningful materials, finding retroactive interference to increase with the degree of similarity. Melton and Von Lackum (16) report the same result for nonsense syllables. McGeoch and McGeoch (14) and Johnson (10) find the same result to hold for transfer when this paradigm is used.

An important experiment by Gibson (6) also fits this paradigm. Her materials and procedures were identical with those reported above for Hamilton (7). The Gibson experiment was actually the first of the series. Visual stimulus forms were varied through independently measured degree of generalization, as was the case in Hamilton's study, but here responses were different and neutral. Negative transfer and retroactive interference were obtained, their magnitudes decreasing as stimulus similarity decreased and approximating zero with neutral stimuli. It should be noted that in both studies approximately zero transfer or retroaction was found when stimuli were neutral, regardless of response identity or difference. The empirical law for this paradigm: *when both stimulus and response members are simultaneously varied, negative transfer and retroactive interference are obtained, the magnitude of both increasing as the stimulus similarity increases.*

There are a considerable number of substantiating studies which have not been cited here, but if this writer's survey of the literature has been adequate, *there are no exceptions to the above empirical laws.* There are few studies where more than one relation is systematically explored, with the same materials, procedures and subjects, and for this reason it is difficult to quantify these relations. An exception is a study by Bruce (1). One set of nonsense pairs (such as *req-kiv*) was learned by all subjects and transfer to several variations was measured: where stimuli were varied and responses were constant (*zaf-kiv* or *reb-kiv*) positive transfer was found as compared with a control condition, the amount being greater when stimuli were more similar: where responses were varied and stimuli were constant (*req-vor*), negative transfer was found. The condition in which stimuli were constant and responses were highly similar (*req-kib*) was slightly superior to the control condition (both members neutral). Although this result appears to contradict the empirical law for this paradigm, it will be found to fit the hypothesis presented in the latter part of this paper: if ordinary learning is to be theoretically feasible, high degrees of response similarity must yield facilitation.

Attempted Integrations of the Data

A series of attempts to integrate the facts of transfer and retroaction can be traced in the history of this problem. As early as 1919 Wylie (24) had made a distinction between stimulus and response activities, stating that the transfer effect is positive when an "old" response is associated with a new stimulus but negative when an "old" stimulus must be associated with a new response. "Old" in this context merely means that the member in question has previously been associated with another stimulus or response. This principle is valid, of course, within the limits of its gross differentiation. But (a) it takes account of neither stimulus nor response similarities and (b) it leaves the fundamental paradox untouched. Since successive responses are never precisely identical, even in ordinary learning, we are always associating stimuli with "new" responses and hence should inevitably get negative transfer.

Robinson was one of the first to perceive clearly this paradox and in 1927 he offered what is now known as the Skaggs-Robinson Hypothesis as a resolution. As shown in Figure 2, this hypothesis states that facilitation is greatest when successively practiced materials are identical (point *A*); facilitation is least, and hence interference maximal, with some moderate degree of similarity (point *B*); and facilitation increases again as we move toward neutrality (point *C*) but never attains the original level. Note that while point *A* defines maximum similarity (identity) and point *C* defines minimum similarity (neutrality), point *B* actually specifies no degree of similarity at all, but merely says that somewhere there is a low point in the

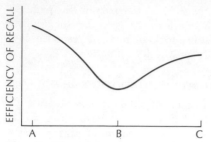

Fig. 2. The Skaggs-Robinson Hypothesis: point A specifies maximum similarity (identity) and point C minimum similarity (neutrality) among the successively practiced materials; point B merely indicates the low point in the curve for efficiency of recall.

facilitation curve. Several experiments (3, 4, 8, 11, 19) combine to give rough validation to this poorly defined hypothesis, especially the A-B sector of it.

The series of studies by McGeoch and his associates (10, 13, 14) ran into direct conflict with this hypothesis and the experimental evidence supporting it. Using meaningful words, they consistently found that as the judged similarity of the original and interpolated materials increased, interference also increased. The highest degree of similarity they could obtain, where close synonyms appeared on the two serial lists, yielded the most interference. There was no evidence here of facilitation as one approached identity. In *The Psychology of Human Learning* (12) Mc-Geoch offered two alternative rapprochements between his data and the Skaggs-Robinson Hypothesis: (1) He distinguished "similarity of meaning" and "degrees of identity" as two different dimensions of similarity, each having a different interference function. This distinction was suggested by the fact that some of the experiments supporting the hypothesis (8, 11, 19) had employed numeral and letter combinations with similarity indexed by the number of identical elements. Unfortunately, in other substantiating studies, materials were used in which identical elements

were no more readily specifiable than with meaningful words. Dreis (4), for example, used code-substitution, and Watson (22) used card-sorting. Furthermore, this type of resolution implies an analysis of meaningful similarity that would segregate it from identity of elements, and this has not been done. (2) At a later point, McGeoch tried to resolve the difficulty by stating that his results applied only to the portion of the Robinson Curve ebtween B and C, i.e., that the maximum similarity of his materials only reached point B. However, given the multidirectional shape of this theoretical function and the fact that point B defines no degree of similarity, not only could any obtained data be fitted to some portion of it, but it could always be argued that the similarity of one's materials fell *anywhere* between A and C. In other words, this second suggestion is incapable of either proof or disproof.

Perhaps the clearest experimental evidence against either of McGeoch's resolutions appears in the results of a recent experiment by the writer (17). *Also* using meaningful materials in the tradi-tional retroaction paradigm, interference was found to *decrease* as the meaningful similarity among the response members increased. Not only would these results seem to fit "degrees of identity" rather than "similarity of meaning" as the functioning dimension, despite the nature of the materials used, but they fall within the A to B sector of the theoretical curve.

Quite apart from the apparent negative evidence in the McGeoch studies, the Skaggs-Robinson Hypothesis is inadequate on several grounds. It does, to be sure, allow ordinary learning to occur. But (a) it contains a dual function of facilitation in relation to similarity without specifying at what degree of similarity the shift occurs; (b) no specification is made of the locus of similarities

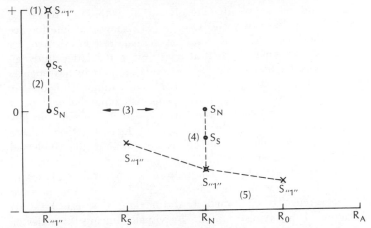

Fig. 3. Allocation of experimental data: vertical, direction and degree of either transfer or retroaction; horizontal, degrees of response similarity. Numbers in parentheses refer to step in analysis followed in text.

within the materials practiced (whether among stimulus members, response members or both), and we have seen that both the direction and the degree of either transfer or retroaction are empirically predictable from such specification. One of the most recent attempts to integrate these data has been made by Gibson (5). She followed Wylie's lead in differentiating between stimulus variation and response variation, and she added to this picture the refinement of stimulus generalization, derived from Pavlovian conditioning principles. Gibson's two theoretical laws were: (1) if responses are *identical* facilitation is obtained, its amount increasing with the degree of stimulus generalization (similarity); (2) if responses are *different* interference is obtained, its amount increasing with the degree of stimulus generalization (similarity). These hypotheses fit much of the data in the field and further serve to integrate the phenomena of human learning with those of the animal laboratory. But they are insufficient. (a) No account is given of the *degree* of response similarity, and this appears as one of the relevant variables. (b) We have one function

(increasing interference) when responses are different and another (decreasing interference) when responses are "identical"; and one would anticipate, therefore, a strange, abrupt shift in function somewhere along the line as the degree of response difference is reduced. (c) The fundamental paradox remains: responses can never be truly identical but must always be different to some degree, yet ordinary learning can occur.

THE TRANSFER AND RETROACTION SURFACE

The formulation proposed here makes full use of Gibson's analysis, but, utilizing data which have recently become available, goes beyond it. It is quite literally constructed from the empirical laws presented above, and this can be demonstrated by use of Figure 3, which provides a rational framework within which the data can be integrated. The vertical dimension represents the direction and degree of *either* transfer or retroaction; degrees of response similarity are distributed along the horizontal dimension. The parenthetical numbers refer to the sequence of steps to be followed in allocating the data.

Let us first consider the ordinary learning of an association, the case in which the same materials are used for original and interpolated activities. Here functionally identical stimuli and responses are successively repeated and maximal facilitation is obtained, allowing us to locate the first point as shown (number 1). The phenomena of positive transfer (stimulus generalization) and retroactive facilitation when responses are identical and stimuli varied are represented by the series of open circles (number 2): as the degree of stimulus similarity decreases from "identity" less and less facilitation is obtained, effects of zero magnitude being found when stimuli are neutral. Data reported by Hovland (9) and Hamilton (7) are typical. As pointed out earlier, the fact that Hamilton and Gibson (6) used the same materials and procedures, with the single exception that responses were the same in the former case and different in the latter, provides an extremely useful comparison (see number 3); where stimulus members are neutral, effects of approximately zero magnitude are obtained in both experiments, allowing us to link the Gibson and Hamilton data together on the zero-effect base line. In other words, variations in the relation between response members are of no consequence when stimulus members are completely unrelated. The Gibson experiment itself, along with other substantiating studies, provides data for the condition in which responses are different and neutral while stimulus similarity is varied. Here negative transfer and retroactive interference are regularly obtained, increasing in magnitude as the similarity of the stimulus members increases, and these data are represented by the series of solid circles (see number 4). There remains to be included the condition in which stimuli are constant and response similarity is varied. The fact that "identity" of stimulus and variation of response yields negative transfer and retroactive interference is amply testified to by a number of studies (1, 6, 21). Experiments in which the *degree* of response similarity is sys-

tematically varied, as those by Bruce (1) and Osgood (17), show that interference is *less* for similar responses than for neutral ones. Since the latter study included a condition in which responses were neutral and stimuli functionally identical, thus matching the final point of the Gibson data, it is possible to link the two sets of facts together. These data are represented by the connected series of X's (number 5).

The pattern of empirical points established here sharply limits the possible theoretical functions that can be generated. By visually tracing the series of X's, for example, including the point for ordinary learning, a fairly well-defined curve becomes apparent, this curve representing the functions for stimulus "identity." A family of such stimulus-relation curves has been constructed to fit both these empirical points and the requirements of common sense, and they appear in Figure 4. The function for *stimulus neutrality* is a straight line of zero effect, reflecting the reasonable fact that response variations are of no consequence when successive stimulus situations are completely unrelated. Given this as a zero-effect base line, increasing the similarity among stimuli yields a progressive maximization of *both* facilitation and interference, the actual direction of the effect being dependent upon response relations. The greatest facilitation and the greatest interference are possible only with functional *stimulus identity*. Intermediate transfer and retroaction effects fall between these limits depending upon degrees of stimulus similarity. The points for antagonistic responses, showing a final, sharp increase in interference, are admittedly hypothetical. However, the writer has recently reported (18) evidence for a special form of *reciprocal inhibition* associated with the successive learning of meaningfully opposed responses. The assumption is made here that this in-

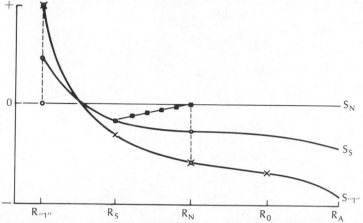

Fig. 4. Family of stimulus-relation curves constructed from data in Fig. 3; series of open squares represents data obtained by McGeoch and his associates (see text).

hibitory effect is maximal when responses are directly antagonistic.

But how do the classic findings of McGeoch and his associates fit this hypothesis? In a real sense, they serve as a crucial test of it, being both well substantiated and in apparent conflict with other results. It will be remembered that these investigators employed a method wherein the similarity of *both* stimuli and responses varied simultaneously and through the same degrees, actually from neutrality of both to high similarity (but not identity) of both. As may be seen from the row of open squares in Figure 4, the present hypothesis *must* predict gradually increasing amounts of interference under these conditions, and this is precisely the result obtained in these studies.

Although Figure 4 provides a useful method of demonstrating the congruence of empirical data and theoretical functions, it does not offer a clear picture of the hypothesis as a whole. To do so requires a three dimensional form, representing stimulus similarity, response similarity and degree of effect as simultaneously interrelated variables. Figure 5 presents what may be termed *the trans-*

fer and retroaction surface. The vertical dimension represents the direction and degree of either transfer or retroaction, both having been shown to have identical functions of similarity; the width of the form represents stimulus similarity, from functional identity to neutrality; its length represents response similarity, varying from functional identity, through neutrality, to direct antagonism. The median horizontal plane indicates effects of zero magnitude, and it may be seen that the condition of stimulus neutrality is co-extensive with this plane regardless of response variations while the remainder of the surface intersects this plane at a point between response "identity" and response similarity. Finally, it is apparent that we have here a smooth, unbroken sequence of transfer and retroaction functions, facilitative relations rising above the median plane and interfering relations falling below it. There are no reversals in these functions nor any abrupt shifts between identity and similarity. Identity becomes merely the limiting case of maximal similarity.

Certain Advantages of This Hypothesis

By way of summary, certain advantages which this hypothesis offers in comparison with those which have preceded it may be indicated. (1) *All existing*

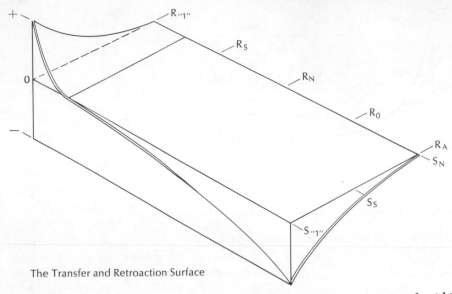

The Transfer and Retroaction Surface

The Transfer and Retroaction Surface
FIG. 5. The transfer and retroaction surface: medial plane represents effects of zero magnitude; response relations distributed along length of solid and stimulus relations along its width.

empirical data in the field are consistent with it and find representation upon the transfer and retroaction surface. This statement is by necessity limited to those data wherein the locus of the similarities is specifiable and also by the adequacy of the writer's survey of the literature. The first limitation is not a serious one. If results can be shown to be lawful, and hence predictable, when such specification of the similarity relations is possible, the conflicting and confused results obtained under unspecifiable conditions are presumably attributable to unanalyzable variations in the paradigms employed. Witness the conclusive inconclusiveness on the question of formal discipline! This state of affairs illustrates why it is so difficult to make recommendations for efficient human learning in practical situations. What, for example, are the loci of similarities when the student simultaneously studies French and Spanish?

(2) *The phenomena of both transfer and retroaction are integrated within a single framework, in so far as the similarity variable is concerned.* It is common textbook procedure to study transfer under learning and retroaction under forgetting, as if these processes were somehow different in kind. The present analysis, it is felt, is a step in the direction of integrating the problems of human learning. Another step in the same direction is also suggested here: distinctions are often made in terms of meaningful vs. nonsense materials, meaningful similarity vs. degrees of identity, and so on. It should be pointed out that data substantiating each of the three empirical laws derived above have been obtained with meaningful and nonsense materials, with materials varying in terms of meaningful similarity as well as degrees of identity. There is here, of course, the underlying problem of defining similarity. It may be defined operationally in terms of generalization (*cf.* Gibson, 5), although this definition is inherently circular since the phenomenon of generalization is nothing other than a case of positive transfer with functionally identical responses. Any precise behavioral definition of similarity will re-

quire much more knowledge of the nervous system than we have at present. In practice, degrees of similarity have been specified informally by experimenters or formally by a sample of judges, which probably suffices for our present rather gross purposes.

(3) *Although constructed directly from existing empirical evidence, this hypothesis does go considerably beyond it, predicting phenomena that have not as yet been observed.* For one thing that portion of the transfer and retroaction surface where increasing similarity of response (high degrees) is accompanied by increasing facilitation remains to be explored by standard procedures, the Robinson group of studies having used a memory span technique.[1] It will also be noticed that the theoretical surface requires that, regardless of the degree of stimulus similarity, all functions must become facilitative at precisely the same degree of response similarity, somewhere between identity and high similarity. In other words, just as the degree of response variation is inconsequential when stimulus members are neutral, so there must exist (according to this hypothesis) some definite degree of response similarity for which all variations among stimuli will yield zero effect. This is a novel but necessary prediction from theory that sets an intriguing experimental problem. It is not inconceivable that this common shift-over from facilitation to interference at a certain degree of variation among responses may reflect a basic characteristic of the nervous system,—but this is all assuming that the present hypothesis will be found valid in terms of constantly accruing facts.

(4) Finally, *this hypothesis resolves the fundamental paradox with which this paper began—the fact of ordinary learning becomes theoretically feasible.* The transfer and retroaction surface describes a system of curves within which the condition of ordinary learning, with func-

tionally identical stimuli and responses in the materials successively practiced, is continuous with other relations. Identity is here merely the limiting case of maximal similarity, and no abrupt shifts of function are required to account for the fact that learning occurs.

1. BRUCE, R. W. Conditions of transfer of training. *J. exp. Psychol.*, 1933, **16**, 343-61.
2. BUGELSKI, B. R. Interferences with recall of original responses after learning new responses to old stimuli. *J. exp. Psychol.*, 1942, **30**, 368-79.
3. CHENG, N. Y. Retroactive effect and degree of similarity. *J. exp. Psychol.*, 1929, **12**, 444-9.
4. DREIS, T. A. Two studies in retroaction: I. Influence of partial identity. II. Susceptibility to retroaction at various grade levels. *J. gen. Psychol.*, 1933, **8**, 157-71.
5. GIBSON, E. J. A systematic application of the concepts of generalization and differentiation to verbal learning. *Psychol. Rev.*, 1940, **47**, 196-229.
6. ———. Retroactive inhibition as a function of degree of generalization between tasks. *J. exp. Psychol.*, 1941, **28**, 93-115.
7. HAMILTON, R. J. Retroactive facilitation as a function of degree of generalization between tasks. *J. exp. Psychol.*, 1943, **32**, 363-76.
8. HARDEN, L. M. A quantitative study of the similarity factor in retroactive inhibition. *J. gen. Psychol.*, 1929, **2**, 421-30.
9. HOVLAND, C. I. The generalization of conditioned responses: I. The sensory generalization of conditioned responses with varying frequencies of tone. *J. gen. Psychol.*, 1937, **17**, 125-48.
10. JOHNSON, L. M. Similarity of meaning as a factor in retroactive inhibition. *J. gen. Psychol.*, 1933, **9**, 377-388.
11. KENNELLY, T. W. The role of similarity in retroactive inhibition. *Arch. Psychol.*, N. Y., 1941, **37**, No. 260.
12. McGEOCH, J. A. *The psychology of human learning.* New York: Longmans, Green and Co., 1942.
13. ———, & McDONALD, W. T. Meaningful relation and retroactive inhibition. *Amer. J. Psychol.*, 1931, **43**, 579-88.
14. ———, & McGEOCH, G. O. Studies in retroactive inhibition: X. The influence of similarity of meaning between lists of paired associates. *J. exp. Psychol.*, 1937, **21**, 320-29.
15. McKINNEY, F. Quantitative and qualitative essential elements of transfer. *J. exp. Psychol.*, 1933, **16**, 854-864.
16. MELTON, A. W., & VON LACKUM, W. J. Retroactive and proactive inhibition in retention: evidence for a two-factor theory of

1. An as yet uncompleted investigation by Mark W. Harriman at Johns Hopkins University appears to be filling in this gap in our empirical knowledge. With functionally identical stimulus members, responses on original and interpolated lists are varied by extremely small degrees, such as having the singular and plural of the same word on two lists, and the predicted results seem to be forthcoming.

retroactive inhibition. *Amer. J. Psychol.*, 1941, **45**, 157-173.

17. Osgood, C. E. Meaningful similarity and interference in learning. *J. exp. Psychol.*, 1946, **36**, 277-301.

18. ————. An investigation into the causes of retroactive interference. *J. exp. Psychol.*, 1948, **38**, 132-154.

19. Robinson, E. S. The "similarity" factor in retroaction. *Amer. J. Psychol.*, 1927, **39**, 297-312.

20. Siipola, E. M. The relation of transfer to similarity in habit-structure. *J. exp. Psychol.*, 1941, **28**, 233-261.

21. Underwood, B. J. The effect of successive interpolations on retroactive and proactive

inhibition. *Psychol. Monogr.*, 1945, **59**, No. 273.

22. Watson, B. The similarity factor in transfer and inhibition. *J. educ. Psychol.*, 1938, **29**, 145-157.

23. Wickens, D. D. The transference of conditioned excitation and conditioned inhibition from one muscle group to the antagonistic muscle group. *J. exp. Psychol.*, 1938, **22**, 101-123.

24. Wylie, H. H. An experimental study of transfer of response in the white rat. *Behav. Monogr.*, 1919, **3**, No. 16.

25. Yum, K. S. An experimental test of the law of assimilation. *J. exp. Psychol.*, 1931, **14**, 68-82.

32 / Mixed vs. Unmixed Lists in Transfer Studies

HELEN M. TWEDT AND BENTON J. UNDERWOOD,[1] *Northwestern University*

In relatively recent years there has been an increase in the frequency with which mixed lists (ML) have been used to study transfer with verbal materials. In ML a single group of Ss may be used. Each S learns only two lists in which different relationships between subgroups of items allow the simultaneous observation of the transfer effects produced by these different relationships. Thus, if each of two lists consisted of nine paired associates, three pairs in each list could form the A-B, A-C paradigm, three the A-B, C-B, and three an A-B, C-D paradigm.

The ML procedure may be contrasted with the classical one in which unmixed lists (UL) are used. With UL the relationships between all items in the two lists are the same. Thus, if the paradigm was A-B, A-C, all stimuli in the two lists would be the same and all responses different. Obviously, to study transfer effects for more than one paradigm requires as many different sets of lists as there are paradigms.

Certain contradictions in the facts of transfer could be attributed to the possibility that UL and ML produce different transfer effects. The clearest example of this possibility is seen in the work of Mandler and Heinemann (1956) and

Porter and Duncan (1953). In both of these studies an A-B, A-C paradigm was used, and also a paradigm that will be called A-B, A-Br. In this latter paradigm the same stimuli and same responses are used in both lists (UL) or among a subgroup of items in the two lists (ML), but they are re-paired in the second list. Porter and Duncan, using UL, found poorer second-list performance on A-B, A-Br than on A-B, A-C, while Mandler and Heinemann found just the opposite. There are other differences between the two studies over and above UL vs. ML which could account for this discrepancy. Indeed, a study (1958) published after the present one was completed essentially confirmed the Porter-Duncan results using ML. Therefore, other differences between the studies may be responsible for the different results. In other contradictions in the literature (e.g., Bugelski and Cadwallader [1956] vs. Osgood [1946]) ML vs. UL is again one of several possible factors involved. Therefore, a direct test of the transfer effects for the two kinds of lists is indicated to decide whether or not ML vs. UL is a

From the *Journal of Experimental Psychology*, 1959, **58**, 111-16, with permission of the authors and publisher.
1. We are grateful to R. W. Schulz for his critical reading of the manuscript.

variable of importance in the study of transfer. The major purpose of the present study is to make such a test.

There was an a priori reason to suggest that ML vs. UL is a variable influencing the relative amount of transfer among different paradigms. This may be seen by considering the situation in which S learns A-B, A-C with UL. While this paradigm can produce negative transfer, it has always been puzzling why (*a*) the negative effects are small, and why (*b*) so few B responses intrude during the learning of A-C. This would be less puzzling if it is assumed that two relatively independent response systems are maintained, differentiated by temporal or first and second list distinctions. If this differentiation is possible, S could instruct himself *not* to give responses from the first list and a relatively small amount of negative transfer would be expected. However, if the ML procedure is used in which some of the first-list responses are appropriate in the second list (A-B, C-B or A-B, A-Br) and some are not (A-B, A-C), the maintenance of the independent response systems is not possible. The prediction would be, therefore, that negative transfer would be greater for ML than for UL in the A-B, A-C paradigm. It is also possible that other interactions among effects of other paradigms could occur in ML and not in UL.

METHOD

Lists.—The transfer effects for four paradigms were studied, each by the use of both UL and ML. If A-B represents the first list, the four paradigms may be symbolized in the second list (UL), or in subgroups of items in the second list (ML), as A-C, A-Br, C-B, and C-D. The last paradigm may be considered the control condition, in that no systematic identities obtain between the items in the two lists (UL) or between the particular subgroup of items for ML.

The materials were paired-associate lists of 12 pairs of two-syllable adjectives. All Ss in all conditions with both UL and ML

learned exactly the same *second* list. Therefore, any differences in transfer resulting from ML vs. UL cannot be attributed to differences in list or pair difficulty. This second list consisted of the following 12 pairs: *honest—frantic, senior—rotten, certain—aloof, ready—severe, human—unshut, complex—valiant, single—noonday, zigzag—absurd, lukewarm—stubborn, profane—bitter, famous—exact, filthy—rising.* These 12 pairs were selected by use of a table of random numbers from a pool of 24 pairs used by Young (1955) in his low-similarity conditions. The items forming the remaining 12 pairs were used as necessary to construct the first list: for UL, all 12 pairs were used for the A-B, C-D paradigm, none was used for A-B, A-Br, and 12 items were necessary for A-B, A-C, and A-B, C-B.

For ML, with 4 conditions and 12 pairs in a list, each condition was represented by 3 pairs. The use of four groups of Ss for ML made it possible to use all 12 pairs in the second list for each paradigm. Thus, in UL, four groups of Ss were needed, each group having a given paradigm, and this paradigm held between all 12 pairs in the two lists. In ML, four groups were also used, and for all four groups combined, the relationship between the first and second lists was exactly the same as for UL.

Procedure.—The first list was presented until one perfect trial was attained. After 1 min. the second list was presented for 10 trials. Learning was by the anticipation method, with the stimulus being presented for 2 sec. and the stimulus and response together for 2 sec., as timed by a Hull-type memory drum. The intertrial interval was 4 sec. Three different orders of the lists were used to minimize serial learning. In ML the three pairs representing a given paradigm were not grouped; that is, the ordering of the pairs was such that those representing one paradigm were mixed up with those representing other paradigms. In neither ML nor UL was S instructed concerning the nature of the relationships between the two lists.

Four groups of 18 Ss each learned under the ML procedure and four other groups of the same number learned under the UL procedure. An order of conditions was made up such that each of the eight conditions was represented once by each block of eight Ss. Within each block the ordering was random. The Ss were simply assigned in order of their appearance at the laboratory. All Ss had previous experience in verbal-learning experiments.

It should be emphasized that all Ss learned the same second list. Therefore, it is of little or no consequence whether or not first lists differed in difficulty; this would be true for comparisons within UL and within ML, and it would be true for comparisons between UL and ML. In actual fact, for eight groups, the over-all mean number of trials to learn the first list was 12.7 trials, with a range of from 10.5 to 15.2. An analysis of variance yielded an F of 1.46, which is far from significant. This does not mean, of course, that these first lists did not differ in difficulty since possible ability differences among groups and possible list differences are confounded.

RESULTS

The results will be presented first in graphical form and then attention will be given to statistical analyses. In Figure 1, the mean total correct responses on the 10 transfer trials are shown for each condition for both UL and ML. For UL, each condition represents the mean performance of 18 Ss on 12 pairs. For ML, each condition represents the performance of 72 Ss, each learning three pairs. To coordinate the values for UL and ML, the total correct responses were summed for successive groups of four Ss each on ML, such that all 12 items representing a condition for UL were likewise represented for each subgroup of four Ss in ML. Thus, in a sense, 18 Ss were "constructed" out of the 72 Ss learning under ML, and this was done for each transfer condition.

In Figure 1, it may first be noted that differences between UL and ML are very small. The second fact shown in Figure 1 is that if C-D is considered the control condition, all three other conditions show negative transfer, the amount

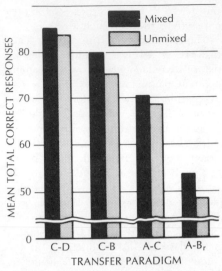

FIG. 1. Total correct responses over 10 transfer trials as a function of mixed and unmixed lists and four transfer paradigms.

of this negative transfer increasing from C-B, to A-C, to A-Br.

In Figure 1, the values represent the total correct responses over all 10 transfer trials. It is conceivable that a different ordering of the conditions could occur at various stages in learning the second list. That this is not true is shown by Figure 2, where it is seen that the ordering of conditions remains relatively constant throughout all 10 trials. Also, Figure 2 shows quite clearly that the differences between UL and ML are of small consequence. The coordination between UL and ML was handled the same way for Figure 2 as for Figure 1.

The first statistical analysis consists of a direct test of the results for UL vs. ML. The measure used was the number of correct responses over the 10 transfer trials. These comparisons were made for the total correct for each group of three items. For example, in ML one group of 18 Ss had a particular group of three pairs for A-Br. These same three pairs were also learned by 18 Ss in UL. Four t tests could be made for each condition, therefore, and

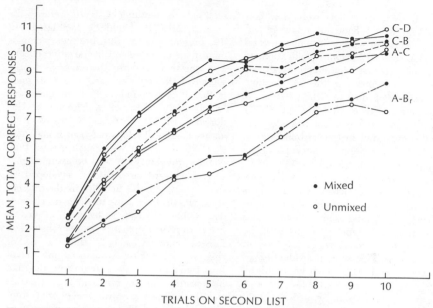

FIG. 2. Acquisition curves over 10 transfer trials as a function of mixed and unmixed lists and four transfer paradigms.

these four tests would exhaust all 12 items used for that condition. With four conditions (A-Br, A-C, C-B, and C-D) and four tests for each condition, a total of 16 *t* tests was involved. The results were that not a single *t* was significant, using the .05 significance level. Thus, it may be concluded that for the present materials and conditions, whether UL or ML is used is of no consequence in determining the amount of transfer.

The statistical analysis of results for the UL procedure alone was straightforward. Simple analysis of variance showed conditions to be a highly significant source of variance. Several *t* tests (using the pooled estimate for the error term) show the following facts: (*a*) If C-D is considered the control condition, A-C and A-Br resulted in significant negative transfer whereas C-B did not. The *t* values were 6.29, 2.68, and 1.52, respectively, with 34 *df*. (*b*) The amount of negative transfer produced by A-Br is greater than that produced by A-C. The *t* is 3.61. A comparable analysis performed on the mean correct responses on Trials 1 and 2 did not change the conclu-

sions reached for the analysis of the total correct over all 10 trials.

For the statistical analysis of the results for ML alone, direct-difference *t* tests were used among conditions, each based on 72 Ss, with each S having three items learned under each condition. Comparing C-D with each of the other three conditions gave *t* values of 10.09, 4.59, and 2.40, for A-Br, A-C, and C-B, respectively. The only conclusion which differs from those reached for UL is that in ML the C-B condition resulted in significant negative transfer (the *t* of 2.4 is at the .02 significance level).

For the A-C and A-Br conditions, a count was made of intrusions of first-list responses during the learning of the second. These were counted only if they occurred to the stimulus with which they had been paired in the first list. For A-Br, the total intrusions over 10 trials was 182 for ML and 154 for UL. For A-C, the values were 5 for ML and 4 for UL. Thus, the nature of the list does not appear to seriously affect intrusion-making tendencies.

DISCUSSION

The results have shown that UL and ML produced essentially the same transfer

results. Indeed, it is not likely that correspondence would have been higher had
the two experiments used the same method
(either UL or ML). One implication of
these results is that contradictions in the
facts of transfer, noted in the introduction,
are probably not due to ML vs. UL. A
second implication is that the possibility
that S maintains independent response systems (also suggested in the introduction) in
the A-B, A-C paradigm is untenable. The
third implication is that it appears that investigators may choose either ML or UL procedures, depending upon circumstances
which make one more desirable than another
for a particular investigation, without serious
concern that the transfer results will be
affected by this choice. It is possible, of
course, that the present near-identity of
results for UL and ML will not hold with all
materials, e.g., consonant syllables, although
there is no obvious reason why they should
not.

Concerning the transfer effects, the present experiments confirm Porter and Duncan (1953) and Besch and Reynolds (1958)
in showing that A-Br produces more negative transfer than A-C. That Mandler and
Heinemann (1956) actually found positive
transfer with A-Br and negative transfer
with A-C may be attributed (as suggested
by Besch and Reynolds) to the low meaningfulness of the responses used by Mandler
and Heinemann. However, this matter will
not be pursued here. It is sufficient to say
that it does not appear that the source of
contradiction is in the nature of the lists
(ML vs. UL).

The one finding that does not fit current
theory or previous findings is that the A-B,
C-B paradigm produced negative transfer
when evaluated against A-B, C-D. It is true
that the amount of negative transfer is small,
but it is consistent in both experiments
and is present throughout most of the 10
transfer trials. Furthermore, there is reason
to believe that the negative factor (or factors) may be greater in extent than actually
appears in the performance. It is known
(Underwood, Runquist, & Schulz, 1959) from
other research that teaching S responses
before learning a list of paired associates
will facilitate the learning. In effect, when
S learns A-B he has learned the responses

required in learning C-B; therefore, the
learning of C-B should be facilitated. In
the present results, this positive factor is
more than counteracted by negative effects.
The question remains, therefore, as to the
source of this interference. The best guess
is that it results indirectly from backward
learning. It is known (Feldman & Underwood, 1957) that as S learns A-B,
an association develops between B and A so
that B will elicit A with much greater than
chance probability. It may be assumed that
such backward associations developed in
the learning of the first list in the present
study; B will have some tendency to elicit A.
The S then proceeds to learn C-B. As this
association develops, it is possible that when
C is presented it makes S "think of" B, but
that B (via backward association) makes
him think of A (the stimulus in the first
list) leading to an erroneous "conclusion"
that B does not go with the present stimulus—C. It would not require many such
confusions to produce the negative transfer
observed.

SUMMARY

This study was designed to investigate
the transfer effects in verbal paired-associate learning using a mixed design (in which
subgroups of pairs in the second list form
various transfer paradigms with pairs in the
first) and an unmixed design (in which all
pairs in the second list relate in the same
way to the pairs in the first). Four paradigms were studied by each of these two
procedures: A-B, A-Br (second-list pairs
constitute a repairing of first-list pairs); A-B,
A-C; A-B, C-B; and A-B, C-D. The latter
paradigm constituted the control condition.
For all paradigms for both mixed and unmixed designs all Ss learned the same second list. The various paradigms were formed
by changing the pairs in the first list. Eight
groups of 18 Ss each were used. The first
list of paired adjectives was presented until
all items were correctly anticipated on a
single trial; the second or transfer list was
presented for 10 trials.

The results show no difference in the
transfer effects as a function of mixed vs.
unmixed lists. Thus, the use of various
paradigms among subgroups of items within

a single list does not produce interactions among the transfer effects for the various paradigms. It was concluded, therefore, that investigators may use either type of design without serious concern that the transfer effects will be different.

Using A-B, C-D as a control, the results show that all paradigms produce negative transfer throughout the 10 trials on the second list. The greatest negative transfer was produced by A-B, A-Br, the next greatest by A-B, A-C, and the least by A-B, C-B. A possible source of interference in the latter paradigm was discussed.

BESCH, N. F., & REYNOLDS, W. F. Associative interference in verbal paired-associate learning. *J. exp. Psychol.*, 1958, **55**, 554-8.

BUGELSKI, B. R., & CADWALLADER, T. C. A reappraisal of the transfer and retroaction surface. *J. exp. Psychol.*, 1956, **52**, 360-66.

FELDMAN, S. M., & UNDERWOOD, B. J. Stimulus recall following paired-associate learning. *J. exp. Psychol.*, 1957, **53**, 11-15.

MANDLER, G., & HEINEMANN, S. H. Effect of overlearning of a verbal response on transfer of training. *J. exp. Psychol.*, 1956, **52**, 39-46.

OSGOOD, C. E. Meaningful similarity and interference in learning. *J. exp. Psychol.*, 1946, **36**, 277-301.

PORTER, L. W., & DUNCAN, C. P. Negative transfer in verbal learning. *J. exp. Psychol.*, 1953, **46**, 61-4.

UNDERWOOD, B. J., RUNQUIST, W. N., & SCHULZ, R. W. Response learning in paired-associate lists as a function of intralist similarity. *J. exp. Psychol.*, 1959, **58**, 70-8.

YOUNG, R. K. Retroactive and proactive effects under varying conditions of response similarity. *J. exp. Psychol.*, 1955, **50**, 113-19.

33 / Implicit Verbal Chaining in Paired-associate Learning [1]

WALLACE A. RUSSELL AND LOWELL H. STORMS, *University of Minnesota*

The role of covert symbolic processes in behavior determination has been emphasized by many psychological theorists, but the relative lack of supporting experimental evidence for this influence has been noted by several writers (**2, 8**, p. 110). Among the various factors deemed relevant to the operation of mediational or symbolic processes, the verbal habits of the individual have been prominently suggested. The work of Foley and Cofer (**3**) on verbally mediated generalization, and of Bousfield (**1**), Jenkins and Russell (**6**), and others working with recall, have established that the influence of such verbal associations can be studied effectively under experimental conditions.

While the mediational role of word associations has been demonstrated in several performance situations, there are surprisingly few studies which report positive findings with regard to the effects of mediated associations upon learning. Bugelski and Scharlock, using paired-associate learning and nonsense syllables, have provided what they term a "reasonably clear-cut demonstration of mediated

association in the learning of verbal material" (**2**, p. 37). Their Ss showed facilitated learning of A-C associates when another term, B, presumably intervened between A and C as a consequence of previous learning of associations A-B and B-C. The term B, then, provided an implicit common term which was elicited by A and which in turn tended to elicit C. This mediation of the correct response C occurred even though Ss did not report deliberate use of the common term as a mnemonic device. The Bugelski and Scharlock data provide a much clearer instance of mediation than did the earlier experiments of Peters (**12**). Although the latter obtained some positive results, the majority of his test situations failed to demonstrate mediational effects.

Both Bugelski and Scharlock and

From the *Journal of Experimental Psychology*, 1955, **49**, 287-93, with permission of the authors and publisher.

1. This study is part of a larger series of studies of verbal behavior being conducted at the University of Minnesota. The series is being sponsored by the Office of Naval Research (Contract No. N8 onr-66216) under its policy of encouraging basic research.

Peters worked with associations learned within the context of the experiment and neither considered situations involving more than one intervening term. Nevertheless, applications of the mediation hypothesis have frequently referred to existing language habits and have almost always involved reference to a "chain" of several intervening terms which are linked on an associative basis. Uniprocess theorists who, according to Harlow (**4**, p. 452), maintain that "thinking is dependent only upon the formation and appropriate elicitation of a vast number of simple associations" have most commonly assumed that (*a*) mediational effects can occur across several intervening terms, and (*b*) these influences are at least as strong for associations between real words as between nonsense syllables. Hull's concept of pure stimulus acts (**5**), Miller's extension of the notion of verbally mediated generalization (**10**, p. 181), and Osgood's discussion of thinking (**11**, p. 638) are but a few examples in which one or the other of these assumptions has been made. However,

lists: List 1 established A-B associations; List 2, B-C associations; and List 3 tested for mediation effects in the learning of A-C associations. In the study reported here, real words were used rather than nonsense syllables, and two implicit terms rather than one linked the pairs learned on the test trials. Here, the learning of List 1 established A-B associations. The B term was in each case a stimulus word from the Kent-Rosanoff association test (**7**). Recently obtained norms for responses on this test [2] then made it possible to infer certain B-C associations without establishing them experimentally. Similarly, other unpublished studies provided normative data concerning the most frequent associative responses (D) made to the C terms. Thus, once the A-B associations were learned, it was possible to infer an associative chain leading from A to B to C to D. The test for mediational effects was made by requiring Ss to learn a list containing A-D pairings and appropriate control pairings (A-X) of nonchained terms. It was hypothesized that the A-D pairings would be learned more easily than the A-X pairings. The manner in which associative chains might facilitate the elicitation and learning of A-D pairs is schematically illustrated as follows:

	List 1	Associations Inferred from Norms ($B_1\rightarrow C_1\rightarrow D_1$)	List 2 (Test List)
Chaining Paradigm	$A_1 \ldots > B_1$		$A_1 \ldots\ldots\ldots > D_1$
			($B_1\rightarrow C_1$)
Control Paradigm	$A_2 \ldots > B_2$	($B_2\rightarrow C_2 D_2$)	$A_2 \ldots\ldots\ldots\ldots > X_2$
			($B_2\rightarrow C_2\rightarrow D_2$)

neither Peters nor Bugelski and Scharlock provide a basis for these assumptions.

The purpose of this experiment was to test the adequacy of the above assumptions by observing the effects of mediating verbal processes on paired-associate learning when the mediating process is implemented in part by pre-existing language habits and extends over more than one implicit verbal term.

METHOD

Design.—The design of this study was similar to that of Bugelski and Scharlock (2). Their Ss learned three paired-associate

Broken arrows indicate the association to be learned in each list. Solid arrows represent associations established before a list is learned. It can be seen that associations existing before the learning of the test list provide an indirect linkage of the A and D terms which must become associated in the chaining paradigm. In the control paradigm, a similar linkage exists between A and D, but no such connection can be inferred between the A-X pairs which are to be learned.

Construction of paired-associate lists.—

2. Revised norms for 100 words from the Kent-Rosanoff word-association test were obtained from 1008 students in beginning psychology classes at the University of Minnesota. This work was carried out as part of a larger project on verbal behavior. Information concerning these norms may be obtained from the authors.

TABLE 1. *Associative frequencies of the three most frequent responses to ten Kent-Rosanoff stimulus words (Based on R's from 1008 Ss)*

Stimulus	Primary R	f	Secondary R	f	Tertiary R	f
STEM	FLOWER	402	PLANT	224	LEAF	125
MEMORY	MIND	119	REMEMBER	99	FORGET	80
SOLDIER	ARMY	187	SAILOR	182	MAN	101
TROUBLE	BAD	89	SHOOTER	49	WORRY	45
WISH	WANT	124	DREAM	118	DESIRE	112
JUSTICE	PEACE	250	LAW	182	COURTS	163
THIEF	STEAL	286	ROBBER	138	CROOK	69
OCEAN	WATER	314	SEA	233	BLUE	111
COMMAND	ORDER	196	ARMY	102	OBEY	78
FRUIT	APPLE	378	VEGETABLE	114	ORANGE	94

Tables 1 and 2 contain the associative frequencies from the norms [3] for the three most frequent responses to the words relevant to this experiment. Table 1 provides this information for the ten Kent-Rosanoff stimulus words employed and Table 2 provides analogous data for the most frequent responses to those ten words.

Table 3 contains the nonsense syllables, the particular associative chains, and the control words used throughout the experiment. List 1 (A-B pairings) was made up of the nonsense syllables in Column A and the corresponding words in Column B. Columns B, C, and D list the verbal associative chains (B → C → D) derived from the normative tables. Two test lists were formed. One combined the first five nonsense syllables of Column A with the five corresponding words of Column D and the last five nonsense syllables with the corresponding words of Column X. The other combined the first five nonsense syllables in Column A with the five corresponding words of Column X and the last five nonsense syllables with the

five corresponding words of Column D. Thus the two lists were counterbalanced and each contained five A-D and five A-X pairs. The response words of Form 1 of the test list are followed by a "1" in the table; the remaining words made up Form 2.

The ten nonsense syllables of Column A were selected from Melton (9), and all had Glaze association values of 0%. The ten verbal chains listed in Columns B, C, and D of the table were selected so that as far as the complete norms would indicate, no word in any chain appeared among the ten most frequent responses to any word in any other chain. In addition, no final word (D) in a chain appeared as a response to the first word (B) more than seven times in the 1008 responses to that word in the norms. It may be noted that while Column C is essential to the construction of the ten associative chains, no words in that column appeared in any of the experimental lists. The control words in Column X were chosen from the Kent-Rosanoff list such that none

3. See footnote 2.

TABLE 2. *Associative frequencies of the three most frequent responses to ten primary responses to Kent-Rosanoff stimulus words (Based on R's from 100 Ss)*

Word	Primary R	f	Secondary R	f	Tertiary R	f
FLOWER	SMELL	15	ROSE	12	PRETTY	12
MIND	BRAIN	15	MATTER	14	THINK, SOUL	12
ARMY	NAVY	39	SERVICE	7	SOLDIER, MAN	4
BAD	GOOD	71	EVIL	4	MEAN	3
WANT	NEED	27	DESIRE	19	HAVE	8
PEACE	WAR	42	DOVE	10	QUIET	8
STEAL	TAKE	14	THIEF	10	ROB	8
WATER	DRINK	19	THIRSTY	14	WET	11
ORDER	DISORDER	14	COMMAND	6	STOP	5
APPLE	TREE	16	RED	14	ORANGE	13

TABLE 3. *Nonsense syllables, associative chains, and control words used in forming the paired-associate lists*

A	B	C	D	X
Non-sense Syl-lable	First Chained Word	Second Chained Word	Final Chained Word	Control Word
CEF	STEM	FLOWER	SMELL (1)	JOY
DAX	MEMORY	MIND	MATTER (1)	AFRAID
YOV	SOLDIER	ARMY	NAVY (1)	CHEESE
VUX	TROUBLE	BAD	GOOD (1)	MUSIC
WUB	WISH	WANT	NEED (1)	TABLE
GEX	JUSTICE	PEACE	WAR	HOUSE (1)
JID	THIEF	STEAL	TAKE	SLEEP (1)
ZIL	OCEAN	WATER	DRINK	DOCTOR (1)
LAJ	COMMAND	ORDER	DISORDER	CABBAGE (1)
MYV	FRUIT	APPLE	RED	HAND (1)

Note.—The words and syllables were presented in capital letters exactly as above. The response words of Form 1 of the test list are followed by a "1."

appeared among the ten most frequent responses to any of the chained words and no chained word appeared among the ten most frequent responses to a control word. Finally, the control words were matched with the final words of each chain on the basis of Thorndike-Lorge (13) frequency as a partial equalization of difficulty between control and experimental words.

Procedure. — Twenty-seven sophomore women from a beginning psychology class served as Ss.

Following general instructions on paired-associate learning, each S learned List 1 on a standard Hull-type memory drum. Each stimulus word was exposed for 2 sec. before the response word appeared beside it for another 2-sec. period. The next stimulus word followed immediately, except that 4 sec. elapsed after each complete trial through the list. The S was required to learn the ten pairs in List 1 to a criterion of three consecutive trials in which all response words were correctly anticipated. To control for serial position effects, the list was presented in three successive random orders of pairs before the first order was repeated. Three Ss failed to reach the criterion on List 1 within 40 min. and were not used further in the experiment.

After a pause of 4 min., each remaining S was presented with either Form 1 or Form 2 of the test list. The Ss were instructed that the procedure was exactly the same as for

List 1 and were urged to do their best on the test list. Since one S failed to reach the criterion of one trial in which all the response words were correctly anticipated, there remained 23 Ss for the final analysis of results. Twelve of these learned Form 1 of the test list and 11 learned Form 2.

For each S, all correct anticipations and errors were tabulated for both List 1 and the test list. Measures used in the final analysis were: (a) the number of trials required to reach the criterion on List 1; (b) the number of mediated (D) and unmediated (X) responses occurring in the first five different correct anticipations by each S; (c) the total number of correct responses made for the mediated (D) and unmediated (X) words during the test trials.

Control experiment.—Twelve additional female Ss from the same population were used in a subsequently performed control experiment designed to allow a comparison of the learning of A-D and A-X pairs in a situation where associative chaining could not differentially contribute to the learning of the pairs. Instead of learning List 1, these Ss first learned either Form 1 or Form 2 of the test list. The second list was the other form of the test list. Thus, in the control experiment, associative facilitation due to A → B → C → D linkages was not possible because the A-B associations of List 1 were not learned by any S. The analysis of results for the control Ss was based on measures similar to those of the main experiment.

RESULTS

Since two forms of the test list and two groups of Ss were involved in the design, the equivalence of the two lists and the two groups must be established before the combined results can be dealt with. An analysis of the mean number of trials required to reach the criterion of learning on List 1, which all Ss learned, indicated that the 12 Ss who subsequently learned Form 1 of the test list did not differ significantly ($t = .52$) from the 11 Ss who subsequently learned Form 2 of the test list. The mean for the former group was 25.00

$(SD=9.17)$; for the latter it was 22.91 $(SD=9.30)$. With respect to performance on the two forms of the test list, the mean number of correct anticipations per S during learning did not differ significantly between Forms 1 and 2. The means for Forms 1 and 2 were, respectively, 67.08 $(SD=30.75)$ and 58.09 $(SD=17.04)$. The Behrens-Fisher d of .87 did not allow rejection of the null hypothesis concerning form differences.

As a consequence of these comparisons, the results from Forms 1 and 2 of the test list were combined. In order to determine whether the response terms for A-D pairs, for which associative chaining was possible, were more easily elicited during the early trials, an analysis was made of the first five different correct responses made by each S. Of the 115 responses in this analysis, 67 were members of "chained" A-D pairs and 48 were from "unchained" A-X pairs. The normal curve approximation to the binomial indicates that a result this large and in this direction would occur by chance less than 4 times in 100 if the probabilities of successes for A-D and A-X pairs were equal. Of the 23 Ss in this part of the experiment, 19 showed more chained than unchained responses in their first five different correct responses. The same one-tailed binomial test indicated that this result would occur by chance only 1 time in 1000 if the probabilities of successes for all pairs were equal. The conclusion that chained words were more easily elicited during the early trials of learning seemed warranted.

The major purpose of the experiment, however, was to compare the ease with which chained and unchained pairs were learned. The design allowed this comparison to be made with each S acting as her own control. Since each S learned an equal number of chained (A-D) and unchained (AX) pairs, the total number of correct anticipations by each S for the unchained pairs was subtracted from the corresponding total for chained pairs. If there is facilitation of the learning of chained pairs (i.e., S has a larger number of correct anticipations on the A-D than on the A-X pairs) this difference will be positive. Over all Ss the mean difference between chained and unchained pairs was 3.74 $(SD=5.32)$. A t of 3.30 $(.01 > p > .001)$ leads to rejection of the null hypothesis, and the conclusion that there was facilitation of learning of A-D pairs as contrasted with the learning of A-X pairs.

A secondary analysis of performance on Form 1 and Form 2 separately revealed that the direction of the difference between chained and unchained pairs was positive for both forms (Form 1, M $= +4.92$, $SD=5.85$; Form 2, M$= +2.45$, $SD=4.31$). For Form 1, the t of 2.79 was significant at the .02 level of confidence. For Form 2, the t of 1.80 was between the .15 and .10 levels.

It was recognized that, if for reasons other than associative chaining, the A-D pairs were as a group intrinsically easier to learn than the A-X pairs, the results obtained here could be accounted for on the basis of that factor alone. The control study was run to provide information about the relative difficulty of A-D and A-X pairs in a situation where chaining of A-D pairs was not possible. The 12 Ss in the control experiment learned both Forms 1 and 2 of the test list. The performance of these Ss on whichever form was learned last provided the basis for the analysis of the control experiment. First, the mean number of correct anticipations of the response word was determined for the ten A-D and the ten A-X pairs. The means were 7.06 and 7.35 respectively, with SD's of 1.29 and 1.39. This difference did not approach significance and the direction of difference is unfavorable to the hypothesis that the A-D pairs were easier to learn than the A-X pairs. Finally, the two major analyses of the main experiment were repeated here. As Table 4 indicates, neither of the differences tested was significant, and in each case the direction of difference did not favor the A-D pairs.

TABLE 4. *Summary of major results*

Experi-ment	Initial Successful Anticipations (First 5 Different Correct R's for Each S)			Total Correct Responses: Mean of Chained Minus Unchained	
	Chained	Un-chained	Signifi-cance of Differ-ence	(3)	Signifi-cance
Main	67	48	.04	+ 3.74	.01
Control	30	30		− 0.50	

In the absence of the possibility of associative chaining, then, there was no evidence of easier learning of the A-D pairs used in this experiment.

DISCUSSION

Statistically, these results provide stronger evidence for mediational effects in learning than do the results of Bugelski and Scharlock (2). This is true in spite of the fact that the present experiment involves one more step in the chain of associations mediating the facilitated learning. Instead of an A-B-C sequence contributing to the learning of A-C, an A-B-C-D chain contributed to the learning of A-D. This demonstration of mediational influences extending over more than one intervening term, and involving language habits established prior to the experiment, offers some confirmation for theoretical explanations of thinking, problem solving, etc., which have postulated the operation of such complex implicit associative sequences.

Of course, the highly significant results obtained here, in the face of less convincing evidence obtained in schematically simpler situations (2), raise the problem of accounting for this stronger effect. Two possibilities occur to the writers. First, it is probable that this experiment allowed a more efficient analysis by removing variability due to individual differences in learning ability. Although Bugelski and Scharlock endeavored

to have each S act as his own control, their technique of analysis admittedly left some individual difference factors operating. Our procedure of using within-individual differences removed this variable and may have allowed mediational effects to be revealed more sensitively. Furthermore, it is at least conceivable that the pre-existing verbal habits of this experiment were stronger than the associations learned during the Bugelski-Scharlock experiment. It is probable that such strong associations, if such they were, brought about mediational effects more readily than weaker associations would have done.

The mere demonstration of mediational influences in learning, however, does not explain how the effect is achieved. The most plausible explanation would hold that the presence of an associative chain between the stimulus term and the response term in paired-associative learning increases the probability that the response term will be elicited in the learning situation. Any such elicitation would presumably have two effects. First, it would increase the total number of correct responses made during learning. This would be a performance change influencing the criterion measures used in this study. Second, there would be an influence on learning. The performance change, of course, does not necessarily reflect a change in the underlying learning process itself. Nevertheless, such a learning change is implied, since any factor which increases the frequency of occurrence of a correct response would increase the number of reinforced trials and thus indirectly influence the amount of learning.

Less obvious is the possibility that the differences between the mediated and unmediated pairs are due to interference effects in the learning of the control (A-X) pairs. Although interference due to the tendency for the A terms to elicit B was controlled by the design, possible differential interference effects may be seen when the entire A-B-C-D sequence is considered. If the probability of the elicitation of D is enhanced by the presence of A, as is stated above, then this tendency would compete with the elicitation of the correct response X in the unmediated pairs and possibly delay learning. It is conceivable that the associative chains here produced both a facilitative effect upon mediated pairs and an interference effect upon unmediated pairs. The possibility that these two effects of associative chains do operate is amenable to experimental test, although the design of this experiment and that of Bugelski and Scharlock (2) do not allow an analysis which would separate them.

Whatever the explanation of the mediational effect may be, there can be little doubt that it is the phenomenon underlying the superior performance of Ss on the A-D pairs. The controls inherent in the main experiment plus the additional information from the control experiment leave little room for alternative hypotheses. Such factors as serial position, idiosyncrasies of words and Ss, etc. operated equally for the mediated and nonmediated pairs and could not account for the differences obtained.

The fact that questions following the experiment yielded no evidence that Ss could verbalize the mediating terms only emphasizes the Bugelski-Scharlock conclusion that mediated association may be "unconscious."

Summary

This experiment was designed to study the effects of mediating verbal processes on paired-associate learning when the mediating process is implemented in part by pre-existing language habits and extends over more than one implicit verbal term.

First, ten chains of word associations, B-C-D, were constructed from normative data on association frequencies. Twenty-three female college Ss then learned a list of A-B pairs where the A terms were nonsense syllables and the B terms were the initial members of the chains described above. The test situation required that Ss learn another list consisting of A-D and A-X pairs. The D terms were the final members of the associative word chains, and the X terms were not associated with any of the chains. A control experiment revealed that the A-D and A-X pairs did not differ in difficulty in the absence of chaining possibilities.

It was found that the A-D pairs were learned significantly faster, and elicited in learning, than the A-X pairs. It was concluded that implicit verbal chains of more than one link mediated these effects. Reasons for these results being even more clearcut than those of schematically simpler previous experiments were discussed.

1. BOUSFIELD, W. A. The occurrence of clustering in the recall of randomly arranged associates. *J. gen. Psychol.*, 1953, **49**, 229-40.
2. BUGELSKI, B. R., & SCHARLOCK, D. P. An experimental demonstration of unconscious mediated association. *J. exp. Psychol.*, 1952, **44**, 334-8.
3. FOLEY, J. P., JR., & COFER, C. N. Mediated generalization and the interpretation of verbal behavior: II. Experimental study of certain homophone and synonym gradients. *J. exp. Psychol.*, 1943, **32**, 168-75.
4. HARLOW, H. F. Thinking. In H. Helson (Ed.), *Theoretical foundations of psychology*. New York: D. Van Nostrand, 1951. Pp. 452-500.
5. HULL, C. L. Goal attraction and directing ideas conceived as habit phenomena. *Psychol. Rev.*, 1931, **38**, 487-506.
6. JENKINS, J. J., & RUSSELL, W. A. Associative clustering during recall. *J. abnorm. soc. Psychol.*, 1952, **47**. 818-21.
7. KENT, G. H., & ROSANOFF, A. J. A study of association in insanity. *Amer. J. Insanity*, 1910, **67**, 37-96, 317-90.
8. MCGEOCH, J. A., & IRION, A. L. *The psychology of human learning*. New York: Longmans, Green, 1952.
9. MELTON, A. W. Materials for use in experimental studies of the learning and retention of verbal habits. Unpublished manuscript, Univ. of Missouri, 1940.
10. MILLER, G. A. *Language and communication.* New York: McGraw-Hill, 1951.
11. OSGOOD, C. E. *Method and theory in experimental psychology.* New York: Oxford Univ. Press, 1953.
12. PETERS, H. N. Mediate association. *J. exp. Psychol.*, 1935, **18**, 20-48.
13. THORNDIKE, E. L., & LORGE, I. *The teacher's word book of 30,000 words.* New York: Teachers Coll., Columbia Univ., 1944.

34 / Associative Factors in Verbal Transfer [1]

JARVIS BASTIAN,[2] *University of Minnesota*

In the two decades since the publication of Gibson's (1940) well-known analysis of verbal transfer in terms of generalization and differentiation, an impressive amount of research has been directed towards tracing out the effects of verbal generalization in a wide range of transfer situations. These efforts have produced a body of results of sufficient breadth and uniformity to permit the construction of fairly general statements of the experimental effects of verbal generalization, such as those provided by Osgood (1953) and Underwood (1949).

However, comparatively little has been done to determine the underlying processes responsible for these effects. It is generally conceded that verbal generalization, aside from that which is ascribable to the phonetic or orthographic properties of the experimental materials, is the result of processes quite different from those governing primary generalization. Nevertheless, the feeling persists that there must be parallels between the two phenomena, particularly in regard to the roles played by similarities in the verbal domain and the physically specifiable similarities associated with primary generalization.

It is perhaps for this reason that the notion of "meaning" is so often invoked in theoretical discussions of verbal generalization, because "similarities in meaning" apparently provide a basis for verbal generalization that is analogous to the similarities in physical attributes involved in primary generalization.

In spite of the extremely formidable logical and linguistic problems that are involved in the notion of "similarities of meaning," its use in this context has been strengthened by a considerable amount of experimental evidence clearly relating the degree to which verbal materials are judged to be similar in meaning to the degree of generalization obtaining between these materials. Haagen (1943), Morgan and Underwood (1950), and Underwood (1951) have all reported transfer results in paired associate training which indicate that generalization effects increase as a function of the degree to which words in comparable interlist positions are judged to be similar in meaning.

However, the results of these studies are possibly contaminated by another, uncontrolled, factor in the experiments. The experimental variable, degree of similarity in meaning, was manipulated in all of these experiments by selecting words from a set of 400 pairs of adjectives for which Haagen (1949) had collected ratings of degree of synonymity. But Haagen also obtained, from a separate group of judges, ratings of the degree of associative connection between these same word pairs. The correlation between the scale values derived from the two sets of ratings was .90, which was only slightly less than their individual reliability coefficients. Thus, in the experiments cited, the generalization results can be attributed as much to the associative factor as to the similarities in meaning, if, indeed, these appear as separate factors in these studies.

Although degree of semantic similarity and degree of associative connection are evidently highly correlated, it might be possible to manipulate them separately because of the considerably broader range of interverbal relations covered by associative tendencies. The exploration of this possibility is highly desirable, for McClelland and Heath (1943) and Russell and Storms (1955) have reported transfer experiments which suggest that associative factors may be fundamentally involved in the production of verbal generalization. These studies both demonstrated

From the *Journal of Experimental Psychology*, 1961, **62**, 70-79, with permission of the author and publisher.
1. This report is based on part of a PhD dissertation presented to the Graduate School of the University of Minnesota. The author is deeply indebted to W. A. Russell and J. J. Jenkins for their advice and encouragement.
2. Now at Haskins Laboratories, New York, New York.

pronounced generalization effects across paired associate lists containing words in analogous interlist positions which were linked by associative tendencies, as inferred from word association norms, but which were not semantically related in any acceptable sense.

The present experiment was designed to assess the separate and combined generalization effects produced by the two different interverbal relations in order to provide some further information that might lead to a clear conceptualization of the factors mediating verbal generalization.

METHOD

The strategy of this research required a situation that provided a sensitive index of verbal generalization, and one in which the factors of associative strength and similarity of meaning could be separated and their effects compared. For this purpose a transfer of training situation was selected that involved the successive learning of two lists of paired associates containing identical stimulus elements. The basis for the selection of this experimental situation is that in the successive learning of paired-associate lists, each containing the same set of stimulus items, but different response items, generalization between the responses results in positive transfer, whereas the lack of generalization results in negative transfer (cf. Osgood, 1953; Underwood, 1949). In addition, parallel experiments conducted by Haagen (1943) have indicated that this situation is more sensitive to generalization effects than those in which responses are held constant across lists and stimuli varied, or those in which both stimulus and response elements are varied.

Materials.—With these considerations in mind, lists of 12 paired associates were constructed with the same set of words appearing as stimulus elements in each. The response elements in List 1 were taken from the stimulus words used in the Kent-Rosanoff free association test.

Each response element in the other lists was related to a given response element in

List 1 by one of the following three relationships: Type A elements were highly frequent word associates of the List 1 response words, but were judged to bear little or no similarity to them in meaning; Type S elements were very infrequent word associates of the List 1 response words, but were judged to be highly similar to them in meaning; Type C elements were control words which were neither associates of, nor judged to be similar in meaning to the List 1 response words.

The measure of frequency of association between the List 1 response words and the response words in the other lists was obtained from the frequency with which these words appeared as responses to the List 1 words in the Kent-Rosanoff norms provided by Russell and Jenkins (1954). The measure of similarity of meaning between the List 1 response words and those in the other lists was obtained from median judgments provided by a group of 32 judges not otherwise participating in the experiment. The judges were asked to rate each pair of words on a four-point scale ranging from a minimum at "0" (defined for them as: "no similarity or even opposite in meaning") to a maximum at "3" (defined as: "identical or very similar in meaning").

From a much larger pool of word pairs for which these measurements were available, 36 words were selected which most closely matched the properties of each of the Type A, S, or C relationships to the List 1 response words. (It turned out to be exceptionally difficult to discover words which met these combined requirements. Evidently, if a pair of words in general use is judged to be similar in meaning, it is also quite likely that each will be evoked by the other in a word association test.) Lists 2, 3, and 4 were then constructed by pairing each of these words with the same stimulus word that had been paired with their counterparts in List 1, so that Lists 2, 3, and 4 each contained four response words representing each of the three types of interlist relationships. The composition of the lists and the type of relation each of the response words in Lists 2, 3, and 4 bore to the List 1 response words are presented in Table 1.

All words were carefully screened to eliminate any other associative or semantic

TABLE 1. *Composition of lists and interlist relations*

Stimulus Words All Lists	List 1 Responses	List 2 Responses	Type	List 3 Responses	Type	List 4 Responses	Type
BREAD	HIGH	LOFTY	S	LEFT	C	LOW	A
COLD	STEM	TRUNK	S	FLOWER	A	PROVE	C
EAGLE	SICKNESS	HEALTH	A	BROOK	C	DISEASE	S
FRUIT	QUIET	LOUD	A	HAND	C	SILENCE	S
HAMMER	SOUR	SWEET	A	ACID	S	NARROW	C
JUSTICE	DREAM	IMAGINE	S	MARKET	C	SLEEP	A
MUTTON	LONG	SAND	C	SHORT	A	TALL	S
NEEDLE	KING	QUEEN	A	CHIEF	S	CLOSE	C
OCEAN	BOY	NORTH	C	LAD	S	GIRL	A
SLOW	LIGHT	MINE	C	DARK	A	GAY	S
TABLE	MAN	CONTAIN	C	HUMAN	S	WOMAN	A
THIRSTY	HARD	DIFFICULT	S	SOFT	A	LITTLE	C

relations within or between the lists, and to eliminate orthographic similarities and words having low frequencies of usage.

In order that differences in the extent of generalization might be confidently inferred from differences in performance in the transfer task, it would first be necessary to establish that such differences in performance could not be attributed to intrinsic differences in the ease with which different types of pairs are learned, irrespective of the effects of the prior learning of the related pairs. For this reason it was desirable to have different groups of Ss learn the lists in two different sequences (Sequences I and II) so that the subsequent task in one sequence would be the same as the prior task in the other sequence. It was also thought desirable to investigate the generalization effects produced by the various interlist relations in the recall of the original pairs. Therefore, the order of tasks presented in

Sequence I was: learn List 1; learn List 2, 3, or 4; recall List 1. The comparable order in Sequence II was: learn List 2, 3, or 4; learn List 1; recall List 2, 3, or 4.

However, it should be appreciated that the associative relation is not necessarily symmetric. That is, the extent to which Word A evokes Word B as an association response is not necessarily the same as the extent to which Word B evokes Word A. Thus it was necessary to determine the frequency with which the response words in List 1 tended to be given as association responses to their counterparts in List 2, 3, or 4. This frequency was inferred from additional association norms collected by Russell and Jenkins (1956) and from norms collected by E from 139 Ss not otherwise participating in the experiment.

Table 2 presents the interlist association and similarity properties in both sequences for words in each type of interlist relation.

TABLE 2. *Percentage association and median rating of similarity to List 1 response words for words in each type of interlist relation*

Type A	Association Seq. I	Association Seq. II	Similarity	Type S	Association Seq. I	Association Seq. II	Similarity	Type C	Association Seq. I	Association Seq. II	Similarity
DARK	64.2	82.2	0.53	ACID	0.2	6.5	1.92	BROOK	0.0	0.0	0.50
FLOWER	39.9	1.0	0.84	CHIEF	0.1	0.0	2.38	CLOSE	0.0	0.0	0.52
GIRL	76.2	69.8	0.57	DIFFICULT	0.5	65.5	3.11	CONTAIN	0.0	0.0	0.53
HEALTH	37.3	24.8	0.53	DISEASE	0.1	19.4	2.44	HAND	0.0	0.0	0.50
LOUD	34.5	6.7	0.52	GAY	0.0	0.0	2.07	LEFT	0.0	0.0	0.50
LOW	67.0	64.0	0.53	HUMAN	0.3	36.0	1.65	LITTLE	0.0	0.0	0.50
QUEEN	74.5	71.0	0.99	IMAGINE	0.0	22.3	2.53	MARKET	0.0	0.0	0.53
SHORT	75.2	33.3	0.52	LAD	0.5	69.1	3.16	MINE	0.0	0.0	0.50
SLEEP	44.9	4.7	0.94	LOFTY	0.1	64.0	2.99	NARROW	0.0	0.0	0.52
SOFT	66.9	44.1	0.52	SILENCE	0.6	53.2	3.27	NORTH	0.0	0.0	0.50
SWEET	56.3	43.1	0.53	TALL	0.5	0.7	1.82	PROVE	0.0	0.0	0.53
WOMAN	76.1	61.1	0.57	TRUNK	0.7	0.0	2.25	SAND	0.0	0.0	0.50
Mean	59.4	42.8	0.63		0.4	28.1	2.47		0.0	0.0	0.51

It can be seen that on the average the properties of the interlist relations in the converse order (Sequence II) were different from those obtaining in Sequence I in that the response words participating in the Type S relation were characterized by a substantial degree of interlist associative linkages, whereas the associative linkages between the words of Type A were somewhat weaker than those in Sequence II. Since of necessity, the similarity in meaning relation is symmetric, the words representing the Type S interlist relation in Sequence II combined to a considerable extent the properties of both Type A and Type S relations.

Procedure.—Seventy-two Ss, students in an introductory psychology course, participated in the experiment, 36 learning the lists in each sequence. In order to obtain a measure of the effect of the different lists, Ss were further divided into three equal groups within each sequence, according to the particular lists they were to learn during the different phases of the experiment. In Sequence I Ss in Groups 1, 2, and 3 learned Lists 2, 3, and 4, respectively, as their second lists, and in Sequence II Lists 2, 3, and 4 were learned as their original lists by Groups 1, 2, and 3, respectively.

After a short period of pretraining on a practice list of nonsense syllable-digit paired associates, Ss proceeded to learn two of the experimental lists by the anticipation method, with instructions to pronounce aloud both stimulus and response words on all occasions. The materials were presented on a Hull-type memory drum arranged so that the stimulus words were exposed for 2 sec. and then were joined by the response words for another 2 sec. Two seconds intervened between the presentation of each pair, and 8 sec. separated successive trials. The 12 pairs in each list were presented in five different orders.

The Ss were instructed to correct all mistakes aloud and to continue practice on the lists until all response words had been correctly anticipated in a single trial. When this criterion had been reached on the original list, a shutter arrangement on the apparatus was shifted to expose the second list, and after a brief period for instructions lasting approximately 1 min., practice began immediately on the second list and continued until the same criterion was met. Then, immediately following an instructional period of the same duration in which Ss were told to recall as many of the original responses as possible on the first trial, the shutter arrangement was shifted back to the original list, and the recall test began and continued until all responses had been correctly anticipated in one trial.

RESULTS

Original list learning.—The number of trials required to reach the criterion of correctly anticipating all responses in the original lists was analyzed for any overall differences in the ease with which the lists were learned, irrespective of the types of interlist relations in which their component responses would subsequently participate. The mean numbers of trials needed to attain this criterion for Groups 1, 2, and 3 in learning List 1 in Sequence I were 13.17, 11.83, and 12.67, respectively. The groups learning Lists 2, 3, and 4 in Sequence II required 14.38, 11.92, and 11.00, respectively. The differences among the group performances on these lists cannot be considered reliable ($F=.92$, $df=2/66$), nor were the other sources of variation significant.

The total numbers of correct anticipations given by all Ss in learning the original lists in each sequence were analyzed for differences among the different types of interlist relations. Since each list contained words from each category, measurements of Ss' performance on them cannot be considered independent. Therefore, Collier's (1958) modification of the model for the analysis of observations correlated on one dimension presented by Kogan (1948) was applied.

The mean total correct anticipations of response words of Types A, S, and C, respectively, were 31.69, 31.89, and 32.39 in Sequence I, and 32.00, 31.91, and 31.08 in Sequence II, and 31.84, 31.90, and 31.73 for the two sequences combined. The differences among these means cannot be considered reliable, nor were any reliable differences found between groups or sequences (all $Fs < .80$).

However, significant Type × Group interaction effects did appear in the combined sequence analysis ($F = 15.11$, $df = 4/132$, $P < .01$) and in the analyses of each sequence separately. For Sequence I, in which the groups were all learning List 1, $F = 10.53$, $df = 4/66$, $P < .01$, and for Sequence II, $F = 7.08$, $df = 4/66$, $P < .01$. The appearance of this effect, even when the groups were learning the same list, suggests that it was due to the considerable differences in the ease with which individual paired associates were learned. In Sequence I, the difficult pairs in List 1 were variously classified as Types A, S, and C, according to the interlist relations they would form when the groups subsequently learned the other lists. These differences in learning the individual paired associates were somehow related to the stimulus component of the lists, since certain pairs sharing the same stimulus words were uniformly more difficult to learn in all the lists.

This same interaction also appeared in analyses of the number of trials required to reach the criterion of correctly anticipating all responses of a given type on a single trial ($F = 8.82$, $df = 4/66$, $P < .01$ in the combined sequence analysis). The mean trials required to reach this criterion for Types A, S, and C, respectively, were 8.34, 8.95, and 9.23 in Sequence I, and 8.92, 8.26, and 9.34 in Sequence II. Neither these differences, nor those due to other sources in the analysis, can be considered reliable (all $Fs < 1.80$). Thus any type differences in performance appearing when these lists were presented in the transfer test can be assumed to be the differential effect of previous learning.

Second list learning.—The possibility that the use of Ss' performance in learning the original list as a covariance con-

trol might effect greater precision in the analysis of the results of the transfer and recall tests had to be rejected, as the regression coefficients between original list performance and the other measures were uniformly small and could not be regarded as reliably different from zero.

The number of trials required to reach the criterion of correctly anticipating in a single trial all responses in the second lists, regardless of type memberships, was analyzed for over-all differences in the learning of the lists. For the groups learning List 1 as their second list in Sequence II, 9.83, 8.67, and 10.50 trials were required, respectively. The groups learning Lists 2, 3, and 4 in Sequence I needed 10.67, 9.00, and 9.00 trials, respectively. These group performances cannot be regarded as different ($F = .58$, $df = 2/66$), nor were the other sources of variance significant.

Differences in verbal generalization related to differences in interlist relations have typically been found to be greatest in the initial stages of second list learning and original list learning and original list relearning (cf. Haagen, 1943; Morgan & Underwood, 1950; Osgood, 1946, 1948; Underwood, 1951). Therefore, performances on the first anticipation trial on the second lists were examined. The results of these analyses are presented in Table 3.

A Type × Group interaction effect appeared in this analysis as it had in analyses of performances in the original learning of these same lists. The different types of interlist relations were also an appreciable source of variation.

In order to compare the Type means in the two sequences, Snedecor's (1956) procedure for testing comparisons among all means was followed, using the variance estimate from the combined sequence analysis to establish confidence intervals about the means. This indicated that all differences within and between

Tᴀʙʟᴇ 3. *Analysis of variance of performances in learning second lists*

Source	df	Correct Anticipations First Trial		Correct Anticipations All Trials		Trials to Criterion	
		MS	F	MS	F	MS	F
Within Ss	144						
Types	2	31.60	43.89°°	753.50	48.30°°	71.30	10.45°°
Types × Seq.	2	1.85	2.57	173.40	10.45°°	34.90	5.12°°
Types × Groups	4	3.72	5.17°°	452.55	29.01°°	76.30	11.19°°
Types × Groups × Seq.	4	.90	1.25	9.98	.64	1.10	.16
Error 1	132	.72		15.60		6.82	
Between Ss	71						
Sequences	1	1.50	1.35	65.50	.16	10.20	.30
Groups	2	2.20	1.98	216.05	.52	50.10	1.46
Seq. × Groups	2	3.05	2.75	117.70	.28	30.30	.88
Error 2	66	1.11		418.22		34.31	

°° $P < .01$.

sequences were significant at the .05 level, except for the difference between the Type A means in the two sequences, and the difference between the Type A and S means in Sequence II, which could not be considered reliable. The Type means for each sequence are presented in Table 4.

In order to examine the effect of the interlist relations beyond the first trials, an analysis of the total correct anticipations produced throughout the course of learning the second lists was performed. In addition, the number of trials required to reach the criterion of correctly anticipating all words of a given type within a single trial was also analyzed. The results of these analyses are also presented in Table 3.

In both analyses the Type effect continued to be significant. Again, the Type × Group effect appeared in each, and the Type × Sequence effect also attained significance in these analyses. The Type

means within each sequence in both analyses are presented in Table 4.

Applying Snedecor's procedure to the means of the total correct anticipations produced on all trials revealed that all Type differences within each sequence were significant, except for that between Types A and S in Sequence II. All Type differences between sequences were significant except for those between Type S in Sequence I and Types A and S in Sequence II.

In the analysis of the trials required to reach criterion, all differences within Sequence I were found to be significant, but in Sequence II Types A and S were different from Type C but not from each other. Between sequences, all differences were reliable except for those between Type S in Sequence I and Type A in Sequence II and between the two Type S means.

Recall and relearning of original lists. —The relearning of the original lists was

Tᴀʙʟᴇ 4. *Performances on words of each type in learning second lists*

Type	Correct Anticipations First Trial				Correct Anticipations All Trials				Trials to Criterion			
	Sequence I		Sequence II		Sequence I		Sequence II		Sequence I		Sequence II	
	Mean	SD	Mean	SD	Mean	SD	Mean	SD	Mean	SD	Mean	SD
A	1.97	.99	1.78	.97	33.00	11.97	31.42	13.68	5.56	3.82	6.56	4.60
S	1.27	.94	1.56	1.23	30.39	11.08	30.78	12.71	6.64	4.34	6.12	4.09
C	.36	.63	.78	.26	23.72	12.14	28.22	12.23	8.81	3.59	7.23	4.16

TABLE 5. *Analysis of variance of performances in recalling and relearning original lists*

Source	df	Correct Anticipations Recall Trial		Correct Anticipations All Trials		Trials to Criterion	
		MS	F	MS	F	MS	F
Within Ss	144						
Types	2	17.00	20.24°°	59.60	4.53°	12.85	3.34°
Types × Seq.	2	.20	.24	4.20	.32	1.20	.31
Types × Groups	4	6.75	8.04°°	94.40	7.18°°	29.78	7.74°°
Types × Groups × Seq.	4	.90	1.07	6.20	.47	2.72	.71
Error 1	132	.84		13.15		3.85	
Between Ss	71						
Sequences	1	.00	.00	.00	.00	17.20	1.28
Groups	2	2.60	1.50	156.10	.48	10.90	.81
Seq. × Groups	2	.50	.29	32.05	.10	5.45	.40
Error 2	66	1.73		323.31		13.48	

° $P < .05$.
°° $P < .01$.

a comparatively easy task for all Ss. The numbers of trials needed in Sequence I to reattain criterion on List 1 were 4.75, 5.00, and 6.08 for Groups 1, 2, and 3, respectively, while in Sequence II the groups relearning Lists 2, 3, and 4 required 5.92, 6.17, and 7.50 trials, respectively. The differences between these groups cannot be considered significant ($F = .89$, $df = 2/66$), nor were the other sources of variance significant.

The analyses of the number of correct anticipations for words of each type on the recall trial are presented in Table 5. Both Type and Type × Group interaction effects were found. Within both sequences Types A and S differ significantly from Type C, but not from each other. None of the Type A and S differences between sequences were reliable, but each was significantly different from either Type C means. The type means from sequences are presented in Table 6.

Performance on relearning the original lists was measured by the total correct anticipations given on all trials and by the number of trials required to reattain criterion. Analyses of these performances are presented in Table 5. Both Type and Type × Group effects appeared in each analysis. The Type means in each Sequence obtained from analysis of both measures of relearning are presented in Table 6.

In the analysis of the number of correct anticipations produced throughout relearning, it was found that, within both sequences, Types A and S were both reliably different from Type C, but not from each other. As in the recall test, none of the Types A and S differences between sequences were reliable, but each was itself significantly different from either Type C means.

The analysis of the number of trials required to reach the relearning criterion in Sequence I indicated that the Type A

TABLE 6. *Performances on words of each type in recalling and relearning original lists*

Type	Correct Anticipations Recall Trial				Correct Anticipations All Trials				Trials to Criterion			
	Sequence I		Sequence II		Sequence I		Sequence II		Sequence I		Sequence II	
	Mean	SD	Mean	SD	Mean	SD	Mean	SD	Mean	SD	Mean	SD
A	2.94	1.00	2.81	1.02	16.28	9.27	15.86	9.81	2.86	2.00	3.78	3.06
S	2.69	1.02	2.69	1.10	16.36	9.91	16.25	9.93	3.03	1.74	3.64	3.36
C	1.92	1.16	1.96	1.22	14.36	9.76	14.89	10.95	3.92	2.71	4.08	2.89

and S means were each reliably different from the Type C mean, but not from each other. None of the differences among the Sequence II means were significant. Type A in Sequence I differed from all Sequence II means and Type S in Sequence I differed from Types A and C in Sequence II, but none of the other between-sequence differences were reliable.

DISCUSSION

All analyses of second-list learning and first-list recall and relearning clearly indicate that associative interlist relations are sufficient to produce verbal generalization. Indeed, the results of the most sensitive test of interlist transfer indicate that words participating in associative relations, irrespective of any attendant semantic affinities, were more easily anticipated than words linked only by semantic relations. This suggests that associative relations may even be a necessary factor in interverbal generalization, and that words having semantic relations typically yield generalization effects only because they are usually associated or that they are particularly susceptible to being temporarily associated.

If this were so, the manner in which associative factors operate might be as follows. At the start of learning the pairs in the transfer tests, the responses most likely to occur upon the initial presentations of the stimulus words are those which have been paired to these same words in the initial lists. But because of the establishment of associative connections prior to the experiment, there exists a substantial tendency for these responses, intruding from the preceding lists, to evoke the correct responses in the transfer tests. Hence, these presumably implicit interlist intrusions facilitate the learning of the second list, as their occurrences act as mnemonic aids to learning the transfer list.

This formulation has considerable appeal because it is readily extendable to other generalization situations, and because the mediating processes referred to are exclusively verbal. Thus, they are presumably subject to rather direct assessment and manipulation, and require no supplementary

theoretical treatments of semantics or other philosophically redoubtable topics.

In spite of its appeal, this formulation of verbal generalization does not seem to account for the positive transfer found for words participating in the Type S interlist relation in Sequence I, where the required associative connections between lists were apparently lacking. However, this failure may not be in the formulation itself, but in the index of associative connection used in this experiment. The strength of some of the interlist associative connections between the words of Type S in Sequence I may have been considerably greater in the experimental situation than had been inferred from the word association test norms. That is, there may have been features of the experimental situation which produced a temporary increase in the strength of the interlist connections between some of the words of Type S sufficient to account for the limited positive transfer found.

A study reported by Storms (1958) provides evidence for the possibility that temporary supplemental strengthening of associative connections does occur under conditions similar to this. A list of words was read aloud to a group of Ss who were told they were to be subsequently tested for their retention of these words. The list contained a number of words which appeared with very low frequency as associative responses to a set of stimulus words in an association test (median frequency was 1%). When the association test was administered under these conditions, the median net increase in responding with the words which had recently been heard was 18%. Evidently, these conditions made the usually weak response "more available" for association.

The present experiment provides a situation in which the strength of some of the associative connections between the words of Type S in Sequence I, although very low under most conditions, may have been temporarily supplemented in a manner similar to that found by Storms, for on the first exposure to the transfer list, Ss were told to read the words aloud and try to anticipate them correctly thereafter. This possibility is empirically meaningful, for it may be possible to discover associative connections that are not susceptible to supplemental strengthening, or to present materials in generalization tests which do not provide the conditions for supplemental strengthening of weak associations.

Summary

Transfer and recall of lists of paired associates were compared in situations in which the original and subsequent lists had identical stimulus words but in which the response words were variously related. The response words in the different lists were either strongly associated but not similar in meaning, highly similar in meaning but not associated, both similar in meaning and associated, or neither similar in meaning nor associated.

The results indicated that positive transfer occurred whenever the words were linked by associative connections, irrespective of semantic relations. Some positive transfer also occurred to a lesser extent across words highly similar in meaning but only weakly associated. It was suggested that the latter result was due to a temporary supplementation of some of the interlist associations connecting these words.

The results suggested a formulation of verbal generalization in which the tendency for the occurrence of the generalized responses is increased because of their associative connections to the responses learned in the original task. On the basis of this formulation, generalization between words judged to be similar in meaning occurs only because associative tendencies connecting them are usually present in Ss' verbal behavior.

Collier, R. O., Jr. Analysis of variance for correlated observations. *Psychometrika*, 1958, 23, 223-36.

Gibson, E. J. A systematic application of the concepts of generalization and differentiation to verbal learning. *Psychol. Rev.*, 1940, 47, 196-229.

Haagen, C. H. Learning and retention as a function of the synonymity of original and interpolated tasks. Unpublished doctoral dissertation, State University of Iowa, 1943.

Haagen, C. H. Synonymity, vividness, familiarity, and association value ratings of 400 pairs of common adjectives. *J. Psychol.*, 1949, 27, 453-63.

Kogan, L. S. Analysis of variance: Repeated measurements. *Psychol. Bull.*, 1948, 45, 131-43.

McClelland, D. C., & Heath, R. M. Retroactive inhibition as a function of degree of association between original and interpolated activities. *J. exp. Psychol.*, 1943, 33, 420-26.

Morgan, R. L., & Underwood, B. J. Proactive inhibition as a function of response similarity. *J. exp. Psychol.*, 1950, 40, 592-603.

Osgood, C. E. Meaningful similarity and interference in learning. *J. exp. Psychol.*, 1946, 36, 299-301.

Osgood, C. E. An investigation into the causes of retroactive interference. *J. exp. Psychol.*, 1948, 38, 132-54.

Osgood, C. E. *Method and theory in experimental psychology.* New York: Oxford Univer. Press, 1953.

Russell, W. A., & Jenkins, J. J. The complete Minnesota norms for responses to 100 words from the Kent-Rosanoff Word Association Test. *ONR tech. Rep.*, 1954, No. 11. (Contract No. N8onr-66216, Univer. Minnesota)

Russell, W. A., & Jenkins, J. J. Associative frequenciees for Kent-Rosanoff stimuli and responses under various conditions. *ONR tech. Rep.*, 1956, No. 12. (Contract No. N8onr-66216, Univer. Minnesota).

Russell, W. A., & Storms, L. H. Implicit verbal chaining in paired-associate learning. *J. exp. Psychol.*, 1955, 49, 287-93.

Snedecor, G. W. *Statistical methods.* (5th ed.) Ames: Iowa State Coll. Press, 1956.

Storms, L. H. Apparent backward association: A situational effect. *J. exp. Psychol.*, 1958, 55, 390-95.

Underwood, B. J. *Experimental psychology: An introduction.* New York: Appleton-Century-Crofts, 1949.

Underwood, B. J. Associative transfer in verbal learning as a function of response similarity and degree of first list learning. *J. exp Psychol.*, 1951, 42, 44-53.

35 / Transfer of Verbal Paired Associates [1]

EDWIN MARTIN,[2] *University of Iowa*

From the current literature it is possible to identify 2 processes underlying the acquisition of verbal paired associates: response learning and association formation. It is also apparent from the literature that a complete treatment of association formation must take into account association directionality. Altogether, then, 3 "things" are seen to evolve during the acquisition of a paired-associate list: response availability, forward associations, and backward associations. The thesis of the present research is that what is transferred from the 1st to the 2nd task in a paired-associate transfer situation is some combination of these 3 effects. Utilizing the coordinate system invented by Osgood in which all the transfer paradigms can be arranged, 3 transfer surfaces are proposed which describe how each of the 3 effects is transferred individually. Applications to extant transfer literature are made. It is found that the principal results of nearly all experiments utilizing the A-B, C-D control paradigm can be accounted for.

The problem of transfer of verbal paired associates originated with Müller and Schumann (1894), whose law of associative inhibition was essentially a specification of the negative transfer paradigm A-B, A-D, and Müller and Pilzecker (1900), who developed the method of "right associates." A closely related problem, one with which transfer is, in many respects, inextricably intertwined, is that of retroactive inhibition, which also originated with Müller and Pilzecker (1900) in conjunction with their perseveration theory of reproduction inhibition. In 1949, Osgood attempted to organize the many facts and insights that had been accruing in this general problem area since Müller's time by proposing a transfer and retroaction surface. Thus the period from Müller to Osgood is a historical package, so to speak, with the most articulate summary being Osgood's paper. The purpose of the present paper is a reorganization based on additional facts and insights, some of which have accumulated since 1949, with the restriction that only transfer problems will be considered.

In an analysis of the effects of having learned one set of paired associates on the subsequent learning of another, four experimentally controllable variables emerge for which there are sufficient data to draw definitive conclusions. Two of these, interlist stimulus and interlist response similarity, have received considerable attention and were incorporated into Osgood's (1949) transfer theory. The other two, degree of first-task learning (L_1) and response meaningfulness (M), have been treated experimentally but not explained theoretically. To grasp the empirical relationships

among these four variables, it seems best to first examine Osgood's theory and then to describe how L_1 and M underlie systematic departures.

Osgood's (1949) contribution to transfer theory can be seen to resolve into two components: (*a*) the invention of a coordinate system in which all paired-associate paradigms can be arranged, and (*b*) a summary of available data in the form of a surface which describes how amount of transfer and position in the coordinate system are related.[3] The coordinate system has the important feature of formally distinguishing the separate roles of interlist stimulus and interlist response dissimilarity. These two variables are expressed as orthogonal axes, the X_S and X_R axes of Figure 1F, with the origin representing complete similarity, or identity. Thus, for example, A-B, A-D has the coordinates $X_S = 0$ and X_R some sufficiently large value to indicate complete dissimilarity (or unrelatedness) between the responses of the first- and transfer-task lists. All transfer paradigms are assigned a unique position in joint accordance with the dissimilarity between the stimuli and the dissimilarity

From the *Psychological Review*, 1965, **72**, 327-43, with permission of the author and publisher.
1. This article derives in part from a doctoral dissertation submitted to Graduate College, University of Iowa. The author gratefully acknowledges the advice and guidance of R. W. Schulz. The valuable comments of A. W. Melton are also recognized. Preparation of the manuscript was supported by the Advanced Research Projects Agency, Department of Defense, monitored by the Air Force Office of Scientific Research, under Contract No. AF 49 (638)1235 with the Human Performance Center, University of Michigan.
2. Now at Human Performance Center and Department of Psychology, University of Michigan.
3. At approximately the same time, and apparently independently, Underwood (1949) made an equivalent proposal based on the same data, plus expectations from generalization theory, in the form of four curves. His curves are essentially the surface edges given by Osgood.

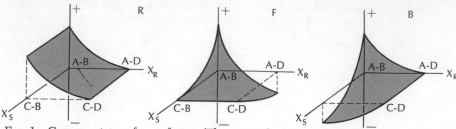

FIG. 1. Component transfer surfaces. (The surfaces R, F, and B represent the transfer of response availability, forward associations, and backward associations, respectively.)

between the responses of the two lists. Surface points above the X_S-X_R plane represent positive transfer; points below, negative transfer.

A matter to be taken into account before proceeding further is that of the so-called "opposed" relationship between the two tasks. With stimuli identical, for example, the responses of the first and transfer tasks can be identical (A-B, A-B paradigm), similar (A-B, A-B′), neutral (A-B, A-D), or opposed. A number of investigators, including Osgood, have used this last condition. As an example of the opposition relationship, *sickly* is similar to *pale,* but *healthy* is opposed. Usually, response opposition produces less negative transfer than the neutrality relationship of the A-B, A-D paradigm (e.g., Bugelski & Cadwallader, 1956; Wimer, 1964).

If two items are judged opposite in meaning, they must perforce be related; otherwise, opposition could not be established. Generally speaking, the axes of Osgood's coordinate system are seen as representing similarity in meaning. However, it would be more consonant with the present status of interference theory to suppose that the axes represent associative relatedness. Similarity would clearly be included; but, more importantly, opposition would thereby be placed at points on the axes between identity and complete dissimilarity in-

stead of beyond the complete dissimilarity point. To so recognize opposition as a category of relatedness achieves two reasonable objectives: (*a*) It places data points arising from opposition relationships (between Tasks 1 and 2) in an area of the coordinate system where transfer is known to be less than maximally negative. In the experiment by Bugelski and Cadwallader (1956), the response-opposition condition would thus interpose between the identical (A-B, A-B) and similar (A-B, A-B′) conditions, but closer to the similar condition; in the Wimer (1964) experiment, the response-opposition condition would fall between the similar (A-B, A-B′) and unrelated (A-B, A-D) conditions. (*b*) It would more completely link interference interpretations of verbal learning to the transfer situation by removing the restriction that the only relationship represented by the coordinate axes is that of strict similarity. Associative relatedness is the basis for both synonymity and antonymity. There can thus be no paradigm on the dissimilarity axes beyond the completely unrelated paradigms (A-B, C-B for simuli; A-B, A-D for responses). This is somewhat of a departure from Osgood's original conceptualization, but a departure which nevertheless seems necessary if thinking about what is transferred is to square with current thought on what is acquired when learning takes place.

At positions where the surface is either above or below the X_S-X_R plane, positive or negative transfer, respectively, is supposed to obtain. A perusal of the transfer studies whose designs constitute a test of Osgood's surface, however, reveals that although the general shape of the surface is fairly well substantiated, there are a number of systematic discrepancies which can be attributed to specific experimental factors, namely, L_1 and response M. (In the ensuing discussion, only experiments utilizing the A-B, C-D control paradigm for nonspecific effects will be cited; thus amount and sign of transfer at other positions in the coordinate system are always with respect to transfer-task performance at the A-B, C-D position.)

The effect on transfer-task performance of increasing L_1 is either to decrease positive transfer or to increase negative transfer, depending upon the position in the coordinate system. Bruce (1933) found that as L_1 increased from 6 trials to 12, the amount of positive transfer in the A-B, C-B paradigm decreased, while in the A-B, A-D paradigm the amount of negative transfer increased. In Jung's (1962) experiment, transfer progressed from positive to negative in the A-B, C-B paradigm and became more negative in the A-B, A-D paradigm as L_1 increased from a 3/6 to a 6/6+5 criterion. Dean and Kausler (1964) have shown striking shift from positive transfer with a first-task criterion of $L_1 = 3/6$ to negative transfer with $L_1 = 6/6+5$ in the A-B, C-B paradigm. Further substantiation of this role of degree of L_1 is provided by Spiker (1960) for the A-B, A-D paradigm and by Postman (1962b) for several paradigms.

If overlearning of the first task is considered, the foregoing clear picture of the role of degree of L_1 becomes somewhat clouded. Postman (1962b), while reporting an increase in negative transfer with a change from a 6/10 to a 10/10 criterion for L_1 in both the A-B, C-B and A-B, A-D paradigms, finds a sharp reduction in amount of negative transfer for a 10/10+50% criterion.

Mandler and Heinemann (1956) report negative transfer in the A-B, C-B paradigm after 10 errorless L_1 trials but positive transfer after 30 and 50 such trials, with a return to negative transfer after 100 trials. In the A-B, A-D paradigm, transfer remains negative throughout but shows fluctuation similar to that in the A-B, C-B. These results are difficult to reconcile both with each other and with data not involving overlearning. Mandler (1962) has presented a systematic argument for negative transfer as a V-shaped function of degree of L_1, transfer becoming more negative then less negative in the A-B, A-D paradigm. It should be noted, however, that in making that argument, Mandler cites his own data (Mandler & Heinemann, 1956) but leaves out the data point for his greatest-degree-of-overlearning condition, a data point which denies the V-shaped function. Other data cited by Mandler in support of a V-shaped function are not relevant in the present context because they do not include A-B, C-D control paradigms for nonspecific effects. Thus, although degree of L_1 inversely affects transfer in the A-B, A-D and A-B, C-B paradigms in a regular manner at ordinary degrees of L_1, a definitive conclusion regarding the role of over-learning does not seem possible at this point.

Where M is taken as a generic term referring to the core attribute of verbal units reflected by such highly inter-correlated scales as meaningfulness, association value, and pronunciability (Noble, 1963), the effect of first-list response M on transfer-task performance is to increasingly impede that performance as M is increased. Jung (1963) showed that when responses are low-M trigrams, considerable positive transfer and barely negative transfer are observed in the A-B, C-B and A-B, A-D paradigms respectively; but when responses are high-M trigrams, transfer in the A-B, C-B becomes nearly zero, and transfer in the A-B, A-D becomes very negative. Varying M over three levels (low—CCCs, medium—CVCs, high—words), Merikle and Battig (1963) showed that as M increases, transfer in the A-B, A-D paradigm decreases from barely negative to considerably negative.

Further evidence on this matter can be had by categorizing available data according to whether transfer is positive or negative in the A-B, C-B paradigm. If this is done, it turns out that all studies yielding positive transfer involve trigrams as responses (Bruce, 1933; Jung, 1963; Mandler & Heinemann, 1956), whereas those yielding negative transfer involve meaningful responses, such as adjectives (Dallet, 1962; Harcum, 1953; Kausler & Kanoti, 1963; Keppel & Underwood, 1962; Twedt & Underwood, 1959; Wimer, 1964). An exception to this categorization is the Bugelski and Cadwallader (1956) study, which reports positive transfer at the A-B, C-B position with words as response materials. Their procedure involved dropping out pairs from the first-task list once given correctly twice in succession. Further, they used visual patterns as stimuli.

Thus degree of L_1 and response M appear to be major experimental factors responsible for systematic deviations from Osgood's surface. There are, of course, other factors whose effects will eventually have to be accounted for, for example, intralist similarity, list length, and time between L_1 and the transfer task. At the present time, little is known about the effects of the first two on the transfer task; and, adhering to the restriction of considering only transfer data which includes the A-B, C-D control, only one study, Newton and Wickens (1956), is known to the present writer concerning the last. If one is willing to compare percent saving (the percent the difference in the number of trials to criterion for the two tasks is of the number for the first task) in the A-B, A-D para-

digm (their Experiment I) with percentage of saving in the A-B, C-D paradigm (their Experiment II), it turns out that the differences obtained by subtracting the latter from the former for intertask delays of 0, 24, and 48 hours is -26, -8, and $+5$. Thus for the A-B, A-D paradigm there is evidence that the associations which are to interfere during transfer-task learning are lost over time. The studies customarily cited on this phenomenon, however, either do not employ the A-B, C-D control for nonspecific effects (Bunch & McCraven, 1938) or deal only with the nonspecific effects of the A-B, C-D paradigm (Hamilton, 1950).

Essentially, while the coordinate system is definitional in nature, the surface proposed by Osgood is an empirical law, an induction from the facts. In view of the growing complexity of the facts as revealed, at least, by the roles of L_1 and M, however, a revised induction does not seem feasible; instead it would appear easier to turn to the implications embedded in already extant verbal learning theory for an improved formalization of transfer phenomena. On this view, two developments are of special interest: the two-phase conceptualization of verbal learning and the notion of association bidirectionality.

The idea that verbal learning may profitably be viewed as more than one process seems to have originated with Thorndike (1932), who notes that "other things being equal, connections are easy to form in proportion as the response is available [p. 343]" and that "much of learning consists in making certain responses more available [p. 347]." Current expression of this notion is well exemplified by Underwood and Schulz (1960): "Logically speaking, the acquisition of a serial or paired-associate list can be divided into two stages. The first will be called *response-learning* or *response-recall* stage. It occurs temporally prior to the second stage which will be called the *associative* or *hook-up stage* [p. 92]."

The utility of distinguishing two phases of the total verbal learning process is readily discernible in the literature. For example, Underwood, Runquist, and Schulz (1959), Horowitz (1961), and Carterette (1963) have demonstrated that the two phases can be discriminated experimentally on the grounds that a single variable differentially affects certain response measures separately identifiable with the two phases. It was found that while variations in intralist response similarity had a direct effect on response learning (as measured by recallability), association formation (as measured either by responding to specific stimulation or by ordering performance) was inversely affected.[4] A more detailed consideration of these two components of learning, plus others, has been given by McGuire (1961): He argues cogently for their utility and demonstrates experimentally their distinguishability.

Since it is meaningful to view the acquisition of verbal paired associates as a composite of two processes, response learning and association formation, it makes sense to conclude that at the end of L_1 in a transfer situation there are at least two "things" available for transfer to the second, or transfer, task; namely, response availability and associative connections, the former being the product of first-task response learning, the latter of first-task association formation.

Admitting that associative connections are available for transfer from task to task entails a consideration of the rather extensive literature on backward associations. Cognizance of this problem apparently begins with Ebbinghaus (1885), who wrote that "as a result of the learning of a series certain connections of the members are therefore actually formed in a reverse as well as in a forward direc-

tion [p. 112]." Most of the early interest in backward associations was centered on the problem of remote associations in serial learning, the first application to transfer apparently not occurring until the appearance of Harcum's paper in 1953. Harcum's finding that backward associations are transferred has since been confirmed by Murdock (1958) with different materials, with further evidence provided by Keppel and Underwood (1962); hence a generality seems to be in order. The conclusion, then, is that backward associative connections are a component of what is transferred in a transfer situation and must be included in a formalization of transfer phenomena.

A COMPONENT-SURFACES CONCEPTUALIZATION

It has been argued that there are three components to that which is transferred from one paired-associate task to another, namely, response availability, forward associations, and backward associations. An immediate implication of this position is that all of the ordinary measures of transfer (number of trials to criterion on the transfer task; number of correct responses, or errors, in so many transfer-task trials; etc.) reflect what is best called a net effect. In other words, a

---

4. Caution must be exercised in claiming that high intralist response similarity facilitates response learning. When similarity among items is produced by means of either (*a*) generating a list of trigrams from a limited alphabet or (*b*) basing similarity on the notion of synonymity, the possibility exists that given one response some of the others can be inferred. In such situations, it becomes problematic whether observed facilitation is effected by current learning or by transfer of previously acquired rules or strategies.

It is not reasonable to suppose that response learning is the sole source of the response availability measured by recall. Strictly speaking, response learning is the serial acquisition of the elements of the response (and hence is itself an association-formation process). Response availability, however, involves also the contextual associations that support recall. Thus the recall measure is not a pure measure of response learning. In the transfer situation, context associations which tend to elicit responses are indistinguishable from specific transferred associations, hence in future references to response availability what is intended is availability arising from response learning only.

single transfer surface whose ordinate values are given by any one of the standard measures is essentially a net transfer surface and presumably can be analyzed into other, more specific component surfaces. This means that, since there are three effects transferred, there should be three transfer surfaces, each describing how its particular effect is transferred as a function of position in the coordinate system. The specification of such a triad of surfaces, at least schematically, follows from general paired-associate interference theory.

Consider first how response availability (that due to response learning) transfers from one paired-associate task to another. Any response learning evolved during the first task must transfer maximally to the transfer task of paradigms at positions in the coordinate system where first- and transfer-task responses are identical. This transfer is not perfect to the extent that response availability includes context and/or other nonparadigmatic associations not carrying over; in fact, such associations may even be a source of interference. Response availability due to first-task response learning, however, has a maximum and equal positive effect along the X_S axis, that is, at all positions from A-B, A-B to A-B, C-B. At the other extreme, none of the response learning of the first task is appropriate to the transfer task of paradigms involving completely new transfer-task responses. Response availability acquired extraexperimentally may certainly apply but not response availability from first-task learning. Therefore, a surface representing the transfer of first-task response learning must coincide with the X_S-X_R zero-transfer plane at positions from A-B, A-D to A-B, C-D.

Regarding positions between the maximally positive-transfer loci from A-B, A-B to A-B, C-B and the zero-transfer loci from A-B, A-D to A-B, C-D, intermediate amounts of response availability

obtain. These varying degrees of transferred response availability are seen as arising from the applicability of first-task response learning to whatever characteristics or components of the transfer-task responses are responsible for the similarity (relatedness, including opposition) between the first- and transfer-task responses. This argument can be summarized by a hypothetical surface, called the R surface for response availability, and is shown in Figure 1R.

The second component of paired-associate acquisition, forward association, requires some degree of similarity between first- and transfer-task stimuli in order to induce a nonzero effect. If associations A-B are acquired in the first task, then to the extent to which the stimuli of the transfer task are similar to A, the associates of A from the first task are elicited in transfer-task learning. Thus, those positions on a line between A-B, C-B and A-B, C-D cannot involve transfer of forward associations because completely new stimuli characterize the transfer task. In progressing from the A-B, C-B position toward the A-B, A-B position in the coordinate system, first-task forward associations become increasingly more useful in the transfer task, until the A-B, A-B position is reached where the transfer task is but a continuation of the first task.

As the A-B, A-D position is approached (from any direction), however, the forward associations acquired in the first task become increasingly stronger sources of interference in transfer-task learning. This interference is inferred from the fact that acquisition of A-D associations involves the extinction of A-B associations (Barnes & Underwood, 1959; Briggs, 1954; Postman, 1961, 1962a). As will be pointed out below, the literature is unanimous that relative to the A-B, C-D control paradigm the A-B, A-D yields negative transfer. The point to be made here is that this negativity cannot be due to either transferred response availability or transferred backward associations (because the responses of the transfer task are completely new) and hence must be due to interfering forward associations. The F surface, depicting the transfer of forward associations, is shown in Figure 1F. It is essentially the surface proposed by Osgood (1949).

The third, and final, component to be considered is that of backward association. The surface to represent this effect must necessarily be symmetric in general form, if not in magnitude, with the F surface where the axis of symmetry is the line between the A-B, A-B and A-B, C-D positions. Arguing in the reverse direction, there must be some degree of similarity (relatedness, including opposition) between the responses of the first and transfer tasks in order for backward associations acquired in the first task to be elicited in the transfer task. Now it has already been pointed out that backward associations are a component of what is acquired in paired-associate learning; hence if, as in the A-B, C-B paradigm, the backward B-A associations of the first task are elicited during transfer-task learning, then the acquisition of the backward B-C associations will be impeded. Thus the surface representing the transfer of backward associations must be negative at the A-B, C-B position. At the A-B, A-B position, however, the backward associations to be acquired in the transfer task are the same as those already practiced in the first task, hence the surface there must be positive. On a line between A-B, A-D and A-B, C-D, the responses are completely different in the transfer task, that is, the stimuli capable of eliciting the backward associations of the first task are absent, hence the surface must coincide with the X_S-X_R zero-transfer plane. Such a surface is shown in Figure 1B.

The three surfaces of Figure 1 are not entirely empirical (as was Osgood's single surface) because the three concepts represented by them are indeed primarily concepts. The surfaces are intended to be representative of expectations as to the nature of the components of the two-task paired-associate situation (transfer) arising from the general interference theory of the single-task paired-associate situation.

The locus of action of the experimental variables L_1 and M can now be seen somewhat more clearly. In the degenerate case where $L_1 = 0$, that is, where no first-task learning obtains, all surfaces collapse into the X_S-X_R zero-transfer plane: Nothing is transferred. With successive first-task trials, the associations which are to transfer become stronger, and the F and B surfaces assume their characteristic curvature. For example, at the A-B, C-B position, as L_1 increases, the negativeness of the B surface increases, presumably asymptotically, until a maximum is reached (see earlier discussion of over-learning). With respect to the R surface, L_1 trials serve also to develop its curvature. In situations where first-task responses are of the highest M (e.g., familiar nouns), only a few trials are required for full development of the R surface. Thus L_1 and M enter the analysis as factors determining the developmental (over trials) dispositions of the surfaces *relative to the X_S-X_R zero-transfer plane*. These relationships will emerge more clearly when applications of the model are discussed below.

Each surface is thus a different function of the same two variables, X_S and X_R. For example, the R surface would be described by some function, f, as

$$R = f(X_S, X_R; M, L_1),$$

where M and L_1 are parameters representing the response-M and degree-of-L_1 characteristics, respectively, of the transfer situation. If response M, say, were to be studied functionally at some fixed position in the coordinate system, then resulting variations in response availability would be represented by

$$R = f(M; X_S, X_R, L_1),$$

where f is the same function as before, but M is now taken as the variable and X_S, X_R, and L_1 as the parameters. Thus there are multiple experimental approaches to the ultimate specification of the three functions relating the component surfaces to X_S and X_R. The most formidable obstacle between the present state of transfer theory and such a goal, however, is the unavailability of a suitable similarity (relatedness) measure for the X_S and X_R dimensions. If such a measure cannot be evolved, then the Osgood coordinate-system view of transfer phenomena cannot develop into a quantitative theory.[5]

The decomposition of transfer phenomena into component effects has been given brief consideration by Postman (1962b). He distinguishes four sources of transfer: (a) learning to learn and warm-up, or nonspecific effects; (b) response learning, which is represented by the R surface in the present formulation; (c) associative interference, which has here been formally subdivided into the F and B component surfaces; and (d) differentiation between lists, a characteristic of transfer tasks represented by the X_S and X_R values assigned to the paradigm involved. Regarding the last source, if X_S and X_R are to adequately represent differentiation between lists, they must necessarily include more than scaled dissimilarity. Undoubtedly, Postman means to include the type of differentiation characterized by increased certainty as to which of the two tasks a given response item belongs. Postman draws further attention to the fact that second-task learning also has two phases and that the several effects being transferred from the first task should be

expected to differentially affect them.

Before proceeding to applications of the component-surfaces conceptualization to specific transfer situations, it is necessary to take one more step on the theoretical level: In addition to the defined coordinate system and the assumed component surfaces, there needs to be a statement about the temporal relationship between the two phases of learning. The role of such a statement would be to provide a conceptual mechanism by means of which the parameters of the transfer problem can specify dispositions of the component surfaces *relative to each other*. For example, suppose it were assumed that the response-learning phase precedes the association-formation phase; then for a sufficiently low degree of L_1 very little association formation could occur. Therefore, at a position such as the A-B, C-B where the sign of transfer depends upon the net effect of the positive R and the negative B effects (see Figure 1), positive transfer would be predicted because no B effects could have developed. But this is an example of a successful application of the complete component-surfaces conceptualization to actual data and hence is putting the cart before the horse, so to speak. If the original plan of attack is to be adhered to, a statement about the temporal relationship between the two phases should be evolved outside of transfer theory.

The facts insist that there is no clear temporal distinction between the response-learning and association-formation phases in verbal acquisition. Three studies of particular interest on this score are those of Peterson and Peterson (1959,

5. It is of interest to note that in a component model for stimulus compounding and generalization presented by Atkinson and Estes (1963) a statement can be derived which says that in general the similarity relation between two verbal units is not symmetric; for example, *abc* may be more similar to *ab* than *ab* is to *abc*. If this is in fact the case, it would make a difference which list goes into which task in a transfer problem, hence introducing directionality into dissimilarity measure.

Experiment II), Crothers (1962), and Mc-Guire (1961). Peterson and Peterson studied the short-term retention of consonant syllables and discovered that the dependent probabilities of subsequent letters being correct, given that the preceding letters were correct, increased with the number of repetitions before recall. In other words, parts of a unit may become available before the unit is available as a whole. Crothers, working in a paired-associate situation, found that when response items comprise more than one component, association formation may begin between the stimulus and whatever components are available before the entire response is available as a unit. This conclusion for the paired-associate situation finds further exemplification in the work of McGuire. The import of these studies is: Although response learning and association formation may be effectively distinguished, they nevertheless overlap; for association formation may begin as soon as at least one of the components of the response item is available.

Certainly the entire response unit must be available before a correct response can be accredited, and certainly association formation continues after responding has become correct; but these two arguments say nothing about when, relative to each other, the bulks of the two processes occur. An adequate analysis of this problem requires first an agreement as to what is meant by "the bulks of." Pending such a step, it might be noted in the Underwood, Runquist, and Schulz (1959) data that whereas the effects of intralist response similarity on recall of the response items disappear after the first half-dozen trials, the effects on over-all learning carry on to the end, an indication that response learning may be a more rapid process than association formation in some situations. For theoretical purposes, it will be assumed that, in general, response learning precedes, but overlaps, association formulation. Vindication of this step will emerge as applications are considered.

The coordinate system, the component surfaces, and the assumption just made comprise a clearly asymmetric formulation: No mention has been made of stimulus learning or integration. In view of the limited role of experimentally manipulated stimulus availability in subsequent paired-associate learning (e.g., Schulz & Martin, 1964; Schulz & Tucker, 1962), and because of the small effect of stimulus M relative to response M (e.g., Underwood & Schulz, 1960), it does not seem profitable at the present time to develop an accommodating structure within transfer theory. That certain stimulus factors will prove to be of considerable importance in paired-associate learning is clear from the work of McGuire (1961) and Shepard (1963); however, the implications for transfer situations are not yet clear.

APPLICATIONS

In order to see how the foregoing proposed conceptualization applies to extant data and generates expectations, several of the more thoroughly studied paradigms will be considered separately.

A-B, C-D. First, it is clear that the analysis of the net surface into component surfaces leaves the A-B, C-D position as the appropriate control for all other positions; in fact, its naturalness as a control is emphasized. Since the transfer task involves new responses, none of the backward associations formed in L_1 is elicited; nor is there any "head start" on transfer-task response learning since the response familiarization effected in L_1 is completely irrelevant. Similarly, since the transfer task involves new stimuli, none of the forward associations formed in L_1 is elicited. On the other hand, the transfer task does benefit from the nonspecific transfer effects common to all the paradigms. Certainly the measure of transfer used, and hence the choice of a control, depends upon the intent of the investigator; but if the specific effects of response availability and forward and backward associations are being studied, use of the A-B, C-D control seems imperative.

A complication alluded to by Postman (1962b) regarding the adequacy of the A-B, C-D position as a control when low-M material is used should be mentioned. Although not so stated by him, the cause for concern arises when the items are, say, consonant trigrams (CCCs), thus making it very difficult to satisfy the stipulation (required for the adequacy of the A-B, C-D position as a control) that first- and transfer-task stimuli and responses are completely dissimilar. Due to the limited number of letters (21) from which CCCs can be formed, at least some formal similarity between lists of any length will obtain.

A-B, C-B. Of the three effects, R, F, and B, available for transfer at the end of L_1, only R and B are actually transferred at the A-B, C-B position. Since the transfer task involves new stimuli, forward associations are not elicited, hence leaving in opposition the positive R and negative B effects. This much is based simply on the assumed component surfaces. In order to form an expectation as to the circumstances in which the net R-B effect will be positive or negative, it is necessary to evoke the assumption that response learning precedes association formation. Thus when degree of L_1 is sufficiently low, only response learning will have occurred, to the exclusion of association formation, thereby allowing only R effects to evolve. Increasing the degree of L_1 permits the opposing negative B effects to develop. As degree of L_1 goes from low to high, the net R-B effect shifts from positive to negative. In this way, the theory can account for the observed variations in transfer at the A-B, C-B position as a function of degree of L_1.

A similar use of the R and B component surfaces and the assumption regarding the temporal order of response learning and association formation leads to an explanation of the role of response M in transfer at the A-B, C-B position. When low-M first-task responses are used for a given degree of L_1, L_1 is primarily taken up with response learning and only secondarily with association formation; but when high-M responses are used, such an extensive response-learning phase is not necessary, allowing more emphasis on the formation of the backward associations which will cause interference in the subsequent transfer task. An increase in response M, then, means an increased opportunity for the development of negative B effects, hence either a decrease in positive transfer or an increase in negative transfer, depending on the given degree of L_1.

The foregoing theoretical treatment of the effects of degree of L_1 and level of response M at the A-B, C-B position is intended as an explanation of the data cited earlier as discrepant from Osgood's single surface. Several predictions for situations in which there are as yet no data can also be generated. One of these has to do with the effect of variations in first-task intralist response similarity. Since it is well known that high intralist response similarity tends to impede over-all paired-associate learning but to facilitate response learning (e.g., Feldman & Underwood, 1957; Underwood, Runquist, & Schulz, 1959), decreasing amounts of negative transfer should be associated with increasing intralist response similarity. In comparing two groups, one with high and one with low first-task intralist response similarity, during L_1 the former will have evolved more response availability (stronger R effects) than the latter in equal numbers of trials. This is because high similarity facilitates response learning. (In addition, the difference between these two groups should be larger for low-M response materials than for high.) Further, in the group with high intralist response similarity, acquisition of the associative connections (B effects) which will subsequently produce interference in the transfer task will be impeded to a greater extent than in the group with low similarity. This is because response similarity impedes association formation. Thus the high similarity group should not only have stronger positive R effects, but also less developed negative B effects, and therefore should show positive transfer relative to a low-similarity group.

Other predictions attach to the several ways of varying response M or variables relating to response M. For example, one should be able to independently manipulate the R surface by such expediencies as varying the number of "chunks" (Melton, 1963) in the first-task response members or administering varying amounts of response familiarization prior to beginning the first task. The consequences of such procedures would be differential emphases on association formation during L_1 and hence variations in the net R-B effect.

A-B, A-D. At the A-B, A-D position, one sees from Figure 1 that neither R effects nor B effects are transferred, leaving only the interfering forward associations acquired during L_1. This unqualified expectation of negative transfer is unanimously borne out by studies using the A-B, C-D control. In order to explain the roles of degree of L_1 and level of response M at this position, it is again necessary to evoke the assumption that response learning precedes association formation.

Variations in degree of L_1, regardless of position in the coordinate system, entail variations in degree of asso-

ciation formation: Since response learning precedes association formation, the time allotted to the formation of the forward associations which subsequently cause interference during transfer-task acquisition depends directly upon the amount of L_1 in excess of that required for the response-learning phase. Thus as degree of L_1 increases, the amount of negative transfer at the A-B, A-D position should increase.

A similar argument leads to the expectation of increased negative transfer with increased M of first-task responses. Although the R surface is inoperative at the A-B, A-D position, variations in response M differentially delay (inversely according to level of M) the association-formation phase of L_1.

The foregoing derivations regarding degree of L_1 and level of response M are in complete accord with the data cited earlier.

A result which can be accounted for in terms of component surfaces but not by the single transfer surface is that of the Young and Underwood (1954) response-predifferentiation study. They studied three paradigms situated along the edge of the surface from A-B, A-D to A-B, A-B. Half of the subjects were given predifferentiation training on the response items of their first- and transfer-task lists by means of a verbal discrimination task, the other half receiving irrelevant predifferentiation training. Those in the latter category yielded the expected gradient of decreasing positive transfer with decreasing interlist response similarity; those receiving relevant response predifferentiation yielded a markedly modified gradient, best represented by a horizontal line. In other words, relevant response predifferentiation eliminated the gradient. Now response predifferentiation can be seen to have two effects in such a situation. First, mere repetition (during the verbal discrimination task) of the items which are subsequently to be responses raises the R surface, that is, increases response availability, with the maximum effect occurring at the A-B, A-D position. Second, the X_R value for the paradigm involved is increased; this is because predifferentiation serves to increase the distinction between the responses of the two lists. The net effect of these two factors should be negative for paradigms close to the A-B, A-B position since changes in the R surface are less effective there (R is at its maximum at A-B, A-B), but the fast dropping F surface would bring about a considerable negative shift with the increase in X_R. On the other hand, the net effect on paradigms near the A-B, A-D paradigm should be positive: Paradigms near there receive nearly the full effect of increased response availability but only a negligible negative effect due to increased X_R.

Table 1 summarizes the signs of the three components of the net transfer effect for the three paradigms discussed, plus the A-B, A-B. Note that Table 1 is a tabular restatement of Figure 1 for the four positions listed.

TABLE 1. *Direction of component transfer effects*

Paradigm	Component effect		
	R (Response availability)	F (Forward associations)	B (Backward associations)
A-B, A-B	+	+	+
A-B, C-B	+	0	−
A-B, A-D	0	−	0
A-B, C-D	0	0	0

A-B, A-Br.[6] Although the Osgood coordinate system is entirely adequate for providing a position for every paired-associate transfer paradigm, an examination of the A-B, A-Br paradigm leads to the conclusion that the component-surfaces formulation proposed in this paper cannot be applied to a certain class of paradigms of which the A-B, A-Br is a member. Three peculiarities of this para-

digm seem of importance. First, because the exact same stimuli and responses appear in both tasks, it must be that, for this paradigm, $X_S = X_R = 0$, and hence that the A-B, A-Br is assigned the same position as the A-B, A-B. But the latter represents a maximum positive-transfer situation while the former typically involves considerable negative transfer. This is because in the A-B, A-Br the transfer-list re-pairings require transferred F and B effects to be negative. Therefore, in spite of the fact that the A-B, A-B and A-B, A-Br paradigms occupy the same position in the coordinate system, the same triad of component surfaces cannot describe the transfer effects of both.

Second, although each transfer-list stimulus has a new response, the responses are not new in the sense that they are in the A-B, A-D paradigm; and further, the old responses are still present somewhere in the list, not completely removed as in the A-B, A-D paradigm. To understand the import of such an arrangement, consider a single transfer-task pair where the stimulus member is the same as it was in the first task but where the response member is different. There are two kinds of response items which may be assigned: a completely *new* response item, that is, an item not used in the first task (1); or an *old* response item, one already used with a different stimulus in the first task (2). But both of these kinds of response items may be assigned to the stimulus under either of the following two conditions: (a) where the original response item, the one that went with this stimulus in the first task, is completely *removed* from the transfer list; or (b) where the

6. This paradigm designates transfer situations where the stimulus and response members of the transfer task are identical with those of the first except that they are repaired. The notation was introduced by Porter and Duncan (1953), the first to study this paradigm using verbal materials. Gagné, Baker, and Foster (1950) discuss a similar situation in motor transfer problems under the name of complete reversal learning.

original response item is *retained* elsewhere in the transfer list as the response to some other stimulus. The four combinations, 1*a*, 1*b*, 2*a*, and 2*b*, form a 2×2 table where across the top, say, is denoted which kind of response member the transfer-task pair has, new (1) or old (2), and down the side is denoted the transfer-task status of the original (first-task) response, removed (*a*) or retained (*b*). This table is shown as Table 2. Conditions 1*a* and 2*b* are the usual A-B, A-D and A-B, A-Br paradigms, respectively.

As can be seen from the signed transfer effects listed in Table 2, the A-B, A-Br paradigm involves not only a positive R effect and negative F and B effects, as would be expected from a simple consideration of the three component effects, but an additional negative F effect. This is because the presence of old, first-task responses tends to elicit backwardly the interfering forward associations acquired in the first task, thus causing these associations to be more resistant

TABLE 2. *Breakdown of transfer effects in the A-B, A-D and A-B, A-Br Paradigms*

Status of original response	Type of second-list response	
	New (1)	Old (2)
Removed (*a*)	(A-B, A-D) R: 0 F: − B: 0	R: + F: − B: − (A-B, A-Br)
Retained (*b*)	R: 0 F: −,− B: 0	R: + F: −,− B: −

and Wetzel (1962) with results consonant to extinction.[7] An experiment utilizing essentially the design of Table 2 has been conducted by Besch, Thompson, with expectations based on the table.

The third peculiarity attaching to the A-B, A-Br paradigm which has theoretical significance is that transfer in an A-B, A-Br situation must necessarily be a list phenomenon: The repairing operation cannot be carried out on a single pair. Transfer theory as discussed in this paper prior to the treatment of the A-B, A-Br is in no way contingent upon a distinction between transfer from a first to a second list and transfer from a first to a second pair.

From the preceding observations, two queries come to mind in quick succession. First, since it is clear that the noted peculiarities of the A-B, A-Br paradigm arise from the operation of re-pairing, is it not plausible to suppose that such an operation can define a whole new set of transfer paradigms? And second, since a system of component surfaces clearly serves well to account for transfer phenomena in unre-paired (ordinary) paradigms, is it not reasonable to wonder if an equally serviceable conceptualization might not be devised for the re-paired paradigms?

The set of re-paired paradigms is not difficult to characterize. In the first place, they will be as numerous as the ordinary paradigms because for any ordinary paradigm a re-paired paradigm can be obtained by simply carrying out the re-pairing operation. Re-paired paradigms involving completely new transfer-task stimuli and/or responses would not, of course, be distinguishable from their corresponding ordinary paradigms. This means that for such indistinguishable paradigms any system of transfer surfaces designed to handle the re-paired paradigms must coincide with the system of surfaces shown in Figure 1. The loci of coincidence would be along the edges from A-B, C-B to A-B, C-D and from A-B, C-D to A-B, A-D.

Another characteristic of such a system of re-paired paradigms is that the re-paired F and B surfaces must be negative for all positions where first-task forward and backward associations are

7. That first-list associations are extinguished during second-list learning has been adequately established. For evidence and discussion on this point, see Briggs (1954), Barnes and Underwood (1959), and Postman (1961, 1962a).

elicited in the transfer task. The R surface, however, would be the same in both the re-paired and ordinary cases. As far as the present writer knows, the only data pertaining to re-paired transfer situations is that involving the A-B, A-Br paradigm: There have been no studies in which nonzero values of X_S and X_R have been utilized.

As a final remark on the A-B, A-Br paradigm, it is of interest to note that compared to the A-B, A-D the A-B, A-Br involves (besides its extra negative F effect) the net R-B effect, the opposing positive and negative effects of transferred response availability, and backward associations. This opens up the possibility of expecting *less* negative transfer using the A-B, A-Br paradigm than the A-B, A-D for experimental specifications generating a sufficiently positive net R-B effect. Such a situation would arise whenever either very-low-M response materials were used and/or very few trials of L_1 were given, thus making response learning the predominant first-task process. In fact, using trigrams as responses with L_1 taken to a 3/6 criterion (approximately 3.7 trials), Jung (1962) reports transfer in the A-B, A-Br paradigm to be less negative than that in the A-B, A-D; that is, he reports a positive R-B net effect. At a higher degree of first-task learning (a 6/6+5 criterion), the crossover has occurred and the A-B, A-Br paradigm is more negative than the A-B, A-D. The corresponding role of first-task response M was demonstrated by Merikle and Battig (1963): When first-task responses were low M (CCCs), approximately zero transfer was observed in the A-B, A-D paradigm but considerable positive transfer in the A-B, A-Br; however, as M increased, transfer in the A-B, A-Br paradigm became even more negative than the increasingly negative A-B, A-D. In general, studies using adjectives as responses report more negative transfer in

the A-B, A-Br than in the A-B, A-D paradigm (Besch & Reynolds, 1958; Besch, Thompson, & Wetzel, 1962; Kausler & Kanoti, 1963; Keppel & Underwood, 1962; Porter & Duncan, 1953; Postman, 1962b; Twedt & Underwood, 1959), whereas those using trigrams report less (Jung, 1962; Mandler & Heinemann, 1956). Thus the net R-B effect plays the same role in the A-B, A-Br paradigm as in the A-B, C-B paradigm.

ATKINSON, R. C., & ESTES, W. K. Stimulus sampling theory. In R. D. Luce, R. R. Bush, & E. Galanter (Eds.), *Handbook of mathematical psychology*. Vol. 2. New York: Wiley, 1963. Pp. 121-268.

BARNES, J. M., & UNDERWOOD, B. J. "Fate" of first-list associations in transfer theory. *J. exp. Psychol.*, 1959, 58, 97-105.

BESCH, N. F., & REYNOLDS, W. F. Associative interference in verbal paired-associate learning. *J. exp. Psychol.*, 1958, 55, 554-8.

BESCH, N. F., THOMPSON, V. E., & WETZEL, A. B. Studies in associative interference. *J. exp. Psychol.*, 1962, 63, 342-52.

BRIGGS, G. E. Acquisition, extinction, and recovery functions in retroactive inhibition. *J. exp. Psychol.*, 1954, 47, 285-93.

BRUCE, R. W. Conditions of transfer of training. *J. exp. Psychol.*, 1933, 16, 343-61.

BUGELSKI, B. R., & CADWALLADER, T. C. A reappraisal of the transfer and retroaction surface. *J. exp. Psychol.*, 1956, 52, 360-66.

BUNCH, M. E., & MCCRAVEN, V. G. The temporal course of transfer in the learning of memory material. *J. comp. Psychol.*, 1938, 25, 481-96.

CARTERETTE, E. C. A replication of free recall and ordering of trigrams. *J. exp. Psychol.*, 1963, 66, 311-13.

CROTHERS, E. J. Paired-associate learning with compound responses. *J. verb. Learn. verb. Behav.*, 1962, 1, 66-70.

DALLET, K. M. The transfer surface reexamined. *J. verb. Learn. verb. Behav.*, 1962, 1, 91-4.

DEAN, M. G., & KAUSLER, D. H. Degree of first-list learning and stimulus meaningfulness as related to transfer in the A-B, C-B paradigm. *J. verb. Learn. verb. Behav.*, 1964, 3, 330-34.

EBBINGHAUS, H. *Memory: A contribution to experimental psychology.* Leipzig: Duncker & Humboldt, 1885. (Trans. by H. A. Ruger) New York: Teacher's College, Columbia Univer., Bureau of Publications, 1913.

FELDMAN, S. M., & UNDERWOOD, B. J. Stimulus recall following paired-associate learning. *J. exp. Psychol.*, 1957, 53, 11-15.

GAGNÉ, R. M., BAKER, K. E., & FOSTER, H. On the relation between similarity and transfer of training in the learning of discriminative motor task. *Psychol. Rev.*, 1950, 57, 67-79.

HAMILTON, C. E. The relationship between length of interval separating two learning tasks and performance on the second task. *J. exp. Psychol.*, 1950, 40, 613-21.

HARCUM, E. R. Verbal transfer of overlearned forward and backward associations. *Amer. J. Psychol.*, 1953, 66, 622-5.

HOROWITZ, L. M. Free recall and ordering in trigrams. *J. exp. Psychol.*, 1961, 62, 51-7.

JUNG, J. Transfer of training as a function of degree of first-learning. *J. verb. Learn. verb. Behav.*, 1962, **1**, 197-9.

JUNG, J. Effects of response meaningfulness (*m*) on transfer of training under two different paradigms. *J. exp. Psychol.*, 1963, **65**, 377-84.

KAUSLER, D. A., & KANOTI, G. A. R-S learning and negative transfer effects with a mixed list. *J. exp. Psychol.*, 1963, **65**, 201-5.

KEPPEL, G., & UNDERWOOD, B. J. Retroactive inhibition of R-S associations. *J. exp. Psychol.*, 1962, **64**, 400-404.

MANDLER, G. From association to structure. *Psychol. Rev.*, 1962, **69**, 415-27.

MANDLER, G., & HEINEMANN, S. H. Effect of overlearning of a verbal response on transfer of training. *J. exp. Psychol.*, 1956, **51**, 39-46.

McGUIRE, W. J. A multiprocess model for paired-associate learning. *J. exp. Psychol.*, 1961, **62**, 335-47.

MELTON, A. W. Implications of short-term memory for a general theory of memory. *J. verb. Learn. verb. Behav.*, 1963, **2**, 1-21.

MERIKLE, P. M., & BATTIG, W. F. Transfer of training as a function of experimental paradigm and meaningfulness. *J. verb. Learn. verb. Behav.*, 1963, **2**, 485-8.

MÜLLER, G. E., & PILZECKER, A. Experimentelle Beiträge zur Lehre vom Gedächtniss. *Zeitschrift für Psychologie*, 1900, **1**, 1-300.

MÜLLER, G. E., & SCHUMANN, F. Experimentelle Beiträge zur Untersuchung des Gedächtnisses. *Zeitschrift für Psychologie*, 1894, **6**, 81-190, 257-339.

MURDOCK, B. B., JR., "Backward" associations in transfer and learning. *J. exp. Psychol.*, 1958, **55**, 111-14.

NEWTON, J. M., & WICKENS, D. D. Retroactive inhibition as a function of the temporal position of the interpolated learning. *J. exp. Psychol.*, 1956, **51**, 149-54.

NOBLE, C. E. Meaningfulness and familiarity. In C. N. Cofer & B. S. Musgrave (Eds.), *Verbal behavior and learning*. New York: McGraw-Hill, 1963. Pp. 76-119.

OSGOOD, C. E. The similarity paradox in human learning: A resolution. *Psychol. Rev.*, 1949, **56**, 132-43.

PETERSON, L. R., & PETERSON, M. J. Short-term retention of individual verbal items. *J. exp. Psychol.*, 1959, **58**, 193-8.

PORTER, L. W., & DUNCAN, C. P. Negative transfer in verbal learning. *J. exp. Psychol.*, 1953, **46**, 61-4.

POSTMAN, L. The present status of interference theory. In C. N. Cofer (Ed.), *Verbal learning and verbal behavior*. New York: McGraw-Hill, 1961. Pp. 152-79.

POSTMAN, L. Retention of first-list associations as a function of the conditions of transfer. *J. exp. Psychol.*, 1962, **64**, 380-87. (a)

POSTMAN, L. Transfer of training as a function of experimental paradigm and degree of first-list learning. *J. verb. Learn. verb. Behav.*, 1962, **1**, 109-18. (b)

SCHULZ, R. W., & MARTIN, E. Aural paired-associate learning: Stimulus familiarization, response familiarization, and pronunciability. *J. verb. Learn. verb. Behav.*, 1964, **3**, 139-45.

SCHULZ, R. W., & TUCKER, I. F. Stimulus familiarization and length of the anticipation interval in paired-associate learning. *Psychol. Reps.*, 1962, **12**, 341-4.

SHEPARD, R. N. Comments on Professor Underwood's paper. In C. N. Cofer & B. S. Musgrave (Eds.), *Verbal behavior and learning*. New York: McGraw-Hill, 1963. Pp. 48-70.

SPIKER, C. C. Associative transfer in verbal paired-associate learning. *Child Development*, 1960, **31**, 73-87.

THORNDIKE, E. L. *The fundamentals of learning*. New York: Columbia Univer. Press, 1932.

TWEDT, H. M., & UNDERWOOD, B. J. Mixed vs. unmixed lists in transfer studies. *J. exp. Psychol.*, 1959, **58**, 111-16.

UNDERWOOD, B. J. *Experimental psychology*. New York: Appleton-Century-Crofts, 1949.

UNDERWOOD, B. J., RUNQUIST, W. N., & SCHULZ, R. W. Response learning in paired-associate lists as a function of intralist similarity. *J. exp. Psychol.*, 1959, **58**, 70-78.

UNDERWOOD, B. J., & SCHULZ, R. W. *Meaningfulness and verbal learning*. New York: Lippincott, 1960.

WIMER, R. Osgood's transfer surface: Extension and test. *J. verb. Learn. verb. Behav.*, 1964, **3**, 274-9.

YOUNG, R. K., & UNDERWOOD, B. J. Transfer in verbal materials with dissimilar stimuli and response similarity varied. *J. exp. Psychol.*, 1954, **47**, 153-9.

PSYCHOLINGUISTICS

This section considers a relatively new sub-area of psychology, or more properly, a new interdisciplinary enterprise. Psycholinguistics is the psychological investigation of language behavior. Its independent variables are characteristically linguistic in conception, and its materials are words, sentences, or items with language-like aspects.

The problems facing investigators are challenging. Among them are such questions as: how does the average speaker generate novel and appropriate sentences with such apparent ease, does one's language determine one's perceptions of the world, what is the specific mechanism whereby meaning is conveyed, and what is the psychological status of rules of grammar? The facts of language behavior have not yielded in a satisfactory manner to approaches based upon direct applications of animal conditioning principles. In an excellent critical review, Chomsky (1959) trenchantly spelled out the weaknesses and inadequacies of one ambitious attempt to analyze verbal behavior through an operant conditioning paradigm. Even more complex associationistic approaches, such as the mediational theory of reference offered by Mowrer (1954), have encountered difficulties upon closer examination. It is expected that any workable theory of language production will have to employ constructs that reflect the generative and rule-following characteristics exemplified in the behavior of language users. In describing some unique properties of language behavior and their implications for theory, Miller (1965, p. 20) stated:

If the hypothetical constructs that are needed seem too complex and arbitrary, too improbable and mentalistic, then you had better forgo the study of language. For language is just that—complex, arbitrary, improbable, mentalistic—and no amount of wishful theorizing will make it anything else.

The following readings are illustrative of both empirical and theoretical contributions offered by the psychologists in the area. It will be apparent that the theoretical efforts in this field are relatively programmatic, and that the systematic experimental testing of deductions has only just begun.

The paper by Aborn, Rubenstein, and Sterling examined the role of contextual constraint upon words in sentences. A sentence is an ordered, not a random, sequence of words. The probability of appearance of particular words is influenced by the other words in the sentence. This context sets limits to the number and class of words that can conceivably occupy a given sentence position. Using a "cloze" procedure, Aborn *et al.* found that the length, distribution, and grammatical structure of the context were all influential in constraining performance. The effect of sequential dependencies upon free recall was first shown by Miller and Selfridge (referred to in the Introduction to Section V), whose article is also pertinent to psycholinguistics. A further experimental analysis is given by Treisman (1965), who shows the independent effects of grammatical and semantic sources of constraint.

Epstein's paper investigated the effect of syntactic structure upon the rate of learning of lists of items. A familiar example of material which has syntactic structure but almost no meaning is the "Jabberwocky" poem. " 'Twas brilling, and the slithy toves did gyre and gimble in the wabe," is semantic nonsense which nonetheless has the smack of language about it. Such lists are learned more rapidly than those which lack familiar grammatical tags. Along these same lines, Miller and Isard (1963) measured the accuracy with which three types of word strings were able to be perceived. The materials were meaningful grammatical sentences, anomalous sentences (syntactically sound, but semantically distorted), and ungrammatical strings (both semantically and syntactically distorted). Results showed that the intelligibility of these materials was inversely related to the degree of violation of linguistic rules that each embodied.

Miller's paper deals with the psychological significance of syntactic structure. The existence of difficult self-embedded sentences was cited to indicate the need for a model of grammar that could accommodate such complex structures. A simple Markovian model would be inadequate. A transformational grammar was described, and data were presented to suggest that complex transformations take more time to perform than do simpler ones, and that sentences are psychologically stored as a kernel-plus-transformation code. This latter position has generated a sustained series of experimental tests designed to explore its plausibility.

The paper by Osgood is a comprehensive theoretical statement. It begins with an account of various theoretical approaches to the problem of the generation and understanding of sentences. Examination of finite state, phrase structure, and transformational grammar models developed by linguists all showed certain short-comings. Similarly, psychological learning theories of the single-stage and two-stage mediation type were found to be inadequate. The rest of the paper contains a general description of a three-stage mediation theory with a three-component process of sentence understanding.

Fodor's paper presents a closely reasoned criticism of theories that attempt to explain linguistic reference, or meaning, through a mediational paradigm. The analysis shows that such attempts are fundamentally no improvement in principle over non-mediational accounts in meeting the demands of linguistic reality. The psychology of semantics is probably one of the least understood areas in the entire field of human learning.

CHOMSKY, N. Review of B. F. Skinner, *Verbal behavior. Language*, 1959, **35**, 26-58.

MILLER, G. A. Some preliminaries to psycholinguistics. *Amer. Psychologist*, 1965, **20**, 15-20.

MILLER, G. A., & ISARD, S. Some perceptual consequences of linguistic rules, *J. verb. Learn. verb. Behav.*, 1963, **2**, 217-28.

MOWRER, O. H. The psychologist looks at language. *Amer. Psychologist*, 1954, **9**, 660-92.

TREISMAN, A. Verbal responses and contextual constraints in language. *J. verb. Learn. verb. Behav.*, 1965, **4**, 118-28.

36 / Sources of Contextual Constraint upon Words in Sentences [1]

MURRAY ABORN, *Division of Research Grants, National Institutes of Health*
HERBERT RUBENSTEIN, *Operational Applications Laboratory,*
Air Force Cambridge Research Center
AND
THEODOR D. STERLING, *Kettering Laboratory, University of Cincinnati*

This study investigated the constraint upon words attributable to the length, distribution, and structure of context consisting of incomplete sentences. The measure of constraint employed was single-guess word predictability. The positive relationship between length and constraint has already been demonstrated in the case of letters (Burton & Licklider, 1955; Shannon, 1951). While there is no reason to believe that this relationship will not hold where word rather than letter predictability is employed, there may well be a difference in the length of context required for maximum constraint. For letter prediction, this length has been reported to be 32 letters (Burton & Licklider, 1955). The present study afforded an opportunity to observe the constraint on words in contexts well beyond the 32-letter limit.

The relationship between constraint and the distribution of context, i.e., whether the context totally precedes, follows, or is situated on both sides of the dependent (the word to be predicted), has not received much attention from investigators. The results of studies by Kaplan (1950) and Miller and Friedman (1957) indicate that bilateral distribution exerts greater constraint than either form of unilateral distribution. The present study attempted to confirm this for contexts encompassing whole sentences.

Of the relationship between constraint and the structure of context, little is known beyond Kaplan's (1950) finding that short contexts (1–4 words) consisting entirely of articles, prepositions, conjunctions, etc. (*particle contexts*) exert less semantic constraint than contexts containing at least one noun, verb, adjective, or adverb (*substantive contexts*). Since Kaplan's characterization of contexts as

From the *Journal of Experimental Psychology*, 1959, **57**, 171-80, with permission of the authors and publisher.
1. This paper is based upon research carried out while the first two authors were with the Air Force Personnel and Training Research Center and the third was principal investigator of Contract AF 41(657)-137. The work was done under ARDC Project No. 7730, Task No. 17125, in support of the research and development program of the Air Force Personnel and Training Research Center, Lackland Air Force Base, Texas. Permission is granted for reproduction, translation, publication, use, and disposal in whole or in part by or for the United States Government.

particle or substantive is unfortunately inapplicable to longer contexts—almost all contexts longer than four words would be substantive—the difficulty of classifying structures so that the classification bears some relation to the degree of constraint is still unresolved. Thus, structure was investigated in the present study only in a very indirect way; namely, through the effect of the grammatical class of words on their predictability. The connection between the grammatical class of the dependent and the structure of the context would lie, of course, in the fact that the structure of the context determines the class to which its dependents belong. Although this relationship is attenuated by the fact that most contexts will admit more than one class of dependents, one class will in general be predominant; that is to say, the most frequent dependents will generally belong to the same class. Certain inferences may thus be drawn between the structure of the context—defined in terms of the class of its most frequent dependents—and its contribution to constraint. Therefore, if nouns turn out to be less predictable than verbs, it may be inferred that contexts having a structure such that the most frequent dependents are nouns exert less constraint than contexts in which the most frequent dependents are verbs.

METHOD

Materials

About 3,000 printed English sentences exactly 6, 11, and 25 words long were drawn randomly from a number of back issues of a representative selection of popular magazines. Contractions were counted as two words, hyphenated words as one. Sentences punctuated with a semicolon, containing dots to show omission, or appearing as captions to pictures were excluded. Other than that, no restrictions were placed on the punctuation, structure, or content of the sentences that could be drawn.

Word classification.—Each word of every

sentence in the sample was classified as belonging to one of six classes: noun, verb, adjective, adverb, pronoun, or function word. The class of function words includes articles, conjunctions, prepositions, auxiliary verbs, interjections, and quantity words.

Although they bear familiar designations, these classes differ somewhat from the traditional classes in that they are based on Fries' (1952) system of analysis with two important modifications: First, the pronoun was treated as a separate class apart from the noun. This was advisable since it appeared likely that the pronoun would be found to differ from the noun in predictability and since Aborn and Rubenstein (1957) had already observed it to be statistically distinct. Secondly, all of Fries' groups of function words were combined into one class —both for the sake of simplicity of design and because all are highly dependent upon context. Other differences between the classification used in the present study and Fries' system have been taken up in detail in the Aborn and Rubenstein study (1957).

Position of omission.—Four positions were selected from which a single word would be omitted in the experimental sentences, i.e., those sentences of the entire sample that were to be administered to Ss. Since the sentences were of three different lengths, two of the four positions of omission were comparable rather than identical from one length to the next. The positions selected were: *sentence initial, early medial* (the third word in 6-word sentences, the fourth word in 11-word sentences, and the eighth word in 25-word sentences), *late medial* (the fourth word in 6-word sentences, the eighth word in 11-word sentences, and the seventeenth word in 25-word sentences), and *sentence final.* (Recalling that contractions were originally counted as two words, any contraction appearing in a position of omission was rewritten as two separate words.)

Experimental sentences.—The entire sample of 6-word sentences was divided into six groups according to the class of the first word. Twenty sentences were then chosen from each group. The sentences were chosen at random, but those having a proper noun or a numeral in the position of omission were discarded in favor of some other sentence. (The names of persons, places, or numbers are nearly impossible to predict in sentence-length contexts and their inclusion would merely serve to reduce the proportion of correct responses.) The remainder of the 6-word sentences were arranged and rearranged three times more, once according to the classification of words in the early medial position, once according to the classification of words in the late medial position, and once according to the classification of words in the final position. Each time, 20 sentences were chosen randomly (under the same restrictions as before) from each of the six word-class groups. There was one exception: Since function words occur very infrequently in the last position of the sentence (in printed English at least), sentences were chosen with only five classes represented in that position.

The entire procedure for selecting the experimental sentences from the 6-word sample was repeated for the 11- and 25-word samples. When the procedure was complete, there were 1,380 experimental sentences divided into three treatments of length (with 460 sentences each), within which were four treatments of position (with 120 sentences each except in sentence final), within which were six treatments of word class (with 20 sentences each) minus one class in sentence final at each length, giving, in all, 69 treatment combinations capable of testing the effects of any one variable under controlled conditions of the other two.

Test booklets.—Copies of each sentence, with an underlined blank space appearing in place of the omitted word, were mimeographed on separate sheets of paper. Each sheet bore a code number identifying the combination of treatments represented by the sentence. The sheets were assorted into stacks of 20 and separated into groups representing the 69 treatment combinations. The sheets were then collated into booklets in accordance with a previously prepared table of permutations which arranged the code numbers into groups of 20 sets of 69, with no duplications. In brief, the test booklets were made up of 69 sentences each, every booklet containing one sentence from each combination of treatments, arranged in sets of 20 so that each set exhausted all 1,380 sentences, with the sentences appearing in a different sequence in each booklet.

Subjects

The experimental sentences were administered to 24 second-semester freshmen at the University of Alabama.[2] An attempt was made to secure a relatively homogeneous group with regard to academic proficiency in general and high verbal ability in particular. Subjects were selected from students scoring in or very near the top decile of both the English placement test and the reading comprehension test given by the university. In addition, candidates for S were administered the School and College Aptitude Test, and only those achieving total or verbal scores falling within the upper quartile of the national norms were chosen.

Procedure

The Ss met as a group for twenty 1.5-hr. testing sessions conducted over a period of four weeks. Each time they met, each S completed one of the 20 booklets in the set assigned to him. The following directions were read to the group at the beginning of every session:

"Each sentence has a word missing in it. The missing word is indicated by an underlined blank space. One, and only one, word is missing from the sentence. It may occasionally be a hyphenated word, but it is never two words, it is never a contraction (don't, won't, shouldn't, can't, etc.), and it is never the name of a person, the name of a place, or a number.

"Read each sentence carefully. Think about the sentence before you fill in the missing word. These are real sentences taken from popular magazines. Write in the word you think was most likely to have occurred in that sentence.

"Don't be disconcerted if many sentences suggest the same missing word to you. Don't deliberately strive for variation among your guesses. Always guess what was most likely the word missing from the sentence at hand, regardless of your guesses on other sentences.

"Be sure to complete every sentence in the booklet. Leave no sentence out. When you are finished, go back and count to see if you have completed all 69 sentences in the booklet.

2. This phase of the study was carried out under Contract AF 41(657)-137.

"The underlines indicating the missing word are all the same size. The length of the underline is absolutely no indication of whether the missing word was a long or a short word.

"Write in your guess in any part of the empty page below the sentence. Don't try to crowd it into the blank space itself. Write legibly. We cannot give you credit for a word we cannot read."

To help motivate Ss, double pay was offered to those achieving the 10 highest scores.

Scoring.—A response was scored as correct only if it reproduced the missing word exactly as it originally appeared in the sentence. Variations in number, tense, or person were scored as incorrect. Misspellings, however, were disregarded if the response was unambiguous.

RESULTS AND DISCUSSION

The differences in predictability occurring under the 'various treatments of word class, position of omission, and sentence length are shown by the means in Table 1. These means were obtained by summing the number of correct predictions in each treatment combination and dividing by 24, the number of Ss. In order to test the significance of the main effects directly from these data, each mean was taken as a single score representing a maximum likelihood estimate of an S's performance on 20 sentence replications. Since it was theoretically possible for each of these scores to have assumed any value between 0 and 20, the scores could be regarded as a random variable over a subset of the continuous interval 0 to 20. The distribution of means was approximately Poisson, and the square-root transformation was used as the most appropriate transform for normalizing the distribution for analysis of variance (Bartlett, 1947).

As shown in Table 1, there were three cells for which no scores existed: function word in the final position of the 6-, 11-, and 25-word lengths. In order to evaluate all of the data in a single analysis, the mean squares of the treatment and residual variances were modified by estimating the missing variates by the Yates (1933) procedure.[3]

Table 2 summarizes the results of the analysis performed with the data shown in Table 1, as modified. It should be noted that 3 *df* were lost by the approximation of the missing variates. The correct estimate of the within variance turns out to be the pooled mean square for all interactions because replications have been eliminated and the

---

3. As a check on the possible bias introduced by estimating the missing data variance, an analysis of the scores was made with all values for sentence final omitted. This analysis yielded treatments and error mean squares that differed from those of Table 2 by no more than one decimal.

TABLE 1. *Mean number of words correctly predicted in each combination of treatments*

Position of Omission	Sentence Length	Word Class					
		Noun	Verb	Adj.	Adv.	F.W.	Pro.
Initial	6-word	3.79	9.00	1.46	3.04	9.04	8.58
	11-word	3.21	5.83	4.25	5.38	12.92	11.46
	25-word	3.92	5.79	4.08	3.21	11.96	11.71
Early medial	6-word	4.54	6.17	4.00	7.25	13.08	8.83
	11-word	6.25	8.79	5.63	4.79	11.96	13.25
	25-word	7.46	10.75	5.25	5.00	13.88	14.63
Late medial	6-word	5.29	5.46	5.50	9.96	11.67	7.83
	11-word	5.63	7.88	6.08	8.46	14.46	11.46
	25-word	3.17	10.58	5.17	4.83	13.54	15.83
Final	6-word	5.54	3.63	1.46	7.46		5.96
	11-word	6.33	8.29	3.29	7.17		10.71
	25-word	3.75	6.71	4.54	9.63		11.25

TABLE 2. *Analysis of variance of transformed maximum likelihood estimates for treatment combinations*

Source of Variation	df	MS	F
Word Class (C)	5	4.442	26.284°
Position of omission (P)	3	.467	2.763°°
Sentence length (L)	2	.544	3.219°°
C × P	15	.203	—
C × L	10	.206	—
P × L	6	.164	—
C × P × L	27	.137	
Pooled error	58	.169	
Total	68		

Note.—The total number of *df* is 71. Since estimates of three missing values were used, however, 3 *df* had to be subtracted.
° $P < .001$.
°° $P < .05$.

interactions of the lower order fail to yield significant *F* values (Edwards, 1950, pp. 255-6). The results indicate that the obtained differences in predictability among word classes were highly significant and that the obtained differences among positions of omission and sentence lengths were acceptably significant. As noted above, none of the interactions was significant, indicating that each of the three variables is capable of producing differences in constraint independently of the constraining effects of the other two.

Word class.—The results pertaining specifically to word class are summarized in Table 3. The data in the table are derived from data already presented in Table 1. In the case of Table 3, however, the number of correct predictions for the various word classes was taken without regard to position of omission, and the cells are based on 80 sentences (60 sentences for function words) rather than 20, as in the case of Table 1. To avoid confusion with the figures in Table 1, the entries in Table 3 are given as percentages rather than means.

Table 3 shows quite clearly that, beyond the matter of the reliability of the differences, differences in the predictability of words belonging to different word classes were of considerable magni-

TABLE 3. *Percentage of words correctly predicted by class*

Sentence Length	Word Class					
	Noun	Verb	Adj.	Adv.	F.W.	Pro.
6-word	24	30	16	35	56	39
11-word	27	39	24	32	66	59
25-word	23	42	24	28	66	67
Mean %	25	37	21	32	63	55

tude. Function words, for example, were on the whole about three times as predictable as adjectives; pronouns, about twice as predictable as nouns. The differences are not only large, but appear to be inverse to the size of the class of the omitted word. We would expect these differences to be related to the relative size of the classes—reasoning that the larger the class of the omitted word, the greater the number of alternatives admitted by the context and consequently the lower the probability of correct prediction.

In this connection, it should be noted that great differences in size exist among the various word classes. French, Carter, and Koenig (1930), for example found that among 2,240 different words in a sample of 79,390 words of telephone conversation, 46% were nouns, 28% were adjectives or adverbs, 20% were verbs (excluding auxiliaries), and 6% were pronouns and words classified as function words in the present study. Similarly, Fries (1952) found in 1,000 different words of telephone conversation that 39% were Class 1 words (nouns and pronouns), 25% Class 2 words (verbs), 17% Class 3 words (adjectives), 12% Class 4 words (adverbs), and 7% function words. The descending hierarchy of classes according to size, then, is: noun, verb, adjective, adverb, function word, and pronoun. Comparing this with the ascending hierarchy according to predictability—adjective, noun, adverb, verb, pronoun, and function word—there would indeed appear to be some degree of inverse relationship, but disturbed by reversals. Not too much significance can be placed upon the finding that function words are more predictable than pronouns. Both are such small classes—there are about 50 pronouns and 150 function words in the language—that the difference in size is probably too slight to be detected by a single-guess measure of predictability. The unexpectedly low predictability of the adjective and adverb, however, is a more serious matter. For some reason, the number of alternatives from which Ss selected their responses was greater in the case of omitted words which were adjectives or adverbs than we would expect from the sizes of these classes. One possible explanation is that in contexts where the omitted word was an adjective or adverb, Ss tended to draw their responses from other classes as well. To test this possibility the number of responses disagreeing with the class of the omitted word was determined (Table 4). While showing that the amount of disagreement was generally low, Table 4 clearly indicates that the tendency for Ss to draw responses from a class other than that of the omitted word was most pronounced in the case of the adjective and adverb. In other words, the grammatical constraint exerted by the context is weakest for the adjective and adverb. The following sentences may serve as examples of contexts in which the adjective or adverb might be replaced by a different word class: *Good* (adjective) or *That* (function word) *cheese is expensive. The big* (adjective) or *store* (noun) *window was broken. He was sick* (adjective) or *killed* (verb). *Quietly* (adverb) or *Discouraged* (adjective) *he left the room. They found him there* (adverb) or *working* (verb). *He read quickly* (adverb) or *it* (pronoun).

The effects due to differences in grammatical constraint were eliminated by analyzing the data of only those sentences where Ss all drew their responses from the class of the omitted word. The following means overall sentence lengths and overall positions but initial (there were too few such sentences for adjectives and adverbs in initial position) were then obtained: nouns 30%, adjectives 30%, verbs 38%, adverbs 46%, pronouns 59%, and function words 69%. Apparently, the low predictability of the adverb is due to the lower grammatical constraint exerted on it. It is equally clear from these figures that the low predictability of the adjective, on the other hand, involves something besides class size and grammatical constraint. It may

TABLE 4. *Percentage disagreement with the word class of the omitted word*

Position of Omission	Sentence Length	Word Class					
		Noun	Verb	Adj.	Adv.	F.W.	Pro.
Initial	6-word	42	8	62	21	22	8
	11-word	33	14	48	20	12	5
	25-word	30	21	49	29	7	16
Early medial	6-word	15	1	32	18	8	10
	11-word	21	0	11	23	10	15
	25-word	16	0	19	15	4	9
Late medial	6-word	10	6	12	29	8	18
	11-word	9	4	16	21	11	12
	25-word	9	2	14	17	4	3
Final	6-word	3	3	25	28		15
	11-word	2	6	15	15		20
	25-word	2	7	22	16		24
Mean %		16	6	27	21	10	13

be that adjective alternatives have a greater tendency toward equiprobability or, possibly, that authors tend toward a greater avoidance of clichés in the use of adjectives than in the use of other word classes. At any rate, the data of the present experiment do not permit a convincing answer one way or the other.

Position of omission.—The results pertaining specifically to position of omission are summarized in Table 5. As in

TABLE 5. *Percentage of words correctly predicted by position*

Sentence Length	Position of Omission				Mean %
	Initial	Early Medial	Late Medial	Final	
6-word	29	37	38	24	32
11-word	36	42	45	36	40
25-word	34	48	44	36	40
Mean %	33	42	42	32	

Table 3, the data in Table 5 are derived from data already presented in Table 1. In Table 5, however, the number of correct predictions for each position of omission was taken without regard to word class, and the cells are based on 120 sentences (100 sentences for sentence final) rather than 20, as in the case of Table 1. To avoid confusion with the figures in Table 1, the entries in Table 5 are given as percentages rather than means.

Table 5 shows that words in the medial positions of omission were more predictable than words in the initial or final position. It is evident that a bilateral context exerts greater constraint than a unilateral context of the same length—regardless of whether the context precedes or follows. Similar findings have been reported by Miller and Friedman (1957) and by Kaplan (1950). Kaplan found that a bilateral context consisting of one word on each side of the dependent exerted greater constraint than either two words preceding or two words following. The present study indicates that a bilaterally distributed context exerts greater constraint in much longer sequences as well. It would seem, therefore, that the proximity of segments of context to the dependent is a more powerful factor in constraint than the length of context per se. Table 5 shows, for example, that a bilateral context of three words on one side and two words on the other exerts constraint equal to that exerted by a unilateral context of 10–24 words either preceding or following the dependent.

Sentence length.—The data in Table 5 indicate that predictability increases with sentence length regardless of sentence position. This is in accord with the observation of information theorists that constraint increases with the increase in context (Shannon, 1951). The data of the present experiment, however, confirm another observation too: namely, that the relationship between constraint and length of context does not go on indefinitely. There is a point beyond which increasing context will not further increase constraint. Thus, Table 5 shows no appreciable difference in predictability between 11- and 25-word sentences. The implication is that the effect of context attains its maximum somewhere between a length of 5 words and one of 10 words. It is interesting to observe that this interval—between 23 and 45 letters, if one takes the average word length as 4.5 letters—includes the limit of 32 letters suggested by Burton and Licklider (1955). Apparently, then, the amount of context required for maximum constraint is roughly of the same order for letter and word prediction—at least when the words are predicted within sentences of fixed length.

Predictability when word class is uncontrolled.—As an estimate of how predictability might vary from one position of omission to the next in a sample of sentences in which the frequency of word classes in each position was uncontrolled, the prediction scores were weighted according to the probability of occurrence of each word class (Aborn & Rubenstein, 1957) at the position in question. More specifically, the weighting was carried out as follows: Each entry in Table 1 was multiplied by the probability of the class in the given condition. The sum of these products for each position and sentence length (the mean number of correct responses per S in 20 sentences) was then divided by 20 and multiplied by 100 to yield the precentage of correct predictions in the total number of responses.

It is apparent from the data presented in Table 6 that, when the frequencies of the word classes are left uncontrolled, all positions except the final show about the same predictability. These results

TABLE 6. *Percentage of words correctly predicted by position after weighting*

Sentence Lenth	Position of Omission			
	Initial	Early Medial	Late Medial	Final
6-word	38	41	43	26
11-word	50	46	51	34
25-word	50	53	48	25
Mean %	46	47	47	28

are most easily explained in terms of the relative frequency of the highly predictable pronoun and function word. The low predictability of the final position is due to the almost complete absence of function words and the low probability of occurrence of pronouns (only about .05–.08). The equal probability of the initial and medial positions—despite the advantage of bilateral context in the case of medials—results from the fact that function words and pronouns have a combined probability of .7 in initial position but only .45 in medial positions.

These data permit a rough comparison between the predictability of letters omitted randomly and the predictability of letters constituting a word. Miller and Friedman (1957) tested the ability of Ss

to reconstruct passages originally 300 letters in length when various percentages of the letters were randomly deleted (omitted with the position of omission indicated), abbreviated (omitted without indication of omission), or replaced by other letters. We may regard the omission of words in the present study as an abbreviation of letter sequences—abbreviation rather than deletion since position of omission is indicated only for the first letter. If the mean word length is taken to be 4.5 letters, the omission of one word in an 11-word sentence is roughly a 9% abbreviation while the omission of one word in a 6-word sentence is roughly a 17% abbreviation. With 9% random abbreviation, Miller and Friedman found that Ss could correctly predict about 98% of the missing letters; and with 17% random abbreviation, that Ss could correctly predict about 80% of the missing letters. According to the results of the present study, Ss could correctly predict about 47% of the missing words in 11-word sentences and about 38% of the missing words in 6-word sentences (see Table 6). To employ these figures as indices of letter predictability, it was necessary to incorporate the percentage of letters correctly predicted even when the total word was scored as incorrect. Examination of the data revealed that 7% of letters (averaged over all positions in the word) were correctly predicted under this circumstance. In all, then, the percentage of letters correctly predicted was 54% in 11-word sentences and 45% in 6-word sentences. The predictability of letters constituting a word is therefore little more than half as great as the predictability of letters omitted randomly.

SUMMARY

In order to test the constraint exerted upon words in sentences by three properties of context, 1,380 sentences were selected from about 3,000 sentences drawn randomly from a number of popular magazines. One word was omitted from each sentence in a way that yielded three treatments of sentence length, within which were four treatments of position of omission, within which were six treatments of word class of the omitted word. The sentences were administered to 24 Ss, who were instructed to predict the missing word in each sentence with a single guess. Analysis of the predictability scores showed that:

1. The length, distribution, and grammatical structure of context are all independently effective sources of constraint on words in sentences.

2. The predictability of words belonging to a given word class is, in general, inversely related to the size of that class. However, this relationship is disturbed in instances where the context exerts so little grammatical constraint that more than one class may occur with near-equal probability.

3. Increasing the context beyond 10 words does not increase predictability. The length at which context attains maximum effectiveness lies between 5 and 10 words.

4. A bilaterally distributed context exerts greater constraint than a totally preceding or totally following context of the same length. This generalization holds true for long as well as short contexts.

5. When the frequency of word-class occurrence is left uncontrolled, words have almost the same predictability in all positions in the sentence except the final, where predictability is much lower.

6. The predictability of letters constituting a word is only about half as great as the reported predictability of letters omitted randomly.

ABORN, M., & RUBENSTEIN, H. Word-class distribution in sentences of fixed length. *Language*, 1957, **32**, 666-74.

BARTLETT, M. S. The use of transformations. *Biometrics*, 1947, 3(1), 39-52.

BURTON, N. G., & LICKLIDER, J. C. R. Long-range constraints in the statistical structure of printed English. *Amer. J. Psychol.*, 1955, **68**, 650-53.

EDWARDS, A. L. *Experimental design in psychological research.* New York: Rinehart, 1950.

FRENCH, N. R., CARTER, C. W., & KOENING, W. The words and sounds of telephone conversations. *Bell System Tech. J.*, 1930, **9**, 290-324.

FRIES, C. C. *The structure of English.* New York: Harcourt, Brace, 1952.

KAPLAN, A. An experimental study of ambiguity and context. *Rand Corp.*, P-187, Nov., 1950.

MILLER, G. A., & FRIEDMAN, E. A. The reconstruction of mutilated English texts. *Information and Control*, 1957, **1**, 38-55.

SHANNON, C. E. Prediction and entropy of printed English. *Bell System Tech. J.*, 1951, **30**, 50-64.

YATES, F. The analysis of replicated experiments when the field results are incomplete. *Emp. J. exp. Agr.*, 1933, **1**, 129-42.

37 / The Influence of Syntactical Structure on Learning [*]

WILLIAM EPSTEIN, *University of Kansas*

This experiment was designed to study the role of syntactical structure in verbal learning. Syntax can be defined as the generalized pattern or schema which is imposed upon the reservoir of available words and determines the sequences of these words. The fact that verbal messages in ordinary usage are encoded according to a set of grammatical rules may make the learning of natural linguistic units very different from the learning of a series composed of independent items, *e.g.*, a list of nonsense-syllables.

Sequential or transitional-probability orderings and syntactical arrangements must be distinguished at the outset. A sentence usually entails a high degree of transitional probability among its components. Nonetheless, a sentence cannot be defined simply as a highly probable sequence of words. The distinction is clearly expressed by Deese,[1] and also by Chomsky. Concerning this point, Chomsky writes: "If we rank the sequences of

From the *American Journal of Psychology*, 1961, **74**, 80-85, with permission of the author and publisher.
[*] Received for publication December 28, 1959. This study was supported by Grant M-3600 from the United States Public Health Service.
1. James Deese, *The Psychology of Learning*, 2nd ed., 1958, 331.

a given length in order of statistical approximation to English, we will find both grammatical and ungrammatical sequences scattered throughout the list; there appears to be no particular relation between order of approximation and grammaticalness." [2]

The ability to produce and to recognize grammatical utterances, therefore, is not based on any notions of transitional probability. Nor does the experience of syntactical structure depend on semantic meaningfulness or familiarity. Grammatical structure can be recognized easily even in an arrangement of nonsense-syllables.[3] It should be possible, therefore, to study the influence of syntactical structure independently of meaningfulness, familiarity, or sequential probability.

Some evidence bearing on this factor is cited by Osgood, one of whose students "compared the ease of learning nonsense sequences that retained the structure of the English sentences from which they were derived, for example, *The maff vlems oothly um the glox nerfs*, with matched materials in which the grammatical cues had been eliminated, for example, *maff vlem ooth um glox nerf*." [4] The structured series were learned more easily than random lists. Further evidence is provided by the present investigation in which the learning of structured material and matched, unstructured material was compared.

Materials

Six categories of material were composed, each consisting of two "sentences." Category I contains two sentences composed of nonsense-syllables in combination with two functional words which have no referential meaning, *e.g.* articles,, conjunctions, and prepositions. Grammatical tags, such as *ed* on past tense verbs and *s* on plural nouns, were appended to the syllable-stems to simulate the requirements of English syntax. The result is a series of nonsense-syllables which is readily perceived to be grammatically

structured. In Category II, these syllable-stems are presented again in the same order but without the appended grammatical tags. Category III repeats the material contained in Category I, but the items are arranged in random order. As a consequence of the omission of the tags in Category II and the randomization of items in Category III, the four sentences comprising these two categories are devoid of any discernible syntactical structuring.

In Category IV, the identity of the original syllable-stems and the order with which they are presented in Category I are retained. The only difference between the two categories is in the position of the appended grammatical endings. In the fourth category, the positions of the tags have been shifted in an effort to induce the formation of a competing syntactical pattern, that is, a structure which is not congruent with customary English usage.

For purposes of comparison, the remaining two categories consist of meaningful words. These words are arranged in an order which is *sententially* meaningless and within which there exists a very low level of transitional probability between neighboring words. Category V contains two series of words so ordered as to meet the demands of syntactical structure. Category VI contains the same words in random, unstructured order.

The sentences were typed separately on 5×8-in. index cards in a horizontal line, as is customary for written material in English. To enhance the grammatical character of the material in Categories I, IV, and V, the first word in each of these sentences was capitalized and each sentence was closed with a period. In the remaining three categories both the capital letter and the period were omitted. The material is reproduced in Table I.

2. Noam Chomsky, *Syntactic Structures*, 1957, 17.
3. I do not mean to imply that the listener or reader must be aware of the grammatical aspects of the message to respond to the information provided by syntax.
4. C. E. Osgood, A behavioristic analysis of perception and language as cognitive phenomena, in J. S. Bruner, *et al.*, *Contemporary Approaches to Cognition*, 1957, 88. I am indebted to Dr. Osgood for making available an unpublished report of this work, by Swanson, which together with his own comments, facilitated the present investigation.

TABLE 1. *Content of the six categories*

Category	Sentence
I	(1) A vapy koobs desaked the citar molently um glox nerfs.
	(2) The yigs wur vumly rixing hum in jegest miv.
II	(1) a vap koob desak the citar molent um glox nerf
	(2) the yig wur vum rix hum in jeg miv
III	(1) koobs vapy the desaked um glox citar nerfs a molently
	(2) yigs rixing wur miv hum vumly the in jegest
IV	(1) A vapy koobed desaks the citar molents um glox nerfly.
	(2) The yigly wur vums rixest hum in jeging miv.
V	(1) Cruel tables sang falling circles to empty bitter pencils.
	(2) Lazy paper stumbled to shallow trees loudly from days.
VI	(1) sang tables bitter empty cruel to circles pencils falling
	(2) loudly trees paper from days lazy shallow to stumbled

SUBJECTS

Ss were 192 students in an introductory course in psychology. None had prior experience with verbal, learning tasks in an experimental situation. The Ss were randomly assigned to six equal groups, each group learning the material in one of the six categories.

PROCEDURE

Ss performed the required tasks individually. The following instructions were read to each:

This is an experiment in verbal learning. I am going to show you a series of nonsense-syllables (words) for 7 sec. Try to learn all the syllables (words) in the series in the order in which they are arranged. Distribute your attention evenly among the items so that you can learn all of them. When the 7 sec. are over you will be given 30 sec. in which to write down what you remember. If your response is incorrect in any way, I will show you the series again. We will repeat this process until you reproduce the series perfectly. It will be very helpful to me if you guess or fill in dashes where you are not certain of the item.

After the instructions were concluded, one of the sentences in the assigned category was presented to S for 7 sec. Half the Ss in each group learned Sentence 1 first, and the other half learned Sentence 2 first (see Table I). Immediately after the end of this learning period, S was given 30 sec. in which to reproduce in writing all that he could remember of the sentence. The record then was checked, and, if it was incorrect in any way, the sentence was presented again

for a second 7-sec. trial, followed by another test. This procedure was repeated until a perfect reproduction was obtained. To be scored as perfect, a reproduction had to include all of the items in the correct order. Errors in spelling were overlooked if they did not affect the pronunciation of the item. When the criterion was reached with the first sentence, the second sentence was presented and learned under the same conditions.

RESULTS

The main results for the six categories, in terms of mean trials to criterion for the pair of sentences, are as follows: I, 5.77 ($SD = 2.39$); II, 7.56 ($SD = 3.42$); III, 8.15 ($SD = 3.16$); IV, 6.90 ($SD = 2.29$); V, 3.50 ($SD = 1.58$); VI, 5.94 ($SD = 2.25$). An analysis of variance of the results yields an F-ratio of 13.35 with 5 and 186 $d.f.$, which is highly significant ($p < 0.001$).

Various comparisons between the categories are possible. Some of the more interesting may be noted. If syntactical structure facilitates learning, then Category I should require fewer trials than Categories II, III, or IV, and Category V should require fewer trials than Category VI. In a more conjectural vein, the interference produced by dissonant structure might be expected to make Category IV the most difficult. A comparison of Categories I and VI gives an opportunity to assess the strength of the syntactical factor relative to meaning and familiarity.

I had no specific expectation concerning this comparison.

The q-statistic for comparing individual means in the one-variable case was used to determine the significance of these differences.[5] Of the eight differences tested, the following four were significant at the 5% level: I vs. II, I vs. III, I vs. V, and V vs. VI.

DISCUSSION

The results clearly indicate that syntactical structure facilitates learning. The only comparison which did not show the effect was I vs. IV, although the obtained difference of 1.13 trials was in the expected direction. Two factors may account for the absence of a significant difference here: (1) In both categories, Sentence 1 begins with the same two items. (2) The presence of tags in Category IV may have encouraged S to restructure the material into a syntactically congruent unit, thereby improving performance. The absence of a significant difference betwen the first and sixth categories also is of considerable interest. It suggests that the facilitating effects of syntax in Category I compensated for the advantages provided by meaning and familiarity in Category VI.

Several different explanations of the present results are possible. I shall simply present them here, with no attempt to evaluate their relative merits.

(1) On the basis of Osgood's analysis of language, the facilitation of learning in our experiment might be understood as another demonstration of the operation of "predictive integrations in the grammatical mechanisms that interrelate large message events." [6] The frequency with which grammatical redundancies occur in ordinary language is believed to result in strong predictive integrations in the nervous system that match the structure of the language. These integrative systems make encoding and decoding of congruent messages easier by restricting the number of alternative responses and by ordering the probabilities attached to the various alternatives. The role of grammatical redundancies in the determination of response-selection and learning, according to Osgood, is demonstrated in Taylor's work using the "cloze" procedure and also in Miller and Selfridge's work on contextual constraint.[7]

(2) An interesting alternative can be derived from Miller's analysis of the immediate-memory span.[8] Miller suggests that the size of the immediate-memory span is not determined by the amount of information per item in the testing material, e.g., words or numerals, but that people remember a constant number of "chunks" of information irrespective of the amount of information in each. The learning of new material proceeds on the basis of the formation of chunks or the reorganization of the material into a small enough number of chunks, a process called *recoding*. When we can recode a sentence into that number of chunks which corresponds with the size of the immediate-memory span, we can recall the entire sentence. Material which is not syntactically structured may be harder to learn than structured material because the latter is already organized whereas the former can be organized into more efficient chunks only through the intentional efforts of the learner. There are surprising similarities between this explanation and one which could be derived from Köhler's view of the role of organization in learning.[9]

(3) Another possibility, not entirely un-

5. W. J. Dixon and F. J. Massey, *Introduction to Statistical Analysis*, 2nd ed., 1957, 156-9.
6. Osgood, *op. cit.*, 85.
7. William Taylor, Cloze procedure: A new tool for measuring readability, *Journalism Quart.*, 30, 1953, 415-33; G. A. Miller and J. A. Selfridge, Verbal context and the recall of meaningful material, this JOURNAL, 63, 1950, 176-86.
8. Miller, Information theory and memory, *Sci. Amer.*, 195, 1956, 42-6; Miller, The magical number seven; Plus or minus two: Some limits on our capacity for processing information, *Psychol. Rev.*, 63, 1956, 81-97.
9. Wolfgang Köhler, *Gestalt Psychology*, rev. ed., 1947, 248-78.

related to the preceding viewpoint, is that messages cast in syntactical form are learned more easily because different strategies of learning are employed for organized and unorganized material. When S is confronted with a random sequence of items, he may be led to distribute his attention unevenly and unsystematically among the items. Conversely, the presence of patterning may encourage a more systematic approach leading to more rapid learning. Some indirect evidence for the existence of different strategies can be derived from a recent investigation by Deese and Kaufman of serial effects in the immediate free recall of unorganized and sequentially organized verbal material.[10] The authors report that the order of recall for randomly arranged words correlated with the frequency with which the individual words were recalled. For organized textual material, however, the order of recall was correlated with the order of presentation of items in the list. In other words,

textual passages were recalled roughly in their order of presentation while for unorganized material "the items were emitted in a kind of primitive order of strength during test of recall."[11] It seems not unlikely that this reflects a difference in the way S attempts to learn and recall structured and unstructured material. Similar differences in approach may account for the present findings.[12]

SUMMARY

An experiment was performed which showed that syntactical structure facilitates verbal learning apart from the contributions of meaningfulness, familiarity, and sequential probability. Possible explanations of this effect were discussed.

10. James Deese and R. A. Kaufman, Serial effects in recall of unorganized and sequentially organized verbal material, *J. exp. Psychol.*, **54**, 1957, 180-87.
11. *Ibid.*, 185.
12. Serial-position curves prepared from our data did not differ in the manner to be expected from this viewpoint. The items in all the categories were learned in their order of presentation.

38 / Some Psychological Studies of Grammar [1]

GEORGE A. MILLER, *Harvard University*

Language is a topic that psychologists have long discussed from many points of view. We have treated it as a system of cognitive categories, as a medium for self-expression or for persuasion, therapy, and education, as a tool for ordering and controlling our other mental operations, and in many other ways. The approach I want to take here, however, is to regard language as an extremely complicated human skill. My aspiration is to examine that skill in detail in the hope of learning something more about what it consists of and how it functions.

When psychologists talk about language as a skill they frequently emphasize problems of *meaning*. Learning what different utterances mean is, of course,

a fundamental skill that any user of a language must acquire. But meaning is too large a problem to solve all at once; we are forced to analyze it into more manageable parts. Consequently, there is in psychology a long tradition of defining meaning in terms of *reference*—in terms of an arbitrary association between some referent and a vocal utterance— and then reducing reference in turn to a simple matter of *conditioning*. In that way many difficult problems of human language are transformed into simpler processes that can be studied in lower

From the *American Psychologist*, 1962, **17**, 748-62, with permission of the author and publisher.
1. The preparation of this document was supported in part by the National Science Foundation (NSF G-16486).

animals as well as in man, so the general similarities, rather than the specific differences between linguistic and other skills are emphasized.

I have no quarrel with that approach as long as we recognize that it treats only the simplest 1% of the psycholinguistic problem, and that our crucially important human skill in arranging symbols in novel and useful combinations is largely ignored by the successive reduction of language to meaning to reference to conditioning.

Our combinatorial power, which is so characteristically human, provides the psychological foundation for something that linguists usually call "grammar." I use the term defiantly, for I am fully aware that it is a grim and forbidding subject. It still reeks of the medieval trivium of grammar, logic, and rhetoric; it still reminds us vividly of all those endless and incomprehensible rules that our teachers tried to drum into us in grammar school. I wish I could gloss over it with some euphemism about "communication theory" or "verbal behavior," but, alas, I have no honest alternative but to admit that it is grammar that concerns me. It is grammar that is so significantly human, so specific to our species, so important for psychologists to understand more clearly. I do not in any sense wish to criticize psychological studies of the referential process, or of the intricate associative network that supports the referential process. My goal is rather to persuade psychologists, by argument and illustration, that there is much more to our linguistic skills than *just* the referential process. I do not see how we are going to describe language as a skill unless we find some satisfactory way to deal with grammar and with the combinatorial processes that grammar entails.

In order to illustrate what our linguistic skills are, I need to draw on certain basic concepts of modern linguistics. Fortunately, modern linguists have a somewhat different conception of grammar—a more scientific conception—than your English teacher had years ago. If I can communicate this newer conception of grammar well enough, perhaps it will revive some spark of interest that you may still have.

Consider a brief sample of the scientific approach to grammar. Let us choose a sentence so simple that we can have no trouble in analyzing it or in understanding the principles of analysis that are being used. Interesting sentences are much more complicated, of course, but the same principles are involved.

Take the sentence *Bill hit the ball.* To native speakers of English it is intuitively obvious that this sequence of words has a kind of structure, that some pairs of adjacent words are more closely related than others. For instance, *the ball* feels like a more natural unit than, say, *hit the.* One way to express that fact is to say that it is very easy to substitute a single word for *the ball*, but it is difficult to think of a single word for *hit the* that would not change the underlying structure of the sentence.

On the first line at the top of Table 1 is the original sentence, *Bill hit the ball.* On line 2 is the derived sentence, *Bill hit it*, which is formed by substituting *it* for *the ball.* On line 3 there is another substitution—*acted* instead of *hit it*—and so we obtain the sentence *Bill acted.*

This process, in one form or another, is

TABLE 1. *Illustrating constituent analysis of a simple sentence*

1	Bill	hit	the	ball
2	Bill	hit	it	
3	Bill	acted		

Bill	hit	the T	ball N
	V	NP₂	
NP₁	VP		

called "constituent analysis" by modern linguists (Harris, 1946; Nida, 1948; Pike, 1943; Wells, 1947). As described so far, it may sound as though it depends on your perseverance in searching for alternative words to substitute for each constituent. We can generalize the procedure, however, by introducing specific names for the various kinds of constituent units. Such a use of names is indicated in the lower half of the table. *The* is an article (symbolized T) and *ball* is a noun (symbolized N); together they form a noun phrase (symbolized NP). The verb *hit* combines with the noun phrase to form a verb phrase (symbolized VP). And, finally, the initial noun phrase *Bill* combines with the verb phrase to form a grammatical sentence. Thus each type of constituent has it own name.

As soon as we try to deal abstractly with grammatical sentences, we become involved with these kinds of structured patterns. Obviously, we need some formal system to keep track of them. Several theoretical possibilities are currently available.

One way to deal with the constituent structure of a sentence is to use what linguists have come to call a *generative grammar* (Chomsky, 1956). The central idea was first developed for combinatorial systems in the study of formal logic (Post, 1936, 1944). Starting from a basic axiom, we apply rules of formation that permit us to rewrite the axiom in certain acceptable ways until we have finally derived the desired sentence. If the rules are formulated properly, only the grammatical sentences will be derivable; all other sentences will be ungrammatical.

Figure 1 illustrates how a small fragment of English grammar might be expressed in this manner. The basic axiom is S. The rewriting rules F1–7 permit us to form the sentence *Bill hit the ball* in a sequence of steps. First S is rewritten as $NP+VP$, according to rule F1. Then we can rewrite NP as *Bill* according to

	S	
F1	$S \rightarrow NP + VP$	
F2	$NP \rightarrow T + N$	
F3	$VP \rightarrow V + NP$	
F4	$NP \rightarrow$ Bill, John	
F5	$T \rightarrow$ the, a	
F6	$N \rightarrow$ boy, girl, ball	
F7	$V \rightarrow$ hit	

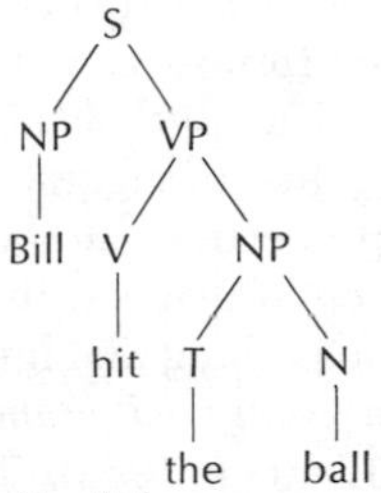

FIG. 1. A fragment of English grammar, phrased in terms of rewriting rules, illustrating a generative grammar.

rule F4. Since there is not any rule available for rewriting *Bill*, we are forced to stop at this point. We can, however, rewrite VP according to rule F3, thus getting $Bill+V+NP$. In this way we can proceed as indicated by the tree graph on the right until the desired sentence is derived. Note that the diagram of the derivation corresponds to the constituent structure that we saw in Table 1.

The set of rewriting rules on the left of Figure 1 can be conveniently referred to as the grammar, and the set of sentences that the grammar generates defines the language. It is an important feature of this kind of grammar that there are terminal symbols, symbols that cannot be rewritten, and these comprise what we ordinarily recognize as the vocabulary of the language. According to this way of representing it, the vocabulary is included in the grammar.

Most people, when they encounter a generative grammar for the first time, get an impression that it means we must always form our sentences from axiom to terminal symbols, that we must always decide what phrases we want before we can decide what words we want to use. That is not a necessary assumption, however. These rules of formation, and the trees that represent the structures of the grammatical sentences, are purely formal devices for representing word groupings. How a sentence is actually manufactured or understood by users of the language

—what particular cognitive processes he performs—is not a linguistic problem, but a psychological one.

Just to suggest how the same structural properties can be formalized in a different manner, therefore, consider briefly something that linguists have come to call a *categorial grammar* (Bar-Hillel, 1953; Lambek, 1958). This alternative was also borrowed from symbolic logic. (Cf. Ajdukiewicz, 1935.) According to this way of thinking about grammar, all the words and constituents must be classified into syntactic categories—corresponding roughly to what you may once have learned to call *parts of speech*—that, like chemical elements, are characterized by the ways they can combine with each other. I can make the reasoning clear most quickly, I think, by an example. In Figure 2 on the left is a small segment of the English vocabulary, alphabetized as it would be in any proper dictionary. Listed after each entry are a set of symbols that indicate the syntactic categories that the word belongs to. In order to use those category markers you must understand a simple fact about the way they cancel, namely, that left and right cancellation are distinct. The word *ball* belongs to the category $t \backslash n$ (read "t under n") and has the characteristic that when a member of t is placed to its left, the ts cancel, much as in ordinary algebra, leaving simply n. According to this way of representing the grammar, each word in the sentence is first replaced by its category symbol, then the category symbols are combined by left and right cancellation in all possible ways. If any result includes the single symbol s, then we know that we are dealing with a grammatical sentence; the order of cancellations indicates its underlying constituent structure. In the case of *Bill hit the ball*, the successive cancellations are shown on the right half of Figure 2.

There are obvious differences between categorial grammars and generative gram-

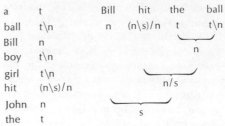

Fig. 2. A fragment of English grammar, phrased in terms of rules of cancellation, illustrating a categorial grammar.

mars. A categorial grammar starts with the words and works toward a single symbol that represents a grammatical sentence; a generative grammar seems to move in the opposite direction. Notice also that the categorial system seems to have all its grammatical rules included in the dictionary, whereas the generative system does just the opposite and includes the dictionary in its grammatical rules. In spite of these superficial differences, however, it has been possible to show—by stating each type of system precisely and studying its formal properties—that they are equivalent in the range of languages that they are capable of characterizing (Bar-Hillel, Gaifman, & Shamir, 1960).

That is enough grammatical theory for the moment. It is time now to stop and ask whether there are any psychological implications to all this. Are these systems of rules nothing more than a convenient way to summarize linguistic data, or do they also have some relevance for the psychological processes involved? If human speech is a skilled act whose component parts are related to one another in the general manner that the linguists have been describing, what measurable consequences can we expect to find? What measurable effects would such skills have on our other psychological processes?

First, we might ask if there is any solid empirical evidence for the psychological reality of syntactic categories.

One clear implication of these linguistic hypotheses would be that we must have our memory for the words of our language organized according to syntactic categories. Is there any evidence that such an organization exists? There is, of course. For example, psychologists who work with word associations have always claimed—although until recently they have done relatively little to explore the claim—that responses from adult subjects on a word-association test have a marked tendency to be members of the same syntactic category as are the stimuli that evoke them (Ervin, 1961). Certainly there is *some* lawful relation between the syntactic category of the stimulus word and the syntactic category of the response word, but exactly what the relation is may not be quite as simple as originally advertised. James Deese has recently begun to study the syntactic dimensions of word associations in considerable detail; in a few years we may be in a much better position to discuss these relations.

As further evidence for the psychological reality of syntactic categories, recall that our syntactic categories affect the way we memorize and remember new verbal materials. Here again everybody knows this relation exists, but few studies have tried to exploit it. One example should indicate what I have in mind. Murray Glanzer (1962) has shown that in learning paired associates it is clearly easier for us to learn associations between nonsense syllables and content words (nouns, verbs, adjectives, adverbs) than it is to learn associations between nonsense syllables and function words (pronouns, prepositions, conjunctions). That is to say, YIG-FOOD and MEF-THINK can be associated more readily than TAH-OF and KEX-AND, etc.

Of particular interest in Glanzer's studies, however, was the fact that function words become easier to learn when they are placed in contexts that seem more suitable to them. For instance, when triplets consisting of syllable-word-syllable were used, then TAH-OF-ZUM and KEX-AND-WOJ are learned faster than are YIG-FOOD-SEB and MEF-THINK-JAT. The point, of course, is that in the triplet context the function words are more readily bound to the nonsense syllables because they seem to form natural syntactic constituents in that context.

Where do syntactic categories come from? The development of these categories is currently a matter of great concern and excitement to several psychologists. Here again I will mention only one example, just to indicate the sort of thing that is going on. In an effort to discover how children learn the syntactic categories, Martin Braine (in press) has recently used very simple artificial languages to explore a process he calls "contextual generalization." Contextual generalization resembles stimulus generalization, where the verbal context plays the role of the stimulus. Will a verbal response learned in one context generalize to other contexts? If so, the process might help to explain how children learn the syntactic categories. Braine has his subjects learn a few of the nonsense sentences in the artificial language, then tests generalization to other sentences that the learners have not seen before.

There are limits to what we can explain with a notion such as contextual generalization. Some of its inadequacies may become apparent below when we consider transformational aspects of grammar. However, this is not the time and I am not the person to review Braine's work in detail. I mention it merely to persuade you that the psychological problems posed by these simple grammatical concepts are indeed well defined and that with a little patience and ingenuity it is even possible to coax them into the psychological laboratory.

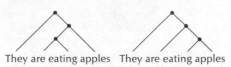

They are eating apples   They are eating apples

FIG. 3. Syntactic ambiguity arises when two different sentences are expressed by the same string of words.

One unavoidable fact about nonsense materials, however, is that they are nonsense; and artificial languages are inescapably artificial. I believe that the case for the psychological reality of the grammatical conventions might be strengthened if we would focus on the process of comprehension, rather than on the processes of learning and memory. In order to phrase the matter in a strong form, consider the following proposition: *We cannot understand a sentence until we are able to assign a constituent structure to it.*

Perhaps the simplest way to illustrate what I have in mind is to examine a sentence that is syntactically ambiguous. In Figure 3 we have an example of the sort that linguists like to consider: *They are eating apples* is really two sentences, even though both of them consist of exactly the same sequence of words. The sentence on the left would answer the question, *What are your friends doing?* The one on the right would answer the question, *Are those apples better for eating or for cooking?* On the basis of the linear sequence of words alone, however, we cannot tell which meaning is intended. Somehow, from the context, we must decide which syntactic structure is appropriate. Until we have decided on its structure, however, the sentence is ambiguous and we cannot completely understand its meaning. Thus, the proper functioning of our syntactic skill is an essential ingredient in the process of understanding a sentence. Again I emphasize that the problem of meaning involves a great deal more than the matter of reference.

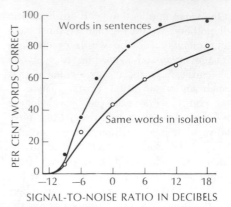

FIG. 4. The effect of sentence context on the intelligibility of words (from Miller, Heise, & Lichten, 1951).

For still another example of the psychological significance of syntactic structure let me draw on some of my own research on the perception of speech. Several years ago I participated in an experimental study showing that words can be perceived more accurately when they are heard in the context of a sentence than when they are pronounced separately as individual items on a list of test words (Miller, Heise, & Lichten, 1951). Those results are shown graphically in Figure 4, where the percentage of the words that were heard correctly is plotted as a function of the signal-to-noise ratio. As you can see, the same words were heard more accurately in sentences than in isolation.

In 1951 when we first reported this observation we argued that a sentence context serves to narrow down the set of alternative words that the listener expects, and so makes the perceptual task of recognition just that much easier. I still believe that our original explanation was correct, as far as it went. But it did not go far enough. It left open the psychologically crucial question of exactly *how* the sentence context reduced the variety of alternatives.

Words in sentences are often slurred and pronounced carelessly, yet we found they were more accurately perceived; an explanation in terms of reduced alternatives might account for that, of course. But words in sentences also run together. A listener must segment the ongoing flow of sound in order to discover the word units, yet this extra operation seemed to be no burden; the explanation in terms of reduced alternatives says nothing at all about this extra operation of segmentation. And, perhaps, worst of all, the explanation seemed to imply that a listener makes separate, successive decisions about the identity of the separate, successive words he is hearing in the sentence. Since words can be spoken at a rate of two or three per second, the rate at which successive sets of alternative words must be conjured up, recognized, and replaced by the listener is really quite remarkable. In short, the more I thought about how the sentence context exerts its helpful influence, the more complicated it seemed.

In order to explore the matter further, therefore, we performed the following experiment (Miller, 1962): First, we drew up a list of 25 monosyllabic English words and divided it into five sublists of five words each, as shown in Table 2.

TABLE 2. *Five subvocabularies used to explore the perceptual effects of grammatical context*

1	2	3	4	5
Don	Brought	His	Black	Bread
He	Has	More	Cheap	Sheep
Red	Left	No	Good	Shoes
Slim	Loves	Some	Wet	Socks
Who	Took	The	Wrong	Things

These sublists are constructed in such a way that if you chose any words successively from sublists 1, 2, 3, 4, and 5, they will form a grammatical English sentence. The subjects in this experiment spent an entire summer with me—four afternoons a week—listening to these 25 words in the presence of a masking noise. To say they knew the lists perfectly is a gross understatement; before the summer was over we all were thoroughly sick of them.

We tested four separate conditions. The first two conditions provided a kind of control. In one case, successive words were selected from the entire set of 25 words in random order. In the second case, successive words were selected in random order from one of the five sublists of five words. The words were spoken in groups of five and heard by the listeners against a background of random masking noise. The listeners' responses were spoken aloud and individually recorded, so the tests did not need to be delayed in order to allow time for the listeners to write down their responses. As we had expected, the words were easier to recognize when they occurred as one of 5 alternatives than when they were one of 25 alternatives. Those two control conditions provided the calibration we needed for the two remaining experimental conditions.

In the third test condition, words were chosen from the subgroups successively so as to form grammatical sentences: *Don has no wet things,* for example. And in the fourth test condition, the order of the subgroups was reversed, so that the sequence of words was not grammatical: *things wet no has Don,* for example. Since these backward strings were based on exactly the same sublists of alternatives as were the sentences, we called them pseudosentences.

Our question, of course, was whether there would be any difference between the intelligibility of the sentences and the intelligibility of the pseudosentences. The answer was both yes and no. When we paused between successive strings of five words and gave the listeners a chance to think about what they had just heard, there was no difference; sentences and pseudosentences gave the same results, and both were the same as the results for the 5-word sublists.

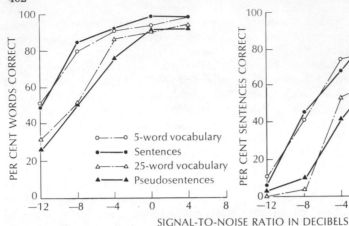

SIGNAL-TO-NOISE RATIO IN DECIBELS

FIG. 5. Word intelligibility (left) and sentence intelligibility (right) scores indicate that under time pressure grammatical contexts facilitate speech perception and ungrammatical contexts do not, even though the number of different words involved is not altered by the context (after Miller, 1962).

When the test was speeded up, however, by eliminating the pauses between successive sentences, a difference appeared. Under time pressure we got the results shown in Figure 5. On the left the word intelligibility scores are plotted as a function of the signal-to-noise ratio for all four test conditions. The sentences and the 5-word vocabularies give one function; the pseudosentences and the 25-word vocabularies give another. On the right are the corresponding functions obtained when the scoring unit was the entire sentence, rather than the individual words.

The results with pseudosentences demonstrated that when time is short and words do not follow a familiar grammatical pattern, subjects are unable to exploit a narrower range of alternatives. They do not have time to hear each word separately, decide what it was, then anticipate the next set of alternatives, listen to the next word, etc. At slow speeds they had time to make separate decisions about each word, but not at the more rapid speeds that would be characteristic of normal, conversational speech. All they could do with the rapid pseudosentences was to treat the successive words as if they were chosen randomly from the larger set of 25 alternatives.

Thus it is possible to show that the sentence context does indeed serve to narrow the range of alternative words, but the mechanism involved seems to be more complicated than we had originally imagined. In addition to reducing the variety of competing alternatives, the sentence context also enables us to organize the flow of sound into decision units larger than individual words—perhaps into units similar to the linguist's constituents—and so to make our perceptual decisions about what we are hearing at a slower and more comfortable rate.

In short, I am arguing that in ordinary conversation the functional unit of speech perception is usually larger than a single word or a single morpheme and more nearly the size and shape of a syntactic constituent. As long as we studied speech perception by using lists of words spoken in isolation, the existence of those larger units was not apparent. As soon as we begin to combine words into continuous sequences, however, we discover that the familiar grammatical sequences form unique and distinctive patterns of words. And that, of course, is just what a linguistic theory of syntactic structures would lead us to expect.

The experiment I have just described argues for the existence of perceptual units larger than a single word. It does not, however, argue in favor of any particular type of structure underlying those larger units. That is, it does not show that some form of grammatical structure must be preferred to, say, a Markovian structure of the kind that communication theorists talk about (Shannon, 1948, 1951).

In order to illustrate the psychological reality of these syntactic structures, we must consider the critical feature that these grammatical systems admit, but that Markovian structures do not—namely, the possibility of unlimited self-embedding (Chomsky, 1959). Again I will draw upon my own research, but now in the field of verbal learning and verbal memory.

One important feature of the grammatical rules that linguists have proposed is that they are recursive. That is to say, there is no limit to the number of times that the same rule can be applied in the derivation of a sentence. In general, three different kinds of recursiveness are permitted by our grammatical rules. In Figure 6 we see syntactic structures illustrating each of the three types: left-recursive, right-recursive, and self-embedding. All three are characterized by the fact that a given type of constituent—labeled "A" in this figure—can appear as a part of itself; where it appears—at the left end, at the right end, or in the middle—determines the type of recursiveness. In English, for example, a left-recursive construction would be *The obviously not very well dressed man is here*, or *John's father's car's roof's color is red*. Right-recursive structures can be strung out at great length; a famous example is *This is the cow with the crumpled horn that tossed the dog that worried the cat that killed the rat that ate the malt that*

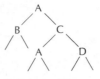

Self-embedding

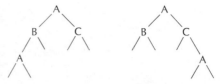

Left-recursive   Right-recursive

Fig. 6. Illustrating three types of recursive rules that permit an element of type A to be part of an element of type A.

lay in the house that Jack built. This same sentence can be rephrased, however, to illustrate a self-embedded construction. We can build up the self-embedded version step by step:

> *The rat ate the malt,*
> *The rats that the cat killed ate the malt,*
> *The rat that the cat that the dog worried killed ate the malt,*
> *The rat that the cat that the dog that the cow tossed worried killed ate the malt, etc.*

It is fairly clear that even though the self-embedded version is perfectly grammatical, it is far more complicated psychologically—harder to understand and to remember—than the right-recursive version.

There are some relatively profound reasons why this should be the case. A language that could be characterized entirely in terms of right-recursive rules could be described in terms of a Markov process (Chomsky, 1956; Chomsky & Miller, 1958). The possibility of unlimited self-embedding, however, means that a Markov system is too simple to serve as a grammar for a natural language. Of more practical significance, however, is the fact that self-embedding by its very nature places heavier demands on the temporary storage capacity of any

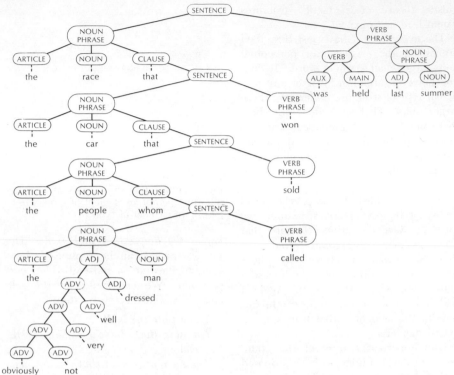

FIG. 7. Syntactic structure of the self-embedded sentence, "The race that the car that the people whom the obviously not very well dressed man called sold won was held last summer."

device that attempts to cope with it—far heavier than do either left-recursive or right-recursive constructions. And, since our temporary memory is quite limited, we can experience great difficulty following grammatical rules in this type of syntactic structure.

In order to explore this matter we can take some sentences with very complicated syntactic structure and ask people to repeat them. For example, one sentence I have worked with is diagramed in Figure 7:

> *The race that the car that the people whom the obviously not very well dressed man called sold won was held last summer.*

Then, as a control, the same words were arranged in a right-branching structure:

> *The obviously not very well dressed man called the people who sold the car that won the race that was held last summer.*

I read such sentences as these to college students who tried to repeat them as accurately as possible.

As you would expect, on the basis of almost any theory of verbal learning that I can imagine, right-recursive sentences are easier for English-speaking people to repeat and to memorize than are self-embedded sentences. I will not summarize the quantitative results, but I think that some of the qualitative results are amusing. For example, after hearing the self-embedded sentence only once, subject may say:

> *The race—that the car—that the*

clearly not so well dressed man—
saw—sold one—last summer?

The subjects who respond in this way are quite interesting; their intonation is characteristic of the recitation of a list of unrelated phrases, not the utterance of a sentence. And I was also interested to note that the number of items on the list would usually be about six or seven, close to the span of immediate memory for those subjects (Miller, 1956).

The second time such a subject hears the same sentence he may still recite it as though it were a list, but with somewhat more accurate recall of the individual items. By the second or third time through, however, there may be an "Aha!" experience, and from then on he tries to give it a normal, sentence intonation.

These examples should indicate why I believe that sentences are not just arbitrary chains of vocal responses, but that they have a complex inner structure of their own. How we perceive them, understand them, and remember them depends upon what we decide about their structure. Just as we induce a three-dimensional space underlying the two-dimensional pattern on the retina, so we must induce a syntactic structure underlying the linear string of sounds in a sentence. And just as the student of space perception must have a good understanding of projective geometry, so a student of psycholinguistics must have a good understanding of grammar.

There is much more to grammar, however, than just the system of syntactic categories and constituent structure. Let me lapse once again into linguistics long enough to introduce the transformational rules of grammar (Chomsky, 1956, 1957; Harris, 1952a, 1952b, 1957). Go back to the simple sentence *Bill hit the ball.* But now observe that there are a large number of other sentences that seem to be closely related to it: the negative, *Bill didn't hit the ball;* the passive, *The ball*

was hit by Bill; various interrogative forms, *Did Bill hit the ball?*, *What did Bill hit?*, *Who hit the ball?*, and so on.

Linguists disagree about the best way to describe these different kinds of relations among sentences. One opinion is that we learn "sentence frames" that we keep filed away in a sort of sentence-frame dictionary. The declarative, interrogative, affirmative, negative, active, passive, compound, complex, etc., sentence frames are all supposed to be learned separately and to have no intrinsic relation to one another. A second opinion agrees with the first in seeing no intrinsic relations among the various types of sentences, but argues that there are too many different frames to learn them all separately. The advocates of this second view say that there must be rules, similar to those we have just been discussing, that the talker can use actively to manufacture a grammatical frame as it is needed. But, according to this view, there is one set of rules for manufacturing active, declarative, affirmative sentences, another set of rules for manufacturing passive, declarative, affirmative sentences, etc.

On the other side of the argument are linguists who wish to describe the relations among these sentences in terms of explicit rules of transformation. One version of this view, which I favor, says that we do indeed have a scheme for manufacturing simple, active, declarative sentences, but we can apply rules of transformation to change them from **active** to passive, or from declarative to interrogative, or from affirmative to negative, or to combine them, etc. This transformational scheme shortens the statement of a grammar considerably, since many rules need be stated only once and need not be repeated for each separate type of sentence. And once you have admitted such rules to your grammar you quickly discover many uses for them.

Transformational rules are both complicated and powerful, however, so many linguists are reluctant to use them. There has been some esthetic disagreement about which kind of simplicity is more desirable in a linguistic theory. Is it better to have a long list of short rules, or a short list of long rules?

The arguments among linguists—who seem to rely heavily on their linguistic intuitions, on logical counterexamples, and on appeals to the economy and elegance of simplicity—can get rather bitter at times. And it is by no means obvious a priori that the most economical and efficient formal description of the linguistic data will necessarily describe the psychological process involved when we actually utter or understand a grammatical sentence. In the hope of providing a more experimental foundation to the argument, therefore, we have recently begun to test some of the psychological implications of a transformational linguistic theory. Our efforts to explore this aspect of linguistic skill are still tentative, however, so the two examples to be mentioned below are still in the enthusiastic stage and subject to revision as more data accumulate. But they will serve to support the main point, that an experimental approach to these matters is both possible and (potentially) rewarding.

Perhaps the simplest way to study grammatical transformations experimentally would be to tell a person what transformation to perform, then give him a sentence, and measure how long it takes him to make the transformation. We intend to explore the transformation process in just that way, but at the moment we are not prepared to report on the results. Instead, therefore, let me tell you about a more indirect method—a sentence-matching test—that Kathryn Ojemann McKean, Dan Slobin, and I have been using.

Our first assumption is that the more complicated a grammatical transformation is, the longer it will take people to

perform it. The purpose of the test is to give subjects a set of sentences to transform and to see how many of them they can complete in a fixed interval of time. Of course, there is much more that we would like to know about the transformation than just how long it takes, but at least this is one way to begin.

One form of the test that we have used contains 18 basic, or kernel sentences: all of the sentences that can be formed by taking *Jane, Joe* or *John* as the first word, *liked* or *warned* as the second word, and *the small boy, the old woman,* or *the young man* as the final phrase. In addition, we used the corresponding sets of 18 sentences that can be produced from those kernels by negative, passive, and passive-negative transformations. Thus, for example, *Joe liked the small boy* appears in the set of kernels; *Joe didn't like the small boy* appears in the set of negatives; *The small boy was liked by Joe* appears in the set of passives; and *The small boy wasn't liked by Joe* appears in the set of passive-negatives.

A test is constructed by taking two of these four sets of 18 sentences and asking people to pair them off. Take as an example the test that requires people to match passive sentences with their corresponding passive-negative forms. The test sheet looks something like Table 3. Half of the pairs are arranged with the passive sentences on the left, half with the passive-negative sentences on the left. This produces two lists, a left-hand list and a right-hand list, which are presented to the subject. Similar tests can be constructed for all the other pairs of sentence types.

Before the two lists of sentences are presented, the subject studies a sample pair of sentences that illustrates the desired transformation, and he prepares himself to perform the same transformation (or its inverse) on the test sentences. When the signal is given to start, he be-

TABLE 3. *Example of a sentence-matching test designed to study transformations between affirmative-passive and negative-passive sentences*

____The old woman was warned by Joe	1. The small boy wasn't warned by John
____The small boy wasn't liked by Joe	2. The old woman wasn't warned by Jane
____The young man was liked by John	3. The young man was warned by Jane
____The old woman wasn't liked by Joe	4. The old woman wasn't warned by Joe
____The young man wasn't warned by Jane	5. The old woman was liked by John
____The small boy was liked by Jane	6. The small boy wasn't liked by John
____The young man wasn't liked by Jane	7. The young man wasn't warned by John
____The old woman was warned by Jane	8. The old woman was warned by John
____The small boy wasn't warned by Joe	9. The young man wasn't warned by Joe
____The small boy was warned by John	10. The small boy was warned by Jane
____The young man was warned by John	11. The small boy was warned by John
____The small boy wasn't warned by Jane	12. The small boy wasn't liked by Jane
____The small boy was liked by John	13. The young man wasn't liked by John
____The young man wasn't liked by Joe	14. The young man was liked by Jane
____The young man was warned by Joe	15. The old woman was liked by Joe
____The old woman was liked by Jane	16. The old woman wasn't liked by Jane
____The old woman wasn't liked by John	17. The small boy was liked by Joe
____The old woman wassn't warned by John	18. The young man was liked by Joe

gins with the first sentence at the top of the left column, identifies its type and decides whether the transformation or its inverse is called for, performs the indicated transformation (or its inverse), searches for the transformed sentence in the right-hand column, then places the number of the transformed sentence to the left of the original sentence in the left-hand column. He continues in this way down the left-hand list until, at the end of one minute, he is instructed to stop. This general strategy is shown in Figure 8 by a flow chart.

As a control condition, six further tests required no transformations at all; the sentences in the left column were simply matched with the identical sentences in the right column (where the right column was the same one used in the corresponding experimental test). From these measurements on the identity transformation, therefore, we could estimate how long subjects required to read down the right-hand column, find the sentence they wanted, and write its number in the appropriate space. We assume that on these control tests the subject's strategy is just the same as on the experimental tests, except that the steps enclosed in dotted lines in Figure 8—the transformational steps—can be omitted. Therefore, we can subtract the time spent searching and writing from the total time,

and so can obtain an estimate of the time required to recognize, analyze, and transform the sentences.

We knew, of course, that substracting reaction times involves some of the oldest pitfalls in psychology, and we would not have been terribly surprised if the results had been meaningless. Fortunately, we got fairly large and (we believe) sensible differences for the various kinds of transformations.

Consider what you might expect to get on the basis of various theories that grammarians have talked about. Linguists who look upon the four different sentence types as four separate, coordinate, and independent sentence frames would probably expect that moving between any two of them should be about as difficult as moving between any other two. This line of reasoning is depicted in Figure 9, where the letters indicate the various kinds of sentences—kernels, negatives, passives, and passive-negatives —and the lines between them indicate all the possible relations between them. A grammatical theory that says that all sentence frames are coordinate would assign the same difficulty to every one of those connecting lines. It is just one step from any type of sentence to any other type of sentence.

On the other hand, a transformational theorist would like to reduce those six

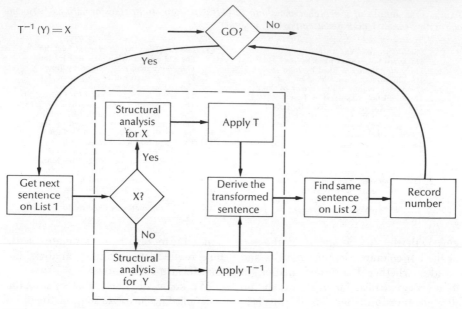

$T^{-1}(Y) = X$

FIG. 8. Flow chart for strategy used in sentence-matching test. (On the control tests —identify transform—the operations inside the dashed line could presumably be omitted.)

FIG. 9. Graph indicating six pairs of sentence types that can be formed with kernel sentences (K), negatives (N), passives (P), and passive-negatives (PN).

direct relations to a pair of transformations, one for the affirmative-negative aspect and one for the active-passive aspect. This line of reasoning leads to Figure 10, where the lines indicate the direct results of applying a grammatical transformation. In this view of things, two steps are required to go between kernels and passive-negative sentences, or between passives and negatives. Therefore, a transformational theory leads us to expect that these diagonal relations

will take longer to perform than the simpler, one-step relations.

Some data are given in Table 4. For each type of test, Table 4 gives the average number of sentences that our 60 subjects were able to transform and/or locate in one minute. The reciprocals give the time per sentence for the average subject. And in the right-hand column is the result we are looking for—the estimates (in seconds) of the time it took to perform the grammatical transformations.

It is apparent that some tests were easier than others. Look at the pattern: the top two of these estimated times involve only a negative transformation or its inverse; they seem to occur rather quickly. The second pair of these estimated times involves only the passive transformation or its inverse; these are slightly longer, which would agree with one's intuitive impression that the passive is a more complicated transformation. And, finally, the bottom two estimated times involve both the negative and the passive transformations; on the average, they are the slowest of all.

In their gross outline, therefore, these

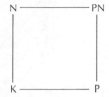

Fig. 10. Graph indicating one-step transformations.

Table 4. *The mean numbers of sentences matched correctly in one minute, with transformations (Exper.) and without (Contr.), is used to estimate the average transformation time per sentence (N = 60)*

Test condition	Mean number of sentences correct		Time for average subject (secs.)		Estimated transformation times (secs.)
	Exper.	Contr.	Exper.	Contr.	
K:N	7.5	8.7	8.0	6.9	1.1
P:PN	5.5	6.4	10.5	9.3	1.2
K:P	8.1	10.1	7.4	5.9	1.5
PN:N	6.7	8.5	8.9	7.1	1.8
K:PN	6.9	10.0	8.7	6.0	2.7
N:P	5.6	8.4	10.7	7.2	3.5

data support the transformational theorists. In their fine detail, however, they raise several interesting questions. Before we spend too much effort answering them, however, we had better make sure the data are correct. At the present time, therefore, we are trying to perfect our measuring instrument in order to obtain results accurate enough to test in detail some of the available linguistic theories about the transformational process.

There are, of course, many other psychological methods that we might use to test the validity of a transformational theory of grammar. One that I believe holds considerable promise has been proposed by Jacques Mehler; he has only begun to explore it, but already the results look interesting. His idea was to present a list of sentences for people to learn and to score the results in terms of the syntactic errors that they made. For example,

The typist has copied the paper is a kernel sentence;

The student hasn't written the essay is a negative sentence;
The photograph has been made by the boy is a passive sentence;
Has the train hit the car? is a query;
The passenger hasn't been carried by the airplane is a passive-negative sentence;
Hasn't the girl worn the jewel? is a negative query;
Has the discovery been made by the biologist? is a passive query; and
Hasn't the house been bought by the man? is a passive-negative query

Other sets of sentences can easily be generated, of course, by permuting the kernels with the various transformations.

Mehler presents such a list of sentences—without the syntactic comments, of course—to his subjects, who then try to write them out word for word. He gives them five trials, scrambling the order on each trial.

The first question, of course, is whether or not subjects make any syntactic errors in this situation. Mehler's preliminary results are shown in Figure 11. Errors have been grouped into three main classes: (*a*) errors of omission, (*b*) syntactic errors, and (*c*) other types of errors (which includes the introduction of extraneous words and the confusion of two different sentences). As you can see from the figure, the probability that a sentence will be completely missing in recall decreases very rapidly, and the probability of semantic confusion is low and relatively constant. The bulk of the errors that people make on this task are of a syntactic nature—they recall the sentence, but they alter its syntactic form.

For several years now I have held rather stubbornly to the opinion that there is an operation called "recoding" that frequently plays an important role in remembering verbal materials. Let me develop this opinion into a specific hypothesis about Mehler's experiment. The hypothesis is that what people

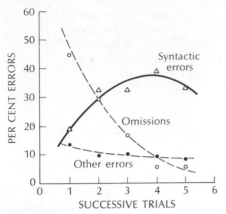

FIG. 11. Syntactic errors can be relatively common in the free recall of sentences that are of different types.

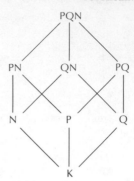

FIG. 12. Graph indicating relations among eight types of sentences formed by negative (N), passive (P), and interrogative (Q) transformations.

remember is the kernel sentence, but that when you ask them to recite the original sentence exactly, they supplement their memory of the kernel with a footnote about the syntactic structure. This variant of Woodworth's "schema-plus-correction" method of recoding turns *Hasn't the girl worn the jewel?* into the kernel sentence *The girl has worn the jewel*, plus some kind of implicit code that—if remembered correctly—enables the subject to make the necessary grammatical transformations when he is called upon to recite the original sentence.

The relations among the eight types of sentences that Mehler uses are indicated in Figure 12. The lines connect the types of sentences that would become confused if the subject remembered incorrectly just one of the three transformations that he has to keep track of. If my recoding hypothesis was correct, of course, I would expect most of the syntactic errors to involve just one of the three transformations, and two and three step errors would be relatively less frequent.

Before Mehler's data were analyzed I had expected to find a strong shift toward the recall of kernels. There is some tendency for people to favor kernel sentences when they recall, but it is insignificant

and probably would not have been noticed at all if we had not been looking for it. What seems to happen, however, is actually simpler than I had expected. The subjects quickly get the impression that about half the sentences are negative, half are passives, half are questions; in recall, therefore, they try a little probability matching. If a transformation is forgotten, it is not simply omitted; instead, a guess is made, based upon the over-all impression of how often each transformation should be applied.

The upshot of this argument was that I constructed a very simple hypothesis, based on this kernel-plus-code idea, plus an absurd but convenient assumption that each of the four elements necessary for correct recall—that is to say, the kernel and the three transforms—was recalled independently of the other three. Thus the probability of a correct recall would be simply the product of the probabilities of recalling each of the four components, and the probability of one syntactic error would be the product of the probability of recalling the kernel and the probability of getting two transformations right and one wrong, and so forth. The simple result of this line of reasoning is the following equation. Given these definitions:

k = probability of recalling the kernal;

$p = 1 - q$ = probability of recalling transforms to be recalled; P_i=probability of recall with i syntactic errors; then, on the assumption of independent recall of the kernels and the several transformations, we have:

$$P_i = k \binom{m}{m-i} p^{m-i} q^i.$$

Now by lumping together all of Mehler's 15 subjects on all trials for all sentences, we can estimate the necessary probabilities and then see if the assumption of independence will predict the observed distribution of errors. The results are shown in Table 5. The estimated

TABLE 5. *Distribution of Syntactic errors in free recall of sentences*

Errors:	0	1	2	3
Calculated P_i	0.34	0.25	0.06	0.01
Obtained P_i	0.36	0.20	0.09	0.01

probability of recalling the kernel was 0.66. The estimated probabilities for getting each of the transformations correct were all very close to 0.80, so that a single value was used for all three. And when we put these parameter values into the equation for P_i, we obtain fairly good agreement between data and hypothesis. Or to state the matter more carefully, on the basis of Mehler's preliminary evidence, we cannot reject the hypothesis that sentences were recoded and that each of the four components of the kernel-plus-code was remembered correctly or incorrectly independently of the others.

Here again our work has only begun and so my report of it is still colored by all the natural enthusiasm and prejudices that seem to accompany every programmatic statement. My colleagues and I now see syntactic structure as an important variable to explore. The logicians and linguists are currently defining the theoretical issues with great precision, so that the full range of our experimental and psychometric methods can be brought to bear. I am enthusiastically convinced that such studies have an important contribution to make to the science of psychology.

In the course of this work I seem to have become a very old-fashioned kind of psychologist. I now believe that mind is something more than a four-letter, Anglo-Saxon word—human minds exist and it is our job as psychologists to study them. Moreover, I believe that one of the best ways to study a human mind is by studying the verbal systems that it uses. But what I want most to communicate here is my strong conviction that such a program is not only important, but that it is also possible, even now, with the relatively crude and limited empirical weapons that we have already developed. In the years ahead I hope we will see an increasing flow of new and exciting research as more psychologists discover the opportunities and the challenge of psycholinguistic theory and research.

AJDUKIEWICZ, K. Die syntaktische Konnexität. *Stud. phil.*, 1935, **1**, 1-27.

BAR-HILLEL, Y. A quasiarithmetical notation for syntactic description. *Language*, 1953, **29**, 47-58.

BAR-HILLEL, Y., GAIFMAN, C., & SHAMIR, E. On categorial and phrase-structure grammars. *Bull. Res. Council Israel*, 1960, **9F**, 1-16.

BRAINE, M. D. S. On learning the grammatical order of words. *Psychol. Rev.*, in press.

CHOMSKY, N. Three models for the description of language. *IRE Trans. Inform. Theory*, 1956, **IT-2**, 113-24.

CHOMSKY, N. *Syntactic structures.* 's-Gravenhage: Mouton, 1957.

CHOMSKY, N. On certain formal properties of grammars. *Inform. Control*, 1959, **2**, 137-67.

CHOMSKY, N., & MILLER, G. A. Finite state languages. *Inform. Control*, 1958, **1**, 91-112.

ERVIN, S. M. Changes with age in the verbal determinants of word-association. *Amer. J. Psychol.*, 1961, **74**, 361-72.

GLANZER, M. Grammatical category: A rote learning and word association analysis. *J. verbal Learn. verbal Behav.*, 1962, **1**, 31-41.

HARRIS, Z. S. From morpheme to utterance. *Language*, 1946, **22**, 161-83.

HARRIS, Z. S. Discourse analysis. *Language*, 1952, **28**, 1-30. (a)

HARRIS, Z. S. Discourse analysis: A sample text. *Language*, 1952, **28**, 474-94. (b)

HARRIS, Z. S. Co-occurrence and transformation in linguistic structure. *Language*, 1957, **33**, 283-340.

LAMBEK, J. The mathematics of sentence structure. *Amer. math. Mon.*, 1958, **65**, 154-69.

MILLER, G. A. The magical number seven, plus or minus two. *Psychol. Rev.*, 1956, **63**, 81-97.

MILLER, G. A. Decision units in the perception of speech. *IRE Trans. Inform. Theory,* 1962, **IT-8,** 81-3.

MILLER, G. A., HEISE, G. A., & LICHTEN, W. The intelligibility of speech as a function of the context of the test materials. *J. exp. Psychol.,* 1951, **41,** 329-35.

NIDA, E. A. The analysis of immediate constituents. *Language,* 1948, **24,** 168-77.

PIKE, K. L. Taxemes and immediate constituents. *Language,* 1943, **19,** 65-82.

POST, E. L. Finite combinatory processes: Formulation I. *J. symb. Logic,* 1936, **1,** 103-5.

POST, E. L. Recursively enumerable sets of positive integers and their decision problems. *Bull. Amer. Math. Soc.,* 1944, **50,** 284-316.

SHANNON, C. E. A mathematical theory of communication. *Bell Sys. tech. J.,* 1948, **27,** 379-423.

SHANNON, C. E. Prediction and entropy of printed English. *Bell Sys. tech. J.,* 1951, **30,** 50-64.

WELLS, R. S. Immediate constituents. *Language,* 1947, **23,** 81-117.

39 / On Understanding and Creating Sentences [1]

CHARLES E. OSGOOD, *University of Illinois*

It was exactly a decade ago that Hobart Mowrer (1954) offered this Association his Presidential Address on "The Psychologist Looks at Language." At the core of his paper was the insightful proposition that "in communication we are not transferring meanings from person to person so much as we are transferring meanings *from sign to sign* within a given person, within a single mind [p. 663]." And he went on to say that "The communicative act, in its most salient and significant aspect, lies . . . in the combination, juxtaposition, or association of the meanings thus aroused in *novel, 'informative' ways* [pp. 663-4]." The means for accomplishing this was the *sentence,* and Mowrer proposed that, psychologically, the sentence is essentially a conditioning device. Many, many words about words have flowed through the psychological literature in the decade since then, and it seems necessary, as well as appropriate, to take another look at the psychology of the sentence.

Toward the close of his address, Hobart Mowrer also had this to say:

One can hardly think of a more exciting, yet arduous, scientific undertaking than would be involved in a joint exploration by grammarians [linguists] and learning theorists of the innumerable psychological functions which, over countless centuries, have become imbedded in the structural forms of the world's major and minor languages [p. 690].

What with linguists like Roman Jakobson, Joseph Greenberg, and Noam Chomsky to the left of me and with psychologists like Fred Skinner, Jack Carroll, Jim Jenkins, and Roger Brown to the right of me—not to mention George Miller, who is usually ahead of me—I feel that I have been rather in the thick of psycholinguistics. This paper is my attempt to meet a challenge from the linguists that has become completely explicit in the past few years: *Can our psychological theories incorporate and render comprehensible the way human beings understand and create sentences?* If not, then our theories are at best insufficient and at worst erroneous.

THE PROBLEM

So that you will appreciate the nature of the problem, I must ask you to return with me, for just a little while, to grammar school. We will start with a simple, unanalyzed string of words—THE MAN HITS THE COLORFUL BALL—and trace through a series of increasingly powerful linguistic models designed to analyze them and define their sentence-hood.

We may begin with the finite state grammar, a model generally familiar to psychologists. Since sentences have a

From the *American Psychologist,* 1963, **18,** 735-51, with permission of the author and publisher.
1. Address of the President to the Seventy-First Annual Convention of the American Psychological Association, Philadelphia, September 1, 1963.

REWRITE RULES   TREE DIAGRAM

Fɪɢ. 1. Illustration of phrase structure analysis.

way of proceeding sequentially (or from left to right on the printed page), it seems intuitively reasonable that each succeeding word should be probabilistically dependent upon the preceding words, and hence that a Markov-type sentence generating machine should be sufficient. The probabilities at each transition point would depend upon the machine's previous experience with sentences, this experience providing both its lexicon and its rules of transition (or grammar). The linguist Chomsky (1957) has argued that such a finite-state generator could not produce the potentially infinite set of grammatical sentences, including novel ones, that characterizes any natural language, and Miller, Galanter, and Pribram (1960) have pointed out that, assuming an ordinary vocabulary and an upper limit of 20 words per sentence, it would take a childhood lasting 100 years to be exposed just once to each of the possible sentences. Chomsky also demonstrates that a Markov-type generator could not handle the potentially infinite imbedding

that characterizes sentences in natural languages, as for example in the sentence *The man who said that I know that John is the one who left the party that we had earlier is here*—a difficult but by no means inconceivable utterance.

A model that seems to resolve these difficulties, and the one commonly employed by linguists, is the phrase structure grammar. As shown in Figure 1, our sample sentence (S) is first resolved into its immediate constituents, a noun phrase (NP) plus a verb phrase (VP), these in turn are resolved into their immediate constituents, and so on—gradually generating a hierarchically organized "tree." Now you are certainly convinced that you're back in grammar school! This is nothing other than what we once studied under the name of "parsing" or "diagraming" a sentence. But there is more to this than meets the eye.

Note first that each shift from one level to the next can be represented by a rewrite rule, and each rewrite rule is restricted to a linear segregation or amalgamation of the units at the subordinate level. Note second that such grammatical trees, as contrasted with the Markov model, clearly specify "what goes with what" along the terminal strings (thus *the man* or *the colorful ball* form wholes, whereas *hits the* definitely does not). Finally, note that the rewrite rules are of quite different kind than what I have called the dictionary rules: The rewrite rules are analogous to the principles in a scientific theory, with the symbols (S, NP, V, etc.) serving as the theoretical constructs; but the dictionary rules are like those of identification, where we assign construct status to events in the real world in order to operate on them in the theory. Thus the sentence *A boy rings an ancient bell* is equivalent in grammatical theory to the sentence we have diagramed here.

Contrary to usual linguistic practice, in which the rewrite arrows and sequences within the tree are unidirectional (left-to-right and up-to-down), I have deliberately shown bidirectional arrows. The linguist's way of doing things reflects his too exclusive concern with the speaker, I think—that is, with generating or encoding sentences. The listener, in the position of interpreting or decoding sentences, begins with strings of words, combines them into large units and, finally, understands the sentence as a whole. In other words, sentence creators start at the trunk and end with the leaves, whereas sentence understanders begin with the leaves and hopefully end up at the trunk. At the very bottom of this diagram I have suggested the humble status of the finite state sentence generating model.

Is this phrase structure model sufficient for linguistic purposes? The problem is one of efficiency, simplicity, and elegance. Not only does this grammar require a different representation for every modification of each basic sentence, but, since no account is taken of the derivational history of sentences, it cannot disambiguate ambiguous sentences like *The shoot-* *ing of the hunters was terrible*—without knowing whether this sentence was derived from *the hunters shoot* or from *they shot the hunters*, we do not know whether to say "They should practice more" or "They should have been wearing red jackets!" Chomsky's major contribution to linguistics has been his elaboration of the rationale for a transformational grammar. One set of transformation rules will carry our diagramed kernel sentence into the passive (*The colorful ball is hit by the man*); another set carries it into negation (*The man does not hit the colorful ball*); a combination of these two sets of rules carries it into a passive-negation construction (*The colorful ball is not hit by the man*); and so forth. The power of this theory lies in its capacity to generate an infinite set of grammatical sentences, and no ungrammatical ones, from a minimally finite set of kernels and a minimally finite set of transformations.

But what about meaning? Linguists have had relatively little to say about semantics; indeed, one could fairly say that they have avoided it like the plague. The most rigorous attempt to apply linguistic methods to the semantics of sentences of which I am aware is to be found in a recent paper by Katz and Fodor (1963) titled "The Structure of Semantic Theory." Their basic proposition is that *semantics equals linguistic description minus grammar*. What does grammar leave for semantics? In the first place, we note that any grammar will provide identical structural descriptions for sentences that obviously differ in meaning (*Man bites dog* versus *Dog bites man*, for example) and different descriptions for sentences that are the same in meaning (*The dog bit the man* versus *The man was bitten by the dog*). There are also sentences that are structurally unambiguous but semantically ambiguous, like *He will get the case* (of beer? at law? in the railroad station?), sentences that are structurally unambiguous but semantically anomalous, like *He was aware of the subliminal stimulus* (I realize that a number of psychologists have failed to recognize the anomaly here!), and sentences that are paraphrases of each other and yet structurally different, as the sentence *She is my mother-in-law* is to *She is my wife's mother.*

What, according to Katz and Fodor, are the necessary components of a semantic theory, i.e., necessary for an understanding of the fluent native speaker's ability to interpret sentences? The first component is a dictionary—the grammar of a language cannot account for differences in interpretation that depend solely upon substitution of lexical alternatives within otherwise identical frames. It means something quite different to say *A scorpion bit me* than to say *A mosquito bit me.* The second necessary component is a set of projection rules which take account of relations between words in the sentence and between syntactic structure and meaning alternatives—a dictionary usually provides more semantic alternatives for a word than are possible in the context of the given sentence.

Now let us return to the sample sentence diagramed in Figure 1 and subject it to semantic analysis *à la* Katz and Fodor. Such a sentence, along with its structural description as diagramed, is the input and a semantic interpretation is the output. Since we are dealing with the interpretation (decoding) of this sentence we proceed upward, successively amalgamating the branches under each node. The structural analysis predetermines the grammatical alternatives we select from the dictionary—thus *man* (N) rather than *man* (V) and *hits* (V) rather than *hits* (Npl)—but it does not select semantic alternatives within the same form class. Combining the two dictionary alternatives for *colorful* ("abounding in contrasting bright colors" versus "having distinctive character") with the three

dictionary meanings of *ball* ("large assembly for the purpose of dancing" versus "having globular shape" versus "solid missile for projection by engine of war"), and applying a semantic rule which eliminates anomalous compounds, Katz and Fodor retain four viable amalgamations of *the + colorful + ball.* Looking up *hits* in our dictionary, and following only the grammatical path marked V (verb), we find two alternatives: "collides with an impact" versus "strikes with a blow or a missile." Combining these alternatives with the four viable alternatives for *the colorful ball* and again using a rule of anomaly, all alternatives using *ball* in the sense of "large assembly for the purpose of dancing" are eliminated. The final combination of *the man* with *hits the colorful ball* does nothing further to disambiguate this sentence, and Katz and Fodor conclude (*a*) that this sentence is not semantically anomalous and (*b*) that it is four ways semantically ambiguous.

I have gone through this rather laborious analysis to make two critical points: First, *semantic analysis of this type takes no account of the varying probabilities of alternative interpretations.* I take it to be intuitively obvious that the four alternatives here differ markedly in the probability of what was intended by the speaker or writer, and this can be shown by paraphrasing the alternative readings:

1. *the man strikes the colorful round object with a blow* (very high probability);

2. *the man collides with the colorful round object* (conceivable, but it would have to be a pretty big ball!);

3. *the man strikes the colorful solid missile with a blow* (conceivable, but not probable in this day and age);

4. *the man collides with the colorful solid missile* (all one could say to this would be, "What, is Tom Thumb drunk again?").

Second, *semantic analysis of this type is*

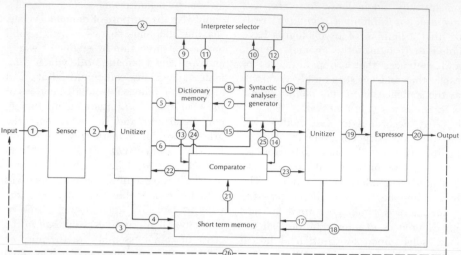

Fig. 2. Hypothetical sentence machine.

unable to select among ambiguities and resolve them. If such an innocuous sentence as *The man hits the colorful ball* is open to no less than four unresolvable interpretations, I suspect that the vast majority of sentences we encounter in everyday life would remain ambiguous after analysis—and if this were the best fluent speakers and listeners could do, communication would be in an even worse state than it is now.

The reason for this sorry state of affairs, of course, is precisely what Katz and Fodor must leave out in order to make their analysis rigorous in the linguistic sense—knowledge on the part of users of a language about the nature of their world and about the momentary situational, motivational, and linguistic contexts in which particular sentences occur.

I have asked my colleagues in linguistics and computeristics what would be the minimum equipment required for a sentence understanding and creating machine. The result of this inquiry is shown in Figure 2. It is just a bit overwhelming. I am not going to lead you along the paths of this flow diagram—it would take too much time—but I would like you to note the types of equipment

needed: For sentence decoding we need SENSORS, UNITIZERS, SHORT-TERM MEMORIES, DICTIONARY MEMORIES, SYNTACTIC ANALYZERS, COMPARATORS, and INTERPRETERS; for sentence *encoding* we would need SELECTORS, DICTIONARIES, SYNTACTIC GENERATORS, COMPARATORS, UNITIZERS, and EXPRESSORS. Computer models of this kind are exercises in problem setting rather than problem solving. Terms like DICTIONARY, UNITIZER, COMPARATOR, and SYNTACTIC GENERATOR merely point to processes that must be accounted for in an ypsychological theory, rather than providing explanations in and of themselves—and besides, I think we can do the job more economically.

NEO-BEHAVIORISM AND PSYCHOLINGUISTICS

So let me turn now to a bit of psychological theory. I will be very brief about it, both because I have presented these ideas *in extenso* elsewhere (cf. Osgood, 1955, 1956, 1957, 1963), and because I am eager to get on with the psychology of the sentence. In complete agreement with B. F. Skinner (1957), I believe that an adequate theory of language behavior must be a learning theory, but that we neither wish nor require any special theory for language. The goals of psycholinguistic theory include those of linguistics—since, after all, the rules of grammar are part of the lawfulness of human behavior—but must go beyond to encompass relations between linguistic and nonlinguistic events (semantics and pragmatics). We will consider several models of behavior in general, each of increasing complexity—a complexity forced by the criterion of sufficiency.

Of course, there are differences between linguistic and psychological approaches to language that go beyond the question of inclusiveness. It was the linguist Ferdinand de Saussure who first made the oft-cited distinction between *la langue* and *la parole*. *La langue* refers to language as an abstract system; *la parole* refers to language as actualized speech events. The linguist is characteristically interested in the former, the psychologist in the latter. Chomsky's conception of the grammar of a language as a theory which will generate an infinite set of sentences that are grammatical and none that are ungrammatical is clearly in the realm of *la langue*. When one listens to spontaneous speech with an ear toward how things are being said rather than what is being said, however, it appears that well-formed, grammatical sentences are an exception to the rule. Here is a literal transcription from the taped spontaneous speech of someone whom I consider to be a normally fluent speaker of English:

As far as I know, no one yet has done the // in a way obvious now and interesting problem of / doing a // in a sense a structural frequency study of the alternative / syntactical ///[a] in a given language, say, like English, the alternative /[a] possible structures, and how // what their hierarchical / probability of occurrence structure is.

Lest some of my colleagues in psycholinguistics suspect this might be an excerpt from their speech, let me hasten to say that this was a bit of my own verbal behavior at a Social Science Research Council conference on content analysis.

If one wishes to travel over a terrain, and he builds a kiddie-car to do it in, this is fine if it gets him everywhere he wants to go efficiently and economically. In fact, it is then a most parsimonious device. So when I refer to Skinner's single-stage behaviorism as a "kiddie-car model" I am not being derogatory—merely descriptive. In his book *Verbal Behavior*, Skinner (1957) sets himself the task of describing the antecedent conditions which determine the emission of verbal responses, that is, lawful dependency relations between classes of stimuli and classes of responses (operants). That his is a very mechanistic and deterministic conception of man's highest achievement is not the issue. The question is one of sufficiency. There are some psychological peaks and linguistic jungles which the kiddie-car simply cannot negotiate.

There is the securely documented phenomenon known as semantic generalization: Having learned a novel response to the word JOY (for example, lifting the forefinger to escape shock), the normal adult speaker of English will promptly transfer this response to the word GLEE —but not to the physically more similar word BOY. The basis for the transfer is obviously similarity of meaning, but there is no place for such symbolic processes in Skinner's behaviorism. There is also the phenomenon of semantic satiation which Wallace Lambert and Leon Jakobovits (1963) are busily pinning down: When subjects rapidly repeat the words CANOE or NEGRO, semantic profiles for these words shrink toward meaninglessness; but equally massed repetition of the nonsense syllables NÚKA or GRONÍ (which have the same overt response form as CANOE or NEGRO) produces no semantic satiation. And then there are the jungles of grammar and syntax, which Skinner tries to explore armed with little more than the autoclitic (a special form of intraverbal operant); according to Chomsky's (1959) incisive review, this excursion is a monumental failure.

The *two*-stage mediation model had its origins in Hull's notion of the "pure stimulus act," an act whose function is to produce distinctive self-stimulation rather than to be instrumental in itself. At that time, 1930, Hull noted that such a mechanism could serve as the basis for symbolic processes, but he did not fully explore this possibility himself. Along with many others, I have proposed the mediation model as the characteristic, rather than the exceptional, case in behavior, and I have tried to use it as the basis for a psychological theory of meaning. We might dub this the "horse-and-buggy model"—at least it has the advantage of putting the driver inside.

The essential nature of mediation can be understood in terms of Figure 3. *Whenever some originally neutral stimulus* (sign-to-be), $\boxed{S}$ *is repeatedly contiguous with another stimulus* (significate), $\dot{S}$, *which regularly and reliably elicits a particular pattern of total behavior,* R_T, *the neutral stimulus will become associated with some portion,* r_m, *of this total behavior as a representational mediation process.* This is a conditioning postulate with a significant difference—namely, that the mediating reaction to the sign is not the same as the reaction to the significate, but rather consists of those most readily conditionable, least effortful, and least interfering components of the total original reaction. Such a process is representational because it is part of the very same behavior made to the thing signified; it is mediational because the distinctive self-stimulation, s_m, can become associated selectively with various instrumental acts, R_X, which are appropriate to, or take account of, the thing signified.

What has been done here, in effect, is to break the behavior sequence between overt S and overt R into two indepen-

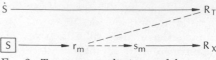

Fig. 3. Two-stage mediation model.

dently variable parts, decoding habits and encoding habits. All of the conceptual machinery of single-stage S-R theory—generalization, inhibition, and the like—is assumed to apply to each of the stages of the mediation model. This separation greatly increases the explanatory power of behavior theory: The phenomena of semantic generalization and semantic satiation are readily incorporated, and we have the beginnings of a theory of meaning and the symbolic processes. But there are at least two regions where this horse-and-buggy model cannot travel. The first of these is the territory of perceptual organization, long the stronghold of Gestalt theory and the Waterloo of S-R theory. The second is the territory of motor skill organization. In both cases we appear to be dealing with closure and integration phenomena, either of S-S or R-R nature, and no strictly S-R model will suffice.

Therefore, let us investigate the possibilities in a *three*-stage mediation-integration model. At the APA meetings last year, two of our award winning members, J. J. Gibson (1963) and Donald Hebb (1963), agreed on the need to separate sensation from perception but also on the identification of perception with meaning. Let me suggest that on both input and output sides we are dealing with a three-level system, as suggested in Figure 4. On the input side, the lowest level, which I shall call *sensory*, begins with the receptors and ends with sensory signals at the termini of the projection systems, providing a faithful mirror of "what is." The second level, which I shall term *perceptual*, begins with these patterns of sensory signals and ends with the most probable integration of their more central correlates as

LEVEL PROCESS

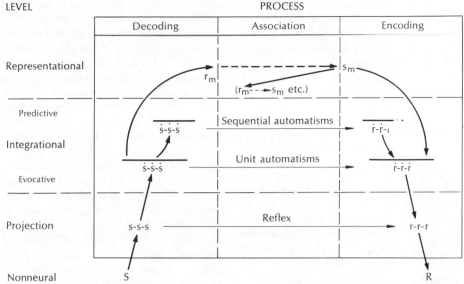

| | Decoding | Association | Encoding |

Fig. 4. Three-stage mediation-integration model.

determined by redundancies in past experience—thus, a mirror of "what ought to be." The third level, which I shall call *meaningful*, begins with these meaningless sensory integrations and ends with the most probable representational mediation processes with which they have been associated—a mirror of "what it signifies" in terms of past experience with behavioral outcomes. Similar analysis of behavioral output yields *execution* (projection), *skill* (integrational), and *intention* (meaningful) level.

What now requires some explication is the integration level. Let me borrow, rephrase, and simplify a notion developed by Hebb (1949) in his analysis of cell assemblies and phase sequences, and call it the Integration Principle: *The greater the frequency with which stimulus events (S-S) or response events (R-R) have been paired in input or output experience of the organism, the greater will be the tendency for their central correlates to activate each other.* One critical variable here is redundancy among input or output events; another

is frequency; yet another is temporal contiguity. But I think this is all—motivation and reinforcement seem to have nothing to do with the formation of S-S or R-R integrations.

All of the extensive literature relating visual and auditory thresholds for words to their frequencies of usage testifies to the role of frequency—high frequency and contiguity yield evocative integrations (units which display closure) whereas lower frequency or less contiguity yield merely predictive integrations which help to override the "noise" in everyday decoding and encoding. A recent experiment by Vernon Tyler (1962) tested the assumption that sensory integrations are formed independently of reinforcement; results were as predicted.

This model must appear quite complicated in comparison with most S-R theories. I'm afraid complexity is the price we must pay for sufficiency. However, since I am by no means convinced that even this "monster" is sufficiently complex to handle language behavior, I merely dub it "the Model-T Ford theory." Also, I realize that there are many who will conclude that, despite the fancy chrome and the three-tone horn, this is still just the little old kiddie-car at heart. In a sense this is true, and that is as it should be. The question before us is whether this souped-up kiddie-car will enable us to navigate the domain of The Sentence.

DECISION AND CONTROL IN BEHAVIOR

Now I want to discuss the problem of decision and control in behavior. It will be useful for us to think in terms of two quite different types of hierarchies: sequential hierarchies (horizontal, left-to-right), relating antecedent to subsequent events; and simultaneous hierarchies (vertical, up-to-down), relating subordinate events to supraordinate events. The former are clearly Markovian or probabilistic in nature; the latter clearly are not.

Viewed in the abstract, there are two different kinds of sequential hierarchies, convergent and divergent: A pure convergent hierarchy exists when multiple antecedent events are associated with a single subsequent event; a pure divergent hierarchy exists when a single antecedent event is associated with multiple subsequent events. As we know from transfer and interference studies, convergent hierarchies are facilitative whereas divergent hierarchies are competitive. But behavior does not transpire in the abstract, of course, and in practice convergent and divergent hierarchies involving the same sets of events operate simultaneously. Let me make two simple, and I hope clarifying, assumptions here: First, "decision" in behavior is simply selection of the momentarily most probable alternative within any divergent hierarchy. There is nothing necessarily "cognitive" or "volitional" involved; it is a probabilistic business going on at all levels in decoding, associating, and encoding. Second, "control" over behavior is simply the way in which combination and patterning within convergent hier-archies modifies the momentary probabilities of dependent alternatives. This, too, is a strictly probabilistic business, having nothing to do with "purpose" or "will," except as these notions may be redefined in these terms. It is the way context influences outcomes at choice points throughout the behavior system.

The notion of simultaneous, vertical hierarchies of units within units within units has been about as foreign to psychologists as the notion of probabilistic sequential hierarchies has been to linguists. The only psychologists I know who have made full use of the notion of hierarchical "trees" in a general theory of behavior are Miller, Galanter, and Pribram (1960) in their book on *Plans and the Structure of Behavior*, but this conception is consistent with the way complex operations are programed on a computer and with the phrase structure grammar employed by linguists. The problem is to identify the functional units at each level of organization. One of the rules of the game is that the units at each supraordinate level must be exhaustively divisible into units at all subordinate levels, with no leftover pieces, and vice versa.

The two inner columns in Figure 5 present what I think are the minimum and sufficient levels of units in language decoding and encoding. Units which do not seem to have psychological reality—regardless of their linguistic reality and usefulness—are bracketed. Psychological correlates of each unit are suggested in the outer columns. A major division is indicated between meaningful and meaningless levels of organization, and within each a distinction is made between spatially and temporally patterned events. Thus phonemes at the meaningless level and words at the meaningful level are represented as simultaneous "bundles" of distinctive, differentiating features.[2]

2. The figure is not quite accurate with regard to phonemes.

		ψ Correlate	ℒ Decoding	ℒ Encoding	ψ Correlate
MEANINGFUL	Temporal pattern	Interpretations	SENTENCES	SENTENCES	Intentions
		Kernel amalgamation	(PHRASES)	(PHRASES)	Kernel differentiation
	Spatial pattern	Meanings	WORDS	WORDS	Meanings
MEANINGLESS	Temporal pattern	Forms	WORDS	WORDS	Forms
		?	(MORPHEMES)	(MORPHEMES)	?
		Perceptual skill components	PHONEMES	SYLLABLES	Motor skill components
	Spatial pattern	Sensory signals	DISTINCTIVE FEATURES	DISTINCTIVE FEATURES	Motor signals

Fig. 5. Units of decoding and encoding.

There are several rather radical proposals embodied in this diagram. One is that the units of decoding and encoding are not necessarily the same—the syllable, for example, is plainly evident in speaking but seems to have no representation in listening. Another is that the morpheme, so crucial in linguistic analysis, is psychologically nonexistent; compare *boys* with *noise*—the former is two morphemes, [boy] + [s-pl.] and the latter is one, yet there is no sense of the morpheme boundary in the former case. Perhaps the most radical suggestion is the double role given the *word*—incidentally, a unit which linguists have great trouble defining even if native speakers do not. Here the humble word is shown as Janus faced; at meaningless levels it serves as the most inclusive unit whereas at meaningful levels it serves as the minimal unit. I will have more to say on this anon.

Now we are in position to reconsider the Markov versus Chomsky controversy. The Markovian model of language behavior provided a happy meeting ground for information theorists and learning theorists, and the past decade has witnessed an outpouring of descriptive and experimental demonstrations of the stochastic nature of language behavior at all levels. Yet, you will recall, Chomsky demonstrated the insufficiency of the Markov model on several logical grounds, and many of his adherents have interpreted "insufficient" to mean "erroneous." Actually, the evidence for nonchance, transitional dependencies in language behavior is impressive and neither trivial nor irrelevant; it must also be taken into account in any complete psycholinguistic theory.

I detect what I believe are two ambiguities in Chomsky's (1957) arguments. The first is what I shall call the unilevel fallacy: Many of his criticisms of the Markovian model involve the tacit assumption that stochastic processes operate only on one level of units at a time—usually on the terminal strings of grammatical trees, i.e., the word level. There is nothing about the model itself that sets this restriction. The second is what I shall call the decision fallacy: Chomsky's generative grammar, even in its full-blown transformational form, says nothing whatsoever about decision making. For example, what determines whether the speaker will select a simple kernel sentence form or transform it into a passive or a question form? As a matter of fact, such decisions are what Chomsky (1959) himself has termed the

REWRITE RULES   TREE DIAGRAM

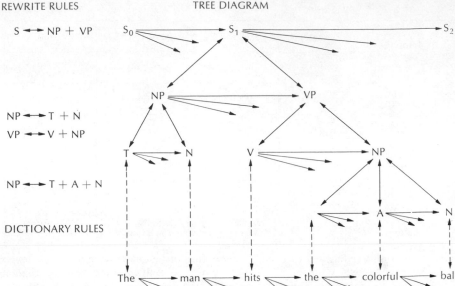

$S \longleftrightarrow NP + VP$

$NP \longleftrightarrow T + N$
$VP \longleftrightarrow V + NP$

$NP \longleftrightarrow T + A + N$

DICTIONARY RULES

FIG. 6. Integration of sequential and simultaneous hierarchies.

"optional rules of grammar"; not only are these options by no means trivial, as Chomsky agrees, but they appear to be precisely the points of articulation between the Markovian and Chomskian models.

Figure 6 suggests how sequential (probabilistic) and simultaneous (unitizing) hierarchies can be integrated. You will recognize this as the "tree" diagram with which we began, but with some modifications and additions. Divergent sequential hierarchies have been substituted for the +'s in the old diagram, to indicate that what follows what within the noun phrase or within the verb phrase is in part optional and therefore probabilistically determined. Both an antecedent sentence (S_0) and a subsequent sentence (S_2), which could have been produced either by the same or a different speaker, have been added, to indicate that sentences as wholes do not appear out of nowhere but rather are themselves linked probabilistically to other units at their own level. Transitional decisions at supraordinate levels modify the probabilities of units at subordinate levels, but only partially; not that the noun class of *man* in the diagramed sentence is jointly dependent upon its vertical relation to NP and its horizontal relation to T.

A very recent experiment by Neal Johnson (1963) is particularly a propos here. He had subjects learn sentences of the two grammatical types shown in Figure 7. In the first, linguistic analysis would locate one major juncture between *boy* and *saved;* in the second, there would be a minor break between *house* and *across* and a major one between *street* and *is.* Johnson predicted that probability of transitional error in recall would be greater across phrase boundaries than within. The bars in this figure give the relative probabilities of errors at each word-to-word transition. Note, first, that as predicted sentence Type (a) has one peak of transitional error between *boy* and *saved* whereas sentence Type (b) has a minor peak between *house* and *across* and a major peak between *street* and *is.* But note, second, that within each phrase there is an almost linear decrease in transitional errors running

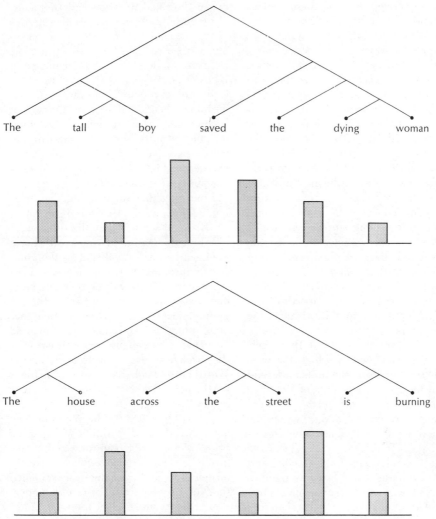

FIG. 7. Frequency of transitional errors in two types of sentences (after Johnson, 1963).

from left to right. These data appear to confirm rather strikingly the idea that simultaneous and sequential hierarchies combine in the understanding and creating of sentences.

COMPONENTS OF A THEORY OF THE SENTENCE

Now I would like to suggest three essential components or processes in a psychological theory of the sentence. Al-though I will give them fancy names for communication purposes, this will be no special theory of language behavior, since in each case I shall try to show that these functions require nothing more, mechanismwise, than is available in the three-stage, mediation-integration model of behavior in general.

First, we have the Word Form Pool. The term "pool" has at least two meta-phorical usages: (*a*) as a reflecting sur-face on which ephermal patterns can be displayed and (*b*) as a supply of entities or the place where they are stored. I intend to convey both of these notions simultaneously. What I have termed the sensory and motor integration systems are modifiable in terms of the redundancy, frequency, and contiguity of their inputs and outputs respectively; thus they can come to "mirror" in their own neural organization regularities in the past experience of the organism. Being convergent, probabilistic systems, they have the additional, most important property of closure—sketchy input information is internally elaborated into the most probable wholes. By virtue of the reverberatory property of cell assemblies, these systems provide a "reflecting surface" on which the elements for sentence building can be displayed; they are thus functionally equivalent to the notion of "temporary storage" as used by those who think in terms of computers. They are also "unitizers" of input or output, by virtue of the closure property.

But what *are* the units at this level? Given the principles by which the integration systems work, the units must tend toward the largest segments of language that are (*a*) highly redundant, (*b*) very frequent in occurrence, and (*c*) within the temporal limits of cell-assembly reverberation. Some short sentences (like *How do you do* and *What do you know*) and many trite phrases will fit these requirements, but most *words* in a person's active vocabulary obviously do. *I am therefore led to propose the word as the characteristic unit of perceptual forms in language.* The morpheme fits neither the requirements nor the data—witness the fact that the tachistoscopic threshold for MOTHER is lower than that for either of its morphemic components, [MOTH] and [ER], despite the fact that their total frequency of occurrence must be higher since they appear in many words besides MOTHER.

What about my assertion that word units in the Form Pool are meaningless? First note that the lawful relation be-

tween threshold duration and frequency of usage only obtains when all instances of the same form, regardless of meaning, are summed. The word form TAKE is given no less than 69 meanings in *Webster's Collegiate Dictionary,* yet there is no sensory clue as to its particular meaning when it is flashed on the screen. Second, note that in semantic satiation the subject must repeatedly and discriminately perceive the word form and vocalize the word form, as a single-stage "texting operant" in Skinner's terms, yet it is the meaning that satiates, not the "texting." The meaningless status of words at this level implies that the number of discriminable units in the Word Form Pool can be much smaller than the number of meaningful words in a speaker's vocabulary. There will be only one *play,* one *player,* one *plays* and so forth; the grammatical fact that *plays* can be either noun plural or verb and the semantic fact that *play* can be in the theatre or the backyard has no relevance in the Word Form Pool, but this *is* the focus for the next stage in sentence understanding and creating.

Let us turn, then, to the Semantic Key Sort. A little demonstration will help us bridge the gulf between form and meaning. I am going to give you a perfectly meaningful and grammatical sentence that you may have a bit of trouble understanding: LIGHT LIGHTS LIGHTLY LIGHT LIGHT LIGHTS. I imagine few readers could give a satisfactory paraphrase. The reason is that each of the three word-form units is ambiguous as to both grammatical and semantic coding. But now let me provide a paraphrase along with a situational context: It is a balmy summer evening, we are sitting in a Japanese garden, and I say, PALE FLAMES GENTLY ILLUMINATE AIRY LANTERNS, or, LIGHT LIGHTS LIGHTLY LIGHT LIGHT LIGHTS. As a form in the Word Pool, LIGHT could activate any combination of three grammatical codings (N, V, or A) each with

Base probabilities	Form pool sort	Grammatical sort	Associational sort	Affective sort	Denotative sort

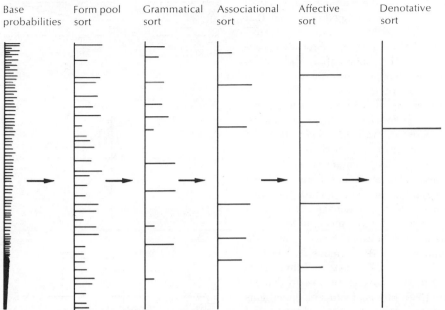

Fig. 8. Operation of a hypothetical Semantic Key Sort.

some five semantic codings, yielding at least 15 high-probability alternatives. Disambiguation requires independent representation of these alternatives and probabilistic selection among them.

Imagine now a very large box of edge-punched key sort cards. There must be one card for each discriminable usage. Thus, whereas there was only one *play* in the Word Form Pool, in the Semantic Key Sort there will *be play$_1$* (verb, to frolic), *play$_2$* (verb, to act), *play$_3$* (verb, to wager), *play$_{11}$* (noun, recreation), *play$_{12}$* (noun, drama), *play$_{13}$* (noun, game event), *play$_{111}$* (adjective, make-believe), and so on through many more discriminable interpretations and intentions. I have only indicated grammatical and semantic (denotative) coding, but the cards would also have to have "fields" for gross affective coding and associative coding. And finally—or perhaps we should say first—each card would have to be coded for its representation in the Word Form Pool, since this exercises a

major selective effect. Let me hasten to point out that, although my analogy with a key sort implies a physical place of storage (as do terms like "dictionary" or "permanent memory"), the actual behavioral model will deal with semantic selection as a process, involving multiple usage of (hopefully) a relatively small number of components.

But first let's see how such a Semantic Key Sort might operate. Figure 8 illustrates a series of sortings, even though I'm sure they would be simultaneous for maximum efficiency. I assume that the cards would be ordered according to their base probabilities of usage, but given the large number of items having at least some probability, the differences here would be very small. Now imagine that our human computer scans this sentence, *The play got rave reviews in "Variety" this week,* and word forms *the* and *play* appear first in the Pool. The "needle" for the meaningless form *play* selects all cards coded appropriately, this representing a great reduction in uncertainty. Utilizing the unfolding grammatical information in the Word Form Pool, here the

T——V frame, the grammatical N needle sorts the *play* cards again, and all that are not nouns drop out. The needle sensitive to the REVIEW-*play* associative coding reduces the probabilities of *play* as in gambling, games, or puns; affective needles do their work; and finally the discriminative denotative needles, sensitive to the restrictive effects of *the, review,* VARIETY, and *this week* select that one *play* card punched for "specific dramatic product, contemporary."

Now, since I do *not* think semantic coding would actually operate this way, let me return to behavior theory. I will use the affective meaning system as a model, not because it is the most important system for sentence understanding and creating but because I think more about it. We have been able to demonstrate three bipolar factors or dimensions which account for a large share of the variance in affective meaning and appear to be common to all people, regardless of differences in both language and culture. Figure 9 illustrates how a concept (represented by the black dot) must project simultaneously onto all of the dimensions. Now, as shown in the diagram, if in theory we identify each bipolar factor with an independent, reciprocally antagonistic reaction system, then we have here three independent affective components of meaning. In other words, representational mediation processes (r_m) are assumed to be just as complexly componential as the total behaviors from which they are derived. My general suggestion is this: *In a fashion strictly analogous to the way a phoneme is defined as a bundle of simultaneous phonetic features, so may a meaning be defined as a bundle of simultaneous semantic features.* And just as recombination of a relatively small number of distinctive phonetic features generates a relatively large number of phonemes, so may recombination of semantic features generate large numbers of meanings. The problem

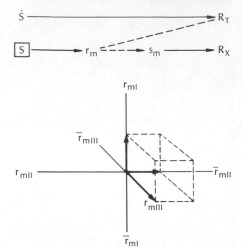

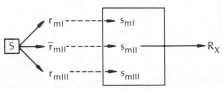

FIG. 9. Differentiation of the affective meaning of a concept in terms of three bipolar components.

is to identify all of the semantic features, or components, of r_m, including the grammatical ones. Needless to say, we are far from solving this problem, particularly for denotative meaning.

Is there any support for my assumption that grammatical distinctions are at base semantic in nature? Although the trend in contemporary linguistics has been to enforce an absolute separation between grammar and meaning, no less an authority than Roman Jakobson (1959) states approvingly that "It was clear to Boas that any difference of grammatical categories carries semantic information." For some grammatical categories the semantic information is clear (for example, when we hear the plural [-s] morpheme on a concrete noun, we look for more than one of it), but for others it is less so (for example, what is the semantics of *to* in the infinitive form *to go?*). In any case, it is clear that grammatical coding would have to operate on clues available in the strings of meaningless word forms, including affixes, function words, word orders, and guesses about ambiguous items. Tannenbaum and Stolz (1963) have reported recently that a computer programmed to assign grammatical form classes to strings of words in newspaper English on just this basis does so as well as college sophomores!

The notion of a semantic "field" or "sphere" is familiar to historical linguists, to philologists, and to psychologists who have worked with aphasic patients. Semantic change over time seems to operate componentially (psychologically, a special case of mediated generalization), and aphasics seem to make errors on a similar basis (e.g., saying *violin* for *trumpet*, *smoke* for *pipe*, and so on)—in other words, shifts appear to be stepwise within the same semantic sphere. In a more experimental vein, Pollio (1963) had subjects produce serial association and then compared rapid versus slow "bursts" in terms of both the associative overlap among the words involved and their mean distances in semantic profiles. He found that the more closely related words are in either associative or affective meaning, the more likely they are to appear together in rapid bursts. Research by Arthur and Caroline Staats on verbal operant conditioning (cf. Staats, Staats, Finley, & Minke, 1961) and by Susan Ervin (1961, 1963) and James Deese (1962) on word association also suggests that common semantic coding is the basis for formation of verbal response classes. It would appear, then, that rather than a deck of key sort cards in any permanent memory or "dictionary" we have a system for multiple, simultaneous, differential coding of words, and it is this which gives them meaning.

The third component of a psychological theory of the sentence is what I shall call a Cognitive Mixer—but this, too, is really

a process. Let us return to Hobart Mowrer's (1954) notion of the sentence as a conditioning device and his now-classic example, *Tom is a thief*. Mowrer saw the predicate, *thief*, functioning as the unconditioned stimulus, and the subject, *Tom*, functioning as the conditioned stimulus. There are several difficulties with this formulation:

1. It doesn't explain how we understand momentarily the meaning of the novel utterance *Tom is a thief*, without necessarily believing it, on a single presentation or trial.

2. It doesn't take grammatical structure into account—simple conditioning in the sentence *Tom is a perfect idiot* should lead to cancellation of the *Tom is perfect* and *Tom is an idiot* effects.

3. It doesn't account for the fact that the predicate may be modified as much as or more than the subject, as in the sentence *President Kennedy favors a test-ban treaty*.

But Mowrer's essential insight—that a sentence communicates by producing a dynamic interaction in the mind of the receiver—remains as valid now as it was a decade ago. The problem is to specify the nature of the interaction.

In 1955 Percy Tannenbaum and I (Osgood & Tannenbaum, 1955) proposed the Congruity Hypothesis as means of explaining some very systematic data on attitude change. The underlying notion was that, since the meaning system can do only one thing, assume only one "posture" at a time (cf. meaning as a simultaneous "bundle" of semantic components), *if* this meaning system is driven in two or more directions at once it must reach a compromise on every factor or component. The formal statement is as follows: *Whenever two signs are related by an assertion, the mediating reaction characteristic of each shifts toward congruence with that characteristic of the other, the magnitude of the shift being inversely proportional to the intensities of the interacting reactions.* In other words, more meaningful items have greater "pulling power." Note that the signs must be related by "an assertion" —which is our entrée to grammatical structure and the fundamental notion of the sentence as a propositionalizing device. But assertions can be perceptual as well as verbal; the sight of TOM DIPPING HIS HAND IN THE TILL is just as much an assertion as the sentence *Tom is a thief.* And note, finally, that assertions may be either associative or dissociative; the impact upon *Tom* must be quite different in the sentence *Tom is a thief* than it is in the sentence *Tom is not a thief* (which, incidentally, is another count against the simple conditioning model).

The general hypothesis states that meaning shifts are always toward congruence—but what or where is congruence? It is intuitively evident that the assertion *Tom is a thief* is already congruous to the policeman who caught him with his hand in the till, but not to Tom's mother; there should be no shift in meaning in the first case, but a cruel if momentary cognitive twist toward semantic fusion of *Tom* and *thief* in the mother's mind. It is also intuitively apparent that the assertion *Tom is not a thief* would already be congruent to his mother, but incredibly incongruent to the officer who had just taken Tom's hand out of the till; here there should be no meaning shift produced in the mother, but a gasping if momentary cognitive effort toward semantic dissolution of the meanings of *Tom* and *thief* on the part of the earnest officer of the law. Our general principle can be extended formally as follows: *Whenever two signs are related by an assertion, they are congruent to the extent that their mediating reactions are equally intense, either in the same* (compatible) *direction of excitation in the case of associative assertions or in opposite* (reciprocally antagonistic) *direc-*

tions in the case of dissociative assertions. Thus cognitive interaction is fusive for associative assertions and dissolusive for dissociative assertions.

In a paper bearing the intriguing title, "Computer Simulation of 'Hot Cognition'," Robert Abelson (1963) criticizes the Congruity Hypothesis on the ground that it makes meaning change complete and inexorable and, through repeated fusions, must leave people "adrift in a sea of neutrality." It certainly is true that if word meanings were completely at the mercy of "instant conditioning," one's semantics would be reduced to a hopeless, meaningless shambles by the end of a paper like this—if it is not anyhow for other reasons! But Abelson fails to note that dissociative assertions tend to push meanings outward—the wily politician keeps pushing himself off from such stable evils as Communism, Sin, and Higher Taxes. In fact, I think there is a general pressure toward polarized opposition, simple flip-flop binaries being easier to deal with cognitively than finely graded distinctions. Going back to my key sort analogy, I assume that an assertion pulls a couple of cards from the deck, which are already semantically punched, cognitive interaction produces some momentary compromise, which is necessary for sentence understanding, and then the cards are replaced in the file—slightly indented by the momentary collision but not permanently repunched. Of course, if the same assertion is repeated again and again—as was the case with *Fifth-Amendment Communist* during the heyday of Senator McCarthy— then repeated indenting yields permanent repunching, or meaning change.

Now we are in position to inquire into the dynamics of phrase interpretation. In 1956, for the rather practical purposes of content analysis, Sol Saporta, Jum Nunnally, and I (Osgood, Saporta, & Nunnally, 1956) applied the Congruity Hypothesis to gauging attitudes from message materials, by what we called "evaluative assertion analysis." Each complex sentence had to be transformed by a set of rules into an exhaustive set of "kernel assertions," all of the subject-copula-object form and together being semantically equivalent to the original sentence. Although we did not realize it then, since this was in the pre-Chomskian era, we had fallen into a kind of transformational grammar—by no means as elegant as Chomsky's formal system and different in several crucial respects, but crudely serviceable for psycholinguistic purposes.

Take for illustration the fairly complex sentence *the clever young thief was severely sentenced by the rather grim-faced judge* given in the following display:

—and each follows a different rule of cognitive interaction, the former homeostatic and the latter multiplicative. Examples of qualifying phrases, and their transformations, would be: *Castro's Cuba* (Cuba belongs to Castro); *volatile Castro* (Castro is volatile); *American promises* (promises are American); *dependable promises* (promises are dependable). Interactions here should be predictable from the Congruity Hypothesis. Examples of quantifying phrases would be: $V \times AUV$ (*used to steal*, which weakens the assertion); $V \times AV$ (*works hard*, which strengthens the assertion); $N \times Q$ (*some men*, which reduces the intensity of men); $A \times AV$ (*very kind*, which intensifies the adjective). Interactions here should follow a multiplicative function.

Is there any evidence for these specula-

S

THE CLEVER YOUNG THIEF WAS SEVERELY SENTENCED BY THE RATHER GRIM-FACED JUDGE

Kernel Assertions

[THE THIEF] [WAS] [CLEVER]

[THE THIEF] [WAS] [YOUNG]

[THE JUDGE] [WAS] [RATHER GRIM FACED]

[THE JUDGE] [SENTENCED SEVERELY] [THE THIEF]

As shown, under assertion analysis this sentence breaks down into the following kernels: [*the thief*] [*was*] [*clever*]; [*the thief*] [*was*] [*young*]; [*the judge*] [*was*] [*rather grim faced*]; [*the judge*] [*sentenced severely*] [*the thief*]. You can judge for yourself whether or not these kernels preserve the total meaning of the original sentence, albeit in primitive, childlike form. Now note that there are two basic types of phrases implicit in my bracketing—between-bracket phrases (like *the thief was clever*) and within-bracket phrases (like *rather grim faced*). My proposal here is this: *There are two essentially different types of phrase analyzing processes psychologically—qualifying operations* (between brackets) *and quantifying operations* (within brackets)

tions? Interactions of the qualifying type (between brackets) were investigated by Tannenbaum (cf. Osgood & Tannenbaum, 1955); assertions like *The Chicago Tribune condemns Modern Art* were imbedded in news type messages, and meaning changes for sources and concepts were predicted from the Congruity Hypothesis—results were as predicted. Osgood and Ferguson (cf. Osgood, Suci, & Tannenbaum, 1957) predicted the meanings of adjective/noun combinations (like *listless nurse, sincere scientist, and average husband*) from the meanings of their components (*listless, sincere, nurse, scientist,* and so forth) with reasonable success, except that there was evidence for adjective dominance and negative polarization.

Interactions of the quantifying have been studied by Norman Cliff (1959), using intensive adverb/adjective combinations like *somewhat evil, quite ordinary,* and *very charming,* and by Edmund Howe (1963), using probabilistic adverb/adjective combinations like *possibly evil, probably ordinary,* and *certainly charming;* both types of combination were found to obey a multiplicative function. Howe went further and combined probabilistic and intensive modes of quantifying (e.g., *certainly quite angry*); he concluded that "the data satisfactorily indicate . . . that content-free adverbs of the two classes used here systematically combine with each other [with] predictable multiplicative effects upon adjectives." Of course, there are many other types of phrases that require such quantitative analysis, but a pattern seems to be emerging.

tion of the basic kernel sentence, thereby yielding a uniquely modified meaning of the subject or "topic" of the sentence. So let us now see what, in theory, should happen to our sample sentence as it unreels in the meaningless Word Form Pool. I shall assume that "storage" in the Word Form Pool is limited in duration and that the meaning system can do only one thing at a time—and therefore that phrases will tend to be resolved as units in the order of their appearance. I shall also assume that within-bracket (quantifying) phrases are resolved prior to between-bracket (qualifying) assertions whenever the same sentential material is involved.

A hypothetical series of operations upon inputs from the Word Form Pool which generate semantic modifications as outputs is shown in the following display: [3]

	Input	*Operation*	*Output*
(1)	THE CLEVER YOUNG . . .	—	—
(2)	THIEF WAS . . . [CLEVER]	$N_1^0 \xrightarrow{+} A_1^0$	N_1^1
(3)	$[N_1^1]$ [YOUNG]	$N_1^1 \xrightarrow{+} A_2^0$	N_1^2
(4)	$[N_1^2]$ [WAS] SEVERELY . . .	—	—
(5)	$[N_1^2]$ [WAS] [SEVERELY] SENTENCED BY . . .	$V_1^0 \times AV_1^0$	V_1^1
(6)	$[N_1^2]$ $[V_1^1]$ THE RATHER . . .	—	—
(7)	$[N_1^2]$ $[V_1^1]$ [THE] [RATHER] GRIM-FACED . . .	$A_3^0 \times AV_2^0$	A_3^1
(8)	$[N_1^2]$ $[V_1^1]$ $[A_3^1]$ JUDGE	$N_2^0 \xrightarrow{+} A_3^1$	N_2^1
(9)	$[N_1^2]$ $[V_1^1]$ $[N_2^1]$	$N_2^1 \xrightarrow{+} N_1^2$	N_2^2
(10)	$N_2^2 =$ the momentary meaning of JUDGE		

Finally, let us look at the cognitive resolution of sentences as wholes. It was Hobart Mowrer's insight, as well as Edward Sapir's, that sentences "interpret" their subjects. Sapir referred to the sentence as being essentially a "topic" plus "commentary." If this is the case, then understanding a sentence psychologically should be a series of phrase resolving interactions terminating in a final resolu-

The then *clever* then *young* (1) appear as meaningless word forms which serve to elicit sequentially their corresponding bundles of semantic features. Until *thief* appears there is no cognitive interaction, since no qualitative or quantitative asser-

---

3. Subscripts indicate specific items; superscripts indicate operations already performed; brackets indicate items in temporary storage; $\rightarrow$ indicates qualifying operation; $\times$ indicates quantifying operation; $+$ indicates associative assertion.

tion has been formed—hence *clever* and *young* are stored temporarily. *The thief was clever* (2) resolves into *thief* once modified [N_1^1] and *The thief* (once modified) *was young* (3) resolves into *thief* modified [N_1^2] which is temporarily stored —but presumably now a rather dynamic thief! Sensory integrations in the Word Form Pool are continuing to be formed; *severely* (4) is differentiated but no interaction is required, and then *sentenced by* appear (5)—promptly yielding the multiplicative $V \times AV$ resolution, which is stored [V_1^1]. Occurrence of *the* and *rather* (6) produce no dynamics, but *grim-faced* (7) generates another multiplicative $A \times AV$ resolution. In Stage (8), *judge was grim faced* is resolved. Now, in Stage (9), we have stored noun *thief* twice modified, verb phrase *was sentenced by* once modified, and noun *judge* once modified. This is the final assertion to be resolved, and I make the dubious assumption (as Chomsky does) that passives must be transformed to actives— hence, that *judge* is the real "topic" of the sentence. This final qualifying assertion resolves into *judge* twice modified —which is the momentary meaning or "image" of *judge* communciated by this sentence.

Does all this seem extraordinarily, perhaps even frighteningly, complicated? Of course it does. But one would not expect Man's unique and highest achievement—sentence understanding and creating—to be exactly simple. The question is whether such complexity is necessary and sufficient to handle the phenomenon, and I suspect my model is not complex and subtle enough. However, it should be kept in mind that the computer program for even a simple operation, such as generating a finite series of numbers according to some rule, looks pretty complicated—yet the computer, once programmed, can complete the entire operation within less than a second. The human brain is a pretty efficient computer, too.

THE QUESTION OF SUFFICIENCY

By way of concluding, let me return to the question of sufficiency. I have no illusions whatsoever about what I have presented here being a complete theory of the sentence. For one thing, I have said less about creating sentences than I will say in an extended version; for another, space limitations have forced me to cut out much of the substantiating data. But even with these items added, my account would remain nothing more than a sketch of what I consider to be some of the essentials in a very complicated process.

Psycholinguists are now busily filling in details of the sketch—an architect's version of a sentence interpreting and generating machine. And there are many architects. George Miller, both in his Presidential Address before the Eastern Psychological Association last year (1962) and in his more recent paper at the International Congress in Washington, has described some extremely significant experiments—one, for example, demonstrating that we can measure the increased time required for sentence understanding as the number of grammatical transformations is increased. In our own laboratory at the Institute of Communications Research, George Kent and Merrill Garrett are following up a lead given them by Ladefoged and Broadbent (1960) —that the apparent occurrence of a "click" given to one ear is displaced toward the syntactic boundaries of a sentenced being fed simultaneously into the other ear; Kenneth Forster is trying to separate the contribution of syntactic variables from both grammatical and semantic sequential dependencies, by using nonsense sentences like *the siths who ouberelled the entis theatly esiled the ongel raton*, under both serial learning and whole learning conditions. And this, of course, is only a small part of the role.

The thing we must avoid, I think, is "explaining" sentence understanding and creating by simply putting a new homunculus in our heads—in this case, a little linguist in every brain. It is true that speakers produce novel sentences all the time, but the semantics *and* the grammatics cannot both be simultaneously novel, or we fail to comprehend. What is novel is the combination, and this is a familiar psychological problem. It is also true that sentences may be ambiguous without syntactic analysis—witness the sentence *They are cooking apples.* But also note the fact that the speaker is never ambiguating (except when he is deliberately punning, i.e., using a metalanguage) and the hearer is never ambiguated in ordinary discourse (he sees the cooks stirring the apples). If the only claim for a little linguist in our heads were disambiguation, then I am sure we are not in trouble—because the very contextual factors the linguist must leave out are the psychologist's strength in dealing with language "as she is spoke." Let us therefore strive for psychological theories of the sentence which are part of our theories of behavior in general.

ABELSON, R. P. Computer simulation of "hot cognition." New Haven: Yale University, 1963. (Mimeo)

CHOMSKY, N. Syntactic structures. The Hague: Mouton, 1957.

CHOMSKY, N. Review of B. F. Skinner, *Verbal behavior. Language*, 1959, **35**, 26-58.

CLIFF, N. Adverbs as multipliers. *Psychol. Rev.*, 1959, **66**, 27-44.

DEESE, J. On the structure of associative meaning. *Psychol. Rev.*, 1962, **69**, 161-75.

ERVIN, S. M. Changes with age in the verbal determinants of word-association. *Amer. J. Psychol.*, 1961, **74**, 361-72.

ERVIN, S. M. Correlates of associative frequency. *J. verbal Learn. verbal Behav.*, 1963, **1**, 422-31.

GIBSON, J. J. The useful dimensions of sensitivity. *Amer. Psychologist*, 1963, **18**, 1-15.

HEBB, D. O. *The organization of behavior. A neurophysiological theory.* New York: Wiley, 1949.

HEBB, D. O. The semiautonomous process: Its nature and nurture. *Amer. Psychologist*, 1963, **18**, 16-27.

HOWE, E. S. Probabilistic adverbial qualification of adjectives. *J. verbal Learn. verbal behav.*, 1963, **1**, 225-42.

HULL, C. L. Knowledge and purpose as habit mechanisms. *Psychol. Rev.*, 1930, **37**, 511-25.

JAKOBSON, R. Boas view of grammatical meaning. *Amer. Anthropologist*, 1959, **61**, 139-45.

JOHNSON, N. F. Linguistic models and the functional units of language. Unpublished manuscript, University of Ohio, 1963.

KATZ, J. J., & FODOR, J. A. The structure of a semantic theory. *Language*, 1963, **39**, 170-210.

LADEFOGED, P. & BROADBENT, D. Perception of sequence in auditory events. *J. exp. Psychol.*, 1960, **12**, 162-70.

LAMBERT, W. E., & JAKOBOVITS, L. A. The case for semantic satiation. Montreal: McGill University, 1963. (Mimeo)

MILLER, G. A. Some psychological studies of grammar. *Amer. Psychologist*, 1962, **17**, 748-62.

MILLER, G. A., GALANTER, E., & PRIBRAM, K.H. *Plans and the structure of behavior.* New York: Holt, 1960.

MOWRER, O. H. The psychologist looks at language. *Amer. Psychologist*, 1954, **9**, 660-94.

OSGOOD, C. E. A behavioristic analysis of perception and meaning as cognitive phenomena. *Symposium on cognition. University of Colorado, 1955.* Cambridge: Harvard Univer. Press, 1957.

OSGOOD, C. E. Behavior theory and the social sciences. *Behav. Sci.*, 1956, **1**, 167-85.

OSGOOD, C. E. Motivational dynamics of language behavior. In M. R. Jones (Ed.), *Nebraska Symposium on Motivation: 1957.* Lincoln: Univer. Nebraska Press, 1957.

OSGOOD, C. E. Psycholinguists. In S. Koch (Ed.), *Psychology: A study of a science.* New York: McGraw-Hill, 1963.

OSGOOD, C. E., SAPORTA, S., & NUNNALLY, J. C. Evaluative assertion analysis. *Litera*, 1956, **3**, 47-102.

OSGOOD, C. E., SUCI, G. J., & TANNENBAUM, P. H. *The measurement of meaning.* Urbana: Univer. Illinois Press, 1957.

OSGOOD, C. E., & TANNENBAUM, P. H. The principle of congruity in the prediction of attitude change. *Psychol. Rev.*, 1955, **62**, 42-55.

POLLIO, H .R. Some semantic relations among word-associates. *Amer. J. Psychol.*, 1963, in press.

SKINNER, B. F. *Verbal behavior.* New York: Appleton-Century-Crofts, 1957.

STAATS, A. W., STAATS, C. K., FINLEY, J. R., & MINKE, K. A. Mediating responses in the operant conditioning of word classes. Technical report No. 21, 1961, 2794(02), Office of Naval Research.

TANNENBAUM, P. H., & STOLZ, W. S. Markov chains in the grammatical structure of English. Madison: University of Wisconsin, 1963. (Mimeo)

TYLER, V. O., JR. Sensory integration with and without reinforcement. *J. exp. Psychol.*, 1962, **63**, 381-6.

40 / Could Meaning Be an r_m?[1]

JERRY A. FODOR, *Massachusetts Institute of Technology*

This paper is primarily devoted to an investigation of the cogency of mediational accounts of linguistic reference. As Chomsky (1959) has extensively discussed the inadequacies of so-called "single-stage" accounts of language, I shall not review at great length the history of attempts to accommodate verbal behavior within learning theory by equating learning the meaning of a word with establishing a simple S-R connection. Since, however, it has been the failure of such attempts that has prompted psychologists to adopt mediational models, a brief review of the nature of their inadequacies is in order. Suffice it to recall the single-stage models have invariably suffered from three defects that are jointly sufficient to establish the inadequacy of simple S-R theories of meaning.

First, though there can be no objection to considering the verbalizations of fluent speakers to be "linguistic responses," one must not suppose that, in this context, "response" means what it usually means: "A stimulus-occasioned act. An (act) correlated with stimuli, whether the correlation is untrained or the result of training" (Kimble, 1961, glossary). On the contrary, a striking feature of linguistic behavior is its freedom from the control of specifiable local stimuli or independently identifiable drive states. In typical situations, what is said may have no obvious correlation with conditions in the immediate locality of the speaker or with his recent history of deprivation or reward. Conversely, the situations in which such correlations do obtain (the man dying of thirst who predictably gasps "Water") are intuitively highly atypical.

Indeed, the evidence for the claim that linguistic responses are responses *in the strict sense* would appear to be non-existent. There is no more reason to believe that the probability of an utterance of "book" is a function of the number of books in the immediate locale than there is to believe that the probability of an utterance of the word "person" or "thing" is a function of the number of persons or things in view. Lacking such evidence, what prompts one to these beliefs is, first, a confusion of the strict sense of "response" ("a stimulus-correlated act") with the loose sense in which the term applies to *any* bit of behavior, stimulus-correlated or otherwise; and second, a philosophy of science which erroneously supposes that unless all behavior is held to consist of responses in the strict sense some fundamental canon of scientific method is violated. But the claim that behavior consists solely of responses cannot be established on methodological grounds alone. On the contrary, such a claim constitutes an extremely general empirical hypothesis about the degree to which behavior is under the control of specifiable local stimulation.

The second inadequacy of simple S-R models of language is also a consequence of the identification of verbalizations with responses. In laboratory situations, an organism is said to have mastered a response when it can be shown that it produces any of an indefinite number of functionally equivalent acts under the appropriate stimulus conditions. That some reasonable notion of functional

From the *Journal of Verbal Learning and Verbal Behavior*, 1965, 4, 73-81, with permission of the author and publisher, Academic Press, Inc.
1. This work was supported in part by the United States Army, Navy, and Air Force, under Contract D.A. 36-039-AMC-03200 (E), The National Science Foundation (Grant G.P.-2495), The National Institutes of Health (MH-04737-04), The National Aeronautics and Space Administration (N.s.G.-496); and in part by the United States Air Force (E.S.D. Contract A.F. 19(628)-2487). This paper although based on work sponsored by the United States Air Force, has not been approved or disapproved by that Agency.

equivalence can be specified is essential, since we cannot, in general, require of two actions that they be identical either in observable properties or in their physiological basis in order to be manifestations of the same response. Thus, a rat has "got" the bar-press response if and only if it habitually presses the bar upon food deprivation. Whether it presses with its left or right front paw or with three or six grams of pressure is, or may be, irrelevant. Training is to some previously determined criterion of homogeneity of performance, which is another way of saying that what we are primarily concerned with are functional aspects of the organism's behavior. We permit variation among the actions belonging to a response so long as each of the variants is functionally equivalent to each of the others. In short, a response is so characterized as to establish an equivalence relation among the actions which can belong to it. Any response for which such a relation has *not* been established is *ipso facto* inadequately described.

We have just suggested that it is not in general possible to determine stimuli with which verbal responses are correlated. It may now be remarked that it is not in general possible to determine when two utterances are functionally equivalent, i.e., when they are instances of the same verbal response. This point is easily overlooked since it is natural to suppose that functional equivalence of verbal responses can be established on the basis of phonetic or phonemic identity. This is, however, untrue. Just as two physiologically distinct actions may both be instances of a bar-press response, so two phonemically distinct utterances may be functionally equivalent for a given speaker or in a given language. Examples include such synonymous expressions as "bachelor" and "unmarried man," "perhaps" and "maybe," etc. Conversely, just as an action is not an instance of a bar-press response (however

much it may resemble actions that are) unless it bears the correct functional relation to the bar, so two phonemically identical utterances—as, for example, utterances of "bank" in (1) and (2)—may, when syntactic and semantic considerations are taken into account, prove to be instances of quite different verbal responses:

(1) The bank is around the corner.
(2) The plane banked at forty-five degrees.

It appears, then, that the claim that verbal behavior is to be accounted for in terms of S-R connections has been made good at neither the stimulus nor the response end. Not only are we generally unable to identify the stimuli which elicit verbal responses, we are also unable to say when two bits of behavior are manifestations of the same response and when they are not. That this is no small difficulty is evident when we notice that the problem of characterizing functional equivalence for verbal responses is closely related to the problem of characterizing such semantic relations as synonymy; a problem for which no solution is at present known (cf. Katz and Fodor, 1963).

Finally, the identification of verbalizations with responses suffers from the difficulty that verbalizations do not admit of such indices of response strength as frequency and intensity. It is obvious, but nevertheless pertinent, that verbal responses which are equally part of the speaker's repertoire may differ vastly in their relative frequency of occurrence ("heliotrope" and "and" are examples in the case of the idiolect of this writer), and that intensity and frequency do not covary (the morpheme in an utterance receiving emphatic stress is not particularly likely to be a conjunction, article, preposition, etc., yet these "grammatical" morphemes are easily the most frequently occurring ones). What is perhaps true is

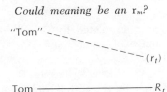

Tom ——————————— R_t

FIG. 1. Pattern of conditioning responsible for the understanding of the word "Tom" (after Mowrer, 1960).

that one can vary the frequency or intensity of a verbal response by the usual techniques of selective reinforcement.[2] This shows that verbal behavior can be conditioned but lends little support to the hypothesis that conditioning is essential to verbal behavior.

Faced with these and other difficulties, a number of learning theorists have acknowledged the necessity of abandoning the simpler S-R accounts of language. What has not been abandoned, however, is the belief that *some* version of conditioning theory will prove adequate to explain the characteristic features of verbal behavior, and, in particular, the referential functions of language. I wish to consider the extent to which more complicated versions of conditioning theory may succeed where simple S-R models have failed.

The strength of single-stage S-R theories lies in the fact that they produce an unequivocal account of what it is for a word to refer to something. According to such theories, w refers to x just in case:

(3) There is a response R such that the presentation of x increases the probability of R, and such that R is nonverbal;

(4) the utterance of w increases the probability of R being produced by a hearer;

(5) the presentation of x increases the probability of the utterance of w.

Thus, on the S-R account, "apple" refers to apples just because

(6) there is some non-verbal response (reaching, eating, salivating, etc.) the probability of which is increased by the presentation of apples, and

(7) the utterance of "apple" tends to increase the probability of that response being produced by a hearer;

(8) the presentation of apples tends to increase the probability of the utterance of "apple."

The weakness of the single-stage S-R theory lies largely in the failure of words and their referents to satisfy conditions (4) and (5). That is, utterances of words do not, in general, serve as stimuli for gross, nonverbal responses, nor can such utterances in general be viewed as responses to specifiable stimuli. What is needed, then, is a version of conditioning theory which provides an account of reference as explicit as that given by single-stage S-R theories; but does not require of verbalizations that they satisfy such postulates as (4) and (5). It has been the goal of much recent theorizing in psycholinguistics to provide such an account in terms of mediating responses.

Consider, for example, the following passage from Mowrer (1960, p. 144).

As Figure 1 shows, the word "Tom" acquired its meaning, presumably, by being associated with, and occurring in the context of, Tom as a real person. Tom himself has elicited in John, Charles, and others who have firsthand contact with him a total reaction that we can label R_t, of which r_t is a component. And as a result of the paired presentation of occurrence of "Tom"-the-word and Tom-the-person, the component, or "detachable," reaction, r_t, is shifted from the latter to the former.

It is clear that this theory differs from S-R theories primarily in the introduction of the class of constructs of which r_t is a member. In particular, it is with r_t the "detached component," and not with R_t,

2. It is possible to raise doubts about the possibility of operant conditioning of verbal behavior. Cf. Krasner (1958).

the gross response, that Mowrer identifies the meaning of the word "Tom."

The differences between r_t and R_t thus determine the difference between Mowrer's approach to verbal behavior and single-stage theories. In particular,

(9) while R_t is an overt response, or, at any event, a response that may have overt components, r_t is a theoretical entity; a construct postulated by the psychologist in order to explain the relation between such gross responses as R_t and such stimuli as utterances of "Tom." Hence,

(10) occurrences of mediating responses, unlike occurrences of overt responses, are not, in general, directly observable. Though it *may* be assumed that progress in physiology should uncover states of organisms the occurrence of which may be identified with occurrences of mediating responses, r_t and other such mediators are, in the first instance, functionally characterized. Hence, whatever evidence we have for the correctness of the explanatory models in which they play a role, is *ipso facto* evidence for their existence.

(11) The relation of r_t to R_t is that of proper part to whole. It is important to notice that for each r_i and R_i, $r_i \neq R_i$ is a basic assumption of this theory. In each case where it does not hold, mediation theory is indistinguishable from single-stage theory. To put it the other way around, single-stage theory is the special case of mediation theory where $r_i = R_i$.

It is clear that the introduction of mediating responses such as r_t will render a learning-theoretic approach to meaning impervious to some of the objections that can be brought against single-stage theories. For example, the failure of verbalizations to satisfy (4) and (5) is not an objection to theories employing responses, since it may be claimed that verbalizations do satisfy (12) and (13).

(12) If r_i is a mediating response

related to w_i as r_t is related to "Tom"; then the utterance of w_i increases the probability of r_i.

(13) If S_i is an object related to R_i as Tom is related to R_t, and if r_i is a mediating response related to R_i as r_t is related to R_t; then the presentation of S_i increases the probability of r_i. Since mediating responses are not directly observable, and since the psychologist need make no claim as to their probable physiological basis, such postulates as (12) and (13) may prove very difficult to refute.

The result of postulating such mediating events as r_t in the explanation of verbal behavior is, then, that an account of reference may be given that parallels the explanation provided by single stage S-R theories except that (4) and (5) are replaced by (12) and (13). Roughly speaking, a word refers to an object just in case first, utterances of the word produce in hearers a mediating response that is part of the gross response that presentation of the object produces and second, presentation of the object produces in speakers a mediating response which has been conditioned to occurrences of the relevant word.

A rather natural extension of Mowrer's theory carries us from an explanation of how words function as symbols to an account of the psychological mechanisms underlying the understanding and production of sentences:

What, then, is the function of the sentence "Tom is a thief?" Most simply and most basically, it appears to be this. "Thief" is a sort of "unconditioned stimulus" . . . which can be depended upon to call forth an internal reaction which can be translated into, or defined by, the phrase "a person who cannot be trusted," one who "takes things, steals." When, therefore, we put the word, or sign, "Tom" in front of the sign "thief," as shown in Figure 2, we create a situation from which we can predict a fairly definite result. On the basis of the familiar principle of conditioning, we would expect that some

"Tom (is a) thief"

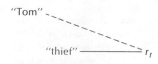

FIG. 2. Pattern of conditioning responsible for the understanding of the sentence "Tom is a thief" (after Mowrer, 1960).

of the reaction evoked by the second sign, "thief," would be shifted to the first sign, "Tom," so that Charles, the hearer of the sentence, would thereafter respond to the word. "Tom," *somewhat as he had previously responded to the word "thief"* (p. 139).

Or, as Mowrer puts it slightly further on,

[The word "thief" is] presumed to have acquired its distinctive meaning by having been used in the presence of, or to have been, as we say, "associated with" actual thieves. Therefore, when we make the sentence, "Tom (is a) thief," it is no way surprising or incomprehensible that the r_t reaction gets shifted . . . from the word, "thief" to the word, "Tom" (p. 144).

It thus appears to be Mowrer's view that precisely the same process that explains the shifting of r_t from occasions typified by the presence of Tom to occasions typified by the utterance of "Tom" may be invoked to account for the association of the semantic content of the predicate with that of the subject in such assertive sentences as "Tom is a thief." In either case, we are supposed to be dealing with the conditioning of a mediating response to a new stimulus. The mechanism of predication differs from the mechanism of reference only in that in the former case the mediating response is conditioned from a word to a word and in the latter case from an object to a word.

Thus, a view of meaning according to which it is identified with a mediating response has several persuasive argu-

ments in its favor. First, it yields a theory that avoids a number of the major objections that can be brought against single stage S-R theories. Second, it appears to provide an account not only of the meaning of individual words, but also of the nature of such essential semantic relations as predication. Third, like single-stage S-R theories, it yields a conception of meaning that is generally consonant with concepts employed in other areas of learning theory. It thus suggests the possibility that the development of an adequate psycholinguistics will only require the employment of principles already invoked in explaining non-verbal behavior. Finally, these benefits are to be purchased at no higher price than a slight increase in the abstractness permitted in psychological explanations. We are allowed to interpose s-r chains of any desired length between the S's and R's that form the observation base of our theory. Though this constitutes a proliferation of unobservables, it must be said that the unobservables postulated are not different *in kind* from the S's and R's in terms of which single-stage theories are articulated. It follows that, though we are barred from direct, observational verification of statements about mediating responses, it should prove possible to infer many of their characteristics from those that S's and R's are observed to have.

Nevertheless, the theory of meaning implicit in the quotations from Mowrer cited above is thoroughly unsatisfactory. Nor is it obvious that this inadequacy is specific to the version of the mediation theory that Mowrer espouses. Rather, I shall try to show that there are chronic weaknesses which infect theories that rely upon mediating responses to explicate such notions as reference, denotation, or meaning. If this is correct, then the introduction of such mediators in learning-theoretic accounts of language cannot serve to provide a satisfactory answer to the charges that have been brought against single-stage theories.

In the first place, we must notice that Mowrer's theory of predication at best fails to be fully general. Mowrer is doubtless on to something important when he insists that a theory of predication must show how the meaning of a sentence is built up out of the meanings of its components. But it is clear that the simple conditioning of the response to the predicate to the response to the subject, in terms of which Mowrer wishes to explain the mechanism of composition, is hopelessly inadequate to deal with sentences of any degree of structural complexity. Thus, consider:

(14) "Tom is a perfect idiot."

Since what is said of Tom here is not that he has the properties of prefection and idiocy, it is clear that the understanding of (14) cannot consist in associating with "Tom" the responses previously conditioned to "perfect" and "idiot." It is true that the meaning of (14) *is,* in some sense, a function of the meaning of its parts. But to understand (14) one must understand that "perfect" modifies "idiot" and not "Tom," and Mowrer's transfer of conditioning model fails to explain either how the speaker obtains this sort of knowledge, or how he employs it in understanding sentences. Analogous difficulties can be raised about

(15) "Tom is not a thief."

Lack of generality is, however, scarcely the most serious charge that can be brought against Mowrer's theory. Upon closer inspection, it appears that the theory fails even to account for the examples invoked to illustrate it. To begin with, the very fact that the same mechanism is supposed to account for the meaning of names such as "Tom" and of predicates such a "thief" ought to provide grounds for suspicion, since the theory offers no explanation for the obvious fact that names and predicates are quite different kinds of words. Notice, for example, that we ask:

(16) "What does 'thief' mean?"
but not
(17) "What does 'Tom' mean?"
and

(18) "Who is Tom?"
but not
(19) "Who is thief?"

All this indicates what the traditional nomenclature already marks: there is a distinction to be drawn between names and predicates. A theory of meaning which fails to draw this distinction is surely less than satisfactory.

Again, it is certainly not the case that, for the vast majority of speakers, "thief" acquired its meaning by "having been used in the presence of . . . actual thieves." Most well-brought-up children know what a thief is long before they meet one, and are adequately informed about dragons and elves though encounters with such fabulous creatures are, presumably, very rare indeed. Since it is clearly unnecessary to keep bad company to fully master the meaning of the word "thief," a theory of language assimilation must account for communication being possible between speakers *who have in fact learned items of their language under quite different conditions.* Whatever it is we learn when we learn what "thief" means, it is something that can be learned by associating with thieves, reading about thefts, asking a well-informed Englist speaker what "thief" means, etc. Though nothing prevents Mowrer from appealing to some higher-level conditioning to account for verbal learning of linguistic items, it is most unclear how such a model would explain the fact that commonality of response can be produced by such strikingly varied histories of conditioning.

Nor does the mediation theory of predication appear to be satisfactory. It is generally the case, for example, that conditioning takes practice, and that continued practice increases the availability of the response. But, first, there is no reason to suppose that the repetition of simple assertive sentences is required for understanding, or even that it normally facilitates understanding. On the contrary, it would appear that speakers are capable of understanding sentences they have never heard before without difficulty, that the latency for response to novel sentences is not strikingly higher than the latency for response to previously encountered sentences (assuming, of course, comparability of length, grammatical structure, familiarity of vocabulary, etc.), and that repetition of sentential material produces "semantic satiation" rather than increase of comprehension. Second, the conditioning model makes it difficult to account for the fact that we do not always believe what we are told. Hearing someone utter "Tom is a thief" may, of course, lead me to react to Tom as I am accustomed to react to thieves; but I am unlikely to lock up the valuables *unless I have some reason to believe that what I hear is true.* Though this fact is perfectly obvious, it is unclear how it is to be accounted for on a model that holds that my understanding of a sentence consists in having previously distinct responses conditioned to one another. It might, of course, be maintained that the efficacy of conditioning in humans is somehow dependent upon cognitive attitude. This reply would not, however, be of aid to Mowrer, since it would commit him to the patently absurd conclusion that a precondition for understanding a sentence is believing that it is true; and, conversely, that it is impossible to understand a sentence one does not believe. Third, if my understanding of "Tom is a thief" consists of a transference of a previously established reaction to "thief" to a previously established reaction to "Tom," it is difficult to account for the fact that I, a speaker who does not know Tom and therefore has no previously established response to utterances of the word "Tom," am perfectly capable of grasping that sentence. It is clear what the story ought to be: I know that "Tom" is a name (a bit of information which, by the way, I did *not* pick up by hearing "Tom" uttered "in the presence of . . . or, as we say 'associated with'" names), and I therefore know that the sentence "Tom is a thief" claims that someone named Tom is a thief. What is not clear, however, is how a story of this sort is to be translated into a conditioning model.

Some more serious difficulties with mediation theories of reference now need to be investigated.

According to our reconstruction, the mediation theorist wishes to hold, in effect, that a sufficient condition of w_i

standing for S_i is that it elicits a response r_i such that r_i is part of R_i. It is clear, however, that such a theory will require at least one additional postulate: namely, that each fractional response which mediates the reference of an unambiguous sign belongs to one and only one gross response. For, consider the consequence of rejecting this postulate. Let us suppose that the unambiguous word w_i evokes the mediating response r_i and that r_i is a member of both R_i and R_j, the functionally distinct unconditioned gross responses to S_i and S_j, respectively. The assumptions that R_i and R_j are functionally distinct and that w_i is univocal, jointly entail that S_i and S_j cannot both be referents of w_i. But if S_i and S_j are *not* both referents of w_j, then the principle that membership of a fractional response in a gross response is a sufficient condition for the former to mediate references to stimuli that elicit the latter has been violated. For, since r_i belongs to both R_i and R_j, applying this principle would require us to say that w_i refers both to S_i and S_j. Hence, if we are to retain the central doctrine that a sufficient condition for any w to refer to any S is that it elicit a part of the relevant R, we will have to hold that the fractional responses which mediate unambiguous signs are themselves unambiguous, i.e. that they belong to only one gross response. If, conversely, we do *not* adopt this condition—if we leave open the possibility that r_i might belong to some gross response other than R_i —then clearly the elicitation of r_i by w_i would at best be a *necessary* condition for w_i referring to S_i.

The same point can be made in a slightly different way. All the learning-theoretic accounts of meaning we have been discussing agree in holding that "The essential characteristic of *sign behavior* is that the organism behaves towards the sign . . . in a way that is somehow 'appropriate to' something other than itself" (Osgood, 1957, p. 354), i.e. that signification depends upon transfer of behavior from sign to significate. The distinctive characteristic of mediation theories is simply that they take it to be sufficient for signification if *part* of the behavior appropriate to the significate transfers to the sign. Partial identity is held to be adequate because the mediating response is simply those ". . . reactions in the total behavior produced by the significate . . . [that] . . . are more readily conditionable, less susceptible to extinctive inhibition, and hence will be called forth more readily in anticipatory fashion by the previously neutral [sign] stimulus" (p. 355). In short, mediators are types of anticipatory responses and they act as representatives for the gross responses they anticipate.

But notice that, just as the single-stage theorist must postulate a distinct sort of appropriate behavior (i.e. a distinct gross response) for each distinct significate, so the mediation theorist must postulate a distinct anticipatory response (i.e. a distinct mediator) for each distinct gross response. If this condition were not satisfied, there would exist mediators which can anticipate many different gross responses. Given an occurrence of such an ambiguous mediator, there would be no way of determining *which* gross response it is anticipating. From this it follows that there would be no way of determining the significance of the sign that elicited the mediator. For, the theory only tells us that the significate is that object to which the gross response anticipated by the mediator is appropriate, and this characterization of the significate is informative only if the relevant gross response can be unequivocally specified, given that one knows which mediator has occurred.

Having established the result that the membership of r_i in more than one R is incompatible with the assumption that w_i is unambiguous, we can now generalize the argument to include the case of ambiguous signs. Since no sign is *essentially* ambiguous (i.e no sign is in principle incapable of being disambiguated) there must always be some set of conditions that, if they obtained, would determine which R is being anticipated by a mediating response elicited by an ambiguous sign. This fact permits us to treat each ambiguous w as a family of univocal homonyms. Each member of such a family is assigned a distinct r such that the specification of that r includes whatever information would be required to choose it as the correct disambiguation of a given occurrence of w. Thus a word like "bat" would be associated with two mediators the specification of one of which would involve information adequate to certify an occurrence of that word as referring to the winged mammal, while the specification of the other would involve information adequate to certify an occurrence of that word as referring to sticks used in ball games. Each of these mediators would thus correspond to precisely one R.

The treatment of ambiguous signs thus differs in no essential respect from the treatment of univocal ones; an ambiguous sign is simply a set of univocal signs all of which happen to have the same acoustic shape. It thus follows that the same arguments that show that the relation of r's to R's must be one to one if mediation theories are to provide a coherent analysis of the reference of univocal signs also show that the relation must be one to one in the case of the r's that mediate the reference of each of the homonymous members of an ambiguous sign. In either case the assumption of a one to one correspondence avoids the possibility that r_i could be part of a response other than that elicited by S_i, since for each linguistically relevant r it is now assumed that there is one and only one R of which it is a part. We can now securely adopt the cardinal principle of mediation theories of reference viz. that w_i refers to S_i just in case r_i belongs to R_i.

Though the adoption of the postulate of a one to one correspondence between mediating and gross responses is clearly necessary if mediation theories are to propose sufficient conditions for linguistic reference, that postulate is subject to two extremely serious criticisms.

In the first place, it would appear that the sorts of response components that become "detached" from gross responses, and which are thus candidates for the position of r_m, are not of a type likely to be associated with R's in a one to one fashion. Rather, they appear to be rather broad, affective reactions that, judging from the results obtained with such testing instruments as the semantic differential, would seem to be common to very many distinct overt responses. Second, even if it should turn out that the detachable components of R's can be placed in one to one correspondence with them, the following difficulty arises on the assumption that such a correspondence obtains.

If we assume a one to one relation between gross and mediating responses, the formal differences between single-stage and mediation theories disappears. So long as each r_i belongs to one and only one R_i, the *only* distinction that can be made between mediation and single-stage views is that, according to the former but not the latter, some of the members of stimulus-response chains invoked in explanations of verbal behavior are supposed to be unobserved. But clearly this property is irrelevant to the explanatory power of the theories concerned. It is thus not possible in principle that mediation theories could represent a significant generalization of single-stage theories so long as the mediating responses in terms of which they are articulated are required to be in one to one correspondence with the observable responses employed in single-stage S-R theories.

To put it slightly differently, two theories that explain the event e_n by claiming that it is causally contingent upon a set of prior events $e_1, e_2, \ldots e_{n-1}$, give substantially identical explanations of e_n if they differ only on the question whether all members of $e_1 \ldots e_{n-1}$ are observ-

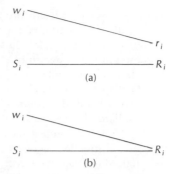

FIG. 3a, 3b. Schematic representation of difference between mediational and single-stage theories of the pattern of conditioning underlying the understanding of the sign w_i. See text.

able. But it would appear that once a one to one association is postulated between mediating responses and the gross responses of which they are a part, precisely this relation obtains between single-stage and response-mediation explanations of verbal behavior. To put it still differently, once we grant a one to one relation between r's *and* R's, we insure that the former lack the "surplus meaning" characteristic or terms designating *bona fide* theoretical entities. Hence, *only* observability is at issue when we argue about whether our conditioning diagrams ought to be drawn as in Figure 3a or as in Figure 3b.

If this argument is correct, it ought to be the case that, granting one to one correspondence between r's and R's, anything that can be said on the mediation-theoretic view can be simply translated into a single-stage language. This is indeed the case since, in principle, nothing prevents the single-stage theorist from identifying the meaning of a word with the most easily elicited part of the response to the object for which the word stands (viz., instead of with the whole of that response). Should the single-stage theorist choose to make such a move, his theory and mediation theory would be literally indistinguishable.

In short, the mediation theorist appears

to be faced with a dilemma. If his theory is to provide a sufficient condition for linguistic reference, he must make the very strong assumption that a one to one correspondence obtains between linguistically relevant mediators and total responses. On the other hand, the assumption that each mediator belongs to one and only one total response appears to destroy any formal distinction between mediation and single-stage theories, since, upon this assumption, the explanations the two sorts of theories provide are distinguished *solely* by the observability of the responses they invoke. It is, of course, possible that some way may be found for the mediation theorist to simultaneously avoid both horns of this dilemma, but it is unclear that this has been achieved by any version of mediation theory so far proposed.

CHOMSKY, N. Review of Skinner's *Verbal behavior.* *Language,* 1959, **35**, 26.

KATZ, J., & FODOR, J. The structure of a semantic theory. *Language,* 1963, **39**, 170-210.

KIMBLE, G. A. *Hilgard and Marquis' Conditioning and learning.* New York: Appleton-Century-Crofts, 1961.

KRASNER, L. Studies of the conditioning of verbal behavior. *Psychol. Bull.,* 1958, **55**, 148-70.

MOWRER, O. *Learning theory and the symbolic processes.* New York: Wiley, 1960.

OSGOOD, C. Motivational dynamics of language behavior. *Nebraska symposium on motivation,* 1957, 348-424.

CONCEPT FORMATION

Research in the area of concept formation concerns itself with a process which is at least one step more complex than that visualized for rote learning. Basically, this process is one of determining and applying rules of selection to a universe of entities. The subject in a concept formation experiment is typically faced with the task of classifying stimuli in a manner which accords with the experimenter's criteria. Through the procedure of being exposed to a variety of stimuli, and being given some information about their class membership, he is expected to arrive at the criteria for their membership. If he is successful, he can correctly classify all future instances of such stimuli, and may also be able to verbalize the basis for their inclusion. He is then said to be using the correct concept.

Traditional logic affords a sound framework for referring to the concept formation task. Let us say that a name has two properties, specifically, denotation and meaning. The denotation of a name is that set of entities to which it applies. The meaning of a name is the rule which determines its correct application to all possible instances. Thus, the name "triangle" is denoted by the set of all triangles, and its meaning is the rule that all three-sided plane figures are members of that denotative set. If we substitute the term "concept" for the term "meaning," it is evident that a concept is a classification rule. This type of terminology has been adopted by Hunt (1962) in his excellent book on concept learning. In the usual concept formation procedure therefore, the subject encounters members of a denotative set as well as non-members of that set (negative instances), and eventually discovers the concept appropriate to the set.

In an operational sense concept attainment requires the attachment of the same response to a number of different stimuli. However, if a paired-associates list has several randomly chosen stimuli each paired with the same response, and the rest paired with another common response, it does not automatically constitute a concept-formation situation. What is essential is that the stimuli be paired with a common response by virtue of some general *rule* which permits their inclusion. Otherwise, there is only denotation but no concept, and the commonality of responses is just a superficial resemblance to a true conceptual problem.

It is the task of psychologists to delineate the variables governing the rate of concept formation, and to provide a theory of the underlying processes. Some variables which have been investigated are the type of concept (conjunctive, disjunctive, etc.), the number of irrelevant dimensions, the number of redundant dimensions, the use of negative instances, previous practice, and certain details of procedure. The apparatus for concept studies is minimal. It can consist simply of a deck of cards, each portraying a given level of each of a number of orthogonal dimensions. For instance, the deck may have three dimensions (color, shape, size), each at two levels (red and blue, square and circle, large and small), making a total of eight cards. The subject must place each card in one of two boxes, and he is told whether his placement was correct or not. Eventually he makes all placements correctly and can state the rule that squares go to the left and circles to the right. Such is the basic procedure, with variations which may include the assignment of names to cards, verbalization of momentary hypotheses, instructions about the type of concept, shifts in the correct concept, and so forth. Strictly speaking, most experiments are concerned with concept *identification* rather than concept *formation*, since the possible dimensions of the stimuli are either obvious or else described beforehand by the experimenter. In a relevant paper, Hovland (1952) calculated the least number of positive and negative instances necessary for correct identification, as a function of the number of dimensions and values used.

The readings below tend to stress theoretical contributions over sheer empirical findings. Four of the articles are concerned with the theoretical implications arising from the results of the reversal shift procedure. The reversal shift had its origin in the continuity-noncontinuity controversy cited in the introduction to Section IV, where it was used with infra-human subjects and called the discrimination reversal problem. It has been a most fruitful device for the analysis of concept identification processes.

The article by Kendler and Kendler considers dual processes in problem solving. The basic data discussed came from comparisons of reversal vs. nonreversal shifts made across species as well as in the developing child. It is suggested that increased facility in executing reversal shifts is associated with linguistic development, which in turn permits the use of efficient mediation processes. A pertinent analysis of mediation in concept formation is also found in Goss (1961).

The Isaacs and Duncan article reports a comparison of reversal versus two types of nonreversal shifts, with proper controls for nonspecific transfer effects. A mediation theory would predict positive transfer for the reversal shift, but the results showed negative transfer. A previous experiment by Harrow and Friedman (1958) provided some of the inspiration for this study.

Restle's article develops a mathematical model for concept identification. It is cognitive in that it assumes a strategy-selection approach. Restle shows that so far as errors are concerned, it makes no difference whether a subject considers one strategy (hypothesis) at a time, all strategies at a time, or a random sample of strategies.

The Bower and Trabasso article examines the all-or-none vs. incremental hypotheses (discussed in Section IV) within the context of concept identification. With a reversal-nonreversal shift procedure reminiscent of the early experiment by Prentice (1949), the results clearly supported the all-or-none position.

The intriguing paper by Bogartz shows that the familiar superiority of reversal over nonreversal shifts can be obtained even in the absence of *dimensions* among the stimuli. It would seem that the role of dimensions in concept identification needs further elucidation.

Goss, A. Verbal mediating responses and concept formation. *Psychol. Rev.*, 1961, **68**, 248-74.

Harrow, M., & Friedman, G. B. Comparing reversal and nonreversal shifts in concept formation with partial reinforcement controlled. *J. exp. Psychol.*, 1958, **55**, 592-8.

Hovland, C. D. A "communication analysis" of concept learning. *Psychol. Rev.*, 1952, **59**, 461-72.

Hunt, E. B. *Concept learning: An information processing problem.* New York: John Wiley & Sons, 1962.

Prentice, W. C. H. Continuity in human learning. *J. exp. Psychol.*, 1949, **39**, 187-94.

41 / Vertical and Horizontal Processes in Problem Solving [1]

HOWARD H. KENDLER, *New York University*
AND TRACY S. KENDLER, *Barnard College*

The present paper is concerned with *an* approach—and not *the* approach—to the universally appealing but nevertheless unpopular research area of problem solving. Problems of problem solving have proved to be particularly refractory to psychologists. More often than not the uncommon researcher with the temerity to attack some aspect of reasoning retreats to more secure and conventional problems when he discovers that his sorties fail to achieve any impressive victory. As a result the literature of problem solving is almost chaotic because it is so heavily sprinkled with isolated bits of information (Duncan, 1959).

Perhaps the present stage of development of psychology does not justify the strategy of investigating such a complex phenomenon. Fortunately, nor not, science has no built-in traffic lights to inform investigators when to proceed. It may be a risky and potentially unfruitful gambit to investigate problem solving but then again it may not be. In addition to the intrinsic interest of the area it does

From the *Psychological Review*, 1962, **69**, 1-16, with permission of the authors and the publisher.
1. An earlier version of this paper was delivered by Howard H. Kendler as an invited address to the 1960 meeting of the Eastern Psychological Association, which was held in New York City. The authors are indebted to the Office of Naval Research and the National Science Foundation for their support of the research reported in this paper.

offer a challenge to those psychologists who are interested in testing the generality of any set of theoretical principles stemming from other areas of behavior (e.g., learning, perception).

This paper initially will make fleeting references to some methodological problems with which a researcher in the field of reasoning must contend. Then a simple pretheoretical model of problem solving will be described, followed by a report of research which the model generated, and which in turn is shaping the model itself.

METHODOLOGICAL PROBLEMS IN PROBLEM SOLVING RESEARCH

Anybody who does research is—or should be—aware that every decision he makes cannot be justified by facts or logic. Some decisions must be made on the basis of personal intuition. This is particularly true for the researcher in problem solving who must make three strategic decisions which cannot help but have profound influences on his research and the ideas they generate (Kendler, 1961). These decisions, which are not completely independent, are related to the place of problem solving in psychology, the use of complex or simple experimental tasks, and the selection of a pretheoretical model to guide research. Considering the volitional nature of these problems, as well as the current status of psychological knowledge, it would be both inappropriate and erroneous to consider these methodological problems as offering only one sensible alternative. Adopting this point of view would do much to minimize the needless disputation that seems to perennially surround matters of research strategy.

Accepting the principle that a basic research strategy is not simply an outgrowth of logical and factual considerations does not reduce one to making decisions in either a haphazard or random manner. A given strategy can be adopted on the basis of rational considerations as long as it is realized that other reasonable attitudes might lead to the adoption of different decisions.

The history of problem solving in particular and psychology in general suggests that problem solving can best be conceptualized not as a basic psychological process, but instead as one that reflects the interaction of more fundamental processes (e.g., learning, perception, and motivation).

If problem solving is not viewed as a unitary process, how is an appropriate experimental situation selected to investigate it? One possibility is that a problem can be selected from a "true life" situation such as troubleshooting electronic equipment. Or problems can be invented (Duncker, 1945; Maier, 1930) that capture the flavor, if only partially, of problems we meet in everyday life.

A more analytical approach can be taken to the selection of an experimental situation to investigate problem solving. If problem solving is compounded of elementary behavioral processes, then it may be more strategic to devise some simple problems in which the relationships of fundamental psychological mechanisms to problem solving are highlighted. That is, tasks should be devised not to duplicate or imitate everyday problems, but instead to isolate and magnify the basic mechanisms that operate in such complex tasks.

This analytical approach which is favored by the authors suffers from one major drawback. How is it possible to know the basic mechanisms of problem solving prior to their discovery? Obviously, excepting divination, there is no method. But this does not prevent the analytical approach from operating. The researcher can prejudge theoretical issues by formulating a model of what he guesses problem solving to be like. The model can guide the investigator in selecting the hypotheses to test, as well as the experimental situations in which to test them.

This brings us to the third and most important decision a problem solving researcher has to make: his choice of a pretheoretical model (Koch, 1959). A pretheoretical model is not equivalent to a theory. The criterion of validity cannot properly be applied to it because essentially a pretheoretical model is an informal conception that operates as an analogy (Lachman, 1960). It is conceivable that different models (e.g., learning, perception, information theory) can all lead to fruitful and valid theories of problem solving.

Psychologists have many possibilities from which to choose their model. These models can be conveniently divided into two main categories: the empirical model that springs primarily from experimental data, and the formal model that is usually generated by mathematical or logical systems. Among the empirical models that have achieved some acceptance are those that are based on introspective findings (e.g., the four successive stage model of "preparation," "incubation," "inspiration," and finally "verification"), the facts of perception, and those of learning. Some formal models used are those dependent upon stochastic models, game theory, and the operation of computers.

The present authors adopted an S-R learning pretheoretical model. The decision no doubt was influenced by professional training and past research efforts. But other considerations entered. For the past 4 decades S-R learning psychologists have probably been the most active experimental and theoretical group in psychology. To some, if not a large, extent this can be attributed to the fruitful and cleansing effect S-R language has upon designing, reporting, and interpreting research. S-R language forces the psy-chologist to focus his attention on objectively defined environmental and behavior variables and thus encourages the collection of data and the testing of ideas. The efforts of S-R learning psychologists have supplied a host of facts, concepts, and hypotheses that can be exploited in an exploratory excursion into the realm of problem solving.

The facts and theories of learning, however, do not spontaneously coalesce to form a model that can guide research in problem solving. Some selection must be made. S-R learning theory does not represent a single organized formulation. Anyone who is familiar with the systematic orientations of Hull (1952), Guthrie (1952), Spence (1956), and Skinner (1953) is aware of this. Many of these systematic differences, however, become attenuated and some even disappear when viewed from the distance of problem solving behavior. It is possible and perhaps even profitable to develop a learning model for problem solving that ignores many of the points of disagreement among S-R theories.

Much of the objection to S-R language stems from the apparent discrepancy between active, flowing behavior and the inert, static, single S-R association. Using S-R language does not mean that complex behavior *actually* consists of S-R connections. After analyzing the concept of light, Toulmin (1953), concludes: "We do not *find* light atomized into individual rays: we *represent* it as consisting of such rays" (p. 29). Applying the same idea to the concept of the S-R association: "We do not *find* behavior atomized into individual S-R associations: we *represent* it as consisting of such S-R associations." The concept of the S-R association, therefore, must be judged not in terms of its ability to provide a clear image of behavior, but rather in its capacity to represent the facts of behavior.

PRETHEORETICAL MODEL OF PROBLEM SOLVING

An S-R model needs to represent two important characteristics of problem solving behavior. These characteristics are behavior is continuous, and at any one time behavior consists of several habits. The terms "horizontal" and "vertical" are used to refer to these processes; horizontal to the continuity of behavior against the dimension of time, and vertical to the assumption that independent levels of behavior (i.e., S-R units) occur simultaneously.

The assumption that S-R associations do not occur in isolation, but instead are linked together to form integrated, continuous behavior goes back many years (e.g., Watson, 1913). Today the process is most commonly referred to as chaining. Skinner (1953) and his associates have developed powerful techniques that shape behavior into long, complicated chains. The mass of data they have collected suggests important principles governing habit chaining. There is little doubt that when their quasitheoretical system is exploited fully with autoinstructional devices that important insights into problem solving behavior will emerge, particularly in relation to how an added bit of knowledge can trigger problem solution. The kind of chaining with which the Skinnerians have dealt (i.e., adding new S-R units to an already functioning chain) does not exhaust all the problems associated with the horizontal processes of problem solving. Of particular importance to problem solving is the *spontaneous* integration of separate habits which occurs when an organism infers the consequences of combining previously independent S-R units. This kind of chaining was investigated in Kohler's (1925) classical studies of insight and in the more controlled reasoning experiments of Maier (1930). More recently the authors (Kendler & Kendler, 1956, 1961; Kendler,

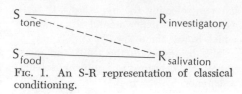

FIG. 1. An S-R representation of classical conditioning.

Kendler, Pliskoff, & D'Amato, 1958) have tried to identify some of the important variables that enable children to combine separate experiences in order to solve an inference-type problem. Much of the research reported in this paper will be concerned with how mediated stimulus and response events aid in the formation of problem solving chains.

The assumption of vertical processes, i.e., the organism responds several different ways at any one time, is also not a novel one. Every psychologist is aware that organisms make several different responses simultaneously, although typically only one is attended to. Sometimes the different responses are interrelated, as is the case between the heart and respiration rates of a fearful organism. In other cases the different responses are independent, e.g., a person's conversation is uninfluenced by his tugging at his ear lobe. The best laboratory example of vertical processes, and one that has much relevance to problem solving, is shown in Figure 1. Those familiar with introductory psychology textbooks will recognize this diagram as representing classical conditioning. Notice that the two solid lines indicate independent S-R units which are operating simultaneously. One is the tone that initiates the "investigatory" response, and the other is the food which elicits salivation. Initially these two associations operate in a *parallel* fashion, but as a result of their simultaneous occurrence an *interaction* takes place which is expressed by the broken line representing the acquired conditioned response.

Obviously the brief reference to horizontal and vertical processes in which it is assumed fundamental S-R principles operate (e.g., discrimination, generalization, etc.) presents at best the barest skeleton of a model of problem solving. It needs the flesh and skin of experimental facts to give it solidity and theoretical principles to clothe it in scientific respectability. Let us now review some of the progress that has been made in this direction.

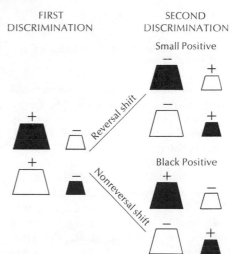

FIG. 2. Examples of a reversal and a nonreversal shift.

CONCEPT LEARNING AND UTILIZATION

Although the primitive model just described fails to generate any research by itself, it does suggest that individual experiments cannot be directed at *problem solving in its entirety*. There are too many aspects to this phenomenon. The researcher, in designing an experiment, must scan the entire problem solving process and then focus upon that segment that promises to yield fruitful results and is also amenable to investigation.

For reasons that will become evident, it was decided to compare reversal and nonreversal shifts in a simple concept learning task. Figure 2 characterizes each kind of shift by showing a *simplified* version of an experimental situation used with children. The stimuli (cups) for their first discrimination differed simultaneously on two dimensions (size and brightness). The subject is rewarded for responses to one dimension (e.g., large cup is positive, small cup is negative). The other dimension is irrelevant. After learning the first discrimination, the subject is forced to shift to another response. In a reversal shift the subject is required to respond to the same dimension on which he was originally trained, but his overt choice has to be reversed, e.g., he has to shift from a *large* cup to a *small* one. For a nonreversal shift the previously irrelevant dimension becomes relevant, e.g., black

becomes positive after large had been positive.

Buss (1953) reported that college students executed a reversal shift more rapidly than a nonreversal shift. He attributed this superiority to the intermittent reinforcements that retard the progress of a nonreversal shift. For example, in Figure 2,[2] when a subject is making a nonreversal shift from large positive to black positive, he is reinforced when choosing the large black cup in preference to the small white cup. This fortuitous reinforcement of the choice of the large cup helps maintain the size discrimination and hence retards the learning of the brightness discrimination. The reversal shift group, on the other hand, receives no reinforcement of the previously correct responses, since they are 100% *non*reinforced.

This analysis is at best incomplete. The work of Kendler and Vineberg (1954) suggested that adult human con-

2. The purpose of Figure 2 is to clarify the meaning of both a reversal and nonreversal shift. It would be misleading to believe that it represents *exactly* the methodology of "reversal-nonreversal" studies reported in this paper. For all experiments reported, except that of Buss (1953), designs were used that controlled for fortuitous intermittent reinforcements effects in a nonreversal shift.

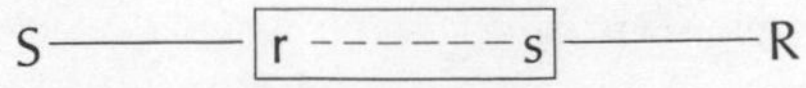

S ——————— | r − − − − − s | ——————— R

FIG. 3. A schematic representation of the mediational hypothesis.

cept learning cannot be represented adequately by a single-unit S-R theory in which the external stimulus is directly connected to the overt response. Instead, a mediational mechanism (see Figure 3) is required which assumes that the external stimulus evokes an implicit response which produces an implicit cue that is connected to the overt response.

It would be useful to digress for a moment to comment about the epistemological status of these inferred stimulus and response events which are enclosed in the rectangle to emphasize their hypothetical character. Although not directly observable, they are "tied to" environmental and behavioral events. The basic assumption of the mediational hypothesis, at least for the time being, is that the implicit stimulus and response events obey the same principles that operate in observable S-R relationships.

The mediational hypothesis has generated confusion. Perhaps the following brief statements will clarify some possible areas of misunderstanding.

1. The mediational hypothesis is neither new nor revolutionary. Meyer (1911) and Watson (1913) referred to it, and Hull (1930) gave it a more formal status by coining the concept of the "pure stimulus act." Guthrie (1952) has always laid heavy stress on a mediational-type hypothesis when emphasizing the importance of proprioceptive stimulation in learning.

2. The implicit stimulus and response events *need not* be conceived as having an existence independent of their relation to independent and dependent variables. These implicit events are theoretical constructs. Their epistemological status is closer to such concepts as drive and habit than to directly observable stimulus and response events.

Some mediating events can conceivably and probably will be coordinated to introspective reports, language behavior, muscular movements, and other observable events. Coordinations of this sort can be useful in developing mediational theory. But such coordinations are not *essential* to mediational theory. The fact that genes are not directly observable (at least according to the geneticists consulted) does not interfere with their theoretical and practical usefulness. Even if it were possible to observe a gene directly, it would be necessary to distinguish between it as an observable entity and as a concept

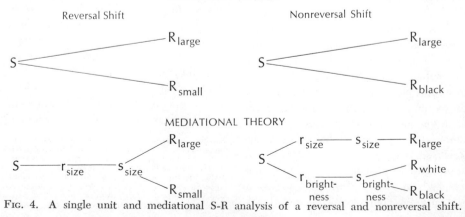

FIG. 4. A single unit and mediational S-R analysis of a reversal and nonreversal shift.

within a nomological network. It would be unwise, and strategically shortsighted, to *identify* mediational events with introspective reports or language behavior, or other observable events. The "validity" of the mediational mechanism does not depend on being coordinated with observable events, but depends instead on being utilized in a successful explanatory system.

Figure 4 characterizes reversal and nonreversal shifts in terms of both a single unit S-R analysis and a mediational one.[3] It would be predicted, according to a single unit hypothesis, that if fortuitous intermittent reinforcements were eliminated from a nonreversal shift, it would occur more rapidly than a reversal shift. The reason for this is that at the time of the shift the difference between the strength of the dominant incorrect habit and the to-be-correct habit is much greater for the reversal, as compared to the nonreversal shift. Consequently more training will be required to make the correct habit dominant in a reversal shift. According to the mediational theory the situation is entirely different. A reversal shift enables the subject to utilize the same mediated response. Only the overt response has to be changed. A nonreversal shift, on the other hand, required the acquisition of a *new* mediated response, the cues of which have to be attached to a *new* overt response. Because the old mediational sequence has to be discarded and a new one formed, the nonreversal shift should be executed more slowly than a reversal shift.[4] Thus, if it were possible to eliminate fortuitous intermittent reinforcements, then the stage would be set for a crucial experiment testing the conflicting implications of the single-unit and mediational S-R theories. The results of a series of such crucial experiments (Buss, 1956; Harrow & Friedman, 1958; Kendler & D'Amato, 1955) have

TABLE 1. *Mean number of trials to criterion on test discrimination for subjects scoring above and below the median on the training discrimination*

Group	Performance on training discrimination	
	Above Median (slow learners)	Below Median (fast learners)
Reversal	24.4	6.0
Nonreversal	9.0	15.5

been consistent with the mediational formulation in showing that college students execute a reversal shift more rapidly than a nonreversal shift. It is important to note that in a similar kind of problem rats find a nonreversal shift easier than a reversal shift (Kelleher, 1956). Thus, one is forced to conclude that a single unit S-R theory accurately represents the behavior of rats, while mediational S-R theory is required for the concept learning of articulate humans.

The discontinuity between the behavior of rats and college students directs one's attention toward the conditions

3. Figure 4 highlights the problem of what are the effective stimuli that are associated to the overt response in both a reversal and nonreversal shift. It is not intended to be a detailed analysis of which there may be several alternatives. For example, in a single unit theory the habit to choose the large container might result from learning two separate specific habits (e.g., the choice of a large black container when coupled with a small white one and the selection of a large white container when paired with a small black one). Another possibility, which would be consistent with Spence's theory (1936), is that the response is to the effective stimulus *large* since responses to the other features of the environment are not consistently reinforced. Similarly adult subjects in a reversal shift might use the mediator *size* or *large* or both. The effective stimulus which is controlling the organism's response must be determined by experimentation. The point made here is that the general implications of the single unit and mediational theories, as discussed in this paper, would be the same for a number of different effective stimuli. 4. There are two possible ways of analyzing the superiority of a reversal shift over a nonreversal shift within an S-R mediational framework. One is to simply count the number of new associations that have to be formed. As Figure 4 indicates only one new association has to be formed in a reversal shift while two have to be formed for a nonreversal shift. Another possibility is that a mediating response is more difficult to extinguish than is an overt response. For the present the formulation can remain open-ended until information relevant to these two alternatives is gathered.

responsible for the development of mediational processes. Somewhere on a hypothetical evolutionary dimension between the rat and college student there should be a point where a transition is made from a single unit to mediational control. An obvious place to locate this point would be in the behavior of young children.

A study with kindergarten children (Kendler & Kendler, 1959) showed that these children as a group executed a reversal and nonreversal shift at approximately the same rate. One might conclude that the point in human development was discovered which was psychologically halfway between the white rat and the college student, since the kindergarten children were neither responding in a single unit nor mediational manner, but instead in some compromise fashion. Another possibility is that the children had reached a transitional stage in development, in which the task to which they were subjected led some to function on a single unit basis, and others to operate with a mediational mechanism. If half of the subjects respond in each way, the total results would have revealed no difference between the two kinds of shifts.

The second alternative seems to fit the data. When the kindergarten children were divided into fast and slow learners on the basis of their performance in the first problem (training discrimination), slow learners performed during the second problem (test discrimination) according to the single unit theory; like rats they found a nonreversal shift easier. Fast learners, on the other hand, performed in accordance with the mediational theory; like college students, they found a reversal shift easier. These results were interpreted as demonstrating that these kindergartners, taken as a group, were in the process of developing mediating responses relevant to this task, and that

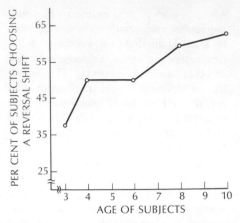

FIG. 5. Percentage of children responding in a reversal shift manner as a function of age.

some were further along than others.

If this interpretation be correct, then it would follow that for a group of younger (i.e., preschool) children a still smaller proportion should develop appropriate mediating responses. It would be expected that such a group, taken as a whole, would show clearcut evidence of the superiority of a nonreversal over a reversal shift. An experiment (Kendler, Kendler, & Wells, 1960) designed to test this hypothesis produced results consistent with this prediction; like rats, nursery school children found a nonreversal shift to be easier than a reversal shift.

In a very recent study the experimental procedure was modified so that after learning the initial discrimination, the children of 3, 4, 6, 8, and 10 years of age who served as subjects, had a choice of either responding in a reversal or a nonreversal manner. Under such circumstances, it would be expected that the proportion of children who respond in a reversal manner would increase with age. Figure 5 shows that the percentage of children who chose a reversal shift rose gradually from 37.5 at 3 to 62.5 at 10.

Generalizing from all of these results,

it would seem that in their early development, children tend to respond in a manner consistent with a single unit S-R theory. With age, they develop a tendency to respond in a mediational manner. The last study cited suggests that it is, or will soon be, possible to ascertain the lawful relationship governing the course of this development.

The point of these experiments is not to classify children into one of two categories: rat-like or human-like. Their aim is to lay the groundwork for experiments designed to investigate the mediational process itself. It one wants to investigate mediational processes, does it not seem sensible to scrutinize them at the time when they are developing? Answering this question in the affirmative, it was decided to investigate the relationship between the hypothesized mediational processes and verbal behavior—a relationship everybody assumes to be intimate and important.

Particularly relevant to this attempt to coordinate verbalization with mediation were observations that during the course of the experiments just described, it was not uncommon for children to verbalize spontaneously the correct solution while simultaneously making an incorrect choice. A few children did this for many consecutive trials. This observation is relevant to the concept of vertical processes. Two chains of habits are occurring simultaneously. One has to do with verbal response; the other with the overt choice. For these children the two chains are parallel, that is, they do not interact.

Luria (1957), the Russian psychologist, made somewhat similar observations in his research with children. He explains this sort of phenomenon in the following way:

In the early stages of child development, speech is only a means of communication with adults and other children. . . . Subsequently it becomes also a means whereby he organizes his own experience and regulates his own actions. So the child's activity is mediated through words (p. 116).

These observations and their interpretations of noninteracting parallel processes point to the complex interrelationships existing between verbal behavior on the one hand and problem solving on the other. If nothing else, they destroy the illusion that it is reasonable to describe an organism as verbal or nonverbal without considering the problem with which it is confronted. The terms verbal and nonverbal become meaningful—and fruitful—when related to specific problem solving tasks.

It would seem fruitful to investigate the cue function of words for children of two age levels. One possibility is that age influences problem solving only in so far as it leads to the acquisition of words. If younger children, say 4 years of age, could acquire the same words as 7-year-olds, they would solve a simple concept-learning problem the same way. The other possibility is that the acquisition of the verbal label by itself is not sufficient; the word must be integrated with other behavior chains to influence problem solving behavior. And for this to happen some developmental changes must first take place.

In order to test these two alternatives, children of 4 and 7 years of age were presented with another variation of the reversal shift problem as shown in Figure 6. They initially learned a simple discrimination between a pair of stimuli that varied simultaneously in size and brightness. In the illustration provided in Figure 6, the large black square is correct. While they were learning, the children were required to verbalize aloud the stimuli to which they were responding. One-third learned to say "large" (or "small" as the case may be) by the simple device of instructing them to tell the experimenter which was correct, the large

FIRST
DISCRIMINATION

SECOND
DISCRIMINATION

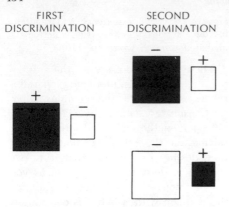

FIG. 6. The experimental procedure used to study the influence of verbal habits on a reversal shift.

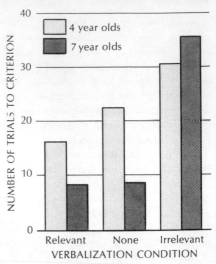

FIG. 7. The effect of verbalizations on a reversal shift for 4- and 7-year-old children.

or the small one. Another third learned to say "black" (or "white") in a corresponding way. The remaining third was not required to say anything. After learning the discrimination, all subjects were presented with a reversal shift. In the example depicted in Figure 6, the shift is to small regardless of size. Thus, the group that initially described the correct stimulus as "large" had verbalized the relevant dimension. The verbal response of "black" was irrelevant to this reversal shift.

Figure 7 shows the results of the three experimental groups for the two age levels. If developmental processes affect the utilization of verbal responses in problem solving, then it would be expected that the three verbalization conditions (which produced a significant main effect) would influence the behavior of the two age groups, differently. These results suggest, but not quite at a significant level, that there is an interaction effect. Figure 7 shows that the younger children profited by making the kind of verbal response appropriate to a reversal shift, while they were hindered by learning inappropriate verbal responses. With no verbalization the 7-year-old children who presumably were responding largely in a mediational manner, accomplished

a reversal shift much more rapidly than their younger counterparts. But unlike the 4-year-olds, they did not profit from being trained to make the relevant responses. At 7 years of age they are capable of making the response themselves and outside help appears to be of little use. In contrast, the influence of irrelevant verbalizations is marked. The performance of the 7-year-olds was even poorer than that of the 4-year-olds, suggesting that the interfering effects of being given an inappropriate mediated response are greater when one is capable of spontaneously generating the correct one (7-year-olds) than when one is not (4-year-olds).

How are these data to be explained? Attributing differences to developmental factors is not sufficient. It is necessary to represent developmental differences in terms of the concepts of the behavior model that is being used. That is, if a verbal label for a young child does not possess the same cue function as it does for an older child, then it becomes necessary to specify how and why this comes about. To some extent this has been done by emphasizing the transi-

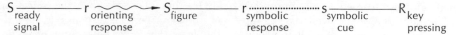

S——————— r ⌣⌣⌣→ S———————— r ·············· s———————— R
 ready   orienting   figure   symbolic   symbolic   key
 signal   response   response   cue   pressing

FIG. 8. The hypothesized behavioral chain operating at the time the subject was being shifted to the second concept. (Capital letters refer to directly observable stimulus and response events, while small letters refer to those that are inferred.)

tion from a single unit to a mediational system, as well as suggesting that with age an increase occurs in interaction among chains of different vertical levels. But obviously this analysis of the developmental process demands further theoretical and empirical development.

These studies are intimately related to the oft-reported finding that many species of subhuman animals are able to make a fairly rapid reversal shift *if* they receive a previous series of such shifts. Rats (Buytendijk, 1930; Krechevsky, 1932) show a marked improvement in executing successive reversals. They finally reach a point (Dufort, Guttman, & Kimble, 1954), in a **T** maze, where they learn to go to a new rewarded goal after making only one error. Even more dramatic are the rapid discrimination reversals exhibited by Harlow's (1949) monkeys. But fish (Wodinsky & Bitterman, 1957) exhibit only a slight improvement in successive reversals, while isopods (invertebrates) show no improvement (Thompson, 1957).

Because of the necessity to use somewhat different experimental procedures for different species, it is difficult to draw an unqualified conclusion about the ability of different species to transfer what has been learned from previous reversal shifts to a new one. But the suggestion is strong that as you ascend the evolutionary scale organisms acquire a greater capacity to generate cues that enable them to make rapid reversal shifts. This behavior, according to our analysis, borders on the language responses of humans. The main difference is that our human subjects, except

those of a very young age, exhibit rapid reversals without any previous reversal training. Whereas the human automatically seems to generate a mediated response that provides the basis for his rapid reversal, the animal subject must gradually acquire an ability to respond appropriately to some response produced cue resulting from nonreinforcement of a previously correct response.

Up to now, the reversal and nonreversal technique has been used to investigate mediational and developmental variables. It has proved sufficiently flexible to be used in a study (Kendler, Glucksberg, & Keston, 1961) which was designed to lengthen a problem solving chain so that the interaction between various segments could be observed. In this study a perceptual orienting S-R unit was added on to the mediational chain already described. Figure 8 illustrates in an oversimplified manner the behavior sequence involved in this study in which subjects had to learn to press the correct button when two physically discrete and spatially separate stimulus patterns were projected on a screen at such a rapid rate that only one could be perceived on any trial. During the learning of each of two successive concepts (involving either a reversal or nonreversal shift), the subject had to pay attention to the relevant stimulus pattern while ignoring the irrelevant one. Thus, in order to make the correct overt response consistently, a subject initially had to make the appropriate orienting response in order to perceive the relevant stimulus pattern to which he had to make the correct mediational response which served as the cue for the key-pressing act.

An experimental design was used in which, at the time of the shift from the first to the second concept, one group had already learned the appropriate orienting response as well as the appropriate mediating act. They needed only to learn a new terminal key-pressing response. The shift, for them, was easy to make. In contrast, the behavior of three other experimental groups was significantly worse. One group had to learn a new orienting response, e.g., look to the left instead of the right. Another group had to learn a new mediated response (i.e., they were required to make a non-reversal shift). The last group had to acquire both a new orienting and mediated response. The fact that the groups which were missing one or both of the necessary behavior units (orienting and mediated responses) did not differ significantly among themselves, as well as being much poorer than the group that had both, highlights the problem of synchronizing the S-R units in a behavioral chain. The advantage in this study of having one appropriate unit without the other is at best negligible. The reason for this is that reinforcement is only achieved consistently when both the appropriate orienting and mediating responses are operating. This particular study points to the need for discovering laws associated with the strengthening and weakening of independent S-R units in a problem solving chain, as well as the principles governing their synchronization.

This study also highlighted a very basic problem in all of these reversal studies. This problem has to do with the very first correct response following the reversal shift. After discovering that the previous mode of responding is erroneous, what makes the subject change his response, i.e., push the button that was previously wrong? Introspective reports fail to provide any clearcut answer and even if they did they would be in need of explaining (Kendler, 1961).

One hypothesis is that the selection of the new correct response is due to the operation of a behavioral chain in addition to the one described in Figure 8. The first nonreinforcement in a reversal shift sets off a chain, the consequence of which is to select the response other than the one that was previously correct. This may result from a number of different reasons (e.g., logical considerations, forgetting, etc.). The important point, however, is that the new key-sorting response occurs contiguously with the implicit mediational response appropriate to a reversal shift. As a result, a new association is formed between the old implicit cue and the new key-pressing response.

In essence, what is being stated is that adult subjects, when making or deciding to make the first correct post-shift response, do not adopt the *principle* underlying a reversal shift. Instead, it is assumed processes are operating which encourage the selection of the correct response while an implicit cue appropriate to a reversal shift is operating. This sort of an analysis was described previously (Kendler & Mayzner, 1956) as

sort of a James-Lange theory of problem solving . . . one makes the overt correct . . . response and if the appropriate symbolic cue is present, then problem solution will occur (pp. 247–8).

Guthrie (1959) says the same thing more neatly: "*What is being noticed becomes a signal for what is being done*" (p. 186).

Again the authors would like to guard against giving the impression of oversimplifying a terribly complex problem. They do not believe the contiguous occurrence of an implicit cue from one chain with the correct overt response from another tells the whole story. This new association in order to persist must be reinforced and in some manner "fit into" the subject's ongoing behavioral chains. The emphasis on this vertical connection between a cue and a response from different chains is related in a distant way to Hebb's (1958) stressing the role of "chance" in problem solving:

There are few scientists who have not had the experience of setting out to solve problem A and ending up instead with the solution to B. . . . This is serendipity, the art of finding one thing while looking for another (p. 215).

According to the present analysis, serendipity results from the adventitious and contiguous occurrence of a cue and a response which are themselves segments from different behavior chains. Theoretically it should be possible to demonstrate this point experimentally by training subjects to respond simultaneously to two separate tasks. A problem then would have to be presented that requires for its solution the combination of a stimulus from one chain with the response from the other. In such an experimental situation, controlling the time relationship between the two should have an important effect on problem solving. Presumably contiguity between the two should provide the most optimal conditions for problem solving (Underwood, 1952). The development of this kind of experimental procedure should allow for parametric studies of the basic variables of the phenomenon which has commonly been called "insight," as well as throw light upon issues raised by others (e.g., Cofer, 1957; Maltzman, 1955; Saugstad, 1957).

The pretheoretical model that guides the present research has many more facets that can be exploited. Only one will now be mentioned. Glucksberg (1962), for example, extended neobehavioristic drive theory (Spence, 1956) to problem solving. He used a functional-fixedness problem (Adamson, 1952, Duncker, 1945) in which the correct response in the habit hierarchy could either be made to be low or high. If the correct habit was low, it would be expected

that a strong drive would retard problem solving because it would retard the extinction of the dominant incorrect response (Kendler & Lachman, 1958; Perin, 1942). Since drive energizes behavior, a high drive should facilitate problem solving performance when the correct habit is dominant. The findings were consistent with this analysis.

Because functional-fixedness problems are often represented in perceptual terms, Gluckberg was interested in seeing whether the same drive model could be applied to a simple perceptual recognition problem in which subjects were instructed to identify tachistoscopically presented words as rapidly as possible. The results were similar to those reported for the functional-fixedness study: when the correct response was dominant, an increase in drive improved performance, i.e., the visual duration threshold was lowered. In contrast, increasing drive when the correct response was low in the hierarchy raised the threshold.

There is obviously still much more work, both empirical and theoretical, needed to develop the model that has been described. At this point it may be appropriate to summarize the major points of this paper.

There is not just one way to investigate problem solving. The researcher who is interested in problem solving has several different pretheoretical models from which to choose. This paper reported the results of a research program based on an S-R model in which the importance of horizontal and vertical processes were emphasized. Horizontal processes refer to the linking of successive S-R units into a behavioral chain, while vertical processes refer to the assumption that independent chains occur simultaneously. A series of experiments was reported, the implications of which supported postulating a mediational mechanism within a behavioral chain. By comparing the behavior of human subjects of different ages, as well as relating their results to lower animals, it was possible to infer that as a child matures he makes a transition from responding on the basis of a single unit S-R mechanism to a mediational one. Additional data were cited that suggest the full impact of verbal behavior on problem solving depends on developmental processes that encourage interaction between chains at different vertical levels. It was also suggested that problem solving begins in a simple concept learning task when a correct overt response from one behavioral chain occurs contiguously and adventitiously with the appropriate implicit cue from another chain. The paper was concluded by citing findings that suggested the neobehavioristic drive theory which assumes that the effect of different levels of drive depends on the position of the correct response in the habit hierarchy is applicable to a functional fixedness problem as well as a perceptual-recognition task.

If nothing else, it is hoped that the present paper demonstrates that it is possible to investigate problem solving in a systematic fashion. If more psychologists accepted this possibility and were willing to expend their research energies in the field of problem solving, progress in this area would be greater than it is today.

ADAMSON, R. E. Functional-fixedness as related to problem solving. *J. exp. Psychol.*, 1952, **44**, 288-91.

BUSS, A. H. Rigidity as a function of reversal and nonreversal shift in the learning of successive discrimination. *J. exp. Psychol.*, 1953, **45**, 75-81.

BUSS, A. H. Reversal and nonreversal shifts in concept formation with partial reinforcement eliminated. *J. exp. Psychol.*, 1956, **52**, 162-6.

BUYTENDIJK, F. J. J. Über das Umlernen. *Arch. Néerl. Physiol.*, 1930, **15**, 283-310.

COFER, C. N. Reasoning as an associative process: III. The role of verbal responses in problem solving. *J. gen. Psychol.*, 1957, **57**, 55-8.

DUFORT, R. H., GUTTMAN, N., & KIMBLE, G. A. One trial discrimination reversal in the white rat. *J. comp. physiol. Psychol.*, 1954, **47**, 248-9.

DUNCAN, C. P. Recent research on human problem solving. *Psychol. Bull.*, 1959, **56**, 397-429.

DUNCKER, K. On problem solving. *Psychol. Monog.*, 1945, **58**(5, Whole No. 270).

GLUCKSBERG, S. The influence of strength of drive on functional fixedness and perceptual recognition. *J. exp. Psychol.*, 1962, in press.

GUTHRIE, E. R. *The psychology of learning.* (Rev. ed.) New York: Harper, 1952.

GUTHRIE, E. R. Association by contiguity. In S. Koch (Ed.), *Psychology: A study of a science.* Vol. 2. New York: McGraw-Hill, 1959. Pp. 158-95.

HARLOW, H. F. The formation of learning sets. *Psychol. Rev.*, 1949, **56**, 51-65.

HARROW, M., & FRIEDMAN, G. B. Comparing reversal and nonreversal shifts in concept formation with partial reinforcement controlled. *J. exp. Psychol.*, 1958, **55**, 592-7.

HEBB, D. O. *A textbook of psychology.* Philadelphia: Saunders, 1958.

HULL, C. L. Knowledge and purpose as habit mechanisms. *Psychol. Rev.*, 1930, **37**, 511-25.

HULL, C. L. *A behavior system.* New Haven: Yale Univer. Press, 1952.

KELLEHER, R. T. Discrimination learning as a function of reversal and nonreversal shifts. *J. exp. Psychol.*, 1956, **51**, 379-84.

KENDLER, H. H. Problems in problem solving research. In, *Current trends in psychological theory: A bicentennial program.* Pittsburgh: Univer. Pittsburgh Press, 1961.

KENDLER, H. H., & D'AMATO, M. F. A comparison of reversal shifts and nonreversal shifts in human concept formation behavior. *J. exp. Psychol.*, 1955, **49**, 165-74.

KENDLER, H. H., GLUCKSBERG, S., & KESTON, R. Perception and mediation in concept learning. *J. exp. Psychol.*, 1961, **61**, 186-91.

KENDLER, H. H., & KENDLER, T. S. Inferential behavior in preschool children. *J. exp. Psychol.*, 1956, **51**, 311-14.

KENDLER, H. H., KENDLER, T. S., PLISKOFF, S. S., & D'AMATO, M. F. Inferential behavior in children: I. The influence of reinforcement and incentive motivation. *J. exp. Psychol.*, 1958, **55**, 207-12.

KENDLER, H. H., & LACHMAN, R. Habit reversal as a function of schedule of reinforcement and drive strength. *J. exp. Psychol.*, 1958, **55**, 584-91.

KENDLER, H. H., & MAYZNER, M. S., JR. Reversal and nonreversal shifts in card sorting tests with two or four sorting categories. *J. exp. Psychol.*, 1956, **51**, 244-8.

KENDLER, H. H., & VINEBERG, R. The acquisition of compound concepts as a function of previous training. *J. exp. Psychol.*, 1954, **48**, 252-8.

KENDLER, T. S., & KENDLER, H. H. Reversal and nonreversal shifts in kindergarten children. *J. exp. Psychol.*, 1959, **58**, 56-60.

KENDLER, T. S., & KENDLER, H. H. Inferential behavior in children: II. The influence of order of presentation. *J. exp. Psychol.*, 1961, **61**, 442-8.

KENDLER, T. S., KENDLER, H. H., & WELLS, D. Reversal and nonreversal shifts in nursery school children. *J. comp. physiol. Psychol.*, 1960, **53**, 83-8.

KOCH, S. *Psychology: A study of a science.* Vol. 1, *Sensory, perceptual, and physiological formulations.* New York: McGraw-Hill, 1959.

KOHLER, W. *The mentality of apes.* New York: Harcourt, Brace, 1925.

KRECHEVSKY, I. Antagonistic visual discrimination habits in the white rat. *J. comp. Psychol.*, 1932, **14**, 263-77.

LACHMAN, R. The model in theory construction. *Psychol. Rev.*, 1960, **67**, 113-29.

LURIA, A. R. The role of language in the formation of temporary connections. In B. Simon (Ed.), *Psychology in the Soviet Union.* Stanford: Stanford Univer. Press, 1957. Pp. 115-29.

MAIER, N. R. F. Reasoning in humans: I. On direction. *J. comp. Psychol.*, 1930, **10**, 115-43.

MALTZMAN, I. Thinking: From a behavioristic point of view. *Psychol. Rev.*, 1955, **62**, 275-86.

MEYER, M. F. *The fundamental laws of human behavior.* Boston: Gorham, 1911.

PERIN, C. T. Behavior potentiality as a joint function of the amount of training and the degree of hunger at the time of extinction. *J. exp. Psychol.* 1942, **30**, 93-113.

SAUGSTAD, P. An analysis of Maier's pendulum problem. *J. exp. Psychol.*, 1957, **54**, 168-79.

SKINNER, B. F. *Science and human behavior.* New York: Macmillan, 1953.

SPENCE, K. W. The nature of discrimination learning in animals. *Psychol. Rev.*, 1936, **43**, 427-49.

SPENCE, K. W. *Behavior theory and conditioning.* New Haven: Yale Univer. Press, 1956.

THOMPSON, R. Successive reversal of a position habit in an invertebrate. *Science*, 1957, **126**, 163-4.

TOULMIN, S. *The philosophy of science.* London: Hutchinson Univer. Library, 1953.

UNDERWOOD, B. J. An orientation for research on thinking. *Psychol. Rev.*, 1952, **59**, 209-20.

WATSON, J. B. Psychology as the behaviorist sees it. *Psychol. Rev.*, 1913, **20**, 158-77.

WODINSKY, J., & BITTERMAN, M. E. Discrimination-reversal in the fish. *Amer. J. Psychol.*, 1957, **70**, 569-75.

42 / Reversal and Nonreversal Shifts within and between Dimensions in Concept Formation

I. DAVID ISAACS AND CARL P. DUNCAN, *Northwestern University*

In a number of studies of concept learning in human adults (Buss, 1953, 1956; Harrow & Friedman, 1958; Kendler & D'Amato, 1955; Kendler & Mayzner, 1956), Ss were first reinforced for different responses to two stimuli varying on some dimension (e.g., circle vs. square, form dimension) while the stimuli simultaneously varied on one or more momentarily irrelevant dimensions (e.g., color). After mastery of this task (hereafter, the training task), some Ss were shifted to a transfer task in which each of the two stimuli that had been reinforced in training was now paired with the opposite response (reversal shift). Thus, in transfer, reversal Ss had to learn two re-paired S-R associations. Other Ss were shifted to a transfer task provided by reinforcing the stimuli (e.g., red vs. blue) on a previously irrelevant dimension (nonreversal shift to a different dimension). All of the studies using human adults as Ss (those cited above, the only ones of concern here) consistently found that nonreversal shift to a different dimension provided a more difficult transfer task, in terms of trials to learn, than reversal shift.

This finding has been used to support a mediation theory of the way human adults learn and transfer in such concept tasks (for details, see, e.g., Goss, 1961; Kendler & D'Amato, 1955). However, mediation theory also predicts, according to Kendler and D'Amato, that the reversal condition should yield positive, not negative, transfer in comparison to a control group that learns only the transfer task. Since it is usually found that re-pairing of S-R associations produces negative transfer (e.g., Porter & Duncan, 1953), it is important to determine if this prediction can be confirmed. Of the three studies that used a control group, one (Kendler & D'Amato, 1955) did find that the reversal group learned the transfer task more quickly than the control group; one (Buss, 1953) found the control learned faster than the reversal group; and one (Harrow & Friedman, 1958) found no difference. This disagreement among the studies is probably unimportant because, it is suggested here, none of the studies actually used

From the *Journal of Experimental Psychology*, 1962, 580-85, with permission of the authors and publisher.

an appropriate control group. In all cases the control group learned only the transfer task; no attempt was made to equate control and experimental groups on nonspecific transfer variables (e.g., learning to learn, warm up) which would be developed in the experimental groups by the training task. Since nonspecific transfer factors are likely to have a net positive transfer effect, performance of control groups in the three cited studies was probably poorer than would have been the case if nonspecific transfer had been controlled. So, the present study is a further comparison of reversal shift (R) and nonreversal shift to a different dimension (NRD) in transfer, along with an attempt to provide a more appropriate transfer control for these groups.

In addition to the usual NRD condition, it is also possible, as Harrow and Friedman (1958) point out, to provide another kind of nonreversal shift in transfer, viz., nonreversal shift on the same dimension that was relevant in training (NRS). Harrow and Friedman suggest that this NRS condition should also, like the R condition, be easier to learn, in transfer, than NRD. This prediction is also tested in the present study.

METHOD

Apparatus.—The S and E, seated on opposite sides of a table, were separated by a vertical plywood panel 29 in. high, 48 in. wide. The side of the panel viewed by S was painted gray and contained a plastic window 2½ in. high, 4½ in. wide, centered in the panel 11 in. above the table. Two lights, one on each side of the window, were used to provide reinforcement. Two push buttons were fixed to the table, one below each light. If S pushed either button, the light above it came on to signal a correct choice, provided that E had previously set a mercury switch on E's side of the table.

On E's side of the panel a deck of stimulus cards was pressed against the window by means of a drawbar and springs. Thus, when E removed the card appearing in the window, the next card was immediately revealed.

Stimuli.—For Ss in experimental groups the stimuli varied on two dimensions, form and number (of forms), one or the other of which was relevant at some time during the experiment for all Ss. In addition, the stimuli varied in color (all forms on any one stimulus card were either red or blue), a dimension that was always irrelevant. All stimuli were drawn with colored pencils on white 3 × 5 in. cards. Cards were inserted in plastic envelopes.

There were four values on the form dimension (circle, square, hexagon, triangle), and four on the number dimension (one, two, three, or four forms on a card). At any one time during the experiment S had to respond to just two of the values, on one of the dimensions, paired against each other, e.g., circle vs. square. Only the following pairs were used: circle vs. square, hexagon vs. triangle, one vs. three forms, two vs. four forms.

The training stimuli for the control group were vertical arrows, colored black, drawn on 3 × 5 in. cards. These control stimuli also varied on two dimensions, each relevant for some Ss: direction (up-pointing or down-pointing arrowhead), and height (¾ in. or 2 in.). There was also a dimension that was always irrelevant, width: an arrow was either ⅛ in. or ½ in. wide. There was only one arrow on each card.

Conditions.—The design is shown in Table 1. There were three experimental groups and a control group, all given different training tasks but the same transfer task. As may be seen in Table 1, all four combinations formed by putting together a pair of stimuli from one dimension and a pair from the other dimension were used, for different Ss within each group, in both training and transfer tasks. Group R was trained on a form discrimination, either circle vs. square, or hexagon vs. triangle. Group NRD was trained on a number discrimination, either one vs. three, or two vs. four forms. Group NRS was, like Group R, trained on forms but was transferred to different forms, whereas Group R was transferred to the same forms reversed. Group C (control) was trained either on direction (up- or down-pointing arrow), or on height (tall or short

TABLE 1. *Stimuli and experimental design*

Group	S	Training		Transfer	
		Left	Right	Left	Right
R (Reversal to same dimension)	1	C1, C3	S1, S3	S2, S4	C2, C4
	2	C2, C4	S2, S4	S1, S3	C1, C3
	3	H1, H3	T1, T3	T2, T4	H2, H4
	4	H2, H4	T2, T4	T1, T3	H1, H3
NRD (Nonreversal to different dimension)	1	1S, 1C	3S, 3C		
	2	2S, 2C	4S, 4C	Same as for Group R	
	3	1H, 1T	3H, 3T		
	4	2H, 2T	4H, 4T		
NRS (Nonreversal to same dimension)	1	H2, H4	T2, T4		
	2	H1, H3	T1, T3	Same as for Group R	
	3	C2, C4	S2, S4		
	4	C1, C3	S1, S3		
Control	1	UX, UZ	DX, DZ		
	2	XU, XD	ZU, ZD	Same as for Group R	
	3	UX, UZ	DX, DZ		
	4	XU, XD	ZU, ZD		

Note.—C, S, H, T, — circle, square, hexagon, triangle; 1, 2, 3, 4 = number dimension, number of forms on a card; U or D = up-pointing or down-pointing arrow: X = short arrow, Z = tall arrow. Symbols in bold face print indicate reinforced stimuli or dimension. Left and right indicate responses.

arrow). All groups were transferred to the *same* form discrimination.

Table 1 also shows that for Group NRD, partial reinforcement on the transfer task was controlled. When this group was shifted to the transfer task, the previously rein-forced values on the number dimension were changed to new values so S would not receive partial reinforcement (by continuing to respond to the training stimuli) in transfer. A more detailed presentation of this partial reinforcement issue in concepts shifts is given by Harrow and Friedman (1958). Since, for Group NRD, shifting from training to transfer involved changing stimulus values on one dimension while not changing values on the other dimension, it was decided to use this same "degree of change" for all three experimental groups, as may be seen in Table 1.

There is one more important feature of the design shown in Table 1. It can be seen that in both Group R and Group NRS, any particular form discrimination (e.g., in Table 1, C1, C3, vs. S1, S3) required of some one S (subject) during training, was also required of some other S during transfer. Therefore, when the training task for either Group R or Group NRS is taken as a whole (ignoring the counterbalancing of stimuli for individual Ss), each of these training tasks provides a measure of difficulty of the transfer task in

the absence of nonspecific transfer from a prior task. In other words, performance of Groups R and NRS during training is a measure of how an inappropriate control group (not corrected for nonspecific transfer) would perform on the transfer task.

Subjects.—The Ss were students in intro-ductory psychology courses, assigned to groups in trun. Each of the three experi-mental groups (R, NRD, NRS) was assigned 32 Ss. Two Ss in Group NRD failed to reach criterion on the training task and were replaced.

It soon became clear that for Ss in Group C, discrimination of height of arrows was much more difficult than discrimination of direction. Therefore, 48 Ss were run in Group C, 24 Ss on the height discrimination (Group Ch), 24 on direction (Group Cd). Ten Ss failed to learn the height discrimina-tion and were replaced.

Procedure.—For half the Ss in each group, the stimuli reinforced by pressing the left or the right button are shown under the Left or Right columns in Table 1. For the re-maining Ss this was reversed; stimuli ap-pearing under Left were reinforced for pressing the right button, etc.

With stimuli varying on two dimensions, plus an always irrelevant dimension, a deck of 8 cards was necessary to represent all possible combinations for either experimental or control Ss. Two such decks were prepared, so 16 cards in all were available. Four different orders of these 16 cards were used. This permitted presentation of each of the four combinations of possibly relevant stimuli, number and form (or height and direction of arrow in Group C), equally often as the first card shown an S. Then, for each S, the second card presented revealed the other values of number and form (or height and direction) that had not appeared on the first card. Thus, in the first two cards presented S saw all possibly relevant stimulus values and dimensions that were to appear in the particular task on which he was working. Four different random orders were used to determine the order of presentation of the remaining 14 cards, with the restriction that the 8 different stimulus cards be shown before any card was repeated.

The instructions to S essentially told him to press the left or right button for each card appearing in the window, and that if he were correct, the light above the button would come on.

For both training and transfer tasks, S was required to reach a criterion of six successive correct responses. If S had not met criterion after three presentations of the pack of 16 cards (six presentations of the 8 different stimulus cards), S was dropped as a nonsolver.

The S was allowed to proceed at his own pace; on the average, about 7 sec. elapsed between presentation of successive cards. There was no interruption between training and transfer tasks.

RESULTS

Training.—The left portion of Table 2 summarizes performance on the training task as measured by number of trials to the criterion of six successive correct responses. The six criterion trials are not included in the data. Although 32 Ss were taken to criterion on the training task in Groups R, NRD, and NRS, 1 S in Group NRS and 1 S in NRD failed to reach criterion on the transfer task. These 2 Ss were eliminated, and 1 S in Group R, with median performance in training was also eliminated

to reduce N to 31 in each of the three experimental groups.

There was no significant difference among the three experimental groups (top three lines in Table 2) on the training task ($F < 1$). Hartley's test indicated that the group variances were homogeneous ($F_{max} = 1.87$, $df = 3/30$).

It was noted earlier that it was necessary to run separate subgroups in Group C because of differential difficulty of the dimensions of training stimuli. The difference between the mean (see Table 2) of the subgroup that discriminated direction (Group Cd) and the subgroup that discriminated height (Group Ch) was highly significant ($t = 4.06$).

When Group Ch was included with the three experimental groups in analysis of variance of training means, F was 3.22 ($P < .05$, $df = 3/113$). By t test, the mean for Group Ch differed significantly from the means of each of the three experimental groups at the 5% level or less. Analysis of variance of Group Cd and the experimental group yielded $F < 1$. Hereafter, Group Cd will be considered the more appropriate control group.

Transfer.—Mean trials to criterion on the transfer task are shown in Table 2.

TABLE 2. *Mean trials to criterion in training*

Group	N	Training		Transfer	
		Mean	σM	Mean	σM
R	31	7.03	1.70	7.52	1.72
NRD	31	8.81	1.98	13.77	2.10
NRS	31	7.00	1.45	3.03	.93
Cd	24	4.67	1.63	2.67	.49
Ch	24	13.83	1.63	7.42	1.76

Again, the means do not include the six criterion trials. Since the variances of the three experimental groups were heterogeneous ($F_{max} = 5.03$, $P < .01$), and since the distributions were also positively skewed, the scores were transformed to log ($X + 1$). This eliminated the heterogeneity of variance and produced approximately normal distributions. Analysis of variance of the transformed scores of the experimental groups gave $F = 19.4$ $(P < .001, df = 2/90)$. By t test, Group R differed significantly from Group NRD $(t = 3.14)$, and from Group NRS $(t = 3.32)$. Groups NRD and NRS also differed significantly $(t = 6.46)$. The fact that Cond. R was easier than Cond. NRD is in agreement with all previous studies that have made this comparison. The new finding is that Cond. NRS was easiest of all.

Analysis of variance of transformed scores of experimental groups and Group Cd yielded $F = 16.6$ $(P < .001, df = 3/113)$. By t test, Group Cd differed significantly from Group R $(t = 2.42)$ and from Group NRD $(t = 5.35)$ but not from Group NRS $(t < 1)$.

Errors.—The number of trials on which S pressed the wrong button (errors), divided by the number of trials to criterion, was computed for each S. These error ratios for both training and transfer are summarized in Table 3. There

TABLE 3. *Mean error ratios*

Group	N	Training		Transfer	
		Mean	σM	Mean	σM
R	31	.52	.013	.70	.020
NRD	31	.53	.009	.49	.007
NRS	31	.43	.013	.42	.029
Cd	24	.50	.029	.44	.022
Ch	24	.50	.004	.66	.020

were no significant differences among groups in training. Analysis of variance of the transfer data for experimental groups and Group Cd yielded $F = 4.80$ $(P < .01, df = 3/113)$. By t test, Group R differed significantly from Group NRD $(t = 2.53)$, from Group NRS $(t = 3.39)$, and from Group Cd $(t = 2.92)$. Other comparisons were not significant.

DISCUSSION

The data show that Group R, operating under a negative transfer paradigm, did in fact show significant negative transfer when compared to a control group in which nonspecific transfer was controlled. Group R also showed the highest error ratio in transfer, another index of intertask interference.

The need to control for nonspecific transfer in studies of this kind is indicated by the powerful effects such transfer had in the present study. Recall that for a group of Ss as a whole, the training task for both Groups R and NRS was identical to the transfer task for all groups; therefore, performance of these groups in training yields a measure of difficulty of the transfer task for Ss not provided with training for nonspecific transfer. This measure was essentially the same for both Groups R and NRS (7.03 and 7.00 mean trials to criterion in training, respectively). Nonspecific transfer was presumably controlled in Group Cd, and this group required a mean of only 2.67 trials (transfer mean) to learn the same task. It seems likely that in the studies of Buss (1953), Harrow and Friedman (1958), and Kendler and D'Amato (1955), the reversal groups would have shown negative transfer had the control groups been trained so as to minimize nonspecific transfer.

Most of the data on reversal shifts in concept learning in human adults has been interpreted in terms of "mediating mechanisms" or "implicit cues" (Goss, 1961; Harrow & Friedman, 1958; Kendler & D'Amato, 1955). The interpretation of the present data, which follows, avoids this particular theoretical language. Instead, the interpretation is based largely on a single, and presumably fairly simple, assumption.

Assume that Ss reinforced on a particular dimension and extinguished on all other dimensions during training, tend to continue to respond, initially, to the reinforced dimension during transfer. If so, then Group NRS (trained on forms, transferred to new forms) would have responded primarily to the two new forms on the transfer task. Since the two new forms would have had roughly equal probabilities of association with the two responses, the transfer task would essentially reduce to a simple two-choice discrimination for these Ss. Group NRS should, and did, learn the transfer task very rapidly.

According to the same assumption, Group

R (trained on forms, transferred to the same forms re-paired with the responses) should also have continued to respond to stimuli on the form dimension early in transfer. But because the forms available to these Ss had been differentially reinforced in training, and were re-paired in transfer, initial probability of association between the forms and responses would not be equal. Thus, although Group R was also faced, it is assumed, with only a two-choice discrimination in transfer, the training associations had to be extinguished before the transfer task could be learned. Group R should, and did, transfer more slowly than Group NRS, and should make many errors. And as has been shown, Group R should and did transfer more slowly than an appropriate control group.

Still following the basic assumption, Group NRD (trained on number, transferred to forms) would continue to respond to the number dimension during transfer. Since no number stimuli, new or old, were consistently reinforced during transfer, the task for these Ss became quite difficult. First, responses to stimuli on the number dimension had to be extinguished. There now remained two dimensions, form and color, from which to choose; since both these dimensions had been extinguished during training, there was no basis for choosing between them. So Group NRD next had to discover that it was forms, not colors, that was being reinforced during transfer. Finally, these Ss had to discover which form went with which response. It seems clear that the total number of alternatives from which to choose was greater for Group NRD than for any other group (Goss, 1961, has come to the same conclusion), and Group NRD showed the poorest performance of all in transfer. Viewed this way, it is not surprising that Group NRD should be inferior to Group Cd and Group NRS. But in this and in all previous studies that have made the comparison, Group NRD also learned the task more slowly than even the negative transfer group (R). This finding simply shows that having to deal with several stimulus alternatives that have previously been subjected to differential reinforcement and extinction is more difficult than having to deal with a re-paired situation involving basically only two associations,

a difference in task difficulty that would seem to have little theoretical import.

SUMMARY

In a study of human concept formation, two experimental groups were trained on a two-choice form discrimination, with number and color stimuli irrelevant. For one group (reversal shift) the transfer task consisted of re-pairing the training stimuli with the responses; for the other group (nonreversal shift to the same dimension), two new forms were used as transfer stimuli. A third experimental group (nonreversal to a different dimension) was trained on number stimuli and transferred to forms. A control group was trained on stimuli differing from any of those used for experimental groups, then transferred to forms. The same two-choice form discrimination, with number and color irrelevant, was used as the transfer task for all groups.

The results showed three significantly different levels of performance (in terms of trials to learn) on the transfer task. In order of best to poorest performance, the levels were: (a) nonreversal to same dimension, and control; these groups did not differ, (b) reversal shift, and (c) nonreversal to different dimension. As compared to the control, the reversal group showed significant negative transfer. It was suggested that performance of all groups could largely be accounted for by a combination of two factors: nonspecific transfer, and a specific tendency to continue to respond in transfer to the dimension of stimuli reinforced in training.

Buss, A. H. Rigidity as a function of reversal and nonreversal shifts in the learning of successive discriminations. J. exp. Psychol., 1953, 45, 75-81.

Buss, A. H. Reversal and nonreversal shifts in concept formation with partial reinforcement eliminated. J. exp. Psychol., 1956, 52, 162-6.

Goss, A. E. Verbal mediating responses and concept formation. Psychol., Rev., 1961, 68, 248-74.

Harrow, M., & Friedman, G. B. Comparing reversal and nonreversal shifts in concept formation with partial reinforcement controlled. J. exp. Psychol., 1958, 55, 592-8.

Kendler, H. H., & D'Amato, M. F. A comparison of reversal and nonreversal shifts in human concept formation behavior. J. exp. Psychol., 1955, 49, 165-74.

KENDLER, H. H., & MAYZNER, M. S., JR. Reversal and nonreversal shifts in cardsorting tests with two or four sorting categories. *J. exp. Psychol.*, 1956, 51, 244-8.

PORTER, L., & DUNCAN, C. P. Negative transfer in verbal learning. *J. exp. Psychol.*, 1953, 46, 61-4.

43 / The Selection of Strategies in Cue Learning [1]

FRANK RESTLE, *Michigan State University*

In a cue learning problem (discrimination learning, concept formation, and maze learning) the subject chooses one of two or more responses on each trial. The correctness of the response depends on some aspect of the situation at the time of response.

In this paper it is assumed that subjects have difficulty with cue learning problems to the degree that they tend to use strategies (habits, patterns of response) which conflict with the strategy intended by the experimenter. It is often assumed that the subject must also associate correct responses with cues in the situation. However, in most cue learning experiments the subject is instructed or pretrained to make the desired responses before the cue learning process begins. Furthermore, the experimental situation constrains the subject to make exactly one of the available responses per trial. It seems reasonable to assume that cue learning is not so much a matter of the formation as of the selection of responses. The present theoretical discussion begins with a set of strategies and is concerned with the mechanisms by which the subject might select out those strategies intended, and consistently rewarded, by the experimenter.

The term "strategy" is employed in a sense related to the more common terms, "habit" and "hypothesis," to designate a particular pattern of responses to stimuli. Consider, for example, a rat being trained to jump to the larger of two white circles in a Lashley Jumping Stand. Some possible strategies include;

jumping to the left side, jumping to the right side, jumping alternately left and right, jumping always to the side last reinforced, jumping to the side which last was punished, jumping in the direction the rat was placed down on the stand, jumping toward the circle with less (or more) acute curvature, jumping toward the side with more white area, jumping toward the side which reflects more total light, and so forth. Each such pattern of behavior, if it occurs in isolation for a sufficiently long sequence of trials, can be identified by the experimenter. It will be seen that there are ordinarily a large number and variety of possible strategies in a cue learning problem, and that a number of strategies may be perfectly confounded. In the example above, jumping to the circle with less acute curvature will always lead to the same result as jumping to the side which reflects more light, since these will both be jumps to the larger circle.

THREE MODELS OF THE SELECTION OF STRATEGIES

The general idea developed here is that the problem gives rise to a set of strategies. The subject uses these various strategies, which at first are selected at random, and attempts to select strategies which will consistently lead to correct responses. For simplicity the discussion is limited to problems in which

From the *Psychological Review*, 1962, 69, 329-43, with permission of the author and publisher.
1. This research was facilitated by the author's tenure as Faculty Research Fellow of the Social Science Research Council, 1959-61.

there are at least some strategies which are always correct.

Let H be the set of strategies available to the subject at the beginning of the problem. Suppose that some subset C of these strategies are always correct, another subset W are always wrong, and the remainder, I, are sometimes correct and sometimes wrong. For simplicity of presentation, begin with a problem in which the strategies of I are correct and wrong on successive trials with independent probabilities all of which are ½, and restrict attention to the two-choice problem.

Presentation of the theory of this conventional discrimination learning problem will begin with a special case in which one strategy is used on each trial. Then an alternative theory will be proposed, in which the subject uses all strategies at once and attempts to narrow down to the correct one. Third, a model will be proposed in which the subject chooses a random sample of all strategies and attempts to narrow down to the correct strategies within his sample. These three models will be shown to be essentially equivalent, in a theorem which may be called the "indifference to sample size" theorem. Following proof of that theorem, some empirical implications of the theory will be derived and compared with relevant data.

One strategy at a time. On the first trial of the experiment, the subject selects a certain single strategy from H at random and makes the indicated response. If the response is correct, the same strategy is used on Trial 2. If it is again correct, it is used again on Trial 3, and so forth. If, on any trial, the response is incorrect, the subject returns his strategy to the set H and then chooses a strategy again at random. It is considered possible that the same strategy may be resampled, so that the sampling process is with replacement. Imagine that an error occurs on Trial 2. Then

a new strategy is chosen and this strategy is used on Trial 3. If it is correct it is used again on Trial 4. If the response on Trial 3 is wrong, the subject again chooses an hypothesis at random for Trial 4.

Notice that if the subject chooses a correct strategy, he will make no more errors. The correct strategy leads to correct responses, and when the response is correct the subject does not change strategy. Thus, the learning process is terminated by the choice of a correct strategy.

Since sampling is with replacement, the probabilities of choosing a correct, a wrong, or an irrelevant strategy are constant from trial to trial. Let these three probabilities be c, w, and $i = 1 - c - w$.

At the beginning of training the subject chooses a strategy of one of the three types, which have probabilities c, w, and i. After each error he also chooses a strategy, with probabilities c, w, and i. Thus an error is an event which returns the subject to exactly the same condition (in terms of the probabilities of future events) with which he started—it resets the process and makes it begin over. Such an event is called a "recurrent event" (Feller, 1950). Since our experimental interest centers around errors and correct responses, we can limit attention to errors and thus to the theory of recurrent events.

Imagine that at some Trial n the subject makes an error. There is a certain probability f_1 that the next error occurs at Trial $n+1$, a probability f_2 that the next error occurs at Trial $n+2$, and in general a probability distribution f_j that the next error after Trial n occurs at Trial $n+j$. In a model of recurrent events like the present one, the distribution f_j is the same for all Trials n on which an error occurs, and is the same as the distribution of probabilities that the first error occurs on Trial 1, 2, etc.

The random process and all of its properties are specified by the distribution f_j. However, the analysis of the process from the distribution f_j will be postponed until two steps have been completed; first, calculation of the distribution f_j for the one-strategy-at-a-time model, and second, the formulation of two other models, very different in assumptions, which also lead to systems of recurrent events with the same distribution. When these steps are completed, the generality of the f distribution will be apparent, and derivations of properties of the process will be justified.

First, f_1 is the probability of an error immediately following another error. The second error can occur because a wrong strategy was chosen (with probability w) or because an irrelevant strategy was chosen and turned out to be wrong (with probability $\frac{1}{2}i$). These are mutually exclusive events and exhaust the possibilities, so that:

$$f_1 = w + \tfrac{1}{2}i.$$

An error occurring on the second trial after the last one, with a correct response intervening, cannot result from the selection of a wrong strategy for the wrong strategy would not lead to an intervening correct response. If the error does occur on the second trial we know that the strategy chosen was not correct. Hence it must be an irrelevant one which led first to a correct and then to a wrong response. In simple discrimination learning, the probability that an irrelevant strategy would lead to a correct and then a wrong response is $\frac{1}{2} \cdot \frac{1}{2} = (\frac{1}{2})^2$. The probability of choosing an irrelevant strategy which gives this sequence, correct-wrong, is therefore:

$$f_2 = i(\tfrac{1}{2})^2$$

By the same reasoning, any value of f_j, $j > 2$, implies that an irrelevant strategy was chosen and then led to $j-1$ correct responses followed by a wrong response. The probability of a string of exactly $j-1$ correct responses each with probability $\frac{1}{2}$, followed by an error with probability $\frac{1}{2}$, is $(\frac{1}{2})^j$. Hence, for $j \geq 2$:

$$f_j = i(\tfrac{1}{2})^j$$

Summarizing the results we have the distribution:

$$f_1 = w + \tfrac{1}{2}i$$
$$f_j = i(\tfrac{1}{2})^j$$

for all $j \geq 2$. The distribution f_j is not a proper probability function because it does not sum to unity. Notice that:

$$\sum_{j=1}^{\infty} (f_j) = w + i \sum_{j=1}^{\infty} (\tfrac{1}{2})^j = w + i = 1 - c$$

In Feller's terms this means that errors are *uncertain* recurrent events for with probability c the subject chooses a correct strategy and never makes another error. Some of the probability of the f distribution is located at the (improper) point ∞, and the proportion so located is c. This merely reflects the fact that learning occurs in the present model and the subject can eliminate errors. The fact that f_j is not a probability function does not place any serious difficulties in the way of analysis.

All strategies at once. We now consider a second model of a subject working on the same discrimination learning problem discussed above, with exactly the same set of strategies H divided into correct (C), wrong (W), and irrelevant (I) subsets. Since a strategy corresponds to any specific cue in the situation and these cues are numerous and finely divisible, consider that the set of strategies consists of a fairly sizeable (though finite) number of strategies, each of which is as likely to be used, and has as much influence on behavior, as every other.

In the all-strategies-at-once model we imagine that the subject begins the learning process by considering the entire set H of strategies simultaneously. In informal terms, he then attempts to narrow down to the correct strategy by a process of elimination. However, we suppose that the subject has only a limited memory and cannot remember all of the strategies at once, but only those with which he is presently concerned. The main disability of the subject in this model is that he may accidentally eliminate the correct strategies. When this happens he is unable to remember what they were, for he can remember only the ones he is still using. When the correct strategies have been lost the subject has no recourse but to begin over with the whole set of strategies. This general idea is now stated more precisely.

On the first trial the subject considers all strategies and chooses his response. The correct strategies and some of the irrelevant ones lead toward a correct response, the wrong strategies and the remainder of the irrelevant ones lead to an error. We suppose that the probability of a response is equal to the proportion of the strategies which lead to that response, so that, if we let N_c, N_w, and N_i be the number of strategies in sets C, W, and I, and if we let N_i^- be the number of irrelevant strategies which

$$f_j = \frac{N_c + N_i - N_{n,1}}{N_c + N_w + N_i} \cdot \frac{N_c + N_i - N_{n,1} - N_{n,2}}{N_c + N_i - _{n,1}} \cdots$$
$$\cdot \frac{N_c + N_i - N_{n,1} - \ldots - N_{n,j-2} - N_{n,j-1}}{N_c + N_i - N_{n,1} - \ldots - N_{n,j-3} - N_{n,j-2}} \cdot \frac{N_{n,j}}{N_c + N_i - N_{n,1} - \ldots - N_{n,j-1} - N_{j-1}}$$

lead to an error on the next trial, the probability of an error is:

$$f_1 = (N_w + N_i^-)/(N_w + N_c + N_i).$$

When the subject makes this first response we suppose that he eliminates or sets aside all the strategies he does not use. Suppose, for example, that he chooses a correct response. He at the same time eliminates all the wrong strategies and the irrelevant strategies which would have led him to the opposite response. On the next trial he will have only the correct strategies and the surviving irrelevant strategies left.

To complete the discussion and generalize it somewhat we introduce notation for the set of irrelevant strategies which, following any Trial n, first lead to a wrong response on Trial $n+j$. Let $N_{n,j}$ be the number of irrelevant strategies which lead to correct responses on trials $n+1$, $n+2$, . . . , $n+j-1$, and an error on trial $n+j$. Now we can write the probability of an error after an error as:

$$f_1 = (N_w + N_{n,1})/(N_c + N_w + N_i).$$

After one correct response, the only strategies which will lead to an error are those $N_{n,2}$ irrelevent strategies which first lead to an error on the second trial. The total strategies left are N_c correct and $N_i - N_{n,1}$ irrelevant strategies which have not already led toward a wrong response. Thus, the probability of an error following one correct response which follows a given error is:

$$f_2 = (1 - f_1)(N_{n,2}/[N_c + N_i - N_{n,1}])$$
$$= \frac{N_c + N_i - N_{n,1}}{N_c + N_w + N_i} \frac{N_{n,2}}{N_c + N_i - N_{n,1}}$$

Extension of this line of argument shows that in general:

In this expression the numerator of each term except the last cancels with the denominator of the following term, so that:

$$f_j = N_{n,j}/(N_c + N_w + N_i)$$

In our ideal experiment, $N_{n,j}$, the number of strategies which first lead to a wrong response on Trial $n+j$ after a given error on Trial n, is independent of n and is given by $N_i(\frac{1}{2})^j$. This statement follows from the idea that irrelevant strategies are correct and wrong with independent probabilities of $\frac{1}{2}$. Actually, $N_i(\frac{1}{2})^j$ is the expected number of irrelevant strategies which first lead to an error on Trial $n+j$, but the derivation to follow does not hinge on the distinction.

If we substitute $N_i(\frac{1}{2})^j$ for $N_{n,j}$ in the expression for f_j and simplify, letting i be the proportion of irrelevant strategies in H, we obtain:

$$f_j = i(\frac{1}{2})^j.$$

A similar substitution in the expression for f_1 gives:

$$f_j = w + \frac{1}{2}i.$$

These two results are in agreement with the one-strategy-at-a-time model. We have shown that the one-strategy-at-a-time and the all-strategies-at-once models are both systems in which errors are recurrent events, and we have shown that f_j is the same in both systems. Hence, so far as errors are concerned, the two models are identical.

One remark is in order. In the one-strategy-at-a-time model, the probability of a correct response on any trial is 1, $\frac{1}{2}$, or 0 depending on whether a correct, irrelevant, or wrong strategy is being used. The probability of a correct response in the all-strategies-at-once model can take a variety of values; if there are a great many strategies, the possible values of this probability are numerous and closely packed. The two models are not at all alike in the probabilities involved, and the theorem that they give indistinguishable sequences of errors is by no means obvious on intuitive grounds, even though the proof is easy.

The correspondence of the models extends to the interpretation of the parameters. In the one-strategy-at-a-time model the parameters c, w, and i are the probabilities of selecting a correct, wrong, or irrelevant strategy. In the all-strategies-at-once model the parameters c, w, and i are the proportions of correct, wrong, and irrelevant strategies, where elementary strategies are taken to have equal weight. In terms of experimental

realizations of the models, these two sets of parameters are not distinguishable.

It is still possible, of course, to tell which model is more reasonable by any technique which goes beyond the choice data. One might, for example, ask human subjects which strategies they are using, or one might use memory tests to see what parts of the situation have been employed. The equivalence of the models is asserted only for the acquisition of a single problem, and only with respect to the overt choices made: the writer will suggest, in subsequent work, that recognition and transfer tests may permit differential predictions.

A random sample of strategies. The two models discussed above are extremes. One would intuitively imagine that the subject would use, not all strategies and not just one, but some sample of strategies. The third model, called the random-sample-of-strategies model, supposes that on the first trial and after each error the subject draws a random sample of all strategies. So long as he makes no errors the subject discards wrong and irrelevant strategies by the same mechanism as that invoked in the all-strategies-at-once model. If the subject makes an error he takes a new independent sample from H and begins the process over.

The theorem to be proved is, if the sampling process is random in a strict sense to be described below and excludes the possibility that the subject might choose the empty sample, then the random-sample-of-strategies model generates a system of recurrent events which is the same as the other two models given above.

We again consider the set H of strategies, composed of equally potent elementary strategies. Suppose that there are N strategies in H of which N_c are correct, N_w are wrong, and N_i are irrelevant. We shall interpret N_c/N as c, the proportion of correct strategies, N_w/N as w, and N_i/N as i.

In a random sampling model of learning one may assign a fixed probability of being sampled to each element and let the sample size vary randomly, or assign a fixed sample-size, supposing that all such samples are equally probable (Estes, 1959.) To eliminate the possibility of the empty sample it is desirable to deal with a fixed sample size n. The random-sampling specification is that all samples of size n are equally probable.

The total number of samples of size n which can be drawn from a population of N elements is:

$$\binom{N}{n} = \frac{N!}{n!(N-n)!}$$

Similarly, one can draw $\binom{N_c}{n_c}$ samples of n_c correct strategies from the population of N_c strategies. For each of these samples of n_c correct strategies, there are $\binom{N_w}{n_w}$ samples of n_w wrong strategies, so that there are $\binom{N_c}{n_c}\binom{N_w}{n_w}$ ways of drawing n_c correct and n_w wrong strategies. For each of these combinations there are $\binom{N_i}{n_i}$ ways of drawing n_i irrelevant strategies. Hence the total number of ways one could obtain n_c correct, n_w wrong, and n_i irrelevant strategies is:

$$\binom{N_c}{n_c}\binom{N_w}{n_w}\binom{N_i}{n_i}$$

where, of course, it is assumed that $n_c + n_w + n_i = n$. Since every sample of size n is assumed to be as likely as any other, the probability of drawing a sample of exactly n_c correct, n_w wrong, and n_i irrelevant strategies is:

$$P(n_c, n_w, n_i) = \frac{\binom{N_c}{n_c}\binom{N_w}{n_w}\binom{N_i}{n_i}}{\binom{N}{n}}$$

which is the three-category generalization of the hypergeometric distribution (Feller, 1950).

It was asserted, in the statement of the model, that once the subject has chosen a sample his performance follows the rules of the all-strategies-at-once model. Hence, after any error and the choice of a sample with n_c, n_w, and n_i strategies, we can construct the f_j distribution. We may write the f distribution conditional on the constitution of the sample as:

$f(j|$sample with n_c, n_w, n_i strategies)

$$= \begin{vmatrix} (n_w + \tfrac{1}{2}n_i)/n & \text{for } j=1 \\ (\tfrac{1}{2})^j n_i/n & \text{for } j>1 \end{vmatrix}$$

directly from our results on the all-strategies-at-once model. To obtain the unconditional f_j we multiply each conditional f by the probability of the sample, and sum. This gives us the expectation of the conditional f. For f_1 we have:

$$f_1 = \mathbf{E}[(n_w + \tfrac{1}{2}n_i)/n]$$
$$= \mathbf{E}(n_w/n) + \tfrac{1}{2}\mathbf{E}(n_i/n)$$

However, in the hypergeometric distribution the mean proportion of wrong strategies in samples of size n is just the proportion of wrong strategies in the whole population. That is, $\mathbf{E}(n_w/n) = N_w/N = w$. Similar equations hold for irrelevant and correct strategies. Hence:

$$f_1 = w + \tfrac{1}{2}i$$

and, by the same argument:

$$f_j = (\tfrac{1}{2})^j i$$

for j greater than 1. Thus it is shown that the random-sample-of-strategies model with fixed sample size n is a system of recurrent events (this point is obvious and is not proved above) with the same f distribution found in the one-strategy-at-a-time and the all-strategies-at-once models. At this point one can see that the one-strategy-at-a-time model is a special case of the random-sample-of-strategies model with sample size $n=1$; and similarly, the all-strategies-at-once model is a special case with sample size $n = N$.

One further generalization is possible. Since the final equations of the random-sample-of-strategies model contain no reference to the sample size n, one would get a system of recurrent events with the given f distribution from any mixture of systems which use different sample sizes. One can withdraw the assumption that the sample size is fixed, permitting the possibility that samples are of all different sizes. The only restrictions are that for any n, all samples of size n are equally likely; and there are no empty samples.

The strategy-sampling model differs from Estes' stimulus-sampling model (Estes, 1959) in an important respect. Let the total number of elements (strategies or, in Estes' case, stimulus elements or patterns) be N and the sample size be n. In Estes' formulations, n/N is analogous to the learning rate θ and controls the rate of learning and all the statistical characteristics of the acquisition data. In the present model, learning is independent of the sample size n/N and depends solely on the composition of the basic set H; namely, the proportions of correct, wrong, and irrelevant strategies in H. Thus while the sampling process invoked in this strategy-sampling theory is one of those used by Estes, its place in the theory is entirely different.

In this section it has been shown that three models of the selection of strategies all lead to the same system of recurrent events. Whether or not this is of interest depends largely on whether the resulting description fits the data of cue learning experiments, a question which is considered in the remainder of the paper.

STATISTICAL PROPERTIES OF THE RAW DATA

The discussion above has been restricted to the distribution f_j, the probability that an error follows the last error by exactly j trials. The f distribution can be estimated directly from raw data, but this is neither a conventional nor a very interesting way of describing the data of cue learning. In this section the data generated by this model are analyzed in several of the ways commonly employed by experimenters. Details are given in Restle (1961).

Learning curve(s). Consider three versions of the learning curve. One is the succession of correct and wrong responses by an individual subject. A second is the average learning curve of a group of subjects. The third is a corrected or idealized form of the learning curve computed by adjusting a group learning curve (Vincentizing) or by averaging the data of subjects who are selected after the fact for similarity of over-all performance (Spence, 1956).

According to the present theory, the individual data are composed of a sequence of correct and wrong responses in irregular order, followed by an infinite sequence of correct responses. If $w > 0$, there will be somewhat more errors than correct responses on the resolution trials, and there will be a tendency for errors to follow other errors more often than errors follow correct responses. The probability of an error following an error will be $(w + \frac{1}{2}i)/(w + i)$ whereas the probability of an error following a correct response is $\frac{1}{2}$. An individual subject will produce such below-change behavior for some block of trials and then abruptly, after some errors, will either happen on a correct strategy (in the one-strategy-at-a-time model) or will begin a process of elimination which ends up with all correct strategies. This is an extreme form of the "discontinuous" or insightful learning curve. Unfortunately it is difficult to decide whether any individual subject does or does not exhibit this pattern, so data are usually combined.

The group learning curve is merely

the average of a set of (theoretically) discontinuous individual curves. If all subjects have the same parameters c, w, and i, they will nevertheless happen to master the problem at different trials, so that the average learning curve is gradual. Its mathematical form is complex but in general appearance, the group learning from this theory resembles the common "growth" curve (Restle, in 1961).

If one selects, from a larger group of subjects, those who make the same number of total errors, or those who reach criterion at the same time, and averages their learning curves; or if one rescales learning trials as by the Vincent-curve method, the resulting curve will usually be S shaped. The writer has investigated this question by generating data which arise directly from the assumptions of the present model, by use of tables of random numbers. When, from a large set of such data, one selects a subgroup of "subjects" who all make the same number of errors, or who reach criterion at about the same trial, and average the performance within such a subgroup, the result is an S shaped curve. Exact Vincentizing produces a flat (stationary) learning curve before criterion.

The reason for the S shaped curves is not difficult to find; the above methods of selecting or rearranging the data tend to put the (theoretically random) times of solution close together. If the times of solution are put exactly together a step-function should result, but if the times of solution are only grouped close to one another, the step is blurred and an S shaped curve results (Spence, 1956).

Summary statistics of the data. In the present theory the actual trial on which learning takes place is not in any way fixed, but depends upon the random outcome of the process of selecting strategies. The result is large intrinsic variance in the acquisition phase, which can most conveniently be described in terms of the total errors made by each subject.

If each subject is trained until a long sequence of consecutive correct responses has been obtained, one is reasonably sure that the number of errors made approximates the theoretical total errors.

On the first trial or after any error the subject may either make another error, sometime later, or he may make no more errors. The probability that the subject will make at least one more error, the first one in exactly j trials, is f_j. Thus the total probability of at least one more error is:

$$\sum_{j=1}^{\infty}(f_i)=1-c$$

With probability c the subject never makes another error at all. From this it is not difficult to show that the probability of exactly k errors is $(1-c)^k c$. This is the geometric distribution which has mean:

$$\mathbf{E}(k)=(1-c)/c$$

and variance:

$$\mathrm{Var}(k)=(1-c)/c^2.$$

The standard deviation of the distribution of error scores should be nearly equal to its mean, according to the theory, and the distribution should show an extreme positive skewness.

Provided that irrelevant strategies are correct just half the time at random, trials-to-criterion behaves very much like total errors.

Methods of estimating the parameters w *and* c. An important step in any mathematical development of a learning theory is the estimation of parameters. Fortunately, in the present model quite simple and efficient estimates are available. A maximum-likelihood estimator of c is given by:

$$\hat{c}=1/(\overline{T}+1)$$

where $\overline{T}$ is the mean total error score of a group of subjects. The variance of this estimate, with N subjects in the group, is:

$$\mathrm{Var}(\hat{c}) = c^2(1-c)/N$$

It is also possible to estimate w by the maximum-likelihood method. As was mentioned earlier, a high frequency of consecutive errors in the presolution phrase is an indication of a relatively large proportion of wrong strategies, whereas a chance frequency of consecutive errors is an indication that there are relatively few wrong strategies; provided that the irrelevant strategies are correct and wrong strictly at random. The method is to count "Trial 0," an imaginary trial before training begins, as an error. Then for each subject divide this expanded set of errors into M_0 errors which are followed by correct responses and M_1 errors which are followed by errors. Then computing the means of these statistics one has:

$$\hat{w} = \frac{\overline{M}_1 - \overline{M}_0 + 1}{\overline{M}_0 + \overline{M}_1}$$

as a maximum-likelihood estimator of w (Restle, 1961).

Some Variations of the Basic Model

The theory stated above is so restrictive in its assumptions that it cannot be applied with success to a great many experimental data. For example, with the theory above, one must expect the standard deviation of error scores to be just slightly less than their mean, and this is not observed with any great regularity. Furthermore, animal subjects often show a strong tendency to remain with one strategy even if it is wrong or irrelevant, for a fairly long string of trials. The model given above says that the subject starts over after each error, and this simply is not a plausible assumption for animal studies.[2]

Perseveration. The model is quite easily generalized to take some account of perseveration of strategies. In place of the assumption that the subject always resamples after an error, one supposes that resampling occurs with some probability r, which may be considered a constant for given experimental conditions and also a constant during the presolution period. The subject chooses some strategy or sample of strategies at Trial 1, whence the probability of making zero errors is c. The probability that any actual error is the last one is only rc, the joint probability that (a) the subject resamples and (b) having resampled, hits on a correct strategy (in the one-strategy-at-a-time model) or goes into a terminal process of narrowing down (in the all-strategies-at-once or the random-sample-of-strategies models). For this model with perseveration the distribution of total error scores is:

$$P(0) = c$$
$$P(T) = (1-c)(1-rc)^{T-1}rc.$$

where $T > 0$. The value of this model in fitting animal data is illustrated by analyzing a set of error scores reported in detail by Harlow, Harlow, Rueping, and Mason (1960), (See Restle, 1960). Harlow's distributions show a relatively high frequency of solutions with zero errors, along with a spread to very large error scores, in original learning by baby monkeys. The result is that the standard deviations of the distributions are somewhat larger than the means. Harlow et al. remarked on the high degree of perseveration shown by some monkeys. Even more striking is Warren's investigation (Warren, 1959b) of the discrimination learning of cats, which show strong perseverative tendencies and which give distributions of error scores with standard deviations much larger than the corresponding means.

It is not at all sure that perseverative effects can be reduced to the single parameter r, and the writer's investigations are entirely insufficient to support the assumption. Within the model there are

2. The writer is indebted to Marvin Levine for pointing out the importance of this factor in animal discrimination learning.

several symptoms of perseveration; a high frequency of zero error scores relative to the remainder of the distribution, higher standard deviation than mean errors, and consecutive runs of responses which follow a wrong or irrelevant strategy, such as a position habit, object preference, etc. One can imagine that perseverative tendencies would be strong whenever the incentive for learning is not entirely effective, or when the subjects (perhaps from partial reinforcement) have developed an expectation that rewards cannot always be attained. Something of this last effect, in college students, is suggested by the results of Morin (1955).

Complexity of correct strategies. In the model above it is tacitly assumed that the problem can be solved on the basis of a single correct strategy. This seems a reasonable assumption in the case of simultaneous discrimination. However, when two situations are presented on successive trials it is a question whether complete solution involves learning one strategy (turn right to white and left to black) or two strategies, one for each situation. If two strategies are learned independently and with the same parameters, then the distribution of errors is the distribution of the sum of two random variables (total errors in each situation) each of which has a geometric distribution. This results in a negative binomial distribution (see Restle, 1961) with mean:

$$E(T) = 2(1-c)/c$$

and variance:

$$Var(T) = 2(1-c)/c^2.$$

These statements follow at once from the fact that the mean of the sum of two independent variables is the sum of the means, and the variance of the sum is the sum of the component variances. With small c the standard deviation will be about $1/\sqrt{2}$ or about 0.7 of the mean.

An interesting fact can be brought forward in favor of this argument, though the writer has not been able to make an exhaustive test. In a case of successive size discrimination by college students (Restle, 1955) the writer found ratios of standard deviation/mean of 1.1 and 0.9 for two problems—both very close to unity, hence in agreement with the original model and with the notion that a single strategy is sufficient to solve the problem. In a comparable study using rats in a successive black-white discrimination, Amsel (1952) obtained data on three groups in which the ratio of standard deviation to mean was 0.65, 0.68, and 0.72. The rat results are in excellent agreement with the hypothesis that the rats had to use two separate strategies to solve the problem. One might guess that rats do not integrate the two habits, right turn to white and left turn to black, into a single cognitive structure, whereas humans might make just such an integration. The present analysis may be useful in throwing further light on the nature of successive discriminations for various species of subjects.

ADDITIVITY OF CUES

In several papers regarding another theory the writer has discussed the additivity of cues (Restle, 1955, 1957, 1958, 1959a; see also Bourne & Restle, 1959, and Trabasso, 1960). In simple terms the experiment involves three groups; one learns a problem based on a set A of cues, the second learns a problem based on the set B of cues, and the third learns a problem which can be solved using either A or B cues disjunctively. If the sets A and B are separate then the third set $A \cup B$ should have measure $m(A \cup B) = m(A) + m(B)$, (see Trabasso, 1960). Experimental results have been reconciled with an S-R theory involving adaptation of irrelevant cues (Restle, 1955).

Generally speaking, the calculations from the present model are in good numerical agreement with those from the "adaptation" model. Reanalysis of three of the most satisfactory sets of data used before, and one set not previously used, are reported here. The other data previously discussed are so fragmentary that analysis will hardly be fruitful; and Trabasso (1960) used such difficult problems that many of his subjects failed to learn at all on the more difficult problems, making analysis by the present model unsatisfactory. In general, the estimates reported below are not the maximumlikelihood estimates because the subjects were not run to a strong criterion. However, since learning was nearly complete, the approximate estimates are adequate.

Scharlock (1955; see also Restle, 1957) ran a place-versus-response experiment with rats in which the relative weight of correct place (extra-maze) and correct response (intra-maze) strategies can be estimated. He also ran one group with both place and response strategies correct, and a group with response strategies correct and no place cues present. In the calculations below it is assumed that the number of wrong strategies of a given type (place or response) equals the number of correct strategies. This is a symmetry assumption which, while not strictly appropriate for Scharlock's experiment, is needed to permit prediction, since separate estimates of wrong strategies cannot be made on the available data.

Rats learned to go to the same place (using extra-maze cues), with response cues irrelevant, making an average of 9.7 errors. Using the estimate $c = 1/(1 + \bar{T})$, one estimates that the correct place strategies make up $1/10.7 = .093$ of the total set of strategies. Other rats learned to make a constant response to different places, averaging 6.7 errors. We estimate that correct response strategies constitute $1/7.7 = .130$ of the total set.

The simplest interpretation of the experiment is that when both place and response strategies would work, the proportion of correct strategies would be the sum of the proportions of place and re-

sponse strategies, since the same total set of strategies is available. One predicts that with place-plus-response learning, $c = .093 + .130 = .223$. We have the formula that the expected errors to solution is $(1 - c)/c$. Hence the expected mean errors is $.777/.223 = 3.4$; the obtained mean was 4.0, which is adequately close. The discrepancy can partly be explained by the fact that the place-learning and response-learning groups were not run to a high criterion and probably would have made more errors if tested longer. The fast-learning place-plus-response group would likely not have made more errors, since their performance was excellent at the end of the training given.

Another group learned a fixed response in the absence of any good place cues. We assume that this group simply had neither correct nor incorrect place strategies. Its predicted proportion of correct strategies is $.130/1 - 2(.093) = .130/.814 = .160$. The expected errors is $.840/.160 = 5.25$; the observed mean was 5.0 Both predictions are close to the obtained results, well within sampling deviations.

Warren (1959a) has reported data on monkeys in an experiment analogous to Scharlock's study of rats. Warren's monkeys had to learn position habits in some problems and object-discriminations in other problems. Warren also used a response-plus-object problem (object discrimination with the objects left in the same place each trial) and a pure response problem (e.g., choose the left one of two indistinguishable objects.) Predictions followed the same formulas as above, and were extremely accurate; the proportions of object and response strategies were estimated from behavior on object (position-varied) and position (object-varied) problems. When these values were added to predict object-plus-position, the prediction was a mean of 0.67 errors, whereas Warren observed 0.63. For pure response learning, the model predicted 3.25 mean errors and the observed value was 3.04. These agreements between theory and data are well within the range of probable sampling error.

Similar results were obtained by analyzing Warren's experiment on the additivity of color, form, and size cues (Warren, 1953). The analysis is substantially the same as that given in a previous paper (Restle, 1958). Learning data are collected on problems involving only color, only form, or only size differences between the objects. These data are used to calculate the proportional weights of the three sources of strategies, and the resulting values are recombined to compute predicted learning rates for problems involving two or more dimensions; for example, discrimination of a red triangle from a green circle involves color plus form cues. In each calculation account is taken of the greater total number of strategies involved in problems with added cues, and it is assumed that whenever a set of correct strategies is introduced by adding cues, an equally large set of wrong strategies also enter the situation.

Calculations on Warren's (1953) data afforded four predictions of total errors to solution. The four predictions were wrong by -17, 0, 5 and 10 percent respectively, and all of the errors can reasonably be attributed to sampling variations.

The hypothesis of additivity of cues has also been applied to human learning (Restle, 1959a) in an experiment which required subjects to learn differential verbal responses to consonant syllables. The procedure was simple concept formation with individual letters of the syllables used as cues, and the same sort of additivity of cues as above. The adaptation model gave quite accurate predictions and the present model is, if anything, slightly more accurate; it predicts (given data on the two cues separately) that the added-cue group should make an average of 5.26 errors, whereas the observed mean was 5.25. Considering the variability of the data, the extreme closeness is coincidental.

COMPARISON WITH OTHER THEORIES

The three models of the selection of strategies are conceptually similar to the writer's adaptation theory of discrimination learning (Restle, 1955). The "strategies" of the present model resemble the "cues" of the earlier theory. The strategy-selection model has, as a theorem, that the rate of learning depends upon the proportion of correct strategies. A similar idea is expressed in the adaptation model in which it was assumed that the rate of learning (θ) would depend upon the proportion of relevant cues.

Several of the serious faults of the adaptation theory are corrected in the theory of strategy-selection. First, in the adaptation theory the subject was supposed to begin conditioning relevant cues and adapting irrelevant cues, with a rate θ equal to the proportion of relevant cues, right from the first trial of training. Of course, at that first trial the subject has no possible way of knowing which cues will turn out to be relevant—it would be possible for the experimenter to change his mind after the first trial is complete. Hence, the adaptation theory could apply only to a prescient subject. The selection-of-strategies theory does not have the subject treat different strategies differently except on the basis of trials already completed, hence avoids the absurdity. Second, the idea that the structure of the problem (proportion of relevant cues or correct strategies) controls the rate of learning was only a simplifying assumption, with no justification, in the adaptation model; but is an inescapable theorem of strategy-selection. Third, the adaptation theory yielded a determinate learning curve in the sense that $p(n)$ was exactly specified for a given θ and $p(1)$. The variance of typical data was in large part left unexplained by the adaptation model and had to be attributed to individual differences, even though it is notoriously difficult to find any strong predictor of such learning. In the strategy-selection model learning itself is a random event and the model generates variability comparable with that obtained in the data.

Despite these important differences, the present theory is close enough to the adaptation theory to make it possible to carry over many of the theoretical insights, though in modified form. The one type of prediction discussed in this paper was additivity of cues, but other ideas such as the proposed basis of learning sets (Restle, 1958) and various quantitative relationships in concept identification (Bourne & Restle, 1959) can be recast in the mold of the selection of strategies. The many similarities and few differences in predictions must be studied in detail and cannot be discussed here, except to mention that most of the results of the Bourne and Restle paper can be reproduced using the strategy-selection model.

In more general terms, it may be remarked that the strategy-selection model is similar to the ideas of Lashley (1928) and Krechevsky (1932) in general intent. In comparison with stimulus-sampling theories (Restle, 1959b) the strategy-selection model is like theories of the observing response (Atkinson, 1959a, 1959b; Wyckoff, 1952), except that in the strategy-selection model there is no conditioning, only observing (selecting). The mathematical structure of the model is very close to that of Bower's (1960) one-element association model.

Summary

A stochastic model for the solution of cue learning problems by the selection of strategies was stated and developed. Errors were shown to constitute a system of uncertain recurrent events in Feller's sense. Three models, one-strategy-at-a-time, all-strategies-at-once, and a-random-sample-of-strategies, were formulated and shown to yield the same system of recurrent events, to be identical in terms of data. This is the independence-of-sample-size theorem. The basic distribution of the recurrent-events system was used to generate a description of the data, and also a method for estimating the proportions of correct and wrong strategies in a problem. Variations of the model which take account of perseveration and complex strategies, were indicated. Experimental evidence, mainly on the additivity of cues, was discussed.

AMSEL, A. Rate of learning a visual brightness discrimination as a function of discriminanda duration. *J. Comp. physiol. Psychol.*, 1952, **45**, 341-6.

ATKINSON, R. C. The observing response in discrimination learning. Technical Report No. 4, 1959, University of California, Los Angeles, Contract Nonr 233(58). (a)

ATKINSON, R. C. A theory of stimulus discrimination learning. Technical Report No. 1, 1959, University of California, Los Angeles, Contract Nonr 233(58). (b)

BOURNE, L. E., JR., & RESTLE, F. Mathematical theory of concept identification. *Psychol. Rev.*, 1959, **66**, 278-96.

BOWER, G. H. Properties of the one-element model as applied to paired associate learning. Technical Report No. 31, 1960, Stanford University, Contract Nonr 225(17).

ESTES, W. K. Component and pattern models with Markovian interpretations. In R. R. Bush & W. K. Estes (Eds.), *Studies in mathematical learning theory*. Stanford: Stanford Univer. Press, 1959.

FELLER, W. *An introduction to probability theory and its applications.* (1st ed.) New York: Wiley, 1950.

HARLOW, H. F., HARLOW, M. K., RUEPING, R. R., & MASON, W. A. Performance of infant Rhesus monkeys on discrimination learning, delayed response, and discrimination learning set. *J. comp. physiol. Psychol.*, 1960, **53**, 113-21.

KRECHEVSKY, I. "Hypotheses" in rats. *Psychol. Rev.*, 1932, **39**, 516-32.

LASHLEY, K. S. *Brain mechanisms and behavior.* Chicago: Univer. Chicago Press, 1928.

MORIN, R. E. Factors influencing rate and extent of learning in the presence of misinformative feedback. *J. exp. Psychol.*, 1955, **49**, 343-51.

RESTLE, F. A theory of discrimination learning. *Psychol. Rev.*, 1955, **62**, 11-19.

RESTLE, F. Discrimination of cues in mazes: A resolution of the "place-vs.-response" question. *Psychol. Rev.*, 1957, **64**, 217-28.

RESTLE, F. Toward a quantitative description of learning set data. *Psychol. Rev.*, 1958, **65**, 77-91.

RESTLE, F. Additivity of cues and transfer in

discrimination of consonant clusters. *J. exp. Psychol.*, 1959, **57**, 9-14. (a)

RESTLE, F. A survey and classification of learning models. In R. R. Bush & W. K. Estes (Eds.), *Studies in mathematical learning theory.* Stanford Univer. Press, 1959. (b)

RESTLE, F. A note on the "hypothesis" theory of discrimination learning. *Psychol. Rep.* 1960, **7**, 194.

RESTLE, F. Statistical methods for a theory of cue learning. *Psychometrika,* 1961, **26**, 291-306.

SCHARLOCK, D. P. The role of extramaze cues in place and response learning. *J. exp. Psychol.,* 1955, **50**, 249-54.

SPENCE, K. W. *Behavior theory and conditioning.* New Haven: Yale Univer. Press, 1956.

TRABASSO, T. R. Additivity of cues in discrimination learning of letter patterns. *J. exp. Psychol.,* 1960, **60**, 83-8.

WARREN, J. M. Additivity of cues in visual pattern discriminations by monkeys. *J. comp. physiol. Psychol.,* 1953, **46**, 484-6.

WARREN, J. M. Solution of object and positional discriminations by monkeys. *J. comp. physiol. Phychol.,* 1959, **52**, 92-3. (a)

WARREN, J. M. Stimulus perseveration in discrimination learning by cats. *J. comp. physiol. Psychol.,* 1959, **52**, 99-101. (b)

WYCKOFF, L. B. The role of observing responses in discrimination learning. Part 1. *Psychol. Rev.,* 1952, **59**, 431-42.

44 / Reversals Prior to Solution in Concept Identification [1]

GORDON BOWER AND THOMAS TRABASSO,[2] *Stanford University*

These studies investigated the effects of reversal and nonreversal shifts before solution upon performance in a later concept indentification task. In 2 experiments, a reversal or a nonreversal shift after an error on a critical trial had no interfering effect upon subsequent learning. The reversal and nonreversal groups made about the same number of errors and required as many trials to learn as did controls who were not shifted. In a 3rd experiment, 1 group of Ss received reversals on every alternate error, but still made the same number of informed errors as did controls who learned with no shifts. These results support the hypothesis that learning is insightful or an all-or-nothing event in simple concept identification.

In the typical two-category concept identification experiment, S is shown a series of complex patterns which vary in several, binary attributes. As each pattern is presented, S attempts to anticipate the correct classification; following his response, he is informed of the correct response. The patterns are divided into two mutually exclusive classes, R_1 and R_2. If, say, color (red or blue) is the relevant attribute, then red objects might be assigned to Response Class R_1 and blue objects to Class R_2. We will refer to this rule as a particular S-R assignment.

In recent studies (Bower & Trabasso, 1963a; Trabasso, 1963) of this situation with college students, Ss appeared to learn suddenly. Backward learning curves were horizontal at the chance level of 50% correct classifications over all trials until S's last error before solving. The performance of an S might be characterized by saying that on any given trial

he is either in the presolution state or in the solution state, with corresponding probabilities of .50 or 1.00 of correctly classifying the stimuli. According to this two-state description of the performance, learning would be identified as a discrete, one-trial transition from the initial, presolution state into the terminal, solution state.

The theories of cue-selection learning proposed by Restle (1962) and Bower and Trabasso (1963a) imply this two-state description of individual performance. These theories assume that S is selectively attending to or sampling

From the *Journal of Experimental Psychology*, 1963, **66**, 409-18, with permission of the authors and publisher.

1. This research was supported by Grant M-3849 to the first author from the National Institute of Mental Health. The same agency provided the second author with a post-doctoral fellowship, MPD-18070, during which time the work was done. Thanks are due to Milton Kielsmeier who assisted us in obtaining Ss for Exp. III.

2. Now at University of California, Los Angeles.

cues from the stimulus display and that he is testing hypotheses regarding the relevance of these cues to the correct solution. If S's response is correct, it is supposed that he continues to use the same hypothesis; if his response is incorrect, he resamples at random from the set of possible hypotheses. Assume further that the proportion of correct hypotheses is c whereas the remaining proportion $1-c$ is irrelevant hypotheses which lead to correct and incorrect responses half the time. By these assumptions, the probability that S solves the problem after any given error is a fixed constant, c. This elementary theory has been used successfully in predicting quantitative details of several sets of data (Bower & Trabasso, 1963a).

The present studies investigate whether S acquires partial knowledge about the solution to the problem. The all-or-nothing theory supposes that he does not. Specifically, it says that when S makes an error, he has not yet learned anything of relevance regarding the correct concept. Three experiments were performed to provide tests of this assumption; the first two are described now.

Experiments I and II

Experiments I and II are identical in design; Exp. II was a replication of Exp. I with an easier problem and different stimulus materials. The design resembles that used in several animal experiments conducted on the continuity-noncontinuity issue in discrimination learning theory (e.g., Krechevsky, 1938; McCulloch & Pratt, 1934). Control Ss in Group C learned a problem with the same S-R assignments throughout (Cue A-R_1 Cue B-R_2). Two other groups worked on different S-R assignments initially and then were transferred to the assignments of the control group. This transfer occurred immediately after S made an error following a critical trial of the initial series. Group R, a reversal group, was trained initially with the opposite assignments, A-R_2 and B-R_1. Group NR, a nonreversal-shift group, was trained initially with Cues A and B present but irrelevant while another set of cues was relevant (C-R_1, D-R_2).

The question of interest is whether the initial wrong-way training retards performance of Ss in Groups R and NR who are shifted to the final, transfer problem before solving their initial problem. If Ss partially learn responses to the initially relevant cues before the shift, then such partial learning should induce negative transfer on the final problem. However, if S's error initiating the shift indicates that nothing of importance has yet been learned, then the performance on the final problem should be the same for the three groups, independent of the initial S-R assignments.

Method

Experimental design.—A schematic outline of the design is presented in Table 1. Only two of the several stimulus attributes are represented in the left columns of Table 1. The rows give the combinations of stimulus values in the patterns and the correct responses to each pattern are listed under each condition. The Control and Reversal groups had Cues A and B relevant but they had opposite response assignments during initial training (10 trials in Exp. 1 and 5 trials in Exp. II). The Nonreversal group had one of the other dimensions (Cues C and D) relevant during initial training.

The Ss who made an error on Trial 10 in Exp. I or Trial 5 in Exp. II or soon thereafter were immediately shifted to the final problem listed in the right hand column of Table 1. We wished to compare on this final problem only those Ss who had not yet learned their initial problem by Trial 10 (or 5 in Exp. II). Consequently, if an S in any group began a criterion run of 16 consecutive correct responses on or before the critical trial (10 or 5), he was not shifted but was, as a result, excluded from the critical comparison between those Ss who did get put onto the final problem. According to the theory, these

TABLE 1. *Design for Exp. I and II*

Patterns		Response Assignments			
		Initial Trials			Final Problem
Dimension 1	Dimension 2	Control	Reversal	Nonreversal	
A	C	R_1	R_2	R_1	R_1
A	D	R_1	R_2	R_2	R_1
B	C	R_2	R_1	R_1	R_2
B	D	R_2	R_1	R_2	R_2

latter Ss were equalized at the start of the final problem since each S made an error before the shift was effected.

Procedure.—The same instructions were read to all Ss. The S was to classify a set of patterns into two classes. In Exp. I, the classificatory responses were MIB and CEJ; in Exp. II, the numerals 1 and 2. The S was told that the patterns could be classified by a simple principle.

Patterns were presented one at a time on a card holder. The S paced his verbal responses and E then stated the correct classification. The S was allowed 4 sec. to view the pattern after reinforcement. A different order was presented each S by shuffling the cards before the session. Cards were reshuffled at the end of every 64 trials if S had not yet reached the learning criterion of 16 successive correct responses.

Stimulus materials.—For Exp. I, patterns were constructed by sampling a single letter from each of four pairs of letters, (v or w), (F or G), (x or y), (Q or R). Thus, VFYQ was a pattern, WVXR was not. The four letters were printed in a diamond shape on a 3 × 5 in. card. The letters appeared fixed in the order given above, but their locations at the four diamond corners rotated randomly from trial to trial. Location was an irrelevant cue. For Groups C and R, the letter pair (v, w) was relevant; the classification depended on which one of the letters was present on the card. One of the other letter pairs was selected randomly to be initially relevant for each S in Group NR, whereas (v, w) was irrelevant. The final problem was with (v, w) as the relevant cues with response assignments V-MIB and W-CEJ.

For Exp. II, the stimuli were geometric figures drawn in crayon pencil from templates on white 3 × 5 in. file cards. There were six binary dimensions: color (red or

blue); size (large or small); shape (square or hexagon); number (three or four figures); position (figures arranged along right or left diagonal); and colored area within figure (upper-right and lower-left or upper-left and lower-right quadrants). There was one relevant dimension and five irrelevant dimensions for each group. Color was relevant for Groups C and R. One of the other five dimensions was randomly selected and made relevant during initial training for each S in Group NR.

Subjects.—For Exp. I, the Ss were 65 students in the introductory psychology course at Stanford University. Eleven Ss began a criterion run on or before Trial 10; there were 4, 3, and 4 Ss in Groups C, R, and NR, respectively. These Ss do not enter into the comparison on the final problem since they were not transferred. Setting aside these Ss, 18 Ss (13 males and 5 females) remained in each group.

For Exp. II, the Ss were 46 students in the introductory psychology course at Stanford University. Since the problem was easier, a larger proportion of Ss was expected to solve within a few trials. Hence, fewer initial training trials (five) were used so that the majority of Ss would not have to be set aside. Sixteen Ss, 5 in Group C, 4 in Group R, and 7 in Group NR, began a criterion run on or before Trial 5. These Ss were excluded from comparisons on the final problem. There remained 10 Ss (6 males and 4 females) in each group for comparison on the final problem.

Results

In Exp. 1, one S in Group C and one in Group NR failed to reach criterion within 140 trials on the final problem; all other Ss solved within 140 trials.

In Exp. II, all Ss solved the final problem. Comparisons among groups on final-problem performance refer to trials following the error trial that initiated the shift to the final problem for a given S. Average errors and trial of last error are shown in Table 2 for the three conditions in both experiments.

or partial elimination of irrelevant cues (cf. Group NR). Effectively, we may rely upon a single error by S to indicate that he is "naive" about the correct solution. An error in this situation has the properties of an uncertain recurrent event (Restle, 1962); when S commits an error, we may, so to speak, reset him back to

TABLE 2. *Mean errors and trial of last error, SDs, and c estimates for the final problem*

Group	N		Mean Errors	SD	Mean Trial of Last Error	SD
		Exp. I				
Control	18	.052	19.11	19.01	38.33	32.50
Reversal	18	.052	19.11	16.42	39.56	32.27
Nonreversal	18	.055	18.28	19.28	36.94	38.23
		Exp. II				
Control	10	.078	12.90	8.42	28.60	20.82
Reversal	10	.067	14.90	9.77	29.00	19.71
Nonreversal	10	.071	14.00	14.15	26.90	26.45

The group differences on mean errors and mean trial of last error on the final problem were negligible in both experiments. The learning-parameter estimates (reciprocal of mean errors) are shown in Table 2; a likelihood ratio test for equality of c's was nonsignificant in both experiments. Further, a likelihood ratio test that each S's learning parameter, c_i, was equal to a common c was tested for all 65 Ss in Exp. I and for all 45 Ss in Exp. II. In each case, the null hypothesis could not be rejected—for Exp. I, χ^2 (64)=53.3, $p > .05$; for Exp. II, χ^2 (45)=42.4, p > .05 (Bower & Trabasso, 1963b). Thus, the data were consistent with the hypothesis of a common c for Ss in each experiment; the differences among Ss' error scores could be attributed to the variability inherent in the theoretical process.

The lack of group differences indicates that performance on the final problem was unrelated to the response assignments reinforced during the initial series. Correspondingly, there was no evidence for partial learning of the relevant cues

the starting point from which he began working on the problem. It should be noted that the null effects of reversal and nonreversal shifts before solution differ from the effects of such shifts after initial solution has occurred (Kendler & Kendler, 1962). What differs in the two cases is that after solution, S has a strong bias to attend to the formerly relevant cue, whereas before solution he is sampling cues at random to test (Kendler, Glucksberg, & Keston, 1961).

Presolution analyses.—The data prior to the last error of each S were analyzed according to the expectations of the all-or-none theory. In theory, the presolution responses of S may be represented as a stationary and independent binomial process. To test for a constant probability of success prior to the last error, backward learning curves (Hayes, 1953) were constructed. These were stationary near .50 in each experiment. Pooling the two experiments, the probabilities of a correct classification on Trials $-1, -2 \cdots -8$ backwards from the last error were .50, .50, .52, .53, .54, .49, .51, and .50. Furthermore, the curve was flat when analyzed in two-trial blocks for 40 trials backwards from criterion, $\chi^2(19) = 19.31$, $p > .05$.

Successive correct or incorrect responses prior to the last error were also statistically independent. For Exp. I, the conditional probability of a success was .52 following a success and .53 following an error; in Exp. II, the conditional probabilities were .50 and .52, respectively. Neither set of data permits rejection of the hypothesis of independence.

If presolution responses approximate a binomial series, then the number of successes between two successive errors should be geometrically distributed as qp^n, where p is the probability of a success and $q = 1 - p$. Figure 1 shows that this random variable has a geometric distribution in the data of the two experiments.

A number of numerical predictions has been made accurately for these data, and they are reported elsewhere (Bower & Trabasso, 1963a). The distribution of total errors should be geometric, i.e., $\Pr\{T = k\} = c(1 - c)^{k-1}$, and this was observed in both experiments. The geometric distribution implies that the SD will be large but slightly less than the mean. Pooling all Ss in Exp. I from Trial 1, the mean errors were 20.85; the observed σ was 18.49 with 20.30 predicted. Pooling all Ss in Exp. II from Trial 1, the mean errors were 11.45; the observed σ was 11.02 with 10.96 predicted.

A criticism that might be made is that the theory asserts the null hypothesis,

and what has been shown is that our experiments had inadequate power to reject the null hypothesis. The methodological status of such matters has been discussed elsewhere (Binder, 1963; Grant, 1962). Our opinion is that if the partial learning is of such small magnitude that it does not appear with a combined total of 28 Ss in each condition, then indeed it may be considered a negligible effect. To provide a more severe test of the theory, Exp. III was conducted by extending the presolution reversal design. In Exp. III, the S-R assignments were reversed after every second error that S made. Thus, as S proceeded along through his series of trials, the S-R assignments were switching repeatedly back and forth.

EXPERIMENT III

The procedure will be illustrated briefly in order to make the theoretical predictions meaningful. Table 3 shows the first 14 trials for a hypothetical S.

TABLE 3. Correct (C) and error (E) responses of a hypothetical S in the reversal group

Alternating S-R Assignments	1	2	3	4	5	6	7	8	9	10	11	12	13	14
Red-VEK / Blue-CEJ	C	E	C	E ↓						↑ C	E	E ↓		
Blue-VEK / Red-CEJ					C	C	E	C	E				C	E

The stimulus patterns vary in five binary dimensions. Color is the relevant attribute and this S begins with the assignments "Red in Class VEK, Blue in Class CEJ." Suppose that his responses to the patterns on Trials 1 and 3 are correct according to these assignments, whereas his responses to the patterns on Trials 2 and 4 are wrong. The second error, occurring on Trial 4, initiates an immediate reversal of the S-R assignments, and S is told "Correct" for his response on Trial 4. According to the reversed assign-

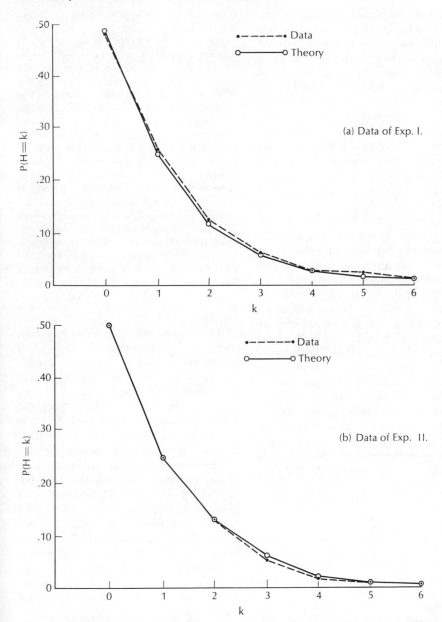

FIG. 1. Distribution of numbers of successes intervening betwen two adjacent errors.

ments, the responses on Trials 4, 5, and 7 are correct whereas those on Trials 6 and 8 are errors. The second error of this subseries, occurring on Trial 8, initiates another immediate reversal back to the original S-R assignments, and the response on Trial 8 is called "Correct." The series of reversals on every second error continues in this fashion until S produces a string of 10 consecutive correct responses since his last reversal. A second group of control Ss was never reversed; they simply learned a fixed set of S-R assignments by the conventional training procedure in which they were informed of every error.

The prediction from the theory is that the number of *informed* errors (those not arrowed in Table 3) before learning for the Reversal Ss will be equal to the number of informed errors before learning made by the Control Ss. That is, no interference should result from the multiple reversals that occur during training. This prediction follows from the assumptions that learning occurs in one trial, that opportunities for giving up an irrelevant hypothesis, and hence learning, occur only after *informed* errors, and that the probability of learning following an informed error is not affected by the past S-R assignments for the relevant cues. The point of the last statement might be phrased in terms of the cues to which S is attending: if S is selectively attending to irrelevant cues and is not "noticing" the color, then his behavior when he starts noticing color is unaffected by the past history of changing correlations between the reinforced responses and the unnoticed color values. In contrast to the equality prediction above, if any one of the three assumptions is wrong, the Reversal Ss should make more informed errors than do the Control Ss.

Method

Subjects.—The Ss were 33 paid volunteers from elementary history and psychology classes at Foothill Junior College who were randomly assigned to two groups (10 or 11 males and 6 females each).

Procedure.—The instructions were the same as those used in Exp. I and II. The classificatory responses were VEK and CEJ. The learning criterion was 10 successive correct responses.

Stimuli.—The patterns were identical to those used in Exp. II with the exception that the area which was colored within each figure was kept constant. Thus, there were one relevant and four irrelevant binary

dimensions. Color was the relevant dimension for both groups.

Design.—The Control group of 16 Ss learned a problem with fixed S-R assignments throughout. For 8 of these Ss, the assignments were Red-VEK and Blue-CEJ; the other 8 Ss had the opposite pairings. The Reversal group of 17 Ss learned the same color-relevant problem but the response assignments were reversed on every second error that each S committed. On alternate errors, S's response was confirmed (called 'Correct") in accord with the instantaneous reversal of the assignments which E made as soon as S's second error of a subseries occurred. The procedure was discussed above in connection with Table 3. By this procedure, it would not be feasible to reverse S on every error since he would always be told "Correct" and E would forfeit any control over what S learns.

Results

All but two Ss, one in each group, met the learning criterion. The two nonsolvers arrived late for their experimental session and had less time than the other Ss to complete the problem; therefore, they are excluded from the following analyses. Since both Ss made about the same number of errors, their exclusion does not affect the comparisons.

The remaining 16 Ss in the Reversal group averaged 7.00 reversal shifts before meeting criterion. The average numbers of informed errors were nearly equal for the two groups. For the Reversal group, the average number of informed errors was 7.81; for the Control group, it was 8.00. The *SD* of errors for the Control group was 8.22. Thus, the difference of .19 informed errors is not significant.

Two Ss in each group learned after only one error. As a result, two Ss in the Reversal condition were never reversed because they learned their initial response assignments. Removing these two Ss from each group, the mean number of reversals was 8.00; the mean number of informed errors was 8.79 for the Reversal group and 9.08 for the Control group, a nonsignificant difference.

On those trials where a reversal occurred, S was told "Correct" when in fact he made an error. Such a procedure should serve to maintain an irrelevant hypothesis for at least one more trial. The net effect of this procedure would be to produce more "correct" responses before the last error for the Reversal Ss than for the Controls. The mean numbers of correct responses prior to criterion for the Reversal and Control groups were 21.1 and 9.6, respectively, $t(29) = 1.99$, $p = .05$.

The mean trial of last error can be predicted for both groups once the mean errors for the Control group are known. These predictions are made to rule out the possibility that (a) length of success runs increased over trials in the Control groups and (b) successive reversals tended to become more spaced out in the Reversal group over trials. For both predictions, the probability of a success prior to the last error is assumed to be constant and the a priori one-half. Let T_c be the total errors made by an S in the Control group; then his expected trial of last error is $2T_c$. The predicted mean trial of last error for the Control group was 16.00; the observed was 17.60. The difference was not significant by a matched t test, $t(14) = 1.75$, $p > .05$.

For the Reversal group, let T_r be the number of informed errors and r be the number of reversals before learning. Then the average trial of last error, n', for the Reversal group should be

$$n' = T_r + r + 1 + 2(T_r - 1). \qquad [1]$$

The first two terms, T_r and r, in Equation 1 count the number of informed error trials plus the reversal trials. The additional terms $1 + 2(T_r - 1)$ are the expected number of correct responses for an S who makes T_r informed errors in the Reversal group. The T_r informed errors partition the successes as follows:

there is an average of one success before the first error, and an average of two successes between each of the $T_r - 1$ remaining informed errors. By hypothesis, the informed errors should be the same for both groups, so that $T_c = T_r$. Secondly, r is related to T_r, for if S makes T_r informed errors, then his number of reversals should be $T_r - 1$, assuming that he makes one more error after his rth and final reversal. (Note that the average number of reversals was 7, or exactly $T_c - 1$.) Substituting into Equation 1 the relations $r = T_r - 1$ and $T_c = T_r$, the following relation is obtained between T_c and the average trial of last error for the Reversal group.

$$n' = 4T_c - 2. \qquad [2]$$

Substituting the observed $T_c = 8.00$ into Equation 2, the predicted mean trial of last error (n') is 30.00. For the 16 solvers in the Reversal group, the observed value was 28.81; the SD was 26.09. The prediction is thus not significantly discrepant from the data.

The results of Exp. III favor a one-step, all-or-none interpretation of two-category concept identification in adult Ss. In addition, the results indicate that the effective information promoting learning in these problems occurs on informed error trials. Finally, the results are consistent with the notion that S's probability of solving after any given informed error is unaffected by the past history of inconsistent reinforcements to the relevant cue on which he solves.

Again the criticism may be lodged that our experiment had inadequate power to reject the null hypothesis. To provide further power for the test, we presently are running the design of Exp. III with larger groups of Ss, a different problem, and more explicit instructions to S regarding the dimensions of the stimuli, the form of the solution, etc. To date, with 24 Ss in each condition, the mean numbers of informed errors in the Control and Multiple Reversal groups are 8.22 and 7.94, respectively. Thus, the qualitative results of Exp. III are being replicated.

DISCUSSION

The Reversal and Control conditions in Exp. I and II resemble the standard ones used with this design on the continuity-noncontinuity issue. Judging from the review by Blum and Blum (1949), nearly all of the previous studies involved rats learning simultaneous discriminations with a small number of cues. On balance, that evidence favored a continuity position supplemented by constructs such as receptor orienting acts (e.g., Ehrenfreund, 1948). Whether such results should have a crucial bearing on a situational theory of adult human concept identification is a moot question. Writing for the continuity position, Spence (1940) pointed out early that the results from the animal studies may not be directly relevant to adult human learning mediated by complex symbolic mechanisms. Such mechanisms evidently are used by adults in solving concept problems, and current theorizing emphasizes such mechanisms (e.g., Bower & Trabasso, 1963a; Hunt, 1962; Kendler & Kendler, 1962; Underwood & Richardson, 1956). Our working hypothesis is that the extent to which an S's discrimination learning fits the all-or-none as opposed to the incremental description depends on the extent to which symbolic mediating responses are available to S.

It would appear that one reason why the all-or-nothing model predicts accurately in these experiments is that the conditions promote "focus sampling" (Bruner, Goodnow, & Austin, 1956) because the memory load on S is otherwise overwhelming. The random-cue selection postulate implies that S's selection following an error of a new focus sample of cues to test is not affected by the past history of response assignments for the various cues. Such random selection of a sample focus is reasonable only if S's memory of specific past information is in some way impoverished. The experimental conditions presumably responsible for such poor memory include (a) the complexity of the stimuli, here 5 or 6 bits plus the 1-bit response, (b)

the relatively rapid rate of presentation of this information (average time viewing each card was approximately 6 sec.), and (c) S has a specific set to identify the relevant cue, not to memorize and later recall the information he is seeing. In other experiments by us, direct tests of recall of specific information under these conditions showed the memory for six-card series to be very poor. Judging from the limited capacity of Ss for quickly processing and storing such large amounts of information, it is not surprising to find that they resort to focus sampling of specific cues to test.

The present results extend previous findings (Trabasso, 1963) that single-cue concept problems can be characterized as a one-step learning process. However, it is clear that not all varieties of concept learning can be so simply described. Our aim was to explore initially the most elementary form of concept learning, in a situation similar to a conventional discrimination learning procedure. Obviously, the simple all-or-nothing model must be elaborated and extended before it will account for learning of compounds of simpler concepts (e.g., conjunctions of several cues). Such extensions are currently under investigation (Trabasso & Bower, in press).

BLUM, R. A., & BLUM, J. S. Factual issues in the "continuity controversy." Psychol. Rev., 1949, 56, 33-50.

BINDER, A. Further considerations on testing the null hypothesis and the strategy and tactics of investigating theoretical models. Psychol. Rev., 1963, 70, 107-115.

BOWER, G. H., & TRABASSO, T. R. Concept identification. In R. C. Atkinson (Ed.), Studies in mathematical psychology. Stanford: Stanford Univer. Press, 1963, in press. (a)

BOWER, G. H., & TRABASSO, T. R. Working paper on concept identification. Unpublished manuscript, Stanford University Library, 1963. (b)

BRUNER, J. S., GOODNOW, J. J., & AUSTIN, A. A study of thinking. Wiley: New York, 1956.

EHRENFREUND, D. An experimental test of the continuity theory of discrimination learning with pattern vision. J. comp. physiol., 1948, 41, 408-22.

GRANT, D. A. Testing the null hypothesis and the strategy and tactics of investigating theoretical models. Psychol. Rev., 1962. 69, 54-61.

HAYES, K. J. The backward curve: A method for the study of learning. Psychol. Rev., 1953, 60, 269-75.

HUNT, E. B. Concept learning. New York: Wiley, 1962.

KENDLER, H. H., GLUCKSBERG, S., & KESTON, R. Perception and mediation in concept learning. J. exp. Psychol., 1961, 61, 1-16.

KENDLER, H. H., & KENDLER, T. S. Vertical and

horizontal processes in problem solving. *Psychol. Rev.*, 1962, **69**, 1-16.

KRECHEVSKY, I. A study of the continuity of the problem-solving process. *Psychol. Rev.*, 1938, **45**, 107-33

McCULLOCH, T. L., & PRATT, J. G. A study of the pre-solution period in weight discrimination by white rats. *Psychol. Rev.*, 1934, **18**, 271-90.

RESTLE, F. The selection of strategies in cue learning. *Psychol. Rev.*, 1962, **69**, 329-43.

SPENCE, K. W. Continuous versus noncontinuous interpretations of discrimination learning. *Psychol. Rev.*, 1940, **54**, 223-9.

TRABASSO, T. R. Stimulus emphasis and all-or-none learning in concept identification. *J. exp. Psychol.*, 1963, **65**, 398-406.

TRABASSO, T. R., & BOWER, G. H. Component learning in the four-category problem. *J. math. Psychol.*, in press.

UNDERWOOD, B. J., & RICHARDSON, J. Verbal concept learning as a function of instructions and dominance level. *J. exp. Psychol.*, 1956, **51**, 229-38.

45 / Effects of Reversal and Nonreversal Shifts with CVC Stimuli

WILLIAM BOGARTZ, *University of Kansas*

An experiment was performed comparing performance on reversal and nonreversal shifts after training to a criterion of one perfect trial or 50% overlearning on the first task. The Ss were 48 undergraduates. Stimuli were eight CVCs which had no relevant attribute in common. Learning was by a standard paired-associate method. Reversal shift was superior to nonreversal shift, and overlearning facilitated performance on the second task. It was concluded that mediating responses to stimulus dimensions are not necessary for the shift effect. Alternative explanations in terms of partial reinforcement, mediated association, and extraexperimental transfer were considered.

There has been a great deal of interest recently in experiments comparing reversal and nonreversal shifts (Kendler & D'Amato, 1955; Kendler & Mayzner, 1956; Kendler & Kendler, 1959, 1962). One characteristic of the basic procedure underlying these experiments is that in the nonreversal shift the correct responses to half the stimuli remain unchanged, so that a simple association theory would be constrained to predict better performance than in the reversal shift, where all of the stimuli must be associated with different responses. Still, the consensus of results has been that adult human Ss learn the reversal-shift task more easily. This is interpreted to mean that some sort of multi-stage mediation process must be at work.

At this point, however, some divergence of views is possible. Kendler and Kendler (1962) have concluded that it is a verbal response to the relevant dimension which serves to mediate correct responding in the reversal shift. While this explanation is plausible, it carries the assumption that it is the variation of the *dimensions* and the responses, and not some other property of the situation, which is responsible for the observed effect. This assumption has not yet been tested. Since all experiments dealing with the shift effect have used stimuli characterized by clearly defined dimensions such as color and size, it is premature to conclude that the effects would not also be observed were these dimensions absent.

The present research was designed to investigate the above issue by constructing an analogue of the basic shift experiment in such a way as to eliminate the role of dimensions. The experiment reported below differs from previous studies in that the stimuli were CVCs, and those stimuli for which a given response was correct shared no clear common attribute. No control for partial reinforcement (Buss, 1953, 1956; Kelleher,

From the *Journal of Verbal Learning and Verbal Behavior*, 1965, **4**, 484-8, with permission of the author and publisher, Academic Press, Inc.

1956) was attempted, for reasons to be treated in the discussion. In all other respects, the S-R relationships characteristic of reversal and nonreversal shifts were present.

METHOD

Materials. Eight CVCs from Noble's (1961) list, ranging from 2.42 to 2.51 in m', were printed on 4×6-inch white plastic cards. On the left side of each card was a CVC, and on the right side a symbol representing the correct response, either a dot or a cross. Four lists were prepared, designated 1, 1R, 2, and 2R, in each of which four stimuli had the dot response and the other four the cross response, but differing in the particular assignments. Beginning with list 1, half of the dots and half of the crosses were interchanged to make list 2, and all responses on each of these two lists were reversed to yield lists 1R and 2R. All consonants in the CVC stimuli were different, while four vowels each occurred twice, but were orthog-

task was then begun without interruption and continued to a criterion of one perfect trial.

Design. The experiment was a $2 \times 2 \times 4$ factorial design in three randomized blocks, with the 16 Ss in each block randomly assigned to treatments. The factors were Shifts (reversal or nonreversal shift), Training (criterion or 50% overlearning on Task I), and Lists (particular list learned in Task II). The pairs of lists employed for the two tasks were for the reversal condition: 1-1R, 2-2R, 1R-1, or 2R-2; for the nonreversal condition: 1-2R, 2-1R, 1R-2, or 2R-1. As indicated above, the two lists in a reversal shift differed in all their responses, while those in a nonreversal shift differed in exactly half of both dots and crosses.

RESULTS

Mean errors to criterion, trials to criterion, and errors per trial for each of the four main treatment groups are summarized in Table 1.

TABLE 1. *Mean trials to criterion, errors to criterion, and errors per trial on Task II*

Training	Shift	Trials to criterion		Errors to criterion		Errors per trial	
		Mean	SD	Mean	SD	Mean	SD
Criterion	R	7.33	3.58	16.00	2.66	2.33	.75
	NR	8.83	5.46	25.92	15.94	3.36	1.32
Overlearning	R	2.67	1.23	5.08	2.25	1.94	.58
	NR	7.08	6.56	20.00	20.16	3.07	.93

onal to the dots and crosses in all lists. Each list was used to construct three decks of eight cards, each arranged in a different order.

Subjects. The Ss were 48 students from the introductory psychology course.

Procedure. The Ss were run individually, under standard instructions for paired-associate learning. Stimuli were presented in a Hunter Cardmaster at a 2:2-sec rate, with a 20-sec intertrial interval (once through an eight-item deck was considered a trial). The CVCs appeared in three different orders, which were randomly varied from trial to trial. Training on the first task was continued to a criterion of one perfect trial or for half again as many overlearning trials, as explained in the next section. The second

Analysis of variance of errors to criterion, after a logarithmic transformation, yielded significant effects of Shifts, $F(1,39) = 16.41$, $p < .001$, and Training, $F(1,39) = 13.99$, $p < .001$. Interaction of these two variables was not significant at the .05 level, $F(1.39) = 3.35$, $p < .08$. Analysis of trials to criterion showed substantially the same effects, with significant Shifts, $F(1,39) = 4.86$, $p < .05$, and Training, $F(1,39) = 5.72$, $p < .05$, but no significant interaction ($F = 1.19$).

Because of the theoretical inmportance of any asymmetry in the shift effect as a function of training, and in view of the suggested interaction in the error data, further comparisons were made between all pairs of treatments by the Newman-Keuls procedure for *a posteriori* test (Winer, 1962). The results may be summarized as follows: the over-learning-reversal condition was superior to all others both in errors to criterion ($p < .01$) and trials to criterion ($p < .05$), but the other three conditions did not differ. In particular, reversal shift superiority was significant in the overlearning condition on both errors, $q(3,39) = 5.88$, $p < .01$, and trials, $q(2,39) = 3.29$, $p < .05$, but there was no significant shift effect in the criterion condition for either errors, $q(3,39) = 2.22$, $p > .10$, or trials, $q(2,39) = 1.50$, $p > .10$. Thus, while the data do not provide clear evidence of an interaction between Shifts and Training, they do indicate that the hypothesis of no shift effect in the criterion condition may not be rejected.

These findings confirm the results of Ludvigson & Caul (1964), for shifts with two response categories with "dimensional" stimuli, which also indicated a significant shift effect with overlearning but not with criterion training.

Analysis of errors per trial gave somewhat different results. For this variable, Shifts was significant, $F(1,39) = 17.68$, $p < .001$, but there was no appreciable effect of Training ($F = 1.01$) or its interaction with Shifts ($F = .00$). These results mean that overlearning affected errors to criterion and trials to criterion proportionately, while the shift effects were disproportionate, that is, changed one measure relatively more than the other. This must be the case in order for a difference to be produced in the ratio of errors to trials.

In order to evaluate the data in more detail, errors in the nonreversal condition were subjected to a further analysis. These errors could occur either on shifted (S) items, whose responses had been changed in Task II, or on unshifted (U) items. A repeated-measures analysis of

variance was performed on the data for the first three post-shift trials.

This analysis yielded significant effects of Items, $F(1,22) = 42.00$, $p < .001$, Trials, $F(2,44) = 6.29$, $p < .005$, Items × Trials, $F(2,44) = 9.28$, $p < .001$, and Items × Training, $F(1,22) = 7.31$, $p < .025$. These effects indicated that more errors were made on S items, errors diminished over trials, the difference between errors on S and U items diminished over trials, and the difference between S and U items was greater in the overlearning condition.

Of special interest is the interaction of S versus U errors with trials. The mean numbers of errors on S items were, for the three trials, 3.46, 2.08, and 1.54. Mean errors on U items were .88, 1.04, and 1.17. That is, errors on the unshifted items, which of course represent responses which were incorrect in both tasks, did not extinguish as rapidly as those on shifted items, and even appeared to show a slight increase, or at least no decrease. Precisely the opposite would be expected from the standpoint of a simple association, partial reinforcement, or response-to-dimension hypothesis.

Discussion

It is clear that under the present conditions differential performance occurred in the absence of the dimensions central to the interpretation proposed by Kendler and Kendler (1962). It is therefore necessary to consider alternative explanations for the shift effect.

Partial reinforcement. Since in the non-reversal shift responses to half of the stimuli remain unchanged, Buss (1953) argued that responses to irrelevant cues would be partially reinforced, and that this might delay acquisition in Task II and thus account for the shift effect. In the present experiment it is assumed that the only pertinent cues were the letters of which the CVCs were composed. The consonants, of which no two were alike, were relevant in both tasks, and the vowels were always orthogonal to the dot and cross responses, and hence irrelevant in both tasks. There was thus no basis for the partial reinforcement proposed by Buss.

Mediated association. If it is assumed that stimuli which are associated with a common response in Task I will tend to become associated with each other (Jenkins, 1963) or equivalent (Katz, 1963; Petre, 1964), then when in Task II a new response must be associated with a given stimulus, this response should generalize to the other stimuli with which it was associated in Task I. This process would produce correct responses in the reversal shift and incorrect responses in the nonreversal shift.

It would appear that part of the variation in this experiment is attributable to mediated association (MA), but the results are far from clear. The interaction between trials and item type in the nonreversal condition is perhaps the best support, since it is at variance with the alternative hypotheses but can be explained by generalization of responses from shifted to unshifted items. The MA hypothesis also implies a greater shift effect in the overlearning condition, since the amount of generalization should vary with degree of mastery of Task I. On this point the data are inconclusive, since there was no significant interaction of Shifts and Training. Nevertheless, the effects actually observed were in the predicted relation, and in view of the similar results reported by Ludvigson and Caul (1964), there is at least a presumption that the hypothesis may have some substance. Further replication is indicated.

Extraexperimental transfer. The reversal shift is isomorphic with a habit which may often be present in S's preexperimental repertoire, which has several names, such as "doing the opposite," "switching," or the term "reversal" shift,

and which might produce positive transfer by providing a means for recoding the contingency between Tasks I and II. This notion receives some support from the fact that 15 of the 24 Ss in the reversal condition responded to a nonspecific query after the experiment by reporting that they "just did the opposite," or words to that effect. This sort of data has its limitations, but deserves to be considered.

The hypothesis of extraexperimental transfer can also successfully account for two findings which are accommodated only with difficulty by the Kendler's explanation, namely that reversal shift superiority tends to vanish when there are four response categories instead of two (Kendler & Mayzner, 1956; Ludvigson & Caul, 1964), and that young children do not learn the reversal shift more easily (Kendler & Kendler, 1959). The former follows immediately from the fact that "doing the opposite" cannot generate correct responses exclusively when there are four alternatives, and the latter would of course be the case for a given S at any time before this particular concept has been learned.

Conclusion. The one clear conclusion to be drawn from this experiment is that mediating responses to dimensions of the stimuli are not necessary for the shift effect. This finding neither contradicts previous results nor implies that stimulus dimensions are never a basis for transfer, but it does indicate the need for further analytic experiments with homogeneous stimuli.

Buss, A. H. Rigidity as a function of reversal and nonreversal shifts in the learning of successive discrimination. *J. exp. Psychol.*, 1953, **45**, 75-81.

Buss, A. H. Reversal and nonreversal shifts in concept formation with partial reinforcement eliminated. *J. exp. Psychol.*, 1956, **52**, 162-6.

HARROW, M. Stimulus aspects responsible for the rapid acquisition of reversal shifts in concept formation. *J. exp. Psychol.*, 1964, **67**, 330-34.

JENKINS, J. J. Mediated associations: paradigms and situations. In Cofer, C. N. (Ed.), *Verbal behavior and learning.* New York: McGraw-Hill, 1963.

KATZ, PHYLLIS A. Effects of labels on children's

perception and discrimination learning. *J. exp. Psychol.*, 1963, **66**, 423-8.

KELLEHER, R. T. Discrimination learning as a function of reversal and nonreversal shifts. *J. exp. Psychol.*, 1956, **51**, 379-84.

KENDLER, H. H., AND D'AMATO, M. J. A comparison of reversal and nonreversal shifts in human concept formation behavior. *J. exp. Psychol.*, 1955, **49**, 165-74.

KENDLER, T. S., AND KENDLER, H. H. Reversal and nonreversal shifts in kindergarten children. *J. exp. Psychol.*, 1959, **58**, 56-60.

KENDLER, H. H., AND KENDLER, T. S. Vertical and horizontal processes in problem solving. *Psychol. Rev.*, 1962, **69**, 1-16.

KENDLER, H. H., AND MAYZNER, M. S. Reversal and nonreversal shifts in card-sorting tasks with two or four sorting categories. *J. exp. Psychol.*, 1956, **51**, 244-8.

LUDVIGSON, H. M., AND CAUL, W. F. Relative effect of overlearning on reversal and nonreversal shifts with two and four sorting categories. *J. exp. Psychol.*, 1964, **68**, 301-6.

NOBLE, C. E. Measurement of association value (*a*), rated associations (*a'*), and scaled meaningfulness (*m'*) for the 2100 CVC combinations of the English alphabet. *Psychol. Rep.*, 1961, **8**, 487-521.

PETRE, R. D. Concept asquisition as a function of stimulus-equivalence pretraining with identical and dissimilar stimuli. *J. exp. Psychol.*, 1964, **67**, 360-64.

WINER, B. J. *Statistical principles in experimental design.* New York: McGraw-Hill, 1962.

SECTION X

CONDITIONING OF VERBAL RESPONSE CLASSES

The two areas of verbal operant conditioning and rote verbal learning represent basically different approaches to the study of human learning insofar as their heritage and emphases are concerned. Both monitor the verbal utterances of subjects in a controlled situation and involve the presentation of a predetermined environmental event that permits learning to take place. Nevertheless, their differences are more salient than their similarities.

The traditional rote learning approach reflects the influence of its pioneer ancestor, Ebbinghaus. The emphasis is upon accurate memorization. Except for special purposes, the materials are fixed lists of unrelated items presented for successive trials to a subject whose task is clearly specified. Although prompt feedback is provided at every turn of the memory drum, the fast pace of the machine tends to restrict effective development of strategies or organized attacks upon the material. The result is *rote* learning.

The conditioning of verbal operants appears to be more recent in origin. It might be traced to Thorndike's work upon the effects of symbolic rewards and punishments. The data and theory bearing upon that problem have been thoroughly analyzed in Postman's (1962) excellent review. But verbal operant conditioning appears to be nothing less than an enlargement of experimental activity beyond the confines of the Skinner box, to the human organism, with a different class of operants and a different set of reinforcers. Instead of memorization, the emphasis is upon changes in the rate of broadly defined responses. The basic paradigm is familiar. When a response from a preselected operant class is emitted, a stimulus contingent upon that emission is presented, and depending upon the consequences for rate of responding, the stimulus is either called a reinforcer or it is not. In contrast to the more restricted rote learning situation, there is no pacing and no prescribed set of materials, and the instructions are rather vaguely permissive ("just say words"), so that the subject is not directed to any clearcut goal. Beyond this basic paradigm, the entire range of associated phenomena can be explored. Awaiting the experimenter's contingencies are the discriminated operants, intermittent reinforcement schedules, response chaining, superstitions, and so forth. Whether such a prospect offers any more profitable a route to a firm under-

493

standing of human learning than does the memory drum, is a question whose answer mainly serves to exercise the speakers' biases.

As will be seen, the challenging simplicity of the operant conditioning model has led to a somewhat mentalistic counter-proposal. Critics have asked whether the nature of the subjects' awareness of the situation helps determine the learning outcome. Being so loosely instructed, perhaps the subject tries to find out what is really going on, if anything, and engages in tests of various hypotheses. Such a notion is foreign to the operant conditioning vocabulary, but it seems inevitable that whenever human subjects are introduced, a cognitive interpretation is not far behind.

A promising practical application of Skinner's approach to verbal learning is the teaching machine. The operation of this device is partially predicated upon the assumption that immediate reinforcement is most effective. However, even this premise is not without detractors, for Cook (1963) plainly suggests that the strict conception of reinforcement is out of place in verbal learning. The question of the relationship between rote learning principles and human learning in general, is discussed in a recent contribution by Underwood (1964).

The following readings are presented in their chronological order of appearance in the literature. They display the progression of early findings and hopes, followed by inevitable complications highlighted by increasing focus upon the problem of awareness.

The article by Greenspoon describes the reference experiment in this area whose methodology is a faithful translation of the Skinnerian technique used with infra-human organisms. It was found that the contingent stimulus "Mmm-hmm" was a reinforcer governing the rate of emission of plural nouns. Through post-experimental inquiries it appeared that the effect occurred without the subjects being aware of the reinforcing contingency. It was evidently a case of automatic action of a reinforcer. Other verbal conditioning attempts were reported at this time, such as that by Hildum and Brown (1956), which showed the possibility of influencing the outcome of attitude surveys.

The Verplanck article demonstrated conditioning of rate of opinions through agreement and paraphrase. Conducted in naturalistic settings, with subjects who were unaware of its purpose, the study dramatically implied that one's very conversation can be deliberately manipulated in a manner so subtle as to arouse no suspicion.

The article by Salzinger and Pisoni has relevance for the clinical interview situation. It shows that the rate of self-referred affect statements of schizophrenic patients can be reliably conditioned by the interviewer's agreement responses.

Dulany's article inquired whether verbal conditioning is strictly a matter of the automatic influence of reinforcers, or whether it is mediated by the subject's hypotheses concerning the task. Two related experiments lent support to the latter alternative. Pertinent to problems of post-experimental inquiry is Orne's (1962) discussion of "demand characteristics" and their effects.

Although several studies showed a relationship between awareness of the reinforcing contingency and the probability of conditioning, the issue remained of whether this awareness came about as a *consequence* of verbal conditioning itself. The article by DeNike tested this possibility. The clearcut outcome of the experiment strongly suggested that performance gains were mediated by awareness.

It would appear that the one-stage conception of verbal operant conditioning is being strongly challenged by a cognitive account.

COOK, J. O. "Superstition" in the Skinnerian. *Amer. Psychologist*, 1963, **18**, 516-18.

HILDUM, D. C., & BROWN, R. W. Verbal reinforcement and interviewer bias. *J. abnorm. soc. Psychol.*, 1956, **53**, 108-11.

POSTMAN, L. Rewards and punishments in human learning. In L. Postman (Ed.), *Psychology in the making: Histories of selected research problems.* New York: Alfred A. Knopf, 1962. Pp. 331-401.

ORNE, M. T. On the social psychology of the psychological experiment: With particular reference to demand characteristics and their implications. *Amer. Psychologist*, 1962, **17**, 776-83.

UNDERWOOD, B. J. The representativeness of rote verbal learning. In A. W. Melton (Ed.), *Categories of human learning.* New York: Academic Press, 1964. Pp. 47-78.

46 / The Reinforcing Effect of Two Spoken Sounds on the Frequency of Two Responses

JOEL GREENSPOON, *Indiana University*

The reinforcing effects of various stimuli presented immediately following a response have been investigated largely with infra-human Ss. In the context of experiments using the operant conditioning paradigm, the accepted definition of the reinforcing stimulus is a stimulus introduced following a response that increases the probability of occurrence of that response. Despite this research utilizing infra-human Ss, there has been relatively little effort to identify reinforcing stimuli for human Ss. Many investigators have conditioned humans, but they have used only a few reinforcing stimuli. Thorndike demonstrated the effectiveness of "right" and "wrong" in increasing the frequency of different responses.[1] Hurlock demonstrated that praise and reproof significantly affected performance in the classroom situation.[2] Other investigators have demonstrated that various stimuli would increase the probability of responding.[3] Most of the research involving reinforcing stimuli with human Ss has, however, been designed to test problems other

From the *American Journal of Psychology*, 1955, **68**, 409-16, with permission of the author and publisher.

° Accepted for publication October 1, 1954. This article is based upon a dissertation submitted to the Department of Psychology of Indiana University in partial fulfillment of the requirements for the Ph.D. degree. This research was supported in part by a grant from the Graduate School of Indiana University. Appreciation is expressed to Dr. C. J. Burke for his aid in the statistical analyses and to Dr. T. A. Sebeok for his aid in the phonetic analysis of the contingent stimuli.

1. E. L. Thorndike. *The Psychology of Wants, Interests, and Attitudes*, 1935, 10-305.
2. E. B. Hurlock, The evaluation of certain incentives used in school work, *J. Educ. Psychol.*, 16, 1925, 1-49.
3. A. J. Mitrano, Principles of conditioning in human goal behavior, *Psychol. Monog.*, 51, 1939 (No. 230), 1-55; Louis Long. Conceptual relationships in children: The concept of roundness, *J. Genet. Psychol.*, 57, 1940, 289-315; A. B. Warren and R. H. Brown, Conditioned operant response phenomena in children, *J. Gen. Psychol.*, 28, 1943, 161-207; K. W. Estes, Some effects of reinforcement upon verbal behavior of children, Unpublished

than the identification of reinforcing stimuli for human Ss. The primary purpose of this research was to investigate the effect of the introduction and omission of two spoken sounds following a pre-determined response on the frequency of occurrence of that response.

PROCEDURE

The experiment was simple in design. S was asked to say words, and as he went along, some of the words were followed by a spoken sound from E. Conditioning and, later, extinction were both obtained.

The experiment was conducted in a small room, $7 \times 7 \times 7$ ft., with sound-insulated walls, and lighted by one 75-w. ceiling bulb. The room contained a small table and two chairs. S sat in one chair placed beside the table and was unable to see E who sat behind him in the other chair. A small red light was placed on table where it could be seen by S. He could also see a microphone that was attached to a Peirce Wire Recorder. The recorder sat on a small stand out of sight during the experiment, but it was visible to S when he entered the experimental room. A stop watch was used to record time.

Seventy-five undergraduate students in elementary psychology and speech classes at Indiana University were randomly assigned to five different groups of 15 Ss each. Each S was tested individually.

The two contingent stimuli were "mmm-hmm" and "huh-uh." [4] The phonetic construction of these sounds was: ʔm,³hm² and ¹hã²ʔã́.[4] The indication of stress is Pike's.[5] The stress and phonetic pattern represent the norm as each one was not pronounced in exactly the same way each time.

Two responses were defined for use in the experiment. One response included any plural noun. The second response included all verbal responses except plural nouns and is called non-plural responses. The defining characteristic of the plural and non-plural responses was based on common grammatical usage.

The experimental session was 50 min. in length. S first entered the experimental room and seated himself. A brief, casual conversation, to acclimate S to E and to the experi-

mental room, preceded the following instructions:

"What I want you to do is to say all the words that you can think of. Say them individually. Do not use any sentences or phrases. Do not count. Please continue until I say stop. Go ahead."

No additional instructions were given during the remainder of the experimental session. S received no information about the correctness of his response or the significance of the contingent stimulus that was introduced.

For Groups I and II the contingent stimulus was introduced following each plural response during the first 25 min. For Group I the contingent stimulus was "mmm-hmm" and for Group II it was "huh-uh." For Groups III and IV the contingent stimulus was introduced following each non-plural response during the first 25 min. For Group III the contingent stimulus was "mmm-hmm" and for Group IV it was "huh-uh." Ss in all groups continued to respond for an additional 25 min. during which the contingent stimulus was omitted. One control group was used, in which no contingent stimulus was introduced during the entire 50 min. session. At the end of the 50 min. of responding each S was asked the following questions: (1) What do you think it was all about? (2) Did you notice any change in the kind of words you were saying? (3) What do you think the purpose of the "mmm-hmm" (or "huh-uh") was? (4) How long do you think you were saying words?

RESULTS

The first step in the treatment of the data was to eliminate those Ss who were able to verbalize the relationship between

doctor's dissertation, University of Minnesota, 1945; P. R. Fuller, Operant conditioning of a vegatative human organism, this JOURNAL, 62, 1949, 587-90; E. J. Hovorka, A study of stimulus-generalization in human operant behavior, Unpublished master's thesis, Indiana University, 1950; B. D. Cohen, H. I. Kalish, J. R. Thurston, and E. Cohen, Experimental manipulation of verbal behavior, J. Exper. Psychol., 47, 1954, 106-10.
4. The two stimuli used in this experiment, "mmm--hmm" and "huh-uh," are called contingent stimuli rather than reinforcing stimuli since one of the purposes of the experiment was to determine whether or not these two stimuli were reinforcing stimuli.
5. K. L. Pike, American English Intonation, 1946, 1-135.

the contingent stimulus and the response which it followed. One S in Group I and nine Ss in Group II reported that they noted the relationship of the contingent stimulus and the response it followed. The elimination of these 10 Ss reduced to 65 the number for whom the data were further analyzed.

The second step in the analysis was to determine the ordinal position of the first plural response. The control group and the two experimental groups in which the plural response was the measured response were compared. The mean ordinal position of the first plural response of Groups I and II and the control group is presented in Table I. The three values did not differ significantly as an F of 0.0626 with 2 and 32 degrees of freedom was obtained. The groups of Ss were probably selected from the same population with respect to the readiness to give the first plural response. No corresponding analysis was made for Groups III and IV.

The total 50 min. of responding was divided into ten 5-min. periods for purpose of

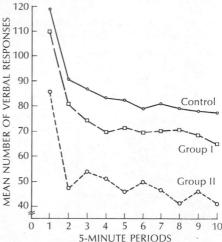

Fig. 1. Mean number of verbal responses for successive 5-min. periods of the control groups and the experimental groups in which the contingent stimulus was introduced following each plural response. (The contingent stimulus was omitted during the last five periods of the experimental groups.)

TABLE I. *Mean ordinal position of first plural response of control group and experimental groups in which contingent stimulus was introduced following each plural response*

Control Group (No stimulus)	Group I ('Mmm-hmm')	Group II ('Huh-uh')
21.13	23.71	20.83

the additional analyses. The data of the control group and the experimental groups in which the contingent stimulus was introduced following each plural response are presented first. Both periods, during which the contingent stimulus was introduced and omitted, are included.

A graphic presentation of the mean frequency of all verbal responses, both plural and non-plural, is given in Figure 1 for the control group and Groups I and II. There is a progressive decline in the mean number of verbal responses for all groups.

The mean number of plural responses for each 5-min. period by Groups I and II and the control group is presented in Table II, with the corresponding standard deviations. The generalized analysis of variance was applied separately to the plural responses during the periods

when the contingent stimulus followed each plural response and when it was omitted.[6]

The between-group-variance for the periods 1–5 when the contingent stimulus was introduced for the experimental groups was significant beyond the 1-% level of confidence. The between-group-variance was significant between the 5-%

6. The generalized analysis of variance was developed by C. J. Burke of Indiana University. It can be applied to those cases in which there is correlation between measurements within the various groups. The test is designed to evaluate variance and co-variance simultaneously. The measurements in successive periods of the groups used in this experiment are presumably correlated since they are made on the same Ss. If the result is significant, then t-test can be used to find the locus of the differences. The results of this analysis are presented in terms of the confidence level from conversion tables developed by Burke. The information necessary to compute the statistic was obtained through personal communication.

TABLE II. *Mean number and standard deviation of plural responses for successive 5-min. periods for control group and for experimental groups in which contingent stimulus was introduced following each plural response*
(Stimulus omitted last five periods of experimental groups)

5-min. periods	Control Group (No stimulus)		Group I ('Mmm-hmm')		Group II ('Huh-uh')	
	Mean	SD	Mean	SD	Mean	SD
1	15.47	11.60	25.50	22.80	11.33	5.62
2	11.20	9.22	22.07°	13.53	7.17	5.50
3	11.00	6.83	22.43°	16.90	2.83°	2.68
4	10.53	7.74	19.07°	13.19	4.83	3.85
5	8.40	8.93	20.86†	11.36	3.83	3.19
6	8.13	5.77	16.21°	12.18	7.33	6.90
7	8.27	6.50	11.64	9.24	4.83	5.46
8	10.87	10.30	10.50	8.68	3.00	4.40
9	6.67	6.48	11.43	10.11	7.33	6.13
10	8.33	7.94	9.50	7.38	4.83	5.88

° Mean difference between experimental and control groups significant between the 5-% and 1-% level of confidence.
† Mean difference between experimental and control groups significant beyond 1-% level of confidence.

and 1-% level of confidence during the remaining periods when the contingent stimulus was omitted.

The *t*-test was applied to determine the locus of the differences in the mean number of plural responses between the experimental groups and the control group; every 5-min. period was examined separately. The results of this analysis show that Group I had a significantly greater mean number of plural responses than the control group for the last four periods in which the contingent stimulus was introduced and for the first period in which the contingent stimulus was omitted. Group II had a significantly smaller mean number of plural responses than the control group in one period in which the contingent stimulus "huh-uh" was introduced and in none of the periods in which the stimulus was omitted.

Substantially the same analysis was made of the data for Groups III and IV, in which non-plural rather than plural responses were followed by the contingent stimulus. The mean frequency of all responses for successive 5-min. periods is presented in Figure 2, and again there is a continuous decline in the rate of responding.

The mean number of non-plural responses with corresponding standard de-

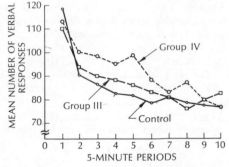

FIG. 2. Mean number of verbal responses for successive 5-min. periods of the control group and the experimental groups in which the contingent stimulus was introduced following each non-plural response. (The contingent stimulus was omitted during the last five periods of the experimental groups.)

viations for each 5-min. period for the two experimental groups and the control group is presented in Table III. The generalized analysis of variance indicated that the difference among the groups when the contingent stimulus was introduced was significant beyond the 5-% level of confidence. The difference was not statistically significant during the periods when the contingent stimulus was omitted. The analysis by means of the *t*-test showed none of the mean differences to be statistically significant.

TABLE III. *Mean number and standard deviation of non-plural responses for successive 5-min. periods of control group and experimental groups in which contingent stimulus was introduced following each non-plural response*
(Stimulus omitted last five periods of experimental groups)

5-min. periods	Control Group (No stimulus)		Group III ('Mmm-hmm')		Group IV ('Huh-uh')	
	Mean	SD	Mean	SD	Mean	SD
1	102.67	34.50	93.93	39.33	95.07	40.50
2	79.40	28.01	84.33	34.99	87.60	37.46
3	75.40	26.49	82.13	36.59	87.00	36.75
4	72.27	26.79	80.80	35.46	84.60	35.38
5	73.60	29.96	79.33	35.46	90.47	41.10
6	70.47	28.11	75.93	34.23	80.20	26.53
7	72.47	26.53	74.73	33.53	76.07	33.47
8	67.73	24.70	70.27	30.67	77.60	32.70
9	70.87	25.03	71.60	33.16	71.20	29.70
10	68.93	28.05	72.87	35.11	68.87	24.47

DISCUSSION

The results obtained from the introduction of "mmm-hmm" were consistent for both of the responses, plural and non-plural. Since, according to the initial definition of the reinforcing stimulus, any stimulus introduced following a response that increases the probability of occurrence of that response is a reinforcing stimulus, we may conclude that "mmm-hmm" is a reinforcing stimulus. Additional support for this conclusion comes from the results that were obtained when "mmm-hmm" was omitted. The frequency of plural responses declined to the point where the difference between the mean number of plural responses of the control group and Group I was not statistically significant.

The results obtained from the introduction of "huh-uh" following the plural response were significantly different from the results obtained when "huh-uh" was introduced following non-plural responses. The results were obtained, however, from only 6 Ss in Group II who did not verbalize the relationship between "huh-uh" and plural responses. This represents a rather small sample. The apparently diverse results in the case of "huh-uh" may clarify some of the thinking about reinforcing stimuli. It would appear from these results that one of the factors that may determine whether or not a particular stimulus will be a reinforcing

stimulus is the response following which the stimulus is applied. An examination of the two responses used in this experiment reveals some differences. Plural responses are a smaller and more narrowly defined class in that all members of the class were plural nouns. The data from the control group indicate that approximately 11% of the verbal responses were plural nouns. Non-plural responses form, therefore, a much larger class. They also presumably differ from the plural responses in being more heterogeneous. All parts of speech other than nouns, and also non-plural nouns, are included. Thus, either the relative size or the heterogeneity of the class, or both, may be factors in determining whether or not a particular stimulus will be a reinforcing stimulus.

It should be noted that there was little tendency for the Ss to repeat a particular word that had been followed by one of the contingent stimuli. It was possible for S to make responses which differed in many respects but were the same in that they were all plural nouns or were non-plural responses. Thus, the importance of the class is emphasized by this experiment. E limits the extent of the class by his use of the reinforcing stimulus; but, the extent of the class may in turn determine whether a stimulus has reinforcing effects.

The small differences in the number

of non-plural responses between the control and experimental groups may be a function of the fact that the frequency of non-plural responses of the control group approaches a maximum. Any possible increase in frequency of non-plural responses is restricted when compared to the possible increase in the frequency of plural responses. This restriction in the size of the possible difference between the control and experimental groups may have reduced the statistical significance of the differences as well.

SUMMARY

The purpose of this experiment was to determine the effect of two operations on two different verbal responses. The Ss were 75 undergraduate students at Indiana University. Each S served individually. Data from 10 Ss who verbalized the relationship between the contingent stimulus and the response it followed were eliminated from further analyses. The operation performed was to present one of two stimuli, "mmm-hmm" or "huh-uh," after one of the two responses, plural nouns or any word not a plural noun. In a control group no stimulus was introduced following the response.

The S was instructed to say singly all the words, exclusive of sentences, phrases and numbers, that he could think of for 50 min. One of the contingent stimuli was introduced immediately following each response of a predetermined class during the first 25 min. and omitted during the second period of 25 min.

The results indicated that "mmm-hmm" increased the frequency of plural responses and "huh-uh" decreased the frequency of plural responses. Both stimuli tended to increase the frequency of non-plural responses. Thus, the contingent stimulus, "mmm-hmm," had the same effect on both responses. The stimulus, "huh-uh," had different effects on the two responses. This differential effect on the two responses suggested that the nature of the response is a determinant of the reinforcing character of the stimulus.

---

47 / The Control of the Content of Conversation: Reinforcement of Statements of Opinion [1]

WILLIAM S. VERPLANCK, *Harvard University* [2]

Some kinds of human behavior have seemed to be resistant to experimental investigation because of both their complexity and their apparent variability. One such class includes the commonplace activities of people—for example, whatever the reader was doing just before he picked up this journal. Perhaps talking to someone.

This paper describes the successful experimental application of some principles of operant conditioning in this area; specifically to conversation between two people. The experimental procedure is based on two assumptions (2, 3). (*a*)

Apparently heterogeneous human verbal behavior falls into comparatively simple operant response classes; hence, any one is susceptible to conditioning. The class of verbal behavior chosen is the *stating of opinions*. (*b*) Classes of environmental events can be isolated that have the property of altering any behavior on

From the *Journal of Abnormal and Social Psychology*, 1955, **51**, 668-76, with permission of the author and publisher.
1. The first experiments on this subject were carried out by Mr. Ronald M. Dworkin, as an experimental project in an undergraduate course. His exploratory results were indispensable in setting up the procedures followed in this experiment.
2. Now at Stanford University.

which their occurrence has depended, i.e., some events are reinforcing stimuli. Specifically, under our conditions, statements of *agreement* or *paraphrase* are hypothesized to be reinforcing stimuli for the verbal behavior of a speaker. According to these assumptions, if someone agrees with every opinion of a speaker, the speaker should show a sharp increase in his rate of stating opinions. The *stating of opinions* has been conditioned.

Since it is both interesting and important to obtain changes in behavior that correspond to those termed conditioning when the subject is not aware that he is "being conditioned" (or, indeed, that his behavior is being manipulated in any way) the present experiments were conducted under conditions in which the occurrence of such "insight" was extremely unlikely.

METHOD

General plan of the experiment. The experiment was carried out in a series of ordinary conversations between two people, the subject (S) who was not informed in any way that he was taking part in an experiment, and the experimenter (E). The conversations lasted at least a half-hour which was divided into three 10-minute periods.

During the first 10-minute period, once the conversation was under way, E did not reinforce any statement made by S, but determined his operant level of "stating opinions" by ticking off the total number of statements and the number of opinion-statements made by S in successive one-minute intervals. This treatment for the first 10-minute period is labeled O in the first column of Table 1.

In the second 10 minutes, every opinion-statement S made was recorded by E and reinforced. For two groups, E agreed with every opinion-statement by saying: "Yes, you're right," "That's so," or the like, or by nodding and smiling affirmation if he could not interrupt. This treatment is labeled A, for agreement, in the second column of Table 1. For two other groups, E reinforced by repeating back to S in paraphrase each opinion-statement that S made (labeled P in the second column of Table 1).

In the third 10-minute period, the Es attempted to extinguish the opinion-statements of two groups by withdrawing *all* reinforcement, that is, by failing to respond (labeled E for extinguish in the third column of Table 1) in any way to S's speech, and of two other groups by disagreeing with each opinion stated (labeled D in the third column of Table 1).

The design of the experiment is depicted in Table 1. Of the four O-groups of the first period, two become groups

TABLE 1. *Treatments followed by experimenters*

N	First 10 Minutes	Second 10 Minutes	Third 10 Minutes
5	O—Measure operant level	A—Reinforce each opinion-statement by agreement	D—Extinguish by disagreeing with each opinion-statement
2	O—Measure operant level	A—Reinforce each opinion-statement by agreement	E—Extinguish by failing to respond to any statement of S (silence)
6	O—Measure operant level	P—Reinforce each opinion-statement by paraphrase	E—Extinguish by disagreeing with each opinion-statement
4	O—Measure operant level	P—Reinforce each opinion-statement by paraphrase	E—Extinguish by failing to respond to any statement of S (silence)
7	A_1—Reinforce each opinion-statement by agreement	E—Extinguish by failing to respond to any statement of S (silence)	A_2—Reinforce each opinion-statement by agreement

in which reinforcement came by agreement (A-groups) in the second period, and two became groups in which reinforcement came by paraphrase (P-groups). In the third period, one of the A-groups was extinguished by disagreement (D-group) and one by E's silence (E-group). A similar division was made for the P-groups. Thus, each of the four groups can be designated by the combination of treatments provided in the three consecutive periods of conversation.

In a fifth, control group (A_1EA_2), run to insure that any changes in S's rate of stating opinions could not be attributed to the passage of time during the experiment, E reinforced by agreement S's opinion-statements in the first and third 10-minute periods, and withdrew all reinforcement during the second period.

During the first (O) period for the first four groups, and the E period for the fifth group, E asked a "neutral" question ("What did you say?") if S's rate of speaking showed signs of declining. Few such were necessary.

Experimental situation. The Es performed the experiment when and where they could, restricted by only three criteria: (a) that only two persons be present, (b) that there be a clock, and the paper and pencil required for recording, and (c) that enough time be available to both S and E for them to talk for at least a half hour. The Es did not suggest to Ss at any time that an experiment was being carried on, and in the rare cases in which an S showed signs of suspicion that this was not an ordinary conversation the experiment was terminated (although the conversation was carried on).

Seventeen Ss were run in student living quarters, two in restaurants, two in private homes, and one each in a hospital ward, in a public lounge, and over the telephone. In one experiment, contrary to instructions, a third (but uninformed) person was present.

The topics of conversation ranged from the trivial to the "intellectual" and included dates, vacations, Marxism, theory of music, man's need for religion, architecture, Liberace.

Experimenters. Seventeen members of a course [3] in the Psychology of Learning served as Es. Twelve were Harvard undergraduates, two were Radcliffe undergraduates, and three (two women and one man) were students in the Graduate School of Education. All the experimenters had had extensive experience in the techniques of conditioning bar-pressing in the rat, and of conditioning chin-tapping in the human (3). Of the 17 students who undertook the experiment, all were able to collect one or two sets of data as the design demanded.

Subjects and experimental groups. Of the 20 men and four women who served as Ss, 13 were described by the Es as friends, seven as roommates, one a date, one an uncle, and one a total stranger. In all but four conversations, S and E were of the same sex. All but six Ss were of college age; of these six, four were in the thirties, and two were 55 and 60, respectively.

These Ss were distributed over the four experimental groups as follows: OAD, 5; OPD, 6; OPE, 2; OAE, 4; and A_1EA_2, 7.

There were 20 students in the class, and the design called for N's of 5 and 10, but 3 students reported that they were unable to undertake the experiment,[4] and of the 17 Es, one placed himself in the wrong group.

The response conditioned. The re-

---

3. An experiment of this sort very probably could not be successfully performed *de novo* in a laboratory situation suitably equipped for tape-recording and concealed observation. The present strategy was dictated by the need to determine whether positive results could be obtained in conversations on a variety of topics, carried on in a wide variety of situations, and especially in a situation in which it was most unlikely that S would suspect that an experiment was being carried on.

4. That three Es found themselves unable to undertake the experiment is in itself interesting. A fourth resorted to the telephone, with good results.

sponse selected for reinforcement was the uttering by S of a statement or "sentence" beginning: "I think . . .," "I believe . . .," "It seems to me," "I feel," and the like. The Es were instructed to be conservative in classifying a statement as an opinion, and to do so only if one or another such qualifying phrase began the statement. (Es were aware that the experiment was designed to investigate Ss' behavior, and not their own.) No attempt was made to define what constituted a statement or a "sentence" except that E should not expect grammatical sentences (1). These instructions proved adequate; no E had difficulty in counting such units of verbal behavior, although doubtless many speech units counted would not parse.

Reinforcing stimuli. Two classes of reinforcing stimuli were used by the Es. The first was *agreement* (A), defined as the experimenter saying "You're right," "I agree," "That's so," or the like, nodding the head, smiling (where E did not want to interrupt). The second was repeating back to S in paraphrase (P) what he had just said. No further attempt was made to specify paraphrasing. *Extinction* was carried out in one of two ways. In some groups E simply refrained from responding in any way to a statement by S (E) and in others, he disagreed (D) with each opinion-statement.

The Es did not speak, except to reinforce, to disagree, or to "prime" S with a question during operant-level determination. They contributed nothing new to the conversation.

Recording. A clock, or watch with sweep-second hand, a pencil, and something to write on were necessary for the recording. One E was able to record the whole conversation on a tape-recorder. The Es ticked off each statement occurring in successive one-minute intervals by making a series of doodles incorporating marks, or by making marks on the margin or text of a book or magazine. Different

marks were used for opinions and other statements. Recording proved inconspicuous, and in only one or two cases did an E have to terminate an experiment because S seemed to notice his recording.

Although problems arose occasionally, Es by and large had no difficulty in arriving at and maintaining a criterion for a "sentence" or "statement," i.e., for the unit of speech that they counted, and for the subclass, statement of opinion.

The criteria varied from experimenter to experimenter, in that the rates of speaking of two subjects reported by the same Es are correlated, and the reported rates are a function not only of the subject's rate of speaking, and of E's rate of speaking in reinforcing, but also of the criterion for "statements" adopted by E.

In only one case did an S comment on E's recording: during extinction he asked E what she was doodling, and was satisfied when she showed him her scribbles. The Es also noted S's general behavior during extinction, and the mode of termination of the experiment.

Execution. In a few cases, the experiment was begun, and then terminated by phone calls, third persons entering the room, or because E feared that S had noticed that he was recording. All the experiments completed are reported in this paper, except one from group A_1EA_2, whose data could not be accurately transcribed. Under questioning, no experimenter reported that he terminated the experiment because results did not seem satisfactory to him.

Two Es carried out operant-level determination for only 9 minutes, and one went overtime. Four went overtime during reinforcement. The greatest variability appeared during extinction; seven Ss failed to continue talking for 10 minutes following the beginning of disagreement, or of nonreinforcement, either leaving the room or falling into silence. Eight Es carried on the conversation past the 10-minute minimum extinction period. Since

Es were not consistent in continuing to record or to converse past this time, data are reported only on the first 10 minutes.

In summary, the experiment is designed to determine whether a person, in conversation with another person, can manipulate the second person's conversation by agreeing or disagreeing, or by paraphrasing. The experimenter himself, it should be noted, contributes nothing new to the content of the conversation.

RESULTS

Awareness. No S ever gave any evidence that he was "aware" that he was

Distributions were made of the number of opinion-statements (N_{opin}) and of all statements (N_{all}), and their cumulative values (CN_{opin} and CN_{all}) for each minute of the three experimental periods. From the latter, mean rates of making statements were computed. Relative frequencies of opinions ($RF_{opin} = CN_{opin}/CN_{all}$) were determined for each S for each period.

Rates. The rates of making statements (CN_{all}/t) showed no significant changes as a function of reinforcement. Table 2 gives, in the upper portion, data on the distribution of these rates for each inter-

TABLE 2. *Median and ranges for each 10-minute period*

	10-Minute Period	Groups OAE, OAD, OPE, OPD combined			Group A_1EA_2		
		Proc.	Median	Range	Proc.	Median	Range
Rate (statements/minute)	1st	op	5.3	2.2–12.8	cond	7.1	2.4–14.0
	2nd	cond	5.7	3.2–17.1	ext	6.3	1.9–11.0
	3rd	ext	5.2	1.4–12.8	recond	5.8	2.9–14.5
Relative frequency of opinion - statements	1st	op	0.320	.012–.655	cond	0.574	.208–.653
	2nd	cond	0.558	.071–.702	ext	0.302	.094–.526
	3rd	ext	0.333	.048–.643	recond	0.603	.267–.699

serving as a subject in an experiment, that his behavior was being deliberately manipulated and recorded, or that he recognized that there was anything peculiar about the conversation. The only qualification that must be made is this: during extinction, some Ss got angry at E and commented on his disagreeableness, or noted his "lack of interest," and during reconditioning one member of group A_1EA_2 gave E "queer, searching glances," perhaps because of the opinions that E was now agreeing with. These changes of behavior <u>are</u> consistent with those found in other situations when S is undergoing extinction (3).

Conditioning is demonstrated if the appropriate changes appear in the rate of speaking opinion-statements as a function of the conditions of reinforcement. When reinforcement is given, the rate must increase; when it is withdrawn, the rate must decrease.

val. Several nonparametric tests for significance of difference were made, and none showed that the null hypothesis (no difference as a function of period, manipulation, or group) could be rejected. The "priming" of S by means of the question, "What did you say?," seems to maintain the rates in the operant periods, and in the extinction period of group A_1EA_2, although decreases in rate may be obscured by the fact that E is saying little during these times. The rank-order correlation of operant-level rates of speech obtained on two Ss by the same Es was 0.65 ($N = 14$). This figure includes data to be reported elsewhere [5] but obtained under the same conditions.

Relative frequency of opinions. Table 2 (lower portion) presents the medians and ranges of the distributions of RF_{opin}

5. In a paper now in preparation and to be entitled: The control of the content of conversation by reinforcement: topic of conversation.

for each period. Each of the 24 Ss showed an increase in his relative frequency of opinion during the reinforcement period over his operant level, or (for group A_1EA_2) over his preceding extinction period. The probability that this result would have been obtained if there had been no effect of the experimental variable is $(\frac{1}{2})^{24}$. Twenty-one of the 24 showed a *reduced* RF_{opin} in the extinction or disagreement period below that of the preceding period of reinforcement. The probability that fewer than four Ss would not change in the absence of an effect of the experimental variable is 1.1 $(\frac{1}{2})^{13}$. Signed rank tests (4) of the significance of the differences yield p values well below .01.

The magnitude of the effects can be evaluated by determining two ratios for each S: (*a*) that of RF_{opin} obtained during conditioning to RF_{opin} of the operant level or (for group A_1EA_2) RF_{opin} in reconditioning to RF_{opin} in the preceding extinction period, and (*b*) of RF_{opin} during the extinction period to RF_{opin} during the preceding conditioning period. Large values of the former of these ratios are possible only when the operant level RF_{opin} is low. Table 3 presents the mean, median, and range of these values for groupings of the 24 Ss based on the methods of reinforcement and extinction.

An evaluation was made of the rela-tive effectiveness of agreement and para-phrase in conditioning, and of disagree-ment and silence in extinction. Fisher's exact test of independence in contin-gency tables was applied about the me-dians of Table 3A for groups OAD and OAE taken together versus OPE and OPD, and about the medians of Table 3B for groups OAD and OPD against OAE and OPE. No difference in the number of cases falling above and below the medians was significant at the .05 level, although the difference between agreement and paraphrase is significant between the .05 and .10 levels.

Means and variances were also com-puted. An F test of the significance of difference in the variances of OAD and OAE and of OPD and OPE gives 8.239 ($df = 8$, 7), significant at better than the .005 level. Paraphrasing and agreement, although both effective, are not equiva-lent as reinforcing stimuli; paraphrasing is much more variable in its effectiveness (or perhaps the variety of statements made as paraphrases exceeded those called agreements).

The method of extinction also yielded a significant difference in variance: $F = 5.175$ ($df = 10$, 5), significant at the .05 level. Despite these differences in vari-ance, group curves were constructed. All four groups were combined without re-spect to method of reinforcement or ex-

TABLE 3. *Means, medians, and ranges of ratio-index of changes in relative frequency of opinion-statements*

Groups Combined	RF Ratios in Distribution	N	Mean	Median	Range
A. Conditioning Effect (No effect: Ratio-Index = 1.00)					
OAD, OAE	A/O	9	2.27	1.76	1.50– 5.70
A₁EA₂	A₂/E	7	2.29	2.17	1.09– 4.32
OAD, OAE, A₁EA₂	A/O, A₂/E	16	2.28	1.85	1.09– 5.70
OPD, OPE	P/O	8	4.23	2.02	1.05–11.47
All	A/O + A₂/E + P/O	24	2.91	1.85	1.05–11.47
B. Extinction Effect (No effect: Ratio-Index = 1.00)					
OPE, OAE	E/P, E/A	11	0.71	0.70	0.48–0.86
A₁EA₂	E/A₁	7	0.66	0.52	0.45–1.15
OPE, OAE, A₁EA₂	E/P, E/A, E/A₁	18	0.69	0.52	0.45–1.15
OPD, OAD	D/P, D/A	6	0.65	0.62	0.27–1.01
All	E/P, E/A, E/A, D/P, D/A	24	0.67	0.65	0.27–1.15

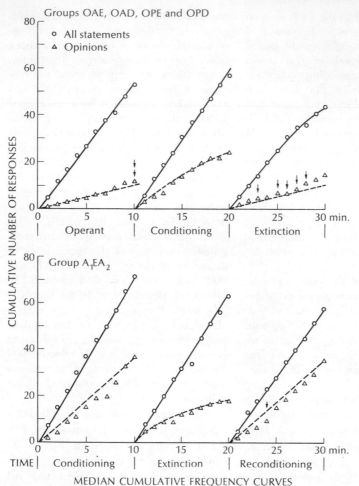

MEDIAN CUMULATIVE FREQUENCY CURVES

FIG. 1. Median cumulative frequency curves of opinion-statements, and of all statements, for each 10-minute period of the experiment

tinction. The median N and CN of opinions, and of all sentences, were then determined for each successive minute of each of the three periods. Figure 1 presents these medians for the groups OAD, OPD, OAE, and OPE, and for group A_1EA_2.

Figure 2 demonstrates that the median curves are indeed representative. In it are plotted the experimental points obtained during the operant level period from (a) the S giving a CN_{op} equaling the median, together with the Ss giving (b) the lowest and (c) the highest values among the 17 Ss of the combined groups, and from the corresponding Ss of group A_1EA_2, chosen about the median of the extinction period. Any other sets of individual data might have been presented, but these give some view of the spread, as well as of the consistency of results of the various subjects.

In summary, the rate of stating opinions changed in accordance with the assumptions made. All Ss increased their rate of stating opinions, regardless of the topic of conversation, its setting, or S's particular relationship with the E. The order of magnitude of the effect depended upon the kind of reinforcement

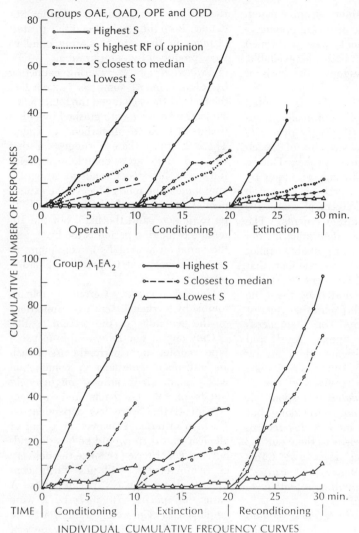

INDIVIDUAL CUMULATIVE FREQUENCY CURVES

FIG. 2. Individual cumulative frequency curves of opinion-statements for each 10-minute period of the experiment, demonstrating the consistency of the effect and its range

For the upper graphs $N = 17$, for the lower, $N = 7$. At each arrow, N on that and successive trials is diminished by one. In the extinction period of the upper graph, each S that dropped out, "had to leave." In the other cases, E discontinued the procedure at the time indicated.

employed. How it may be related to the variables noted above cannot be inferred from the present data.

DISCUSSION

Individual differences in the rates of speech, and of giving opinions, are most striking and highly significant. We have already noted that they are the joint outcome of S's rate of speech, the length of his sentences, of E's discrimination of his speech, and of E's own speech rate. Of the two Ss with the lowest rate of making statements, one was a Finn who spoke English with difficulty, and the other was a young woman who talked very fast and in very long sentences indeed. (She was also the most opinionated, according to our rate of giving opinions.) Since the experiment was performed Fries's (1) work has become available, and a study of it suggests the basis of our Es' criteria.

The statements that the Es counted during the period of reinforcement are evidently identical with Fries's "utterance units" (1, p. 36), i.e., stretches of speech bounded by a change of speaker. During reinforcement and during extinction by disagreement, each stretch of S's speech is bounded by E's delivery of successive reinforcements or disagreements. The cues in S's speech that determine E's delivery of a reinforcement probably cannot yet be specified. However, the facts that the rate of uttering "statements" is stable, and that the rates reported by the same E are correlated with each other suggest that the "statements" or "sentences" counted during the operant level, and during extinction (although these are by definition not Fries's "utterances," since E says nothing) are stretches of speech such that E is *stimulated* to respond (1, p. 49). He does so, not by speaking, but rather by making a mark in his record. If this analysis is correct, then our S's statements are what Fries also terms statements, i.e., "sentences that are regularly directed to eliciting attention to continuous discourse."

Magnitude of the effect. These data do not permit us to draw conclusions about the magnitude of the effect, although it is clearly some function of the values of reinforcement variables. If S rarely states an opinion, it is difficult for the number of reinforcements to become very great, and the effect is necessarily small.

Acquisition effects. The not-quite-significant difference in the median effects of paraphrasing and of simple agreement, and the significant difference in their variances are interesting. Probably many different kinds of paraphrases were employed; the differential effectiveness of

these as reinforcing stimuli needs investigation. Both the smallest and the greatest changes in the rate of stating opinions were produced by paraphrasing.

Extinction effects. During extinction by disagreement, some Ss "marshalled the facts," others changed the topic. Some subjects who were extinguished by either treatment became "disturbed," or angry. There is more than a suggestion that when S undergoes complete nonreinforcement, his speech tends to extinguish and, indeed, he tends to leave the experimental situation earlier ("for study," "to go to dinner," and the like), but the 10-minute extinction period is too brief, and the variation among Es in continuing to record is too great to permit evaluation of this tendency.

General remarks. Certain problems, soluble by further research, set limitations on the generality of the present results.

Only one of our Es was able to use a tape recorder, and clearly, the use of such an instrument, perhaps in conjunction with independent judges, might yield counts of all statements and opinion-statements that were less dependent on E's own criteria. However, it is not at all clear that there would be less dependence on E's criteria (1), since the delivery of reinforcements will necessarily continue to depend on E's speech habits. A variety of specific utterances by E were employed as reinforcing stimuli; a study of the variability in the effectiveness of various kinds of statements by E would be most useful.

The present results do not permit us to state how important is the particular social relationship between S and E. Would agreement by an E whom S disliked reinforce his verbal behavior? These conversations were relatively short, with the result that extinction was carried out to its asymptote in only a few Ss, and hence differences between the effect of disagreement and of complete nonreinforcement, although suggested, cannot be tested. Similarly, neither "satiation" effects of continuous and repeated reinforcement nor complete "talking-out" of S on a topic could occur. (It should be recalled that our procedure does not allow E to contribute anything new to the conversation.)

The topics of conversation were, in only a few cases, such that S might be "ego-involved" in their outcome. Perhaps if S were subjected to these procedures when he was talking about something he "felt deeply" about, the results might differ, e.g., acquisition might be greater and extinction far slower. Orderly *changes* in the topic of conversation should also be observable (see footnote 5 above).

Finally, it should be remembered that our Es were all well trained in conditioning before undertaking this experiment, and this experience may prove necessary for the successful completion of the experiment.

Despite these limitations, this experiment shows that if, in what is ostensibly an ordinary conversation, one agrees with opinions expressed by a speaker, the speaker will give still more opinions, and that returning the speaker's words in paraphrase has the same effect. It also shows that disagreement reduces the number of opinions given, as does ignoring the speaker's statement. The verbal behavior of a speaker, apparently without regard to its content or setting, is under the control, not only of the speaker himself, but also of the person with whom he is conversing.

These results are in accord with the two hypotheses made. But one may ask, is this operant conditioning? By any empirical, non-theoretical definition of conditioning, the changes in behavior found conform with those of conditioning, and the present results may be classified as conditioning. What are some of the alternatives?

Two can be noted, and both suggest that the data depend upon the Es' behavior, rather than the Ss'. The Es may have "made up" the data, since they knew that certain kinds of data were expected of them. This alternative can be rejected without hesitation. The Es' previous performances, and the internal consistency of the data lend it no credulity. A second alternative is that "suggestion" may have altered the Es' discrimination of speech. If this were so, it would itself be a finding of interest. The writer is inclined to doubt very much that this occurred to any extent, in view of the phenomenon of "negative suggestibility," and of the frank skepticism of some Es as to the experiments' outcome before the data were collected and tabulated. Repetition of the experiment, with tape-recording of the verbal behavior of both S and E will permit ready evaluation of both these possibilities.

The results of this experiment make psychological and scientific sense of common-sense descriptions of conversation. ("People like to talk to people who are interested in what they are saying"; "if you ignore him, he'll go away"; "all right, if you don't believe me, here are the facts. . . .") and, indeed, other social and political behaviors. The data suggest that, once the appropriate simplifying assumptions are made, a very high degree of order can be revealed in "complex" situations, and that a still higher degree of order can be introduced into them.

The simplifying hypotheses made here are derived from the concepts of *response* and of *conditioning*, and they have proved experimentally fruitful in the present instance. This complex behavior is available to direct experimental investigation, and the orderliness and lawfulness of the behavior exhibits itself when irrelevant details are ignored. The heuristic advantages of much of present stimulus-response theory, when it is applied in the field of verbal behavior in a social context, are clear.

If our interpretation is correct, experimental work on a wider variety of human social behavior is possible. The isolation in conversation of independent variables susceptible to direct manipulation and of dependent variables showing orderly change, should give a much wider and more significant scope to experimental investigation. The experiments now possible provide new techniques for the investigation of client-therapist relationships and of therapeutic techniques in clinical psychology. They may be applied to the study of the behavior of small groups, and of personality.

They suggest how cooperation may be ensured. They lead to questions such as, "Can one, by pairing oneself with a reinforcing stimulus, come to control effectively the behavior of a total stranger?" That is to say, if a person agrees with everything said by someone whom he has not previously known, will he then have other means of reinforcing, or of exerting other types of control over, the stranger's behavior? The possibilities are interesting.

Summary and Conclusions

Seventeen *Es* carried on conversations with 24 different *Ss*.

Two assumptions are made, (a) that "stating an opinion" is a class of behavior

that acts as a response, and (b) that statements of agreement with, or paraphrases of, such statements of a speaker act as reinforcing stimuli. From these it is inferred that the rate at which a speaker states opinions varies with the administration of agreement or of paraphrase by the person with whom he is conversing. The experimental conversations were carried out on a wide variety of topics of conversation, in a wide variety of places, and in a group of Ss, most of whom were college students. The expected results appeared. Every S increased in his rate of speaking opinions with reinforcement by paraphrase or agreement. Twenty-one Ss decreased in rate with nonreinforcement. Over-all rates of speaking did not change significantly.

In no case was the S aware that he was the subject of an experiment, or that the conversation was an unusual one.[6]

1. FRIES, C. C. *The structure of English.* New York: Harcourt, Brace, 1952.
2. SKINNER, B. F. The generic nature of the concepts of stimulus and response. *J. gen. Psychol.*, 1935, 12, 40-65.
3. VERPLANCK, W. S. The operant conditioning of human motor behavior. *Phychol. Bull.* (in press).
4. WILCOXON, F. *Some rapid approximate statistical Procedures,* New York: American Cyanamid Co., 1949.

6. The writer, after having described the experiment to someone in casual conversation, had the illuminating experience of then being used as S by the person to whom he had described it. He showed the effect and, like, it would seem, *all* Ss in this experiment, was quite unaware that he had been an S.

48 / Reinforcement of Affect Responses of Schizophrenics during the Clinical Interview [1]

KURT SALZINGER AND STEPHANIE PISONI, *Biometrics Research, New York State Department of Mental Hygiene*

Behavior theory has recently expanded its scope to deal with verbal behavior (6). Greenspoon (1) demonstrated the effectiveness of verbal reinforcers upon a subject's rate of utterance of plural vs. non-plural words. Hildum and Brown (2) showed the effect of verbal reinforcement upon attitude statements. Verplanck (7) used verbal reinforcers during conversations to condition opinion statements. Finally, Salzinger (5) investigated the conditioning process in clinical interviews with schizophrenics.

While these studies have supplied evidence for the validity of the application of reinforcement theory to verbal behavior, a good deal of research is still necessary. The present experiment is designed to study (a) reliability of response unit isolation, i.e., to what extent the interviewer can respond reliably with reinforcement to the patient's verbal behavior, (b) the effect of different sources of reinforcements (different interviewers) upon the verbal behavior of the interviewee, and (c) the relationship between the number of reinforcements and the number of responses in extinction.

Since a patient's ability to express affect is usually evaluated through the interview and is considered an important criterion both for diagnosis and prognosis of schizophrenia, the conditions under which affect is evoked by the interviewer might have theoretical importance for arriving at laws describing interview behavior and practical importance in furnishing an objective method for the evaluation of "flatness" of affect. An attempt was made, therefore, to examine the effect of reinforcement upon schizophrenics' output of affect responses in an interview.

METHOD

Subjects. Twenty-four female and twelve male hospitalized schizophrenics from the age of 18 to 50, with a median of 34.3 years, were selected from the admissions to Brooklyn State Hospital. Patients were classified as schizophrenic upon their current admission to the hospital distribution center. One was later rediagnosed as manic-depressive. Nineteen had been previously hospitalized, and 17 had no history of previous hospitalization.

None of the patients received any somatotherapy such as insulin, electric shock, or tranquillizing drugs for at least one week before the first interview or during their participation in the study.

The first 20 patients interviewed were placed in the experimental group. Fourteen were females and six males, with a median age of 32.0 years and a median number of years of education of 10.3. The other 16 patients were placed in the control group. Twelve were females and 4 males with a median age of 34.5 years and a median number of years of education of 11.5.

Experimental procedure. All patients were interviewed one week after their arrival in the hospital. The Ss in the experimental group were interviewed once by a female E and once by a male E on two consecutive days for a period of 30 minutes each. Eleven of the patients were first interviewed by the male; nine were first interviewed by the female E. The Ss in the control group were interviewed once only, nine by the female

From the *Journal of Abnormal and Social Psychology*, 1958, **57**, 84-90, with permission of the authors and publisher.
1. This study was supported by research grant M586(C3) from the National Institute of Mental Health of the National Institutes of Health, Public Health Service. The authors are indebted to J. Zubin and S. Sutton for their constant help and interest in this study and to Suzanne Salzinger for her editing. The authors are also grateful to N. Beckenstein, Director of the Brooklyn State Hospital, A. Glen, L. Olinger, L. Granick, and M. Portnoy for their cooperation in helping to make available the sample used for this study.

511

and seven by the male *E*. All interviews were recorded with the apparatus in full sight of both patient and interviewer.

The interview was presented to the patients as a routine mental hospital procedure. For the first interview, *E* brought the patient into the experimental room and explained that the interview was being conducted to help him. The second interview was introduced by telling the patient that it is helpful to patients to be interviewed more than once despite the fact that this might mean a repetition of their story. All other interview procedures were the same for the second as for the first interview.

The *E* questioned the patient about the following items: name, age, marital status, children, and siblings. The patients answered these questions with little hesitation, thus making it possible for *E* to begin the interview by repeating the answer given, by writing it down, and by saying such words as "mmm-humm," "uhhuh," "I see," etc. This procedure was adopted in an effort to obtain factual information upon which subsequent interview questions could be based and to establish *E* as a source of reinforcement, in this way encouraging the patient to speak in the presence of *E*. The main part of the interview was then initiated with the question, "Would you tell me why you are here in this hospital?"

Interviews with the experimental group were conducted in the following manner: During the first 10 minutes (operant level), the base rate of spontaneous affect responses (see definition below) was determined. The *E* asked questions but did not reinforce any statement made by the patient. Reinforcement was defined as *E*'s verbal agreement through the use of such words as "mmm-hum," "I see," "yeah," etc., with statements made by the patient.

During the second 10 minutes (conditioning), *E* continued to question the patient and reinforced each affect response by immediately following each expression of affect with verbal agreement.

During the third 10-minute period (extinction), *E* withheld all reinforcement but continued asking questions.

Interviews with the control group also lasted 30 minutes, during which time *E* asked questions but did not reinforce any of the patient's responses. This procedure was identical with the operant level phase of the experimental group procedure.

Definition of response. The response class of affect for this experiment was defined as any statement describing or evaluating the state (other than intellectual or physiological) of the patient by himself. The response class therefore included all statements beginning with the pronouns "I" or "we" and followed by an expression of affect. Examples include such expressions as: I am satisfied, I'm happy, We enjoyed it, I like him, I'm very close to him, I was mad at him, We hated her, I'll always be jealous of him, I am upset, I am a lonely person, I was so ashamed, I'm sorry for him, I feel . . . (followed by any words), I was frightened, We coudn't take it, I always suffer, I had a fright, etc.

Quotations in which affect is referred to the speaker, although fitting all other criteria, were excluded on the basis of not being direct expressions of the patient's affect. An example of this was, "My husband said I didn't feel good." Statements like "I am happy and excited" were considered as one affect statement only, since the pronouns "I" or "we" did not precede the second affective word. On the other hand, incomplete (in the sense that the object of the affect is not mentioned) statements like "I love . . ." or "We feared . . ." were viewed as separate responses.

Certain types of private events or internal states were excluded from the response class of affect because they referred primarily to intellectual processes, to actions which are sometimes but not always associated with affect, or to desires which appear to constitute a class of responses different from the affect class as defined here. I am confused, I am confident, I would like to . . ., I want, I was surprised, I am not well, We forgave him, I threaten her constantly, I didn't trust them, etc., are examples.

A count per minute was taken of statements belonging to the general class of self-references (statements beginning with "I" or "We") in order to compare changes in the occurrence of this class with those of the class of self-referred affect statements. In other words, self-referred statements included both self-referred affect statements as well as self-referred nonaffect statements.

Interviewer questions. After the initial question, "Why are you here?" E asked additional questions only when the patient ceased talking for at least two seconds. Some or all of the following topics were discussed during each interview: reasons for being in the hospital and causes for illness; patient's relationships to his parents, siblings, fellow employees, employers, fellow students and teachers, wife or husband, children, friends; patient's activities during free time, and plans for the future. The E made an attempt to balance these topics over the different conditions. For instance, if the patient discussed the symptoms of his illness in the operant level condition, E asked questions regarding the possible causes of the illness during conditioning and brought the patient back to these topics during extinction As long as the topics were approximately balanced over the three conditions, however, E took his cues as to topic from the content of the patient's statements. Both the number of topics and the order in which they were discussed varied from interview to interview.

Questions[2] asking directly for affect such as, "How did you feel about that?" or "Were you happy?" were not used.

RESULTS

Reliability of response unit isolation. A sample of 15 recorded interviews was coded independently for self-referred affect by the two interviewers. Proportions of agreement based on the number of affect statements counted were computed separately for each condition of each interview and ranged from .79 to 1.00. Examination of the disagreements revealed that they were primarily due to poor recording. It was therefore concluded that the affect responses as defined in this experiment can be objectively isolated and counted.

Interviewer differences. The adequacy of the definition of the response was examined by having the two Es who served as interviewers in the experiment independently code the affect responses of the same 15 recorded interviews. This procedure made it possible to test

whether both Es would have reinforced the same responses in identical interviews.

In order to determine whether the two interviewers evoked a different number of affect statements, comparisons were made between the two interviewers on each condition of the initial interviews of the experimental group and the control group interviews. The Mann-Whitney test yielded no statistically significant differences $(p > .05)$, suggesting that the two interviewers evoked approximately the same number of affect statements in their respective interviews. The exact p levels for the experimental group interviews were .79 for the operant level, .54 for the conditioning period, and .52 for the extinction period. For the control interviews, the p levels were considerably lower, although still not significant. The p level for the first 10-minute period was .07, for the second .06, and for the third .22.

Base level of affect. In order to determine whether the experimental and control groups differed initially in the amount of affect spontaneously emitted, a statistical comparison of the number of affect statements given in the first 10 minutes of the control interviews with the number of such statements given during the operant level of the experimental interviews was made. The difference was not statistically significant $(p = .37)$ by the Mann-Whitney test (4).

Conditioning effect. The difference between operant level, conditioning, and extinction for the initial interviews of the experimental group was tested by

2. A pilot study of the effect of interviewer questions of this type of interview was undertaken by the following four graduate students: Ruth Beach, R. S. Feldman, P. Goldberg, and Marilyn G. Hamlin. They found no significant relationship between the conditioning effect and the following: specific vs. nonspecific questions, the introduction of new topics vs. the continuation of old topics, the total number of questions asked, and the number of questions indirectly leading to affect (e.g., How did you react to that?). A larger more definitive study of question effects is presently being undertaken by the authors.

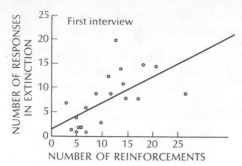

FIG. 1. Number of affect responses during extinction as a function of number of reinforcements in the first interview

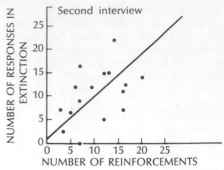

FIG. 2. Number of affect responses during extinction as a function of number of reinforcements in the second interview

Wilcoxon's nonparametric analysis of variance (8) and found to be statistically significant ($p < .01$). The greatest number of affect statements was emitted during conditioning (sum of ranks = 51.0), the next greatest during the operant level (sum of ranks = 39.5), and the least during extinction (sum of ranks = 29.5). The difference between the three conditions of the second interviews of the experimental group was not statistically significant ($.2 > p > .1$). Inspection of the sums of ranks for the three conditions, however, still revealed the greatest number of affect statements in the conditioning period (sum of ranks = 45.0), the next greatest number of affect statements in extinction (sum of ranks = 41.5), and the smallest number during operant level (sum of ranks = 33.5). The fact that the second interview did not yield a statistically significant difference between the conditions appears to be due largely to the greater number of responses emitted during extinction in the second interview in contrast to the first. This is also evident in the comparison of Figures 1 and 2, where responses during extinction were plotted as a function of number of reinforcements, from which one can see the steeper slope in the second than in the first interview. In other words, this result does not indicate a lack of reliability over time but, rather, that apparently fewer reinforcements were necessary for

the same number of extinction responses in the second than in the initial interview. This effect is generally reported for reconditioning.

When the same test was used to compare the three 10-minute periods of control group interviews, no significant number of affect responses was emitted during the last 10 minutes of the interview (sum of ranks = 36.0), the next greatest during the second 10 minutes (sum of ranks = 34.0), and the smallest number during the first 10 minutes (sum of ranks = 32.0).

The Mann-Whitney test was used to compare each 10-minute period of the experimental group interviews to its corresponding period in the control interviews. Comparison of the first 10 minutes of the experimental with the control interviews yielded no significant difference ($p = .37$). Comparison of the last 10 minutes also yielded no significant difference ($p = .92$). The difference between the second 10-minute period of the control-group interviews and the conditioning period of the experimental-group interviews was statistically significant ($p = .03$), using the one-tailed test hypothesis that the experimental group would emit more affect than the control group.

Figures 3 and 4 represent individual cumulative curves of affect responses over the three conditions of the experimental group interviews. Figure 3 shows the

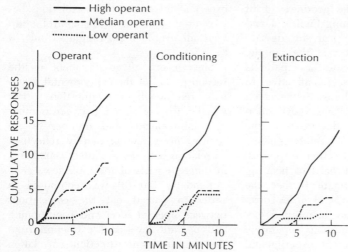

Fig. 3. Individual cumulative response curves for three patients who showed the conditioning effect

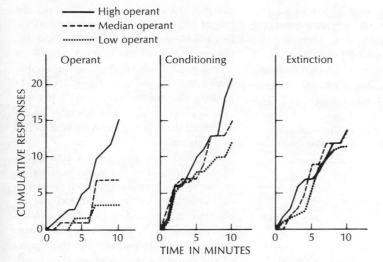

Fig. 4. Individual cumulative response curves for three patients who showed little or no evidence for conditioning

curves of three individuals whose rate of response was modified by reinforcement. These individuals were selected on the basis of being representative of low, medium, and high rates of response in operant level. Figure 4 shows the curves of three individuals whose rates of response were not modified by reinforce-ment. These individuals were also repre-sentative of their group.

In order to gauge the lawfulness of the process of conditioning in the experi-mental group, the number of responses of each patient during extinction was plotted against the number of reinforce-ment in conditioning. It was found that the relationship could be described by a linear equation, i.e., the greater the num-ber of reinforcements administered, the greater the number of responses emitted during extinction. The goodness of fit can be seen by examining Figures 1 and 2. Two patients appear to deviate markedly from the rest of the sample. The diagnosis of one of these patients was changed from schizo-affective to manic-depressive psychosis. She received 13 reinforcements and gave 20 extinction responses. The other deviate from the group, who received 27 reinforcements and gave only 9 extinction responses, was later found to be hard of hearing.

In order to investigate further the effects of reinforcement, rank-order correlation coefficients were computed between every pair of conditions, separately for the first and second experimental interviews and the control interviews. As expected for the experimental group, the highest correlations were found between the number of reinforcements and the number of extinction responses for both the first (.73) and second (.60) interviews. The correlations between all other pairs of conditions were much lower, varying within a restricted range from .41 to .50 (see Table 1). The

TABLE 1. *Rank-order correlations between the three ten-minute periods of the interviews*

| Conditions | Experimental | | Control |
	First Interview	Second Interview	
Conditioning vs. Extinction (2nd vs. 3rd 10 minutes)	.73°°	.60°°	.74°°
Operant level vs. Conditioning (1st vs. 2nd 10 minutes)	.46°	.47°	.85°°
Operant level vs. Extinction (1st vs. 3rd 10 minutes)	.41°	.50°	.70°°

° $p < .05$.
°° $p < .01$.

correlation between the two extinction periods of Interviews 1 and 2 was .41 ($p < .05$) and that between extinction of Interview 1 and conditioning of Interview 2 was .44 ($p < .05$).

In direct contrast to the results of the

experimental group, the correlations between the conditions in the control group were all evenly high, ranging from .70 to .85.

Since every affect statement in the second period of the experimental group was reinforced, the question arises whether the correlation between number of reinforcements and number of responses in extinction merely reflects a correlation between the affect statements in different parts of the interview.

Kendall's tau (3) was computed in order to partial out the correlations between operant level and conditioning and operant level and extinction from the reinforcement-extinction correlation in the experimental group. The tau of .58 ($p = .0002$) between number of reinforcements and extinction responses for the first interview became .53, and the tau of .45 ($p = .002$) for the second interview became .37. When the first 10-minute period of the control interviews was partialed out of the correlation between the second and third 10-minute periods, the tau of .59 ($p = .002$) became .38, a drop of .21, whereas the corresponding drop in the experimental group was only .05.

This indicates that only a small part of the correlation between number of reinforcements and number of responses in extinction can be accounted for by the correlation between operant level and number of reinforcements; the correlation between the second and third parts of the control group, on the other hand, can be accounted for in large part by the correlation between the first and second part of the interview.

The rate of making self-referred statements was found to be invariant over the three conditions of the first and second interviews of the experimental group as well as the interviews of the control group. This was tested by Wilcoxon's (8) nonparametric analysis of variance ($p > .05$). Inspection of the sums of ranks for the first experimental interview (based on an N of 20) indicated a trend toward decreasing frequency of self-referred statements from operant level (sum of ranks = 48.0) to conditioning (sum of ranks = 37.0) to extinction (sum of ranks = 35.0), while in the second interview, the greatest number of self-referred statements appeared in conditioning (sum of ranks = 46.0), the next greatest in extinction (sum of ranks = 39.0), and the smallest in operant level (sum of ranks = 35.0). In the control group (based on an N of 16), the greatest number of self-referred statements was emitted during the first 10 minutes (sum of ranks = 38.5), the next greatest during the third 10 minutes (sum of ranks = 3.5), and the smallest during the second 10 minutes (sum of ranks = 30.0).

DISCUSSION

While it is true that two different interviewers evoked the same number of affect statements within the margin of random error, the fact that two of the comparisons approached the .05 level of significance would seem to indicate that there is still room for greater control of interviewer behavior or that such interviewer characteristics as sex, age, appearance, etc., play an important role in controlling the interviewee's behavior.

While Verplanck (7) was unable to test the constancy of the response used during any one conversation or among different conversations, the recording done in this experiment made it possible to demonstrate that a response class decided upon prior to the interview can be reliably reacted to by different interviewers and coders.

Although this experiment gave definite evidence for conditioning, there was much variability among individuals. This was not surprising in view of the fact that the interviewing was carried out with schizophrenics and the response conditioned one of affect statements.

This variability, both in operant level and in susceptibility to reinforcement, might well provide an objective prognostic measure of degree of flatness of affect. Such a measure would be of value since there are strong indications (10) that marked flatness of affect augurs badly for the outcome of schizophrenia. Follow-up of the patients interviewed in this sample may allow an exact test of the relationship between outcome of illness and flatness of affect.

Perhaps one of the most interesting findings of this study was the linear relationship between number of reinforcements and number of responses in extinction. In a similar study, Williams (9) found that the relationship between number of reinforcements and number of responses during extinction for food-deprived rats was also linear up to about 30 reinforcements. Since fewer reinforcements were administered in the present study, it will certainly be of interest to try to duplicate the rest of Williams' curve for verbal behavior. The results become even more dramatic when account is taken of the fact that flatness of affect, as defined here by frequency of affect statements, appears to vary directly as a function of the interviewer's reinforcing behavior. The implications for the regular psychiatric interview are self evident.

The two patients in the experimental group who showed atypical relationships between reinforcement and extinction, are noteworthy because both deviated in directions that seem sensible on a *post hoc* basis. The hard-of-hearing individual got more reinforcements for the number of responses she emitted in extinction than the Ss in the rest of the sample. This, of course, is exactly what one might expect if S could not hear all the verbal reinforcements given her. The patient whose diagnosis was changed from schizophrenic to manic-depressive psychosis, manic stage, gave many more affect statements in extinction than might be expected from the number of reinforcements she received. This observation suggests the possibility that if a sample of manic-depressives was administered the same number of reinforcements as the schizophrenic group, a linear relationship might similarly be found but with a steeper slope. Manic-depressives may require a smaller number of reinforcements than schizophrenics for the same number of responses in extinction.

The correlation coefficients between all possible combinations of conditions were computed in an attempt to see whether the relationship between number of reinforcements and number of responses during extinction could be explained simply as a correlation that might be obtained between any two 10-minute periods of the same interviews. Table 1 shows that while correlations occurred between all conditions, the highest were between the number of reinforcements and number of responses during extinction in the experimental group. Furthermore, upon partialing out the operant level correlation to study the relationship to be expected between any two 10-minute periods, no substantial change occurred in the correlation between number of reinforcements and frequency of response in extinction. The correlations between the conditions in the control group yield further evidence for the conditioning effect in the experimental group. The fact that they are all approximately equally high, whereas the reinforcement-extinction correlations in the experimental group are outstandingly high by comparison to the operant-extinction and operant-reinforcement correlations, argues strongly for the effect of reinforcement.

A final control on the effect of reinforcement in the interview, that of the rate of self-referred statements, was used in order to check on the possibility that the reinforcement functioned merely to make the patient feel more at ease and therefore talk more about himself. This analysis indicated that the conditioning effect was specific in producing an increase in self-referred affect statements and not in increasing the general class of self-referred statements.

Summary

Thirty-six hospitalized schizophrenics were included in this study. Twenty of them (the experimental group) were interviewed for a period of 30 minutes each on two consecutive days by two interviewers. The other 16 (the control group) were given one interview only, which lasted for 30 minutes. Each interview in the experimental group consisted of a 10-minute operant level, during which E only asked questions necessary to keep up the patient's talk but did not respond to the patient's speech; 10 minutes of conditioning, during which E reinforced by agreement all self-referred affect statements; and, finally, 10 minutes of extinction, during which E withheld all further reinforcement. Each interview in the control group consisted of 30 minutes of operant level only.

It was demonstrated that a difference in interviewers or sources of reinforcement per se need not produce discrepant results during an interview when utilizing a standard procedure for interviewing. It was further shown that a verbal response class can be reliably isolated and reacted to. Conditioning of the response class of self-referred affect statements was found to be possible with schizophrenics during an otherwise usual clinical interview. The relationship *between* number of reinforcements and number of responses in extinction was described by means of a straight line, i.e., the greater the number of reinforcements, the greater the number of extinction responses.

The lawfulness of these findings indicates that the clinical interview is subject to investigation by experimental techniques. Furthermore, a controlled interview may prove useful as a research tool.

1. GREENSPOON, J. The reinforcing effect of two spoken sounds on the frequency of two responses. *Amer. J. Psychol.*, 1955, **68**, 409-16.

2. HILDUM, D. C., & BROWN, R. W. Verbal reinforcement and interviewer basis. *J. abnorm. soc. Psychol.*, 1956, **53**, 108-11.

3. KENDALL, M. G. *Rank correlation methods.* London: Griffin, 1948.

4. MANN, H. B. & WHITNEY, D. R. On a test of whether one of two random variables is stochastically larger than the other. *Ann. math. Stat.*, 1947, **18**, 50-60.

5. SALZINGER, SUZANNE. Rate of affect response in schizophrenics as a function of three types of interviewer verbal behavior. Paper read at East. Psychol. Ass., Atlantic City, March, 1956.

6. SKINNER, B. F. *Verbal behavior.* New York: Appleton-Century-Crofts, 1957.

7. VERPLANCK, W. S. The control of the content of conversation: Reinforcement of statements of opinion. *J. abnorm. soc. Psychol.*, 1951, **51**, 668-76.

8. WILCOXON, F. *Some rapid approximate statistical procedures.* New York: American Cyanamid, 1949.

9. WILLIAMS, S. B. Resistance to extinction as a function of the number of reinforcements. *J. exp. Psychol.*, 1938, **23**, 506-21.

10. ZUBIN, J. Role of prognostic indicators in the evaluation of therapy. Paper read at Conference on the Evaluation of Pharmacotherapy in Mental Illness, Washington, D. C., 1956.

49 / Hypotheses and Habits in Verbal "Operant Conditioning" [1]

DON E. DULANY, JR., *University of Illinois*

Studies of verbal "operant conditioning" (Adams, 1957; Krasner, 1958) raise two fundamental questions: Is this learning without awareness? And how well do empirical operant principles describe the data obtained in a verbal conditioning experiment? Possibly the effects were under the subject's own verbal control.

In the studies most faithful to the operant conditioning paradigm, subjects said words ad libitum and rate of plural nouns increased when followed by a buzzer (Greenspoon, 1951), a light (Greenspoon, 1951; Sidowski, 1954), or a casually murmured "Umhmm" (Greenspoon, 1955; Mandler & Kaplan, 1956; Wilson & Verplanck, 1956). Greenspoon (1955) also showed that Umhmm was an effective reinforcer for other words. It is unsurprising to learn that one can influence the actions of another cooperative human being by informing him when his behavior is judged correct or acceptable. These studies attract attention because they apparently demonstrate learning without awareness in some sense. Some see in this a program for identifying response classes and empirical reinforcers

at the human level through the use of operant conditioning procedures. As Verplanck (1955) puts it, "This is the identification of responses and reinforcing stimuli, and the verification and eduction of laws relating them to one another in human behavior under conditions where the subject is acting as naturally as possible, and where insofar as possible, he is not 'aware' of what is going on" (p. 597). Salzinger (1959), in discussing the verbal conditioning literature, concludes that, "Very little deviation from the approach in animal work has been necessary so far to obtain lawful data in verbal behavior" (p. 70). But those accustomed to wonder about reinforcing mechanisms may think these findings antecedently improbable. Umhmm under several circumstances could be a pleasant thing to hear, but it is unclear how a buzzer or a flash of a 75-watt bulb would

From the *Journal of Abnormal and Social Psychology*, 1961, **63**, 251-63, with permission of the author and publisher.
1. This study was supported by grants from the National Science Foundation and the United States Public Health Service. Richard Erkes collected the data of Experiment I; Janet Pierce and Margo Tuite collected the data of Experiment II and assisted with statistical computations.

activate any of the processes variously assumed to be the basis for a law of effect that is more than empirical. The improbable is not to be dismissed, certainly, but it does invite an examination of alternative explanations—in this case the possibility that the operant conditioning effect was mediated by some kind of verbal control—hypotheses and self-instructional sets, perhaps together with the transfer of prior habits.

There are hints of some alternative in the greater effectiveness of these contingent stimuli in tasks that are puzzling enough to arouse problem solving. When subjects in our laboratory course were asked to say words, and were permitted to express their hypotheses throughout, they seemed to grasp at any figural stimulus, even a light or buzzer, as a sign that would make sense of a silly, meaningless task. Sidowski (1954) found that uninstructed subjects conditioned as well as those advised that the light could be made to blink, and he had reason to believe that the "uninstructed" were self-instructed. With the more meaningful task of telling stories, Ball (1952) found a light to be ineffective as a reinforcer. Neither did a light influence response to a self-acceptance inventory (Nuthmann, 1957) or selection of pronouns while the subject formed complete sentences (Taffel, 1955). And Hildum and Brown (1956) found that Umhmm did not modify response to an attitude questionnaire, again a task the subject usually accepts at face value.

In the first experiment subjects are asked to say words and plural nouns are followed by Umhmm. A number of questions are asked and the subjects are divided into groups depending on what they say that they were supposed to do in the experiment. We should like to know whether these reports of behavioral hypotheses are related to selection of plural nouns as we would in theory expect such hypotheses to be. Theory

in this case is not formal and well-developed, but merely a set of theoretical propositions of long standing—that subjects under selective reinforcement tend to form behavioral hypotheses, that these hypotheses tend to be accompanied by corresponding self-instructional sets (or "intentions"), and that these in turn lead to selection of the corresponding response class.[2] Thus, with the additional hypothesis that subjects tend to report their hypotheses when questioned, subjects who report that they are supposed to say plural nouns should say them. But other behavioral hypotheses as well must be examined for the possibility that they are "correlated hypotheses" (Adams, 1957). Selection of another response class might, because of the subjects' prior organization of habits, also entail selection of plural nouns. If any report of a behavioral hypothesis is found to be related to selection of plural nouns, we shall, in a second experiment, instruct subjects to use the reported response class. Instruction, too, is commonly hypothesized to produce sets, and sets, in turn, to result in response selection. The term, "verbal control," summarizes the set of theoretical propositions involving behavioral hypotheses and instructional sets (self or social). It is used here because it suggests the reporting and manipulating operations used and directs attention to the subjects' verbal processes. The hypotheses and sets under consideration, might, however, be verbal, partially verbal, or entirely cognitive-neural—though in this situation, one would think, verbalizable.[3]

---

2. The hypothesis of association of behavioral hypotheses and self-instructional sets probably requires the assumption of a fair amount of task motivation on the part of the subjects.
3. William James' classical point that language may be inadequate for conveying complex awareness has been applied by Eriksen (1958) to the use of retrospective criteria in studies of this type. The point is most troublesome for claims of learning *without* awareness. In this case, however, "I am supposed to say plural nouns" seems simple to articulate, and failure to do so seems strongly to imply lack of

EXPERIMENT I

METHOD

Subjects. The subjects were 60 male undergraduates in the introductory psychology course, 43 experimentals and 17 controls.

Setting and procedure. The experimental room, similar to that described by the other experimenters, was 8′ × 6′ × 10′, illuminated by a single hanging bulb, and bare except for two chairs and a table with a microphone and tape recorder. The experimenter was a male senior in psychology who was mature in manner and appeared to be in his early twenties. He sat behind the subject and recorded his responses unobserved.

After a few minutes of conversation to establish rapport, the experimenter gave the following instructions taken from Greenspoon (1955): "What I want you to do is to say all the words you can think of. Do not use any sentences or phrases. Do not count. Please continue until I say stop. Go ahead." A few, either baffled or perverse, had to be reminded several times not to give phrases.

The four published experiments of this type have varied in length and manner of scoring. Greenspoon (1955) solicited 50 minutes of responding and plural nouns were tallied by 5-minute periods. In the other three experiments subjects spoke some total number of words, and correct responses were scored by blocks of all responses. The present experiment required five blocks of 55 words of the subject, a chore that took the typical subject about 50 minutes. Scoring by blocks of all words has the advantage of reducing the large variance between subjects in output of plural nouns by eliminating the effect of wide individual differences in overall rate of uttering any words.

For the experimental group the experimenter murmured "Umhmm" after each plural noun in the last four blocks of 55 responses. The intonation of Umhmm varied too much for a meaningful phonetic description, but it could be characterized as noncommittal to warm. While the controls were saying words, the experimenter remained silent. After each block of 55 responses, all subjects were asked, "What do you think the experiment is all about?" At the end of

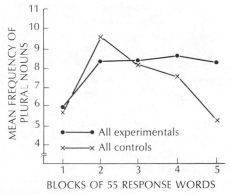

FIG. 1. Frequency of plural nouns in blocks of 55 responses.

the session the experimenter asked that question again and several others: "Did you notice whether I said anything?" ("If so, what?" and "What do you think the significance of that was?") "Was there anything that you were supposed to say in order to be correct?" The entire experimental session was recorded on tape.

Two people independently examined the reports—and, of course, independently of any knowledge of the subject's performance. Their specific object was to sort the subjects into groups on the basis of their reported behavioral hypotheses, with a remaining category for those who reported nothing relevant. Sorting by this single principle proved easier than expected and the two sorts perfectly agreed.

Results and discussion

Manipulations and performance. First, the performance of the entire experimental group was compared with that of the controls (see Figure 1). There was no need to eliminate any subjects from this analysis because none called plural nouns "correct," stated the purpose of the experiment, or said that Umhmm was contingent on plural nouns, the usual criteria of full "awareness" and basis for exclusion. No two of the other studies report the same analysis or the same learning curve, so it is possible

awareness. When reports of awareness are found to be related to behavior in the way awareness should be, the point loses some force.

to replicate their findings here only in the general sense of showing that output of plural nouns came under "control" of the contingent stimulus. An experimental effect is shown most simply by observing that for 35 of 43 experimental subjects, mean frequency of plural nouns, averaged over the four reinforcement blocks, was greater than frequency of plural nouns at the first, nonreinforcement block; and that only 8 of 17 controls show the same increase. A chi square for unrelated groups of 5.48 with a $p < .02$ shows that this increase is significantly associated with experimental treatments.

That the effect does not register as consistent differences in trend over all five blocks can be seen from the insignificant group differences in linear and quadratic components of trend (Lines B and C of Table 1) in Grant's (1956) extension of the Alexander (1946) analysis.[4] Apparently the effect of the reinforcement is to support output of plurals at some phase of reinforcement, but individual fluctuations over the four reinforcement blocks are too irregular and too heterogeneous for significant group differences in trend over all five blocks, either linear or curvilinear. This great heterogeneity must be in response to the reinforcement because the term for linear slopes between individuals is highly significant for the experimental group ($F = 2.96$, 41 and 123 df, $p < .0005$) and insignificant for the controls ($F = 1.35$, 15 and 45 df, $p > .10$) when each is tested against its own term for individual deviations from estimation. With still more heterogeneity in $kind$ of individual curvilinear slope, which is visible in a graph of individual slopes, both the insignificant between-group and between-individual curvilinear trend terms are consistent with the significant chi square for differences in group shift. The lack of an overall mean difference, together with that chi square, also points to heterogeneity. The overall

trend, a rise and fall in output of plurals, is best described by the second order orthogonal component (Line E).

Subjects' reports. The subjects' answers to questioning fell into several conspicuous categories. To Question 1, "What do you think this experiment is all about?," there was a scattering of answers such as "To study how I think," "A vocabulary test," and "I haven't the slightest idea"; but only one had a noticeable frequency. Thirty-four experimental subjects—and 11 controls—replied that the experimenter must be studying their associations, that their task was to run through their associations. In each case the same answer had been given after one or more of the earlier blocks. This is a likely guess, since, as Bousfield (1953) has shown, a subject obliged to produce very many disconnected words usually runs through associated pools; and this is all of much consequence the subjects sees himself doing.

All subjects replied to Question 2 that the experimenter said "Umhmm" and were therefore asked, "What do you think the significance of that was?" They suggested variously that Umhmm was an "encouragement to continue," "A distraction," or "Of no significance," and again only one reply was at all common. Eleven of the above 34 reported that they were supposed to associate in a series or in the same category whenever the experimenter said "Umhmm." These 11 subjects were therefore separable from the others. Typical replies were "I noticed that you appear to say 'umhmm' when I seem to follow a line of more or less synonyms. . . . Your 'umhmms' show me an indication that I'm on the right track. . . . You seemed to be in favor of the more direct associations"; "I think the only thing is you pick at random, like I picked "vege-

---

4. With heterogeneity of variance, the "true" p values could be a little greater than those reported, but all Fs to which interpretative significance is attached have p values of less than .01.

tables,' and you wanted me to talk about that and every time I mentioned some vegetable you'd say 'umhmm'"; "I think you're trying to make me use the same—ehr—stay in the same category . . . you arbitrarily pick subjects and try to make me say what you wanted me to say"; "Well, I think that you're saying 'umhmm' when I say a series of words that are connected together . . . well, like I said before, the only thing I could think of was I'd start relating words to a definite subject and you'd encourage me to do that." Most of these subjects also stated the implied converse: that no Umhmm signaled that they should change categories. None of the controls reported this hypothesis.

Question 3, "Was there anything that you were supposed to say in order to be correct?," was comparatively uninformative, mainly because it had already been answered. Eight of the above 11 restated the hypothesis of "reinforcement for association" and 3 answered, quite consistently, that no particular words or associations were correct. The others replied "No" or that if there were a correct response, they did not know what it was.

Reports and performance.—The experimental subjects, then, divide most naturally into three groups: "reinforcement for association," "associative hypothesis alone," and "no associative hypothesis." They are graphed along with controls in Figure 2. The great rise of the "reinforcement for association" group is reflected in the highly significant *F* for between-group linear slopes (Line B of Table 1). The "associative hypothesis alone" group is hardly distinguishable from the control group and neither of the between group trend terms is significant. There are no significant trend differences between the controls and the "no associative hypothesis" subjects, but this group is significantly *below* the controls in mean output of plurals (Line A). This

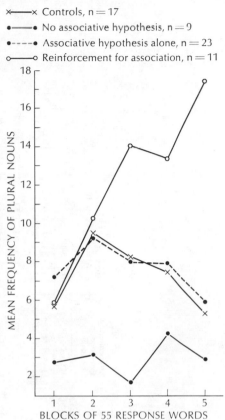

FIG. 2. Frequency of plural nouns in blocks of 55 responses.

is a little puzzling, but a group low in plural output could be selected by their failure to form the associative hypothesis if the Umhmm, which did follow plurals often associatively rendered, had any role in suggesting that the experimenter was interested in associations.

This analysis is obviously *post hoc* in some sense, but it does not thereby capitalize on chance differences. The likelihood of accepting a chance difference is no greater when separating subjects on some principle before inspecting their performance than when separating subjects on some theoretical hypothesis before conducting the experiment. It is only necessary to identify the groups in some clear way independ-

TABLE 1. *Summary of trend analyses*

Source	Error	All Experimentals vs. Controls			Reinforcement for Association vs. Controls			Associative Hypothesis Alone vs. Controls			No Associative Hypothesis vs. Controls		
		df	MS	F	df	MS	F	df	MS	F	df	MS	F
A. Between-group mean	f	1	24.19	0.12	1	824.85	4.78*	1	11.04	0.07	1	538.69	8.01**
B. Between-group linear slopes	g	1	74.83	1.82	1	582.99	11.46***	1	1.35	0.05	1	11.05	0.47
C. Between-group quadratics	h	1	33.85	1.54	1	16.60	0.53	1	11.94	0.51	1	60.73	2.81
D. Overall linear slope	i	1	41.08	0.86	1	207.43	4.08	1	54.02	1.88	1	5.85	0.25
E. Overall-quadratics	h	1	203.06	9.22***	1	163.29	5.20*	1	230.14	9.90***	1	96.07	4.44*
F. Between-individual means	i	58	203.72	10.61****	26	172.61	6.80****	38	159.32	2.58****	24	67.22	4.50****
G. Between-individual linear slopes	i	58	48.03	2.50****	26	50.87	2.00*	38	28.77	1.55	24	23.47	1.57
H. Between-individual quadratics	i	58	22.02	1.15	26	31.43	1.24	38	23.25	1.25	24	21.64	1.45
I. Individual deviations from estimate		174	19.20		78	25.39		114	18.56		72	14.93	

* $p < .05$.
** $p < .01$.
*** $p < .005$.
**** $p < .0005$.

ent of their performance. There does remain some capitalization on chance, but it is by virtue of multiple comparisons. Only three groups are compared with controls, though, and the one significant difference in group slope is very greatly so.[5] The theoretical interpretation of the difference is another matter.

A post hoc hypothesis. In sum, subjects saying nothing that classifies them as "aware" in the usual sense show an acquisition effect in aggregate; those who say that they are to associate in a series when the experimenter says "Umhmm" show a considerable acquisition effect; and the others show none at all. This result is unexpected because unlike the "correct" hypothesis, the "reinforcement for association" (RFA) hypothesis has no immediately obvious relation to saying plural nouns. But let us imagine an experiment in which subjects say words while we reinforce in first one semantic category, then another, tallying as correct all responses falling in the semantic category that is for the moment reinforced. For the RFA subjects this was the perceived pattern of reinforcement, and the experimenter defined a semantic category as correct just as long as plural nouns were forthcoming. It is the tally that differed. If a subject of the imaginary experiment hypothesized that he was to associate in the category of the moment when the reinforcement was "on" and to scan for a new category when it was "off," he should be very well able to increase his tally of correct responses. Association, we know from common sense and an inspection of the Minnesota norms (Russell & Jenkins, 1954), tends to produce semantically related words; and with instruction to associate in the "same category," the tendency should clearly be great. Now it might be that with the same instruction, stimulus and response items would tend also to be grammatically related—to be of the same part of speech or linguistic form class. Words that can take the same position in an utterance conceivably could be linked in some way that would be manifest associatively. The suggestion is that with instruction to associate in the same semantic category, semantic and grammatical associative responses might be correlated—that the RFA hypothesis is a correlated hypothesis.

Subjects of the RFA group report that they are to associate in a series upon presentation of the "Umhmm" and to scan for a new category upon its omission. And a reported hypothesis should tend to be coupled with some self-instructional set. Since the reinforcement in this experiment followed plural nouns we would then infer an associative set after plurals and a nonassociative set after other words. There was no report of this kind from controls and no reason to expect the same alignment of sets for them. In short, it may be that frequency of plural response to prior plural is related to an associative as opposed to a nonassociative set. "Diamonds," when one continues a series, should bring "rubies" or "pearls"—plurals. Scan for a new category and "telephone" might come as easily as "cigarettes." This *post hoc* hypothesis, to be tested in Experiment II, would make sense of the great increase in plural nouns for the RFA group, relative to controls, and the operant conditioning of plural nouns could be attributed to hypotheses which when acted upon are the occasion for manifesting prior verbal habits.

Interpretation of the subjects' reports. We should first consider a possible objection that the questions asked might have suggested the reports obtained.

5. Two systematic replications are now available, though they vary in ways that could have affected the number of subjects reporting the RFA Hypothesis. In one experiment, 8 of 63 report the hypothesis; in the other, 12 of 35. In both, the RFA subjects perform much as do these and differ dramatically from controls. In neither experiment do other subjects differ significantly from controls.

The results lose generality if the RFA hypothesis would not have been formed without the early and repeated question, "What do you think the experiment is all about now?" It seems unlikely, though, that an adult brought to a small room and asked to say words, no phrases or sentences please, would not be provoked to wonder as much. And if this general question could make one hypothesis more likely, it probably would have done the same for the plural noun hypothesis; yet no one called plural nouns correct. Moreover, Sidowski (1954) has reported, and others have implied, that their subjects adopted questioning, problem solving sets without special instructions. The thought that the RFA hypothesis could have been suggested entirely by questioning at the end is embarassed by the coincidence that only the RFA group shows an increase in plurals. Whether or not subjects in other studies, and how many, formed the RFA hypothesis is, of course, unknown; but, in any case, subjects who failed to report that hypothesis in the present experiment do not replicate the verbal conditioning effect.

The present research does not accord unquestioned validity to the subjects' reports or in any way rely upon a phenomenological data language. The concern is to determine whether the subject's report of a behavioral hypothesis is related to response selection in ways that we would in theory expect his hypothesis as construct to be related to response selection. We have considered that a behavioral hypothesis is related to response selection through a self-instructional set. The hypothesis of valid report is but one more proposition within the theoretical network to be evaluated by the data. And these propositions, together with the *post hoc* hypothesis, predict the obtained relation of report to response selection. Moreover, on the common hypothesis that instruction to

perform a response class may arouse a set to do so, it is also important to learn whether the relation of instruction to response selection is like that found for the corresponding report and response selection. The hypothesis of valid report will be further supported if the sets to be induced by the experimenter's instructions in Experiment II are found to be related to response selection in the same way found for the reports from which self-instructional sets were inferred in Experiment I. In short, the subjects' reports are interpretable if they behave as expected from the network of hypothesized relations among instructions, hypotheses, sets, reports, and response selection. The logic of science embodied in discussions of a nomological network and construct validity (Carnap, 1956; Cronbach & Meehl, 1955; Hempel, 1952; Sellars, 1948; Spence, 1958) may be appropriate, not only for the subject's response to a personality questionnaire and extended personal history, but also for his response to questions and more immediate experimental history.

EXPERIMENT II

This experiment tests the *post hoc* hypothesis of Experiment I, that frequency of responding with plural nouns is related to an associative as opposed to a nonassociative set. It also tests the corresponding hypothesis for Other Words, that frequency of responding with Other Words to Other Words is related in the same way to those sets, a possibility that has implications for Greenspoon's (1955) reported conditioning of Other Words. In Experiment I, subjects hypothesized what was expected of them; those hypotheses are the basis for instructing subjects in what is expected of them in Experiment II. By inducing sets in this way, the suspected verbal habits might be manifest in the absence of verbal reinforcement.

Method

One hundred plural nouns and 100 Other Words were drawn at random from the protocols of the first experiment and were used as stimulus words in a word association test. Within each block of 50 stimulus words presented, 25 plural nouns and 25 Other Words were randomly intermixed. The subject responded to each stimulus word in the first and third blocks of 50 words with an associative set and to words of the second and fourth blocks with a nonassociative set. Just before the first and third blocks of words were presented, the experimenter read the following instructions to induce an associative set: "This is a study of word habits. Now listen to each word I read and then tell me the first word you think of that is in the same category, that is related— that would continue in a series." To induce the nonassociative set prior to the second and fourth blocks the experimenter said, "Now listen to each word I read and tell me the first word you think of that is *not* in the same category, that is unrelated— that would not continue in a series." The experimenter, a female graduate student, read each word aloud and recorded the subject's responses. Subjects were run in the same experimental setting as that of Experiment I. At the end of the session the experimenter asked, "Was there anything you were supposed to say in order to be correct?," and the subject's responses were tape recorded.

Subjects of the primary sample were seven male undergraduates, presumably representative of the same population as those of Experiment I. Two others were dropped from the experiment when they failed to follow instructions, in one case by persistently giving simple associations that were not "in a series" (for example, blue-bird rather than blue-green or yellow), in the other case by failure to shift to a non-associative set. In both cases the session was halted and questioning revealed that the subject had not understood the instructions. It is often difficult to judge for a particular response whether or not a subject has followed instructions; it is not so difficult after a series of responses to judge that he consistently does not. An additional five high school students and five graduate students in psychology were also run as a partial check on the generality of the habit. None knew the hypothesis under investigation or the identity of the investigator for whom the assistant collected the data. When questioned none mentioned grammatical categories or replied that a particular kind of response was correct. The graduate students accepted the procedures as an assessment of verbal habits, of a character unknown to them, and expressed some surprise upon being told later that the experimenter was interested in grammatical rather than semantic categories. Most of the others submitted themselves to a "personality test."

Results and discussion

Table 2 presents mean frequency of plural and other responses, for both

TABLE 2. *Mean frequencies of plural response and Other response to plural stimuli and Other stimuli under associative and nonassociative sets*

Subjects	Plural stimuli		Other stimuli	
	Associative set	Nonassociative set	Associative set	Nonassociative set
College undergraduates				
Plural R	32.3	11.6	1.7	4.7
Other R	17.7	38.4	48.3	45.3
High School and graduate students				
Plural R	35.8	13.2	3.6	6.4
Other R	14.2	36.8	46.4	43.6
All subjects				
Plural R	34.4	12.5	2.9	5.7
Other R	15.7	37.5	47.3	44.3

samples, in the several experimental conditions. These values summarize the effects obtained; tests of significance are based on the analysis of individual contingency tables. Phi coefficients and chi squares for the relation of frequency of plural response to plural stimulus (plural vs. other response) with associative vs. nonassociative sets are given in Table 3. Yates' correction was applied to the phi formula when expected frequencies were

TABLE 3. *Association of plural response and Other response with associative and non-associative sets for plural stimuli and Other stimuli*

Subjects	Plural stimuli			Other stimuli		
	ϕ	χ^2	$p<$	ϕ	χ^2	$p<$
College under graduates						
1	.27	7.3	.01	.05	0.3	
2	.40	16.2 [a]	.001	.09	0.9	
3	.40	15.8 [a]	.001	.19	3.4	.10
4	.64	41.2	.001	.13	1.6	
5	.65	42.7	.001	.08	0.7	
6	.28	8.1	.01	.16	2.6	
7	.33	10.9	.001	.07	0.5	
High School and gradu-ate students						
1 HS	.17	3.0	.10	.05	0.3	
2 HS	.22	4.8	.05	.11	1.3	
3 HS	.42	17.4	.001	.11	1.3	
4 HS	.31	9.7	.005	.19	3.5	.10
5 HS	.56	31.6	.001	−.08	0.7	
6 G	.70	49.6	.001	.05	0.3	
7 G	.52	26.5	.001	.15	2.3	
8 G	.38	14.4	.001	.00		
9 G	.82	67.1	.001	.09	0.9	
10 G	.57	32.6	.001	.23	5.4	.02

[a] Phi's to 4 decimal places, which differed before rounding, were used in the computation of chi square.

less than five. All phi coefficients from the undergraduate subjects are positive and all converted chi squares are highly significant. Data from the high school and graduate students (Table 3) are consistent with this. Contrary to common misunderstanding of the "independence" requirement, phi and chi square are appropriately computed upon a single individual's responses. When significant they imply replicability for a particular subject. Generality across subjects can be inferred from 16 individual replications, which, ignoring size of effects, has a chance probability of 2^{-17}. The results clearly support the *post hoc* hypothesis of a relation of plural response to plural stimulus with a set to associate in a series as opposed to a nonassociative set. They suggest a basis for the increase in plural nouns of the RFA group in Experiment I.

Table 3 also presents analogous information for the association of frequency of Other response to Other stimulus with the two induced sets. The tests reported come from contingency tables representing the association of other response vs. plural response with associative vs. non-associative sets. These phi's tend toward zero or low positive relation. Taking both samples, only two of the chi squares for this relation have p values lower than .10, and only one lower than .02. But 15 of the 17 phi's are positive, and by the sign test this outcome has a chance probability of less than .01 (two-sided). The data at least support the possibility that hypotheses and associative habits could have mediated the operant conditioning of Other Words reported by Greenspoon (1955). None of these effects is large, but then Greenspoon (1955) reports a comparatively weaker conditioning effect for Other Words—an F at the .05 level for the three conditions Umhmm, Control, and Uh-huh.

The latter contingency tables can, of course, just as well be interpreted as showing a positive relation between *plural* response to Other Words and a *non*associative set. Viewed in this way, they suggest that scanning for a new category after Other Words, reported by subjects of Experiment I, might also have increased the tendency toward production of plural nouns.

Since categorization may follow many possible attributes, it would be difficult for an observer to judge with great accuracy whether or not the subject's responses were in every instance "in the same category" as the subject would categorize. However, it was only necessary to observe that the associative and nonassociative instructions were generally followed in order to interpret the data of Table 3 as evidence for the correlation of two response classes, responses matched in grammatical category to stimulus and responses matched in semantic category to stimulus.

The verbal association experiment

permits greater control over the manipulation of sets, as well as continuity with a large literature. It does not permit a clear comparison of the magnitude of effects with that of the free response procedure. Nevertheless, the procedure demonstrates the kind of effect hypothesized and shows it to be appreciable under fairly conservative conditions. The number of stimuli is fixed in Experiment II, and it does not provide for cumulative effects of the type possible in Experiment I. Moreover, in the free response procedure, the associative response is often given after a series of two or more plurals and the availability of another plural ought to be even greater in that case than after a single plural. The hypothesis only requires that we find the same kind of relation of instructional sets to behavior that we have found for reports and behavior, reports from which self-instructional sets were inferred. The quantitative effects of instructions uniformly administered and self-instructions irregularly emerging are not fairly compared in any obvious way.

It is worth nothing that the grammatical associative habits transferred without reports by the subjects that they were supposed to produce plurals or Other Words on plural and Other stimulus. This finding agrees with the common view that transfer may occur without awareness even if acquisition may not. And finally, the experiment again calls to mind (cf. Watt, 1905) the importance of instructional sets in the selection of associative habits to be manifest.

GENERAL DISCUSSION

Experiment II supports the interpretation placed on Experiment I. If RFA subjects acted on the hypotheses they reported, they should have increased their output of plural nouns. An associative set after plural nouns should have increased the rate of plural nouns, and

so should have a nonassociative set after Other Words, though much less so. Taken together, the experiments suggest a mechanism of verbal control that may have generality. Subjects may hypothesize what is expected of them and instruct themselves to act accordingly. Acting accordingly may constitute a response or operation as relevant cues are encountered, and the execution of correct responses as the direct manifestation of prior habits. In Experiment I, hypotheses are reported, and we infer corresponding self-instructional sets to associate in series on cue of the reinforcement and to scan for a new category on cue of its omission. With this alignment of sets, to judge from Experiment II, grammatical associative habits are manifest in plural response to prior words uttered.

Relation to other findings. If impressive evidence of verbal operant conditioning without awareness, beyond the effect of Umhmm on plural nouns and Other Words, remains untouched by the implications of this study, then the present findings of course have less significance. Sidowski (1954) reports that a light was effective reinforcement for the conditioning of plural nouns and Greenspoon (1951) reports the same for both a light and a buzzer. Umhmm rather than a light or buzzer was used in the present study not only because it has been used more often, but also for the greater generality of any finding that the contingent stimulus acts as a cue, a source of hypotheses and an occasion for acting on them, rather than as a gratifying social acknowledgment that reinforces without awareness. A light or a buzzer ought to be a less gratifying acknowledgment and a more figural cue.

Greenspoon (1955) also found that Huh-uh decreased the frequency of plural nouns. Though plausible, it would strain a point to suppose that Huh-uh could have signaled "change categories," a hypothesis which Experiment II suggests would depress the frequency of plurals. In any case, the significant effect reported comes from an F for three conditions—Umhmm, Control, and Huh-uh—and the significance of the variance might be due to the effect of Umhmm: the Umhmm group differs by t test from controls at all four reinforcement blocks, the Huh-uh group at only one block. Wilson and Verplanck (1956) add that Umhmm or Good increased the rate of saying adverbs in six of seven cases. Though it should be documented, analogous adverb-to-adverb association habits are a strong possibility, and given the same task used in the present study, their subjects seem no less likely to form the RFA hypothesis. Furthermore, controls were not used and the overall decline in frequency of plural nouns produced by controls here suggests that adverbs might increase in rate without reinforcement. A striking cumulative curve for frequency of pecking with application of a contingent stimulus is compelling evidence for the functional control of that stimulus. A significant shift in output of many human response classes may not be.

Where areas of semantic content such as "travel words" or "living thing words" are reinforced (Wilson & Verplanck, 1956) the RFA hypothesis should be no less likely, and a set to associate in the same category should obviously produce more words in that category. Wilson and Verplanck do acknowledge that many of their subjects stated "correlated hypotheses" (see Adams, 1957), for example, "geographic locations" for "travel words," but they report that these subjects performed no differently than did subjects reporting nothing of relevance. Krasner (1958) and Adams (1957) have reviewed a number of other studies, employing procedures other than the free operant production of single words, in which learning without aware-

ness is reported. Whatever the significance or deficiency of these studies, they are not discussed here beyond observing that both reviewers question the adequacy of criteria for awareness and the exclusion of correlated hypotheses.

The question of learning without awareness. Does Experiment I show learning without awareness? Even to ask the question requires that we specify some conception of awareness. Certainly there are many objects of awareness and the question is not whether unconscious subjects learned. There is no obvious solution in the literature, where investigators describe a number of awarenesses their subjects are said to learn without. But the matter should not be entirely arbitrary if we are interested in other than learning without this-that-and-the-other awareness variously revealed.

Questions of theoretical significance require that we specify some awareness that is theoretically relevant. First of all, we wish a theoretical term for awareness that will enter into theoretical propositions relating it to response selection. A "correct behavioral hypothesis"—the hypothesis that a correct response class is correct—is such a term. It is related to response selection within the theoretical network described. Verbalization of the contingency of the reinforcement on the correct response class, the most favored conception, does not so clearly predict selection of correct responses because it may leave the subject wondering what Umhmm was for and what he was supposed to do. Nor is there a clear inference of verbal antecedents in any number of acceptable statements of the purpose of an experiment or a report that learning occurred.

But the matter is additionally complicated by Adams' (1957) important suggestion that "correlated hypotheses" might account for many of the effects reported. By "correlated hypothesis"

Adams seems to mean any awareness other than of the correct response class that could account for better than chance performance. But this suggestion is not useful enough for prediction and too useful for *post hoc* explanation. The concept begs redefinition by some other specifiable relation to the correct response class. Let us consider instead that a hypothesis is a "correlated hypothesis" if the response class it calls correct is correlated with the response class the experimenter calls correct. Any hypothesis naming some incorrect response class as correct may be related within the theoretical network to selection of the response class it names. If that response class and the correct response class are correlated, then such an hypothesis becomes an antecedent from which to predict selection of the correct response class. To identify a correlated hypothesis, we might instruct the occurrence, then nonoccurrence, of the response class it calls correct, and observe a correlation of presence and absence of those responses with presence and absence of the responses the experimenter calls correct. Or where the hypothesized response class is identified with limited reliability, as is "associating in a series," we might observe a correlation of those instructions with presence and absence of members of the correct response class. This alternative follows on the hypothesis that instruction may induce the hypothesis-related set and response class. On the evidence of Experiment II, then, "I am supposed to associate in a series when you say 'Umhmm'" was identified as a correlated hypothesis for "I am supposed to say plural nouns."

Thus, either a correct or correlated hypothesis—as redefined—should in theory lead to selection of the correct response class, and together they provide a conception of awareness relevant to a second theoretical concern. Since "learning

without awareness" is commonly interpreted as supporting a theory of response selection by automatic action of after-effects (Thorndike, 1933), we should also like a conception of awareness relevant to that theory. The classical theory of automatic strengthening, unqualified by further assumptions, clearly implies that learning should occur in the absence of either a correct or a correlated hypothesis. Any such evidence would tend to support that theory as opposed to some alternative of verbal control. However, with report of a correct or correlated hypothesis as the indicator of awareness, Experiment I presents no evidence for learning without awareness.

But is there a way to recognize that learning occurred only *with* reports of awareness and still hold that it occurred by automatic strengthening? The problem is to account for the relation of reports to performance in a way consistent with that theory.

1. Could the hypotheses and report somehow be in response to the increased usage of plural nouns or to the process of automatic strengthening itself? Perhaps subjects rationalize their plural output as "associating in a series after 'Umhmm,'" or the hypothesis and report might be a phenomenal and verbal emergent of the process of automatic strengthening. These assumptions lack plausibility and generality. With no principle to link selection of plurals with this particular hypothesis and report, we are left to wonder why subjects did not report the opposite, or what a subject would report if we automatically strengthened his adjectives or ear-tugging.

2. There is a more serious variant of this set of assumptions. Suppose that whatever response class is automatically selected, a hypothesis or report of *that* response class follows as a rationalization or as a phenomenal or verbal emergent. And suppose it was associat-

ing in a series after Umhmm that was the response class automatically strengthened. This is probably more consistency than a theory of rationalization can manage—would all subjects who learn need to rationalize their behavior? Or it would require radical augmentation of a classical theory of automatic strengthening. To assume that automatic strengthening entails phenomenal or verbal emergents is, in fact, a new and radical theory, and should be brought forward strongly, if at all, so that it might be evaluated.

3. Most appealing is the thought that both awareness—the RFA hypothesis—and automatic strengthening of "associating in a series" might be consequences of the reinforcement. Perhaps learning occurred only with awareness because enough reinforcement to produce learning is enough to produce awareness. But this assumption must be supported with others. Number of reinforcements was not systematically varied, but programmed alike for all, and those who learned show no initial advantage at the first block which could bring them more reinforcements thereafter ($M_{RFA} = 5.7$; $M_{Other} = 5.9$). Still we might assume that the Umhmm was at the same time made more rewarding and more figural for some, and those subjects learned and reported the correlated hypothesis. Or some unknown kinds of individual receptivities to reinforcement and dispositions to awareness might be correlated.

Explanations 2 and 3 would still require an hypothesis of correlated response classes in order to account for the coincident selection of plural nouns. Explanation 2 does not suggest why some learned automatically and some not. Neither explanation would account for other findings that some subjects report a nonreinforced response class as correct and in fact select it (Dulany, 1960). And, of course, they leave the effects of instruction in Experiment II to be explained in some other way. In summary, a theory of automatic strengthening by aftereffects apparently does not account for these findings without auxiliary assumptions or radical augmentation. A little thought will usually supply assumptions to brace a challenged theory and it is rarely disproved. But the result does not seem a better theory than a theory that subjects report processes prior to and instrumental in response selection. It seems better to interpret the results within a network of simple hypotheses that appear sufficient to account for our findings, and that bring within the same formulation the common relation of reports and of instruction to response selection.

The question of operant conditioning. Neither reports of behavioral hypotheses nor the mechanism of verbal control outlined here enter into the language of operant conditioning as described by Skinner (1938) and extended by many (for example, Salzinger, 1959) to the verbal conditioning literature. Operant conditioning is said to occur when rate of response is brought under the functional control of a contingent stimulus (Skinner, 1938, 1953). How well do empirical operant principles describe the data of subjects in Experiment I? There are, of course, many possible abstractions upon the data, and the fit of empirical operant principles is no less good for uncovering mediating mechanisms. A free operant came under the functional control of a contingent stimulus. Empirical operant principles will describe the performance of subjects with the RFA hypothesis and loosely fit the aggregate behavior of the total experimental group. But the descriptive language of operant conditioning gives no account of the difference in performance of those reporting and those not reporting the critical hypothesis. With attention to the subjects reports there is less mystery that some subjects "condition" and some do not. If there are other resources within Skinner's (1953, 1957) extended system to account for such findings, an accumulation of similar findings would provide a challenge to call upon them. No formulation is obliged to account for irrelevant findings or to answer irrelevant questions. But verbal conditioners, too, apparently see awareness and possible verbal control as critical to their position, and it is they who have raised the question. A lack of awareness has been set as a condition for specifying the laws relating empirical reinforcers and response classes (Verplanck, 1955, p. 597). And most investigators are at pains to report that verbal conditioning occurred without, or unrelated to, reports of some kind of awareness. The languages of operant conditioning and verbal control are alternative formulations in the sense that each may have heuristic value. Wherever, there is evidence of a relation of reported behavioral hypotheses or of behavioral instructions to response selection, they would not seem to be equally adequate accounts of the data.

Still to be considered is the point that, apart from the question of awareness or verbal control, operant conditioning procedures have been shown to "identify" plural nouns as a response class. Identification of response classes is, of course, a clearly stated and fundamental aim of operant analysis, and in the verbal operant conditioning literature this identification is made through the manipulation of a contingent stimulus. Verplanck (1955) rephrases Skinner's (1938) definition of a response class in this way: ". . . a part of behavior (a) that is recurrently identifiable and hence enumerable; and (b) whose rate of occurrence can be determined as a systematic function of certain classes of environmental variables" (p. 595). Salzinger (1959) concurs. By the definition given, however, plural nouns ought to be identified as a response class when subjects are instructed to utter them and do so—voluntarily. That they will is easily shown, and this method of identification has been a routine part of exploratory work preceding this and other of our experiments on the selection of various response classes (Dulaney, 1960). It clearly answers the question whether a collection of possible responses will function as a behavioral variable by showing their rate of occurrence to be a function of presence and absence of instruction.

The empirical relation of plural nouns to a contingent stimulus is interesting and valuable from many standpoints. But though manipulation of a contingent stimulus is a sensible recourse with prelinguistic organisms, for the many human response classes accessible to awareness and capable of verbal control, instruction should be a simpler and more fruitful way of identifying functional response classes. We should not then have to depend upon the emergence of awareness or, alternatively, upon a fragile and disputable finding of "conditioning without awareness." The unsettled empirical question is whether response classes identified so simply will behave as response classes under selective reinforcement in the absence of awareness and verbal control. The present experiments offer no assurance that plural nouns will.

SUMMARY

It is not certain that "verbal operant conditioning" occurs without awareness or is adequately described in the language of operant conditioning.

In the first experiment, subjects said words, and plural nouns were reinforced with Umhmm. In the aggregate, subjects showed a significant shift to plural nouns when compared with controls. Upon questioning, approximately 25% of the experimental subjects reported the hypothesis that whenever the experimenter said "Umhmm" they were to associate in series and that no acknowledgment meant that they were to change semantic categories. This group produced a highly significant acquisition effect, and the remaining subjects none. With motivated subjects these hypotheses should be accompanied by self-instructional sets. For the successful experimental subjects, then, we infer that a "series associative set" tended to follow plural nouns and a "nonassociative set" tended to follow Other Words. None of the controls reported the critical hypothesis. If response after plural nouns brings more plural nouns with a set to continue a series than with a set to find a new category, the present verbal conditioning effect might be ascribed to the mediation of hypotheses, sets, and the transfer of prior verbal habits.

Experiment II presented a word association test with verbal reinforcement excluded. Frequency of plural nouns in response to plural nouns was significantly associated with a set to associate in series as opposed to a set to change categories. Other response to Other Words showed the same, though weaker relation to these sets.

The paper discusses the implications of these findings for some of the reports of verbal operant conditioning, for the question of learning without awareness, and for the adequacy of operant conditioning principles to describe the data obtained, making the following principal points:

1. The "conditioning" of plural nouns in the present study was mediated by a mechanism of verbal control. Subjects may hypothesize that some response class is correct and instruct themselves to respond accordingly. Response to relevant cues as encountered may yield correct responses as the manifestation of prior habits.

2. This mechanism provides a possible account of the verbal conditioning effects obtained in several often-cited experiments.

3. The concept of "correlated hypothesis" requires further explication lest it become too convenient a *post hoc* explanation. To identify a correlated hypothesis we may instruct the occurrence and nonoccurrence of the response class it calls correct and observe a correlation of these instructions (or of the instructed response class) with presence and absence of members of the response class the experimenter calls correct.

4. The question of learning or conditioning without awareness is made more meaningful by specifying an awareness more clearly relevant to theory. On common theoretical propositions, one kind of awareness—a correct or a correlated hypothesis—should lead to selection of the correct response class. And a theory of automatic action of aftereffects implies that learning should occur in the absence of that kind of awareness.

5. With report of the correct or a correlated response class as the criterion of awareness, Experiment I presents no evidence for learning or conditioning without awareness.

6. The language of operant conditioning, as it has been extended to the verbal conditioning experiment, does not describe the differences in performance of those reporting and those not reporting the critical hypotheses.

7. The usefulness of operant conditioning procedures for "identifying" many functional response classes at the human level should be evaluated against the relative ease of identifying response classes by using instructions.

8. The methodological strategy illustrated by these experiments—the joint use of reports and instructions—may be useful in the analysis of verbal control in other learning and conditioning paradigms.

ADAMS, J. Laboratory studies of behavior without awareness. *Psychol. Bull.*, 1957, **54**, 383-405.

ALEXANDER, H. W. A general test for trend. *Psychol. Bull.*, 1946, **43**, 533-57.

BALL, R. S. Reinforcement conditioning of verbal behavior and nonverbal stimuli in a situation resembling a clinical interview. Unpublished doctoral dissertation, Indiana University, 1952.

BOUSFIELD, W. A. The Occurrence of clustering in the recall of randomly arranged associates. *J. gen. Psychol.*, 1953, **49**, 229-40.

CARNAP, R. The methodological character of theoretical concepts. In H. Feigl & M. Scriven (Eds.), *The foundations of science and the concepts of psychology and psychoanalysis.* Minneapolis: Univer. Minnesota Press, 1956. Pp. 38-76.

CRONBACH, L. J., & MEEHL, P. E. Construct validity in psychological tests. *Psychol. Bull.*, 1955, **52**, 281-302.

DULANY, D. E. Reinforcement of verbal behavior. Technical Report No. 1, 1960, National Science Foundation, Grant G-4461.

ERIKSEN, C. W. Unconscious processes. In M. R. Jones (Ed.), *Nebraska symposium on motivation: 1958.* Lincoln: Univer. Nebraska Press, 1958. Pp. 169-227.

GRANT, D. A. Analysis-of-variance tests in the analysis and comparison of curves. *Psychol. Bull.*, 1956, **53**, 141-54.

GREENSPOON, J. The effect of verbal and nonverbal stimuli on the frequency of members of two verbal response classes. Unpublished doctoral dissertation, Indiana University, 1951.

GREENSPOON, J. The reinforcing effect of two spoken sounds on the frequency of two responses. *Amer. J. Psychol.*, 1955, **68**, 409-16.

HEMPEL, C. G. Fundamentals of concept formation in empirical science. Chicago: Univer. Chicago Press, 1952.

HILDUM, D. C., & BROWN, R. W. Verbal reinforcement and interviewer bias. *J. abnorm. soc. Psychol.*, 1956, **53**, 108-11.

KRASNER, L. Studies of the conditioning of verbal behavior, *Psychol. Bull.*, 1958, **55**, 148-71.

MANDLER, G., & KAPLAN, W. K. Subjective evaluation and reinforcing effect of a verbal stimulus. *Science*, 1956, **124**, 582-3.

NUTHMANN, ANNE M. Conditioning of a response class on a personality test. *J. abnorm. soc. Psychol.*, 1957, **54**, 19-23.

RUSSELL, W. A., & JENKINS, J. J. The complete Minnesota norms for responses to 100 words from the Kent-Rosanoff Word Association Test. *Off. Naval Res. tech. Rep.*, 1954, No. 11. (Contract No. N8)

SALZINGER, K. Experimental manipulation of verbal behavior: A review. *J. gen. Psychol.*, 1959, **61**, 65-94.

SELLARS, WILFRIED. Concepts as involving laws and inconceivable without them. *Phil. Sci.*, 1948, **15**, 287-315.

SIDOWSKI, J. B. Influence of awareness of reinforcement upon verbal conditioning. *J. exp. Psychol.*, 1954, **48**, 355-60.

SKINNER, B. F. *The behavior of organisms: An experimental analysis.* New York: Appleton-Century-Crofts, 1938.

SKINNER, B. F. *Science and human behavior.* New York: Macmillan, 1953.

SKINNER, B. F. *Verbal behavior.* New York: Appleton-Century-Crofts, 1957.

SPENCE, K. W. A theory of emotionally based drive (*D*) and its relation to performance in simple learning situations. *Amer. Psychologist*, 1958, **13**, 131-41.

TAFFEL, C. Anxiety and the conditioning of verbal behavior. *J. abnorm. soc. Psychol.*, 1955, **51**, 496-502.

THORNDIKE, E. L. A theory of the action of the after-effects of a connection upon it. *Psychol. Rev.*, 1933, **40**, 435.

VERPLANCK, W. S. The operant, from rat to man: An introduction to some recent experiments on human behavior. *Trans. NY Acad. Sci.*, 1955, **17**, 594-601.

WATT, H. J. Experimentelle Beiträge zu einer Theorie des Denkens. *Arch. ges. Psychol.*, 1905, **4**, 289-436.

WILSON, W. C., & VERPLANCK, W. S. Some observations on the reinforcement of verbal operants. *Amer. J. Psychol.*, 1956, **69**, 448-51.

50 / The Temporal Relationship between Awareness and Performance in Verbal Conditioning [1]

L. DOUGLAS DeNIKE,[2] *Duke University*

Differential predictions concerning the role of awareness in verbal conditioning were tested through an experimental analysis of the temporal relationship between awareness and the inception of performance gains. Female college students were reinforced for "human noun" responses in a word-naming task and Ss' awareness of this response-reinforcement contingency was assessed through ratings of "thoughts about the experiment" which each S recorded during the conditioning trials. Performance gains were found only for aware Ss. Furthermore, increments in perform-

From the *Journal of Experimental Psychology*, 1964, **68**, 521-9, with permission of the author and publisher.

1. This paper was based on a dissertation submitted to the Psychology Department of Duke University in partial fulfillment of the requirements for the PhD degree. The writer expresses deep appreciation to Charles D. Spielberger, now at Vanderbilt University, for his dedicated supervision. The writer is also indebted to K. D. Kroupa, I. H. Bernstein, A. R. Dennison, and R. G. Ratliff for their assistance in the study. This research was supported in part by a grant (MH-7446) from the National Institute of Mental Health, United States Public Health Service, to the dissertation supervisor.

2. Now at the University of Southern California.

ance first occurred on the trial block on which aware Ss first recorded their correct hypotheses (verbalized awareness). The results were interpreted as supporting the hypothesis that performance gains in verbal conditioning are consciously mediated.

In verbal-conditioning experiments, Ss seemingly unaware of the principle by which reinforcement was administered have nonetheless shown systematic changes in their verbal behavior in response to reinforcement. Such changes have been widely accepted as evidence of learning without awareness (see reviews by Greenspoon, 1962; Krasner, 1958; Salzinger, 1959). However, in verbal-conditioning studies reporting learning without awareness, insensitive methods for assessing awareness have typically been employed (Spielberger, 1965). In recent experiments in which awareness was evaluated more thoroughly, the findings have strongly suggested that performance gains in verbal conditioning are consciously mediated (e.g., Dulany, 1961, 1962; Levin, 1961; Spielberger, 1962; Tatz, 1960).

The results of these recent experiments, which support a cognitive interpretation, have included the following: (a) Performance gains were limited chiefly to aware Ss, i.e., to Ss who verbalized hypotheses which, if used as the basis for response selection, would lead to an increased output of the reinforced response class. (b) Performance gains were limited to specific responses for which a given S was aware of a response-reinforcement contingency; e.g., Ss reinforced for constructing sentences beginning with the pronouns "I" and "we," who were aware of the reinforcement contingency for only one of these pronouns, showed conditioning effects only for that pronoun. (c) Initial performance gains for aware Ss tended to occur on the particular trial block identified by S as that on which he first became aware. (d) Instructions which provided information about the presence and/or significance of the rein-

forcement facilitated awareness, and enhanced the performance gains of aware Ss.

However, since awareness is usually assessed through questioning *after* the conditioning trials, it is possible that Ss who then verbalize correct or correlated hypotheses may have conditioned without awareness, and subsequently rationalized their performance by claiming that they developed their hypotheses during conditioning. Thus it would seem that the clarification of the temporal sequence of events in verbal conditioning is crucial to the differentiation between alternative theoretical accounts of this phenomenon. If awareness is a *consequence* of performance gains (Postman & Sassenrath, 1961), or is *suggested* to Ss by questioning (Krasner, 1962), performance gains should begin prior to the time at which Ss develop awareness. But if performance gains are mediated by awareness, acquisition of the reinforced response class should occur only for aware Ss, and only for trials subsequent to their developing correct or correlated hypotheses.

The principal goal of the present study was to examine the temporal relationship between awareness and performance by having Ss write down their "thoughts about the experiment" after each trial block during conditioning. In order to evaluate the comparability of this procedure to customary methods for assessing awareness, a postconditioning interview was also employed.

METHOD

Subjects.—The Ss were 82 female undergraduate students enrolled in the introductory psychology course at Duke University, who volunteered for an experiment on "verbal behavior." Each S received credit toward a course requirement for participating. None of the Ss were previously known to the Es, nor had any of them previously participated in a verbal-conditioning experiment.

Conditioning task and apparatus. The conditioning task, adapted from Greenspoon (1955), required Ss to say words. Human nouns (i.e., nouns denoting a person or persons, such as ARCHITECT, GIRL, PROTESTANTS, SPANIARD, UNCLE) constituted the critical response class to be reinforced. The definition of the critical response class approximated the usage of Matarazzo, Saslow, and Pareis (1960) who found that "human responses" could be reliably scored and readily conditioned. The conditioning procedures were carried out in a small room containing two chairs, a tape recorder, and a 3×5 ft. table bisected across its width by a screen approximately 15 in. in height. The S and E sat at opposite ends of the table. The height of the screen which separated them enabled each to see the other's face, but not the other's writing activity. A 15-w. red light, mounted on a 3×3 in. metal box, stood on the table on S's side of the screen. The switch which operated the light, and the tape recorder, were located on E's side of the screen.

Conditioning procedure.—The E, a male graduate student, initially engaged S in a few moments of casual conversation to establish rapport. Following this, S was seated, and E read these instructions:

We are doing a study on verbal behavior and how people use words. Your job today will be very simple. I want you to say words—any words at all will do, for instance, PIANO, COWS, BARBER, HOUSES, PEOPLE—and there is no time limit, but they must be words; no sentences and no numbers. We will be making a tape recording of the words. As you are no doubt aware, subjects' *thoughts* about an experiment in which they're participating are important to take into account, in order to better understand what they did in the experiment. So I'd like you to write out, briefly but clearly, any thoughts that come to you that have any relation to the experiment. We're not interested in just *any* thoughts you might have—you need not dwell on personal matters—but we would like to get any thoughts that you have about the experiment. After you say a

group of words, this light will go on. (The E operated the switch which turned on the red light.) That's your signal to pause and write down the thoughts that you then have in the space provided on the recording sheet in front of you: Don't feel hurried while you're doing this; take the time necessary to express yourself fully so that it will be clear to us later. Now, have you got something to write with? (The E paused and allowed the S to produce her own writing implement if she had one; otherwise, he provided a sharpened pencil.) When you have finished writing down your thoughts for any particular pause, say "Okay." Then after you see the light go out, go right back to saying words. (The E turned off the red light.) Don't state your thoughts aloud to me. If, between one pause and the next one, no thoughts occur to you, write the word "None" in the space provided for the pause, and then say "Okay." Now, that's quite a mouthful of instructions you've been given; is everything clear? (The E smiled, paused, and, in response to questions, repeated appropriate parts of the instructions in a deliberate manner. Questions concerning the overall purpose of the experiment were answered with the assurance that it would be explained afterward. When S had no further questions, the tape recorder was turned on and E sat down.) All right, ——(S's first name), you can start saying words when you are ready.

Each S was required to say a total of 300 response words and each word was recorded by E as either a human noun or other word. After each trial block of 25 words, the red light was turned on and the tape recorder was stopped while S was writing. The first two trial blocks provided a measure of S's operant rate for saying human nouns. In the first operant trial block, E reinforced S's third response word by saying "Mmm-hmm." This practice was found by Matarazzo et al. (1960) to lessen S's surprise and/or confusion when systematic reinforcement was introduced later. The E remained silent for the other operant trials.

After the operant trials, each S was assigned to the Experimental or the Control group. The first 60 Ss were assigned on a random basis which provided that 3 Ss were assigned to the Experimental group for each S assigned to the Control group. The last 22 Ss were assigned in the same 3 to 1 ratio, but their operant rates were taken into account so that the mean operant rates for the two groups would be approximately equated. Beginning with the third trial block, Ss in the Experimental group ($N = 61$) were reinforced with "Mmm-hmm" for each human noun response. The Ss in the Control group ($N = 21$) were reinforced with 'Mmm-hmm" according to a predetermined random schedule for 10% of their response words. The 10% rate of reinforcement for control Ss approximated the mean operant rate for "human responses" found by Matarazzo et al. (1960).

Postconditioning interview.—Upon completion of the conditioning task each S was directed to a nearby room, where she was interviewed according to a detailed schedule of questions [3] by a second E who had no knowledge of the group to which S had been assigned nor of her performance on the conditioning task. The questions, adapted from those used in previous studies (DeNike & Spielberger, 1963; Spielberger & DeNike, 1962), were designed to detect Ss' hypotheses about the relation of the reinforcement to their verbal responses, and the extent to which Ss wanted the reinforcement and tried to get it. Upon completion of the interview, each S was asked what she had heard about the experiment prior to participation. No S indicated any significant prior knowledge of the procedures. The interviewer then briefly explained the procedures and their rationale, and cautioned S not to talk about the experiment.

RESULTS

Incidence of awareness

Definition of awareness.—The Ss' awareness was determined by examining the "thoughts about the experiment" (notes) which they had written during the conditioning trials. A statement in S's notes that E had responded to the words S said was taken as a reference to the reinforcement whether or not S used the word "Mmm-hmm." The Ss

who recorded in their notes a correct response-reinforcement hypothesis (one which would have yielded essentially 100% reinforcement if acted upon consistently) were rated as *aware*. For example, one S wrote, "The words I said which denoted a human being were responded to by an affirmative murmur from the experimenter." Another wrote, "Oh, for heaven's sake, why didn't you say you wanted names of people. I thought you were clearing your throat." The Ss who did not record correct hypotheses in their notes were classified as *unaware*.

Reliability of awareness ratings.—For the Experimental group four judges independently rated each S's notes for awareness. Two raters were considered to be in *agreement* with respect to a particular S if they both classified her as aware, or if both classified her as unaware. For each possible pair of raters, the percentage of Ss in the Experimental group on whom the two raters agreed was calculated; these percentages of agreement between pairs of raters varied from 90.1% to 95.1% The notes of the 2 Ss for whom there was no consensus (unanimity or a 3 to 1 majority) among the four raters were submitted to a fifth rater. By this process, 21 Ss were judged aware, and 40 unaware. Since the percentages of agreement between pairs of raters were relatively high and since there was unanimity or a 3 to 1 majority among the raters for 59 of 61 Ss in the Experimental group (96.7%), it was concluded that the reliability (objectivity) of the awareness ratings was satisfactory.

---

3. The interview schedule has been deposited with the American Documentation Institute. Order Document No. 8107 from ADI Auxiliary Publications Project, Photo-duplication Service, Library of Congress, Washington, D. C. 20540. Remit in advance $1.25 for microfilm or $1.25 for photocopies and make checks payable to: Chief, Photo-duplication Service, Library of Congress.

Effects of awareness on conditioning

Reliability of scoring of response words.—Performance on the conditioning task was measured by the number of human nouns given during each trial block as recorded by E. In order to assess the reliability of E's tallies of human nouns, the operant trial-block performance of 10 Ss was independently tallied by the writer from the tape recordings. Only responses given during the operant trials were tallied so that the scoring would not be biased by E's "Mmm-hmm." The mean percent agreement between E and the writer for the 10 Ss was 96.8%. The product-moment correlation for the total number of human nouns scored for each S by E and the writer was .97. Thus the findings of the present study confirm the report of Matarazzo et al. (1960) that "human responses" can be reliably scored.

Conditioning performance of aware, unaware, and control Ss.—Prior to the analysis of the conditioning data, the number of human nouns given by each S in the two operant trial blocks was averaged to determine S's operant rate. Since the mean operant rates for the Experimental and Control groups did not significantly differ when statistically evaluated, $CR = 0.15$, it was concluded that the two groups were adequately matched with respect to the number of human nouns emitted prior to the introduction of reinforcement.

In order to assess the influence of awareness on performance, the Experimental group was divided into Aware and Unaware groups. The mean numbers of human nouns given by aware, unaware, and control Ss for the operant trial blocks (averaged) and the 10 subsequent reinforced trial blocks are presented in Figure 1. The Aware, Unaware, and Control groups were quite comparable with respect to their mean operant rates, as may be noted in Fig-

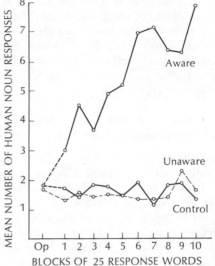

FIG. 1. Performance of aware $(N = 21)$, unaware $(N = 40)$, and control $(N = 21)$ Ss on the conditioning task.

ure 1. When the performance data for the operant trials of these three groups were subjected to analysis of variance (simple randomized design, Lindquist, 1953), it was found that there was no significant differences among the three groups in mean operant rate.

It may be noted in Figure 1 that output of human noun responses in the Aware group increased over trials, whereas the other two groups did not show any performance gains. An analysis of variance of the conditioning data, including the operant trials, resulted in a significant Groups × Trials interaction, $F (20, 790) = 3.74$, p < .001, indicating that the slopes of the curves in Figure 1 differed. The test for linear trend (Winer, 1962, pp. 71–73) was highly significant for the Aware group, $F (1, 200) = 28.46$, $p < .001$, but not for the Unaware group, $F (1, 390) = .65$, nor for the Control group, $F (1, 200) = .13$. When the Unaware group was compared with the Control group by analysis of variance, no significant effects were found (all Fs less than unity). Thus, the performance of unaware Ss as a group was undistinguishable from that of randomly reinforced controls, and only Ss who verbalized a correct response-reinforcement contingency in their notes tended as a group to acquire the reinforced response class.

Performance of aware Ss before and after verbalization of awareness

Some investigators (e.g., Philbrick & Postman, 1955; Postman & Sassenrath, 1961) have reported slight but statistically significant performance gains prior to verbalization of the contingency of reinforcement in Ss who eventually developed correct hypotheses. In order to test for this kind of learning without awareness, the performance of 15 of the aware Ss [4] was examined as a function of the trial block on which each verbalized awareness, i.e., wrote her correct hypothesis in her notes. The mean number of human nouns for these Ss for the operant and reinforced trial blocks are presented as the "raw data" curves in Figure 2. The conditioning data in Figure 2 were arrayed so that the trial blocks on which each S first recorded her correct hypothesis were aligned, and designated the "zero" trial block. The trial blocks prior to and subsequent to the "zero" block were labeled, respectively, with negative and positive integers, after the practice of Philbrick and Postman (1955). Since Ss recorded correct hypotheses at different times, the number of data entries on which the points of the "raw data" curves in Figure 2 were based varied from 9 to 15.

It will be observed in Figure 2 that performance for the preverbalization trial blocks did not rise above the operant level, while performance on the "zero" trial block and later trial blocks was consistently above that level. In order to evaluate these data, the preverbalization trial blocks (−4 to −1) and post-

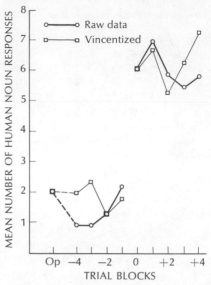

FIG. 2. Performance on the conditioning task for the aware Ss who wrote correct hypotheses between the second reinforced trial block and the final trial block.

verbalization trial blocks (+1 to +4) were Vincentized (Munn, 1950) so that each S's performance contributed to each data point. It may be noted that the curves for the Vincentized data, which are also presented in Figure 2, are similar to the "raw data" curves. The Vincentized data were subjected to three tests of linear trend: (a) over all trial blocks including the "zero" block; (b) over the preverbalization trials (the operant and four preverbalization trial blocks); and (c) over the postverbalization trials (the four postverbalization trial blocks only). The overall trend of the data was highly significant, F (1, 126) = 22.69, $p < .001$, indicating that there was a pronounced tendency for performance to increase over all trials. However, neither the pre- nor the post-

---

4. These Ss recorded a correct hypothesis between the second reinforced trial block and the final trial block. Five Ss who recorded a correct hypothesis immediately after the first reinforced trial block were excluded from this analysis since they had no clearly specifiable preawareness trials. Similarly, one S who recorded the contingency on the final trial block was excluded because she had no clearly specifiable postawareness trials.

verbalization trend *F*s exceeded unity. Thus, there was no tendency for performance to increase *during* the post-verbalization blocks.

On the assumptions that aware Ss (*a*) developed their correct hypotheses during the "zero" trial block, and (*b*) began promptly to select their responses on the basis of these hypotheses, it would be expected that performance gains would begin on the "zero" trial block. In order to test this expectation, the performance data for trial blocks "−1" and "zero" were compared. It was found that performance on the "zero" trial block was significantly above performance on the "−1" block for both the raw data, $t(14) = 2.73$, $p < .05$, and the Vincentized data, $t(14) = 3.08$, $p < .01$.

Thus, it would appear that performance gains first occurred at the trial block on which Ss recorded their correct hypotheses; and that performance for aware Ss was essentially unchanging within the preverbalization, and within the post-verbalization, blocks. Hence, there was no evidence of conditioning prior to verbalization of a correct response-reinforcement contingency.

DISCUSSION

In the present study, only Ss who were aware of a correct response-reinforcement contingency showed performance gains. Moreover, the performance increments of aware Ss first occurred on the trial block for which they wrote their correct hypothesis in their notes; there were no performance gains for these Ss prior to the "zero" trial block. The performance of the systematically reinforced Ss who were unaware of a correct contingency did not differ from that of the randomly reinforced control group. These findings were consistent with the results of other verbal-conditioning experiments in which awareness was carefully assessed, in (*a*) demonstrating relationships between verbal reports and performance, and (*b*) failing to adduce

evidence for learning without awareness. The results support the hypothesis that a cognitive learning process mediates performance gains in verbal conditioning.

Learning theories which posit the direct and automatic strengthening of response tendencies by reinforcement would not explain the complete absence of performance gains for the unaware Ss in the present study, nor the absence of performance gains for the aware Ss on the preverbalization trials. Such theories would predict gradual increments in performance over trials for all Ss. However, a modified theory of automatic strengthening such as that espoused by Postman and Sassenrath (1961) might be invoked to account for the present results. On the hypothesis that "*verbalization of a principle may be considered at the same time a result of past improvement and a condition of further improvement* [Postman & Sassenrath, 1961, p. 124]," it might be speculated that the aware Ss in the present showed initial performance gains without awareness in the early trials of their "zero" blocks, and consequently became aware of the response-reinforcement contingency. However, the specificity of the hypothetical automatic reinforcement effect to the "zero" blocks of aware Ss in the present study would appear incompatible with theories ascribing general trans-situational efficacy to verbal reinforcing stimuli.

Although learning without awareness was not found in this study, it might be argued that the instructions to write "thoughts about the experiment" induced vigilance or self-consciousness in Ss which inhibited the automatic and unconscious influence of reinforcement. Indeed, it is conceivable that Ss' mere knowledge that their behavior was being studied sufficed to vitiate learning-without-awareness effects. Thus, it could still be maintained that in real-life situations reinforcement operates to strengthen automatically the responses it follows, despite the absence of evidence for learning without awareness in better-designed laboratory studies of verbal conditioning. Empirical validation of this line of reasoning, however, is lacking at present and is apparently most difficult to obtain (Azrin, Holz, Ulrich, & Goldiamond, 1961). *Comparison of note-writing and inter-*

view methods for assessing awareness.—In previous investigations of verbal conditioning, interpretations of interview or questionnaire data in terms of mediating cognitive processes have been challenged on the grounds that such verbal reports, gathered by questioning Ss after the conditioning task, may have been unduly influenced by E's suggestion of hypotheses and by S's retrospective distortions. The note-writing procedures employed to assess awareness during the conditioning trials in the present study were clearly less susceptible to such hypothetical biasing factors than were the postconditioning interviews used in most previous verbal-conditioning experiments. Furthermore, awareness ratings made on the basis of Ss' notes agreed with those independently made on the basis of the postconditioning interview for 58 of the 61 Ss in the Experimental group. Thus, it would appear that note-writing and interview techniques yield essentially comparable results in distinguishing between aware and unaware Ss, and that the biasing effects introduced by interviewing Ss after the conditioning period are not large. Additional evidence of the validity of postconditioning interview data as indexes of mediating states is reported in DeNike (1963).

Although aware Ss indicate in the interview that they became aware on the average about one trial block before that on which they recorded their correct hypotheses, no performance gains were found prior to the trial block on which these Ss wrote correct hypotheses in their notes. Thus, it would appear that during the 25 words of their "zero" trial blocks, aware Ss could develop enough confidence in their hypotheses both to begin acting on them and to record them. The finding of a temporal relationship between awareness and performance was generally consistent with the findings of previous verbal-conditioning studies (Spielberger, 1962; Spielberger & Levin, 1962) in which Ss initially showed performance gains on the trial block which they specified during a postconditioning interview as that on which they became aware.

Status of awareness. Since the methods employed in the present study permitted the temporal relationship between awareness and performance gains to be evaluated, and since no performance gains were found prior to awareness, the conclusion that Ss' awareness importantly influenced their subsequent performance appears warranted. The results suggest that the effects of awareness (assessed through ongoing recording of Ss' "thoughts about the experiment") on behavior can be empirically established for at least some experimental contexts. But as Farber (1963) has noted, "This does not mean that the reports obtained need be regarded as the manifest proof of an autonomous cognitive machinery guiding our every action [p. 195]." Whether Ss' awareness under particular conditions should best be conceptualized as mediating behavior, as merely correlated with behavior, or as irrelevant to behavior would appear to be determinable only through appropriate research. It is hoped that the present results may help to stimulate such inquiry by affirming the viewpoint that awareness constitutes a legitimate subject for empirical investigation.

Azrin, N. H., Holz, W., Ulrich, R., & Goldiamond, I. The control of the content of conversation through reinforcement. *J. exp. Anal. Behav.*, 1961, **4**, 25-30.

DeNike, L. D. *Awareness in verbal conditioning: The assessment of awareness from verbal reports written by subjects during conditioning.* (Doctoral dissertation, Duke University) Ann Arbor, Mich.: University Microfilms, 1963, No. 64-8560.

DeNike, L. D., & Spielberger, C. D. Induced mediating states in verbal conditioning. *J. verbal Learn. verbal Behav.*, 1963, **1**, 339-45.

Dulany, D. E. Hypotheses and habits in verbal "operant conditioning." *J. abnorm. soc. Psychol.*, 1961, **63**, 251-63.

Dulany, D. E. The place of hypotheses and intentions: An analysis of verbal control in verbal conditioning. *J. Pers.*, 1962, **30** (Suppl.), 102-29.

Farber, I. E. The things people say to themselves. *Amer. Psychologist*, 1963, **18**, 185-97.

Greenspoon, J. The reinforcing effect of two spoken sounds on the frequency of two responses. *Amer. J. Psychol.*, 1955, **68**, 409-16.

Greenspoon, J. Verbal conditioning and clinical psychology. In A. J. Bachrach (Ed.), *Experimental foundations of clinical psychology.* New York: Basic Books, 1962. Pp. 510-53.

Krasner, L. Studies of the conditioning of verbal behavior. *Psychol. Bull.*, 1958, **55**, 148-70.

Krasner, L. Verbal conditioning and awareness. Paper read at American Psychological Association meetings, St. Louis, September 1962.

Levin, S. M. The effects of awareness on verbal conditioning. *J. exp. Psychol.*, 1961, **61**, 67-75.

Lindquist, E. F. *Design and analysis of experiments in psychology and education.* Boston: Houghton Mifflin, 1953.

Matarazzo, J. D., Saslow, G., & Pareis, E. N. Verbal conditioning of two response classes:

Some methodological considerations. *J. abnorm. soc. Psychol.*, 1960, **61**, 190-206.

MUNN, N. L. *Handbook of psychological research on the rat: An introduction to animal psychology.* Boston: Houghton Mifflin, 1950.

PHILBRICK, E. B., & POSTMAN, L. A further analysis of "learning without awareness." *Amer. J. Psychol.*, 1955, **68**, 417-24.

POSTMAN, L., & SASSENRATH, J. M. The automatic action of verbal rewards and punishments. *J. gen. Psychol.*, 1961, **65**, 109-36.

SALZINGER, K. Experimental manipulation of verbal behavior: A review. *J. gen. Psychol.*, 1959, **61**, 65-94.

SPIELBERGER, C. D. The role of awareness in verbal conditioning. *J. Pers.*, 1962, **30** (Suppl.) 73-101.

SPIELBERGER, C. D. Theoretical and epistemological issues in verbal conditioning. In S. Rosenberg (Ed.), *Directions in psycholinguistics.* New York: Macmillan, 1965, in press.

SPIELBERGER, C. D., & DeNIKE, L. D. Operant conditioning of plural nouns: A failure to replicate the Greenspoon effect. *Psychol. Rep.*, 1962, **11**, 355-66.

SPIELBERGER, C. D., & LEVIN, S. M. What is learned in verbal conditioning? *J. verbal Learn. verbal Behav.*, 1962, **1**, 125-32.

TATZ, S. J. Symbolic activity in "learning without awareness." *Amer. J. Psychol.*, 1960, **73**, 239-47.

WINER, B. J. *Statistical principles in experimental design.* New York: McGraw-Hill 1962.